Routledge Handbook of Space Law

This handbook is a reference work providing a comprehensive, objective and comparative overview of Space Law.

The global space economy reached $330 billion in 2015, with a growth rate of 9 per cent vis-à-vis the previous year. Consequently, Space Law is changing and expanding expeditiously, especially at the national level. More laws and regulations are being adopted by space-faring nations, while more countries are adapting their Space Laws and regulations related to activities in outer space. More regulatory bodies are being created, while more regulatory diversity (from public law to private law) is being instituted as increasing and innovative activities are undertaken by private entities which employ new technologies and business initiatives. At the international level, Space Law (both hard law and soft law) is expanding in certain areas, especially in satellite broadcasting and telecommunications.

The *Routledge Handbook of Space Law* summarises the existing state of knowledge on a comprehensive range of topics and aspires to set the future international research agenda by indicating gaps and inconsistencies in the existing law and highlighting emerging legal issues. Unlike other books on the subject, it addresses major international and national legal aspects of particular space activities and issues, rather than providing commentary on or explanations about a particular Space Law treaty or national regulation.

Drawing together contributions from leading academic scholars and practising lawyers from around the world, the volume is divided into five key parts:

- Part I: General Principles of International Space Law
- Part II: International Law of Space Applications
- Part III: National Regulation of Space Activities
- Part IV: National Regulation of Navigational Satellite Systems
- Part V: Commercial Aspects of Space Law

This handbook is both practical and theoretical in scope, and may serve as a reference tool to academics, professionals and policy-makers with an interest in Space Law.

Ram S. Jakhu is Director of, and a tenured Associate Professor at, the Institute of Air and Space Law at McGill University, in Montreal, Canada, where he teaches and conducts research in International Space Law, Law of Space Applications, National Regulation of Space Activities, and Public International Law. He has served as Director of the McGill Centre for the Study of Regulated Industries from 1999 to 2004 as well as the first Director of the MSS Program (and Senior Faculty Member) at International Space University, Strasbourg, France, from 1995 to 1998.

Paul Stephen Dempsey is Tomlinson Professor Emeritus of Global Governance in Air and Space Law and Director Emeritus of the Institute of Air and Space Law at McGill University. For more than two decades, he held the chair as Professor of Transportation Law, and was Director of the Transportation Law Program at the University of Denver. He was also Director of the National Center for Intermodal Transportation. Earlier, he served as an attorney with the Civil Aeronautics Board and the Interstate Commerce Commission (ICC) in Washington, D.C., and was Legal Advisor to the Chairman of the ICC.

Routledge Handbook of Space Law

Edited by Ram S. Jakhu and Paul Stephen Dempsey

Routledge
Taylor & Francis Group
LONDON AND NEW YORK

First published 2017
by Routledge

2 Park Square, Milton Park, Abingdon, Oxfordshire OX14 4RN
52 Vanderbilt Avenue, New York, NY 10017

Routledge is an imprint of the Taylor & Francis Group, an informa business

First issued in paperback 2019

Copyright © 2017 selection and editorial matter, Ram S. Jakhu and Paul Stephen Dempsey; individual chapters, the contributors

The right of Ram S. Jakhu and Paul Stephen Dempsey to be identified as the authors of the editorial material, and of the authors for their individual chapters, has been asserted in accordance with sections 77 and 78 of the Copyright, Designs and Patents Act 1988.

All rights reserved. No part of this book may be reprinted or reproduced or utilised in any form or by any electronic, mechanical, or other means, now known or hereafter invented, including photocopying and recording, or in any information storage or retrieval system, without permission in writing from the publishers.

Notice:
Product or corporate names may be trademarks or registered trademarks, and are used only for identification and explanation without intent to infringe.

British Library Cataloguing in Publication Data
A catalogue record for this book is available from the British Library

Library of Congress Cataloging in Publication Data
Names: Jakhu, Ram S. (Ram Sarup), 1946- editor. | Dempsey, Paul Stephen, editor.
Title: Routledge handbook of space law / edited by Ram S. Jakhu and Paul Stephen Dempsey.
Other titles: Space law
Description: Abingdon, Oxon [UK] ; New York : Routledge, 2017. | Includes bibliographical references and index.
Identifiers: LCCN 2016029638| ISBN 978-1-138-80771-6 (hbk) | ISBN 978-1-315-75096-5 (ebk)
Subjects: LCSH: Space law—Handbooks, manuals, etc.
Classification: LCC KZD1145 .R68 2017 | DDC 341.4/7—dc23
LC record available at https://lccn.loc.gov/2016029638

ISBN: 978-1-138-80771-6 (hbk)
ISBN: 978-0-367-87045-4 (pbk)

Typeset in Bembo by
FiSH Books Ltd, Enfield

Contents

Contributors	*viii*
Preface, Ram S. Jakhu and Paul Stephen Dempsey	*xviii*

PART I
General principles of international space law   1

1   Sources and law-making processes relating to space activities   3
    Cassandra Steer

2   Legal status of outer space and celestial bodies   25
    Stephan Hobe and Kuan-Wei Chen

3   Legal status of spacecraft   42
    Mark J. Sundahl

4   Liability for damage caused by space activities   59
    Armel Kerrest and Caroline Thro

5   Control over activities harmful to the environment   73
    Jinyuan Su

6   Settlement of disputes and resolution of conflicts   90
    Tare Brisibe

PART II
International law of space applications   107

7   Regulation of telecommunications by satellites: ITU and space services   109
    Yvon Henri, Attila Matas, and Juliana Macedo Scavuzzi dos Santos

8   Regulation of remote sensing by satellites   144
    Sa'id Mosteshar

Contents

9	Regulation of global navigation satellite systems *Michael Chatzipanagiotis and Konstantina Liperi*	160
10	Space traffic management and space situational awareness *Rafael Moro-Aguilar and Steven A. Mirmina*	180
11	Law and military uses of outer space *Setsuko Aoki*	197
12	The intersection between space law and international human rights law *Steven Freeland and Ram S. Jakhu*	225

PART III
National regulation of space activities — 239

| 13 | Law relating to remote sensing – Earth observation
Lesley Jane Smith and Catherine Doldirina | 241 |
| 14 | Law related to space transportation and spaceports
Michael Gerhard and Isabelle Reutzel | 268 |

PART IV
National regulation of navigational satellite systems — 289

15	Regulation of navigational satellites in the United States *Andrea J. Harrington*	291
16	Regulation of navigational satellites in Europe *Michael Chatzipanagiotis and Konstantina Liperi*	295
17	Regulation of navigational satellites in the Russian Federation *Olga A. Volynskaya*	300
18	Regulation of navigational satellites in China *Guoyu Wang*	304
19	Regulation of navigational satellites in Japan *Souichirou Kozuka*	309
20	Regulation of navigational satellites in India *Ranjana Kaul*	313

PART V
Commercial aspects of space law — 319

21 Law related to intellectual property and transfer of technology — 321
    Yun Zhao

22 Commercial satellite programs — 333
    Henry R. Hertzfeld and Alexis M. Sáinz

Index — *352*

Contributors

Md. Tanveer Ahmad is currently an Assistant Professor in the Department of Law, North South University, Bangladesh. He has earned his Doctor of Civil Law (DCL) and Master of Laws (LLM) degrees from the Institute of Air and Space Law, McGill University in 2016 and 2010, respectively. While pursuing his doctoral studies, he held an Assad Kotaite Fellowship of International Civil Aviation Organization and a Boeing Fellowship in Air and Space Law. He obtained his Bachelor of Laws (LLB) (Honors) degree from the University of London, UK, in 2006. He has published in various peer-reviewed law journals, written policy papers, presented papers at various conferences, and has assisted with the editing of Space Monograph Series I, II and III. He has worked on the National Space Legislation Book project as a Research Assistant for Professor Ram S. Jakhu, Institute of Air and Space Law, McGill University, since 2012. He is an Assistant Editor of the *Annals of Air & Space Law* journal.

Setsuko Aoki holds an LLB and an LLM from the Faculty of Law and the Graduate School of Law at Keio University (Japan) and a DCL in Air and Space Law from McGill University. She is Professor of International Law, Keio University Law School and Vice-Director of the Institute of Space Law, Keio University since April 2016. Her previous positions include Professor (since April 2004) and Associate Professor of international Law, Faculty of Policy Management, Keio University (April 1999–March 2016) as well as Associate Professor (since October 1995) and Assistant Professor of Law, School of Social Sciences, National Defence Academy of Japan (April 1994–March 1999). She is currently a member of the Committee on National Space Policy (CNSP) under the Cabinet Office. She is also the Legal Advisor of the Ministry of Foreign Affairs of Japan to the Legal Subcommittee of the Committee on the Peaceful Uses of Outer Space (COPUOS); a member of the Space Law Committee of the International Law Association (ILA); and a member of the Board of the Directors of the International Institute of Space Law (IISL).

Tare Brisibe is currently in private practice. A member of the Nigerian Bar, he was former Chairperson of the Legal Subcommittee – United Nations Committee on the Peaceful Uses of Outer Space, for the biennium 2012 to 2014. He began a career in 1991 practicing in civil litigation, general commercial law, mergers and acquisitions with two leading Nigerian law firms. A former Legal Adviser to the National Space Research and Development Agency of Nigeria, he has served with mobile communications satellite operator Inmarsat Global, as well as aeronautical communications consortium SITA. He previously held an appointment with a Luxembourg based law firm focused on space and communications. He has been involved with multiple expert working groups, notably as: member of the Hague Space Resources Governance Working Group; peer reviewer for the NATO CCD COE Tallinn Manual (version

2.0) on International Law Applicable to Cyber Warfare; member of the Permanent Court of Arbitration, Advisory Group on Optional Rules for Arbitration of Disputes Relating to Outer Space Activities; member of the UNIDROIT Committee of Governmental Experts for preparation of a Space Protocol to the 2000 Cape Town Convention; and Vice Rapporteur of the International Telecommunication Union Development Sector (ITU-D) Study Group Question on Satellite Regulation for Developing Countries. He has been a: Visiting Fellow, Graduate Institute of International and Development Studies, Geneva (2011); Zhang Yong Fellow, Chinese Journal of International Law Research Group (2008); Recipient of the First Prize, Pacific Telecommunications Council Research Essay Contest (1999). He obtained a Master's degree in Space Studies (1999) from International Space University, Strasbourg and a Doctorate in International Law (2006) from Leiden University.

Kuan-Wei (David) Chen holds an undergraduate degree in Law and Politics from the School of Oriental and African Studies (SOAS), University of London, an LLM (*cum laude*) in Public International Law from Leiden University and an LLM in Air and Space Law from the Institute of Air and Space Law, McGill University, where he was also the Boeing Fellow in Air and Space Law. He was previously a Teaching and Research Assistant at the Van Vollenhoven Institute for Law, Governance and Development, Leiden University; and the Co-ordinator of the Telders International Law Moot Court at the Grotius Centre for International Legal Studies. Since 2009, he has been working as a Research Assistant at the Institute of Air and Space Law. In 2014, he became a Course Lecturer at the Faculty of Law of McGill University, and is currently the Deputy Project Manager of the *Manual on International Law Applicable to Military Uses of Outer Space* (MILAMOS) Project. He is also the Assistant Editor of the *Annals of Air and Space Law*, published by McGill University's Centre for Research in Air and Space Law.

Michael Chatzipanagiotis is a practicing attorney in Greece, a legal advisor to the Cyprus Competition and Consumer Protection Service, as well as an adjunct lecturer of aviation law at the European University of Cyprus and of European private law at the University of Cyprus. He specializes in aviation and space law, IPR and consumer protection. He advises various aerospace companies and has worked as an aviation and space law expert in projects with the European Commission, Eurocontrol, the Lufthansa Group and the German Aerospace Center (DLR). The European Aviation Safety Agency has included him in its list of national aviation law experts for Greece and he is an instructor of aviation law at the International Air Transport Association (IATA). He obtained his LL.B from the Law School of the University of Athens, Greece, and his LL.M from the Law School of the University of Cologne, Germany, where he subsequently wrote his PhD on suborbital flights. He holds seminars, presentations and guest lectures on specialized legal issues of aviation law, space law and consumer protection, while he has authored numerous publications on his areas of interest in international law reviews. He is also an active member of the International Institute of Space Law.

Paul S. Dempsey holds a BA in Journalism and an Juris Doctorate in Law from the University of Georgia and then went on to acquire an LLM in International Law from George Washington University and a DCL in Air and Space Law from McGill University. He was Vice Chairman of Frontier Airlines Holdings, Inc., and Chairman of Lynx Aviation, Inc. He Dempsey served as Attorney-Advisor to the Interstate Commerce Commission's Office of Proceedings (1975–1977), Attorney-Advisor to the former Civil Aeronautics Board's Office of General Counsel, and its Bureau of Pricing and Domestic Aviation (1977–1979), and the Legal

Contributors

Advisor to the Chairman of the US Interstate Commerce Commission (1981–1982). He was also the Director of the Transportation Law Program at the University of Denver in Colorado and Director of the National Center for Intermodal Transportation. He has served as Tomlinson Professor of Global Governance in Air and Space Law and Director of the Institute of Air and Space Law at McGill University (2002–2016).

Catherine Doldirina is a consultant to the European Commission on matters related to legal issues regarding access to and use of data. Previously she worked as a researcher at the Joint Research Centre of the European Commission (Italy) focusing on policies and regulations regarding access to and use of geographic and Earth observation data. Catherine's expertise is strongly linked to the research for her PhD thesis "Remote Sensing Data and the Common Good" that she researched at the Institute of Air and Space Law, Faculty of Law McGill University. Her expertise lies in the field of intellectual property law some fields of European law, (geographic) data policies and regulations, as well as general questions of Space Law. She lectures on European competition law, European Copyright Law and Space Law. She has published on various aspects of Space Law and is a member of the International Institute of Space Law.

Steven Freeland is Professor of International Law at Western Sydney University, where he teaches both postgraduate and undergraduate students, and supervises PhD students, in the fields of International Criminal Law, Commercial Aspects of Space Law, Public International Law and Human Rights Law. He is a Visiting Professor at the University of Vienna, Permanent Visiting Professor of the iCourts Centre of Excellence for International Courts, Denmark, a Member of Faculty of the London Institute of Space Policy and Law, and was a Marie Curie Fellow in 2013–2014. He has been appointed to advise the Australian Commonwealth Department of Industry, Innovation and Science on issues related to the regulation of space activities. Among other appointments, he is a Director of the Paris-based International Institute of Space Law, a member of the Space Law Committee of the London-based International Law Association, and a member of the Advisory Board of the Australian Centre for Space Engineering Research. He sits on the Editorial Board of a number of international journals. He has authored approximately 300 publications on various aspects of International Law and has been invited to present over 800 expert commentaries by national and international media outlets worldwide on a wide range of legal and geopolitical issues. He is also a frequent speaker at national/international conferences, having been invited to present conference papers and keynote speeches in over 30 countries.

Michael Gerhard is currently working for the European Aviation Safety Agency (EASA). He joined the Agency in 2008 as a legal advisor and was working in the field of international Aviation Law, EU law, European administrative law and enforcement. Since 2016 he manages the Regulation and Certification Policy Section, being responsible for all regulatory activities related to the initial airworthiness of aircraft. From 1999 to 2008 Dr. Gerhard worked at the German Aerospace Center (DLR). As a legal advisor he was mainly occupied with matters of public international law and administrative law. The main emphasis of his work was to advise the DLR and the federal ministries in matters of national space legislation, insurance and registration of space objects, liability issues, intellectual property issues, security aspects regarding the distribution of remote sensing data and budget law. Furthermore Dr. Gerhard lectures on Aviation Law as well as Space Law to students studying Aerospace Technologies at the Aachen University of Applied Sciences. He has published a book on the topic of national space legislation and more than 50 articles on Aviation and Space law and policy.

Andrea J. Harrington serves on the faculty of the University of Mississippi Law School as Air and Space Law Instructor/Research Counsel and is a licensed Massachusetts attorney. Andrea is an Erin J.C. Arsenault Fellow in Space Governance at the McGill University Institute of Air and Space Law, focusing on insurance and liability issues for the commercial space industry. She served as the Teaching Associate in the Politics, Law, and Economics Department for the International Space University's 2016 Space Studies Program. Andrea holds an LLM, also from the McGill IASL, as well as a JD from the University of Connecticut, an MSc from the London School of Economics, and a BA from Boston University. While at McGill, Andrea has earned numerous awards, including the PEO Scholar Award, the IAWA Scholarship, the SWF Young Professionals IAC Scholarship, and the Setsuko Ushioda-Aoki Prize. She has served as an Assistant Editor for the Annals of Air and Space Law, Jr. Project Manager for Secure World Foundation, and a researcher on projects for the FAA Center of Excellence for Commercial Space Transportation, IAASS, ICAO, and Space Security Index. Prior to transitioning to Air and Space law, Andrea accumulated over five years of experience in the insurance and financial compliance fields.

Yvon Henri is Chief of the Space Services Department (SSD) at the Radiocommunication Bureau of the International Telecommunication Union (ITU), in Geneva (Switzerland). Before joining ITU in 1995, he held various management positions at France Telecom (Paris, France) and INTELSAT (Washington DC, USA) and has been involved in the satellite business for more than 30 years. ITU is a Geneva-based United Nations specialized agency for information and communication technologies (ICTs) and its membership includes 193 Member States and almost 800 Sector Members and private-sector entities and academic institutions. ITU allocates global radio spectrum and satellite orbits, develops the technical standards that ensure networks and technologies seamlessly interconnect, and strives to improve access to ICTs to underserved communities worldwide. Within the ITU, the Space Services Department is responsible for managing the procedures for registration of all space system frequency assignments (satellite and Earth and radioastronomy stations) in accordance with the ITU Constitution and Convention, including the Radio Regulations. The Department is also providing assistance and support to administrations, operators and frequency assignment stakeholders on all issues related to space service frequency management.

Henry R. Hertzfeld is a Research Professor of Space Policy and International Affairs at the Space Policy Institute, Center for International Science and Technology Policy, Elliott School of International Affairs, George Washington University. He is also an Adjunct Professor of Law at George Washington University and teaches the Space Law course. He is an expert in the economic, legal, and policy issues of space and advanced technological development. Dr. Hertzfeld has served as a Senior Economist and Policy Analyst at both NASA and the National Science Foundation, and is a consultant to both US and international agencies and organizations. He is author of many articles on the economic and legal issues concerning space and technology. Dr. Hertzfeld is a member of the Bar in Pennsylvania and the District of Columbia.

Stephan Hobe is Director of the Institute of Air and Space Law, Cologne University and Holder of the Jean Monnet Chair for Public International Law, European Law, European and International Economic Law. He is also the editor of the *German Journal of Air and Space Law* (ZLW); a member of several scientific associations, such as the Board of the International Institute of Space Law, the Board of the European Centre for Space Law, Rapporteur of the Space Law Committee of the International Law Association, Treasurer of the ILA German branch and Board Member of the German Society of International Law. He is the author and editor of over 250 books and articles in the field of International Law, Air and Space Law and teaches Air and Space Law at Cologne University. He is also an Extra-Ordinary Professor at the University of Pretoria, a Honorary Professor at the Beijing Institute of Technology and Gujarat National Law School University.

Ram S. Jakhu is Director of, and a tenured Associate Professor at, the Institute of Air and Space Law, McGill University, Montreal, Canada. He was Director of the Centre for the Study of Regulated Industries (1999–2004) after being Head of the School of Social Sciences and Management, and the first Director of the Masters Program of the International Space University in Strasbourg (1978–1994). Professor Jakhu is a Member of the World Economic Forum's Global Agenda Council on Space Security; Research Director for Space Security Index Project; a Fellow and the Chairman of the Legal and Regulatory Committee of the International Association for the Advancement of Space Safety; Managing Editor of the Space Regulations Library Series; a Member of the Editorial Boards of the *Annals of Air and Space Law* and the *German Journal of Air & Space Law*; and Chair of the Management Board of the McGill Manual on International Law Applicable to Military Uses of Outer Space Project (MILAMOS). In 2016, he received the "Leonardo da Vinci Life-Long Achievement Award" from the International Association for the Advancement of Space Safety and in 2007 the "Distinguished Service Award" from International Institute of Space Law for significant contribution to the development of space law. He obtained B.A., LL.B. and LL.M. (international law) degrees from Panjab University, Chandigarh, India.

Ranjana Kaul is a Partner at Dua Associates, Advocates & Solicitors, in New Delhi, India since 2005. She has a PhD from University of Poona, India and an LLM from the Institute of Air and Space Law, Faculty of Law, McGill University, Montreal, Canada. Ranjana Kaul specializes and advises on several aspects of Indian policy and regulatory framework for commercial space and satellite service businesses. Her legal practice focuses on company laws, IPR, anti-trust and cross border contracts in the aviation, space enabled business and e-commerce sectors, including procedural laws. She is regularly consulted on matters related to Indian law, Aviation Law, law of outer space, and related international contracts. She has served as Counsel for the Union of India at the High Court of Delhi and Counsel for the State of Maharashtra in the Supreme Court of India. She has been consultant to the World Bank and the Indian Council for International Economic Relations, New Delhi. She is member of the Bar Council of India and the International Institute of Space Law. She has published widely and is a Member of the Editorial Board of an international journal specializing in Outer Space matters.

Armel Kerrest is an Emeritus Professor of Public Law. He taught International Public Law, especially Space Law and Law of the Sea at the Universities of Western Brittany and Paris XI. He studied In Germany and Paris. He is a docteur d'état of the university of Paris I. He has taught at other French and foreign universities, published books and articles on European and International Law especially Space Law and Law of the Sea. He advises on Space Law for national and international public institutions as well as private compagnies. He is the Vice chairman of the European Center for Space Law of the European Space Agency (ECSL/ESA), the President of the Association for the Development of Space Law in France, the Chairman of the Institute of Law of International Spaces and Telecommunications (Brittany); a Member of the Space Law Committee of the International Law Association (ILA) and of the Société française de droit aérien et spatial (SFDAS), a Member of the board of the European Centre for Space Law (ECSL)). He is a member of the International Academy of Astronautics and a corresponding member of the Académie de l'Air et de l'Espace.

Souichirou Kozuka (PhD, Tokyo) is Professor of Law at Gakushuin University, Tokyo. He specializes in Commercial Law, Corporate Law and Maritime, Air and Space Law. His recent publications in English include: "An Economic Assessment of the space Assets Protocol to the Cape Town Convention" (co-authored with Fuki Taniguchi) (2011), *Uniform law Review* pp. 927–941; "The Law Applicable on the Continental Shelf and in the Exclusive Economic Zone: The Japanese Perspective" (co-authored with Hideyuki Nakamura), *Ocean Yearbook* Vol. 25, pp. 357–378 (2011); "Insurance Law Issues Due to the Great East Japan Earthquake of 2011", *Zeitschrift für Japanisches Recht* No. 33, pp. 3–11 (2012) and No. 34, pp. 87–94 (2013); "Policy and Politics in Contract Law Reform in Japan" (co-authored with Luke Nottage), in *The Method and Culture of Comparative Law* (Maurice Adams & Dirk Heirbaut (eds.)), pp. 235–253 (2014); "Licensing and Regulation of Japan's Offshore Resources", in Tina Hunter (ed.), *Regulation of the Upstream Petroleum Sector: A Comparative Study of Licensing and Concession Systems* (2015, Edward Elgar). He is a Co-Chair of the Space Law Committee of the International Bar Association (IBA) for 2016 and 2017, correspondent of UNIDROIT (the International Institute for the Unification of Private Law) and an Associate Member of the International Academy of Comparative Law (IACL).

Konstantina Liperi works as a legal officer in the Department of Electronic Communications of the Ministry of Transport, Communications and Works of the Republic of Cyprus. She advises on Telecommunications and Space Law issues and is responsible for drafting legislation relevant to this field. She is the national expert of Cyprus to the EU in relation to the European Global Navigation Satellite Systems (GALILEO and EGNOS). She represents Cyprus on the European Commission's GNSS Programme Committee, on the European GNSS Agency's Administrative Board and in European Space Agency s committees. She obtained a Bachelor of Laws from Sheffield University in the UK and was called to UK (Honourable Society of Middle Temple) and Cyprus Bar (Cyprus Bar Association). She also holds an LLM (Adv) in Air and Space Law from Leiden University in the Netherlands.

Attila Matas serves as Head of the Space Publications and Registration Division at the ITU Radiocommunication Bureau – Space Services Department. He is responsible for the processing and publication of GSO and non-GSO space systems and Earth stations submitted by administrations for inclusion in the formal coordination procedures or recording in the Space Master International Frequency Register (SMIFR). He represents the ITU at the UN COPUOS and ICG and he is an active participant at all World Radiocommunication Conferences (WRC) since 1992. He has served on several WRCs as a secretary for the agenda items related to frequency allocations and regulation of radionavigation satellite services and active and passive space sensors. As of WRC-03 he is a secretary of the RES-609 Radionavigation Satellite Service Consultation meeting in the band 1164–1215 MHz responsible for the coordination of new satellite navigation systems. He holds a degree in radio engineering from the Czech Technical University of Prague.

Steven A. Mirmina has worked in international Air and Space Law for more than 20 years and currently teaches a seminar on Space Law at Georgetown University Law Center in Washington, DC. He has lectured widely and has authored numerous articles. In addition, Professor Mirmina has worked as an attorney at NASA since 1999. He has helped negotiate more than 500 international agreements for missions ranging from human space flight and Mars exploration, to Earth science missions and aeronautics research. Additionally, he is also NASA's lead attorney for telecommunications issues. He has received awards from both NASA and the White House for his work. Before joining NASA, he was an associate in the Aviation Law practice of Crowell & Moring. Professor Mirmina received his first LLM from Leiden University and his second from Georgetown. He is a member of Bar of the Supreme Court of the United States.

Rafael Moro-Aguilar obtained his JD from the Universidad Autónoma de Madrid (Spain) and his LLM from the University of Michigan (USA). He is also a graduate of the International Space University. He worked for seven months at the United Nations Office for Outer Space Affairs, assisting in servicing the official sessions of the UN Committee on the Peaceful Uses of Outer Space (UNCOPUOS). He currently works as the head of legal affairs of Orbspace Engineering, a European aerospace consulting firm. He also advises the Spanish Government on international Space Law issues, having been a member of the delegation of Spain to the UNCOPUOS Legal Subcommittee for the past 15 years. Mr Moro-Aguilar has published a number of papers on various Space Law issues, and he often delivers lectures on these topics in the US, Spain, and elsewhere. He is an active member of the International Institute of Space Law (where he serves as Co-Editor of the annual IISL Proceedings) and the Space Law Committee of the International Law Association (ILA).

Sa'id Mosteshar is Director and Professor of International Space Policy and Law at the London Institute of Space Policy and Law (ISPL), a member of the UK Space Leadership Council, and Advisor to the UK Delegation to the UN COPUOS. He is also a member of the International Association for the Advancement of Space Safety (IAASS), the International Institute of Space Law (IISL) and Fellow of the Royal Aeronautical Society (FRAeS). A practicing Barrister and California Attorney, with degrees also in physics and econometrics, he has advised governments, international agencies and major space corporations on legal and policy matters for about 30 years.

Isabelle Reutzel is Head of the Office of the German Aerospace Center (DLR) in Paris, France. As the permanent representative of DLR in France she is a key partner for any matters relating to space, aerospace, transport, energy and security research in the Franco-German field. As member of the German Delegation to the European Space Agency, her work also encompasses the representation of interests of the Federal Republic of Germany. A lawyer by training, having graduated at the Paris XI University, France, and holding a PhD from the University of Marburg, Germany, she has been working for DLR as a legal advisor since 2007. Her main subjects are international relations and matters relating to national and international Space Law. Isabelle Reutzel has authored several peer-reviewed articles and a book on the subject of national space legislation in Europe.

Alexis M. Sáinz is a Senior Associate in the Washington, DC office of Milbank, Tweed, Hadley & McCloy. Her experience includes representing financial institutions, project sponsors, development and multilateral institutions, export credit agencies, private equity firms, hedge funds, satellite operators, communications companies and other project participants in a wide range of structured financings and investment transactions, including project financings, public offerings, high yield debt, investment grade bonds, mergers and acquisitions, financial restructurings, and in negotiating project contracts. Ms. Sainz earned her JD from the George

Washington University Law School. She received her Master's degree in Computer Science from the American University, and her undergraduate degree from Dartmouth College. She has been admitted to practice law in New York and Washington, DC.

Juliana Macedo Scavuzzi dos Santos is the Chair of Space Policy and Law at the Canadian Space Society (CSS), and the Aviation Environmental Specialist at Airports Council International (ACI). She holds an LLM from the Institute of Air and Space Law at McGill University (IASL) and an MSc in Juridical Science from UNIVALI in Brazil. Juliana is a member of the International Institute of Space Law (IISL), the Brazilian Bar Association (OAB), Women in Aerospace (WIA), and the Brazilian Air and Space Law Association (SBDA), where she is a specialist who contributed to draft a proposal of the Brazilian national legislation for space activities and several other projects in space law. She also completed research at the International Telecommunications Union (ITU), where she studied the impact of harmful interference on satellite communications. She has been an observer advisor of the Brazilian delegation for the UN COPUOS legal subcommittee, where she has been actively contributing to specific subjects such as small satellites. Juliana has also contributed to the National Civil Aviation Authority at the Brazilian Delegation of the International Civil Aviation (ICAO), and to the Environment branch at ICAO. She is particularly interested in developing countries' needs, international cooperation, global governance, UN specialized agencies, harmful interference, small satellites, national space laws, sustainability, greenhouse gas emissions, environmental protection, climate change, aviation and environmental law.

Lesley Jane Smith was appointed Professor of International and European law at the Leuphana University Lüneburg, Germany in 1996, and is a Visiting Professor of Space Law at the University of Strathclyde, Glasgow, and a regular contributor to space programmes with the International Space University and the London Institute of Space Law and Policy. She has been admitted to practice in the UK and Germany, and a partner in the law firm Weber-Steinhaus & Smith in Bremen. Lesley Jane has an extensive command of the field of national and international Space Law, including developments within Europe. She is an expert on commercial space activities, particularly complex contracts, IP licensing, including in the context of Earth observation, as well as procurement. Lesley Jane is on the editorial board of the Brill series Studies in Space Law and a member of the editorial board of the *Journal of Air and Space Law*. She is a corresponding member of the International Academy of Astronautics (IAA), a board member of the International Institute of Space Law (IISL) and a former board member of Women in Aerospace Europe (WIA-E. In 2014, she was appointed General Counsel to the International Astronautical Federation in Paris (IAF).

Cassandra Steer is the Wainwright Fellow at the McGill Faculty of Law. Formerly she was an Erin J.C. Arsenault Postdoctoral Fellow at the McGill Institute of Air and Space Law, and the Executive Director of the Centre for Research at the same institute. Her main research interest is the application of the law of armed conflict to military uses of outer space. Prior to this, she was a Junior Professor at the University of Amsterdam in the Netherlands from 2006–2014, teaching criminal law, international criminal law, public international law, and legal research methods. She holds a BA (Philosophy) from the University of New South Wales, undergraduate and LLM degrees in Dutch Law and International Law from the University of Amsterdam, and a PhD in International Criminal Law. She has interned at the International Criminal Court under Judge Navi Pillay in 2004, and has been a Visiting Researcher at universities in Argentina, Canada, Germany and the US, where she was also a Fulbright Scholar. Currently she is the member for

Canada on the International Law Association Space Law Committee, the Secretary of the IAF Space Security Committee, Executive Director of Women in International Security Canada, and a member of the International Institute of Space Law, Women in Aerospace, the NATO Association of Canada, and the International Society for Military Law and the Law of War.

Jinyuan Su holds a BA in English Language and Literature, an MA in Mass Communication, and a PhD in International Law from Xi'an Jiaotong University, China. He is currently an Associate Professor and Assistant Dean for International Affairs at Xi'an Jiaotong University School of Law. He was an Erin J.C. Arsenault Fellow at the McGill Institute of Air and Space Law between 2014 and 2015, and a visiting research fellow at the Lauterpacht Centre for International Law, University of Cambridge between 2009 and 2010. Dr. Su's research interests lie in outer space law, international aviation law, and the law of the sea. He is a frequent expert in the Chinese delegation to the annual sessions of the UNCOPUOS and its Legal Subcommittee. Dr. Su is a member of the Governance Group of the Space Security Index (SSI), an expert for the project of McGill Manual on International Law Applicable to Military Uses of Outer Space (MILAMOS), a lead drafter for the McGill project of Global Space Governance, and a member (2016–2018) of the Global Future Council on Space Technologies of the World Economic Forum (WEF).

Mark J. Sundahl is a Professor of Law and the Associate Dean for Administration at Cleveland State University's Cleveland-Marshall College of Law where he teaches International Business Transactions and Space Law. Professor Sundahl is a leading expert on the law of outer space and focuses primarily on the business, legal, and policy issues arising from the recent increase in private space activity. He currently serves as a member of the Commercial Space Transportation Advisory Committee (COMSTAC) which advises the Federal Aviation Administration regarding new regulations governing private space activity. The Department of State appointed him as an Advisor to the US delegation to the UN Committee on the Peaceful Uses of Outer Space (COPUOS). He is also a Member (and former Assistant Secretary) of the International Institute of Space Law.

Caroline Thro is currently working for the Launcher and HQ Procurement Division, Procurement Department of the European Space Agency (ESA). Previously, underwent four-month Traineeship in the Legal Department of ESA dealing with Intellectual Property issues in the Institutional Law Division. Afterwards she worked for three months in the Legal Department of the European Aviation Safety Agency (EASA) in Cologne. She graduated 2014 in Space Law at the University Paris South (Faculté Jean Monnet) with a master's in *Droit des activités spatiales et des télécommunications* supervised by Professor Philippe Achilleas. The same year she won the European Round of the Manfred Lachs Moot Court Competition in Wrocław (Poland), dealing with harmful interferences in Outer Space and was Semi Finalist of the World Finals of this same Competition in Toronto (Canada) taking place in the framework of the IAC. She has recently become a member of the Space Law and Policy Group of the Space Generation Advisory Council.

Olga A. Volynskaya is Chief International Law Counsel of the Federal Space Agency of Russia (ROSCOSMOS), a Research Scientist of the Russian Foreign Trade Academy of the Ministry of Economic Development of the Russian Federation, a Permanent member of the Russian delegation to the UN COPUOS, its Scientific and Technical and Legal Subcommittees. She studied international law at the Russian Foreign Trade Academy and the

Moscow State Institute of International Relations of the Ministry of Foreign Affairs of the Russian Federation (MGIMO). She holds a Master degree in EU law of MGIMO and defended her PhD thesis, entitled "Legal aspects of responsibility and liability in the area of space activities", at the Russian Foreign Trade Academy under the supervision of Professor Gennady Zhukov She was a grant scholar of the President of the Russian Federation for distinctive scientific research and achievement. She is the author of 32 scientific publications on various issues of Space Law in the leading Russian and foreign journals in the area of International Law, Space Law and foreign trade. She is the co-author of the Russian treatise "Space Law" edited by Professor Gennady Zhukov and Professor Aslan Abashidze (published in 2014).

Guoyu Wang is Associate Professor, Deputy Director, Institute of Space Law, Beijing Institute of Technology (BIT), China, an Academy Senior Fellow of Chatham House, UK (2014–), a Space Security Consultant of UNIDIR(2015). He has served as a Chinese delegate to the United Nations Committee on the Peaceful use of Outer Space (UNCOPUOS), and on the Inter-governmental Space Debris Coordination Committee (IADC), as well as a Chinese expert on the Long-term Sustainability for Outer Space Activities Working Group of UNCOPUOS. Dr. Wang's expertise includes legal and political analysis of space security issues, including, arms control in outer space, space debris mitigation and remediation, cyber security in outer space, space resources exploitation and space crisis management, space traffic management and space global governance.

Yun Zhao studied at the China University of Political Science and Law in Beijing (LLM and LLB), Leiden University (LLM) and the Erasmus University Rotterdam (PhD). He is currently Head of Department of Law, Professor of Law and Director for the Center for Chinese Law at the Faculty of Law of the University of Hong Kong. He is listed as an arbitrator in several international arbitration commissions. He is also a founding Council Member of Hong Kong Internet Forum (HKIF), a Member of International Institute of Space Law at Paris, a Member of Asia Pacific Law Association and Beijing International Law Society. He sits on the editorial boards of several SSCI journals, including *Hong Kong Law Journal* (as China Law editor), *Journal of East Asia and International Law* (as Executive Editor). He was winner of the 2006 Prof. Dr. I.H.Ph. Diederiks-Verschoor Award from International Institute of Space Law in France, the first winner of the Isa Diederiks-Verschoor Prize in the Netherlands, and also the first winner of the SATA Prize from the Foundation of Development of International Law in Asia (DILA). He has published widely on various topics, in particular Dispute Resolution and Space Law. His recent publications include *Dispute Resolution in Electronic Commerce* (Martinus Nijhoff, 2005), *Liberalization of Electronic Commerce and Law* (Peking University Press, 2005), *Space Commercialization and the Development of Space Law* (Intellectual Property Press, 2008), *Mediation Practice and Skills* (Tsinghua University Press, 2011), *National Space Legislation in China: An Overview of the Current Situation and Outlook for the Future* (Brill, 2015).

Preface

Space Law is robustly changing and expanding, especially at the national level. More laws and regulations are being adopted and adapted by space-faring nations related to activities in outer space. More regulatory bodies are being created, while more regulatory diversity (from public law to private law) is being instituted as increasing and innovative activities are undertaken by private entities which employ new technologies and business initiatives. The 2015 Space Report of the Space Foundation reported that "the global space economy grew by 9% in 2014, reaching a total of $330 billion worldwide. Together, commercial space activities made up 76% of the global space economy, and grew 9.7% in 2014." Consequently, the market for expertise and educational sources in Space Law is expanding.

The McGill University Faculty of Law has spearheaded trans-systemic studies in legal education. Benefiting from this unique approach to legal education, the Institute and Centre for Research of Air and Space Law has over the course of several decades published numerous studies, reports, and compendia, as well as the *Annals of Air and Space Law*, the prominent peer-reviewed journal in the domain. With our interest in pursuing research and dissemination of the knowledge of Space Law, and on the invitation of Routledge in 2014, we undertook this *Handbook of Space Law* to be published by one of the world's leading publishers.

The *Routledge Handbook of Space Law* incorporates a comprehensive analysis of general principles of international Space Law, international law of space applications, and national Space Laws and regulations. Each chapter includes law applicable to the subject-matter followed by, where appropriate, an examination of regulations, jurisprudence, and policy perspectives. Conventional international law is pervasive in Space Law and is incorporated into a number of major multilateral treaties (e.g., the 1967 Outer Space Treaty, the 1968 Rescue Agreement, the 1972 Liability Convention, the 1975 Registration Convention, and the 1979 Moon Agreement as well as the Charter of the United Nations, the ITU Constitution, the ITU Convention, the ITU Radio Regulations, the Partial Test Ban Treaty). Not only the international conventions but also State practice and customary international law are discussed. States implement their international obligations through domestic laws that create national space regulatory administrations that, in turn, promulgate regulations. All of these bodies of law and institutions of law making are discussed in this *Handbook*.

Though some duplication cannot be avoided, the *Routledge Handbook of Space Law* is made meaningfully unique and different from existing publications, especially those that appeared since the initiation of this book project in 2014. It is recognized that there are some other books in the market on Space Law. However, none covers the existing state of knowledge of both international law and national law applicable to space activities in one volume, and nor in an intertwined manner as is envisioned in this *Handbook*. Thus, the uniqueness of the *Handbook* lies in its approach to integrate the multi-dimensional nature of Space Law, which will make it particularly valuable to readers, especially to those engaged in legal practice and in the highly globalized space industry.

The topics covered in this *Handbook* are essentially based on the contents of the Institute's three graduate level Space Law courses, except two subjects (i.e., international space stations and national regulation of satellite communications) that could not be included in order to keep the *Handbook* within the page limits imposed by the publisher. The contents of the courses are regularly revised, updated, and expanded for teaching and research purposes. We believe this to be a valuable reference work providing a comprehensive and comparative overview of Space Law, including contemporary and emerging areas of law, regulation, and public policy in Space Law. This *Handbook* is both practical and theoretical in scope, and should be useful to professors, students (particularly postgraduate students), researchers, lawyers, government and corporate officials, and policy makers. The *Handbook* includes contributions from carefully invited and selected academic scholars and practicing lawyers from around the world. We believe the essays included in this *Handbook* will contribute to the dissemination of and discussion on the subject-matters covered.

This *Handbook* is a labor of love. All author royalties to the book are donated to a fund for the George S. And Ann K. Robinson Space Law Graduate Fellowship in Space Law at the Institute of Air Space Law of McGill University, Montreal, Canada. We express our sincere and special gratitude to the authors of the papers included in this *Handbook* for their intellectual contribution. In editing their papers, we tried to standardize writing and referencing styles, while respecting their individual preferences and without compromising their views. The authors are exclusively responsible for the contents and quality of their papers as well as propriety of any material used in this *Handbook*. The contents of this *Handbook* do not represent the views or opinions of the organizations with which we or each of the authors are affiliated.

Dr. M. Tanveer Ahmad, Andrea J. Harrington and Dr. Michael Chatzipanagiotis provided invaluable assistance in proofreading the texts and in the editing of the papers. We are grateful for the time and effort they devoted to this project.

Ram S. Jakhu & Paul Stephen Dempsey
Co-Editors

Part I
General principles of international space law

1

Sources and law-making processes relating to space activities

Cassandra Steer

Introduction: contextualizing space law

While most people are familiar with the five core space treaties, there is much more to international space law than these five instruments. Because space law is embedded in the larger system of public international law, much of "general international law" applies to space and space activities. Furthermore, as discussed in the introductory chapter, space law is made up of national laws which interact with the international system. In order to understand the larger *corpus juris spatialis,* or body of space law, it is necessary to understand its place in both the international system and the various national systems. Since a comparative analysis of domestic laws is undertaken in Part III of this book, the intention here is to contextualize the different sources of space law and the different law-making processes.

Sources of law can be defined as the systems or processes that allow law to come into being.[1] If a rule or norm is attested by one of the recognized sources, then it may be accepted as part of the system of law.[2] If it cannot be attested by one of these sources, then it is a mere assertion, and cannot be binding on any international actor. Thus, understanding the doctrine of sources in public international law is necessary in order to clarify what is binding in space law and what is mere interpretation or assertion. It is also important to understand the relationship between national space laws and sources of international space law.

Law-making processes in the domestic context

In domestic legal systems, the sources of law are easily recognizable: primary legislation is passed according to the processes prescribed in the constitution of a State, and by the legislative bodies. Domestic space laws are applicable within a State's jurisdiction; for example, in the United States (US), the Federal Aviation Authority (FAA) has been granted certain powers by the federal government to issue launch licenses to US companies as well as to foreign companies

---

1   Ram S. Jakhu & Steven Freeland, *The Sources of International Space Law* (Beijing, 2013) at 461.
2   James Crawford, *Brownlie's Principles of Public International Law* (Oxford: Oxford University Press, 2012) at 20.

wishing to use US launch services. However, even though its legislation may have some effects on foreign companies or on relations between the US and other States, the US cannot legislate extra-territorially or internationally. Every State is sovereign, meaning no State can bind another with its legislation. This is both a limit on national sovereignty and also a protection of it, and, apart from being strongly asserted by States, it is also guaranteed in Article 2(7) of the Charter of the United Nations (UN).[3]

Law-making processes in the international context

In international law, there are no constitutional law-making mechanisms, and no centralized law-making powers.[4] It may therefore not be obvious how law comes into being or who is authorized to make law. In the following section, attention will be paid to each of the traditionally recognized sources of law.

The traditional understanding of international law is that the content and normative force of international law are an expression of the will of States.[5] International law is binding because States have consented to it through the creation and recognition of various obligations and rights. This consensual basis is, for most governments, what gives international law its legitimacy.[6] However in recent decades there are more and more non-State actors, such as international organizations, corporate entities, and individuals, who play an increasingly important role in the international plane in many areas of law, e.g., human rights, environmental law, the law of armed conflict, international investment and trade law. These areas of law are also relevant for space activities. International law today is therefore recognized as an order governing international and transnational relations, including non-State actors.

While a formal understanding of the law-making processes in international law still recognizes States as the only legitimate lawmakers, some theories of law also accept that the law itself can come into being through the participation of non-State actors.[7] One example in space law is the highly influential role played by commercial and private entities as 'sector members' of the International Telecommunications Union (ITU), where regulations are made regarding the registration and protection of orbital slots and radio frequencies.[8] Some would argue that the influence of non-State actors on the content of the regulations is evidence of the fact that international law can be formed beyond the strict limits of State will. Conversely,

---

3   Article 2(7) of the *Charter* provides:

> Nothing contained in the present Charter shall authorize the United Nations to intervene in matters which are essentially within the domestic jurisdiction of any state or shall require the Members to submit such matters to settlement under the present Charter …

4   Crawford, *supra* note 2 at 20.
5   *Ibid.* at 13.
6   Alan Boyle & Christine Chinkin, *The Making of International Law* (Oxford University Press, 2007) at 25.
7   Armin von Bogdandy & Ingo Venzke, eds, *International Judicial Lawmaking, Beiträge zum ausländischen öffentlichen Recht und Völkerrecht* (Berlin, Heidelberg: Springer 2012); Boyle & Chinkin, *supra* note 5; Jean D'Aspremont, "International Law-Making by Non-State Actors: Changing the Model or Putting the Phenomenon into Perspective?" in M Noortmann & C Ryngaet, eds, *Non-State Actors Dynamics in International Law – From Law-Takers to Lawmakers* (Ashgate, 2010); Rosalyn Higgins, *Problems and Process: International Law and How We Use It* (Oxford University Press, 1995); W Michael Reisman, "Theory about Law: Jurisprudence for a Free Society" (1998) 108 Yale Law Journal 935.
8   See Article 3(3) *Constitution of the International Telecommunication Union*, 22 December 1992, 1825 UNTS 331 [*ITU Constitution*].

others would contend that the role of private entities is merely influential, and that the regulations are only binding because they come into being through the Radio Regulations promulgated by the formal processes in the ITU, which was established by State will and consent.

In order to understand this dynamic properly, the traditional sources of international law will be discussed next, with reference to the kinds of space law found in these sources.

Traditional sources of international law

Article 38 of the Statute of the International Court of Justice

Although the international legal order lacks any central constitutional mechanisms, the UN Charter and the Statute of the International Court of Justice (ICJ) are both considered to be constitutive documents. They were drafted immediately following World War II when the UN was conferred certain powers in order to fulfill its primary purpose of promoting and protecting international peace and security.[9] The ICJ is the "principal judicial organ" of the UN,[10] and was established to offer a peaceful means of dispute resolution between States so as to avoid resorting to sanctions or the use of force.[11] The ICJ Statute was primarily written as a document organizing the composition, functioning and jurisdiction of the Court, and Article 38 directs the Court as to what sources it may apply in determining the content of international law.[12] Nonetheless it has come to represent the identification of sources of international law in general; even if it was not intended to "codify" such sources,[13] it is generally seen as the authoritative list of formal sources of binding law.[14]

Article 38 of the ICJ Statute provides:

1. The Court, whose function is to decide in accordance with international law such disputes as are submitted to it, shall apply:
    a. international conventions, whether general or particular, establishing rules expressly recognized by the contesting States;
    b. international custom, as evidence of a general practice accepted as law;
    c. the general principles of law recognized by civilized nations;
    d. subject to the provisions of Article 59, judicial decisions and the teachings of the most highly qualified publicists of the various nations, as subsidiary means for the determination of rules of law.

---

9   Art 1 UN Charter, 1945.
10 Art 1 Statute of the International Court of Justice, 1945.
11 *Ibid.*, Art 36(3).
12 *ICJ Statute, supra* note 10, art 38.
13 Crawford, *supra* note 2 at 22. Article 38 was based on the almost identical article found in the statute of the predecessor of the ICJ, the Permanent Court of International Justice (PCIJ), which had been established by the League of Nations, but was disbanded with the coming of the World War II. See Shabtai Rosenne, "International Court of Justice" in *Max Planck Encyclopedia of Public International Law,* MPEPIL 34 (Oxford University Press, 2006) at 1.
14 While this is the standard view, not all scholars agree that it is an exhaustive list, especially given the increasingly active role of non-State actors on the international plane, and the increased complexity of relationships between them. See e.g. Boyle & Chinkin, *supra* note 5; Higgins, *supra* note 6; Reisman, *supra* note 6; Cassandra Steer, "Non-State Actors in International Criminal Law" in Jean D'Aspremont, ed, *Non-State Participants in the International Legal Order* (Oxford: Routledge, 2011).

Paragraph 1 lists three primary sources, followed by two subsidiary sources under clause (d). Each of the sources listed will be discussed in turn here, with reference to their relevance for space law.

Treaties

Treaties are the first, and arguably 'strongest', source of law listed in Article 38. Agreements, conventions or protocols are all legally binding treaties, and there is no legal difference between any of these terms.[15] The Vienna Convention on the Law of Treaties (VCLT) governs the application and working of all treaties, and it is therefore also applicable to international space law.[16]

International space law relies heavily on its treaties.[17] The most important treaties are the five core treaties, namely the 1967 Outer Space Treaty,[18] the 1968 Rescue Agreement,[19] the 1972 Liability Convention,[20] the 1974 Registration Convention,[21] and the 1979 Moon Agreement,[22] as well as the UN Charter, the 1963 Partial Test Ban Treaty,[23] the VCLT, and the 2010 ITU Constitution and Convention.[24] There are also numerous treaties which do not specifically deal with outer space, but which will come into play with respect to specific space activities, such as the treaties governing the law of armed conflict and prohibiting specific weapons, trade and investment treaties, and human rights treaties.

Treaties act as international contracts between States. They are binding because States explicitly consent to their terms.[25] Usually the terms and provisions of a treaty are negotiated at a convention and is then opened for signature. Often, however, the signature itself is not enough; a State must also ratify the treaty, for instance by enacting it as one of its national laws. For some treaties, although it might be signed by States at a convention, it may not come into legal force until a designated number of States have also ratified it.[26] This is the reason why the 1996 Comprehensive Test Ban Treaty,[27] which was adopted to fill the *lacunae* of the 1963 Partial Test Ban Treaty, has never come into force: although 159 States have ratified it, this is not

---

15 Article 2(1)(a) VCLT.
16 1969 Vienna Convention on the Law of Treaties (Hereinafter VCLT).
17 Ram Jakhu & Steven Freeland, *supra* note 1 at 463.
18 *Treaty on Principles Governing the Activities of States in the Exploration and Use of Outer Space, Including the Moon and Other Celestial Bodies*, 27 January 1967, 610 UNTS 205 [*Outer Space Treaty*].
19 *Agreement on the Rescue of Astronauts, the Return of Astronauts and the Return of Objects Launched into Outer Space*, 22 April 1968, 672 UNTS 119 [*Rescue Agreement*].
20 *Convention on the International Liability for Damage Caused by Space Objects*, 29 March 1972, 961 UNTS 187 [*Liability Convention*].
21 *Convention on Registration of Objects Launched into Outer Space*, 14 January 1975, 1023 UNTS 15 [*Registration Convention*].
22 *Agreement Governing the Activities of States on the Moon and Other Celestial Bodies*, 18 December 1979, 1363 UNTS 3 [*Moon Agreement*].
23 *Treaty Banning Nuclear Weapon Tests in the Atmosphere, in Outer Space and Under Water*, 5 August 1963, 480 UNTS 43 [*Partial Test Ban Treaty*].
24 ITU *Constitution*, *supra* note 8; *Convention of the International Telecommunication Union*, 22 December 1992, 1825 UNTS 390 [*ITU Convention*].
25 Article 11 VCLT.
26 Articles 2(1)(b) and 14 VCLT.
27 *Comprehensive Nuclear-Test-Ban Treaty*, 10 September 1996 (not in force). To view the text of the treaty, see Preparatory Commission for the Comprehensive Nuclear-Test-Ban Treaty (CTBTO), "The Treaty", online: CTBTO www.ctbto.org/fileadmin/content/treaty/treaty_text.pdf.

enough according to the terms of the 1996 Treaty.[28] On the other hand, as soon as a State has signed a treaty, even if it has not ratified it, the State is still obliged to refrain from acts that would defeat the object and the purpose of the treaty.[29] This is often seen as an extension of the rule known as *pacta sunt servanda*, i.e. every State which is bound by a treaty must perform its obligations in good faith.[30] Such good faith must apply from the moment of signature, since this is an international signal of the will of the State to become bound.

A treaty may never bind a third State without its consent.[31] For this reason, the Liability Convention is only applicable to the 100 States that are parties to it, and the Moon Agreement is considered to be only marginally successful, since only 16 States have become parties, with a further four signatories which have not yet ratified it.[32]

If the terms of a treaty allow it, an international organization – for example the UN, the European Union or the African Union – may also sign a treaty. None of the five space law treaties allows this, however the Liability Convention and the Registration Convention may apply to international organizations if they accept the terms of these treaties by declaration.[33] The European Space Agency (ESA) and EUTELSAT have made such declarations with respect to the Liability Convention, and the ESA, EUTELSAT, and EUMETSAT have made declarations with respect to the Registration Convention.[34]

If a State acts in breach of a treaty provision, any other State that is injured by this may demand cessation of the activities, as well as an apology or reparation.[35] If the injurious State fails to respond, the injured State may bring a case before the ICJ. Under Article VI of the Outer Space Treaty, a State is responsible for all national space activities taking place under its jurisdiction. This means that even if a commercial entity acts in breach of a treaty, the State of registry of that entity can be held responsible for that breach. Most of the obligations under the five space treaties can also be considered obligations *erga omnes*, i.e. obligations towards the international community as a whole. In the case of breach of such obligations, any State that is a party to the treaty may bring a claim, without having to prove injury.[36] This may be particularly important in the future as commercial and private entities begin to increase their activities, such as mining asteroids or creating space habitats, where there may be risks of breaching some of the fundamental principles of the Outer Space Treaty.

---

28   Ram Jakhu & Steven Freeland, *supra* note 1 at 464 See www.ctbto.org/fileadmin/content/treaty/treaty_text.pdf (last accessed 13 June 2015). To view the current status of the treaty, see UN, online: UNTC treaties.un.org/pages/showDetails.aspx?objid=0800000280049f7f.
29   Article 18 VCLT.
30   Article 26 VCLT. This is also recognized as a general principle that pre-existed the VCLT.
31   The *pacta tertiis* rule, Article 34 VCLT.
32   *Status of International Agreements Relating To Activities In Outer Space As At 1 January 2015*, A/AC.105/2015/CRP.8, online: www.unoosa.org/oosa/en/SpaceLaw/treatystatus/index.html.
33   Article XXII section 1, 1972 Convention on International Liability for Damage Caused by Space Objects (Liability Convention); Article VII, 1974 Convention on Registration of Objects Launched into Outer Space (Registration Convention).
34   Francis Lyall & Paul B Larsen, *Space Law: A Treatise* (Ashgate, 2009) at 106. See also *Status of International Agreements Relating To Activities In Outer Space As At 1 January 2015*, *supra* note 37.
35   Article 42 (a) *Draft Articles on the Responsibility of States for Internationally Wrongful Acts, Report of the ILC on the Work of its Fifty-third Session, UN GAOR, 56th Sess, Supp. No. 10, p. 43, UN Doc A/56/10 (2001) (ILC Articles on State Responsibility)*.
36   Article 42 (b) ILC Articles on State Responsibility.

Customary law

The second source listed in Article 38 of the ICJ Statute is that of international custom, "as evidence of a general practice accepted as law". There are two elements to customary law: there must be evidence of State practice (the objective element), and this practice must be "accepted as law" (the subjective element). This second element is also known as the requirement of *opinio juris*: a State behaving in a certain way must do so according to a belief that it is bound by law to follow that behavior, before this can be recognized as customary law rather than just a habit or tradition.[37] This subjective element is difficult to prove, since it refers to the "belief" held by an abstract entity, the State. However it is possible to resort to statements made by those representing the State in diplomatic matters or internal political representation. If there is a significant number of States disagreeing with or objecting to such a norm, then it cannot be recognized as custom due to lack of sufficient *opinio juris*.[38]

There is general agreement that many of the principles contained in the Outer Space Treaty are also customary in nature, since they hail from the 1963 UN Declaration of Legal Principles Governing Activities of States in the Exploration and Use of Outer Space (Space Principles Declaration),[39] and these principles themselves have been recognized as customary law.[40] This is not to say that all UN General Assembly resolutions are customary law. These resolutions are not binding and while a resolution may be a reflection of the aspirations and political stances of the countries that vote in favor of it, that is not a reflection of *opinio juris*. More will be said about this below in the section on soft law.

Since many principles of the Outer Space Treaty are considered binding as a matter of customary law, they are also binding on States that have not signed or ratified the Treaty. Whereas treaties are binding in a contractual sense only on States which have signed them, customary law has a broader reach, since it comes into being as a slow process of acquiescence and agreement among all States over time with respect to a specific norm.

One example of customary law in space activities is the emergence of a right of passage into outer space, or the norm that it is acceptable to traverse through the airspace of another State when launching an object into space, without first seeking permission from that State. In the earliest years of space launches, this was the practice that emerged, and it has continued even as the number of States launching and the number of launches per year have continued to increase.[41] Because customary law usually takes a long time to crystallize, it may be questionable as to whether such a form of "instant custom" is entirely legitimate, but the fact that there are no objections may support the claim that this is a recognized right.[42]

The only way for a State to escape the binding nature of a particular norm under customary law is to take an explicit position as a "persistent objector".[43] For instance, the ICJ determined that there was a customary 10-mile rule with respect to marine bays, but that this was not binding on Norway, since it had consistently and publicly objected to this norm, and thus had

37 *North Sea Continental Shelf (Federal Republic of Germany/Netherlands)*, 20 February 1969.
38 Crawford, *supra* note 2 at 25; Boyle & Chinkin, *supra* note 5 at 116.
39 UN GA Res 1962 (XVIII).
40 Lyall & Larsen, *supra* note 24 at 48.
41 Ram Jakhu & Steven Freeland, *supra* note 1 at 466; Manfred Lachs, *The Law of Outer Space: An Experience in Contemporary Law-Making, Reissued on the Occasion of the 50th Anniversary of the International Institute of Space Law*, Re-Issued ed. (Martinus Nijhoff Publishers, 2010) at 126.
42 Lachs, *supra* note 31 at 126. See also the dissenting opinion of Judge Manfred Lachs in the Northsea Continental Shelf Case, ICJ Rep 3, 230; Lyall & Larsen, *supra* note 24 at 161.
43 A "persistent objector" is a State that consistently and persistently lets it be known, through official statements, that it does not agree with a particular rule. See Crawford, *supra* note 2 at 28.

proved itself to be a persistent objector.[44] A single persistent objector cannot veto the emergence of a customary norm; all that the objecting State does is ensure that a specific norm does not apply to it, even while it applies to all other States. Some would argue that such objection in fact undermines *opinio juris,* others maintain that it allows customary norms to emerge while at the same time protecting States against majoritarian tendencies in international law-making.[45]

General principles

The wording under Article 38(c) of the ICJ Statute is very much a product of its time, since it references general principles of law "recognized by civilized nations". Clearly, to make a distinction between 'civilized' and 'uncivilized' nations today would be an anachronism. Even at the time that the Statute was drafted there were voices of dissent, since the intention was to exclude non-Western States, meaning that colonialism ruled the making of international law.[46] This aspect of the text can, therefore, be disregarded.[47]

The intention of including 'general principles' among the sources of international law was to ensure there were no gaps where treaties or custom did not provide clear rules.[48] However they are always by definition general in nature, and are therefore unlikely to offer clear and concrete rules of behavior, or specific rights or obligations.

The drafters of the Statute of the Permanent Court of International Justice – the predecessor to the ICJ and upon which the ICJ Statute was based – had in mind principles such as good faith.[49] This principle is fundamental to the interpretation and application of the space treaties, and to the use and exploration of outer space in general. The underlying principles of the Outer Space Treaty, that the exploration and use of outer space must be "for the benefit and in the interests of all countries", and that space is the province of all humankind,[50] necessitate good faith on the part of all parties in space activities.[51] States must also act in good faith as part of the rather broad obligation in Article IX of the Outer Space Treaty, to conduct their space activities with "due regard to the corresponding interests" of other States.[52] If there were ever a contention between States as to whether this had in fact been fulfilled, "good faith" would be key.

The PCIJ and the ICJ have applied various other general principles in cases before them, many of which may be relevant for future disputes regarding space activities. These include: the

---

44   Fisheries (*UK v. Norway*) ICJ Rep 1951 at 131; Alexander Orakhelashvili, *The Interpretation of Acts and Rules in Public International Law* (Oxford University Press, 2008) at 94.
45   Crawford, *supra* note 2 at 28.
46   Ian Brownlie, *The Rule of Law in International Affairs: International Law at the Fiftieth Anniversary of the United Nations* (Martinus Nijhoff Publishers, 1998); H. Charlesworth, "Law-making and Sources" in: *Cambridge Companion to International Law* 187 (Cambridge University Press, 2012) at 196.
47   It must be noted, however, that when ascertaining general principles, judges and authors still often fail to look beyond the dominant Western legal regimes. See e.g. B. Chimni, "*Third World Approaches to International Law: A Manifesto*", 8 International Community Law Review 3 (2006).
48   Giorgio Gaja, "General principles of law" *Max Planck Encyclopedia of Public International Law* (Oxford University Press, 2013) MPEPIL 1410, online: http://campus.unibo.it/180450/13/EPIL_General_Principles_of_Law.pdf at para 21; Malcolm N Shaw, *International Law* (Cambridge University Press, 2014) at 70; Alain Pellet, "Article 38" *Statute of the International Court of Justice, A Commentary* (Oxford University Press, 2006) at 686.
49   Charlesworth, *supra* note 54 at 196.
50   *Outer Space Treaty*, *supra* note 23, art I.
51   Ram S. Jakhu & Steven Freeland, *supra* note 1 at 468.
52   *Outer Space Treaty*, *supra* note 23, art IX.

fundamental principle of humanity;[53] the principle that no State should knowingly allow its territory to be used by others contrary to the rights of third States;[54] and the principle of self-determination.[55] Other general principles of a more procedural nature applied by these courts include: the determination that an administrative tribunal makes binding decisions the same way other judicial tribunals do (*res judicata*);[56] that if an injured State is unable to provide direct proof of the injury, indirect evidence, such as inferences from facts and circumstantial evidence, is admissible;[57] and that if a party is accused of not fulfilling an obligation, this cannot be held against it where the accusing party prevented the former from doing so.[58]

The question is often raised whether such general principles must be of domestic or international origin.[59] In the list of examples above, all of those in the first group of fundamental principles were determined to be principles of *international* law, whereas those in the second group of more procedural principles were all determined based on their existence in various domestic systems. While either heritage is possible, caution should be exercised before entering a comparative law analysis of domestic laws in order to extract a general principle. National jurisdictions differ due to a diversity of legal traditions, and it could be prejudicial to assert that, because a certain norm appears in a group of jurisdictions, it is "general", when there may be many other jurisdictions which do not share the same norm.[60]

This is important with respect to distilling general principles from national space legislation. Although the work of the UN Committee on the Peaceful Uses of Outer Space (UNCOPUOS) Legal Subcommittee Working Group on National Legislation has provided a very useful comparative table of domestic space legislation, finding commonalities among a relatively small group of nations does not necessarily reflect a general principle.[61]

Judgments and case law – a subsidiary source

Article 38(1)(d) of the ICJ Statute refers to Article 59, according to which judgments of the ICJ are only binding on the parties to the specific case, and do not have any effect of *stare decisis*, which is familiar in common law systems; that is, they do not bind the ICJ nor any other courts to decide the same in any future decisions. At the same time, decisions of the ICJ and of other international tribunals, such as the Permanent Court of Arbitration (PCA), are often referred to as authoritative. The ICJ is recognized *de facto* as authoritatively clarifying and even creating international law.[62] This authority is granted due to the final clause of Article 38(1), according to which reference may be made to judicial decisions wherever treaties, custom, and general principles do not provide a clear answer. This case law is particularly important in areas of

53 *Corfu Channel Case (United Kingdom v. Albania)*, ICJ Decision of 9 April 1949. [1949] ICJ Rep. 4.
54 Ibid.
55 *Western Sahara* Advisory Opinion, 16 October 1975, ICJ Rep 12, ICGJ 214 (ICJ 1975).
56 *Effect of Awards of Compensation Made by the U.N. Administrative Tribunal*, Advisory Opinion, 1954 I.C.J. 47 (July 13)
57 *Corfu Channel Case, supra* note 61 at 22.
58 *Case Concerning the Factory at Chorzów*, [*Germany v. Poland*] Jurisdiction, Judgment, PCIJ Series A No. 9, ICGJ 247 (PCIJ 1927), 26th July 1927, Permanent Court of International Justice.
59 Gaja, *supra* note 36 at 1; Charlesworth, *supra* note 54 at 196.
60 Crawford, *supra* note 2 at 35; Charlesworth, *supra* note 54 at 196.
61 Diane Howard, "Distilling General Principles of International Space Law" in *2013 Proceedings of the International Institute of Space Law* (The Hague: Eleven International Publishing, 2014) 451 at 460.
62 Anthony D'Amato, "Human Rights as Part of Customary International Law: A Plea for Change of Paradigms" (1995) 25 Georgia Journal of International and Comparative Law 47; Anthony D'Amato, "The concept of human rights in international law" (1982) Columbia Law Rev 1110.

international law which have relied upon judicial decisions to explain the terms of treaties, such as human rights, the law of armed conflict, international criminal law, and international trade and investment law.

The general understanding of clause (d) is that it refers to decisions of international courts and tribunals, and not domestic courts. However, in the search for custom and general principles, the ICJ and many international criminal tribunals have sometimes looked to domestic case law.[63] Thus the role of domestic case law may be more important than it once was. Nonetheless, it must be clarified that domestic judicial decisions on *national* space legislation cannot amount to a source of international law, since this legislation is only applicable within a national legal system, and will differ greatly from jurisdiction to jurisdiction. It is for this reason that domestic judicial decisions regarding national laws are also unlikely to amount to evidence of custom or a general principle.[64]

To date, there have been no international judicial decisions regarding contentious application of the space treaties. There was a potential for this to occur when radioactive debris from the USSR Cosmos 954 satellite landed on Canadian territory, and Canada made a claim to the USSR through diplomatic notes under the Liability Convention. Ultimately, however, these two States settled out of court.[65] Judicial decisions are therefore currently not the most influential sources in the direct development of space law. Indirectly, however, there are many judicial decisions which are of importance due to the fact that other areas of international law are applicable in space, such as environmental law, the law on the use of force, the law of armed conflict, and so on.[66]

"The most highly regarded publicists" – a subsidiary source or something more?

Possibly the most controversial of all the formal sources of international law, is the opinion of "the most highly regarded publicists", listed in Article 38(1)(d) as a subsidiary means for determining the law. In the French text of the ICJ Statute, the term *la doctrine* is used, which perhaps reflects the fact that doctrine is considered an important part of domestic law in the European civil law tradition, and this emanates from authoritative scholars. In the debates during the drafting of the Statute of the PCIJ, there was quite a difference of opinion as to whether this should be included. Some States considered doctrine to be recognized as a source of international law, while others considered it as a tool in determining custom. Another group insisted that the writings of scholars had no place in determining the law, arguing it would leave judges too much freedom to be politically selective of authors in order to support a given assertion.[67]

---

63   Cassandra Steer, "Legal Transplants or Legal Patchworking? The Creation of International Criminal Law as a Pluralistic Body of Law" in *Pluralism in International Criminal Law* (Oxford University Press, 2014).

64   This can also be problematic in other fields of law where custom has been asserted based on domestic case law, see e.g. Cassandra Steer, "A Valid International Problem vs. A Valid International Law: Shifting Modes of Responsibility in International Criminal Law" in Marianne Hirsche Ballin *et al.*, eds, *Shifting Responsibilities in Criminal Justice* (The Hague: Eleven International Publishing, 2011).

65   The diplomatic letter making the claim can be found in Cosmos 954 Claim (*Canada v. USSR*) [1979] 18 ILM 899. Stephan Hobe *et al.*, *Cologne Commentary on Space Law: In Three Volumes. Outer Space Treaty* (Carl Heymanns Verlag, 2009) at 143.

66   See "Space Law as part of 'general international law'", *infra*.

67   Michael Peil, "Scholarly Writings as a Source of Law: A Survey of the Use of Doctrine by the International Court of Justice" (2012) 1:3 *Cambridge Journal of International and Comparative Law* 136 at 140.

The final compromise was to include the ambiguous wording we are left with today, without resolving this debate.[68]

Some argue that together with judicial decisions the "teachings of the most highly regarded publicists" are not in fact sources unto themselves, but rather tools for clarifying the content of the law in one of the first three formal sources.[69] Others consider doctrine to be a source unto itself, because it is influential in the development of certain branches of international law.[70]

At the very least, the debate that has continued shows that caution must be exercised in asserting the opinions of any one scholar as authoritative. Even Judge Manfred Lachs, who is often cited as an authoritative scholarly voice in space law, himself stated:

> not even of my heroes, could I say: 'this man made law.' For teachers are not legislators, nor lawmakers in international relations…[but] are only subsidiary means for the determination of the rules of law.[71]

One reason why this caution is necessary is that no scholar ever has a neutral view of the law. Authors are likely to have national biases as well as particular views on the role of law and the content that should be reflected. Since questions of international law are often highly politicized, it is difficult to avoid selective bias when citing only certain authors.[72]

The question, then, is which scholars are "the most highly qualified publicists" with respect to space law? One requirement would be that a scholar is highly qualified not only in space law, but also in public international law in general.[73] Another could be the building of consensus through a high frequency of reference by other scholars.[74] In this respect, there appears to be consensus that Judge Manfred Lachs, Professor Bin Cheng, and Professor Carl Christol have gained this status over time.[75]

Space law as part of "general international law"

From the above discussion, it is clear that there are more sources of international space law than only the five core treaties. It is important to keep in mind that, because space law is a part of public international law, there are also many rules which apply to space activities even when space itself is not referenced. To remove any doubt on the matter, Article III of the Outer Space Treaty underlines this fact:

> States Parties to the Treaty shall carry on activities in the exploration and use of outer space, including the Moon and other celestial bodies, in accordance with international law, including the Charter of the United Nations …[76]

---

68 See ibid. at 141; Pellet, *supra* note 36 at 791.
69 Jakhu & Freeland, *supra* note 1 at 469; Pellet, *supra* note 36 at 781.
70 Peil, *supra* note 56; Steer, *supra* note 10.
71 Manfred Lachs, (1976/III) 151 Hague Recueil 161, at 169. Cited in Peil, *supra* note 56 at 141.
72 Crawford, *supra* note 2 at 43; Charlesworth, *supra* note 54 at 197; Shaw, *supra* note 36 at 106.
73 Jakhu & Freeland, *supra* note 1 at 471.
74 However this could be criticized as a self-reflexive process of reification, since the objective measure of authority is simply a measure of the frequency of subjective authority designated to an author. For a critique of this process see Steer, *supra* note 10.
75 Jakhu & Freeland, *supra* note 1 at 471.
76 *Outer Space Treaty*, *supra* note 23, art III.

One consequence of this wording is that, as mentioned above, the law of treaties applies when it comes to interpreting the space treaties.[77] This will be of particular importance as the business case for commercial entities to mine asteroids or other celestial bodies becomes more viable, since the question of their property rights over whatever they mine or extract will have to be resolved in accordance with a correct interpretation of Article II of the Outer Space Treaty, which prohibits "national appropriation by claim of sovereignty, by means of use or occupation, or by any other means".[78] Treaty interpretation requires first a consideration of the ordinary meaning of the words, second a consideration of the preparatory documents, or *traveaux preparatoires*, in order to determine the intended meaning during negotiations, and finally an interpretation harmonious with the rest of the terms of the treaty.[79] It is also not possible for a State to refer to its own internal law as justification for breach of the terms of a treaty.[80] It would therefore not be possible for a State to legislate such that it allows commercial entities to claim property rights over celestial bodies, given that the Outer Space Treaty prohibits this. Instead, a harmonious interpretation of the treaty terms will have to be sought.

The fact that the UN Charter is mentioned specifically underlines the significance of certain provisions of the Charter, as well as the purpose of the Charter "[t]o maintain international peace and security ... To develop friendly relations among nations ... To achieve international cooperation in solving international problems of an economic, social, cultural, or humanitarian character [...]"[81] Certain provisions in particular are of interest to space activities, e.g., the prohibition of the threat or use of force under Article 2(4), the protection of sovereign equality against interference with matters which are "essentially within the domestic jurisdiction" of a State under Article 2(7), and the provision in Article 103 that, in the case of conflict between different international obligations, obligations under the Charter shall prevail.

With respect to Article 2(4), the only exception to this prohibition of the threat or use of force is that of self-defense. This can include either the right to retaliate if a State has been wrongfully attacked by another party according to Article 51,[82] or the use of force as a form of collective self-defense, where the UN Security Council has so authorized under Article 42.[83] These stringent international rules on the use of force, known as *jus ad bellum,* certainly apply

---

77 Even though the VCLT came into force after the Outer Space Treaty, it is considered to be applicable in all matters of treaty application and interpretation as a matter of customary international law. Treaties can reflect or codify customary law at the time they are negotiated, but they can also come to be seen as reflective of customary law over time. See Crawford, *supra* note 2 at 32.
78 *Outer Space Treaty, supra* note 23, art II.
79 Article 31 VCLT.
80 Article 27 VCLT.
81 Article 1 Charter of the United Nations, 1945 (UN Charter).
82 Self-defense is codified in Article 51 of the UN Charter, however it has a longer history in customary law. Some would argue that the latter is less restrictive than the former, allowing pre-emptive strikes in self-defense, however this is a highly controversial claim. See John Yoo, "International Law and the War in Iraq" (2003) American Journal of International Law 563; William H Taft & Todd F Buchwald, "Preemption, Iraq, and International Law" (2003) American Journal of International Law 557 For the general view that there is essentially little difference between Article 51 and the customary right of self-defense, save in formalities, see; Crawford, *supra* note 2 at 751; Antonio Cassese, "Terrorism is also disrupting some crucial legal categories of international law" (2001) 12:5 European Journal of International Law 993; Josef L Kunz, "Individual and Collective Self-Defense in Article 51 of the Charter of the United Nations" (1947) American Journal of International Law 872; Oscar Schachter, "Self-defense and the Rule of Law" (1989) American Journal of International Law 259; Oscar Schachter, *International Law in Theory and Practice* (Martinus Nijhoff Publishers, 1991).
83 See *Charter*, art 42.

to activities in space as well.[84] A correlative of this is that the entire body of *jus in bello,* otherwise known as the law of armed conflict, or international humanitarian law, also applies to potential hostilities or conflicts either taking place in space, or utilizing space assets as part of a conflict on Earth. The ICJ has confirmed as much in its statement that *jus in bello* "applies to all forms of warfare and to all kinds of weapons, those of the past, those of the present and those of the future".[85]

Beyond the UN Charter, there are other aspects of international law of importance to space activities. For instance, there are some general rules of responsibility and liability under international law which complement the rules of State responsibility under Article VI of the Outer Space Treaty and the Liability Convention.[86] The International Law Commission, a UN body of experts mandated to codify and progressively develop international law,[87] has developed the Draft Articles on State Responsibility, which were adopted by the UN General Assembly in 2001.[88] States have been reticent to finalize this draft as a treaty, however it has nonetheless gained status as an authoritative instrument, as it has been cited in numerous judicial decisions and important international law treatises; in fact, in 2015 the ICJ stated that these Draft Articles have now gained the status of customary law.[89] Similarly, there is a set of Draft Articles on Responsibility of International Organizations,[90] and Draft Articles on Transboundary Harm, both of which may apply to space activities.[91] Given that Article VI of the Outer Space Treaty stipulates that a State shall remain responsible for all of its national space activities, including those undertaken by non-State actors,[92] this body of international law is highly relevant.

---

84 Jackson N Maogoto & Steven Freeland, "From Star Wars to Space Wars – The Next Strategic Frontier: Paradigms to Anchor Space Security" (2008) 33:1 Journal of Air and Space Law 10; Steven Freeland, "In Heaven as on Earth – The International Legal Regulation of the Military Use of Outer Space" (2011) 8 US-China Law Review 272; Michel Bourbonniere, "National-Security Law in Outer Space: The Interface of Exploration and Security" (2005) 70 Journal of Air Law and Commerce 3.

85 Legality of the Threat or Use of Nuclear Weapons, Advisory Opinion, 1996 I.C.J. 259 (July 8). Michel Bourbonniere, "Law of Armed Conflict (LOAC) and the Neutralisation of Satellites or Ius in Bello Satellitis" (2004) 9 Journal of Conflict and Security Law 43; M Bourbonniere & R J Lee, "Legality of the Deployment of Conventional Weapons in Earth Orbit: Balancing Space Law and the Law of Armed Conflict" (2007) 18:5 European Journal of International Law 873; Bourbonniere, *supra* note 70; Kuan-Wei Chen, *The Legality of the Use of Space Weapons: Perspectives from Environmental Law* (Montreal: McGill University Libraries, 2012); Maogoto & Freeland, *supra* note 70; Jackson N Maogoto & Steven Freeland, "The Final Frontier: The Laws of Armed Conflict and Space Warfare" (2007) 23:1 Connecticut Journal of International Law 165; Ramey, Major Robert A, "The Law of War in Space" (2000) 48 Air Force Law Review 1.

86 Ian Brownlie, *State Responsibility* (Oxford University Press, 1983); Boyle & Chinkin, *supra* note 5; James Crawford, *State Responsibility: The General Part* (Cambridge University Press, 2013); James Crawford, *The International Law Commission's Articles on State Responsibility: Introduction, Text and Commentaries* (Cambridge University Press, 2002); Hobe *et al.*, *supra* note 55 at 113.

87 Articles 1 and 2, Statute of the International Law Commission, adopted by UN GA Res 174 (II) of 21 November 1947.

88 UN GA Res 56/83 of 12 December 2001, and A/56/49(Vol. I)/Corr.4.

89 *Application Of The Convention On The Prevention And Punishment Of The Crime Of Genocide (Croatia v. Serbia),* Judgment 3 February 215, at para 128.

90 ILC Draft Articles on the Responsibility of International Organizations, 2011. Yearbook of the International Law Commission, 2011, vol. II, Part Two.

91 ILC Draft Articles on Prevention of Transboundary Harm from Hazardous Activities, 2001. General Assembly resolution 56/82 of 12 December 2001.

92 *Outer Space Treaty, supra* note 23, art VI.

Another body of international law that will apply to certain space activities is that of environmental law. Although the various environmental law treaties have specific applications, such as the prohibition of trade in protected species, or the protection of the Antarctic region, there are some general principles of environmental law which must be applied. For example, the "polluter pays" principle with respect to liability, and the precautionary principle with respect to preventive measures.[93] The latter principle determines that, when probable dangerous, irreversible, or catastrophic events are identified, but scientific evaluation of the potential damage is not sufficiently certain, the need to prevent such potential effects shall inform all decisions made or technologies implemented.[94] This principle will become more relevant as problems of space debris increase, mining extra-terrestrial resources becomes viable, and in the case of attempting to prevent collision with a near-Earth asteroid.

Last, but not least, human rights law is also applicable to space activities. When it comes to space tourism, this body of law will become especially relevant in the near future, and even more so should humans take up residence in space stations on a more permanent basis.[95] As well, principles such as inter-generational equity must come into play as we consider the long-term effects of our use and exploration of space.

Is there a hierarchy of sources?

With all of these various sources and bodies of international law applicable to space activities, what happens if there is disagreement as to interpretation or a clash between two competing obligations? How do we know what law applies in a given situation?

The question of hierarchy among the formal sources

It is unclear from the text of Article 38 of the ICJ Statute whether there is an intended hierarchy between the sources, other than that judgments and the writings of publicists under clause (d) are considered to be subsidiary sources. Some international lawyers believe that the ordering of the other three sources represents a hierarchy, and that in the case of a conflict between obligations, a treaty would be strongest, but customary law would be stronger than a general principle.[96] Others do not consider there to be a hierarchy among these three sources at all.[97] Even without such a hierarchy, it would seem that treaty obligations are likely to be more concrete in formulation, and are enforceable under the law of treaties, and are, therefore, generally stronger obligations.

---

93 The precautionary principle has gained an important place in international environmental law and related trade law, see 1992 Rio Declaration on Environment and Development, United Nations publication, Sales No. E.73.II.A.14 ; and in the 1992 United Nations Framework Convention on Climate Change. See also Article 5.7 of the World Trade Organization's Agreement on Sanitary and Phytosanitary Measures (SPS Agreement) of 1994.
94 Crawford, *supra* note 2 at 357.
95 David Timothy Duval, "Sustainable Space Tourism" in: Micahel C. Hall (ed) *The Routledge Handbook of Tourism and Sustainability* (Routledge, 2015) at 450; Steven Freeland, "Fly Me to the Moon: How Will International Law Cope with Commercial Space Tourism" (2010) 11 Melbourne Journal of International Law 90.
96 Shaw, *supra* note 36 at 88.
97 Crawford, *supra* note 2 at 22; Antonio Cassese, *International Law* (Oxford University Press, 2004) at 198.

There are also many who assert that there is a hierarchy between bodies of law, such that human rights considerations should prevail in the development of other bodies of law.[98] For instance, the UN Committee on Economic, Social and Cultural Rights has declared that the World Trade Organization must take human rights into account in enforcing trade law, and that the realms of trade, finance, and investment are in no way exempt from human rights obligations.[99] The same would therefore apply to space activities, for example labor law as applicable to those working in the space industry, or other human rights applicable to commercial human space flight or to human habitation of space stations.

More generally speaking, if we apply the rules of hierarchy applicable in most domestic legal systems, a "higher" law shall prevail over a "lower" law; a more recent law shall prevail over an older law (*lex posterior derogate priori*); and a special rule shall prevail over a more general rule (*lex specialis derogate legis generalis*). Each of these rules will be discussed here.

Jus cogens – *peremptory norms*

The notion that a "higher" law would prevail over a "lower" one translates to a special rule of hierarchy in international law, where certain norms are considered "peremptory" or non-derogable.[100] These norms are considered to be of such inherent importance that under no circumstances will any other obligation, right or norm prevail over them. The trouble is that it is unclear which norms fall under this category, since this requires "the international community of States as a whole" to agree.[101] In any case, it is agreed that the prohibition of genocide has the status of *jus cogens*,[102] as does the prohibition of torture.[103]

In the specific context of space activities, some have asserted that the right of free access to space, the right of innocent passage through the airspace of another State to reach outer space, and the principle of "province of all humankind" are all *jus cogens* norms.[104] Yet even if they are deserving of this status, the mere desire to have these rights enshrined as non-derogable is not

---

98   Philip Alston & Gerard Quinn, "The Nature and Scope of States Parties' Obligations under the International Covenant on Economic, Social and Cultural Rights" (1987) Hum Rights Q 156; D'Amato, *supra* note 51; Oona A Hathaway, "Do Human Rights Treaties Make a Difference?" (2002) Yale Law J 1935; Bruno Simma & Philip Alston, "The Sources of Human Rights Law: Custom, Jus Cogens, and General Principles" (1988) 12 Australian Yearbook of International Law 82; Dinah Shelton, "Normative Hierarchy in International Law" (2006) American Journal of International Law 291 at 294.

99   UN Comm. on Economic, Social and Cultural Rights, Statement on Globalization, para.5 (May 11, 1998), 6 INT'L HUM.RTS.REP.1176 (1999), available at www.globalpolicy.org/globaliz/define/unstate.htm.

100 These have been given a special place also in the law of treaties, under Article 53 VCLT.

101 Shelton, *supra* note 82 at 300. See also Article 53 VCLT.

102 ICJ referred explicitly to the prohibition of genocide as a *jus cogens* norm in its decision *Armed Activities on the Territory of the Congo* (New Application: 2002) (*Dem. Rep. Congo v. Rwanda*), Jurisdiction and Admissibility, Feb. 3, 2006.

103 Erika De Wet, "The Prohibition of Torture as an International Norm of *jus cogens* and its Implications for National and Customary Law" (2004) 15:1 European Journal of International Law 97 See also *Prosecutor v. Furundzija*, IT-95-17/1-T10 (Dec. 10, 1998), available at www.un.org/icty. It can never be justifiable under any circumstance to torture individuals. The fact that torture still occurs on a disturbing scale, and often at the hands of State agents, is a problem of enforcement, and should not be confused with the normativity of the rule. There are no States that would argue that torture is lawful; they would rather argue that what they are doing is not torture.

104 Carl Q, Christol, "Judge Manfred Lachs and the Principle of Jus Cogens" (1994) 22 Journal of Space Law 33 at 44.

sufficient to raise them to this rank. *Jus cogens* norms form slowly over time with agreement from the majority of States, and can be confirmed in case law. It is difficult to see that these rights have yet gained such an elevated and protected status.

Art 103 of the UN Charter

Another special rule of hierarchy in international law is that of Article 103 of the UN Charter, mentioned above. According to this provision, in the case of a conflict between an obligation under any other source of law and an obligation under the Charter, the Charter shall prevail.[105] This gives special authority to the binding resolutions of the Security Council, which amount to a Charter obligation, and which can authorize the breach of any other obligation, for example, a trade embargo, in the name of peace and security.[106]

This raises interesting questions with respect to the registration by the UN Office of Outer Space Affairs of launches made by the Democratic People's Republic of Korea (DPRK) recently.[107] Given that the UN Security Council has adopted resolutions placing an embargo on arms and anti-ballistic missile technology against the DPRK,[108] some States have raised concerns that these launches are in violation of the resolutions and, thus, that their registration as lawful launches by a UN body is also a violation of these resolutions.[109]

The lex specialis *and* lex posterior *rules*

Finally, the rule that a special norm prevails over a more general norm also applies in international law.[110] This rule may go hand in hand with the *lex posterior* rule in interpreting the apparent dissonance between Article III of the Outer Space Treaty, which uses the language of absolute liability,[111] and the Liability Convention, which distinguishes between absolute and fault-based liability.[112] The Liability Convention should prevail both because it is the more recent, and because it is the more specific. The Liability Convention was negotiated in order to fill out the general terms of Article VII of the earlier Outer Space Treaty.

---

105 The only exception to this is, of course, a norm of *jus cogens* which would also trump a Security Council Resolution. However it is difficult to imagine a scenario in which the Security Council would authorizing something as egregious as torture or genocide.
106 Article 25 of the UN Charter determines that decisions of the UN Security Council may be binding, and Article 41 mandates the Security Council to decide what measures other than use of force are to be implemented in the case of a threat to international peace and security.
107 UN COPUOS Report of the Legal Subcommittee on its fifty-fourth session, A/AC.105/1090 (30 April 2015) at para 71. For earlier similar controversies see e.g. Henry Hertzfeld and Shouping Li, "Registration of the 12 December 2012 satellite launch by North Korea: Should UNOOSA have accepted it?" Space Policy 29 (2013) at 93–94; Jeffrey Lewis, "Is North Korea Gearing Up for more Launches?" 38 North, 2 June 2015, online: http://38north.org/2015/06/jlewis060215/.
108 UN Security Council Resolutions 1718 (2006) 1874 (2009) and 2087 (2013).
109 Report of the Legal Subcommittee on its fifty-fourth session, Vienna, 30 April 2015, A/AC.105/1090, para 71.
110 Michael Akehurst, "The Hierarchy of the Sources of International Law" (1976) 47:1 British Yearbook of International Law 273 at 273; Crawford, *supra* note 2 at 654; Boyle & Chinkin, *supra* note 5.
111 See *Outer Space Treaty*, *supra* note 23, art III.
112 See *Liability Convention*, *supra* note 25, art II, which determines absolute liability for damage caused on the surface of the Earth or to an aircraft in flight; and art III, which determines fault liability for damage caused "elsewhere than on the surface of the Earth" to spacecraft.

Similarly, it could be said that the law of armed conflict – both in treaty form and the norms accepted as part of customary law – shall apply to any conflict that takes place in outer space, or on Earth with the use of space assets, and shall prevail as a matter of *lex specialis* in the case of inconsistency with the space treaties. The law of armed conflict has been developed over a long period of time, and while there may be the need to consider its specific application to space activities, it regulates armed conflict no matter where it takes place.[113]

"Non-traditional" modes of regulation

With respect to sources of international law, it can be argued that there is a division among scholars: some view international law as a body of rules, while others view it as a series of processes that lead to the formation of norms.[114] The first group, which can be termed formalist, generally regards the formal sources discussed thus far as the only valid sources, and tends to place emphasis on the role of States and State consent in the formation of binding rules. The latter group is more interested in the role of multiple international actors in the numerous processes that lead to the formation of norms, not only according to the formal sources, but also in various fora of international engagement. Both of these groups of scholars will generally agree that there is such a thing as "soft law", to be discussed below, however they will place different emphasis on the value of these processes and instruments, and will explain their presence in different ways. This difference in perception can be recognized in the commentaries on space law, and it may be helpful in understanding the mistake made by some space lawyers in asserting that everything which purports to regulate space activities can be considered law.

One thing on which most scholars will agree is that Article 38 of the ICJ Statute is dated and does not reflect the interrelationship between the formal sources that it lists. Critics of the formalist school of thought will go further and contend that it is not reflective of the true processes that lead to the formation of norms either as binding law or in other non-binding forms.[115]

Likewise, there is a political critique with respect to the formal doctrine of sources: the underlying assumption of this doctrine is that the formation of customary law and the identification of general principles is based on an equality of States, but this ignores the inequalities of power that exist.[116] The State practice and *opinio juris* necessary to evidence customary law tend to favor the most powerful States and their assertions. As well, new States and developing States have a less influential voice in the negotiation of treaties, such as the five core space treaties, and in the norms which emerge from the UN General Assembly or as binding resolutions from the UN Security Council.[117]

---

113 Crawford, *supra* note 2 at 654; Bourbonniere, *supra* note 71; Maogoto & Freeland, *supra* note 70; Freeland, *supra* note 70; Maogoto & Freeland, *supra* note 71; Ramey, Major Robert A., *supra* note 71.

114 Bin Cheng, "Nature and Sources of International Law" in Bin Cheng, ed, *International Law: Teaching and Practice* (Stevens, 1982) at 204. For examples of those formalists who see international law as a body of rules, see generally; Crawford, *supra* note 2; Shaw, *supra* note 36 For examples of those who have a more process oriented view of the law, see generally; Higgins, *supra* note 6; Myres Smith McDougal, Harold Dwight Lasswell, & Ivan A Vlasic, *Law and Public Order in Space* (Yale University Press, 1963); Reisman, *supra* note 6.

115 Boyle & Chinkin, *supra* note 5 at 211; Charlesworth, *supra* note 54 at 189; Robert Y Jennings, "The Identification of International Law" in Bin Cheng (ed.), *International Law: Teaching and Practice* (Stevens, 1982) 3 at 9; Steer, *supra* note 10.

116 Brownlie, *supra* note 35 at 33.

117 Boyle & Chinkin, *supra* note 5; Higgins, *supra* note 6 at 11–12.

Regardless of which school of thought one follows, it is undeniable that as international institutions have gained a more influential role in recent decades, the traditional, formal sources of law have been supplemented by some important non-traditional modes of regulation. In space law, this is an area of increasing importance. The difference between the two main schools of thought lies in the acceptance of soft-law norms as sufficient and important contributions to the law (process-oriented), or as merely supplemental and insufficient to be recognized as law (formalist).

"Soft law" in international law

The notion of "soft law" can be confusing as it can be used in different ways. Some refer to weak obligations in otherwise binding, formal sources as "soft law". One example might be the obligation in Article IX to "conduct all activities in outer space ... With due regard to the corresponding interests of all other States Parties to the Treaty".[118] What exactly is entailed in giving due regard to the interests of other States is unclear, and it may be difficult to prove the claim that a State has failed to fulfill this duty. Hence, while the obligation is binding, it is weak. Another example would be the obligation under Article VI of the 1968 Non-Proliferation Treaty on State parties "to pursue negotiations in good faith on effective measures relating to cessation of the nuclear arms race at an early date [...] and on a treaty on general and complete disarmament".[119] The obligation to "pursue negotiations" is one of effort and not of result, since there is no obligation to in fact finalize or to sign a treaty on disarmament, nor to actually disarm by any date. However, such soft obligations are still found in a formal, binding source of law, namely a treaty.

In this handbook the broader and more accepted meaning of "soft law" will be maintained, namely a non-binding instrument that does not fit into one of the formally binding sources discussed above. The contents may include principles, guidelines, aspirational statements or statements of policy agreement. They are something more than merely political arrangements in which there is no precision, yet something less than binding agreements.[120] For example, the long-term sustainability of the use and exploration of space has become a focus of UNCOPUOS, with general guidelines being the outcome rather than a binding treaty.[121]

Some commentators regret the fact that no new space treaties have been negotiated since the 1970s, especially given concerns for space debris and the increased role of commercial and private space actors in general. Because soft-law instruments are not binding, they are not enforceable. Nevertheless, it could be said that they provide incentives in other ways for international actors to modify their behavior, since they represent political agreements and signal requirements of good faith.[122] Sometimes they may even be more effective in reaching a

---

118 *Outer Space Treaty*, supra note 23, art IX.
119 *Treaty on the Non-Proliferation of Nuclear Weapons*, 1 July 1968, 729 UNTS 169, art VI [*Non-Proliferation Treaty*].
120 Kenneth W Abbott & Duncan Snidal, "Hard and Soft Law in International Governance" (2000) 54:3 International Organizations 421 at 422.
121 Proposal by the Chair of the Working Group on the Long-term Sustainability of Outer Space Activities for the consolidation of the set of draft guidelines on the long-term sustainability of outer space activities, A/AC.105/2014/CRP.5 (3 June 2014), online: www.unoosa.org/oosa/en/COPUOS/stsc/ac105-c1-ltd.html
122 Daniel Thurer, "Soft Law" in Max Planck Encyclopedia of Public International Law, (Oxford University Press, 2009) MPEPIL 1469 at para 26.

particular goal with respect to regulating behavior than the slow and politically charged process of negotiating a new treaty.

One example of this is the fact that the consensus-based UNCOPUOS has been politically deadlocked for years on the question whether to pursue treaties on restraining an arms race in space, since some States insist that the Committee is not the venue to discuss military or non-peaceful uses of space. At the same time, the Conference on Disarmament (CD), which would otherwise be the suitable UN body to take up such a task, has also been politically deadlocked on this question.[123] Although China and the Russian Federation have proposed a draft treaty on Prevention of Placement of Weapons in Outer Space (PPWT) before the CD, its further negotiation has not received full support.[124] Concurrently, there have been parallel proposals for a non-binding International Code of Conduct, which received broader international support to begin with, but was recently stymied during meetings in New York in 2015. The intention was to incentivize States to conduct themselves in a similar way as the PPWT aims to achieve. The risk of attempting to negotiate a new treaty is that States can sometimes negotiate to weaken the core provisions in a treaty draft, in order to protect themselves against binding obligations that they feel are restrictive, leaving a binding instrument empty of its original intention. Furthermore, States may sign but not ratify a treaty, preventing it from coming into force.

General Assembly resolutions as soft law

Space law started out as soft law: the first statement produced by the international community was the 1963 UN General Assembly Space Principles Declaration. General Assembly resolutions can be considered to be soft law since they are statements adopted by vote to express international governmental opinion on specific matters, and often contain aspirational calls to action. However, they have no binding force. According to the UN Charter, the General Assembly may only make "recommendations", whereas the Security Council may make binding resolutions.[125]

General Assembly resolutions may still have normative value. As Sir Robert Jennings asserted, "recommendations may not make law, but you would hesitate to advise a government that it may, therefore, ignore them, even in a legal argument".[126] General Assembly resolutions

123 Steven Freeland, "The Role of 'Soft Law' in Public International Law" in Irmgard Marboe, ed, *Soft Law in Outer Space: the Function of Non-binding Norms in International Space Law* (2012) at 22.
124 The original proposal was tabled in 2008, but received much criticism. A new draft was tabled in 2014: UN Conference on Disarmament, "Letter dated 10 June 2014 from the Permanent Representative of the Russian Federation and the Permanent Representative of China to the Conference on Disarmament addressed to the Acting Secretary-General of the Conference transmitting the updated Russian and Chinese texts of the draft treaty on prevention of the placement of weapons in outer space and of the threat or use of force against outer space objects (PPWT) introduced by the Russian Federation and China", CD/1984 (12 June 2014), online: http://daccess-ods.un.org/TMP/7443259.35840607.html. See also "Explanatory Note on the updated draft Treaty on the Prevention of the Placement of Weapons in Outer Space, the Threat or Use of Force against Outer Space Objects", online: http://reachingcriticalwill.org/images/documents/Disarmament-fora/cd/2014/documents/PPWT2014_ExplanatoryNote.pdf.
125 Articles 10 and 11 of the UN Charter mandate the General Assembly to make recommendations on matters within the scope of the Charter; Article 25 determines that States are bound by decisions of the Security Council.
126 Robert Yewdall Jennings & John R Spencer, *What is International Law and How Do We Tell It When We See It?* (Kluwer Law Intl, 1983) at 14 cited in; Steven Freeland, *supra* note 101 at 28.

are adopted by vote, and the vote count can demonstrate the degree to which there is international agreement on a certain matter.[127] When they are adopted without abstentions or dissenting votes, this consensus can have a very strong normative value.

The General Assembly has adopted a series of resolutions of direct importance to space law:

- the 1982 Principles Governing the Use by States of Artificial Earth Satellites for International Direct Television Broadcasting;[128]
- the 1986 Principles Relating to Remote Sensing of Earth from Outer Space;[129]
- the 1992 Principles Relevant to the Use of Nuclear Power Sources in Outer Space;[130] and
- the 1996 Declaration on International Cooperation in the Exploration and Use of Outer Space for the Benefit and in the Interest of All States, Taking into Particular Account the Needs of Developing Countries.[131]

Of these, the resolution on Direct Television Broadcasting was the only one not adopted by consensus, since many States which did not yet have such technology disagreed as to the freedom to broadcast into other States.[132] The Benefit Principles are the most recent, but contain the weakest normative value due to the broad language used in the text, which essentially seeks to expand on Articles I and II of the Outer Space Treaty. The resolution was adopted as a compromise between enabling space-faring nations to progress in their activities while also expressing the concerns of developing nations who wanted to ensure they gained benefits from these activities, and to protect their own future potential space activities.[133]

On the other hand, the principles on Remote Sensing have since been recognized as reflective of customary law, and have thus gained a stronger, binding force in international law.[134] The "norm-creating" language of these principles is an essential part of contributing to this status, since mandatory language can create obligations and rights, whereas the more broad language used in the Benefit Principles does not have this effect.[135] In some cases General Assembly resolutions may be indicative of emerging customary law as they may express evidence of *opino juris,* as the ICJ itself has stated.[136] However, once again, caution should be exercised: this does not mean that all General Assembly resolutions reflect customary law, nor that resolutions are themselves a source of customary law. Rather they can provide evidence of

---

127 UN Charter Article 18. See also Thurer *supra* note 132 at para 11.
128 UNGA Res 37/92, 10 December 1982.
129 UNGA Res 41/65, 3 December 1986.
130 UNGA Res 47/68, 14 December 1992.
131 UNGA Res 51/22, 13 December 1996.
132 Franz Koppensteiner, "The 1982 UN Principles Governing the Use by States of International Direct Television Broadcasting" in Irmgard Marboe, ed, *Soft Law in Outer Space: the Function of Non-binding Norms in International Space Law* (2012) at 170.
133 Gerhard Haffner, "The Declaration on International Cooperation in the Exploration and Use of Outer Space for the Benefit and in the Interests of All States" in Irmgard Marboe, *supra* note 148 at 279.
134 Joanne Gabrynowicz, "The UN Principles Relating to Remote Sensing of Outer Space and Soft Law" in Irmgard Marboe, *supra* note 148 at 185.
135 Jakhu & Freeland, *supra* note 1 at 475.
136 Legality of the Threat or Use of Nuclear Weapons, Advisory Opinion, [1996] ICJ Rep 226 at 254–55. See also Pellet, *supra* note 36 at 709; Ricky J Lee & Steven R Freeland, *The Crystallisation of General Assembly Space Declarations into Customary International Law* (2003).

the opinion of States, especially if they are adopted unanimously. But customary law also requires State practice, so the resolutions alone are not enough.[137]

Standards and guidelines

International norm-creation as soft law can take place in many different international fora. One example is the Inter-Agency Space Debris Coordination Committee (IADC), which was established in 1993 and reports to the UNCOPUOS Scientific and Technical Subcommittee.[138] The IADC does not have any formal law-making capacity. Nevertheless, in 2001, UNCOPUOS asked the IADC to develop a set of space debris mitigation guidelines.[139] UNCOPUOS used these as a basis for its 2007 Guidelines, which were later adopted by the UN General Assembly.[140] The Guidelines are a voluntary measure which encourage States to implement their own national standards dealing with launch and satellite design (to reduce long-term debris), and space safety (to deal with current debris).

The IADC based its original draft guidelines on the prior work of the International Standards Organization (ISO), an independent, non-governmental organization that has representatives from standardization bodies of 163 States.[141] In turn, the ISO works closely with the International Association for the Advancement of Space Safety (IAASS), a non-profit organization "dedicated to furthering international cooperation and scientific advancement in the field of space systems safety",[142] which has observer status at UNCOPUOS. Together these non-governmental organizations can contribute from industry and technical perspectives to the development of soft-law standards and guidelines, which may then be implemented into national space legislation.

Transparency and confidence building measures

There has been a push over recent years to develop soft-law mechanisms in the apparent absence of State will to negotiate binding treaties, particularly with respect to arms control. In 2006 and 2007 the UN General Assembly adopted resolutions on "Transparency and Confidence Building Measures", or TCBMs, stating the need for States and international organizations to create measures that would aid transparency and verification.[143]

TCBMs can take many forms, and are sometimes adopted as standalone actions and sometimes in combination with other instruments. In 2007 the UN Secretary General made a request for concrete proposals, and in response to this, the EU drafted a proposed Code of

---

137   An illustration of this, and of the generally weak normative effect of General Assembly resolutions, are the PAROS resolutions (Prevention of an Arms Race in Outer Space), adopted every year for more than 15 years with almost identical wording and with near unanimity, that have had little effect on the behavior of States and have never been cited as creating an obligation or a customary norm. See Jakhu & Freeland, *supra* note 1 at 475.
138   www.iadc-online.org/.
139   Report of the Thirty-eighth session of the Scientific and Technical Subcommittee, A/AC.105/761.
140   UNGA Res 62/217, 22 December 2007.
141   www.iso.org/iso/home/about/iso_members.htm.
142   http://iaass.space-safety.org/.
143   UN General Assembly Resolution 61/75 (2006), and 62/43 (2007). While TCBMs are aimed at arms control in general, they have begun to play an important part in space arms control in particular, and have featured prominently in discussions before the CD. See Ram S. Jakhu, "Transparency and Confidence Building Measures for Space Security" in: Ajay Lele (ed), *Decoding the International Code of Conduct for Outer Space Activities* (Pentagon Security International, 2012) at 35.

Conduct in 2008.[144] Following criticisms that the process had not been sufficiently transparent and inclusive, the EU held three rounds of multilateral Open-ended Consultations, which led to the 2014 draft International Code of Conduct (ICoC).[145] While this soft-law instrument originally had broad international support, many African and Latin American countries object to the emphasis on a right to self-defense, and feel that accepting a Code could restrict their future space activities.[146] At the recent multilateral negotiations held at the UN Headquarters, the ICoC suffered a major setback as criticisms were repeated that the process was questionable and the text was not representative.[147] In the end no final agreement was reached, and the future of this instrument remains to be seen.

A parallel response to the call for TCBMs has been a joint proposal by China and Russia to develop a binding treaty, the abovementioned PPWT.[148] This proposal has received much criticism from States who do not wish to subject themselves to binding norms, and which would prefer to suffice with the ICoC, in particular from major space-faring nations such as France and the US.[149] Thus, while it may be possible to conceive of TCBMs as a combination

---

144   EU Council Conclusions and Draft Code of Conduct for outer space activities, 17175/08 (17 December 2008), online: http://register.consilium.europa.eu/doc/srv?l=EN&f=ST%2017175%202008%20INIT.

145   Draft International Code of Conduct for Outer Space Activities (31 March 2014), online: www.eeas.europa.eu/non-proliferation-and-disarmament/pdf/space_code_conduct_draft_vers_31-march-2014_en.pdf. (2014 Draft Code of Conduct). Overall 95 UN Member States have participated in the consultation process, and 61 States were present in each round of consultations, see http://eeas.europa.eu/non-proliferation-and-disarmament/outer-space-activities/index_en.htm.

146   Rajeswari Pillai Rajagopalan and Daniel A. Porras, "EU Courts Support for Space Code of Conduct", *Space News* (14 July 2014): http://spacenews.com/41254eu-courts-support-for-space-code-of-conduct/. At the same time the ICoC has received strong support from many countries, see http://reachingcriticalwill.org/resources/fact-sheets/critical-issues/5448-outer-space#CoC.

147   For the agenda and discussion documents, see http://eu-un.europa.eu/articles/en/article_16615_en.htm.

148   The first proposal was presented to the CD in 2002 to mixed responses. http://reachingcriticalwill.org/resources/fact-sheets/critical-issues/5448-outer-space#ppwt. In 2008 the two States presented an updated draft. see UN Conference on Disarmament, "Letter Dated 12 February 2008 From The Permanent Representative Of The Russian Federation And The Permanent Representative Of China To The Conference On Disarmament Addressed To The Secretary-General Of The Conference Transmitting The Russian And Chinese Texts Of The Draft Treaty On Prevention Of The Placement Of Weapons In Outer Space And Of The Threat Or Use Of Force Against Outer Space Objects (PPWT)", CD/1839 (29 February 2008), online: http://daccess-ods.un.org/TMP/6338202.95333862.html. In 2014 a new draft was presented with responses to some of the criticisms to the 2008 draft. See: UN Conference on Disarmament, "Letter dated 10 June 2014 from the Permanent Representative of the Russian Federation and the Permanent Representative of China to the Conference on Disarmament addressed to the Acting Secretary-General of the Conference transmitting the updated Russian and Chinese texts of the draft treaty on prevention of the placement of weapons in outer space and of the threat or use of force against outer space objects (PPWT) introduced by the Russian Federation and China", CD/1984 (12 June 2014), online: http://daccess-ods.un.org/TMP/7443259.35840607.html.

149   *Intervention de M. Louis Riquet, Representant Permanent Adjoint de la France aupres de la Conference du Desarmement «Espace extra-atmospherique»*, Sixty-ninth Session of UN General Assembly First Committee, (27 October 2014), online: www.un.org/disarmament/special/meetings/firstcommittee/69/(td_os_27_oct_France.pdf); Note verbale dated 2 September 2014 from the Delegation of the United States of America to the Conference on Disarmament addressed to the Acting Secretary-General of the Conference transmitting the United States of America analysis of the 2014 Russian-Chinese draft treaty on the prevention of the placement of weapons in outer space, the threat or use of force against outer space objects, CD/1998, (3 September 2014), online: www.unog.ch/80256EE600585943/%28httpPages%29/91543774035C8383C125799F003B295C?OpenDocument.

of hard and soft law, it would seem that, for the moment, the soft-law alternatives may be more successful in creating the kinds of norms necessary for space security.

In this regard, in 2014 the General Assembly adopted a resolution on "No First Placement of Weapons in Outer Space" by consensus.[150] While this resolution expresses support for the proposal to negotiate a PPWT, its more immediate normative force is that it urges all States to adopt a political commitment that they will not be the first to place arms in outer space. At the time of writing, 11 States have made declarations: Argentina, Armenia, Belarus, Brazil, Cuba, Indonesia, Kazakhstan, Kyrgyzstan, Russia, Sri Lanka, and Tajikistan.[151] Notably among these, Russia is the only truly active space-faring nation.

Conclusion

The most important thing to understand about international space law and law-making processes is that these are embedded in public international law as a whole. Thus, the formal sources of international law apply to space law, and these are supplemented by the increasing importance of soft-law mechanisms. In some aspects of space activities, it seems that some States have reached the limit of their will to negotiate formally binding treaties. Nonetheless, this does not mean that space law has come to a halt, or that there is no law that applies. Instead, people interested in space law must first look to the wider body of international law for answers, and may also look to soft-law mechanisms for guiding norms.

The question as to the weight of those soft-law norms may depend on whether one takes the view that international law is a formal body of rules, or that it is rather a process of norm-creation involving multiple actors. The main difference between these views is that a formalist sees soft-law mechanisms as entirely subsidiary to formal law, whereas a process-oriented view may regard soft law as sufficient for international regulation. With respect to space activities, both schools of thought must recognize that as technology develops and our space activities proliferate, the role of soft law mechanisms as supplemental to the formal sources will become increasingly important.

---

150   A/Res/69/85, 2 December 2014.
151   Dr. Alexander Yakovenko, "Russia's No Arms in Outer Space Initiative Gains Support", *RT* (26 November 2014) http://rt.com/op-edge/209027-outer-space-arms-un-resolution/.

2

Legal status of outer space and celestial bodies

Stephan Hobe and Kuan-Wei Chen

Introduction

Outer space as a domain of human activity

Outer space is that part of the Universe which lies beyond air space and is accessible for human activities. Space law governs all human activities related to the use and exploration of outer space, which includes celestial bodies such as the Moon and asteroids.[1] It is a field of international law,[2] and not a self-contained legal regime,[3] which governs and regulates space acvities

---

1 See generally Virgiliu Pop, "A Celestial Body is a Celestial Body is a Celestial Body..." (2001) Proceedings of the Forty-Fourth Colloquium on the Law of Outer Space 100. Celestial bodies should be distinguished from human-made space objects: S Hobe, Article I Outer Space Treaty" in S Hobe, B Schmidt-Tedd & K-U Schrogl (eds), *Cologne Commentary on Space Law, Vol. 1* (2009) at 32.
2 *International Co-operation in the Peaceful Uses of Outer Space,* GA Res 1721(XVI)A, UNGAOR, UN Doc A/RES/1721(XVI) (20 December 1961). As early as 1961, the General Assembly recognized that in the exploration and use of outer space "[i]nternational law, including the Charter of the United Nations, applied to outer space and celestial bodies". The foundations and various customary principles were first identified in *Declaration of Legal Principles Concerning the Activities of States in the Exploration and Use of Outer Space,* GA Res 1962 (XVIII), UNGAOR, 18th Sess, UN Doc A/RES/18/1962 (1963) [*Declaration of Legal Principles*], and later codified in 1967 under the *Treaty on Principles Governing the Activities of States in the Exploration and Use of Outer Space, Including the Moon and Other Celestial Bodies,* 27 January 1967, 610 UNTS 205, 18 UST 2410, TIAS No. 6347, 6 ILM 386 (entered into force on 10 October 1967) [*Outer Space Treaty*].
3 As Bruno Simma points out, whether a regime is a self-contained depends on if it is possible, at all, to "fall-back on the general legal consequences of international wrongful acts": Bruno Simma, "Self-Contained Regimes" (1985) 16 NYIL 111 at 118. For more on self-contained regimes, see International Law Commission, *Fragmentation of International Law: Difficulties Arising from the Diversification and Expansion of International Law,* UN Doc A/CN.4/L.682 (2006). At particularly sect C, para 120, the ILC notes:

> No rule, treaty, or custom, however special its subject-matter or limited the number of the States concerned by it, applies in a vacuum.

as a *lex specialis*[4] in as much as no general rules of international law exist.

Sources of international space law

Space law governs all types of human activities pertaining to the exploration and use of space, including access to and transit through space, space applications, such as telecommunications and use of orbits, mining of celestial bodies, and any space-related activity that is yet to develop in the future. As outer space provides great socio-economic, political and strategic value, and with the shift away from State-led and government-funded space missions to commercial space ventures conducted by an increasing number of private space actors,[5] the formation of space law is naturally thereby shaped by concerns and interests from the public, private and technological, economic, security and political domains. Space law comprises a number of international treaties and resolutions adopted by States under the auspices of the United Nations. Chronologically, the Treaty on Principles Governing the Activities of States in the Exploration and Use of Outer Space Including the Moon and Other Celestial Bodies[6] (commonly known as the Outer Space Treaty) is the first international space law instrument. It contains the basic principles for space activities, provides the basis for the next four treaties,[7] and with 104 ratifications and 25 signatories as of January 2016, the Outer Space Treaty is one of the international treaties with significant support.[8] With widespread support, and the fact that several provisions of the treaty reiterate and codify rules established under an earlier General Assembly resolution,[9] the Outer Space Treaty is considered to contain principles of customary international law which bind not only State parties to the treaty but also non-signatories. In addition, more than 25 countries have enacted their national space legislation which might be seen as an expression of *opinio juris*,[10] if coupled with State practice, can be evidence of custom.

4   In the words of the ILC,

> if a matter is being regulated by a general standard as well as a more specific rule, then the latter should take precedence over the former.

Fragmentation of International Law, ibid., para 56.

5   See Ram Jakhu, "Welcome and Introduction", presentation at the 3rd Manfred Lachs International Conference on NewSpace Commercialization and the Law, 16–17 March, Montreal, Canada, online: McGill University www.mcgill.ca/iasl/files/iasl/2015-lachs-jakhu_welcome_and_intro.pptx.

6   *Outer Space Treaty, supra* note 2.

7   See the *Agreement on the Rescue of Astronauts, the Return of Astronauts and the Return of Objects Launched Into Outer Space*, 22 April 1968, 672 UNTS 119, 19 UST 7570, TIAS No. 6599, 7 ILM 151 (entered into force 3 December 1968) [*Rescue and Return Agreement*] (as of January 2015, 94 ratifications, 24 signatures and 2 declaration of acceptance of rights and obligations); the *Convention on International Liability for Damage Caused by Space Objects*, 29 March 1972, 961 UNTS 187, 24 UST 2389, 10 ILM 965 (1971) (entered into force 1 September 1972) [*Liability Convention*] (as of January 2015, 922 ratifications, 21 signatures and 3 declarations of acceptance of rights and obligations); the *Convention on Registration of Objects Launched into Outer Space*, 6 June 1975, 28 UST 695, 1023 UNTS 15 (entered into force 15 September 1976) [*Registration Convention*] (as of January 2015, 62 ratifications, 4 signatures and 3 declarations of acceptance of rights and obligations); and the *Agreement Governing the Activities of States on the Moon and Other Celestial Bodies*, 5 December 1979, 1363 UNTS 3 (entered into force 11 July 1984) [*Moon Agreement*] (as of January 2015, 16 ratifications and 4 signatures).

8   *Status of International Agreements Relating to Activities in Outer Space, Status of Jan. 1st 2015*, UN Doc A/AC.105/C.2/2015/CRP.8, online: UNOOSA www.unoosa.org/pdf/limited/c2/AC105_C2_2015_CRP08E.pdf.

9   *Declaration of Legal Principles, supra* note 2.

10 Paul S Dempsey, *Space Law* (Dobbs Ferry, NY: Oceana Publications, 2004) (loose-leaf).

The law of outer space can in some aspects be compared to other domains of international law which govern common spaces, such as the law of the sea[11] and the law governing Antarctica.[12] The high seas,[13] deep seabed[14] and the landmass of Antarctica,[15] like outer space, are all excluded from claims of sovereignty. Like the other global commons, due to the particular natural predispositions in space (microgravity and vacuum, high-velocity motion in orbits etc.).[16] Outer space, including celestial bodes, also have physical features which make them unique and therefore subject to a special sub-set of international law that must adapt to rapid technological developments and to activities which are constantly evolving and becoming more complex.

Legal status of outer space

Are there boundaries and where are they?

In order to define where exactly international space law is applicable, a determination needs to be made as to where outer space begins.[17] As outer space is a natural phenomenon, one possible approach would be to orient any legal consideration to its naturally given conditions in relation to the Earth as a starting point for any human activity that is to be regulated. However, no physical boundary exists between air space and outer space. A number of attempts to define where air space ends and outer space begins have been undertaken since the launch of Sputnik I on October 4, 1957. No agreement on the delimitation of air space and outer space exists, despite the fact that this issue has been on the agenda of the United Nations Committee on the Peaceful Uses of Outer Space (UNCOPUOS) for nearly 50 years.[18]

---

11 *United Nations Convention on the Law of the Sea,* 10 December 1982, 1833 UNTS 3 (entered into force 16 November 1994), art 89.
12 *Antarctic Treaty,* 1 December 1959, 12 UST 794, 402 UNTS 71, 19 ILM 860 (1980), UKTS 97 (1961), Cmnd 1535, ATS 12 (1961) (entered into force 23 June 1961), art IV. See in general R Wolfrum, "Die Internationalisierung Staatsfreier Räume", in Armin von Bogdandy, & Anne Peters, *Beiträge zum ausländischen öffentlichen Recht und Völkerrecht, Band 85* (Springer 1984).
13 *UNCLOS, supra* note 11, art 89.
14 Ibid., art 137(1).
15 *Antarctic Treaty, supra* note 12, art IV.
16 For a general technological background for space activities, see, for example: JJ Sellers, *Understanding Space: An Introduction to Astronautics* (New York: Hill-McGraw, 2007).
17 As Max Huber noted in the *Island of Palmas case*:

> Territorial sovereignty is, in general, a situation recognized and delimited in space, *either by so-called natural frontiers as recognized by international law or outward signs of delimitation that are undisputed, … or by acts of recognition of States within fixed boundaries.* […] Territorial sovereignty … *serves to divide between nations the space upon which human activities are employed in order to assure them at all points the minimum protection of which international law is the guardian.*

Island of Palmas case (the Netherlands v. United States of America) (1928) II RIAA 829 at 838–839 [emphasis added]. See also Bin Cheng, "The Legal Status of Outer Space and Relevant Issues: Delimitation of Outer Space and Definition of Peaceful Use" (1983) 11 Journal of Space Law 89 at 89–90.
18 The first mention of the issue of delimitation took place at the *ad hoc* Committeee on the the Peaceful Uses of Outer Space in 1959. Though the Commitee noted there was no consensus on the matter and that "it might eventually prove essential to determine these limits", States "generally believed that the determination of precise limits for air space and outer space did not present a legal problem calling for priorty consideration at this moment". See *Report of the Ad Hoc Committee on the Peaceful Uses of Outer Space,* UN Doc A/4141 (14 July 1959) at 25.

At a theoretical level, one can differentiate between a "functionalist" and a "spatialist" approach.[19] According to the latter, a physical demarcation line between air space and outer space must be set. The Von Kármán line at 100 km above sea level was accepted by the International Aeronautical Federation as a boundary between air space and outer space.[20] The functionalist approach takes into consideration the purpose of a vehicle in flight and its activity: it shall be crucial whether the vehicle is built to operate from Earth to outer space or to fly in airspace.[21] This approach gained more substantial support in the 1970s due to the rapid development of technology.

It appears that a consensus within UNCOPUOS on the delimitation problem cannot soon be expected[22] but it can be affirmed that the functionalist approach has been endorsed by some of the major space-faring nations such as the United States (US).[23] Currently, the lack of a delimitation of outer space does not hamper space activities.[24] So far, no country protested against a space object overflying (during launch or re-entry) its sovereign airspace.[25] However, this question may gain more significant practical meaning if aerospace vehicles start operating because they would be able to fly and operate both in air and in outer space.[26] Leaving the delimitation of outer space unanswered may presently thwart the proper and ordelery governance of outer space and the certainty and strength of international law governing space activities.[27]

Taking into account that there are satellites which can operate in an altitude of about 95–110 km, and the centrifugal force exceeds the aerodynamic lift at 84 km above sea level, it

19   F Lyall & PB Larsen, *Space Law: A Treatise*, (2009) at 165 *et seq*.
20   Australia's *Space Activties Act 1998* (No. 123 of 1998) refers to Wthe distance of 100 km above mean sea level to Earth" in its definition of what is a "launch" and "launch vehicle": see sect 8. See also Dean N Reinhardt, "The Versitcal Limit of State Sovereignty" (2007) 72 J of Air Law and Commerce 65. See also International Aeronautical Federation, "100km Altitude Boundary for Astronautics", online: Fédération Aéronautique Internationale www.fai.org/icare-records/100km-altitude-boundary-for-astronautics.
21   See e.g. RS Jakhu, T Sgobba & PS Dempsey eds, *The Need for an Integrated Regulatory Regime for Aviation and Space. ICAO for Space?* (Springer: New York, 2011) at 58 *et seq*.
22   The issue remains unresolved and was discussed extensively, like in previous years, by the Legal Subcommittee of the UNCOPUOS in 2015: see UNCOPUOS, *Report of the Legal Subcommittee on its fifty-fourth session, held in Vienna from 13 to 24 April 2015,* UN Doc A/AC.105/1090 (2015) at 14 *et seq*.
23   Stephan Hobe & Gérardine Meishan Goh & Julia Neumann, "Space Tourism Activities – Emerging Challenges to Air and Space Law" (2007) J Space L 359 at 363 *et seq*.
24   Manfred Lachs, *The Law of Outer Space* (Leide: Sijthof, 1972) at 58.
25   As all space objects must traverse national air space on its ascent/descent int outer space, Lachs notes the freedom of innocent passage through airspace must be "a necessary corollary"of the freedom to explore and use outer space: Lachs, ibid. at 60–61.

     See also *North Sea Continental Shelf (Federal Republic of Germany v. Netherlands; Federal Republic of Germany v. Denmark)* [1969] ICJ Rep 3, Dissenting Opinion of Judge Lachs at 230.

     The only known protest was when the Democratic People's Republic of Korea launched a rocket that overflew Japanese air space over Okinawa: Tom Phillips, "North Korea Rocket Launch: Satellite Successfully Sent into Orbit", *The Telegraph* (12 December 2012), online: The Telegraph www.telegraph.co.uk/news/worldnews/asia/northkorea/9738806/North-Korea-rocket-launch-satellite-successfully-sent-into-orbit.html. The Security Council, in an unprecedented move, voted uninamously condemned this launch: see UN Security Council Resolution 2087, UN Doc S/RES/2087 (2013).
26   See Ram S. Jakhu & Kuan-Wei Chen, *Regulation of Emerging Modes of Aerospace Transportation* (Centre for Research in Air and Space Law: Montreal, 2014). See also UNCOPUOS, *National Legislation and Practice Relating to Definition and Delimitation of Outer Space*, UN Doc A/AC.105/865/Add.12 (2013).
27   See Cheng, *supra* note 17 at 94 *et seq*.

can be argued that outer space starts somewhere between 80 and 110 km above sea level.[28]

The non-appropriation principle

Whereas a State retains "complete and exclusive sovereignty over the airspace over its territory",[29] outer space, including celestial bodies, similar to other "global commons", is completely excluded from national sovereignty.[30] The so-called "non-appropriation principle" is contained in Article II of the Outer Space Treaty and provides that "outer space, including the moon and other celestial bodies, is not subject to national appropriation by claim of sovereignty, by means of use or occupation, or by any other means".[31] Thus, States Parties to the Outer Space Treaty are prohibited from declaring sovereign or territorial claims over outer space and on celestial bodies.[32] With respect to celestial bodies, the non-appropiation principle is reaffirmed in the Moon Agreement under Article 11.[33]

The exact meaning of the non-appropriation principle, however, is not clear. It does prohibit States to appropriate outer space and celestial bodies,[34] but it is a subject of further interpretation whether only the surface of the celestial bodies or also what lies underneath (such as resources) is protected by this provision.[35] In principle, thus, any appropriation of territory is

---

28 S. Hobe, "Legal Aspects of Space Tourism" (2007) 86:2Nebraska Law Review 439. Vladen Vereschetin notes the concept of "customary delimitation", which is the establishment of a customary lower boundary of outer space based on the lowest perigee of artificial satellites: see Vladlen S Vereshchetin, "Outer Space" in R Wolfrum, ed., *Max Planck Ecyclopedia of Public International Law*, (online edition, updated June 2006), online: Oxford Public International Law http://opil.ouplaw.com/view/10.1093/law:epil/9780199231690/law-9780199231690-e1202?prd=EPIL#law-9780199231690-e1202-div1-4. See also, Bin Cheng, "The Legal Regime of Airspace and Outer Space: The Boundary Problem Functionalism versus Spatialism: The Major Premises" (1980) Annals of Air and Space Law 323 at 351–352; and Nicolas Matte, *Aerospace Law* (London: Sweet and Maxwell, 1969) at 54 *et seq.*
29 *Convention on International Civil Aviation*, 7 December 1944, 15 UNTS 295, ICAO Doc 7300/6 (entered into force 4 April 1947), art 1.
30 Particularly, the high seas, the deep seabed and Antarctica. See *infra* II4b.
31 On the non-appropriation principle see: S Freeland & Ram S. Jakhu, "Article II Outer Space Treaty", in S Hobe, B Schmidt-Tedd & K-U Schrogl (eds), *Cologne Commentary on Space Law*, Vol. 1 (2009) at 50–55.
32 According to Lachs, the phrase "any other means" makes the prohibition of sovereignty absolute:

> neither use, nor occupation, can constitute legal titles justifying the extension of sovereign rigts by any States over outer space, over the moon and other celestial bodies ... [w]hatever criteria one adopts [...] alciams are bound t be considered as devoid of legal foundation.

Lachs, *The Law of Outer Space*, *supra* note 24 at 43.
33 Article 11(2) of the *Moon Agreement*, *supra* note 7, provides:

> The moon is not subject to national appropriation by any claim of sovereignty, by means of use or occupation, or by any other means.

34 Equatorial States Brazil, Colombia, Congo, Ecuador, Indonesia, Kenya, Uganda and Zaire in 1976 attempted to lay claim to the geostationary orbit above their respective territories: see *Declaration of the First Meeting of Equtorial States* (3 December 1976) [*Bogotá Declaration*], ITU Doc WARC-BS (1977) 81-E. States did not recognize such a claim, and the Equatorial States eventually abandoned their stance on this.
35 Cf. Lachs, who notes that non-appropiation must be understood as "including not only sovereign rights but also property rights" and that States "are thus [...] barred from establishing proprietary links in regard to the new dimension" of outer space and celestail bodies. See Lachs, *The Law of Outer Space*, *supra* note 24 at 44.

prohibited. Moreover, the expression "appropriation by use" can be interpreted in the light of Article I which provides for the freedoms of outer space. In November 2015, in an unprecedented detraction from international space law, the US adopted domestic legislation which guaranteed private actors rights in an "asteroid resource or space resource obtained, including the right 'to possess, own, transport, use, and sell the asteroid resource or space resource'".[36]

The non-appropriation principle is a rule of customary international law.[37] However, it might be challenged in the light of its formulation allowing broad interpretation. A systematic interpretation of Article II of the Outer Space Treaty by means of looking at the formulation of Article 11 of the Moon Agreement allows the assumption that exploitation of natural resources is not appropriation *per se* if such activities are governed by a regime established by the international community.[38]

Generally, the non-appropriation principle prohibits claims to ownership in outer space, unless an international regime for exploitation of the resources of the Moon and other celestial bodies is established. A parallel in international law may be found in the UN Convention on the Law of the Sea (UNCLOS), which establishes a regime to govern the exploitation of deep seabed resources.[39] In telecommunications law, which in many instances is interweaved with space law,[40] the allocation of slots in the geostationary orbit (GEO) by the International Telecommunication Union (ITU) represents a regime for governing the exploitation (use) of resources such as the limited orbital slots in GEO.[41] Therefore, the non-appropriation principle which is indeed a fundamental rule not only in space law but also a rule of customary international law, provides room for further elaboration of its exact meaning according to the specific uses which space actors (be they governmental, non-governmental entities or natural persons) aim for.

The freedoms of outer space

The Outer Space Treaty sets out a framework for human activities in space. States are not the only subjects of these provisions. Articles VI and XIII clearly provide that international intergovernmental organizations and private actors are also subject to the provisions of the Outer Space Treaty. "Mankind", which is named in the first paragraph of Article I of the Outer Space Treaty is, however, not a subject of international law.[42] Individuals can benefit from the

---

36 *Spurring Private Aerospace Competitiveness and Entrepreneurship Act of 2015*, HR 2262, Pub L 114–90 [*SPACE Act of 2015*], particularly §§ 51302–51303. Cf. Comments of Ram Jakhu in "US space-mining law seen leading to possible treaty violations", *CBC News* (26 November 2015), online: CBC www.cbc.ca/news/technology/space-mining-us-treaty-1.3339104.

37 It was already affirmed in the *Declaration of Legal Principles, supra* note 2, para 3. See also Lachs, *The Law of Outer Space, supra* note 24 at 44, 47–48.

38 *Moon Agreement, supra* note 7, art 11(7). See also Ram S. Jakhu, S Freeland, & S Hobe, F Tronchetti, "Article 11 (Common Heritage of Mankind/International Regime) MOON", paras 208–212 in S Hobe, B Schmidt-Tedd & K-U Schrogl (eds), *Cologne Commentary on Space Law*, Vol. 2 (2013) at 389 *et seq* [Jakhu, Freeland, Hobe & Tronchetti, "Article 11 MOON"].

39 R Wolfrum, "Die Internationalisierung staatsfreier Räume" in XX Beiträge zum ausländischen öffentlichen Recht und Völkerrecht, Band 85 (Springer 1984), 328 *et seq*. See *UNCLOS, supra* note 11, art 137(1).

40 See Ram S. Jakhu, "The Evolution of the ITU's Regulatory Regime Governing Space Radio-communication Services and the Geostationary Satellite Orbit" (1983) VIII Ann Air & Sp L 381, specifcally at 398–399.

41 *Constitution of the International Telecommunications Union*, 22 December 1992, 1825 UNTS 331, [1994] ATS 28, [1996] BTS 24 (entered into force 1 July 1994) (2011 edition) [*ITU Constitution*], art 12(1).

42 For a discussion on 'mankind' as a subject of international law, see: A Cocca, "Mankind as a New Legal Subject", 13th Colloquium on the Law of Outer Space 211 (1970).

freedoms of outer space but only in as much as States entitle them to do so through national space legislation.[43]

The right, and the scope of such a right, of States (and other subjects of international law) to engage in such activities is confirmed by Article I of the Outer Space Treaty, which gurantees States the freedom to i) explore outer space; ii) use outer space; and iii) to conduct scientific investigation in outer space.[44] It is thus clear that the freedom of exploration, freedom of use and freedom scientific investigation are distinct activities.

The term "freedom" means that all entities which are addressees of these provisions are entitled to use, explore or scientifically investigate in outer space without the need to ask for permission from other States or an international entity.[45] However, also this fundamental provision of space law is formulated in a very broad manner, and a closer look at its exact meaning and legal consequences is needed. Any consideration of the scope of these freedoms should start with an interpretation of the terms used to describe human activities.

Exploration, however, stipulates not so much consuming or profiting from space but rather the discovery of something new or yet unknown. Scientific investigation might, but must not necessarily overlap with "exploration" as scientific activities might be aiming also at already discovered objects or areas.

Freedom of use

The "use" of outer space might include many different types of human activities, which may or may not be aimed at gaining economic profit.[46] For example, every single space operation begins with the launch of the space object from Earth and extends to operations and applications taking place in outer space, which could be gathering information, recording it on a satellite payload and transmitting it back to Earth. The notion of "use" of outer space underlines why clarifying the question of the delimitation of outer space is still relevant, for it is questionable whether operations taking place (partially or fully) in outer space can be considered to be "use" under the terms of Article I of the Outer Space Treaty. It is questionable whether space-related activities taking place on Earth, such as the construction of satellites or even when the space object is transiting through air space on its way to outer space, are also covered by this freedom. An opinion which is also supported by the subsequent State practice, favors the application of Article I for all activities intended for space, thus including Earth-based operations.[47]

---

43 Indeed, the US *SPACE Act of 2015, supra* note 36, is a clear example of private space actors being endowed with the rights to enjoy freedom of use and exploration – some would argue above and beyond the original purpose and intent of the Outer Space Treaty.

44 Respectively, the second and third paragraphs of Article I of the *Outer Space Treaty*.

45 Indeed, the *Lotus* case held that under international law, States are by default free to act and that "restrictions upon the independence of States cannot […] be presumed": *The S.S. Lotus* (France v. Turkey), (1927) PCIJ, A/10 at 18.

46 S Hobe, "Article I (Outer Space Treaty)" in S Hobe, B Schmidt-Tedd & K-U Schrogl (eds), *Commentary on Space Law, Vol. 1* (2009) at 35, para 36.

47 B Cheng "Revisited: International Responsibility, National Activities and the Appropriate State", 27 Journal of Space Law (1998) at 19; F von der Dunk, "Private Enterprise and Public Interest in the European 'Spacescape'" (Leiden University, Leiden 1998) at 13; HA Wassenbergh, "An International Institutional Framework for Private Space Cctivities" (1997) XXIII Annals of Air and Space Law 529 at 533; and HA Wassenbergh, "The Law Governing International Private Commercial Activities" (1983) 12 Journal of Space Law 97 at 108.

Freedom of exploration

The exploration of outer space and its use are different terms but can overlap.[48] However, exploration is a term which emphasizes not so much on the exploitative use or the use aimed at economic benefits. Rather, the term "exploration" as employed in the Outer Space Treaty places emphasis on gaining of knowledge about outer space which enables humankind to develop further its abilities to go to and carry out activities in outer space. In other words, one may circumscribe exploration as covering such activities that aim at the discovery of resources which eventually can be exploited (i.e. used).

Freedom of scientific investigation

This freedom is mentioned explicitly in the third paragraph of Article I of the Outer Space Treaty. Of course, scientific investigation and exploration both mean activities oriented and meant for gaining new knowledge about outer space, and therefore the scope of these distinct activities overlap.[49] The fact that *scientific* investigation is named explicitly reiterates the fact that the drafters of the Outer Space Treaty saw it as a very important activity and stressed its significance by stating that "international co-operation"[50] shall be encouraged.

Limitations to the freedoms of exploration and use

The freedoms of outer space as granted by Article I of the Outer Space Treaty are not without limitations.[51] There are certain exceptions formulated in the *corpus juris spatialis* which provide limitations, under Article I itself as well as in other treaty provisions.[52]

The province of mankind

The first paragraph of Article I of Outer Space Treaty and Article 4 of the Moon Agreement provide the use and exploration of space and celestial bodies are the "province of mankind".[53] There is no elaboration what the term "mankind" encompasses.[54] However, the obligation that space activities must be "carried out for the benefit and in the interest of all States, irrespective of their degree of economic, social or scientific and technological development" does underline

---

48 Hobe, "Article I(Outer Space Treaty)", *supra* note 46 at 35, para 36.
49 Ibid.
50 For details on the principle of cooperation in space law, see below under II.
51 As Lachs opined, the freedom to use outer space "is neither absolute nor unqualified", but is limited by the right and interest of other States: Lachs, *The Law of Outer Space, supra* note 24 at 117.
52 Such as, *inter alia*, the common benefit clause (*Outer Space Treaty*, art I); *ibid*, art III (applicability of international law to outer space activities); art IV (on the military uses of outer space); art VII (international liability); and *Liability Convention*, arts 2 and 3. The UN Charter also contains a provision on the need to ensure mutual respect and benefits for al Member States: *Charter of the United Nations*, 26 June 1945, Can TS 1945 No. 7, 59 Stat. 1031, 145 UKTS805, 24 UST 2225, TIAS No. 7739 (entered into force 24 October 1945), art 2(2).
53 This principle was again reaffirmed, some three decades after the adoption of the Outer Space Treaty in *Declaration on International Cooperation in the Exploration and Use of Outer Space for the Benefit and in the Interest of All States, Taking into Particular Account the Needs of Developing Countries*, GA Res 51/122, UNGAOR, 51st Sess, UN Doc A/RES/51/122 (1996), Preamble, para 9 and para 1 [*Space Benefits Declaration*].
54 See Cocca, "Mankind as a New Legal Subject", *supra* note 42.

interest of all States and all generations (present and future) in the use and exploration of outer space and celestial bodies.[55]

This notion reiterates that in conducting of space activities, the interest of all mankind, without discrimination on the basis of space capabilities of certain nations, must be taken into consideration. The purpose of this limitation is to ensure that no State shall be discriminated in the use and exploration of outer space and that all States are entitled to share the benefits therefrom.[56]

The Common Heritage of Mankind concept

The concept of the Common Heritage of Mankind (CHM) is a principle of international law confined not only to space law.[57] It is also reflected in the UNCLOS[58] and, to a lesser extent, traces of the doctrine be found in the Antarctic Treaty.[59] Its purpose is to provide special protection to and ensure the integrity of areas which lie beyond the limit of any national territory that are of great significance for present and future generations.[60] According to the opinion of leading legal scholars, which is considered a subsidiary source of international law,[61] the specific meaning of CHM in Article 11(5) of the Moon Agreement must be interpreted within the scope of the Moon Agreement, and not in the light of UNCLOS and other international agreements in which it can be found.[62]

In space law, the CHM concept relates to the above-mentioned province of mankind clause and is specifically enshrined in the Moon Agreement. Both notions express the idea that space is an area with a special status which should be open and preserved for all States and the whole of humankind. However, it must be noted that the meaning of CHM under Article I of the Outer Space Treaty and in Article 11 of the Moon Agreement is not fully overlapping.[63] Not only does the Moon Agreement generally prohibit the national appropiation of the Moon and other celestial bodies by any means,[64] it also specifically provides that the surface, subsurface or any natural resources in place cannot become the property of any State or any other entity.[65] Again, the right to explore and use the Moon is "without discrimination of any kind, on the basis of equality and in accordance with international law".[66] To ensure that natural resources are exploited in a way that is non-discriminatory and takes into consideration the interest of all

---

55 See Edith Brown Weiss, "Intergenerational Equity", in R Wolfrum, ed, *Max Planck Encyclopedia of Public International Law*, (online edition, updated February 2013), para 15, online: Oxford Public International Law opil.ouplaw.com/view/10.1093/law:epil/9780199231690/law-9780199231690-e1421.
56 *Space Benefits Declaration, supra* note 53, Preamble, paras 8 and 9, and para 3.
57 Generally, see Rüdiger Wolfrum "Common Heritage of Mankind" in R Wolfrum, ed, *Max Planck Encyclopedia of Public International Law* (online edition, updated November 2009), online: Oxford Public International Law opil.ouplaw.com/view/10.1093/law:epil/9780199231690/law-9780199231690-e1149.
58 UNCLOS, *supra* note 11, art 136. See also Jakhu, Freeland, Hobe & Tronchetti, "Article 11 MOON", *supra* note 38, para 177 *et seq.*
59 *Antarctic Treaty, supra* note 12. See also R Wolfrum, "The Common Heritage of Mankind" (1983) 43 Zeitschrift für ausländisches öffentliches Recht und Völkerrecht 312 at 313.
60 Weiss, *supra* note 55.
61 *Statute of the International Court of Justice*, 26 June 1945, 3 Bevans 1179, 59 Stat 1031, TS 993, 39 AJIL Supp 215 (entered into force 24 October 1945), art 38(1)(d).
62 Jakhu, Freeland, Hobe & Tronchetti, "Article 11 MOON", *supra* note 38 at 394, para 194.
63 Ibid. at 394, para 193.
64 *Moon Agreement, supra* note 7, art 11(2).
65 *Ibid.*, art 11(3).
66 *Ibid.*, art 11(4).

States, once the exploitation of lunar natural resources becomes feasible the Moon Agreement enjoins States to establish an international regime and procedures to govern such exploitation.[67]

Article 11(7) of the Moon Agreement lays down the objectives establishing an international regime to govern the exploitation of the natural resources of the Moon.[68] Though the CHM concept is not expressly stated, in the exploitation of the Moon's resources, States must ensure "equitable sharing" of the benefits derived from those resources and give "special consideration" to the interests and needs of developing countries.[69] This obligation is reflective of the general principle to cooperate when engaging in outer space activities (which will be elaborated below). In summary, it can be assumed that the Moon Agreement does not prohibit the taking of resources *per se* but leaves the distribution of benefits therefrom open for a future determined by a legal regime to be established as soon as this exploitation becomes feasible.[70]

Other limitations

The freedom of action in outer space is further limited by Article III of the Outer Space Treaty, which provides that international law and the UN Charter are applicable to the exploration and use of outer spac. Further, States must ensure that their outer space activities are "in the interest of maintaining international peace and security and promoting international co-operation and understanding". Article III, in effect, denotes principles of space law, and implies that if there are no special laws governing a particular activity in outer space, general international rules are applicable to activities in outer space.

Another important limitation to the use of outer space is contained in Article IV of Outer Space Treaty. This provision limits certain military uses of outer space by specifically prohibiting, *inter alia,* the placement of nuclear weapons and weapons of mass destruction in orbit around the Earth and the establishment of military bases and the testing of weapons on celestial bodies.[71] While States are obliged to use celestial bodies "*exclusively* for peaceful purposes",[72] outer space need only be explored and used for "peaceful purposes".[73] The lack of the word "exclusively" to qualify activties in outer space has been the source of great contention with regards to what "peaceful" in reality entails. The predominant opinion is that peaceful means non-aggressive,[74] signifying that certain military activities are acceptable if exercised lawfully.[75]

67 Ibid., art 11(5).
68 Specifically, Article 11(7)(a)–(7)(c) of the *Moon Agreement* notes the purpose of the international regime includes: the orderly and safe development of the natural resources of the Moon, the rational management and the expansion of opportunities in the use of such resources.
69 *Moon Agreement, supra* note 7, art 11(7)(4).
70 Jakhu, Freeland, Hobe & Tronchetti, "Article 11 MOON", *supra* note 38 at 397, para 194.
71 *Outer Space Treaty, supra* note 2, art IV.
72 Ibid. [emphasis added]. This language is reflective of the *Antarctic Treaty, supra* note 12, Preamble, para 1.
73 *Outer Space Treaty, supra* note 2, Preamble, paras 2 and 4.
74 Carl Q Christol, "The Common Interest in the Exploration, Use and Exploitation of Outer Space for Peaceful Purposes: The Soviet-American Dilemma" (1984) 27 Colloquium on the Law of Outer Space 281 at 282–283.
75 An example would be the right to self-defense under Article 51 of the UN Charter. On the different military doctrines of States for the use of outer space, see K-U Schrogl & J Neumann, "Article IV (OST)" in S Hobe, B Schmidt-Tedd & K-U Schrogl (eds), *Cologne Commentary on Space Law Vol. 1* (2009) at 90 *et seq*. The importance of clarifying scope and legality of military activities that are considered lawful is discussed in Ram S. Jakhu, Cassandra Steer & Kuan-Wei Chen, "Conflicts in Space and the Rule of Law", Space Policy [forthcoming].

The principle of cooperation

Another foundational principle embodied in space law is the principle of cooperation between States. It is found in the Outer Space Treaty under Articles III, IX and X, and was further developed and clarified in the four subsequent treaties on space law.[76]

The infusion of the cooperation principle in space law can be traced to the evolution of international law from its beginnings as a means to "regulate the relations between these co-existing independent communities"[77] to a global governance structure aimed at fostering cooperation between States.[78] This is particularly true in domains, such as outer space, where there are recognized communal interests and obligations necessitating joint efforts of States to realize or enhance.[79] Despite the idealistic spirit of the outer space treaties and resolutions, it was clear from the beginning of the space age that even though all States are endowed with the freedom to explore and use outer space, in reality not all have the economic and technological capabilities to profit from space activities.

However, the body of space law does not provide a definition of the exact scope and meaning of the cooperation principle. It is formulated in the Outer Space Treaty in a rather broad sense, providing that States shall be "guided by" cooperation and mutual assistance and shall carry out space activities with due regard to the activities of other States.[80] In the same text, the need to cooperate appears in the context of the freedom to conduct scientific investigation if outer space,[81] and the provision which obliges States to carry out activities in outer space in accordance with international law, "in the interest of maintaining international peace and security and promoting international co-operation and understanding".[82] To better understand what the obligation to cooperate entails, another interpretation of the term "cooperation" must be sought not only in the provisions of the Outer Space Treaty but also in the texts of other outer space treaties and other legal instruments.

Article IX of the Outer Space Treaty is the basis for environmental protection of outer space. Apart from the principle of non-interference, this provision clearly embodies the cooperation principle and notes in conducting space activities, States must consider the common interest of

---

76 Namely, *Declaration of Legal Principles*, supra note 2, paras 4, 6; *Registration Convention*, supra note 7, art VI; of the *Moon Agreement*, supra note 7, arts 4(2) and 11(7)(d); and generally the *Space Benefits Declaration*, supra note 53.

77 *Lotus*, supra note 45.

78 As ICJ President Bedjaoui notes, "the face of contemporary international society" is being "markedly altered" with the "proliferation of international organizations, the gradual substitution of an international law of co-operation for the traditional international law of co-existence": *Legality of the Threat or Use of Nuclear Weapons*, Advisory Opinion, [1996], ICJ Reports 226, Declaration of President Bedjaoui, para 13. See also Lachs, *The Law of Outer Space*, supra note 24 at 117–118. See generally, *UN Charter*, supra note 52, art 1(3); and *Principles of International Law Concerning Friendly Relations and Co-operation among States in Accordance with the Charter of the United Nations*, Res 2625 (XXV), UN GAOR, 25th Sess., Supp. No. 22, UN Doc. A/2212 (24 October 1970) [*Friendly Relations Declaration*].

79 See generally, *Gabčíkovo-Nagymaros* (Hungary/Slovakia), [1997] ICJ Reports 7, Separate Opinion of Vice-President Weeramantry, 118; Bruno Simma, "From Bilateralism to Community Interest in International Law" (1994) 250 Recueil des cours 217; and in the outer space context, see Ram Jakhu, "Legal Issues relating to the Global Public Interest in Space Law" (2006) 32 Journal of Space Law 31.

80 *Outer Space Treaty*, supra note 2, art IX.

81 Ibid., art I.

82 Ibid., art III.

other States and have due regard to their activities.[83] However, there are no specific requirements or guide to States as to how they can exercise their activities in a manner that would ensure that the standard of care towards activities of other States is considered enough.[84]

The formulations found in the Outer Space Treaty and the Moon Agreement are rather broad and do not provide particular procedural mechanisms to facilitate such cooperation. Due to the fact that there is no central authority to direct and oversee acts of cooperation, it is left to the States how such cooperation as envisaged in the treaties shall be implemented.

As mentioned, there are a number of references to cooperation in the Outer Space Treaty. The term, however, is not specified or interpreted further. An attempt to clarify the duty to cooperate under Article I of the Outer Space Treaty did not bear fruit.[85] Another attempt clarify the meaning and significance of the principle of cooperation in outer space was undertaken in the 1996 Space Benefits Declaration, which empowers States to freely determine "all aspects of their participation in international cooperation in the exploration and use of outer space on an equitable and mutually acceptable basis".[86] In the years of negotiations on the exact formulation of this provision, developing and developed countries could not reach agreement on the modes of international cooperation. The position of the developing countries aimed at, *inter alia*, ensuring that they could benefit from cooperation premised on being subject to "special treatment" by the space-faring nations. This did not meet acceptance by developed nations and agreement was reached only after an approach resembling the positions of the developed countries was adopted.[87] The Space Benefits Declaration provides that the determination of international cooperation shall be based on "an equitable and mutually acceptable basis", which, however, is broadly formulated and leaves room for further interpretation by the concerned States.[88] This shows that the attempts to develop the notion of international cooperation in space and to come to a precise formulation of its structure and implementation did not result in a satisfactory development of the basis laid down in the Outer Space Treaty.

Despite the lack of clarity with regards to the meaning of and framework to realize cooperation, in reality cooperation in outer space has already taken place, especially when one looks at the existing institutionalized forms of cooperation, both at the global and regional level.[89] At the global level, there are bodies in the UN family specifically dealing with space activities, such as the the United Office for Outer Space Affairs (UNOOSA) and the UNCOPUOS). Internationally, there are also organizations that deal with space applications,

---

[83] The due regard principle applies also to the law of the sea (UNCLOS, *supra* note 11, art 87). On the discussion on the interpretation of the "due regard" principle in space law see: S Marchisio, "Article IX (OST)", para 25 in S Hobe, B Schmidt-Tedd & K-U Schrogl (eds), *Cologne Commentary on Space Law Vol. 1* (2009) at 176 *et seq*.

[84] Under general international law, the *Corfu Channel* case is instructive: *Corfu Channel* (United Kingdom v. Albania) [1949] ICJ Reports 4 at 22.

[85] See Joanne Irene Gabrynowicz & Sara M Langston, "A Chronological Survey of the Development of Art. IX of the Outer Space Treaty", Special Topics in Aerospace Law Series, No. 3, A Supplement to the Journal of Space Law, online: University of Mississippi www.spacelaw.olemiss.edu/resources/pdfs/article-ix.pdf.

[86] *Space Benefits Declaration, supra* note 53, para 2.

[87] UNCOPUOS, *Working Paper Submitted to the 30th Session of the Legal Subcommittee of UNCOPUOS by Argentina, Brazil, Chile, Mexico, Nigeria, Pakistan, the Philippines, Uruguay and Venezuela*, Annex, UN Doc A/AC.105/C.2/C.182 (9 April 1991).

[88] S Hobe & F Tronchetti, "Paragraph 2 (Space Benefits Declaration)", marginal note 78 in S Hobe, B Schmidt-Tedd & K-U Schrogl (eds), *Cologne Commentary on Space Law Vol. 3* (2015), at 336–337.

[89] W Balogh, "Institutional Aspects" in C Brünner & A Soucek (eds), *Outer Space in Society, Politics and Law* (Vienna: Springer Wien NewYork, 2011) at 198.

such as the ITU and INTELSAT. At the regional level, organizations such as the European Space Agency (ESA), the Asia Pacific Space Cooperation Organization (APSCO), EUMETSAT, EUTELSAT and ARABSAT are all prominent examples of institutional frameworks that foster the principle of cooperation in space affairs. However, the legal framework of individual forms of cooperation among States needs further elaboration in order to ensure that the general principle of cooperation contained in the *corpus juris spatialis* is effectively applicable.

The responsibility of States for space activities

International responsibility

Under general international law, States,[90] and international organizations,[91] bear international resonsibility for their activities. Responsibility for activities in outer space is laid down in Article VI of the Outer Space Treaty.[92] Article VI can be seen as a further limitation to the freedoms set out under Article I of the same treaty. Whereas States are responsible for national activities, responsibility for space activities conducted under the auspices of international organization rests jointly on the organization and its constituent members. According to Article VI of the Outer Space Treaty, only State parties can bear international responsibility for any kind of national activities in outer space, namely for national activities both by governmental agencies and non-governmental entities. Thereby, private activities in space are allowed but States must provide authorization and continuing supervision in order not to evoke their international responsibility.[93]

Responsibility for internationally unlawful acts must be differentiated from the liability regime set out in Article VII of the Outer Space Treaty[94] and in the Liability Convention, which imposes damages caused by space objects and does not require any unlawfulness of the activity itself.[95] Private entities are not a subject of international law and are not directly bound by international treaties.

What activities, it must be asked, fall under the scope of "space activities" for which States must bear international responsibility and liability? Here it must be considered which activities fall under the scope of Article VI as no definition, specification or enumeration is to be found in this or other articles of the treaties. In the terms of Outer Space Treaty and its foundational provision Article I, any human activity taking place in or intended for space is a space activity. Thereby all activities, from the launching to the operation and re-entry of a space object may entail international responsibility.

---

90 ILC, *Draft Articles on Responsibility of States for Internationally Wrongful Acts*, November 2001, Supplement No. 10 (A/56/10), chp.IV.E.1 [*2001 Draft Articles on State Responsibility*].
91 ILC, *Draft Articles on Draft Articles on Responsibility of International Organizations*, August 2011, Report of the ILC, GAOR 66th Sess, Suppl. 10, Doc. A/66/10.
92 It was first identified under the *Declaration of Legal Principles, supra* note 2, para 5.
93 *Outer Space Treaty, supra* note 2, art VI; and *Declaration of Legal Principles, supra* note 2, para 5.
94 *Declaration of Legal Principles, supra* note 2, para 8.
95 On the differentiation between responsibility and liability in space law, see, F van der Dunk, *Liability versus Responsibility in Space Law: A Misconception or Misconstruction?*, Space and Telecommunications Law Program Faculty Publications, Paper 21 (1992).

State responsibility and national space law

In particular, it is mostly the launching State which bears international responsibility, thereby it is in the interest of countries to ensure that the activity planned by the non-governmental entity will be secure and can be properly supervised. This can be achieved by setting out rules in the national legislation which impose certain requirements on the private entity. In the course of the growing commercialization and privatization of outer space, the duty of States to authorize (license) and supervise activities of their national, non-governmental entities requires more detailed national regulation to outline in more detail how space activities are to be procured. Indeed, the UN has called upon States to enact and implement national laws authorizing and providing for continuing supervision of the activities in outer space of non-governmental entities under their jurisdiction.[96]

Examples of national space laws

Currently, more than 20 States have enacted national space legislation.[97] It is in the interest of the licensing State that the national law provides for the procedures and criteria applicable to the authorized activity, the continuing supervision, for the liability of the launched space object, the registration of the launched space object and to foresee an indemnification and insurance regulation in the context of liability so that the launching State can have adequate coverage if it has recourse against the private entity.[98]

The existing national space laws are different in their scope and extent but there are some similarities. Many of the elements of national space legislation stem from the terms of the United Nations space law treaties themselves. While it is impossible to outline all the specificities of these various countries,[99] below only the legislation of some of the major space-faring countries, namely France, Russia and the United States, are briefly outlined.

France

The French law on space operations[100] contains provisions on the registration of a space object and requires a license by any operator of any nationality who aims at conducting a space operation from French territory or by means of installations located under French jurisdiction. It establishes a system of liability of the operator according to the Liability Convention. However, the liability may be reduced when fault of the victim is proven.

---

96   *Application of the Concept of the Launching State,* G.A. Res. 59/115, UN GAOR, 59th Sess, UN Doc A/RES/59/115 (2004).
97   These States are, *inter alia,* Australia, Austria, Belgium, China, France, Indonesia, Japan, Kazakhstan, the Netherlands, South Korea, Russia, United Kingdom, South Africa, Ukraine, and the US. For the collection of existing national space legislation, see UNOOSA, "National Space Law", online: UNOOSA www.unoosa.org/oosa/en/ourwork/spacelaw/nationalspacelaw/index.html; and ESA, "National Space Legislations", online: ESA www.esa.int/About_Us/ECSL_European_Centre_for_Space_Law/National_Space_Legislations.
98   See PS Dempsey, "The Emergence of National Space Law", (2013) XXXVIII Ann Air & Sp L 303.
99   For further reference, see in general: Ram S. Jakhu (ed.), *National Regulation of Space Activities* (Dordrecht: Springer, 2010); F van der Dunk (ed.), *National Space Legislation In Europe: Issues of Authorisation of Private Space Activities in the Light of Developments in European Space Cooperation* (Leiden: Martinus Nijhof Publishers, 2011).
100 France, French Space Operations Act (*Loi relative aux opérations spatiales*) of June 2008.

Russia

The Russian federal Law on Space Activities of 20 August 1993[101] requires a license for all space activities. The licensing procedure is regulated in the Law on Licensing of Certain Activities and in the Statute on Licensing of Space Activities,[102] and includes provisions on safety standards, technical quality control, including guaranteeing the availibility of qualified and professionally-educated specialists, and the observance of the international obligations of the Russian Federation. It also foresees environmental considerations as space activities should be performed with due regard to the permissible level of human-made contamination of the environment and near-Earth space. Russian law provides for a two-tier system of compulsory and voluntary insurance, which consists of an insurance for the health and life of the cosmonaut, the space infrastructure personnel and for the damage to the life, health or property of third parties. Voluntary insurance should be taken for space equipment and the risk of loss or damage to it.

The United States

The United States has enacted a number of space acts and their national legislation and their contents are by far the most comprehensive. The Commercial Space Launch Act of 1984[103] promotes of commercial space activities and launches by the private sector. It provides for an extensive licensing and foresees that policy and safety approvals from the Federal Aviation Administration (FAA) must be obtained. The Commercial Space Launch Amendments Act of 2004[104] furthermore requires commercial flight operators to make written informal disclosures as to, for example, informed consent of customers the so-called space flight participants.[105] Each license is required to provide the Office of Commercial Space Transportation with specific information for the registration in accordance with Article IV of the Registration Convention. More recently, the United States adopted legislation governing the exploitation of space natural resources.[106]

Suggestions for a model law

At its international conference in Sofia in 2012, the International Law Association adopted a model law for national space legislation.[107] This model law highlights the most important requirements for a national space law.

The ILA's Model Space Law sets out a scope of application and requires a specific (genuine) link for the law to be considered falling under the space activities of a State. This link could be

---

101 Russian Federation, *Law on Space Activities of 20 August 1993*, No. 5663-1.
102 Respectively, Law on Licensing of Certain Activities of 8 August 2001 (as amended) and Statute on Licensing of Space Activities of 30 June 2006.
103 *Commercial Space Launch Act*, Public Law 85-568, 98th Congress, H.R. 3942, 10 December 1984.
104 *Commercial Space Launch Amendments Act Of 2004*, Public Law 108–492, 108th Congress, 118 STAT. 3974, 23 December, 2004.
105 CRF §460.45 (Operator informing space flight participant of risk).
106 *SPACE Act of 2015, supra* note 36.
107 For a full text of the ILA Model Law, "Space Law", Resolution No. 6/2012 [*ILA Model Space Law*]. For the explanatory note, see UNCOPUOS, *Information on the Activities of International Intergovernmental and Non-governmental Organizations Relating to Space law*, UN Doc A/AC.105/C.2/2013/CRP.6, Legal Subcommittee of UNCOPUOS, 52nd Session (26 March 2013).

either the nationality of the natural or the legal person involved carrying out of activities in a certain territory on the national register for ships and aircrafts.[108] Further, the Model Space Law contains a working definition of what falls under the scope of "space activity", and provides that this "includes the launch, operation, guidance, and re-entry of space objects into, in and from outer space and other activities essential for the launch, operation, guidance and re-entry of space objects into, in and from outer space".[109]

The Model Space Law contains provisions governing the requirements and conditions of licensing,[110] including the suspension or withdrawl of a license,[111] and the obligation and procedure to supervise national space activities.[112] Articles 7 and 8 specifically deal with the protection of the requirement and the requirement to mitigate space debris. Further, there are specific provisions dealing with the transfer of space activity and space assets to another operator,[113] addressing the issue of registration,[114] liability,[115] mandatory insurance[116] as well as sanctions for the breach of any provisions of the model law.[117] In line with the requirement for supervision of Article VI of the Outer Space Treaty, Articles 3 and 5 of the Model Law foresee that a respective national authority shall issue license for space activities of national entities and shall supervise them. Article 4 then further enumerates which prerequisites have to be taken into account to make sure that the license applicant will be eligible to carry out the planned activity, for example proof of financial reliability, compliance with the requirements of the treaties on space law national security standards and public safety standards.

The provisions for environmental protection in the Model Space Law are reflective of the obligations under Article IX of the Outer Space Treaty, and requires that an environmental impact assessment before a space activity commences. Article 8 aims at binding States and their national entities to the rules for mitigation of space debris (e.g. by minimizing the potential risks for on-orbit break-ups, and with the post-mission disposal of non-usable space objects prevention of on-orbit collisions in accordance with international space debris mitigation standards) as this question is not regulated in the *corpus juris spatialis* and only non-binding international instruments thereto exist.[118]

It is noteworthy to mention that enacting binding rules for space debris mitigation might be the only avenue available today to prevent and to minimize the growing orbital population of space debris. This issue is very pressing as the risks posed by space debris in the most populated orbits are constantly growing and, according to calculations, might hamper space activities and even make them impossible in the course of the next two or three decades.[119]

---

108 Ibid., art 1.
109 Ibid., art 2 ("Space activity").
110 Ibid., arts 3 and 4.
111 Ibid., art 6.
112 Ibid., art 5.
113 Ibid., art 9.
114 Ibid., art 10. In line with the provisions on registration of space objects in the Outer Space Treaty and the Registration Convention, the Model Space Law also provides with regulation on the information that has to be provided by the launching entity.
115 Ibid., art 11.
116 Ibid., art 12.
117 Ibid., art 13.
118 See UNOOSA, *Space Debris Mitigation Guidelines of the Committee on the Peaceful Uses of Outer Space*, UN Doc A/AC.105/890 (2007), online: UNOOSA www.unoosa.org/pdf/bst/COPUOS_SPACE_DEBRIS_MITIGATION_GUIDELINES.pdf.
119 Darren McKnight & Donald Kessler, "We've Already Passed the Tipping Point for Orbital Debris" (2002), online: IEEE Spectrum spectrum.ieee.org/aerospace/satellites/weve-already-passed-the-tipping-point-for-orbital-debris.

The general liability regime set out in Article VII of the Outer Space Treaty and elaborated in the Liability Convention is concretized by Articles 11 Model Space Law.[120] A regime for a (limited) recourse by the State from the operator is foreseen. A crucial issue related to the authorization of private activities in space is insurance due to the fact that any space activity entails huge financial risks which must be taken into account. Thereby the operator is obliged by the Model Space Law to take out an insurance covering also damage to third parties.[121] This gives more ground to States to effectively exercise their right of recourse.

As to dispute settlement, the Model Space Law foresees that disputes should be judged upon the national court system and provides rules for sanctions in case of violations of the obligations set forth by the national law.[122]

Conclusion

Outer space is the final frontier of human activity, and its vital importance to States, commercial space actors, and indeed humanity, as a whole cannot be underlined enough. The economic, strategic, economic and social benefits space activities and space applications is immeasurable for modern society and life that is so dependent on technology. Therefore, the orderly regulation of space activities under clear and concrete rules of law is essential to fulfill the aspiration of States that space can be a realm to foster greater international cooperation, peace and security.

The foundations of international space law in fact already contain obligations to further those objectives. However, there are many unresolved and definitional issues, such as the delimitation of where outer space begins, the precise meaning of the notion of "non-appropiation" and "cooperation", which continue to trouble jurists to this day. Though these issue remain unsettled, the main *corpus* of space law, and international space law in general, has been been able to guide and facilitate the peaceful uses of outer space to date. National space laws, including the Model Space Law adopted by the ILA, coupled with the practice of States in their conduct of space activities, continually help to refine and concretize definitions and principles in this growing field of jurisprudence and literature.

---

120 For an overview of the discussion on the Model Space Law, see UNCOPUOS, *Information on the Activities of International Intergovernmental and Non-governmental Organizations Relating to Space Law*, UN Doc A/AC.105/C.2/2013/CRP.6 (2013) at 7–8.
121 *ILA Model Space Law, supra* note 106, art 12.
122 Ibid., art 13.

3
Legal status of spacecraft

Mark J. Sundahl*

I Introduction

The treatment of spacecraft under international as well as national law presents a number of issues, many of which continue to be a matter of debate. One of the core questions is which state's law applies to the operation of spacecraft. In the course of its flight, a spacecraft will typically cross the borders of multiple countries as it moves through airspace. And if the launch is successful, the spacecraft will leave the atmosphere and enter the extraterritorial realm of outer space. Throughout this journey, it is important to understand what law applies – which domestic law as well as international law – in order to address issues of regulation of the spacecraft, liability questions, and other legal matters. Other issues taken up in this chapter include the extent to which international law applies to private spacecraft, the legal status of multinational space ventures, and whether air law or space law should govern the flight of suborbital winged spaceplanes.

II Jurisdiction over space objects

Jurisdiction is one of the most fundamental questions in the law of outer space – or for any area of law – since jurisdiction determines the applicable law and the courts that enforce that law. This section provides a brief explanation of the different types of jurisdiction and then explains how this issue affects space objects.

Jurisdiction takes three basic forms: (1) prescriptive jurisdiction; (2) enforcement jurisdiction; and (3) adjudicative jurisdiction.[1] Prescriptive jurisdiction is the right of a state to apply its laws in order to regulate persons and activities.[2] Enforcement jurisdiction refers to a

---

* The author would like to thank his research assistants, Daniel Copfer and Sarah Sexton, for their valuable contributions to this chapter.
1 Cedric Ryngaert, *Jurisdiction in International Law* (Oxford: Oxford University Press, 2008) at 9. See also W Michael Reisman, ed, *Jurisdiction in International Law* (Brookfield, VT: Ashgate/Dartmouth, 1999).
2 Ryngaert, *supra* note 1 at 9, citing *Restatement (Third) of US Foreign Relations Law* §401(a) (1987). Under customary international law, a State has prescriptive jurisdiction if one of the bases of jurisdiction is present. The bases of prescriptive jurisdiction are: (1) territoriality; (2) nationality; (3) effects; (4) national security; (5) passive personality; and (6) universality. Kal Raustiala, "The Geography of Justice" (2004–2005) 73:6 Fordham L Rev 2501 at 2512.

state's right to enforce (or punish non-compliance with) its laws.[3] Adjudicative jurisdiction is the right of a state's courts to subject persons or things to their adjudicative processes and issue a ruling on a matter.[4]

Another way to conceive of the different types of jurisdiction is to distinguish between "jurisfaction" and "jurisaction". Jurisfaction describes the normative element of a state's jurisdiction which entitles a state to "make laws or take decisions, including judicial decisions, with legally binding effect".[5] Jurisaction, in contrast, represents "the concrete element of state jurisdiction which enables a state…to implement and to enforce its laws and decisions".[6]

Jurisdiction can also be "exclusive" or "concurrent". Exclusive jurisdiction exists when a court has sole jurisdiction over a matter and no other court is able to assert its jurisdiction. In contrast, concurrent jurisdiction describes the situation where multiple courts are able to assert their jurisdiction over the same matter.

With this background in mind, the following sections explain how matters of jurisdiction are handled with respect to spacecraft.

A. State of registration to maintain jurisdiction and control

Article VIII of the Outer Space Treaty explicitly grants jurisdiction over a space object to the object's state of registry:

> A state party to the Treaty on whose registry an object launched into outer space is carried shall retain jurisdiction and control over such object, and over any personnel thereof, while in outer space or on a celestial body.[7]

Pursuant to the Registration Convention, when a space object is launched into space, the launching state is required to record the launch in its national registry (as well as provide information about the object to the Secretary-General of the United Nations (UN) to be included in the international register).[8] It is this state of registry that then has "jurisdiction and control" over the object under Article VIII of the Outer Space Treaty.

One interpretation of Article VIII is that the state of registry has exclusive jurisdiction to regulate the space object, personnel thereof, and any related disputes.[9] However, the concept of "jurisdiction" in Article VIII can be more narrowly read at least in two respects. First, Article VIII can be narrowly interpreted as only granting *prescriptive* jurisdiction to the state of registry

---

3   Ryngaert, *supra* note 1 at 9.
4   Ibid. at 10.
5   Bin Cheng, *Studies in International Space Law* (New York: Oxford University Press, 1997) at 480.
6   Ibid.
7   *Treaty on Principles Governing the Activities of States in the Exploration and Use of Outer Space, Including the Moon and Other Celestial Bodies*, 27 January 1967, 610 UNTS 205, art VIII [*Outer Space Treaty*].
8   *Convention on Registration of Objects Launched into Outer Space*, 14 January 1975, 1023 UNTS 15, art II [*Registration Convention*].
9   See e.g. Setsuko Aoki, "In Search of the Current Legal Status of the Registration of Space Objects" in *54th Proceedings of the International Institute of Space Law* (The Hague: Eleven International Publishing, 2011) 245 at 248 ("[j]urisdiction arising from the registration shall be comprehensive, and a State of registry is supposed to hold legislative, judicial and, above all, enforcement jurisdiction"). See also Michael Chatzipanagiotis, *The Legal Status of Space Tourists in the Framework of Commercial Suborbital Flights* (Koln: Carl Heymanns Verlag, 2011) at 48.

over a space object.[10] This would make sense in light of the concept that the state of registry "shall retain jurisdiction and control". It could be argued that Article VIII does not address enforcement or adjudicative jurisdiction.[11] Second, even if Article VIII is read as granting jurisdiction of every form to the state of registry, it can be interpreted as a non-exclusive grant of jurisdiction – thus enabling other states to assert jurisdiction when appropriate under other law.[12] For example, customary international law permits a state to exercise prescriptive jurisdiction if any of the five bases of prescriptive jurisdiction exists (i.e. Territory, nationality, effect, national security, and passive personality).[13] Moreover, Article VI of the Outer Space Treaty suggests that any grant of jurisdiction under Article VIII is non-exclusive,[14] since the duty to supervise national activity under Article VI presupposes that a state retains jurisdiction over the space objects of one's nationals (even if it is not the state of registry).[15]

Article VIII grants jurisdiction not only over the space object but also over any "personnel thereof".[16] This jurisdiction over personnel would conceivably continue when a person leaves the spacecraft, such as during extra-vehicular activity (i.e. a "spacewalk") or when exploring a celestial body outside of the landing craft. A more difficult question is whether the jurisdiction of an astronaut from one flight element of the International Space Station would continue when the astronaut enters a flight element registered by another state. This is discussed in greater detail below in section V.[17]

A state's jurisdiction cannot be easily determined where a space object has not been registered by any state. In such a case, it would be necessary to fall back again onto the customary international law of prescriptive jurisdiction. Under customary law, a state may have the jurisdiction to regulate a space object if:

(1) the object was launched from its territory (territorial jurisdiction);
(2) the object was under the control of its nationals (nationality jurisdiction);
(3) the operation of the object had significant effects on the state (e.g., media broadcasting) (effects jurisdiction); or
(4) the object posed a security threat to a state (national security jurisdiction).

This situation may arise in the case of suborbital spacecraft where the Registration Convention will likely not require registration, since the duty to register only applies to space objects

---

10 Stephan Hobe et al., eds, *Cologne Commentary on Space Law* (Koln: Heymanns, 2009) vol 1 at 159 ("[t]he legal consequence of jurisdiction and control is the applicability of the national law of the State of registry for the object launched into outer space").
11 See e.g. Paul Larsen, "UNIDROIT Space Protocol: Comments on the Relationship between the Protocol and Existing International Space Law" in American Institute of Aeronautics and Astronautics, International Institute of Space Law & International Astronautical Federation, eds, *Proceedings of the Forty-Fourth Colloquium on the Law of Outer Space, 1 October–5 October, 2001, Toulouse, France* (Reston, VA: American Institute of Aeronautics and Astronautics, 2002) 187 at 191 ("Outer Space Treaty is not intended to cover the issue of jurisdiction of national courts").
12 Chatzipanagiotis, *supra* note 9 at 50 ("[i]t has been accepted that the State of registry does not have exclusive jurisdiction").
13 Kal Raustiala, "The Geography of Justice" (2005) 73 Fordham L. R. 2501, 2512.
14 See *Outer Space Treaty*, *supra* note 7, art VI.
15 Hobe et al., *supra* note 10 at 113 ("a State has jurisdiction over any activity that is carried on from its territory as well as over any activity that is carried on by its nationals"). Regarding the duty to authorize and supervise national space activity, see section III, below.
16 *Outer Space Treaty*, *supra* note 7, art XIII.
17 See section V, below.

launched into "earth orbit or beyond".[18] Suborbital vehicles would seem to be outside this scope and, therefore, the question of jurisdiction would have to be resolved under laws other than the space treaties.

B. The effect of transfer of ownership on jurisdiction

The plain language of Article VIII of the Outer Space Treaty implies that jurisdiction remains with the state of registry even after the transfer of the object to another state. The issue arises when the rule of jurisdiction and control under Article VIII faces the reality of commercial space where changes in ownership and control of a space object take place on a fairly regular basis.[19]

Article VIII of the Outer Space Treaty simply assigns "jurisdiction and control" of a space object to the state of registry. The treaty does not provide for any change in this assignment of jurisdiction and control, but contemplates that it will perpetually remain with the original state of registry. While this approach made sense during an age when space objects were only launched by states and the objects were not the subject of subsequent commercial transactions, which would result in the transfer of ownership and actual control to a new party, the current realities of commercial space use have revealed the flaws in the rule under Article VIII. Although it is appropriate for the launching state to have jurisdiction and control over a satellite that it has put into orbit and is operating, it no longer makes sense for the original state of registry to retain jurisdiction and control once this satellite has been transferred to another state. Instead, the transferee state should be granted jurisdiction and be required to exercise control, since this would reflect the reality that the new owner has *de facto* control of the satellite.[20] The transferee state should also have prescriptive jurisdiction under customary international law to regulate the operation of the acquired satellite.

One solution to the problem of jurisdiction remaining with the state of registry following a transfer is to have the state of registry enter into an agreement with the transferee state granting the latter jurisdiction over the satellite.[21] Such agreements are expressly permitted under Article II of the Registration Convention in order to transfer jurisdiction between launching states, but there is nothing preventing a non-launching state from accepting jurisdiction under such an agreement.[22]

---

18 *Registration Convention, supra* note 8, art II. One commentator argues that suborbital spaceplanes would only be exempt from registration if the activity took place entirely within a single country, but that if international borders were crossed, registration would be required. See Frans G von der Dunk, "Beyond What? Beyond Earth Orbit?...!: The Applicability of the Registration Convention to Private Commercial Manned Sub-Orbital Spaceflight" (2012–2013) 43:2 Cal W Intl LJ 269 at 340.

19 See e.g. Michael Chatzipanagiotis, "Registration of Space Objects and Transfer of Ownership in Orbit" (2007) 56:2 ZLW 229 at 230; Julian Hermida, "Transfer of Satellites in Orbit: An International Law Approach" in American Institute of Aeronautics and Astronautics, International Institute of Space Law & International Astronautical Federation, eds, *Proceedings of the Forty-Sixth Colloquium on the Law of Outer Space: 29 September–3 October, Bremen, Germany* (Reston, VA: American Institute of Aeronautics and Astronautics, 2004) 189 at 190. Examples of the transfer of on-orbit satellite include (1) the sale by Telesat Canada of the Anik CI and Anik CII satellites to the Argentine corporation Paracomsat S.A. (2) the sale of the satellite BSB-1A by the United Kingdom to the Swedish company Nordic Satellite AB, and (3) the taking of title by Lloyds of the Indonesian Palapa B satellite following the payment of insurance proceeds to the insured and the subsequent sale of the satellite to a new operator. See Larsen, *supra* note 11 at 190.

20 Chatzipanagiotis, *supra* note 19, at 230; Hermida, *supra* note 19 at 190.

21 Hermida, *supra* note 19 at 190.

22 *Registration Convention, supra* note 8, art II.

Another way of transferring "jurisdiction and control" to the transferee state is for the original state of registry to deregister the space object by removing it from its domestic registry.[23] Although such "de-registration" is not mentioned in the space treaties, there is nothing in the treaties that prohibits such practice.[24] This de-registration is followed by the registration of the object by the transferee state, which would result in the jurisdiction and control being attached to the new state of registry. An example of this process took place in 1997 when four satellites (AsiaSat-1, AsiaSat-2, APSTAR-I, and APSTAR-IA) previously carried on the United Kingdom (UK) registry were deregistered and then subsequently registered by China.[25]

III Authorization and continuing supervision by the appropriate state party

Separate from the grant of jurisdiction to the state of registry under Article VIII of the Outer Space Treaty is the duty prescribed under Article VI of the Treaty that all "non-governmental" space activities "require authorization and continuing supervision by the appropriate state party to the Treaty".[26] This duty follows another provision in Article VI which imposes on states "international responsibility for national activities in outer space … whether such activities are carried on by governmental agencies or by non-governmental entities".[27] Some interpret the duty to "authorize and continually supervise" non-governmental space activity as only clarifying the international responsibility imposed earlier in Article VI by making explicit that this responsibility entails the duty to authorize and supervise the state's national activity.[28] Others see it as a separate imposition of responsibility on a new category of states that qualify as the "appropriate states".[29] Some scholars have posited that only a "launching state" or the state of nationality of the actor should qualify as an "appropriate state".[30] However, others have

---

23 Armel Kerrest, "Remarks on the Notion of the Launching State" in American Institute of Aeronautics and Astronautics & International Institute of Space Law, eds, *Proceedings of the Forty-Second Colloquium on the Law of Outer Space: 4–8 October 1999, Amsterdam, the Netherlands* (Reston, VA: American Institute of Aeronautics and Astronautics, 2000) 308 at 308–09.

24 Ricky J Lee, "Effects of Satellite Ownership Transfers on the Liability of the Launching States" in International Institute of Space Law, ed, *Proceedings of the Forty-Third Colloquium on the Law of Outer Space: 2 October–6 October 2000, Rio de Janeiro, Brazil* (Reston, VA: American Institute of Aeronautics and Astronautics, 2001) 148 at 153.

25 To view information regarding these registrations, see UN, Office for Outer Space Affairs, "Online Index of Objects Launched into Outer Space", online: UNOOSA www.unoosa.org/oosa/osoindex/search-ng.jspx?lf_id= [UNOOSA, "Online Index"]. The index provides links to the following registration documents: ST/SG/SER.E/333 (April 3, 1998); ST/SG/SER.E/334 (April 3, 1998); and ST/SG/SER.E/475 (November 16, 2005). See also Francis Lyall & Paul B Larsen, *Space Law: A Treatise* (Burlington, VT: Ashgate Publishing, 2009) at 92–93.

26 *Outer Space Treaty*, *supra* note 7, art VI.

27 Ibid.

28 Hobe *et al.*, *supra* note 10 at 111.

29 For a thorough discussion of this issue, see Joyeeta Chatterjee, "Reflections on the Concepts of 'Liability' and 'Jurisdiction' in a Privatised Atmosphere" in Mark J Sundahl & V Gopalakrishnan, eds, *New Perspectives on Space Law: Proceedings of the 53rd IISL Colloquium on the Law of Outer Space, Young Scholars Sessions* (The Hague: Eleven International Publishing, 2011), at 194–97.

30 See e.g. Stephen Gorove, "Liability in Space Law: An Overview" (1983) 8 Ann Air & Sp L 377; Vladlen Vereshchetin, "Space Activities of 'Nongovernmental Entities': Issues of International and Domestic Law" in International Institute of Space Law, International Astronautical Federation & American Institute of Aeronautics and Astronautics, eds, *Proceedings of the Twenty-Sixth Colloquium on the Law of Outer Space, October 10–15, 1983, Budapest, Hungary* (New York: American Institute of Aeronautics and Astronautics, 1984) 261.

argued that the term "appropriate state" must, due to its vague nature, be interpreted broadly to potentially include any state that has jurisdiction over the particular space activity (however such jurisdiction arises) or is substantially involved in the operation or control of the space object.[31] It is this duty to "authorize and continually supervise" that requires states to enact appropriate regulatory regimes governing space activity. Examples of such regulations are described below in the section on spaceplanes.

IV The application of international law to private spacecraft

The extension of international treaty obligations to privately-owned spacecraft is difficult to deny. As a starting point, Article VI of the Outer Space Treaty extends the application of the Treaty to private space operations by requiring that states supervise the space activity of *non-governmental entities* and bear responsibility for any failure of non-governmental entities to comply with the Treaty.[32] It also makes good policy to require that all space activity (even if private) observe the duties and obligations that were written into the UN space treaties. As private activities expand, it will become ever more important that these rules are observed by private actors. That said, it is a fundamental rule that private actors are not subject to international law *per se*, so it will fall on states to enact domestic regulations that require private actors to comply with international law.

One widely observed state practice that supports the extension of the international treaties to private activity is the registration of privately-owned satellites by its launching state under the Registration Convention.[33] Similarly, a state is liable for any damage caused by space objects it launches under the Liability Convention whether such objects are owned by the government or a private entity.[34] Finally, a majority of commentators agree to extend to commercial actors the benefits of the duty to rescue personnel and return errant private spacecraft under the Rescue Agreement.[35] The duty to rescue personnel and return spacecraft would seem to apply

---

31 See e.g. William B Wirin, "Practical Implications of Launching State – Appropriate State Definitions" in American Institute of Aeronautics and Astronautics, International Institute of Space Law & International Astronautical Federation, eds, *Proceedings of the Thirty-Seventh Colloquium on the Law of Outer Space: October 9–14, 1994, Jerusalem, Israel* (Washington, DC: American Institute of Aeronautics and Astronautics, 1995) 113; Armel Kerrest, "Remarks on the Responsibility and Liability for Damage Caused by Private Activity in Outer Space" in American Institute of Aeronautics and Astronautics & International Institute of Space Law, eds, *Proceedings of the Forty-Second Colloquium on the Law of Outer Space: 4–8 October 1999, Amsterdam, the Netherlands* (Reston, VA: American Institute of Aeronautics and Astronautics, 2000) 139.

32 *Outer Space Treaty*, supra note 7, art VI.

33 *Registration Convention*, supra note 8, art I. See also UN, Committee on the Peaceful Uses of Outer Space, *Practice of States and International Organizations in Registering Space Objects: Replies from Member States*, UNGAOR, 2004, UN Doc A/AC.105/C.2/L.250/Add.1 (France "registers national satellites, whether they belong to government organizations or private companies" at 3).

34 *Convention on the International Liability for Damage Caused by Space Objects*, 29 March 1972, 961 UNTS 187 [*Liability Convention*]. Regarding the liability of launching States for harm caused by commercial ventures, see Bruce A Hurwitz, "Liability for Private Commercial Activities in Outer Space" in International Institute of Space Law, ed, *Proceedings of the Thirty-Third Colloquium on the Law of Outer Space, October 6–12, 1990, Dresden, Germany* (Washington, DC: American Institute of Aeronautics and Astronautics, 1991) 37 at 39; Ricky J Lee, "Reconciling International Space Law with the Commercial Realities of the Twenty-First Century" (2000) 4 Sing JICL 194 at 230.

35 *Agreement on the Rescue of Astronauts, the Return of Astronauts and the Return of Objects Launched into Outer Space*, 22 April 1968, 672 UNTS 119 [*Rescue Agreement*]. See e.g. IHPh Diederiks-Verschoor & W Paul Gormley, "The Future Legal Status of Nongovernmental Entities in Outer Space: Private

to commercial ventures, since nothing in the text of either the Outer Space Treaty or the Rescue Agreement explicitly excludes commercial venture or limits the scope of the duties to government-sponsored missions. An example of this can be found in Article 2 of the Rescue Agreement:

> If, owing to accident, distress, emergency or unintended landing, the personnel of a spacecraft land in territory under the jurisdiction of a Contracting Party, it shall immediately take all possible steps to rescue them and render them all necessary assistance.[36]

None of the terms in the Rescue Agreement excludes commercial enterprises in their ordinary meaning – in fact, the term "personnel" (as is used in Article 2) is typically used in a commercial context (e.g., cruise ship personnel) as well as in government contexts.[37] This lack of any distinction between private and public spaceflight in the plain language of the Rescue Agreement supports a broad interpretation which would require states to rescue non-governmental personnel and return private spacecraft. Moreover, there have been at least seven instances of space objects being found on Earth resulting in the notification of the UN Secretary-General and the return of the assets to the launching authority as is required under the Rescue Agreement.[38] At least two of these incidents involve the recovery of private spacecraft. Specifically, the governments of Argentina and South Africa, in 2000 and 2004, respectively, notified the UN Secretary-General of the discovery and planned return to the United States (US) of space objects that had been found in their respective territories.[39] In both cases, the governments had determined prior to giving notification that the space objects were parts of Delta II launch vehicles which – although they delivered government payloads – were owned by a private company, namely the Boeing Company.

V The legal status of multinational space objects

Although most satellites and other space objects are typically subject to the jurisdiction and control of a single state, this general rule can be complicated by space objects that involve the

---

Individuals and Companies as Subjects and Beneficiaries of International Space Law" (1977) 5:1&2 J Space L 125 at 155; Frans G von der Dunk, "Space for Tourism? Legal Aspects of Private Spaceflight for Tourist Purposes" in American Institute of Aeronautics and Astronautics & International Institute of Space Law, eds, *Proceedings of the Forty-Ninth Colloquium on the Law of Outer Space: 2–6 October 2006, Valencia, Spain* (Washington, DC: American Institute of Aeronautics and Astronautics, 2007).

36 *Registration Convention*, supra note 8, art II.
37 One example of the use of the term "personnel" to refer to employees can be found in the name of the US Office of Personnel Management (OPM) which oversees the federal workforce. See the OPM website at *www.opm.gov*.
38 Descriptions of these instances of privately-owned space objects being found are provided in Frans G von der Dunk, "A Sleeping Beauty Awakens: The 1968 Rescue Agreement after Forty Years" (2008) 34:2 J Space L 411 at 426–31.
39 UN, Office for Outer Space Affairs, *Note verbale dated 23 March 2004 from the Permanent Mission of Argentina to the United Nations (Vienna) addressed to the Director-General of the United Nations Office at Vienna*, UN Doc A/AC.105/825, 2004, online: UNOOSA www.unoosa.org/oosa/oosadoc/data/documents/2004/aac.105/aac.105825_0.html; UN, Office for Outer Space Affairs, *Note verbale dated 3 July 2000 from the Permanent Mission of the Republic of South Africa to the United Nations (Vienna) addressed to the Secretary General*, UN Doc A/AC.105/740, 2000, online: UNOOSA www.unoosa.org/oosa/oosadoc/data/documents/2000/aac.105/aac.105740_0.html.

participation of multiple states (or their nationals). For example, spacecraft may be constructed out of components manufactured in different states. The construction and launch of a space object may also be a joint venture of multiple companies from different states. Legal obligations may also be shared by multiple states at the same time, which is the case under the Liability Convention which imposes several and joint liability on all "launching states" – a term that captures not only the state that launches (or procures the launch of) the object, but also the state from whose territory or facility an object is launched.[40]

The following sections examine how particular issues in international space law are raised by two multinational ventures: the International Space Station and Sea Launch, the launch service provider.

A. The international space station

The International Space Station (ISS) is the greatest example of international cooperation in outer space. The first module (or "flight element") was placed in orbit in 1998 by Russia and since then numerous other flight elements or other equipment have been contributed by the partner states, namely the US, Canada, Japan, and eleven member states of the European Space Agency (ESA) (Belgium, Denmark, France, Germany, Italy, the Netherlands, Norway, Spain, Sweden, the UK, and Switzerland).[41] Astronauts (and occasionally space tourists) move between the different flight elements as they conduct science and carry out other activities.

The operation of the ISS is governed by the Intergovernmental Agreement on the International Space Station (IGA) which addresses a number of legal topics, such as civil and criminal jurisdiction, intellectual property, and the operational responsibilities of the partner states.[42] The jurisdiction provisions of the IGA are most relevant to the question of legal status and is the focus of this section.

Article 5 of the IGA provides that "each Partner shall register as space objects the flight elements ... which it provides" according to Article II of the Registration Convention.[43] To date, different flight elements have been registered by the US, Russia, Japan, and the ESA.[44] Article 5 goes on to state that "[p]ursuant to Article VIII of the Outer Space Treaty and Article II of the Registration Convention, each Partner shall retain jurisdiction and control over the elements it registers ..."[45] While this portion of Article 5 grants jurisdiction over registered space objects in the same way as the Registration Convention, the jurisdiction over personnel is slightly different under the IGA. Whereas the Registration Convention grants jurisdiction over the space object

---

40 *Liability Convention*, supra note 34, arts I, V(1).
41 For more information on the International Space Station, see US, National Aeronautics and Space Administration, "International Space Station", online: NASA www.nasa.gov/mission_pages/station/main/index.html.
42 *Agreement among the Government of Canada, Governments of Member States of the European Space Agency, the Government of Japan, the Government of the Russian Federation, and the Government of the United States of America concerning Cooperation on the Civil International Space Station*, 29 January 1998, TIAS No. 12927 [IGA].
43 IGA, ibid., art 5(1).
44 Modules and who registered it based on the UN registry: Zarya (US), Unity (US), Zvezda (Russia), Destiny (US), Quest (US), Pirs (Russia), Poisk (Russia), Harmony (US), Tranquility (US), Columbus (ESA), Kibo (Japan), Cupola (US), Rassvet (Russia), and Leonardo (US). See US, National Aeronautics and Space Administration, "International Space Station: Space Station Assembly", online: NASA www.nasa.gov/mission_pages/station/structure/elements/mplm.html.
45 IGA, *supra* note 42, art 5(2).

and the "personnel thereof", the IGA grants jurisdiction to the partner states over their nationals wherever they are "in or on the Space Station".[46] Therefore, a state retains jurisdiction over their nationals even when their nationals are in a flight element registered by another state.

The foregoing jurisdictional rules are modified with respect to criminal jurisdiction. Under Article 22 of the IGA, primary jurisdiction to prosecute an astronaut who has committed a crime on board the ISS and is a national of Canada, Japan, Russia, the US, or one of the European partner states is granted to that state of nationality.[47] Secondary jurisdiction to prosecute the perpetrator is granted to both (1) the state of the victim, and (2) the state that owns the flight element where the crime took place (or where criminal damage occurred to the flight element).[48] This secondary jurisdiction is triggered if the state of the perpetrator's nationality (1) agrees to allow the other state to prosecute or (2) fails to provide adequate assurance that it will prosecute.[49] For example, if a Japanese astronaut commits a crime of violence against a Russian astronaut in a flight element registered by the US, Japan would have jurisdiction to prosecute the perpetrator. However, if Japan either agrees to the jurisdiction of Russia or the US or fails to provide assurance that it will prosecute, either Russia or the US could prosecute the Japanese astronaut.[50]

Special jurisdictional provisions are also provided with respect to intellectual property.[51] The core jurisdictional provision regarding the application of intellectual property law is set forth in Article 21(2), which states that, "for purposes of intellectual property law, an activity occurring in or on a Space Station flight element shall be deemed to have occurred only in the territory of the partner state of that element's registry".[52] This provision returns to the basic rule of the Outer Space Treaty that the jurisdiction of the state of registry applies to each separate flight element. This has the effect of ensuring that discoveries and inventions will be protected by the intellectual property law of the state of registry, while also limiting the applicable law to that of the state of registry.[53] If a discovery or invention occurs in an ESA-registered flight element, any of the ESA partner states may apply its intellectual property laws.[54] However, the holder of any such intellectual property rights may only recover damages for infringement in one ESA partner state.[55]

B. Sea Launch: an example of a multinational private enterprise

Sea Launch is a multinational corporation founded in 1999 that offers launch services. The company was originally composed of five companies: a US company (Boeing), a Russian

---

46 Ibid.
47 Ibid., art 22(1). This list includes those States that have registered flight elements.
48 Ibid., art 22(2).
49 Ibid.
50 For a thorough treatment of criminal jurisdiction on the ISS and references to writings on the topic, see Michael Chatzipanagiotis & Rafael Moro-Aguilar, "Criminal Jurisdiction in International Space Law: Future Challenges in View of the ISS IGA" in International Institute of Space Law, ed, *Proceedings of the International Institute of Space Law* (forthcoming 2015). See also PJ Blount, "Jurisdiction in Outer Space: Challenges of Private Individuals in Space" (2007) 33:2 J Space L 299 at 312–13.
51 See *IGA, supra* note 42, art 21.
52 Ibid., art 21(2).
53 Rochus Moenter, "The International Space Station: Legal Framework and Current Status" (1998–1999) 64:4 J Air L & Com 1033 at 1053.
54 IGA, *supra* note 42, art 21(2).
55 Ibid., art 21(4).

company (Energia), two Ukrainian companies, and a Norwegian company.[56] Sea Launch filed for Chapter 11 bankruptcy reorganization in 2010 during which Energia gained 95 percent of the interest.[57] This left only 2.5 percent of the company equity for both Boeing and the Norwegian company. Sea Launch has its corporate headquarters in Switzerland and is incorporated in the Cayman Islands.[58] The company has two main pieces of equipment: the Odyssey Launch Platform (a converted oil rig where the launches occur), and an Assembly and Command Ship (where rocket and payload are assembled and transported).[59] Sea Launch's homeport is in Long Beach California, where the platform and the Command Ship are docked.[60]

What makes Sea Launch unique is that its launches take place on the high seas in the Pacific Ocean near the Equator.[61] Unlike every other launch site in the world, the Odyssey is not on a state's territory at the time of launch. Launching from the high seas raises the question of what state is a "launching state" for the purpose of allowing for registration of the space objects launched by Sea Launch as well as for the purpose of assigning liability under the Liability Convention. Similarly, launching from non-sovereign territory, such as the high seas, complicates the question of what the "launching authority" is for purposes of returning any lost space objects to the launching authority pursuant to the Rescue Agreement.

The jurisdiction and control over space objects launched by Sea Launch is granted to the state of registration under the Registration Convention.[62] Pursuant to the Convention, only a "launching state" can register a space object. This is where the launching of objects from the high seas creates special issues. Because the high seas are not subject to the sovereignty of any state, there is no launching state on the basis of territory of the launch site. When Sea Launch launches an object, a state can only be deemed a launching state if it can be said to (1) have launched the object, (2) have procured the launch, or (3) own the facility from which the launch takes place.[63] Pursuant to these criteria, there are a number of theories for which states would qualify as a launching state.

- Russia could qualify as a launching state under the theory that it owns the facility from which the launches take place since the Russian company Energia owns 95 percent of Sea Launch.[64] In contrast, the US is unlikely to be a launching state under this theory, since

---

56 See Armel Kerrest, "Launching Spacecraft from the Sea and the Outer Space Treaty: The Sea Launch Project" (1998) 23:1 Air & Space L 16. To learn more about the Sea Launch, see online: Sea Launch www.sea-launch.com.
57 Regarding the Sea Launch bankruptcy filing, see Sea Launch, News Release, "Sea Launch Company Emerges From Chapter 11" (27 October 2010), online: Sea Launch web.archive.org/web/20110927163423/www.sea-launch.com/news_releases/2010/nr_101027.html. Regarding the percentage of ownership, see Nate Raymond, "Boeing Sues Sea Launch Partners for $350 Million", *Reuters* (4 February 2013), online: Reuters www.reuters.com/article/2013/02/04/us-boeing-sealaunch-idUSBRE9130RU20130204.
58 See Sea Launch, "About Sea Launch", online: Sea Launch www.sea-launch.com/about; Kerrest, *supra* note 56 at 16.
59 See ibid.
60 See ibid.
61 See Kerrest, *supra* note 56, and Armel Kerrest, "Launching Spacecraft from the Sea and the Outer Space Treaty: The Sea Launch Project," in (1997) *Proceedings of the 40th Colloquium on the Law of Outer Space* 264.
62 See section II, above.
63 *Registration Convention*, *supra* note 8, art I.
64 Kerrest, *supra* note 56 at 18.

- Boeing, an entity organized in the US, owns only 2.5 percent of the company, thus lacking substantial control over the launch facility.[65]
- The UK might also qualify as a launching state under the theory that it owns the launch facility, since Sea Launch is incorporated in the Cayman Islands, a British Crown Colony.[66]
- Under the theory of procuring the launch, any state that (or state whose company) contracts for Sea Launch's launch services could be treated as a launching state.[67]

A search of the UN Online Index of Objects Launched into Outer Space shows that a number of states have registered satellites placed into orbit by Sea Launch, including the US, Brazil, Japan, and Italy. A state will typically register those satellites that it owns and has procured the launch of them, or those satellites owned by a company of its nationality.[68] The US has asserted jurisdiction over Sea Launch by licensing all of its launches through the Office of Commercial Space Transportation (AST) of the Federal Aviation Administration (FAA), both before and after its reorganization in 2010.[69]

The Liability Convention imposes liability for damage caused by a space object on the "launching state" (or launching states).[70] The definition of "launching state" in the Liability Convention is the same as in the Registration Convention – and, therefore, the analysis of which state qualifies as a launching state for the purposes of assigning liability would follow the same analysis described above.[71]

Pursuant to the Rescue Agreement, in the event of an unintended landing of a space object, the object and any astronauts on board must be returned to the "launching authority".[72] The "launching authority" is defined as the state that is "responsible for launching" the object.[73] The problem with this definition is that a state may not qualify as being "responsible for launching" a space object when the space venture is private in nature (such as Sea Launch). The analysis is further complicated if a launch takes place in non-sovereign territory, such as the high seas. One straightforward solution would be to require the return of a state-owned space object (such as a surveillance satellite) to that state. Likewise, a private space object should be returned to the state where the company is incorporated.

VI Spaceplanes

There are a number of suborbital spaceplanes under development by private companies that will soon be flying passengers, science experiments, and other cargo into suborbital space. The leading companies in this field (with the name of their spacecraft in parentheses) are Virgin Galactic (SpaceShipTwo), XCOR (Lynx), and Swiss Space Systems (SOAR). As the technology

---

65   Ibid.
66   Ibid.
67   Ibid. at 19. See also Kai-Uwe Schrogl & Charles Davies, "A New Look at the 'Launching State': The Results of the UNCOPUOS Legal Subcommittee Working Group "Review of the Concept of the Launching State" 2000–2002" in International Institute of Space Law, ed, *Proceedings of the Forty-Fifth Colloquium on the Law of Outer Space, 10 October–19 October 2002, Houston, Texas* (Reston, VA: American Institute of Aeronautics and Astronautics, 2003) 386.
68   See UNOOSA, "Online Index", *supra* note 25.
69   See US, Federal Aviation Administration, "Data & Research: Launches", online: US Federal Aviation Administration www.faa.gov/data_research/commercial_space_data/launches/?type=Licensed.
70   *Liability Convention, supra* note 34, arts II, III.
71   Ibid., art I.
72   *Rescue Agreement, supra* note 35, arts 4, 5(3).
73   Ibid., art 6.

for this new generation of spacecraft is developed, the legal status of these vehicles is a matter of considerable debate. One question is whether these winged spacecraft that take off and land like airplanes should be subject to international air law or to the law of outer space. Individual states are also struggling with this question on the domestic level, namely whether these spacecraft should be regulated under existing aviation laws or under new laws specifically designed for this new type of space vehicle.

A. Air law vs. space law

Spaceplanes, such as Virgin Galactic's SpaceShipTwo or XCOR's Lynx, traverse airspace on the way to (and when returning from) their apogee at approximately 65 miles (or 105 kilometers) above the Earth.[74] The preliminary legal question regarding such vehicles is whether they should be governed by air law or by space law – or by both. This question has multiple facets. Nonetheless, the initial question is whether a spaceplane that reaches an apogee of 65 miles has entered outer space at all. If not, it is clear that air law should apply. This raises the long-debated question regarding where outer space begins. Two theoretical approaches in determining whether a spaceplane is an aircraft or a space object have also been applied to resolve the question of air law versus space law: the *spatialist* approach and the *functionalist* approach. The following sections explore these questions and theories.

1 The delimitation of outer space under customary international law

In many cases, the answer to the question of whether an object is in outer space will be clear. For example, satellites being sent into orbit will undeniably operate in outer space and will, therefore, qualify as space assets. The more difficult question will involve equipment that is operating on the border of outer space. For example, a court could in good faith raise the question whether a suborbital spaceplane that reaches a maximum altitude of 105 kilometers (just above the von Kármán line, which lies approximately 100 kilometers above the Earth and is widely viewed as the limit of airspace) is a space asset.[75] The same question could be raised with respect to a spaceplane that reaches an altitude of ninety-five kilometers – just short of the von Kármán line.

None of the existing space treaties provide any useful guidance regarding the delimitation of outer space. Although the Outer Space Treaty clearly contemplates its application to activities on the Moon and other celestial bodies, to objects launched into outer space, and to objects placed into orbit around the Earth, the treaty does not explicitly define where "outer space" begins.[76] Both the Liability Convention and the Registration Convention define space object as the "component parts of a space object as well as its launch vehicle and parts thereof".[77] However, the definition only clarifies that "space object" includes its launch vehicle and components. The treaties do not establish the limit of outer space.[78]

---

74 See the Virgin Galactic website at *www.virgingalactic.com/human-spaceflight/your-flight-to-space* and the XCOR website at *spaceexpeditions.xcor.com/the-spaceflight*.
75 See Hobe *et al.*, *supra* note 10 (The "von Kármán line", which bears the name of the Hungarian aerospace engineer Theodore von Kármán, is that point at the edge of the Earth's atmosphere "where aerodynamic lift is exceeded by centrifugal force" at 31).
76 See *Outer Space Treaty*, *supra* note 7, arts I, II, IV, VII, VIII.
77 *Liability Convention*, *supra* note 34, art I(d); *Registration Convention*, *supra* note 8, art I(d).
78 See Ibid.

In the absence of any helpful treaty law, one could look for customary international law regarding the delimitation of outer space. Nonetheless, there is likely not sufficient state practice (or other evidence of customary law) at this point to clearly support an assertion that customary international law exists regarding the boundary of air space and outer space. If a customary international law on this issue were to come into being, the evidence suggests that it will define the boundary of outer space as (or near) the von Kármán line. Evidence of state practice in support of this conclusion can be found in Australian law which suggests that the boundary of outer space lies at 100 kilometers, since the law requires a license only for the launch of space objects above that elevation.[79] In addition, South African law establishes the border of outer space by defining outer space as "the space above the surface of the earth from a height of which it is in practice possible to operate an object in an orbit around the earth".[80] This would place the boundary, under optimal circumstances, in the neighborhood of the von Kármán line. Further support for customary international law may be found in the *Draft Treaty on the Prevention of the Placement of Weapons in Outer Space, the Threat or Use of Force against Outer Space Objects*, submitted in 2008 at the UN Conference on Disarmament by China and Russia to ban weapons in outer space. This draft text defines outer space as "space beyond the elevation of approximately 100 km above ocean level of the Earth".[81] Additionally, the US FAA issued the 2006 Human Space Flight Requirements for Crew and Space Flight Participants ("Human Space Flight Requirements") pursuant to the Commercial Space Launch Amendments Act of 2004.[82] Although these regulations do not define outer space, they are intended to cover the operations of suborbital space tourism companies, such as Virgin Galactic, that are acquiring licenses under the regulations in order to fly their vehicles to 100 kilometers. State practice supporting an even lower elevation for the limit of outer space can be found in the regulations of the US Air Force, which grant an astronaut rating to Air Force officers who fly fifty miles above the Earth's surface.[83]

Briefly stated, there is evidence in state legislation and state practice that could be used to build support for a customary international law of fixing a boundary of space at approximately 100 kilometers above sea level. However, the amount of evidence may not amount to the level that is required to sustain the existence of customary international law.

2 The spatialist and functionalist theories

The question of whether air law or space law should apply to a spaceplane could also be determined through the application of two theories that distinguish an aircraft from a space object. One approach, known as the *spatialist* theory, is to identify the border of outer space on

---

79 *Space Activities Act 1998* (Cth), s 8. See Noel Siemon & Steven Freeland, "Regulation of Space Activities in Australia" in Ram S. Jakhu, ed, *National Regulation of Space Activities* (New York: Springer, 2010) 37 at 51.
80 *Space Affairs Act, 1993* (S Afr), No. 84 of 1993, s 1(xv). See also UN, Committee on the Peaceful Uses of Outer Space, *National Legislation and Practice relating to Definition and Delimitation of Outer Space: Replies received from Member States: Australia*, UNGAOR, 2006, UN Doc A/AC.105/865/Add.1.
81 *Draft Treaty on the Prevention of the Placement of Weapons in Outer Space and of the Threat or Use of Force against Outer Space Objects*, art I(a), online: UNTERM unterm.un.org/DGAACS/unterm.nsf/0f99a7d734f48ac385256a07005e48fb/b8846544f816abf485257922005c37ee.
82 14 CFR Parts 401, 415, 431, 435, 440, 460 (2012); 49 USC §§ 70101–70305 (2011).
83 See US, Air Force, *Air Force Instruction 11–402: Aviation and Parachutist Service, Aeronautical Ratings and Aviation Badges* (5 February 2013) at para 2.3.2, online: US Air Force static.e-publishing.af.mil/production/1/af_a3_5/publication/afi11-402/afi11-402.pdf.

the basis of the natural properties of space.[84] The other approach, known as the *functionalist* theory, is to classify an object as a space object on the basis of its function as such object as opposed to an aircraft.[85]

The most widely-supported proposal under the spatialist theory has been to draw the line between airspace and outer space at the von Kármán line.[86] Among the other possible theories under a spatialist approach are to place the boundary between air space and outer space (1) where there is no longer any atmosphere; (2) where the Earth's gravitational pull is balanced by that of another celestial body (so-called "Lagrange points"); (3) where the lowest possible orbital perigee for a satellite is located; or (4) where the ability of a state to exercise sovereignty ends.[87]

The functionalist approach, though avoids some of the difficulties that come with the spatialist approach, brings its own challenges. Rather than focusing on the identification of a physical boundary between airspace and outer space, the concept behind the functionalist approach is to apply air law to those objects engaged in aviation and apply space law to those objects intended to operate in space.[88] This test would apply regardless of where the object happened to be physically located at the time a legal claim arose. For example, a satellite being launched into space (along with its launch vehicle) would be treated as a space object even if the launch was aborted and the object never reached space. With respect to spaceplanes, the *functionalist* theory provides potentially greater ambiguity than does the *spatialist* theory, since they operate as aircraft while in the atmosphere, but are also designed to enter outer space. It could be contended that the ultimate function of a spaceplane is to enter outer space and, therefore, it should be treated as a space object. However, others might argue that the majority of its flight path takes place in air space and should, therefore, be subjected to air law. A third option might be to apply air law to the vehicle while in air space and space law when it enters outer space.[89]

---

84   For a discussion of the spatialist approach, see Luboš Perek, "Scientific Criteria for the Delimitation of Outer Space" (1977) 5:1&2 J Space L 111.
85   For a discussion of the functionalist approach, see Stephen Gorove, "Aerospace Object – Legal and Policy Issues for Air and Space Law" (1997) 25:2 J Space L 101.
86   Hobe et al., *supra* note 11 at 31; IHPh Diederiks-Verschoor & Vladimir Kopal, *An Introduction to Space Law*, 3rd ed (The Hague: Kluwer Law International, 2008) at 17; Lyall & Larsen, *supra* note 25 at 167–68.
87   Diederiks-Verschoor & Kopal, *supra* note 86 at 17; Lyall & Larsen, *supra* note 25 at 166–69.
88   Diederiks-Verschoor & Kopal, *supra* note 86 at 18–20; Lyall & Larsen, *supra* note 25 at 169–70.
89   For more detailed discussion of the delimitation of space see, in addition to the works cited above, Eilene Galloway, "The Definition of Outer Space", in (1968) *Proceedings of the 10th Colloquium of Outer Space* 268; Vladimir Kopal, "What is 'Outer Space' in Astronautics and Space Law", in (1968) *Proceedings of the 10th Colloquium of Outer Space* 275; Gennady P. Zhukov, "The Problem of the Definition of Outer Space", in (1968) *Proceedings of the 10th Colloquium of Outer Space* 271; Vladimir Kopal, "The Question of Defining Outer Space" (1980) 8 Journal of Space Law 154; Bin Cheng (1983) "The Legal Status of Outer Space and Relevant Issues: Delimitation of Outer Space and Definition of Peaceful Use", 11 Journal of Space Law 89; Oscar Fernandez-Brital (1995) "UNCOPUOS Legal Subcommittee March–April 1993 Meeting and the Limit between Air Space and Outer Space", in *Proceedings of the 37th Colloquium of Outer Space* 244; Robert F.A. Goedhart (1996) *The Never Ending Dispute: Delimitation of Air Space and Outer Space*; Katherine M. Gorove (2000) "Delimitation of Outer Space and the Aerospace Object – Where is the Law", 28 Journal of Space Law 11.

3 The jurisdiction of ICAO

Related to the question of whether space law applies to suborbital spaceplanes is whether the International Civil Aviation Organization (ICAO) has jurisdiction to govern the operation of these vehicles. ICAO is a specialized UN agency concerned with international civil aviation. The primary source of public international air law is the Chicago Convention that established ICAO.[90] The Convention only applies to civil "aircraft".[91] However, the Convention does not define the term "aircraft". The term is defined in the Annexes to the Convention as "[a]ny machine that can derive support in the atmosphere from the reactions of the air other than the reactions of the air against the earth's surface".[92] Some commentators have noted that the mere fact that a spaceplane, which would otherwise satisfy the definition of "aircraft" under the Chicago Convention, briefly enters space does not prevent the application of the Chicago Convention and other instruments of air law.[93] Even if suborbital spacecraft do not come within the definition of "aircraft", the argument can be made that ICAO still has jurisdiction over suborbital spaceflight to the degree necessary to ensure the safety of international civil aviation, as is the stated purpose of the Chicago Convention.[94] Such regulation could, at a minimum, require the incorporation of suborbital flights in the international air traffic management system. If suborbital spacecraft does fall within the jurisdiction of ICAO, then ICAO would have the authority to issue Standards and Recommended Practices (SARPs) to be implemented by ICAO member states. ICAO has formed a "learning group" of industry leaders, academics, and other stakeholders to explore the possible involvement of the organization in the suborbital industry.[95] However, as this book goes to print, this project remains in its early stages.

B. Domestic regulation of human space flight

While the question regarding the application of international air and space law continues to be debated, states have undertaken efforts to develop domestic regulatory regimes to govern suborbital spaceflight. Although the US was the first state to issue regulations on the subject, other states, including the UK, Spain, Sweden, Belgium, and Curaçao, have also undertaken various initiatives with the purpose of developing a regulatory regime for human spaceflight. It should be mentioned that the European Aviation Safety Agency explored the creation of harmonized regulations to apply across the European Union (EU). Those efforts, however, have

---

90   *Convention on International Civil Aviation*, 7 December 1944, 15 UNTS 295, Can TS 1944 No. 36, ICAO Doc 7300/9 [*Chicago Convention*].
91   Ibid., art 3(a).
92   See ICAO (2010) 9 International Standards and Recommended Practices: Annex 6 to the Convention on International Civil Aviation: Part I, International Commercial Air Transport – Aeroplanes, at c 1. For a summary of the Annexes to the Chicago Convention, see ICAO, *The Convention on International Civil Aviation: Annexes 1 to 18*, online: ICAO www.icao.int/Documents/annexes_booklet.pdf.
93   Rafael Moro-Aguilar, "National Regulation of Private Suborbital Flights: A Fresh View" (2015) 10 FIU L. R. 679. 683–684. Regarding ICAO's potential jurisdiction over suborbital spacecraft, see generally Paul Stephen Dempsey & Michael C Mineiro, "The ICAO's Legal Authority to Regulate Aerospace Vehicles" in Joseph N Pelton & Ram S. Jakhu, eds, *Space Safety Regulations and Standards* (New York: Elsevier, 2010) 245.
94   Dempsey & Mineiro, *supra* note 93 at 246–47.
95   Notes of the Author from the October 21, 2015 meeting of the FAA Commercial Space Transportation Advisory Committee.

stalled – leaving the individual member states of the EU to develop their own domestic regulations.[96]

The FAA's Human Space Flight Requirements require that a license be procured by a space vehicle operator intending to launch (or re-enter) a vehicle containing passengers (or "space flight participants").[97] In order to obtain the license and commence launch activity, the operator must comply with a number of provisions contained in the FAA Requirements. These requirements include: (i) showing financial responsibility; (ii) obtaining reciprocal waivers of claims; (iii) complying with certain minimum operational requirements; (iv) crew training; (v) fully disclosing the risks of flight to prospective space flight participants; and (vi) obtaining the informed written consent of space flight participants.[98]

The UK Civil Aviation Authority (CAA) issued a report in 2014 that recommends a temporary regulatory approach to govern suborbital flights in the UK.[99] The report recommends an approach that is in effect very similar to the licensing regime adopted in the US. While the UK CAA determined that suborbital spaceplanes would likely come within the definition of "aircraft" under the Chicago Convention and would, therefore, be subject to existing air law, the proposals for the application of such law resulted in an overall system that resembles the US regime.[100] For example, spaceplanes would be deemed "experimental aircraft", which would exempt them from many of the onerous regulations that otherwise apply to civil aircraft in the UK.[101] While such a designation would typically prevent the transport of private passengers, the report urged that an exception be made to that rule so that paying passengers could be flown on the spaceplanes.[102] Finally, the requirement of "informed consent" of the passengers (the core principle of the US regime) was also adopted in the report.[103]

The Spanish legislature is also considering a bill for the creation of a licensing process for suborbital spaceflight, which is strongly influenced by the US model.[104] Like the FAA regulations, the Spanish proposal allows for the issuance of a launch license upon the showing of compliance with environmental and financial responsibility requirements, and requires the informed consent of all passengers.[105]

---

96 Moro-Aguilar, *supra* note 93.
97 Regarding the Human Space Flight Requirements, see section V.A.1, *above*. For a general description of the Human Space Flight Requirements, see Tracey Knutson, "What is "Informed Consent" For Space-Flight Participants in the Soon-To-Launch Space Tourism Industry?" (2007) 33:1 J Space L 105. See also Stephan Hobe, "Legal Aspects of Space Tourism" (2007–2008) 86:2 Neb L Rev 439.
98 14 CFR Parts 401, 415, 431, 435, 440, 460 (2012).
99 See UK, Civil Aviation Authority, *UK Government Review of Commercial Spaceplane Certification and Operations* (Technical Report, CAP 1189) (July 2014), online: GOV.UK www.gov.uk/government/uploads/system/uploads/attachment_data/file/329758/spaceplanes-tech.pdf; UK, Civil Aviation Authority, *UK Government Review of Commercial Spaceplane Certification and Operations* (Summary & conclusions, CAP 1198) (July 2014), online: GOV.UK www.caa.co.uk/docs/33/CAP1198_spaceplane_certification_and_operations_summary.pdf [*UK Government Review: Summary*].
100 *UK Government Review: Summary*, *supra* note 99 at 33.
101 Ibid.
102 Ibid. at 34.
103 Ibid. at 40.
104 Although the draft bill was not publicly available at time of this publication, a description of the bill can be found in Moro-Aguilar, *supra* note 93.
105 Ibid.

Although a bill has not yet been produced in Sweden, a Memorandum of Understanding was signed in 2007 by Spaceport Sweden and Virgin Galactic, which called for Sweden to develop a regulatory regime that drew on the FAA Human Space Flight Requirements.[106] Curaçao has also embarked on the drafting of a national space law that would accommodate suborbital spaceflight as it prepares to provide the spaceport for commercial flights of XCOR's Lynx spacecraft. As with the UK and Spain, Curaçao has chosen to follow the US model of licensure.[107] In contrast, Belgium has pursued a different path than the aforementioned states in its approach to suborbital flight by deciding to simply treat suborbital spaceplanes as aircraft subject to all of the rules and regulations that govern civil aircraft.[108]

VII Conclusion

As illustrated in this chapter, the issue of the legal status of spacecraft provides a number of difficult questions. Many of these questions arise from the supra-national nature of space travel, the lack of clarity between the border separating air and space law, and the complexity of multinational space ventures. Long-standing concepts of international space law regarding jurisdiction and other issues served well for many years while space activity remained solely in the governmental sphere. However, the growth of private space activity and the evolution of new technologies, such as the spaceplanes being developed by space tourism companies, have raised new legal issues and brought the adequacy of certain aspects of the existing space treaties into question. In response to these new challenges, laws are being drafted and discussions at many levels continue in order to resolve legal uncertainty and pave the way for a new era of private space flight.

---

106 Peter B de Selding & Tariq Malik, "Virgin, Swedish Spaceport Sign Deal for Suborbital Flights", *Space News* (7 February 2007), online: Space News spacenews.com/virgin-swedish-spaceport-sign-deal-suborbital-flights.
107 Moro-Aguilar, *supra* note 90. See also Frans G von der Dunk, "Mixing US and Dutch Approaches: Towards Curaçao's Legislation on Private Commercial Spaceflight" (2013) 62:4 ZLW 740.
108 *Law on the Activities of Launching, Flight Operations or Guidance of Space Objects* (Belgium), online: Belgian Science Policy Office www.belspo.be/belspo/space/doc/beLaw/Loi_en.pdf.

4

Liability for damage caused by space activities

Armel Kerrest and Caroline Thro

Introduction

Legal sources of liability for damage caused by space activities

The issue of liability for space activities caused a lot of ink to flow even before the signature of the Liability Convention[1] and animated hours of debate within the legal sub-committee of the United Nations (UN) Committee on the Peaceful Uses of Outer Space (COPUOS). Only a few days after the first meeting of this sub-committee, the United States (US) submitted a proposal on the issue of liability.[2] The position of the former Soviet Union at that time, which was more focused on the issue of rescue and return of astronauts than on liability for space activities, is interesting. The Soviet Union took that stance because of its belief that "compensation would undoubtedly be payable".[3] This reasoning was coherent with the previous case law.[4] The international community was aware, however, of the high-risk activity, and the necessity of a strict and clear liability regime in case of damage due to space activities. The obligation to pay compensation was not sufficient, since non-space-faring nations were also concerned.[5] As a first step, it has thus to fix the scope of the regime before pointing out its mechanism and procedures.

As soon as human activities are carried out in any space (area), they have to be regulated irrespective of the nature of such activity. Since those activities occur in an international space, international law and, especially, the UN Charter should have a central role to play.

---

1 *Convention on the International Liability for Damage Caused by Space Objects*, 29 March 1972, 961 UNTS 187 *[Liability Convention]*.
2 UN, Committee on the Peaceful Uses of Outer Space, Legal Sub-Committee, *United States Proposal: Liability for Space Vehicle Accidents*, UNGAOR, 1962, UN Doc A/AC.105/C.2/L.4.
3 UN, Committee on the Peaceful Uses of Outer Space, Legal Sub-Committee, *Summary Record of the Fourteenth Meeting*, UNGAOR, 1st Sess, UN Doc A/AC.105/C.2/SR.14 (1962) at 3.
4 *The Corfu Channel Case*, [1949] ICJ Rep 4; *Trail Smelter Arbitration (United States v Canada)* (1938), 3 RIAA 1905, reprinted in 33 AJIL 182 (Arbitrators: Charles Warren, Robert AE Greenshields, Jan Frans Hostie).
5 See Bin Cheng, "Convention on International Liability for Damage caused by Space Objects" in Nandasiri Jasentuliyana & Roy SK Lee, eds, *Manual on Space Law* (New York: Oceana Publications, 1979) vol 1, 84.

Gradually, a *lex specialis* has been created for liability issues in outer space:

1. *Resolution 1348* has stated for the first time that the launching State shall be internationally liable for damage caused by its space object, but has remained silent on the forms of liability.[6]
2. *Outer Space Treaty*[7] has reproduced almost the same wording of Resolution 1348 in its Article VII to describe the specific liability of the launching State(s) for damage caused by a space object. Article VII, however, cannot be read without the correlated Article VI of the Treaty which foresees the international responsibility of States for national space (governmental and non-governmental) activities.
3. It is, however, only in 1972 with the promulgation of the *Liability Convention* that the frame and the scope of a liability regime for damage caused by space objects has precisely been drawn. This convention is the result of the work of the UNCOPUOS[8] which, already in 1959, identified the issue of "liability for injury or damage caused by space vehicle as legal problems susceptible of priority treatment".[9] Owing to the difficulty of the topic and different proposals of the delegations, the draft of the Liability Convention took almost ten years, if Resolution 1348 is taken as a starting point for this issue. At the end, the Liability Convention was adopted containing two different legal regimes depending on the occurrence of the damage, with each time the launching State(s) as designated liable person.

Contrary to the usual solution in case of objective liability, the Liability Convention does not "channel" the liability on the launching State. Article XI opens the possibility for the victim to pursue "a claim in the courts or administrative tribunals or agencies of the launching State".[10]

The aim of the broad approach to the liability issue for space activities comes from one major consideration: should damage occur to a third party due to a space activity, this party should be able to raise a claim against at least one responsible State and get full compensation. The very specific and unique nature of space activities (high technologies, high risks, huge investments, etc.) may lead to important damages which private firms cannot afford. This is why for space activities States play an insurance role in case of damage due to a private activity and pay the remaining compensation amount.

Who is liable?

Under the Liability Convention, the *launching State* is internationally liable for damage caused by its space object(s). It might be surprising that the international liability of a State is engaged even for private activities, which is not the case for any other international regime. As at the time of the Liability Convention's negotiations, the legal nature of outer space was not evident,

---

6 *Declaration of Legal Principles Governing the Activities of States in the Exploration and Use of Outer Space*, GA Res 1962 (XVIII), UNGAOR, 18th Sess, UN Doc A/RES/18/1962 (1963).
7 *Treaty on Principles Governing the Activities of States in the Exploration and Use of Outer Space, Including the Moon and Other Celestial Bodies*, 27 January 1967, 610 UNTS 205 [*Outer Space Treaty*].
8 UN Committee on the Peaceful Uses of Outer Space was established by the UN General Assembly in 1958 as an *ad hoc* committee. See *Question of the Peaceful Use of Outer Space*, GA Res 1348 (XIII), UNGAOR, 13th Sess, UN Doc A.RES/13/1348 (1958).
9 *Report of the Ad Hoc Committee on the Peaceful Use of Outer Space*, UNGAOR, 14th Sess, Agenda Item 25, Annexes, UN Doc A/4141 (1959) at 23.
10 *Liability Convention, supra* note 1, art XI.

since, the rule of State's sovereignty in its air space was established with the Paris Convention[11] and restated in the Chicago Convention.[12] To enforce the liberty of use in outer space, space-faring nations were inclined to accept this specific and strict liability regime. This results also from the above mentioned broad approach and from the fact that outer space is of extreme importance from a strategic point of view. States are thus not inclined to leave it to private entities.

According to the Liability Convention's definition, a launching State is the one:

- Which launches;
- Procures the launch;
- From whose territory the space object is launched; or
- With whose facilities the space object is launched.

These four criteria cover all possible situations and ensure thus the presence of a launching State for any damage caused by any space object. It may have the consequence of a plurality of launching States. According to Article V of the Liability Convention, they shall be jointly and severally liable,[13] meaning that the victim could sue one of the launching States and ask for full compensation. Therefore, the Liability Convention encourages launching States to "conclude agreements regarding the apportioning among themselves of the financial obligation" by leaving any risk-sharing duty to the launching States.[14] As launching States seemed not very keen for signing these agreements, the UN Resolution on the application of the concept of "launching State" pointed out again the high importance of the necessity of signing the agreements on the sharing of risks and financial obligations.[15] In reality, a launching State might not have full control over the respective space activity during the whole process (launch and life in orbit) in case of a joint launch. It would thus make sense to foresee within an agreement the full compensation duty during the launching phase for the State conducting the launch. For any damage occurred during the life in orbit, the State of registration of a satellite, which has effective control over it, would ensure compensation. Only the one having effective control can limit the risks of an accident. Since the victim has no clue on the role of each launching States, the victim is only looking to get its damage repaired by suing one launching State.[16]

The Liability Convention also foresees the case of a damage caused by the collision of two space objects, where two different groups of launching States become jointly and severally liable without knowing it before the occurrence of the accident.[17] Here, the sharing of liability shall be done proportionate to the committed fault or by half, if the fault cannot be determined.[18]

The most important criterion, having regard to a State's liability, is of course the territory criterion, since it can be determined without any doubt.[19] What happens, however, should the

---

11 Convention Relating to the Regulation of Aerial Navigation, 1 June 1922 [Paris Convention].
12 *Convention on International Civil Aviation*, 7 December 1944, 15 UNTS 295, art 1, Can TS 1944 No. 36, ICAO Doc 7300/9 [*Chicago Convention*].
13 *Liability Convention, supra* note 1, art V(1).
14 Ibid., art V(2).
15 See *Application of the Concept of the "Launching State"*, GA Res 59/115, UNGAOR, 59th Sess, UN Doc A/RES/59/115 (2005).
16 This is of course only true for absolute liability, and not for any fault liability.
17 *Liability Convention, supra* note 1, art IV.
18 See ibid.
19 Every seismograph could precisely determine the location of the launch.

launch occur from an international territory, such as the high seas or the airspace above the high seas? Sea Launch, a private consortium, owns launch capabilities on the high seas, that is outside the territorial jurisdiction of any State. The two stages Zenit Rocket are Ukrainian, and the last and third stage the Russian Bock DM Upper. The home port of Sea Launch between the Launch campaigns is Long Beach in California. At the beginning of the project, the Sea Launch Company was incorporated in the Cayman Islands, a British Overseas Territory. Becoming aware of the legal risks and issues of being a launching State of Sea Launch, the United Kingdom (UK) requested the company to register in another State. The company then became American. Boeing Commercial Space Company owns 40 percent of the Sea Launch Company. Since Boeing leads the team, it furnishes the home port and some parts of the launcher and payload accommodations, and commercializes the launch. Thus, the license can be obtained by the US Government in compliance with its Commercial Space Launch Act.[20] As such, the US becomes a launching State of the Sea Launch project, which is also in the interest of the company in case of any damage.

The State procuring the launch is in principle the one having control over the space object, meaning being the owner of the satellite and having registered it.[21] The choice of the State of registration for a private consortium is also determining the law, either national or international, applicable to their operation.

Some argued that no liability of a launching State exists in the case of exclusively private commercial activities.[22] This interpretation goes against the aims, purposes and the spirit of the Liability Convention, and, more specifically, are in contradiction with the context of its Article VI that foresees that States are responsible for "national activities" including public and private operators. It does not reflect the practice of the space-faring States which assume liability also for exclusively private commercial activities. This can been seen in their practice of registration of space object according to the Registration Convention and in the usual provisions of domestic legislation concerning private activities in outer space.

The designation of "launching State" is only valid taking the legal ground of the Liability Convention. Nothing prevents the victim to file a suit against the operator in a domestic court. This solution might be the quickest and easiest one, but will not guarantee all the privileges a victim could have under the Liability Convention: the victim, for example, may have to prove the fault of the tortfeasor which is difficult in the case of space activities.

Here, private international law will determine the applicable law and will judge the case in the same manner as for all tort cases.

This opportunity opens the way of taking the most advantages of various domestic laws which is commonly known as *forum shopping*.

While discussing and debating the issue of liability for space activities to elaborate the Liability Convention, the delegation of the UK, followed by the Australian one, requested the recognition in the Convention of a separate legal personality for international organizations.[23]

---

20   *Commercial Space Launch Act*, Pub L No. 98-575, 98 Stat 3055 (1984) (codified as amended at 51 USC Chapter 509 (2013)).
21   *Convention on Registration of Objects Launched into Outer Space*, 14 January 1975, 1023 UNTS 15, art II [*Registration Convention*].
22   See e.g. Peter van Fenema, "Legal Aspects of Launch Services and Space Transportation" in Frans G von der Dunk & Fabio Tronchetti, eds, *Handbook of Space Law* (Cheltenham, UK: Edward Elgar Publishing, 2015) 398.
23   See e.g. UN, Committee on the Peaceful Uses of Outer Space, Legal Sub-Committee, *Summary Record of the One Hundred and Seventeenth Meeting*, UNGAOR, 8th Sess, UN Doc A/AC.105/C.2/SR.117 (1969) at 12.

International organizations should thus be free/able to make a declaration of acceptance of the agreement, and should not be bound by the declaration of acceptance of its Member States.[24] Some, nonetheless, have argued that, once a majority of its Member States are party to a Treaty, the respective international organization should become *ipso facto* bound by the Treaty.[25]

Ultimately, a consensus on the issue was reached and, as a result, the final wording for the Liability Convention was drafted as follows:

> In this Convention, with the exception of articles XXIV to XXVII, references to States shall be deemed to apply to any international intergovernmental organization which conducts space activities if the organization declares its acceptance of the rights and obligations provided for in this Convention and if a majority of the States members of the organization are States Parties to this Convention and to the Treaty on Principles Governing the Activities of States in the Exploration and Use of Outer Space, including the Moon and Other Celestial Bodies.[26]

For the victim, the inclusion of international organization within the ambit of the Liability Convention does not bring a significant change, since one Member State being Party to the Liability Convention could, at the end of the process, always be held liable for the whole damage. In such a case, the Liability Convention foresees the possibility for the international organization to bring the claim through one of its Member States at the condition that it is also Party to the Liability Convention.[27]

Liable for what?

As already stated in the title, this liability regime only applies to "damage caused by a space object". The term "space object" includes "component parts of a space object as well as its launch vehicle and parts thereof".[28] It appears that the definition of a space object includes the launch vehicle, although the biggest part (upper stage 1 and 2) of the launcher will never enter outer space. This extension of the definition of the space object is employed to broaden the scope of the Liability Convention.

In an attempt to clarify the definition of "object", Article 1 of the Liability Convention includes "component parts of a space object". This was not really useful, since this precision does not clarify the wording. Any object launched in outer space, irrespective of its size or use, is a "space object", and may cause a damage, thus giving rise to the liability of the launching State. If a space object explodes into many objects, these are also space objects according to the Convention.

The European Union is in the process of deploying its own navigation system, called Galileo.[29] Unlike the Global Positioning System (GPS), there will be user-charges for the

24 See e.g. UN, Committee on the Peaceful Uses of Outer Space, Legal Sub-Committee, *Summary Record of the Hundred and Twentieth Meeting*, UNGAOR, 8th Sess, UN Doc A/AC.105/C.2/SR.120 (1969) at 6.
25 UN, Committee on the Peaceful Uses of Outer Space, Legal Sub-Committee, *India: Proposal: Convention concerning Liability for Damage caused by the Launching of Objects into Outer Space*, UNGAOR, UN Doc A/AC.105/C.2/L.32/Rev.2 (1968), art XIII(1).
26 *Liability Convention, supra* note 1, art XXII(1).
27 Ibid., art XXII(4).
28 Ibid., art I(d).
29 See EC, *Regulation (EC) No. 683/2008 of the European Parliament and of the Council of 9 July 2008 on the further implementation of the European satellite navigation programmes (EGNOS and Galileo)*, [2008] OJ, L 196/1.

receipt and use of signal from Galileo; a contract will exist between the service provider and the final user, organizing each party's responsibility in the event of a service interruption.

In any case, it is questionable whether the victim of a navigation service can claim under the Liability Convention, since, for any damage on Earth, the rationale of the Convention is to compensate victims being third parties to any space activity. However, a victim using a navigation service cannot unambiguously be qualified as third party to space activity. Moreover, in the spirit of the Liability Convention, there has to be a physical damage caused by a physical space object, and not by the loss of a signal.[30]

According to Professor Bin Cheng, a space object is a man-made object which is launched or intended to be launched in outer space.[31] During the elaboration of the Convention, a space object was implicitly understood as having material and physical properties.[32] The object causing the damage has to have material and physical properties, and thereby does not include non-material masses, such as signals or electronic interferences.[33] Electromagnetic waves do not constitute a physical means of propagation covered by the Liability Convention.

Furthermore, when launched into Earth orbit or beyond, the space object must be registered according to Article II(1) of the Registration Convention.[34] Since the space signal is not

---

30 Lesley J Smith & Armel Kerrest, "The 1972 Convention on International Liability for damages caused by space objects (Liable)" in Stephan Hobe *et al.*, eds, *Cologne Commentary on Space Law* (Koln: Heymanns, 2009) vol 2, at 83 [Smith & Kerrest, "LIAB article II"].

31 Bin Cheng, "International Responsibility and Liability for Launch Activities" (1995) 20:6 Air & Space L 297 at 297; Eilene Galloway, "International Institutions to Ensure Peaceful Uses of Outer Space" in Nandasiri Jasentuliyana, United Nations Univerisity & International Institute of Space Law, eds, *Maintaining Outer Space for Peaceful Uses: Proceedings of a Symposium held in the Hague, March 1984* (Tokyo: United Nations University, 1984) 165.

32 Carl Q Christol, "International Liability for Damage Caused by Space Objects" (1980) 74:2 AJIL 346 at 354; Armel Kerrest & Lesley J Smith, "Article VII" in Stephan Hobe *et al.*, eds, *Cologne Commentary on Space Law* (Koln: Heymanns, 2009) vol 1, at 126 ; Caroline Videlier, *La responsabilite du fait du signal spatial de navigation par satellite* (Thesis, Universite Toulouse I – Sciences sociales, 2005) at 83 [unpublished]; Ruwantissa Abeyratne, *Space Security Law* (New York: Springer, 2011) at 25; P Rodríguez-Contreras Pérez, "Damage Caused by GNSS Signals in the Light of the Liability Convention of 1972" in Michael J Rycroft, ed, *Satellite Navigation Systems: Policy, Commercial and Technical Interaction: Proceedings of an International Symposium, 26–28 May 2003, Strasburg, France* (Dordrecht: Springer Science+Business Media, 2003) 251; Bin Cheng, "The Commercial Development of Space: the Need for New Treaties" (1991) 19:1 J Space L 17; Vladimir Kopal, "Some Remarks on Issues Relating to Legal Definitions of 'Space Object', 'Space Debris' and 'Astronaut'" in American Institute of Aeronautics and Astronautics, International Institute of Space Law & International Astronautical Federation, eds, *Proceedings of the Thirty-Seventh Colloquium on the Law of Outer Space: October 9–14, 1994, Jerusalem, Israel* (Washington, DC: American Institute of Aeronautics and Astronautics, 1995) 10.

33 Tare Brisibe, *Aeronautical Public Correspondence by Satellite* in Marietta Benkö, ed, Essential Air and Space Law, vol 3 (Utrecht: Eleven International Publishing, 2006) at 190; Lotta Viikari, *The Environmental Element in Space Law: Assessing the Present and Charting the Future* in Frans G von der Dunk, ed, Studies in Space Law, vol 3 (Leiden: Martinus Nijhoff, 2008) at 69; Frank Reda, "Cost, Contractors Liability for Damages" (1967) 1 AFL Rev 33; Kerrest & Smith, "Article VII", *supra* note 34 at 142; David I Fisher, *Defamation via Satellite: A European Law Perspective* (The Hague: Kluwer Law International, 1998) at 21; Stephen Gorove, *Studies in Space Law: Its Challenges and Prospects* in Monograph Series (L.Q.C. Lamar Society of International Law), vol 2 (Leiden: A.W. Sijthoff, 1977) at 126; Henri A Wassenbergh, *Principles of Outer Space Law in Hindsight* (Dordrecht: Martinus Nijhoff, 1991).

34 Bernhard Schmidt-Tedd *et al.*, "Article II REG" in Stephan Hobe *et al.*, eds, *Cologne Commentary on Space Law* (Koln: Heymanns, 2009) vol 2, 244 at 251.

registered in conformity with the Registration Convention,[35] and that it is not launched into Earth orbit or beyond, the space signal cannot be considered as a space object.

Nowadays, there appears to be a specific need for a special liability regime for harmful interferences.[36] Even though the International Telecommunication Union (ITU) Convention and its Radio Regulations strictly prohibit harmful interferences,[37] the ITU has no control procedure upon the States on their use of interferences.

Furthermore, there must exist a *causal link* between the space object and the damage. If the link is too remote, no claim could be raised under the Liability Convention. According to the direct causation theory, the wrongful act must directly lead to the damage.[38] For indirect damage,[39] where the link to the space object is unclear, "it must be such that it would not otherwise have occurred, had the space object not caused the initial damage".[40] The chain of causation should not suffer any interruption.

What kind of liability?

Depending on the damage, the Liability Convention makes a difference on the applicable liability regime. This goes again back to the initial rationale of the liability regime for space activities: it is important to ensure an absolute compensation for a victim stranger to any space activity. Thus, the Liability Convention foresees an absolute liability for damage caused on the surface of the Earth or to an aircraft in flight.[41] On the other hand, concerning damage in outer space, the victim shall prove a fault of the responsible State to establish its liability.[42]

Absolute liability

Since most information in the space sector are highly sensitive and as such, protected, and since fault is almost impossible to prove in the case of damage caused by space activity, the drafters of the Liability Convention felt it important to impose an objective liability. The choice was made in favor of an absolute liability rather than for an objective liability, to avoid any exoneration possibilities. Article II of the Convention provides:

> A launching State shall be absolutely liable to pay compensation for damage caused by its space object on the surface of the Earth or to aircraft in flight.[43]

So here the principle is to designate the liable party/culprit by the Convention without any legal questioning on the way the party carried out its activity.

---

35 *Registration Convention, supra* note 1, art III (the registration must be notified to the UN). The Secretary General maintains a register in which the information notified must be recorded. See Stephan Mick, *Registrierungskonvention und Registrierungspraxis* (Koln: Heymanns, 2007) at 28.
36 Smith & Kerrest, "LIAB article II", *supra* note 30 at para 111.
37 *Convention of the International Telecommunication Union*, 22 December 1992, 1825 UNTS 390, art 45; World Radiocommunication Conference, *Radio Regulations*, 2012 ed, art 15.
38 *Case concerning the Aerial Incident of 3 July 1988 (Islamic Republic of Iran v United States of America)*, Order of 22 February 1996, [1996] ICJ Rep 9.
39 Christol, *supra* note 34 at 359–60.
40 Smith & Kerrest, "LIAB article II", *supra* note 30 at 127.
41 *Liability Convention, supra* note 1, art II.
42 Ibid., art III.
43 Ibid., art II.

The risk of damage on Earth caused by a space object after its launch is rather low. Only huge objects can reach the Earth surface as small ones burn while entering atmosphere. For example, Kosmos 945, a Soviet spying satellite with a nuclear payload, fell on Canadian territory in 1978.

The absolute liability functions without any maximum amount or time. Since States are liable for damage caused by their space objects, there is no need for setting any time limit or amount.[44] Only the victim's "gross negligence" (*faute lourde*) or willful misconduct (*faute intentionnelle*) might limit the respective State's liability.[45]

Fault liability

During the final moments of the adoption of the text of the Liability Convention, Article III was only providing for absolute liability.[46] The Italian position changed the minds of the drafters, and introduced a presumption of fault for collisions in outer space.[47] Article III of the Liability Convention now states:

> In the event of damage being caused elsewhere than on the surface of the Earth to a space object of one launching State or to persons or property on board such a space object by a space object of another launching State, the latter shall be liable only if the damage is due to its fault or the fault of persons for whom it is responsible.[48]

Here, an issue arises with respect to the interpretation of persons for whom the launching State is responsible. Are only agents of the State meant, since it would be the case in general international law?[49] This reasoning would however go against the spirit of international space law. A conformed interpretation would require to take into account Article VI of the Outer Space Treaty, stating that States are responsible for national activities. It is the logical consequence that the launching State is liable for any damage caused by the space activity of one of his nationals, and not only for his State's agents.[50]

It can be argued that liability for damage in orbit has not been efficiently enough dealt with in the Liability Convention. The obligation to prove fault and the absence of special provisions for fault liability may cause some difficulties in the implementation of the provisions of the Convention. If it is the case, the victim would like to sue the operator or even the State, using

44   It is a major difference and interest of the Liability Convention compared to other conventions dealing with liability. For instance, in the 1969/1992 Convention on Civil Liability for Oil Pollution Damage, a limit is set for the liability of the owners of the ship. See *International Convention on Civil Liability for Oil Pollution Damage*, 29 November 1969, 973 UNTS 3, as amended by *Protocol of 1992 to amend the International Convention on Civil Liability for Oil Pollution Damage, 1969*, 27 November 1992, 1956 UNTS 285, art V.
45   *Liability Convention, supra* note 1, art VI(1), (2).
46   UN, Committee on the Peaceful Uses of Outer Space, Legal Sub-Committee, *United States Proposal: Convention concerning Liability for Damage Caused by the Launching of Objects into Outer Space*, UNGAOR, 1964, UN Doc A/AC.105/C.2/L.8, art III.
47   See UN, Committee on the Peaceful Uses of Outer Space, Legal Sub-Committee, *Working Paper submitted by the Italian delegation – Draft convention concerning liability for damage caused by the launching of objects into outer space*, UNGAOR, 1968, UN Doc A/AC.105/C.2/L.40, art 4(2).
48   *Liability Convention, supra* note 1, art III.
49   See *The Corfu Channel Case, supra* note 5; II Yearbook of the international law commission, part II, UN Doc. A/CN.4/SER.A/2001/Add.1 (Part 2) at 93.
50   See e.g. *Loi n° 2008-518 du 3 Juin 2008 relative aux opérations spatiales*, NOR: ESRX0700048L, art 2(2), (3) [*Loi n° 2008-518*].

Liability for damage

another legal basis than resorting to the Liability Convention, domestic law, or general international law.

Exoneration

The particularity of the space liability regime is the principle of *restitutio in integrum*, meaning that no ceiling exists. Like every liability regime, exoneration, however, is possible in specific cases. Concerning absolute liability, no exoneration is possible implying a full compensation for the damage. Only the victim's gross negligence (*faute lourde*) or willful misconduct (*faute intentionnelle*) might limit the delinquent State's liability. This is, however, very difficult to prove and might almost never be the case. In the same line of thinking, it is very difficult to prove the launching State's fault for any damage in outer space. Therefore, it can be contended that the launching State's liability would quite often be excluded for this reason.

The damage

According to the Liability Convention, the term "damage" means "loss of life, personal injury or other impairment of health; or loss of or damage to property of States or of persons, natural or juridical, or property of international intergovernmental organizations".[51] This wording was accepted at the Sixth Session of the Legal Sub-Committee of UNCOPUOS in 1967 while trying to define the term "damage".[52] Nevertheless, no agreement could be reached on the inclusion of an indirect damage in the definition. The best solution was to accept the application of the Liability Convention for damage with an adequate causality.[53] Doubts remained also concerning the approach to be given to nuclear damage. In any case, the fact that *restitutio in integrum* is the basis of indemnification must be taken into consideration when causality is concerned.

Nowadays, the question of liability, which has been raised by some commentators, concerns environmental damage: who can claim them and ask for indemnification? In such cases, the whole mankind suffers a damage. However, the human mankind is not entitled to bring up a claim, since it has no legal personality. The exoneration does not result from the damage itself, but from the victim's nature. If the damage caused to the environment may be connected to a physical or legal person or to a State, the Liability Convention would apply and indemnification must be paid.

This legal gap can, however, be challenging in a case, for instance, where space debris in orbit potentially causes damage to the International Space Station. The increase of space debris in outer space limits the sustainability of use of outer space. In fact, each time a satellite is endangered by a space debris, its operator will have to re-orbit the functioning satellite, which is an expensive operation. This increased collision risks, in a "polluted" zone, will certainly in the future have a negative impact on insurance premium. And as such it could constitute a damage caused by a space object.[54]

---

51   *Liability Convention*, supra note 1, art I(a).
52   UN, Committee on the Peaceful Uses of Outer Space, *Report of the Legal Sub-Committee on the Work of its Sixth Session*, UNGAOR, 1967, UN Doc A/AC.105/37 at para 17.
53   UN, Committee on the Peaceful Uses of Outer Space, Legal Sub-Committee, *Summary Record of the One Hundred and Third Meeting*, UNGAOR, 7th Sess, UN Doc A/AC.105/C.2/SR.103 (1968).
54   But see Frans G von der Dunk, "The 1972 Liability Convention, Enhancing Adherence and Effective Application" in American Institute of Aeronautics and Astronautics & International Institute of Space Law, eds, *Proceedings of the Forty-First Colloquium on the Law of Outer Space: 28 September–2 October 1998, Melbourne, Australia* (Reston, VA: American Institute of Aeronautics and Astronautics, 1999) 366 at 369.

Two ways for the victim to obtain compensation: the dispute settlement mechanism under the liability convention or the recourse before a domestic judge under domestic law

Liability Convention: Under the Liability Convention, this is a State-to-State relationship, unlimited in time and amounts. The biggest impediment of this procedure is exactly this relationship, since the procedure might be time consuming. The victim must address a request for compensation to his/her ministry of foreign affairs which will then forward the demand to the ministry of foreign affairs of the launching State (if more than one launching State can be identified for the space object having caused the damage, the victim's State will have to choose and address to one of the launching States the request of compensation, since they are jointly and severally liable). The State representing the victim might also choose not to act for political reasons. Similarly, the launching State and the victim's State can agree on a partial compensation also for political reasons.

This difficulty has been foreseen by the drafters of the Convention. This is the reason why they decided not to include the requirement of exhaustion of local remedies before instituting any claim for damages under the Convention,[55] The State of the victim is required, however, to act within one year after being aware of the damage.[56] This gives rise to another difficulty: should the claimant choose the internal/domestic recourse, for which the procedure might for sure be longer than a year, the claimant could no longer ask for the diplomatic way in the case of an unsuccessful claim.

It should be noted that if the operator is solvent and the fault easy to prove, the claimant will, it is highly likely, choose domestic law.

The Liability Convention does not apply to "nationals of the launching State" and to foreign nationals having taken part to the launch.[57] In some domestic law, as in the French one[58], the same protections than under the Liability Convention are foreseen for national victims.

According to the Liability Convention, should for any reasons the negotiations remain unsuccessful, the requesting State can ask for the composition of a "Claims Commission".[59] Only if agreed upon by the Parties, the Claims Commission's decision will be binding. Otherwise, it will only have a recommendation character, but must be in any case a motivated decision, meaning that the decision must clearly state the position held by the Claims Commission. The composition of the Claims Commission is mandatory, should the negotiations remain unsuccessful. States can only agree upon the nature of the decision.

Through domestic legal order: Article XI(2) of the Liability Convention, *inter alia*, provides:

> Nothing in this Convention shall prevent a State, or natural or juridical persons it might represent, from pursuing a claim in the courts or administrative tribunals or agencies of a launching State.[60]

The Liability Convention is the international *lex specialis* for the liability regime for damage caused by space objects. It is, however, at the victim's discretion to opt for another basis to claim

---

55 *Liability Convention, supra* note 1, art XI(1).
56 Ibid., art X(1), (2).
57 Ibid., art VII.
58 *Loi n° 2008-518, supra* note 50.
59 It is the same procedure as for an arbitral tribunal: each State choses one judge and both agree on a third one, the President of the Claims Commission.
60 *Liability Convention, supra* note 1, art XI(2).

compensation for damage caused by a space object. By doing so, the victim is able to choose the court in which the claim will be brought and, consequently, which law will apply to settle the dispute. The victim will most probably choose the court and the applicable law that offer the same advantageous protection, and thus full compensation, as the Liability Convention. It can be argued that, having regard to the complexity of the procedure put in place by the Liability Convention, actions will more certainly be brought to national courts rather than on the basis of the Convention.

The consequences of the liability

Any damage caused by a space object(s) obliges the concerned launching State to a *restitutio in integrum*.[61] If this principle cannot be applied, the compensation is made financially. It is, nevertheless, important to take into consideration that principle, since financial compensation is only a second choice. Furthermore, the amount of the financial compensation has to reflect this basic principle.

The necessity of control by potential launching States: As stated previously, Article VII of the Outer Space Treaty cannot be read without Article VI of the Treaty, which provides:

> States Parties to the Treaty shall bear international responsibility for national activities in outer space, ... whether such activities are carried on by governmental agencies or by non-governmental entities ... The activities of non-governmental entities in outer space ... shall require *authorization and continuing supervision by the appropriate State Party* to the Treaty.[62]

Article VII of the Outer Space Treaty and the Liability Convention create another reason for States to control private space activities: they may be liable as a launching State. It is true that there is no special obligation under these treaties on a launching State to control the activities of private entities. Nonetheless, a launching State needs to control the space activities of such commercial entities to avoid being held liable. Therefore, it is the launching State's duty to organize internally an authorization process before any launch and a control procedure upon the operator while conducting the space activity, not only to ensure conformity of such activity with international law, but also to determine the risk of the activity and to reduce the possibility of such risk. Only a State, who has the power to authorize and control, can become the appropriate responsible State for having "the factual means of avoiding liability".[63]

Each State can choose its own way of authorization and control. It is, however, still true that many space-faring nations have yet to enact any domestic space law foreseeing any authorization and control procedures. In such circumstances, it is difficult to know which State has control over a given space object, if no national law foresees any control procedure.

The sharing of risks among launching States: The Liability Convention deals with two different situations. In Article IV, the Convention provides for the case of two space objects colliding and

---

61 See *Case concerning the Factory at Chorzów (Germany v Poland)* (1928), PCIJ (Ser A) No. 17; *The Corfu Channel Case*, *supra* note 5.
62 *Outer Space Treaty*, *supra* note 8, art VI [emphasis added].
63 Michael Gerhard, "Article VI" in Stephan Hobe *et al.*, eds, *Cologne Commentary on Space Law* (Koln: Heymanns, 2009) vol 1, 103 at 115.

causing damage to third parties.[64] Article V considers the incident of a damage caused by one space object, and, hence, addresses plurality of launching States and apportionment of financial obligations among themselves.

In Article IV, the Liability Convention foresees the possibility of two or more launching States who can be held jointly and severally liable, if the collision of their respective space objects have caused a damage to a third party. Here, the Liability Convention organizes their relation, since these launching States could not predict before the launch of the space objects to be jointly and severally liable in the event of damage. Therefore, the Liability Convention provides that these launching States will have equal liability to provide compensation to the third State – the burden of compensation shall be apportioned equally between them – unless one State's fault can be proved. However, as already mentioned, it is difficult to prove fault in the space sector.

According to Article V, since the launching States for one activity can become jointly liable, the victim can claim compensation against only one of these States. In this regard, the latter will be bound to pay, if found liable. However, in such a circumstance, that launching State has a right of indemnity against the other launching State(s). Therefore, the Liability Convention recommends the signature of agreements "regarding the apportioning among themselves of the financial obligation".[65] As for instance, the State from whose territory and with which facilities the launch is procured, must ensure financial compensation for the whole launching procedure, since during that moment the other launching State(s) have no possibility of control over the activity.

The sharing of risks between launching States and private entities: Since most private entities would go bankrupt, domestic law generally provides that the State to whom the private entity belongs takes charge of the remaining amount and will not ask for full reimbursement from the corporatized entity of what it has paid as a launching State. It is thus common for States to require, while granting authorization to the commercial entity for the concerned activity, subscription of an insurance up to the legal ceiling. The State stands as the insurance for the remaining amount. It is questionable whether this ceiling applies also in the case of an action brought by the victim before a domestic court. In this respect, differences between national space laws should be noted.

If the victim claims compensation under the Liability Convention, it is a State-to-State relationship. Nonetheless, the launching State, who has observed its liability engaged, can ask for reimbursement of the amount from the operator. The aim of national laws, if they exist, is to regulate the financial relationship between the launching State and its operator. For the reasons exposed previously, States mainly predict a limitation of such reimbursement.

64 *Liability Convention, supra* note 1, art IV:

> In the event of damage being caused elsewhere than on the surface of the Earth to a space object of one launching State or to persons or property on board such a space object by a space object of another launching State, and of damage thereby being caused to a third State or to its natural or juridical persons, the first two States shall be jointly and severally liable to the third State, to the extent indicated by the following:
> (a) If the damage has been caused to the third State on the surface of the Earth or to aircraft in flight, their liability to the third State shall be absolute;
> (b) If the damage has been caused to a space object of the third State or to persons or property on board that space object elsewhere than on the surface of the Earth, their liability to the third State shall be based on the fault of either of the first two States or on the fault of persons for whom either is responsible.

65 Ibid., art V(2).

France and the US have gone further to protect their launch operators. Both of them have, in their domestic space regulations, agreed with their space industry on the limitation of the operator's liability, thereby maintaining the ceiling irrespective of the procedure chosen by the claimant. This reflects their will to support the space sector, even though, in the case of the US space regulations, the limitation only lasts for 30 days after the launch.

The French space regulation, referring to the French financial law,[66] provides for a warranty for all damage caused during the launching phase.[67] For any damage occurred during the in-orbit phase caused by a space object for which France is the launching State, the warranty plays fully only for damage on the surface of the Earth or to an aircraft in flight.[68]

This provides for a win-win solution. The operator receives the State's warranty for almost all damage and sees its liability limited. On the other hand, the operator has an obligation to obtain a license to conduct space activities conditional on getting an insurance coverage up to the ceiling (after which the State takes the insurer role). An operator carrying out space activities is subject to, like all other companies, bankruptcy, whereas a launching State is considered as being solvent and long-lasting. This justifies that the launching States take over the insurer role up to a certain ceiling. In any case, the insurability would be impossible for the space operator in the absence of a ceiling.

One situation can destabilize this process of control *via* licenses of the launching State upon the operator, namely the transfer of ownership of space object(s) in orbit.[69] This transfer is allowed and has already been foreseen in the Outer Space Treaty:

> Ownership of objects launched into outer space, including objects landed or constructed on a celestial body, and of their components parts, is not affected by their presence in outer space or on a celestial body or by their return to the Earth.[70]

This transfer of ownership should then be followed by the transfer of registration, meaning that the operator being the new owner of the space object has to register it in compliance with the Registration Convention. The Registration Convention limits the possible Registration States to one of the launching States of the space object.[71] This rationale comes from the twofold aims of registration under the Registration Convention: to establish a legal link between a State and an object, and to facilitate a possible claim of a victim, allowing an easier identification of at least one of the liable launching States.

Complications arise when the new owner of the space object is not a national of one of the initial launchings States of this specific space object. A new State will have effective control over the space object and will be responsible according to Article VI of the Outer Space Treaty. However, it cannot register the space object under the Registration Convention, and, thus, will not be liable under the Liability Convention in case of a damage, since the initial owner remains liable according to this text.

66 *Loi n° 2014-1654 du 29 décembre 2014 de finances pour 2015*, JO, 30 December 2014 (rectificatif publié au Journal Officiel du 4 avril 2015).
67 *Loi n° 2008-518, supra* note 50, art 15.
68 Ibid.
69 Armel Kerrest, "Legal Aspects of Transfer of Ownership and Transfer of Activities" (Paper delivered at the IISL/ECSL Symposium "Transfer of Ownership of Space Objects: Issues of Responsibility, Liability and Registration", Vienna, Austria, 19 March 2012) [unpublished] [Kerrest, "Legal Aspects"].
70 *Outer Space Treaty, supra* note 7, art VIII.
71 *Registration Convention, supra* note 21, art II.

To avoid such a situation, national laws,[72] especially the French space regulation,[73] provide for an obligation to secure authorization to transfer ownership of in-orbit space object(s).[74] It may cause difficulties when operators intend to sell their satellites: this may block many transfers and may jeopardize the selling of second-hand satellites.

A solution to counteract the negative effects of the combination of the Liability Convention and the Registration Convention, without modifying any of the conventions, can be to encourage concerned States to enter into bilateral agreements providing for a complete transfer of all international obligations (responsibility, liability, registration, etc.) to the new owner's State.[75]

Concluding remarks

The Liability Convention taken as a whole is a well-thought document which fits in the international space law context from the beginning of the 1970s. However, like all legal instruments, the Liability Convention has limitations to its proper application, especially for the liability regime of damage in orbit.

Additionally, some provisions are not in line with a fault liability. For instance, in the case of a fault liability for damage in orbit, the joint and several liability of the launching States does not make any sense. Again, in the case of damage occurring in orbit caused by space debris, it is not easy to determine the responsible launching State who can be held liable. It should be noted that, due to the presence of space debris in huge amounts, damage frequently occurs in orbit, perhaps more frequently than damage occurring on the surface of the Earth or to an aircraft in flight. In reality, only the US keeps a record/register of some space debris. Nonetheless, in this case, the proof may be influenced, since the register is not neutrally kept by an international organization.

Concerning damage on the surface of the Earth and to aircraft in flight, the Liability Convention fulfills the expectations: a third party to space activities can claim damages. The Liability Convention would certainly fulfill its role of "safety net", by protecting the potential victim and finally making space activities safer "for the benefit and in the interest of all countries".[76]

In current circumstances, any significant modification of the Convention would be very detrimental to the whole system. Alternatively, without modifying the Convention, it is possible, and even necessary, to improve the liability mechanism by practice and by agreements between States, especially launching States.

---

72 See e.g. *Law on the Activities of Launching, Flight Operations or Guidance of Space Objects*, art 13, § 5, online: Belgian Science Policy Office www.belspo.be/belspo/space/doc/beLaw/Loi_en.pdf ("[w]hen the transferee operator is not established in Belgium, the Minister may refuse the authorisation in the absence of a specific agreement with the home State of the third party in question and which indemnifies the Belgian State against any recourse against it under its international liabilities or claims for damages"); Michael Gerhard, "Transfer of Operation and Control with Respect to Space Objects – Problems of Responsibility and Liability of States" (2002) 51:4 ZLW 571 at 578.
73 *Loi n° 2008-518*, *supra* note 50, art 3.
74 See Gerhard, *supra* note 63 at 581.
75 See Kerrest, "Legal Aspects", *supra* note 70.
76 *Outer Space Treaty*, *supra* note 7, art I.

5
Control over activities harmful to the environment

Jinyuan Su

Control of space debris

The amount of orbital debris resulting from human exploration and use of outer space has been steadily increasing in the history of human exploration and use of outer space. Major break-up incidents have resulted in a dramatic increase of space debris.[1] The United States (US) Space Surveillance Network (SSN) currently tracks around 23,000 pieces of debris larger than 10 cm.[2] Those pieces of debris, which travel at very high speed, are one of the primary threats to spacecraft and human space missions.

Law of outer space and international environmental law

The term "space debris" cannot be found in any of the five United Nations (UN) outer space treaties or in any legally binding treaties aimed at protecting the environment. Nevertheless, this does not mean that space debris remain largely unregulated; relevant norms of existing international law, international space law, and international environmental law apply to space debris as one of the environmental issues.

Article IX of the Outer Space Treaty obliges States Parties to, among others, "conduct all their activities in outer space, including the Moon and other celestial bodies, with due regard to the corresponding interests of all other States Parties to the Treaty."[3] The requirement of "due regard", which reiterates the rule of general international law that the legitimate interests of other States must be taken into consideration when a State exercises its right,[4] is viewed as one

---

1   See NASA, "Update on Three Major Debris Clouds", *Orbital Debris Quarterly News* 14:2 (April 2010) 4 at 4, online: NASA orbitaldebris.jsc.nasa.gov/newsletter/pdfs/ODQNv14i2.pdf.
2   Secure World Foundation, *Space Sustainability: A Practical Guide* (updated 2014) at 8–9, online: Secure World Foundation swfound.org/media/121399/swf_space_sustainability–a_practical_guide_2014__1_.pdf.
3   *Treaty on Principles Governing the Activities of States in the Exploration and Use of Outer Space, Including the Moon and Other Celestial Bodies*, 27 January 1967, 610 UNTS 205, art IX [*Outer Space Treaty*].
4   Ram S. Jakhu, "Legal Issues Relating to the Global Public Interest in Outer Space" (2006) 32:1 J Space L 31 at 47.

73

of the limitations on the freedom of outer space.[5] Although what it aims to protect are the "corresponding interests" of other States Parties, it would, nevertheless, contribute to the protection of the space environment. The clause has a "consequence" dimension and a "subjectivity" dimension.[6] First, the creation of a significant amount of space debris, in particular those in the most useful orbits such as Low-Earth Orbits (LEOs) and the Geostationary Orbit (GEO), may jeopardize the "corresponding interests" of other States Parties by posing risks to their activities therein. Second, the conducting State is expected to pay "due diligence" in avoiding unnecessary environmental impacts through, e.g., the implementation of risk assessment and the adoption of cost-effective measures. However, a State is not given the right to subject to its consent another State's activities in outer space based on possible jeopardies to its space activities.[7]

Article IX further requires States Parties to "pursue studies of outer space, including the Moon and other celestial bodies, and conduct exploration of them so as to avoid their harmful contamination".[8] The term "harmful contamination" in its ordinary meaning can be very broad. Whereas the word "contamination" is inherently negative, meaning the act of pollution or infection,[9] "harmful" retains its ordinary meaning of "causing or capable of causing significant harm".[10] Therefore, the introduction of pollutants into outer space, which cause or are capable of causing significant harm, should be regarded as "harmful contamination". It is argued that space debris has become a new form of harmful contamination of outer space.[11] However, States Parties are only obliged to "avoid" it, and adopt "appropriate" measures "where necessary". The ambiguous and subjective nature of establishing a standard for avoiding harmful contamination makes it difficult to assess whether there is a violation of the provision.[12]

Article IX also contains a dual consultation regime. First, if a State Party has reason to believe that an activity or experiment planned by it or its nationals in outer space would cause potentially harmful interference with the activities of other States Parties in the peaceful exploration and use of outer space, it shall undertake appropriate international consultations before proceeding with any such activity or experiment. Second, a State Party, which has reason to believe that an activity or experiment planned by another State Party in outer space would cause potentially harmful interference with its activities in the peaceful exploration and use of outer space, may request consultation concerning the activity or experiment.[13] This regime

---

5   Manfred Lachs, *The Law of Outer Space: An Experience in Contemporary Law-Making* (Leiden: Nijhoff, 1972), at 117.
6   See, e.g., Michael C Mineiro, "FY-1C and USA-193 ASAT Intercepts: An Assessment of Legal Obligations under Article IX of the Outer Space Treaty" (2008) 34:2 J Space L 321 at 340–354, analyzing FY-1C and USA-193 ASAT activities under Article IX as to the consequence and the subjective efforts of the conducting States.
7   This principle, which can also be found in the UN General Assembly Resolution 1962 (XVIII), was originally proposed by the United Kingdom in response to a Soviet Union draft that required prior consent from potentially affected States. See USSR, "Draft Declaration of the Basic Principles Governing the Activities of States in the Exploration and Use of Outer Space" in *Report of the Committee on the Peaceful Uses of Outer Space*, UNGAOR, 18th Sess, Annexes, Agenda Item 28, UN Doc A/5549 (1963) at 11, Annex III, para 6.
8   *Outer Space Treaty*, supra note 3, art IX.
9   Joyce M Hawkins & Robert E Allen, eds, *The Oxford Encyclopedic English Dictionary* (New York: Oxford University Press, 1991) *sub verbo* "contamination".
10 Sergio Marchisio, "Article IX" in Stephan Hobe *et al.*, eds, *Cologne Commentary on Space Law* (Koln: Heymanns, 2009) vol 1, 169 at 177.
11 Ibid.
12 Lotta Viikari, *The Environmental Element in Space Law: Assessing the Present and Charting the Future* in Frans G von der Dunk, ed, Studies in Space Law, vol 3 (Leiden: Martinus Nijhoff, 2008) at 61.
13 *Outer Space Treaty*, supra note 3, art IX.

originally aims to safeguard other States' right to conduct space activities. Ultimately, it would also contribute to the protection of the space environment. However, the obligation to initiate active consultation depends on a subjective determination, which allows a high level of discretion. Even if an affirmative determination is made, there is no guidance as to the procedure and substance of such consultation.[14] In addition, such consultation does not need to achieve certain result(s), and, even if it does, there is no obligation to take into account the result when eventually conducting the concerned space activities.[15]

International law, since its creation, has adhered to no intrinsic geographical limits.[16] Article III of the Outer Space Treaty declares that States Parties are required to "carry on activities in the exploration and use of outer space, ... in accordance with international law, including the Charter of the United Nations".[17] International law, in particular long-established rules of customary international law and basic and explicit tenets of international law, is thus applicable to space activities.[18] The "no harm" principle, namely the "general obligation of States to ensure that activities within their jurisdiction and control respect the environment of other States or of areas beyond national control", is recognized by the International Court of Justice (ICJ) as "part of the corpus of international law relating to the environment",[19] hence applicable to activities in the exploration and use of outer space. The term "respect", which is relative and subjective in nature, echoes the subjectivity element of the "due regard" principle. Applying the "no harm" principle to the control of space debris, it can be concluded that the creation of large amount of debris can cause "damage" to the space environment, and States should pay "due diligence" to avoid debris creation.

---

14 See Mineiro, *supra* note 6 at 338–39.
15 Viikari, *supra* note 12 at 61.
16 Stacey L. Lowder, "A State's International Legal Role: From the Earth to the Moon" (1999) 7 Tulsa J Comp & Int'l L 253 at 256.
17 *Outer Space Treaty*, *supra* note 3, art III.
18 Olivier Bibbelink, "Article III" in Stephan Hobe *et al.*, eds, *Cologne Commentary on Space Law* (Koln: Heymanns, 2009) vol 1, 64 at 67.
19 *Legality of the Threat or Use of Nuclear Weapons Case*, Advisory Opinion, [1996] ICJ Rep 226 at 241 [*Nuclear Weapons Advisory Opinion*]; *Gabčíkovo-Nagymaros Project (Hungry v Slovakia)*, [1997] ICJ Rep 7 at 41. The "no harm" principle traces back to the notion of *sic utere tuo ut alienum non laedas*, i.e. "to use your own property so as not to injure another's". See, e.g., G.A.I., "*Sic Utere Tuo ut Alienum Non Laedas*" (1907) 5:8 Michigan L Rev 673. A few courts and arbitration tribunals had dealt with this principle in the trans-boundary context, but not that of "areas beyond national control". In the *Trail Smelter* case, the Mixed Arbitration Tribunal concluded that "no State has the right to use or permit the use of its territory in such a manner as to cause injury by fumes in or to the territory of another or the properties or persons therein, when the case is of serious consequence and the injury is established by clear and convincing evidence". See *Trail Smelter (USA v Canada)*, Award of 1941, III RIAA 1938, 1965. In the *Corfu Channel* case, the ICJ recognized "every State's obligation not to allow knowingly its territory to be used for acts contrary to the rights of other States". See *The Corfu Channel Case (United Kingdom of Great Britain and Northern Ireland v Albania)*, Merits, [1947] ICJ Rep 4 at 22. The "no harm" principle was recognized in the 1972 Stockholm Declaration and the 1992 Rio Declaration. See *Declaration of the United Nations Conference on the Human Environment*, 1972, in *Report of the United Nations Conference on the Human Environment*, UNESCOR, UN Doc A/Conf.48/14/Rev.1 (1972), Principle 21; *Rio Declaration on Environment and Development*, UN Doc A/CONF.151/5/Rev.1 (1992), 31 ILM 874, Principle 2 [*Rio Declaration*]. The principle has also found expression in the preambles of the Convention on Long Range Transboundary Air Pollution and the UN Framework Convention on Climate Change, and in Article 194 of the UN Convention on the Law of the Sea (UNCLOS). See *Convention on Long-Range Transboundary Air Pollution*, 13 November 1979, 1302 UNTS 217; *United Nations Framework Convention on Climate Change*, 9 May 1992, 1771 UNTS 107; *United Nations Convention on the Law of the Sea*, 10 December 1982, 1833 UNTS 3, art 194(2) [*UNCLOS*].

To summarize, both international space law and environmental law are broad and, paradoxically, vague on the control of space debris. The lack of objective criteria and the emphasis on subjectivity allow a high degree of discretion on the part of conducting States, and make it difficult to hold them accountable for harms to the space environment. As far as subsequent practice in treaty application is concerned, which establishes the agreement of the parties regarding the interpretation,[20] the generation of space debris, even those in tests of anti-satellite weapons, has seldom been alleged of violating the due regard principle, the obligation to avoid harmful contamination, or the "no harm" principle,[21] although there have been accusations of non-fulfillment of the consultation obligation.[22]

UNCOPUOS and IADC Space Debris Mitigation Guidelines

International efforts aimed at addressing the issue of space debris were initiated in the UN Committee on the Peaceful Uses of Outer Space (UNCOPUOS) in the 1990s. However, since the adoption of the 1979 Moon Agreement, States have failed to negotiate any further legally binding agreement relating to outer space under the auspices of the UNCOPUOS. Instead, non-binding instruments are widely being used in the regulation of space activities, and it is the Inter-Agency Space Debris Coordination Committee (IADC), an international governmental forum consisting of major national space agencies,[23] that has first adopted a set of guidelines designed to mitigate the growth of orbital debris population in 2002.[24] The IADC Guidelines then have formed a baseline for the UNCOPUOS to adopt its Space Debris Mitigation Guidelines in 2007,[25] which has been endorsed by the UN in 2008.

The IADC Guidelines cover the overall environmental impact of the space missions with a focus on: (1) limitation of debris released during normal operations, (2) minimization of the potential for on-orbit break-ups, (3) post-mission disposal, and (4) prevention of on-orbit collisions.[26] Organizations are encouraged to use the Guidelines in identifying the standards that they will apply when establishing the mission requirements for planned spacecraft and orbital stages. Operators of existing spacecraft and orbital stages are encouraged to apply the guidelines to the greatest possible extent.[27] The UNCOPUOS Guidelines are overall similar to the IADC Guidelines. Particularly, both Guidelines define "space debris" as "all man-made

---

20 *Vienna Convention on the Law of Treaties*, 23 May 1969, 1155 UNTS 331, art 31.
21 When China brought down its FY-1C in 2007, Japan alleged that China violated the Outer Space Treaty, citing its prohibition of the use of weapons of mass destruction. See Carin Zissis, China's Anti-Satellite Test, online: Council on Foreign Relations www.cfr.org/china/chinas-anti-satellite-test/p12684.
22 After the Chinese test, a few States, regions and international intergovernmental organizations such as the United States, Canada, Japan, Taiwan, India, South Korea, and the European Union protested and called upon China for consultations. See Mineiro, *supra* note 6 at 346–7, citing Theresa Hitchens, "US-Sino relations in Space: From 'War of Words' to Cold War in Space" (2007) 3 China Security 12 at 23. However, neither the United States nor the Soviet Union conducted international consultations in accordance with Article IX prior to conducting kinetic ASAT activities during the Cold War. See Mineiro, *supra* note 6 at 345.
23 See Inter-Agency Space Debris Coordination Committee, "Home", online: IADC www.iadc-online.org/.
24 *IADC Space Debris Mitigation Guidelines*, IADC Action Item No. 22.4, online: IADC www.iadc-online.org/index.cgi?item=docs_pub [*IADC Guidelines*].
25 UN Office for Outer Space Affairs, *Space Debris Mitigation Guidelines of the Committee on the Peaceful Uses of Outer Space* (Vienna: United Nations, 2010) [*UNCOPUOS Guidelines*].
26 See *IADC Guidelines*, *supra* note 24 at 5.
27 Ibid.

objects including fragments and elements thereof, in Earth orbit or re-entering the atmosphere, that are non-functional".[28] However, one of the very few differences between them is that IADC Guidelines recommend a 25-year post-mission orbital lifetime limitation,[29] whereas the UNCOPUOS Guidelines do not.

The IADC Guidelines and the UNCOPUOS Guidelines are a good example of global efforts to counter a common concern amassed from a small number of key players. However, they are limited in a few respects. First, neither of them has retrospective effect: both Guidelines are applicable to mission planning and to the operation of newly designed spacecraft and orbital stages, and existing ones only "if possible" or "to the greatest extent possible".[30] Second, those Guidelines are voluntary, that is not legally binding under international law.[31] Private companies do not have any legal obligation to observe them unless States integrate them into their domestic law, e.g., through a licensing mechanism. Third, those Guidelines do not seem to apply to security-related activities in outer space. Although they have contributed to the mitigation of space debris resulting from civil activities in outer space, the large number of debris caused by military activities would render their efforts in vain. Fourth, there have been observations that it is difficult to comply with the principles, such as the requirement to avoid collision and to limit orbital lifetime, in the case of orbital stages and satellites that do not have a propulsion system.[32]

The IADC Guidelines and the UNCOPUOS Guidelines only state what is to be achieved regarding debris mitigation, without specifying how to achieve those goals. Complementarily, the International Organization for Standardization (ISO) has developed a family of standards addressing debris mitigation. ISO-24113:2011, which is the top-level standard, defines the primary space debris mitigation requirements applicable to all elements of unmanned systems launched into, or passing through, near-Earth space, including launch vehicle orbital stages, operating spacecraft, and any objects released as part of normal operations or disposal actions.[33]

National and regional regulations

International efforts at space debris mitigation were predated and motivated by regulations at the national level, in particular those in the US and Japan. Ever since the adoption of the IADC and UNCOPUOS Guidelines, a growing number of space-faring nations and international organizations have voluntarily made their own orbital debris mitigation guidelines pursuant thereto. In some States, the requirements have been incorporated into their licensing procedure.

Early in 1988, the US firmed up its policy to minimize the creation of space debris, which was binding on the national security and civil space sectors.[34] In 1995, the National Aeronautics and Space Administration (NASA) became the first space agency in the world to issue a comprehensive set of orbital debris mitigation guidelines,[35] which formed the basis of US

28 *UNCOPUOS Guidelines*, *supra* note 25 at para 1; *IADC Guidelines*, *supra* note 24 at 5.
29 *IADC Guidelines*, *supra* note 24 at 9–10.
30 *UNCOPUOS Guidelines*, *supra* note 25 at para 3; *IADC Guidelines*, *supra* note 24 at 5.
31 *UNCOPUOS Guidelines*, *supra* note 25 at para 3; *IADC Guidelines*, *supra* note 24 at 5.
32 International Academy of Astronautics, "Position Paper on Space Debris Mitigation: Implementing Zero Debris Creation Zones", European Space Agency, SP-1301 (February 2006) at 17.
33 See International Organization for Standardization, "Space Systems – Space Debris Mitigation Requirements", ISO 24113:2011, 2nd ed (2011).
34 US, "Presidential Directive on National Space Policy", 11 February 1988, online: NASA www.hq.nasa.gov/office/pao/History/policy88.html.
35 NASA, "Guidelines and Assessment Procedures for Limiting Orbital Debris", NASA Safety Standard 1740.14 (August 1995), online: NASA Orbital Debris Program Office orbitaldebris.jsc.nasa.gov/mitigate/safetystandard.html.

Orbital Debris Mitigation Standard Practices developed by the US Government in 1997.[36] The US Federal Communications Commission (FCC)[37] has also adopted a comprehensive set of rules concerning mitigation of orbital debris.[38] Following the 1995 NASA Guidelines, the National Space Development Agency (NASDA)[39] of Japan adopted its Space Debris Mitigation Standard in 1996.[40]

In 1999, the French national space agency, the *Centre National d'Études Spatiales* (CNES), established the CNES Standard,[41] which served as a basis for the European Code of Conduct for Space Debris Mitigation concluded and signed by the European Space Agency (ESA), and major national space agencies in Europe in 2004.[42] Prior to this Code, the ESA had adopted its European Space Debris Safety and Mitigation Standard and Space Debris Mitigation Handbook, which jointly defined ESA's policies and implementation concepts on space debris mitigation and collision risk reduction for any mission under ESA control.[43] Additionally, the French Space Operation Act, adopted in 2008, provides that "[t]he authorization granted pursuant to the present Act may include requirements set forth for the safety of persons and property, protection of public health and the environment, in particular in order to limit risks related to space debris".[44]

In 2000, the Russian Aviation and Space Agency approved its Space Debris Mitigation Standard.[45] The Requirements are applicable to all space assets production and operation activity by the order of Russian Federal Space Agency (ROSCOSMOS). In 2009, the National Standard of the Russian Federation, titled "General Requirement to Design and Operation of Spacecraft and Orbital Stages on Space Debris Mitigation", came into force.[46] The Standard was harmonized with the UNCOPUOS Guidelines, and applied to newly designed and updated space vehicles (civil, science, commercial, military, and manned missions) of different types at all stages of their life cycle (designing, manufacturing, launch, operation, and disposal).[47]

---

36 NASA, "US Government Orbital Debris Mitigation Standard Practices", online: NASA orbitaldebris.jsc.nasa.gov/library/USG_OD_Standard_Practices.pdf.
37 The FCC is responsible for licensing radio transmissions by private entities in the US. For more information on the FCC, see online: Federal Communications Commission www.fcc.gov.
38 FCC, Mitigation of Orbital Debris, online: FCC https://transition.fcc.gov/ib/sd/ssr/mod.html.
39 NASDA is the predecessor of the Japan Aerospace Exploration Agency (JAXA). For more information, see Japan Aerospace Exploration Agency, "NASDA History", online: JAXA global.jaxa.jp/about/history/nasda/index_e.html; Japan Aerospace Exploration Agency, "JAXA History", online: JAXA global.jaxa.jp/about/history/index.html.
40 See Japan, National Space Development Agency of Japan, "Space Debris Mitigation Standard", NASDA-STD-18 (28 March 1996).
41 France, Centre National d'Études Spatiales, "CNES Standards Collection, Method and Procedure Space Debris – Safety Requirements", RNC-CNES-Q40-512 (1999).
42 *European Code of Conduct for Space Debris Mitigation*, Issue 1.0 (28 June 2004), online: UNOOSA www.unoosa.org/documents/pdf/spacelaw/sd/European_code_of_conduct_for_space_debris_mitigation.pdf.
43 See *European Space Debris Safety and Mitigation Standard*, Issue 1, Revision 0 (2000); *ESA Space Debris Mitigation Handbook* (European Space Agency, 2000) (updated in 2002).
44 *Loi n° 2008-518 du 3 Juin 2008 relative aux opérations spatiales*, NOR: ESRX0700048L, art 5.
45 See *Space Technology Items. General Requirements. Mitigation of Space Debris Population*, Russian Aviation & Space Agency Standard OST 134-1023-2000 (2000).
46 Russia, *General Requirements to Spacecraft and Orbital Stages on Space Debris Mitigation*, GOST R 52925-2008 (2009).
47 See Inter-Agency Space Debris Coordination Committee, "Russian Federal Space Agency (ROSCOSMOS)", online: IADC www.iadc-online.org/members/about_rsa.shtml.

China published the first part of its National Industry Standard – "Requirements on Space Debris Mitigation" – in 2005.[48] The Requirements apply to the design, operational, and post-mission disposal phases of space systems.[49] In December 2009, the State Administration of Science, Technology and Industry for National Defense published the Interim Measures on Administration of Mitigation of and Protection against Space Debris, which are in conformity with the UNCOPUOS Guidelines.[50] China has fully inactivated its Long March rockets, and moved a few aging GEO satellites out of orbit.[51]

Under the Canadian Remote Sensing Act, "[a]n application to the Minister to issue, amend or renew a licence must be made in the prescribed form and manner, be supported by a proposed system disposal plan, [and] proposed guarantee arrangements…".[52] The Minister may not issue a license without having approved that a system disposal plan for the licensed system satisfactory to the Minister that, among other things, provides for the protection of the environment, public health and the safety of persons and property; and arrangements satisfactory to the Minister relating to the guarantee of the performance of the licensee's obligations under the system disposal plan.[53]

Legal issues concerning active debris removal

As the number of orbital debris continues to grow, Active Debris Removal (ADR) has been called for.[54] However, a number of legal issues need to be addressed in advance. First, there is no universally accepted definition of space debris. The definition in the IADC and UNCOPUOS Guidelines, which is based on "non-functionality", is not legally binding. Although States have been encouraged to furnish information to the UN Secretary-General when a space object is no longer functional,[55] universal practice on this matter cannot be observed.

Second, even if a space object becomes space debris, it does not naturally follow that any State other than the State of registration is at liberty to remove it without the consent of the State of registration, since this would amount to an intrusion into the jurisdiction and control of the space object's State of registration.[56] According to the Outer Space Treaty, a State Party on whose registry an object launched into outer space is carried shall "retain jurisdiction and control over such object, and over any personnel thereof, while in outer space or on a celestial body".[57] The formula "shall retain jurisdiction and control" not only refers to the obligation to

---

48 China, *Requirements for Space Debris Mitigation*, QJ3221-2005.
49 See ibid.
50 The Interim Measures on Administration of Mitigation of and Protection against Space Debris is not publicly available. It is currently under revision by the State Administration of Science, Technology and Industry for National Defense.
51 China's Space Activities in 2011, online: China Daily www.chinadaily.com.cn/cndy/2011-12/30/content_14354558.htm.
52 *Remote Sensing Space Systems Act*, SC 2005, c 45, s 7.
53 Ibid., s 9(1).
54 See J-C Liou, NL Johnson & NM Hill, "Controlling the Growth of Future LEO Debris Populations with Active Debris Removal" (2010) 66:5–6 Acta Astronautica 648.
55 See *Recommendations on Enhancing the Practice of States and International Intergovernmental Organizations in registering Space Objects*, GA Res 62/101, UNGAOR, 66th Sess, UN Doc A/RES/62/101 (2007) at para 2(b)(ii).
56 Brian Weeden, "Overview of the Legal and Policy Challenges of Orbital Debris Removal" (2011) 27:1 Space Policy 41.
57 *Outer Space Treaty*, *supra* note 3, art VIII.

exercise jurisdiction and control over the space object, but also the right to exercise sovereignty over it.[58]

Third, in many cases, ADR requires trans-orbit maneuvers and re-entries of satellites, which pose risks to the safety of spacecraft, and of persons and properties on the surface of the Earth or in air. States conducting ADR, and even others falling within the scope of "launching States", may be held liable for damages under Articles VI and VII of the Outer Space Treaty and the Liability Convention. This possible outcome, albeit deriving from a faithful reading of the treaties, would discourage efforts of ADR.

Planetary protection

"Planetary protection" is defined by NASA as "the practice of protecting solar system bodies (i.e., planets, moons, comets, and asteroids) from contamination by Earth life, and protecting Earth from possible life forms that may be returned from other solar system bodies."[59] It covers not only "outward contamination", but also "backward contamination".[60]

International regulations

Outer Space Treaty and Moon Agreement

The issue of planetary protection is addressed in Article IX of the Outer Space Treaty. With respect to "outward contamination", States Parties undertake to "pursue studies of outer space, including the Moon and other celestial bodies, and conduct exploration of them so as to avoid their harmful contamination".[61] Contaminations of the space environment can be from biological, chemical or radiation sources. Biological contamination by materials from the Earth, for instance, could make it difficult to accurately determine if life was present on the planet. As to "backward contamination", States Parties shall avoid "adverse changes in the environment of the Earth resulting from the introduction of extraterrestrial matter".[62] However, the term "adverse changes" has not been defined. It seems, nevertheless, to include only adverse impacts reaching a certain threshold of severity. Furthermore, for both "outward contamination" and "backward contamination", States Parties shall "adopt appropriate measures", "when necessary".[63] However, Article IX does not provide clear guidance as to the circumstances in which "appropriate measures" shall be adopted, granting States Parties the right to determine the existence of such circumstances, and of specific measures that shall be adopted.

The applicability of general international law to activities in the exploration and use of outer space is affirmed by Article III of the Outer Space Treaty.[64] In this connection, the precautionary principle in international environmental law, an evolving principle which has achieved customary status in the context of the European Union but international courts and tribunals

---

58 Bernhard Schmidt-Tedd & Stephan Mick, "Article VIII" in Stephan Hobe *et al.*, eds, *Cologne Commentary on Space Law* (Koln: Heymanns, 2009) vol 1, 146 at 156–58.
59 NASA Office of Planetary Protection, "Overview", online: NASA planetaryprotection.nasa.gov/overview/.
60 See ibid.
61 *Outer Space Treaty, supra* note 3, art IX.
62 Ibid.
63 Ibid.
64 Ibid., art III.

have been reluctant to accept explicitly such a status,[65] should be applicable in the context of outer space, given the high risks associated with space activities and that a stringent interpretation is necessary. According to the principle, where there are threats of serious or irreversible damage, lack of full scientific certainty shall not be used as a reason for postponing cost-effective measures to prevent environmental degradation.[66] The principle is of particular importance in the avoidance of "backward contamination". For instance, returning spacecraft and astronauts, as well as extraterrestrial materials that they brought back, are sterilized and quarantined in practice.

Compared to the Outer Space Treaty, the Moon Agreement lays down more stringent obligations on planetary protection. It provides that States Parties "shall take measures to prevent the disruption of the existing balance of its environment, whether by introducing adverse changes in that environment, by its harmful contamination through the introduction of extra-environmental matter or otherwise".[67] Discarding the term "when necessary", it does not leave so much discretion to States Parties in the adoption of measures when conducting potentially harmful space activities. It has also been observed that "disruption of the environment" is a more extensive concept than "harmful contamination" found in the Outer Space Treaty.[68] The Moon Agreement further requires States Parties to "take measures to avoid harmfully affecting the environment of the Earth through the introduction of extraterrestrial matter or otherwise".[69] "Harmful affection" also seems to be broader than "adverse changes" in the Outer Space Treaty. However, the Moon Agreement only applies to the Moon and other celestial bodies within the solar system, except the Earth.[70] And as of 1 January 2015, there are only 4 Signatory States and 16 Ratifications to the Agreement, compared to 25 and 103 to the Outer Space Treaty.[71]

COSPAR planetary protection policy

The Committee on Space Research (COSPAR), a consultative body to the UNCOPUOS, has been playing a leading role in technical aspects of planetary protection.[72] At the second session of its thirty-fourth meeting, held in Houston on October 20, 2002, the COSPAR Council adopted a revised and consolidated Planetary Protection Policy, and has since been continuing to regularly update and amend the Policy. Whereas the 2002 version of the COSPAR Policy concerned robotic missions, it was amended in March 2011 to include Principles and Guidelines for Human Missions to Mars.[73]

---

65 Philippe Sands, *Principles of International Environmental Law*, 3rd ed (New York: Cambridge University Press, 2012) at 219–28. Some scholars held that the precautionary principle has become a norm of customary international law. See e.g. Owen McIntyre & Thomas Mosedale, "The Precautionary Principle as a Norm of Customary International Law" (1997) 9:2 J Envtl L 221.
66 See *Rio Declaration*, *supra* note 19, Principle 15.
67 *Agreement Governing the Activities of States on the Moon and Other Celestial Bodies*, 18 December 1979, 1363 UNTS 3, art 7(1) [*Moon Agreement*].
68 Viikari, *supra* note 12 at 62.
69 *Moon Agreement*, *supra* note 67, art 7(1).
70 Ibid., art 1(1).
71 *Status of International Agreements Relating to Activities in Outer Space as at 1 January 2015*, UNCOPUOS, Legal Subcommittee, 54th Sess, UN Doc A/AC.105/C.2/2015/CRP.8 (2015), online: UNOOSA www.unoosa.org/pdf/limited/c2/AC105_C2_2015_CRP08E.pdf.
72 To learn more about COSPAR, see Committee on Space Research, "About", online: COSPAR cosparhq.cnes.fr/about.
73 *COSPAR Planetary Protection Policy* 20 October 2002, as amended to 24 March 2011, online: COSPAR cosparhq.cnes.fr/sites/default/files/pppolicy.pdf.

The COSPAR Planetary Protection Policy is being maintained and promulgated as a reference for space-faring nations, both as an international standard on procedures to avoid organic-constituent and biological contamination in space exploration, and to provide accepted guidelines in this area to guide compliance with the wording of the Outer Space Treaty and other relevant international agreements.[74] It makes a distinction between five categories of target body/mission type combinations, and suggests different ranges of requirements for each category.[75] For determinations not covered, advice should be sought through the auspices of the Member National Scientific Institution of COSPAR. If such advice is not available, COSPAR will consider providing such advice through an *ad hoc* multidisciplinary committee.[76] Members are encouraged to inform COSPAR of their establishment of planetary protection requirements for planetary missions, and provide information to it about the procedures and computations used for planetary protection for each flight and about the areas of the target(s) which may have been subject to contamination.[77] The Policy also includes an Appendix of Implementation Guidelines and Category Specifications for Individual Target Bodies.

The COSPAR Policy focuses on organic-constituent and biological contamination in space exploration. Recently, recommendations have been made to expand the framework to address other forms of "harmful contamination" which go beyond biological and organic-constituent contamination.[78]

National and regional regulations

Article IX of the Outer Space Treaty and the COSPAR Policy have been followed by a few major space agencies, such as NASA, ESA, and JAXA. The NASA Planetary Protection Policy is defined by the NASA Policy Directive (NPD), titled "Biological Contamination Control for Outbound and Inbound Planetary Spacecraft".[79] The Directive covers "all space flight missions, robotic and human, which may intentionally or unintentionally carry Earth organisms and organic constituents to the planets or other solar system bodies, and any mission employing spacecraft which are intended to return to Earth and/or its biosphere from extraterrestrial targets of exploration".[80] In order to ensure compliance with the Policy, the NASA Office of Planetary Protection maintains the NASA Procedural Requirements (NPR), entitled "Planetary Protection Provisions for Robotic Extraterrestrial Missions".[81] Crewed planetary missions are currently guided by the NASA Policy Instruction (NPI), titled "NASA Policy on Planetary Protection Requirements for Human Extraterrestrial Missions", which would help

---

74   Ibid., Preamble.
75   Ibid., Policy.
76   Ibid.
77   Ibid.
78   John D Rummel, Margaret S Race & Gerda Horneck, eds, *Report: COSPAR Workshop on Ethical Considerations for Planetary Protection in Space Exploration: Princeton University, Princeton, New Jersey, 8–10 June 2010* (Paris: COSPAR, 2012) at 17–18, online: COSPAR cosparhq.cnes.fr/sites/default/files/ppp_workshop_report_ethical_considerations_princeton_final_v1a_7nov2012.pdf.
79   NASA, *Biological Contamination Control for Outbound and Inbound Planetary Spacecraft*, NPD 8020.7G, online: NASA nodis3.gsfc.nasa.gov/displayDir.cfm?Internal_ID=N_PD_8020_007G_&page_name=main&search_term=8020%2E7.
80   Ibid. at para 2(b).
81   NASA, *Planetary Protection Provisions for Robotic Extraterrestrial Missions*, NPR 8020.12D, online: NASA nodis3.gsfc.nasa.gov/displayDir.cfm?Internal_ID=N_PR_8020_012D_&page_name=main&search_term=8020%2E12.

to obtain scientific information, and to develop the necessary technologies and procedures to draft an NPR for crewed planetary missions.[82]

NASA Planetary protection requirements for each mission are determined on the basis of the type of mission, the nature of destination, and the planetary bodies that may be encountered during the mission. Compliance with formal implementation requirements assigned to each mission is overseen by NASA's Planetary Protection Officer (PPO). The PPO also requests recommendations from internal and external advisory committees, most notably from the Space Studies Board of the National Research Council, on implementation requirements for missions. It is worth mentioning that those requirements are formulated on the basis of the most current scientific information available about the target bodies and about life on Earth, and recommendations on implementation requirements are routinely reassessed as new information becomes available.[83]

ESA Planetary Protection Policy requires the Agency to avoid interplanetary contamination when carrying out activities in outer space, and to comply with the COSPAR Planetary Protection Policy in both crewed and robotic missions.[84] In order to implement the ESA planetary protection requirements,[85] the Agency maintains three technical standards.[86]

In 2012, JAXA established a planetary protection safety review board to be part of its safety review panel, in parallel to the safety review board for rocket payload safety and the safety review board for manned mission safety.[87]

Planetary protection is also regulated domestically through licensing procedure. For instance, the United Kingdom (UK) Outer Space Act requires the licensee to conduct his operations in such a way as to, *inter alia*, "prevent the contamination of outer space or adverse changes in the environment of the earth".[88] The Austrian Federal Law relating to space activities provides that the authorization must be issued if, among other things, "the space activity does not cause harmful contamination of outer space or celestial bodies or adverse changes in the environment".[89]

Control over nuclear radiation and regulation of nuclear power sources

Partial Test Ban treaty

Efforts to negotiate an international agreement to prohibit nuclear tests can be traced back to

---

82   NASA, *NASA Policy on Planetary Protection Requirements for Human Extraterrestrial Missions*, NPI 8020.7, online: NASA planetaryprotection.nasa.gov/documents/.
83   Ibid.
84   ESA Planetary Protection Policy is described in ESA/C(2007)112. See, NASA Policy and Requirements, online: NASA http://science.nasa.gov/media/medialibrary/2011/05/13/10_Conley_-_PP_requirementsv3_TAGGED.pdf.
85   See European Space Agency, *ESA Planetary Protection Requirements*, ESSB-ST-PP-001, Issue 1.
86   They are: European Space Agency, *Material and Hardware Compatibility Tests for Sterilization Processes*, ECSS-Q-ST-70-53C; European Space Agency, *Microbial Examination of Flight Hardware and Cleanrooms*, ECSS-Q-ST-70-55C; European Space Agency, *Bioburden Control of Cleanrooms*, ECSS-Q-ST-70-58C.
87   Yukio Shimizu, "JAXA Has Established a Planetary Protection Safety Review Board for JAXA Deep Space Program" (Paper delivered at the 40th COSPAR Scientific Assembly, held in Moscow, Russia from 2–10 August 2014) [unpublished].
88   *Outer Space Act 1986* (UK), c 38, s 5(2)(e)(i).
89   *Austrian Federal Law on the Authorisation of Space Activities and the Establishment of a National Space Registry (Austrian Outer Space Act*, adopted by the National Council on 6 December 2011), § 4(1)(5), online: UNOOSA www.unoosa.org/pdf/spacelaw/national/austria/austrian-outer-space-actE.pdf.

1955, when the former Soviet Union proposed a cessation of nuclear testing enforced by an international commission as part of an incremental process towards general nuclear disarmament.[90] Concerns over high-altitude nuclear tests conducted in the early years of human exploration and use of outer space, which created electromagnetic pulse (EMP) that brought severe impacts to satellites, apparently accelerated the negotiations. In 1963, the governments of the former Union of Soviet Socialist Republics (USSR), the US, and the UK concluded the Partial Test Ban Treaty,[91] and made it open to other States for signature. The Treaty obliges each of its Parties:

> [T]o prohibit, to prevent, and not to carry out any nuclear weapon test explosion, or any other nuclear explosion, at any place under its jurisdiction or control:
> (a) in the atmosphere; beyond its limits, including outer space; or under water, including territorial waters or high seas; or
> (b) in any other environment if such explosion causes radioactive debris to be present outside the territorial limits of the State under whose jurisdiction or control such explosion is conducted …[92]

States Parties further undertake to "refrain from causing, encouraging, or in any way participating in, the carrying out of any nuclear weapon test explosion, or any other nuclear explosion, anywhere which would take place in any of the environments described, or have the effect referred to," above.[93] The phrase "any other nuclear explosion", as explained by the then US Acting Secretary of State, includes explosions for peaceful purposes, because of the difficulty of differentiating between weapon test explosions and peaceful explosions without additional controls.[94] Underground tests are banned only if the "explosion causes radioactive debris to be present outside the territorial limits of the State under whose jurisdiction or control such explosion is conducted".[95]

After the conclusion of the Partial Test Ban Treaty, the number of underground nuclear tests substantially increased, while that of atmospheric nuclear tests decreased,[96] contributing to the environmental protection of the common areas. Today, the Partial Test Ban Treaty has 91 Signatories, 62 Ratifications, and 36 Accessions.[97]

---

90 Comprehensive Nuclear Test Ban Treaty Organization (CTBTO), "1955–62: From Peace Movement to Missile Crisis", online: CTBTO, www.ctbto.org/the-treaty/history-1945-1993/1955-62-from-peace-movement-to-missile-crisis/.
91 *Treaty Banning Nuclear Weapon Tests in the Atmosphere, in Outer Space and Under Water*, 5 August 1963, 480 UNTS 43 [*Partial Test Ban Treaty*].
92 Ibid., art I(1).
93 Ibid., art I(2).
94 "Nuclear Test Ban Treaty Signed at Moscow, transmitted to Senate for Advice and Consent to Ratification", *The Department of State Bulletin* 49:1261 (26 August 1963) 314 at 319.
95 *Partial Test Ban Treaty*, supra note 91, art I(1)(b).
96 For an overview of worldwide atmospheric and underground nuclear testing between 1945 and 2013, see Preparatory Commission for the Comprehensive Nuclear-Test-Ban Treaty Organization (CTBTO), "Page 6: Nuclear Testing: 1945–2009: Worldwide Nuclear Testing: Atmospheric and Underground 1945–2013", online: CTBTO www.ctbto.org/nuclear-testing/history-of-nuclear-testing/nuclear-testing-1945-today/page-6-nuclear-testing-1945-2009/.
97 See US Department of State, "Treaty on Principles Governing the Activities of States in the Exploration and Use of Outer Space, Including the Moon and Other Celestial Bodies", online: US Department of State www.state.gov/t/isn/5181.htm.

Outer Space Treaty

After the conclusion of the Partial Test Ban Treaty, both the US and the former USSR announced that they had no intention of stationing any objects carrying nuclear weapons or other Weapons of Mass Destruction (WMDs) in outer space.[98] This facilitated the inclusion of the provision prohibiting nuclear weapons in outer space in the Outer Space Treaty without great efforts. Article IV, Paragraph 1 of the Outer Space Treaty provides:

> States Parties to the Treaty undertake not to place in orbit around the Earth any objects carrying nuclear weapons or any other kinds of weapons of mass destruction, install such weapons on celestial bodies, or station such weapons in outer space in any other manner.[99]

Nonetheless, the term "nuclear weapons" has not been defined in the Treaty. The ICJ broadly defined "nuclear weapons" as "explosive devices whose energy results from the fusion or fission of the atom", regardless of the purpose.[100] By this definition, any nuclear explosive devices in outer space should be considered "nuclear weapons".

The threat posed by Near Earth Objects (NEOs) is gaining increasing attention in recent years, and the use of nuclear weapons is regarded as a means of last resort in the mitigation.[101] However, the use of nuclear weapons in planetary defense seems to contradict Article I of the Partial Test Ban Treaty, which prohibits any nuclear explosion.[102] The placement of nuclear weapons in outer space, which is regarded as an important measure for the mitigation of NEOs that have very short warning time such as long-period comets,[103] also seems to be prohibited by Article IV of the Outer Space Treaty if we follow the ICJ's definition of "nuclear weapons". The right to self-defense enshrined in the UN Charter, which is applicable to activities in outer space,[104] can only be invoked "if an armed attack occurs against a Member of the United Nations".[105] The ICJ even opined that the armed attack needs to be conducted "by one State against another State".[106] The right to defend against natural disasters, albeit included in the broad definition of self-defense which literally means "[t]he use of force to protect oneself, one's family, or one's property from a real and threatened attack",[107] is inadequately addressed in the UN Charter and customary international law of self-defense. However, international law does recognize that, in exceptional cases, any State's necessity to safeguard an essential interest threatened by a grave and imminent peril may outweigh its international obligations, thus precluding the wrongfulness for non-compliance.[108] The preclusion, nonetheless, is subject to two conditions: (a) the act must be the

---

98   Ibid.
99   *Outer Space Treaty*, supra note 3, art IV, para 1.
100 *Nuclear Weapons Advisory Opinion*, supra note 19 at 243.
101 Committee to Review Near-Earth Object Surveys and Hazard Mitigation Strategies, National Research Council, *Defending Planet Earth: Near-Earth-Object Surveys and Hazard Mitigation Strategies* (Washington, DC: The National Academies Press, 2010) at 4.
102 See *Partial Test Ban Treaty*, supra note 91, art I.
103 Joseph Packer, Jeffrey A Kurr & Adam Abelkop, "The Policy Trajectory of United States Asteroid Deflection Planning" (2013) 1:1 Timely Interventions 2 at 5.
104 *Outer Space Treaty*, supra note 3, art III.
105 *Charter of the United Nations*, 24 October 1945, 1 UNTS XVI, art 51 [*UN Charter*].
106 *Legal Consequences of the Construction of a Wall in the Occupied Palestinian Territory, Advisory Opinion* [2004] ICJ Rep 136 at para. 139.
107 Bryan A. Garner et al. eds., Black's Law Dictionary, 9th ed. (West, 2009) at 1481.
108 *Draft Articles on Responsibility of States for Internationally Wrongful Acts, with commentaries: 2001*, art 25(1), in "Report of the Commission to the General Assembly on the work of its fifty-third Session" (UN Doc A/56/10) in *Yearbook of the International Law Commission 2001*, vol 2, part 2 (New York: UN, 2001) at 28, 80–84 (UNDOC. A/CN.4/SER.A/2001/Add.1 (Part 2)).

only way for the State to safeguard an essential interest against a grave and imminent peril;[109] and (b) the act shall not seriously impair an essential interest of the State or States toward which the obligation exists, or of the international community as a whole.[110]

Regulation of nuclear power sources

The use of nuclear power in space missions is more advantageous than traditional solar power in at least two respects. First, nuclear power systems function independently of sunlight, enabling spacecraft to operate in areas where there is insufficient solar power. Second, the weight-to-capacity ratio of nuclear power generators is considerably lower than that of solar power systems, thus reducing the cost and increasing the mission length of space missions.[111] However, nuclear power sources (NPS) could present hazards to the terrestrial and extraterrestrial environment in the case of, for example, launch failures, in-orbit leaking or break-ups, post-mission break-ups, or re-entries.[112]

Outer space treaties and nuclear power sources principles

The use of NPS in outer space activities attracts the application of the outer space treaties *ipso facto*. However, those treaties do not adequately address such use of NPS. The re-entry of the former USSR's nuclear-powered Cosmos-954 in 1978, which crashed onto and scattered radioactive debris over northwest Canada,[113] raised international concerns over risks associated with the use of NPS in space activities. Discussions at the UN resulted in the adoption of Principles Relevant to the Use of Nuclear Power Sources in Outer Space (the NPS Principles) by the General Assembly on December 14, 1992. The Principles are applicable to the use of NPS for the generation of electrical power on board space objects, but not to those for propulsive purposes.[114]

The NPS Principles restated many principles and rules that had been well-accepted in international space law prior to its adoption by the General Assembly. For instance, the applicability of international law (Principle 1) can be found in Article III of the Outer Space Treaty.[115] General principles of international environmental law are thus applicable to the use of NPS in outer space. It follows, *inter alia*, that, when using NPS in space activities, States must have due regard to the environment of other States and that of areas beyond national jurisdiction. The obligation of consultation appearing in Article IX of the Outer Space Treaty is reiterated in Principle 6.[116] International responsibility for national space activities, and liability and

---

109 See ibid. Whether these conditions are fulfilled would depend on, among others, the mass of the NEO, the odds of impact, the length of warning time, and accessible means.
110 See ibid. at 81–82. For instance, unsuccessful mitigation which brings damage to States, which could have escaped from such damage in the "no action" scenario, would render the preclusion of wrongfulness inapplicable.
111 Carlos O Maidana, *Thermo-Magnetic Systems for Space Nuclear Reactors: An Introduction* (New York: Springer, 2014) at 6.
112 For a few incidents caused by nuclear-powered spacecraft, see Michael S Straubel, "Space Borne Nuclear Power Sources – The Status of Their Regulation" (1985–1986) 20:2 Val U L Rev 187 at 188–91.
113 See generally Eilene Galloway, "Nuclear Powered Satellites: The U.S.S.R. Cosmos 954 and the Canadian Claim" (1978–1979) 12:3 Akron L Rev 401.
114 *Principles Relevant to the Use of Nuclear Power Sources in Outer Space*, GA Res 47/68, UNGAOR, 1992, UN Doc A/RES/47/68, Preamble [*NPS Principles*].
115 See ibid., Principle 1; *Outer Space Treaty*, *supra* note 3, art III.
116 See *NPS Principles*, *supra* note 114, Principle 6; *Outer Space Treaty*, *supra* note 3, art IX.

compensation for damage, established in Articles VI and VII of the Outer Space Treaty and the Liability Convention,[117] are restated in Principles 8 and 9.[118]

In addition, the NPS Principles developed some of the then existing principles and rules of space law, and general international law, probably due to the higher potential risks associated with NPS. Principle 4, for instance, explicitly requires the launching State, prior to the launch, to "ensure that a thorough and comprehensive safety assessment is conducted", which must cover "all relevant phases of the mission and shall deal with all systems involved".[119]

The NPS Principles also contain some unique principles and rules in response to the unique challenges posed by NPS. For example, Principle 2 adopts a narrower definition of "launching State": "the State which exercises jurisdiction and control over a space object with nuclear power sources on board at a given point in time relevant to the principle concerned".[120] In the context of international liability for damage caused by space objects, the term "launching State" is defined as a State which "launches or procures the launching of a space object", or a State "from whose territory or facility a space object is launched".[121] Thus, the applicability of this definition and rules regarding liability for damage caused by a space object, already provided for in the Outer Space Treaty and the Liability Convention, has been reaffirmed.[122] Whereas the broad definition of "launching State" would enable victims to promptly seek remedies, echoing the victim orientation of the Liability Convention, the narrow definition in the NPS Principles gives more precise guidance as to who bears the special obligation to safely use NPS in outer space. The NPS Principles, therefore, impose additional obligations on States, who are considered as launching States according to the narrow definition under Principle 2, while preserving the general principles for the attribution of liability for damage. Furthermore,

---

117 See *Outer Space Treaty*, *supra* note 3, arts VI, VII; *Convention on the International Liability for Damage Caused by Space Objects*, 29 March 1972, 961 UNTS 187 [*Liability Convention*].
118 See *NPS Principles*, *supra* note 114, Principles 8, 9.
119 Ibid., Principle 4.1. Another example is the obligation to share information and to assist. Principle 5 requires the launching State, in the event that a space object with NPS on board is malfunctioning with a risk of re-entry of radioactive materials to the Earth, to inform States concerned "as soon as the malfunction has become known", update the information "as frequently as practicable", and disseminate the updated information in increasing frequency. See *NPS Principles*, *supra* note 114, Principle 5. Principle 7 requires all States possessing space monitoring and tracking facilities to communicate, in the case of re-entry of a space object containing a NPS, "the relevant information that they may have available on the malfunctioning space object with a nuclear power source on board to" the UN Secretary-General and the concerned State "as promptly as possible". Ibid., Principle 7.1. After re-entry, the launching State, other States, and international organizations with relevant technical capabilities shall promptly offer the necessary assistance. Ibid., Principle 7.2. Whereas the launching State naturally has the obligation to share information and provide assistance so as to minimize the damage, third-party States' obligations to provide information and render assistance in such disasters are not yet widely recognized, although there have been similar examples. According to the Remote Sensing Principles, States participating in remote sensing activities that have identified information in their possession that is capable of averting any phenomenon harmful to the Earth's natural environment shall disclose such information to States concerned. See *Principles relating to Remote Sensing of the Earth from Space*, GA Res 41/65, UNGAOR, 1986, UN Doc A/RES/41/65, Principle X [*Remote Sensing Principles*]. States that have identified processed data and analyzed information in their possession, which may be useful to States affected by natural disasters, or likely to be affected by impending natural disasters, shall transmit such data and information to States concerned as promptly as possible. See *Remote Sensing Principles*, ibid., Principle XI.
120 *NPS Principles*, *supra* note 114, Principle 2.1.
121 *Liability Convention*, *supra* note 117, art I(C); *Outer Space Treaty*, *supra* note 3, art VII.
122 *NPS Principles*, *supra* note 114, Principles 2.2, 9.1.

Principle 3 restricts the use of NPS in space activities to "those space missions which cannot be operated by non-nuclear energy sources in a reasonable way".[123]

IAEA documents

The International Atomic Energy Agency (IAEA) was created in 1957 in response to the deep fear and expectation resulting from the discovery of nuclear energy. The Agency works with its Member States and multiple partners worldwide to promote safe, secure, and peaceful use of nuclear technologies. The IAEA has used non-binding standards to ensure nuclear safety in outer space.

In 1996, the IAEA published the Safety Series Document on Emergency Planning and Preparedness for Nuclear Powered Satellite Re-entry.[124] The document has been prepared to assist States in their response to possible re-entry events in announcement, locating, monitoring, and recovery phases. The document contains nine Annexes.

In 2009, the IAEA and the UNCOPUOS jointly published the Safety Framework for Nuclear Power Source Applications in Outer Space.[125] The Safety Framework, which is voluntary, provides "a foundation for the development of national and international intergovernmental safety frameworks".[126] Its focus is on the protection of people and the environment in Earth's biosphere from potential hazards associated with relevant launch, operation, and end-of-service mission phases of space NPS applications. The protection of humans in space engaged in missions using NPS, and the protection of the environments of other celestial bodies are beyond the scope of the Safety Framework.[127] The Safety Framework lays down guidance for governments and relevant international intergovernmental organizations that authorize, approve or conduct space NPS missions,[128] guidance for the management of the organization involved in space NPS applications,[129] and technical guidance for organizations involved in space NPS applications.[130]

Conclusion

Existing international space treaties appear inadequate to address the challenge posed by the proliferation of space debris, which was not envisaged when the treaties were negotiated. International efforts on space debris mitigation since the late 1980s have contributed to the slow-down of the increase of debris. However, the challenge remains due to the intensified militarization of outer space and the increase and diversification of space actors. The

---

123 Ibid., Principle 3. The NPS Principles also recognize, in its preamble, that "the use of nuclear power sources in outer space should focus on those applications which take advantage of the particular properties of nuclear power sources". Ibid., Preamble.
124 IAEA, "Emergency Planning and Preparedness for Re-Entry of a Nuclear Powered Satellite", Safety Series No. 119, STI/PUB/1014 (October 1996), online: IAEA gnssn.iaea.org/Superseded%20 Safety%20Standards/Safety_Series_119_1996.pdf.
125 UNCOPUOS Scientific and Technical Subcommittee & IAEA, *Safety Framework for Nuclear Power Source Applications in Outer Space*, Doc A/AC.105/934 (Vienna: IAEA, 2009), online: IAEA www.iaea.org/sites/default/files/safetyframework1009.pdf.
126 Ibid. at 1.
127 Ibid. at 2.
128 Ibid. at 2–3.
129 Ibid. at 4.
130 Ibid. at 5.

conduction of active debris removal, which is gaining increasing support in the political and academic circles, will need to be based on not only its technical feasibility and economic viability, but also the resolution of a number of legal and policy issues such as a generally accepted definition of space debris, the sharing of space situational awareness, and the sharing of risks associated with the removal.

Whereas the regulation of planetary protection is similarly ambiguous in the Outer Space Treaty, COSPAR and various leading national space agencies have expounded sets of detailed policies in preventing interplanetary contaminations. It is foreseeable that more attention will be exerted on planetary protection with the further development of space activities, such as lunar exploration and space mining. It is highly recommended that the further elaboration of planetary protection policies should be guided by the precautionary principle, given the high risks associated therewith and potentially irreversible damages caused thereby.

The control over nuclear radiation in outer space is achieved through the prohibition of nuclear tests and nuclear weapons in outer space on the one hand, and the regulation of nuclear power sources on the other hand. Whereas the control has been largely effective in both respects, the question arises as to whether the prohibition of nuclear weapons in outer space would bar States from employing them for the purpose of planetary defense should it become necessary. It is worth noting that general international law does provide moderate flexibilities in this regard.

6
Settlement of disputes and resolution of conflicts

Tare Brisibe

1 Introduction

It is contended, that …"a dispute is a disagreement on a point of law or fact, a conflict of legal views or of interests between two *States*".[1] This echoes the Permanent Court of International Justice (PCIJ) definition in the *Mavrommatis Concessions Cases*[2] that "a dispute is a disagreement on a point of law or fact, a conflict of legal views or of interests between two *persons*." Another definition of dispute, as …"a specific disagreement relating to a question of rights or interests in which the parties proceed by way of claims, counter-claims, denials and so on,"[3] distinguishes same from conflict, which … "is used to signify a general state of hostility between the parties".[4] Yet another definition,[5] considers a dispute as referring to "some disagreement, that is, lack of consensus or the presence of some objection by a party which is regarded as sufficiently significant or substantial to constitute an obstacle to arriving at a decision involving a claim or demand." This proponent asserts, that… "a dispute may relate to any substantive or procedural question, including the proof of damage, problems of causation, the amount of compensation, the method of payment, and any other relevant matter." Furthermore, we should distinguish between disputes and differences of view between governments on issues that may arise during the use and exploration of outer space.[6]

---

1   I. Brownlie, The Wang Tieya Lecture in Public International Law – The Peaceful Settlement of International Disputes, *Chinese Journal of International Law* (2009), Vol. 8, No. 2, p. 268.
2   *Mavrommatis Palestine Concessions, Greece v United Kingdom*, Objection to the jurisdiction of the court, Judgment No. 2, PCIJ Series A No. 2, ICGJ 236 (PCIJ 1924), 30 August 1924. The ICJ, recognized in the *South West Africa* case, ICJ Rep. 1962, p. 319 at 328 that a mere conflict of interests, without more, does not constitute a dispute. See also *Northern Cameroons*, ICJ Reports 1963 pp. 15, 20, 27 and *East Timor (Portugal v Australia)*, ICJ Reports 1995 pp. 90, 99–100.
3   J. Collier & V. Lowe, THE SETTLEMENT OF DISPUTES IN INTERNATIONAL LAW – INSTITUTIONS AND PROCEDURES (2002) p. 1.
4   Id.
5   S. Gorove, Dispute Settlement in the Liability Convention, in SETTLEMENT OF SPACE LAW DISPUTES – THE PRESENT STATE OF THE LAW AND PERSPECTIVES OF FURTHER DEVELOPMENT, Proceedings of an International Colloquium, K. Bocksteigel (ed.), (1979) vol. 1, Studies in Air and Space Law, p. 43.
6   E. Galloway, Which Method of Realization in Public International Law Can be Considered Most Desirable and Having the Greatest Chances of Realization, op. cit., at p. 159.

These distinctions must be made at the outset particularly as it relates to the nature of activities with which this chapter is concerned. Understanding the applicable legal order is pivotal to any consideration of dispute settlement or conflict resolution arising from outer space activities, for various reasons. Summarily, the international legal system establishing the general principle[7] that international disputes be settled peacefully, also establishes *norms, procedures* and *institutions* required to facilitate the avoidance and resolution of international disputes, thereby providing techniques with which States can reach settlements. On the premise[8] that international law including the Charter of the United Nations is applicable to activities in outer space, the main sources of procedures for settlement of disputes arising from outer space activities have traditionally been international principles and treaty provisions including the means set forth in the Charter of the United Nations and of international law in general. Such means or procedures available to States for the settlement of disputes arising from outer space activities, are comprised of: negotiation, inquiry, mediation, conciliation, arbitration, judicial settlement, and resort to regional arrangements or agencies or other peaceful means of the parties' own choice.[9] For outer space activities borne out of a race between superpowers for technological and ideological superiority, the techniques for avoiding, managing and resolving conflict between States, including prior notification and consultation requirements, duties to publish and exchange information and the conduct of impact assessments, are equally important as those techniques required for handling of conflicts and / or disputes that arise despite these preventive methods. Likewise, attention must be paid to composite dispute-settlement mechanisms designed to prevent, to the extent possible disputes from arising, to foster reaching agreed solutions and to put in place efficient dispute-settlement methods when disputes nevertheless arise.[10] Such mechanisms include early warning, partnering, facilitated negotiation, conciliation and mediation, non-binding expert appraisal, mini-trial, senior executive appraisal, review of technical disputes by independent experts, dispute review boards, non-binding arbitration, and judicial proceedings.[11]

The consensual or optional recourse to legal mechanisms by actors at all levels, applies equally in both international and domestic legal systems, albeit without precluding the potential for use of State machinery which may be brought to bear in certain circumstances against the traditional subjects of States. Because international tribunals do not exercise compulsory jurisdiction, any reference to judicial settlement can only be made by agreement of the disputing parties which may be in the form of a rule, decision, agreement, contract, convention, treaty, constituent instrument of an organization or agency, or relationship out of, or in relation to which, the dispute arises. This transpired when the question arose if the PCIJ, i.e., the predecessor of the International Court of Justice (ICJ), could deliver an advisory opinion in relation to obligations of the Soviet Union towards Finland regarding the *Eastern*

---

7   Art. 1, Art. 2 (3), Charter of the United Nations, 24 October 1945, 1 United Nations *Treaty Series*, XVI.
8   UNGA resolution 1721 (XVI) A; Preamble of UNGA resolution 1802 (XVII); UNGA resolution 1962 (XVIII); Art. III, 1967 Treaty on Principles Governing the Activities of States in the Exploration and Use of Outer Space, including the Moon and Other Celestial Bodies (Outer Space Treaty) United Nations, *Treaty Series*, vol. 610, No. 8843.
9   See Article 33 (1) Charter of the United Nations; UNGA resolution 2625 (XXV) para. 5; UNGA resolution 37/10 para. 3 and 10; cited in: United Nations, HANDBOOK ON THE PEACEFUL SETTLEMENT OF DISPUTES BETWEEN STATES, (1992) New York, ISBN 92-1-133428.4.
10 United Nations Publication, A/CN.9/SER.B/4, UNCITRAL LEGISLATIVE GUIDE ON PRIVATELY FINANCED INFRASTRUCTURE PROJECTS (2001) ISBN 92-1-133632-5 at p. 175.
11 Id. pp. 176 to 187.

Carelia case, as the Soviet Union had not given its consent to have this issue resolved through the League of Nations or the Court.[12] The Court held… "it is well established in international law that no State can, without its consent, be compelled to submit its disputes with other States either to mediation or to arbitration, or to any other kind of pacific settlement". Furthermore, as it has been contended,[13] States have proven adept at constructing bespoke systems of dispute resolution concerning particular forms of subject matter or which are operable within particular treaty regimes,[14] or within particular regional contexts or within international organizations.

This said, *procedural mechanisms* for the settlement of disputes arising from outer space related activity in the form in which they arise should not be exclusively governed by public international law, but should also contain elements of private international law.[15] As disputes and conflicts could and do arise from activities of *international persons*, encompassing States, international intergovernmental organizations as well as individuals, recognized in theory and practice as the third category of *international law subjects*. Disputes and conflicts also arise from activities conducted by *subjects of States*, that is, nationals, both "physical" and "juridical" persons. Consequently, this chapter addresses the nature, techniques and particularities associated with settling disputes or resolving conflicts arising from outer space activities between any combination of international persons, or subjects of States, operating within either international or domestic legal systems. Section 2, examines differences between international and domestic legal systems in the context of constituent instruments establishing relationships out of, or in relation to which, disputes arise. An attempt is also made to detail and categorize the nature of disputes and conflicts which could and have in fact arisen from various forms of outer space activity. Section 3 examines techniques for settlement and resolution, in the course of which attention is paid to the Permanent Court of Arbitration 2011 *Optional Rules for Arbitration of Disputes Relating to Outer Space Activities*. Section 4 highlights a number of particularities and concludes the chapter.

2 Typology of disputes and conflict

In considering various instruments establishing relationships out of, or in relation to which disputes arise, there are differences between international and domestic legal systems. In the context of which it is necessary to note the difference between responsibility between States, and liability in private law of one citizen towards another.[16] Concerning the international legal

---

12   *Status of Eastern Carelia (USSR v Finland)* Advisory Opinion (1923) PCIJ Series B no 5 p. 27.
13   Foreward by M. Evans in D. French, M. Saul, N. White (eds) INTERNATIONAL LAW AND DISPUTE SETTLEMENT – NEW PROBLEMS AND TECHNIQUES (2010) vol. 28 Studies in International Law, Hart Publishing, p vii.
14   See the 1972 Convention on International Liability for Damage Caused by Space Objects (Liability Convention) United Nations, *Treaty Series*, vol. 961, No. 13810.
15   T. T. Van Den Hout, Resolving Outer Space Related Disputes, PROCEEDINGS OF THE UN/IIASL WORKSHOP ON CAPACITY BUILDING IN SPACE LAW (2003) ST/SPACE/14 Office for Outer Space Affairs, United Nations Office at Vienna, p. 5. Cf. P. P.C. Haanappel, Private Space Law: Does it Exist and If So, What is It? *Revista del Centro de Investigación y Difusión Aeronáutico-Espacial*, 30 (2012) pp. 11–23.
16   See generally: C. Eagleton, THE RESPONSIBILITY OF STATES IN INTERNATIONAL LAW 3-25 (1928; reprint 1970). Cf. The fact that liability is…"a condition of being responsible for a possible or actual loss, penalty, evil, expense or burden", and as… "the state of being bound or obliged in law or justice to do, pay, or make good something." Bryan A. Garner, (ed.) BLACK'S LAW DICTIONARY, (2014) 10th ed. ISBN 978-0-314-61300-4.

system, the 1967 Outer Space Treaty provides[17] for responsibility[18] and consequent liability of States involved in space activities. Reference to the principle of State responsibility is in the dictum of the PCIJ in *Factory at Chorzow*[19] (Jurisdiction). In respect of which, the court stated: "it is a principle of international law that the breach of an engagement involves an obligation to make reparation." Presumably[20] disputes could include: (a) Disputes occurring from civil space activities; (b) Disputes occurring from criminal acts; (c) A combination of (a) and (b) above; (d) Disputes resulting from the application and interpretation of principles mentioned in international conventions and treaties. Another attempt[21] at categorizing dispute settlement and outer space activities, notes that legal problems can be about outer space, space to earth, and earth to space aspects. Although specifics are discussed in detail in the third section below, the subject matter or issues in related disputes, could concern torts, the environment, antitrust, taxation, intellectual property, insurance, and so on.[22] To date, such subjects or issues associated

17 Note 8 supra, at Art. VI and Art. VII respectively.
18 On state responsibility, see C. Eagleton, Id. Note 16 supra.; K. Zemanek, *Causes and Forms of International Liability*, in B. Cheng and E. D. Brown (Eds.), CONTEMPORARY PROBLEMS OF INTERNATIONAL LAW: ESSAYS IN HONOUR OF GEORG SCHWARZENBERGER ON HIS EIGHTIETH BIRTHDAY pp. 319–321 (1988). On the subject of state obligation and responsibility, *see* A. E. Boyle, State Responsibility and Liability for Injurious Consequences of acts not Prohibited by International Law: A Necessary Distinction?, 39 *International & Comparative Law Quarterly* 1 (1990); T. Street, The Foundation of Legal Liability (1906), cited in Eagleton, supra, at note 16 p. 3; J. L. Brierly, The Basis of Obligation, in H. Lauterpacht and C. H. M. Waldock (eds), INTERNATIONAL LAW AND OTHER PAPERS 1–67 (1958); I. Brownlie, SYSTEM OF THE LAW OF NATIONS – STATE RESPONSIBILITY Part I (1983); E. Jiménez de Arechaga and T. Attila, International State Responsibility, in M. Bedjaoui (ed.), INTERNATIONAL LAW: ACHIEVEMENTS AND PROSPECTS pp. 347–380 (1991); J. Crawford, THE INTERNATIONAL LAW COMMISSION'S ARTICLES ON STATE RESPONSIBILITY – INTRODUCTION, TEXT AND COMMENTARIES (2002); J. Crawford and S. Olleson, The Nature and Forms of International Responsibility, in M. Evans (ed.), INTERNATIONAL LAW 445–472 (2003).
19 1927 PCIJ (Ser. A), No. 9, at 21. For application of the principle, see: *Phosphates in Morocco*, Preliminary, Objections, 1938 PCIJ (Ser. A/B), No. 74, at 28; *Corfu Channel*, Merits, 1949 ICJ Reports 4, at 23; *Military and Paramilitary Activities in and against Nicaragua* (*Nicaragua v. United States of America*), Merits, 1986 ICJ Reports 14, at 142, para. 283, and 149, para. 292; *Gabčikovo-Nagymaros Project* (*Hungary v. Slovakia*), 1997 ICJ Reports 7, at 38, para. 47. On the relationship between the law of treaties and State responsibility, see R. Lefeber, The Gabčikovo-Nagymaros Project and the Law of State Responsibility, 11 *Leiden Journal of International Law* 609 (1998). The ICJ has also referred to the principle of State responsibility in: *Reparation For Injuries Suffered in the Service of the United Nations*, 1949 ICJ Reports 174, at 184; *Interpretation of Peace Treaties with Bulgaria, Hungary and Romania*, Second Phase, 1950 ICJ Reports 221. A number of arbitral tribunals have repeatedly affirmed the principle in: *Dickson Car Wheel Company Case, United Nations Reports of International Arbitral Awards*, IV RIAA 669, at 678 (1931); *International Fisheries Company Case*, IV RIAA 691, at 701 (1931); *British Claims in the Spanish Zone of Morocco Case*, II RIAA 615, at 641 (1925); *Armstrong Cork Company Case*, XIV RIAA 159, at 163 (1953); *Rainbow Warrior (New Zealand v. France)*, XX RIAA 217 (1990).
20 H. Safavi, Cases and Methods of Dispute Settlement in Space Law, (1996) Proc. IISL Coll. IAF/AIAA, at p. 68.
21 I. H. P. Diederiks-Verschoor, The Settlements of Disputes in Space: New Developments (1998) J. Space L. vol., 26 no.1 at p. 44. See also K. Bockstiegel, The Settlement of Disputes Regarding Space Activities After 30 years of the Outer Space Treaty, in G. Lafferranderie and D. Crowther (eds) OUTLOOK ON SPACE LAW OVER THE NEXT 30 YEARS (1997) at pp. 239 to 245 proposing the categorization, as: Disputes between States; Disputes within or Involving International Organizations; and Disputes Involving Commercial Private Enterprises.
22 Id. I. H. P. Diederiks-Verschoor; S. Gorove, The Growth of Space Law Through the Cases (1996) J. Space L. vol. 24 no.1, at p. 44.

with disputes and claims made by States, tend mainly towards *international liability*, protection from *harmful interference, access to orbital resources* and *allocation of radio frequencies*.[23] The principal dispute settlement provisions deriving from international space law and the related multilateral regime can be found in United Nations legal instruments establishing principles on general and specific aspects, including: UNGA Resolution 1962 (XVIII);[24] 1967 Outer Space Treaty;[25] 1972 Liability Convention;[26] 1982 Agreement Governing the Activities of States on the Moon and Other Celestial Bodies[27] (Moon Agreement); UNGA Resolution 37/92;[28] UNGA Resolution 41/65[29] and UNGA Resolution 47/68.[30] Given the predominance of telecommunications in outer space activities, reference to constituent instruments of the International Telecommunication Union[31] (ITU) should be made.

In addition to the aforementioned multilateral instruments, reference can be made to bespoke systems of dispute resolution concerning outer space activities operable within regional contexts,[32] international intergovernmental organizations[33] and thousands of bilateral treaties. Assessing the aforementioned international regime, reveals pertinent considerations amongst which summary include, most notably, the fact that Article IX and Article XIII of the Outer Space Treaty provide for consultations to be undertaken between States party to the Treaty, or by States Parties to the Treaty either with the appropriate international organization or with one or more States members of a relevant international organization, which are Parties to the Treaty. Likewise, in accordance with the Liability Convention's Article VIII paragraphs (1) (2) and (3), States have *locus* to pursue claims, whilst private entities may do so through a State, after having possibly exercised the option of pursuing local remedies. Second, in the absence of an agreement by the States parties to make the decision or award of a Claims

---

23   For a comparable categorization, of international environmental disputes, which could also be applied to outer space, cf R. B. Bilder, The Settlement of Disputes in the Field of the International Law of the Environment (1975) RECUEIL DES COURS at pp. 155 to 156.

24   Declaration of Legal Principles Governing the Activities of States in the Exploration and Uses of Outer Space. (Dispute Resolution provisions in Principle 6).

25   Supra, note 8. (Dispute Resolution provisions in Art. IX, Art. XIII). Cf. Art. III.

26   Supra, note 14. (Dispute Resolution provisions in Art. IX, Art. XI, Art. XIV, et seq.).

27   United Nations, *Treaty Series*, vol. 1363, No. 23002. (Dispute Resolution provisions in Art. 15).

28   Principles Governing the Use by States of Artificial Earth Satellites for International Direct Television Broadcasting. (Dispute Resolution provisions in Annex E: Peaceful settlement of disputes).

29   Principles Relating to Remote Sensing of the Earth from Outer Space (Dispute Resolution provisions in Principle XV).

30   Principles Relevant to the Use of Nuclear Power Sources in Outer Space (Dispute Resolution provisions in Principle 10).

31   Dispute Resolution provisions in Art. 56 of the ITU Constitution and Art. 41 of the ITU Convention; 1992 Optional Protocol on the Compulsory Settlement of Disputes; COLLECTION OF THE BASIC TEXTS OF THE INTERNATIONAL TELECOMMUNICATION UNION ADOPTED BY THE PLENIPOTENTIARY CONFERENCE, 2015; Art. 15, ITU RADIO REGULATIONS (Edition of 2012).

32   For a survey of instruments including regional agreements, see, K. Bocksteigel (ed.), supra note 5 at pp. 206 to 411; INTERNATIONAL AGREEMENTS AND OTHER AVAILABLE LEGAL DOCUMENTS RELEVANT TO SPACE-RELATED ACTIVITIES (1999), prepared as a reference document for member States by the United Nations Office for Outer Space Affairs; PCA Doc. 31641, Survey of Space Law Instruments (2010).

33   Id. For constituent instruments concerning intergovernmental organizations. Post-privatization of several intergovernmental satellite organizations, like INTELSAT, INMARSAT and EUTELSAT, their amended constituent instruments ensure *inter alia* that, in the event of disputes, parties could resort to arbitration (infra section 3).

Commission binding in accordance with the Liability Convention's Article XIX (2), the Liability Convention would not ultimately settle a dispute and provide effective recovery to the claimant party if the Launching State[34] is legally not obliged to abide by the Claim Commission's decision.

Whilst private litigants are as a rule subject to compulsory adjudication of their disputes by courts, or could resort to other means by exercising the voluntary choice of a more flexible, time efficient and cost effective procedure, States are not generally subject to compulsory jurisdiction and would consider all forms of binding dispute settlement a restriction on their freedom.[35] A realistic discussion of dispute settlement and conflict resolution must take account of what has been considered[36] the notorious resistance of sovereign States to any form of international adjudication. This is probably an appropriate juncture to highlight the perception[37] that, despite the aforementioned instruments, the international legal system is inadequate at providing suitable institutions, means or procedures for settlement of disputes arising from outer space activities. Whilst this remains debatable, it can also be argued[38] that relatively, dispute settlement would play a greater role for private enterprises than for States and their institutions because private enterprises do not have recourse to diplomatic and political means. Private enterprises would rather calculate and balance their exposure to costs and evaluate risks associated with fulfillment of contractual obligations. In this regard, as far as contracts are concerned, issues which have arisen, aside a handful of exceptional instances, tend towards *torts*, as well as, *breach* or *performance* obligations mainly in relation to the manufacture, launch and operation of satellites.

The trend[39] is notable, commencing in the early 1980s, towards private sector participation and competition in infrastructure sectors, driven by general as well as country-specific factors. This time line coincides with the start of industry participation in traditional government owned and operated space projects through public-private partnerships (PPPs). It is contended that issues which most frequently give rise to disputes during the life of a project agreement concern possible breaches of the agreement during the construction phase, the operation of the infrastructure facility or in connection with the expiry or termination of the project agreement.[40] One should add that this fairly simplistic description of PPPs, risks underestimating the inherently complex nature of PPPs, because privately financed infrastructure

---

34   The party liable to pay compensation for damage under the Liability Convention's Art. II, is regarded as the "launching State" defined to mean: (i) a State which launches or procures the launching of a space object; (ii) a State from whose territory or facility a space object is launched. Further provision is made under Art. IV, Art. V and Art. VI of the Liability Convention for joint liability when two or more States launch a space object in a collaborative effort.

35   H. Fox, States and the Undertaking to Arbitrate, (1988) vol.37 *International & Comparative Law Quarterly* at p. 160. See also, M. O'Connell (ed.) INTERNATIONAL DISPUTE SETTLEMENT (2003) Ashgate, at p. 160.

36   A. Broches, Experiences from the Practice of an Arbitral Tribunal, in K. Bocksteigel (ed.) Supra Note 5 at p. 28.

37   Which, for instance, inspired establishment of the International Space and Aviation Arbitration Court by the French Air and Space Law Society. See M. G. Bourely, Creating an International Space and Aviation Arbitration Court, in Proc. IISL Coll. (1993) IAF / AIAA, at pp. 144 to 149. Cf. The International Law Association (ILA) *Convention on the Settlement of Disputes Related to Space Activities* (Helsinki 1996) and S. M. Williams, Dispute Settlement and Space Activities: A New Framework Required? in Proc. IISL Coll. (1996) IAF / AIAA, at pp. 61 to 67.

38   K. Bocksteigel in G. Lafferranderie, and D. Crowther (eds) supra note 21, at pp. 237–249.

39   See: UNCITRAL Legislative Guide, supra, note 10 at p. 1.

40   Id. at p. 175.

projects typically require the establishment of a network of interrelated contracts and other legal relationships involving various parties.[41] Such projects must take account of the diversity of relations, which may call for different dispute-settlement methods depending on the type of dispute and the parties involved. This said, the main disputes may be divided into three broad categories, namely: (a) Disputes arising under agreements between the concessionaire and the contracting authority and other governmental agencies;[42] (b) disputes arising under contracts and agreements entered into by the project promoters or the concessionaire with related parties for the implementation of the project;[43] (c) disputes between the concessionaire and other parties.[44]

3 Techniques

3.1 Negotiation and consultation

Negotiation and consultation feature in dispute resolution provisions establishing procedures for settlement of disputes arising from outer space activities. See, procedures to be based on consultations and negotiations pursuant to the Moon Agreement (Article 15), the UNGA Resolution 47/68 (Principle 10) which makes provision for negotiation and application of the United Nations Charter, whilst provisions under UNGA Resolution 37/92 (Annex E) and UNGA 41/65 (Principle XV) invoke established procedures in accordance with the Charter of the United Nations. Consultation also features in UNGA Resolution 1962 (XVIII) (Principle 6) and the Outer Space Treaty (Articles III, IX and XIII), in as much as it is rightly contended[45] that consultation in this regard is geared towards preventing disputes (discussed below), avoiding harmful interference and protecting the environment. Noting also that negotiation can produce a settlement in accordance with legal criteria or in accordance with both legal and political criteria.[46] For instance, regarding international responsibility and potential liability, whilst the 1978 claims against the Soviet Union by Canada, as a consequence of damage caused by the Soviet Cosmos 954 nuclear-powered satellite[47] were made pursuant

---

41   Id. at p. 173.
42   Ibid. Public projects, including those of a space-related nature, could be governed by either administrative law or contract law as supplemented by special provisions developed for government contracts for the provision of public services.
43   Id. at p. 174. Contracts would usually include at least: (i) contracts between parties holding equity in the project company (ii) loan and related agreements (iii) contracts between the project company and contractors; (iv) contracts between the project company and the parties who operate and maintain the project facility; and (v) contracts between the concessionaire and private companies for the supply of goods and services needed for the operation and maintenance of the facility.
44   Ibid. This could include customers of downstream space services such as airlines, airports, marine vessels, etc., or even individual users. Parties to these disputes may not necessarily be bound by any prior legal relationship of a contractual or similar nature. Cf. P. P. C. Haanappel, supra note 15, at p. 12, on the definition of private law and of private space law.
45   I. Herczeg, Provisions of the Space Treaties on Consultation (1967) 10, Proc. IISL Coll., at pp. 141 to 146; J. Sztucki, International Consultations and Space Treaties, op. cit., at pp. 147 to 181; M. Hoskova, Tendencies of Dispute Settlement in Present Eastern European Space Law (1996) Proc. IISL Coll, at p. 83; E. Galloway, supra note 6 at p. 169; S. Marchisio, Article IX, in Hobe, Schmidt-Tedd, and Schrogl (eds) COLOGNE COMMENTARY ON SPACE LAW, vol. I (2009) Carl Heymanns Verlag, at pp. 179 to 180.
46   I. Brownlie, supra note 1, at p. 270.
47   See: P. G. Dembling, Cosmos 954 and the Space Treaties, 6 J. Space L. (1978) pp. 129–136; S. Gorove, Cosmos 954: Issues of Law and Policy, 6 J. Space L. (1978) pp. 137–146; P. P. C. Haanappel, Some Observations on the Crash of Cosmos 954, 6 J. Space L. (1978) pp. 147–149.

to the 1972 Liability Convention and general international law, this landmark dispute involving consultations, resulted in a negotiated settlement.[48]

Other instances to which reference can be made include, international reaction to the United States of America's (USA) 1963 Project West Ford[49] experiment; and reaction by a group of countries[50] concerning information furnished to the United Nations Secretary-General by Russia[51] on the de-orbiting and subsequent disintegration of the Mir Space Station over the Pacific Ocean on 23 March 2001. Likewise, despite detailed procedures available to Member States of the World Trade Organization[52] (WTO), in the matter concerning "Japan and Procurement of a Navigation Satellite" for air traffic management, the European Communities (EC), complaint of 26 March 1997, regarding a procurement tender by Japan's Ministry of Transport (MoT), contended that tender specifications were not neutral but referred explicitly to specifications of the USA. Implying that, European bidders could effectively not participate in the tender which was presumed inconsistent with Annex I of Appendix I of Japan's commitments under the Government Procurement Agreement (GPA), in addition to violating Articles VI(3) and XII(2) of the GPA. This complaint which was resolved by consultations,[53] resulted in a mutually agreed solution, reduced into agreement on 19 February 1998. In this regard, the settlement reached between the European Commission and the MoT saw the establishment of cooperation between the European Tripartite Group (consisting of the European Commission, the European Space Agency and EUROCONTROL) on the one hand and the MoT on the other in the field of interoperability between the MTSAT Satellite-based Augmentation System (MSAS) and European Geostationary Navigation Overlay Service (EGNOS). This cooperation was stated as aimed at jointly contributing to implementation of a global seamless navigation service for aeronautical end-users through interoperability among MSAS, EGNOS and other equivalent systems.[54] Furthermore, whilst multilateral instruments governing space radiocommunications offer various techniques,[55] several disputes concerning

---

48 See Communiqué No. 27 on Settlement of Claim between Canada and the U.S.S.R. for Damages Caused by 'Cosmos 954', 2 April 1981; Protocol between Canada and the U.S.S.R, 2 April 1981; reproduced in SPACE LAW, BASIC LEGAL DOCUMENTS (1990) vol. 1 and 2, K. Böckstiegel and M. Benkö (eds) Martinus Nijhoff Publishers at section A.1X.2.1 and 2 respectively.

49 For the facts, see K. Bockstiegel, Case Law on Space Activities, in N. Jasentuliyana (ed.) SPACE LAW – DEVELOPMENT AND SCOPE (1992) Prager, at pp. 207 citing, UN Doc. A/AC.105/13 and UN Doc. A/AC.105/15, reprinted in SPACE LAW, BASIC LEGAL DOCUMENTS op. cit. note 48 at section A.IX.1.

50 Ministers of Foreign Affairs of the Rio Group expressed concern that …"the common heritage has become an area where dangerous materials are being dumped…". See statement reprinted in SPACE LAW, BASIC LEGAL DOCUMENTS supra note 48 at section A.IX.3.2.

51 UN Doc. A/AC.105/759 (Note verbale dated 23 January 2001 from the Permanent Mission of the Russian Federation to the United Nations Secretary-General); UN Doc. A/AC.105/759/Add.1 (Note verbale dated 28 February 2001 from the Permanent Mission of the Russian Federation to the United Nations Secretary-General).

52 Understanding on Rules and Procedures Governing the Settlement of Disputes, Marrakesh Agreement Establishing the World Trade Organization, Annex 2, 354 (1999), 1869 United Nations *Treaty Series* 401, 33 I.L.M. 1226 (1994).

53 See: WTO Docs WT/DS73/4/Rev.1 and GPA/D1/2/Rev.1 of 14 August 1997.

54 See: WTO Doc. WT/DS73/5 3 March 1998, Notification of Mutually-Agreed Solution from the Permanent Delegation of the European Commission and the Permanent Mission of Japan.

55 See note 31 supra. See generally, A. A. E. Noll, The Various Approaches to Dispute Settlement Concerning International Telecommunications, in PCA International Bureau (ed.) ARBITRATION IN AIR, SPACE AND TELECOMMUNICATIONS LAW – ENFORCING REGULATORY MEASURES (2001) Kluwer, at pp. 161 to 192; Ram S. Jakhu, Dispute Resolution Under the ITU Agreements (2010) discussion paper submitted to the PCA Advisory Group. On file with the author.

access to orbital resources and *frequency allocations*[56] have been resolved mainly by negotiations and consultations. Similar techniques have also been applied regarding alleged deliberate *harmful interference* to radiocommunications. See for instance, the dispute between France and Iran regarding alleged deliberate harmful interference affecting transmissions on EUTELSAT satellites at 7° East and 13° East.[57] Thus in practice, space radiocommunications related disputes between States continue to be resolved in line with procedures for avoiding harmful interference detailed in Art. 15 of the Radio Regulations along with recommendations of the ITU Radio Regulations Board. In all, these interrelated methods for dispute settlement, that is, consultation and negotiation, are widely acknowledged as the first, and in practice constitute the principal technique by which States in particular, have traditionally addressed their differences, given their frequent use with all other methods combined.[58]

3.2 Dispute avoidance

The notion that significant changes have occurred in the structure and content of the space endeavor, reflected in the emergence of new technologies and increasing number of actors at all levels[59] pre-supposes increased activity with a heightened risk of disputes. This said, a tendency towards dispute avoidance in the space sector alongside reluctance to employ adversarial dispute-settlement mechanisms must be noted, given the practices, by either international persons, or subjects of States, that contribute towards eliminating potential conflicts. Evidence of State practice under international instruments applicable to outer space activities, similar to many other areas of international law,[60] indicate a wide adoption of consultation provisions[61] towards dispute avoidance or prevention. It is contended[62] that the long duration[63] of privately financed infrastructure projects makes it important to devise mechanisms to prevent, as much as possible, disputes from arising so as to preserve the business relationship between the parties. Related procedures typically provide for a sequential series of steps starting with an early warning of issues that may develop into a dispute unless the parties take action to prevent them. In most cases, adversarial dispute-settlement mechanisms are only used when the disputes cannot be settled through the use of conciliatory methods. This desire to prevent, as much as possible, disputes from arising so as to preserve the business relationship between the parties is prevalent in the space sector. For instance, under its Space Act authority, the US

---

56   See 1990s controversy concerning Tongasat's ITU application for 16 orbital slots and subsequent lease/auction of 6 orbital slots Tonga secured, absent any specific plan to launch satellites. Cf. frequency co-ordination issues arising from the Zohreh-1 and Zohreh-2 satellites, proposed by Iran, to be deployed at 34° East and 26° East.
57   See: ITU Doc. RRB13 1/8-E, 8 April 2013.
58   C. M. Fombad, Consultation and Negotiations in the Pacific Settlement of International Disputes, (1989) vol.1 *African Yearbook of International and Comparative Law* at pp. 707–724. Reproduced in M. O'Connell (ed.) note 35 supra at, pp. 37 to 54. See also United Nations HANDBOOK, supra note 9 at p. 9 et seq.
59   Para. 9, Declaration on the Fiftieth Anniversary of Human Space Flight and the Fiftieth Anniversary of the Committee on the Peaceful Uses of Outer Space in *General Assembly Official Records Sixty-sixth Session Supplement No. 20* (A/66/20) Appendix.
60   For instance, see consultation provisions of the WTO dispute resolution mechanism, in Art. 4, Understanding on Rules and Procedures Governing the Settlement of Disputes, supra note 52.
61   Infra section 3.1.
62   UNCITRAL Guide, Supra, note 10 at p. 175.
63   Manufacture, launch and in-orbit delivery of a commercial satellite could take anywhere between two to five years at the minimum.

National Aeronautics and Space Administration (NASA) whilst incorporating dispute prevention provisions, has entered into a significant number of agreements with diverse groups of people and organizations, both in the *private* and public sector, in order to meet wide-ranging NASA mission and program requirements and objectives.[64] The Agreement Partner can be a U.S. or foreign person or entity, an educational institution, a Federal, state, or local governmental unit, a foreign government, or an international organization."[65] Likewise, it is notable the European Space Agency's (ESA) practice which is largely based on the ESA Convention,[66] and tailored clauses, favors arbitral tribunals (discussed below) for final disposition of disputes involving ESA. Nonetheless, the agency also promotes multi-layered consultation processes, or a conciliation procedure for resolving disputes between ESA and a contractor, before referring same to arbitration or any another dispute-settlement mechanism.[67]

Outer space activities were born out of a race between superpowers for technological and ideological superiority, in which preventive diplomacy[68] played a critical role in avoiding local struggles from becoming superpower conflicts. In this supposed period of détente, one easily underestimates the value of dispute avoidance, in as much as testing conventional weapons and/or missiles remains lawful in outer space, just as it is lawful on the high seas and in the superjacent airspace.[69] For instance, recent events, intentional and accidental, have resulted in massive debris fallout, giving impetus to proposals for debris removal procedures.[70] In this regard, we will recall, the United Nations Committee on the Peaceful Uses of Outer Space (UNCOPUOS) and its subcommittees have traditionally worked by consensus and for which it is contended[71] that space law disputes requiring legal disposition should not be confused with the process of consensus decision making in UNCOPUOS. Furthermore, ..." Consensus as a method of work cannot always be successful with issues involving extremely sharp and

64 The agency has concluded nearly 1,800 such instruments with domestic and international entities. See National Aeronautics and Space Administration, Office of Inspector General, Report No. IG-14-020, *NASA's Use of Space Act Agreements,* June 5, 2014.
65 See NASA Policy Directive 1050.1I, *NAII 1050-1A NASA Advisory Implementing Instruction, Space Act Agreements Guide.*
66 Specifically with respect to the ESA practice on the conclusion of written contracts, see Annex 1 (Privileges and Immunities), Article XXV of the Conv*ention for the Establishment of a European Space Agency,* 14 I.L.M. p. 864 (1975. For related implementing regulations, see Regulations of The European Space Agency – General Clauses and Conditions for ESA Contracts, ESA/REG/002, rev. 1 Paris, 7 February 2013.
67 See A. Farand, The European Space Agency's Experience with Mechanisms for the Settlement of Disputes, in *Arbitration in Air, Space and Telecommunications Law,* supra note 56 at p. 156; See generally: U.K. Bohlmann, Disputing with ESA, in Proc. IISL Coll. (2014) vol. 56, at pp. 213 to 226.
68 A term supposed to have been first used in 1960 by UN Secretary-General Dag Hammarskjold, with similar approach in 1990 by Boutros-Ghali, another UN Secretary-General. See: J. Nolan-Haley, H. Abramson, P.K. Chew, INTERNATIONAL CONFLICT RESOLUTION: CONSENSUAL ADR PROCESSES (2005) Thomson/West, at p. 279, citing D. A. Hamburg, NO MORE KILLING FIELDS: PREVENTING DEADLY CONFLICT (2002) at p. 117. See definition of Preventive Diplomacy as "action to prevent disputes from arising between parties, to prevent existing disputes from escalating into conflicts and to limit the spread of the latter when they occur" in Boutros Boutros-Ghali, AN AGENDA FOR PEACE (1995) 2nd ed.
69 See: T. Brisibe, The International Normative System and a Code of Conduct for Outer Space Activities, in: A. Lele (ed.) DECODING THE INTERNATIONAL CODE OF CONDUCT FOR OUTER SPACE ACTIVITIES, (2012) Indian Institute for Defense and Security Analysis, Pentagon Press, at p. 127.
70 Ibid. at p. 128.
71 E. Galloway, Consensus Decision Making by the United Nations Committee on the Peaceful Uses of Outer Space (1979) vol. 7 no.1 J. Space L. at p. 171.

seemingly irreconcilable matters, but these often arise from different philosophical concepts of government and are more apt to be political rather than solely legal, and are therefore not justiciable, nor can they be 'settled' by voting".[72] This author is of the view that the UNCOPUOS consensus procedure and outcome may well constitute the results of dispute or conflict settlement procedures by negotiation or consultation. Given that a related question has been considered and judgment rendered in the affirmative by the ICJ in the *South West Africa* cases (Preliminary Objections) diplomacy by conference or parliamentary. Thus, diplomacy[73] has come to be recognized in the past four or five decades as one of the established modes of international negotiation.[74]

3.3 Conciliation

In 1978, claims were made against the Soviet Union by Canada, as a consequence of damage caused by the Soviet Cosmos 954 nuclear-powered satellite.[75] The claims were brought pursuant to a process akin to conciliation[76] provided under the 1972 Liability Convention. That Convention, reveals a number of pertinent issues which include the fact that only States have the *locus* to pursue claims, whilst non-governmental entities may only do so through a State, after having possibly exercised the option of pursuing local remedies, as stipulated under the 1972 Liability Convention's Article VIII. *Second*, in the absence of an agreement by the State parties to make the decision or award of a Claims Commission binding, effective recovery by the claimant party is not an absolute guarantee, if the Launching State (i.e., a State which launches or procures the launching of a space object, or a State from whose territory or facility a space object is launched)[77] has not agreed to abide by the Claim Commission's decision.[78] *Third*, anticipated disputes are limited to those involving damage arising from loss of life, personal injury or other impairment of health; or loss of or damage to property of States or of persons, natural or juridical, or property of international intergovernmental organizations.[79] *Fourth,* while the liability regime for damage caused on earth is no doubt an exception to the general reluctance of States towards rules imposing strict liability, other aspects of liability and responsibility for injurious consequences of outer space activities would depend on the establishment of fault. In respect of which, neither is fault defined, nor are there binding guidelines for standards of care or provisions for imputing negligent conduct to others or for the attribution of vicarious liability. *Fifth*, in determining compensation, the applicable law shall

---

72 Id.
73 See P. Jessup, Parliamentary Diplomacy–An Examination of the Legal Quality of the Rules of Procedure of Organs of the United Nations, (1956) 156 RECUEIL DES COURS at pp. 185 to 318.
74 See note 2 supra, ICJ Reports at p. 346. M. Lachs, International Law, Mediation, and Negotiation, in A. S. Lall (ed.) MULTILATERAL NEGOTIATION AND MEDIATION: INSTRUMENTS AND METHODS (1985) Published for the International Peace Academy, Pergamon Press, at pp. 187, and 190. Cf. Dissenting opinions of Judges Spender and Fitzmaurice, and subsequent views by Judge Fitzmaurice in the *Northern Cameroon's Case*, (Judgement) supra note 2 at p.15.
75 For discussions, see note 47 supra.
76 Defined as … the process of settling a dispute by referring it to a commission of persons whose task it is to elucidate the facts and usually after hearing the parties and endeavoring to bring them to an agreement to make a report containing proposals for a settlement, which is not binding". I. Brownlie, supra note 1 at p. 272, citing H. Lauterpacht, OPPENHEIM'S INTERNATIONAL LAW (1952) vol. II, 7th edn, at p. 12.
77 See note 34 supra.
78 See Liability Convention's Article XIX (2).
79 Id.

be international law and the principles of "equity" and "justice", in order to provide such reparation as will restore the person, State or international organization to the condition which would have existed if damage had not occurred. This derives from provisions of the Liability Convention's Article XII, which could give rise to debate as there is no agreed body of international law providing adequate guides or grounds for determining compensation. Whilst "justice" is considered a term without precise meaning, noting that "equity" is defined in common law and some continental legal systems, its use in measuring compensation in other legal systems is uncertain. There are also unsettled questions concerning the exact scope of what could be construed as "damage" (be it "direct", "indirect" or "delayed") as defined under the Liability Convention.

3.4 Arbitration and adjudication

The object of international arbitration is described[80] as the settlement of disputes between States by judges chosen by the parties themselves and on the basis of respect for law. Accordingly, one of the basic characteristics of arbitration is that it is a procedure which results in binding decisions upon the parties to the dispute. The power to render binding arbitration is thus similar to the method of judicial settlement by international courts whose judgments are not only binding but also, as in the case of the International Court of Justice, final and without appeal. As a consequence, arbitration and judicial settlement (also known as adjudication discussed below) are both usually referred to as compulsory means of dispute settlement. It is contended,[81] that arbitration set up by States to decide a case or a series of cases between them, must be distinguished from another type which deals with disputes in which individuals or corporations are involved as parties, known as private (as opposed to public) international arbitration, or international commercial arbitration. It is perhaps for this reason it has also been contended[82] that it is necessary to distinguish between international arbitration and international disputes, given that the former is governed by conventional or customary international law in respect of both procedure and effect to be given to the outcome of the arbitral process, whilst the latter concerns disputes between and among States (including State agencies) and public international organizations as well as disputes between States and non-State entities. It is argued[83] that whilst public international law is concerned primarily with States, its application is not necessarily exclusive given that international law is a dynamic (not static) decision-making process, in which there are a variety of participants. This is because … "increasingly 'international law' may be specified as the substantive law of a contract, particularly where that contract is with a State or State agency. The reference may be to 'international law' on its own; or it may be used in conjunction with a national system of law". Thus it may be, though perhaps it would be unusual, that the parties could validly agree that a part, or the whole, of

---

80 See: United Nations HANDBOOK, supra note 9 at p. 55, citing the 1899 and 1907 Hague Conventions for the Pacific Settlement of International Disputes. See also N. Blackaby, C. Partasides, A. Redfern and M. Hunter, REDFERN AND HUNTER ON INTERNATIONAL ARBITRATION (2009) 5th edition, at pp. 1 to 2.
81 J. G. Merrills, INTERNATIONAL DISPUTE SETTLEMENT (2005) 4th Edition, Cambridge University Press, at p. 117.
82 A. Broches, supra Note 5 at p. 27.
83 REDFERN AND HUNTER, supra Note 80 at page 207. See also R. Higgins, PROBLEMS PROCESS: INTERNATIONAL LAW AND HOW WE USE IT (1994) Clarendon Press, at p. 39. Citing the statement of a court in *Orion Compañía Española de Seguros v Belfort Maatschappij Voor Algemene Verzekgringeen* [1962] 2 Lloyd's Rep 257, at p. 264.

their legal relations should be decided by the arbitral tribunal on the basis of a foreign system of law, or perhaps on the basis of principles of international law; for example in a contract to which a sovereign State was a party.[84] Suffice it to say that arbitration has become the principal method of resolving disputes between States,[85] individuals, and corporations in almost every aspect of international trade, commerce, and investment.[86]

Activities associated with peaceful uses of outer space are no exception in this regard especially when private individuals and / or corporations have sought binding settlement to the resolution of their disputes. For instance, attempts at resolving an on-going dispute between Antrix (the marketing arm of India's International Space Research Organization (ISRO) and Devas Corporation (a private company) concerning the long-term lease of two ISRO satellites operating in the S-band, are being pursued through arbitration panels. These include a panel constituted under the International Chamber of Commerce (ICC) followed by another panel constituted under the PCA in accordance with the United Nations Commission on International Trade Law (UNCITRAL) Arbitration Rules. The 2003 case involving Loral vs Acatel Space submitted to arbitration and another between Eutelast vs Alcatel Space submitted to the ICC for arbitration also provide good examples.[87] Others include the EchoStar insurance claim[88] submitted to the American Arbitration Association (AAA); the ICC arbitration between New Skies and Astrium;[89] the ICC arbitration initiated against the Boeing Company by insurers in respect of the Thuraya D1 communications satellite, and a similar claim against the Boeing Company by Telesat Canada and its insurers in respect of the Anik F1 satellite.[90] Reference can also be made to the 2009 award[91] by an arbitration panel ordering Sea Launch Co. To pay Hughes Network Systems in a dispute over termination of a launch contract and prelaunch payments. The 2011 AAA award[92] to Avanti Communications in its arbitration against SpaceX relating to Avanti's decision to scrap a planned launch of its Hylas 2 satellite aboard a SpaceX rocket in favor of a launch aboard the Araine 5 vehicle, and more recently, Lockheed Martin Space Systems won an arbitration dispute with SES over contracted performance specifications in respect of anomalies with the A2100 communications satellite.[93]

Regarding arbitration as a preferred technique, on 6 December 2011, the Administrative Council of the PCA comprised of 115 member States adopted Optional Rules for the Arbitration of Disputes Relating to Outer Space Activities[94] (Optional Rules). The text of these Optional Rules, were developed by the PCA's International Bureau in conjunction with an Advisory Group of leading experts in air and space law, relying on the 2010 UNCITRAL Arbitration Rules, as well as multiple sets of PCA procedural rules.[95] Arbitration agreements

84 Id at p. 208.
85 See H. Fox, supra note 35 for a detailed work on States and Arbitration, at pp. 1 to 29.
86 REDFERN AND HUNTER, supra Note 80 at p. 1.
87 See L. Ravillon, *Space Law and Mechanisms for Dispute Settlement*, ECSL News, No. 28, December 2004 at p. 2.
88 P. B. de Selding, *EchoStar to Seek Arbitration Over Insurance Claim*, Space News, July 10, 2000.
89 P. B. de Selding, *Arbitration Court Rules in Favor of New Skies*, Space News, July 27, 2001.
90 P. B. de Selding, *Boeing Found Not Negligent for Solar Array Defects*, Space News, February 10, 2009.
91 P. B. de Selding, *Sea Launch Ordered to Pay HNS $52 Million*, Space News, Thursday, 23 April, 2009.
92 P. B. de Selding, *Avanti Wins Arbitration Award Against SpaceX*, Space News, Wednesday, 20 April 2011.
93 P. B. de Selding, *Arbitration Panel Sides with Lockheed in SES Dispute*, Space News, Thursday, 22 September 2011.
94 F. Pocar, An Introduction to the PCA's Optional Rules for Arbitration of Disputes Relating to Outer Space Activities, (2012) 38 J. Space L. at pp. 171 to 185.
95 Cf. D. P. Ratliff, The PCA Optional Rules for Arbitration of Disputes Relating to Natural Resources and / or the Environment (2001) 14 *Leiden Journal of International Law*, at pp. 887 to 896.

related to settlements discussed above between non-governmental entities, generally provide for arbitration under the UNCITRAL Rules or procedural rules of private arbitration institutions such as the ICC, AAA or London Court of International Arbitration (LCIA). However, these institutional Rules are not necessarily adapted or specific to space related disputes for which States, intergovernmental organizations, non-governmental organizations, corporations and private parties can have recourse, if and when they agree to use them.

In this regard, the following benefits of the Optional Rules should be highlighted. As the title implies, the Rules are optional and flexible, since they only become applicable where parties have agreed that disputes between them in respect of a defined legal relationship, contractual or not, or deriving from various types of legal instruments, shall be referred to arbitration, subject to such modification as the parties may agree.[96] The Optional Rules emphasize autonomy because they remain open to States, international organizations and private entities. More so the characterization of a dispute relating to outer space is not necessary for jurisdiction, if parties have agreed to settle a specific dispute under the said Optional Rules. We will recall, Space technology, being often of a dual-use nature, ensures the influence or role of States (including State agencies) in related activities. State involvement is taken into account by the Optional Rules, which construe consent to arbitration as constituting a waiver of immunity to jurisdiction as would stem from sovereign immunity of States and any immunity to jurisdiction possessed by intergovernmental organizations. Given the confidential and strategic nature of outer space activities, the Optional Rules permit a tribunal, at the request of a party or on its own motion, to appoint a confidentiality adviser as an expert in order to report to it, on the basis of the confidential information on specific issues designated by the arbitral tribunal, without disclosing the confidential information either to the party from whom the confidential information does not originate or to the arbitral tribunal. There is a much welcomed freedom for parties to choose an arbitral tribunal of one, three or five persons from a standing panel of arbitrators, with possibilities for added support from another panel of scientific and technical experts, both maintained by the PCA Secretary-General, without prejudice to the rights of parties to appoint or choose persons outside the lists. The Rules offer services of the Secretary-General and the International Bureau of the PCA provides the distinct benefit of support from an institution with a longstanding tradition of providing registry services and administrative support to international arbitrations involving various combinations of States, State entities, international organizations and private parties. Regarding applicable law, the arbitral tribunal is required to apply the law or rules of law designated by the parties as applicable to the substance of the dispute, failing which the arbitral tribunal shall apply the national or international law and rules of law it determines to be appropriate. This distinction allows parties to designate as applicable to their case, rules of one legal system (i.e., 'law') or those of more than one legal system, including rules of law which have been elaborated on the international level (i.e., 'rules of law') whilst giving the arbitrators, if necessary, the broadest possible scope in determining the applicable law, leading to internationally recognized and enforceable, final and binding awards.

Closely related to arbitration is the possibility of adjudication, for which early compilations

---

96   Cf, the decision of the Supreme Court of India, in Antrix Corp. Ltd vs. Devas Multimedia 2013 (2) ARBLR 226 (SC) on issues concerning the invocation of proceedings and appointment of an arbitrator based on the agreement between the parties which had provided a choice between UNCITRAL or ICC procedures.

and studies[97] categorized disputes before national courts on a thematic basis, such as *torts, the environment, antitrust, taxation, intellectual property, insurance,* and so on. This could be justified, given the paucity of recorded disputes arising from mainly government led and owned space related activities at the time. At present, with the diversification of space activity involving multiple players (State, intergovernmental organizations and non-governmental entities) operating in what has become a vibrant industry underpinned by private international law, public international law and domestic legislation across dozens of countries, dispute-settlement tendencies now require a much broader categorization. More so, it does not generally appear as if activities associated with peaceful uses of outer space are particularly exceptional when private individuals and / or corporations have sought binding settlement to resolution of their disputes. For which, contractual agreements involving private parties that relate to outer space activity alongside contractual agreements involving manufacturers and other contributors to users[98] could be distinguished according to the: (a) *type of deliverable* (i.e., satellites, launcher, equipment, parts; or services) and (b) *type of contract* (i.e., research and development, testing, manufacturing, sale/ supply, services, or licenses/ intellectual property rights). In concluding, a number of particularities are worth highlighting and to which this chapter now turns.

4 Particularities and conclusions

The preceding appraisal of mechanisms and procedures for settlement of disputes, reveals nine particular characteristics[99] in the conduct of outer space activities which require very high investments associated with very high risks. *First,* private enterprises do not have direct access to mechanisms for resolution of disputes in the current, and mainly public, international legal framework governing outer space activities.[100] *Second*, decisions arising from mechanisms for the resolution of disputes in the current public international legal framework governing outer space activities are generally non-binding.[101] *Third*, the sovereign immunity of States could influence the initiation and conduct of proceedings by a tribunal constituted to arbitrate over disputes pertaining to outer space activities, including the enforcement of any awards.[102] For instance, in the matter of *Republic of Serbia* v *Imagesat International NV*[103] a United Kingdom (U.K.) High Court dismissed an application by Serbia to challenge an earlier arbitral award for

---

97   See I. H. P. Diederiks-Verschoor; supra note 21; S. Gorove, supra note 22; and K. Bockstiegel, supra note 49. See also L. S. Kaplan, "Recent Developments in Space Law Litigation" in in Sai'd Mosteshar (ed.) RESEARCH AND INVENTION IN OUTER SPACE: LIABILITY AND INTELLECTUAL PROPERTY RIGHTS (1995), Martinus Nijhoff, at pp. 113 et seq.
98   I. Scharlach, Performance and Warranty Articles in Space Industry Contracts, in L. J. Smith and I. Baumann (eds) CONTRACTING FOR SPACE – CONTRACT PRACTICE IN THE EUROPEAN SPACE SECTOR (2011) Ashgate, at pp. 259–260.
99   The nine characteristics were first advanced by this author in January 2011, concerning the first draft of Optional Rules, in response to an invitation for comments, from the Chair (H. E. Judge Fausto Pocar) of the PCA Advisory Group of Experts. See also T. Brisibe, The 5th Nandasiri Jasentuliyana Keynote Lecture on Space Law – A Normative System for Outer Space Activities in the Next Half Century, in Proc. IISL Coll. (2014) Volume 56, ISBN 978 94 6236 440 0 at pages 25 to 26; T. Brisibe, The Role of Arbitration in Settlement of Disputes Relating to Outer Space Activities, *Financier Worldwide*, December 2012, pp. 48–50.
100 See section 3.3. supra.
101 Id.
102 Cf. provisons for exclusion and waiver of sovereign immunity from jurisdiction in Art. I (3) of the Optional Rules.
103 [2009] EWHC 2853 (Comm), [2010] 1 Lloyd's Rep 324. See in particular paragraphs 119, 120, 126 and 135 respectively.

lack of substantive jurisdiction under Section 67 of the 1996 U.K. *Arbitration Act*, on the ground that Serbia had conferred substantive jurisdiction on the arbitrator by virtue of Terms of Reference. The arbitration arose from a contract between Israeli satellite operator, ImageSat and the State Union of Serbia and Montenegro (the State Union). Shortly after the arbitration was commenced, the State Union split and Serbia responded to the request for arbitration. The arbitrator decided, as a preliminary issue, that Serbia was the continuation of the State Union, rather than a successor State, and was a proper party to the contract and the arbitration. Serbia argued that the arbitrator did not have jurisdiction to determine this issue. The court dismissed the Section 67 challenge, on the ground that Serbia had conferred substantive jurisdiction on the arbitrator, by virtue of the Terms of Reference, to deal with the question whether it was a continuator or successor State. Beatson J (i.e., the presiding Judge) also held that, in the context of this case, that issue was justiciable and *arbitrable* (emphasis mine). However, it is important to highlight the fact that the Judge expressed doubt (*obiter*) about whether such issues would have been justiciable in court proceedings. Imagesat was successful,[104] but the Judge's *obiter* remarks as to whether the question of Serbia's status was justiciable in a non-arbitration context bring into sharp focus the complexities which may arise when private parties enter into commercial contracts or partnerships with States. *Fourth*, the confidential and strategic nature of outer space activities could give rise to challenges associated with adducing evidence before a tribunal constituted to arbitrate over disputes arising from outer space activities. *Fifth*, given the relevance of mandatory laws designed to protect the public interest, particularly in disputes between private entities and the State, an arbitration tribunal addressing a dispute over outer space activities could be faced with possible limitations on the arbitrators' and contractual parties' freedom to choose applicable laws.[105] *Sixth*, there is an established trade (space sector) practice of liability cross-waivers which is summarily defined as a set of promises made by the parties to an agreement in which each of the parties' pledges not to sue the other for damages caused by the other, except in specific circumstances.[106] This has given rise to complex legal issues ranging from matters concerning the establishment of conduct bordering on negligence to consequential damages and establishment of loss, in order to obviate any exclusion of liability provisions between the parties. *Seventh*, the potential for debate on the scope of what constitutes outer space activities could pose significant challenges for ascertaining the jurisdiction of a tribunal established to address a related matter.[107] *Eighth*, the technical nature of outer space activities justifies the need for appropriate legal and scientific expertise in support of related arbitration proceedings.[108] *Ninth*, because pre-dominant actors (i.e., States)

104 It is reported that… "the decision led to a 28 million euro ($38.4 million) arbitration settlement from the government of Serbia and an agreement by Israel Aerospace Industries Ltd of Israel, to buy $81 million worth of ImageSat bonds held by Pegasus Capital Advisors LP, a New York-based private equity investment firm". See Barbara Opall-Rome, *Israel's ImageSat Sheds Some Legal Baggage*, Space News, Friday, 28 January 2011.
105 Cf. provisions for exclusion and waiver of sovereign immunity from jurisdiction in Art. 1(3) of the Optional Rules.
106 See S. Mirmina Cross-Waivers of Liability in Agreements to Explore Outer Space – What They Are and How They Work, *The Scitech Lawyer* (2012) vol. 9, No. 1, American Bar Association; C. du Parquet, Specific Clauses of Launch Service Agreements, in L. J. Smith and I. Baumann (ed.'s) supra note 98 at pp. 387–388.
107 Cf. provisions of the Optional Rules at Article I (1) which provides, inter alia …"The characterization of the dispute as relating to outer space is not necessary for jurisdiction where parties have agreed to settle a specific dispute under these Rules."
108 For a summary of space related disputes resolved by litigation and / or arbitration, along with technical issues arising, see S. Kaplan, supra note 97; and A. Mourre, Arbitration in Space Contracts, (2005) vol 21, issue 1 *Arbitration International* at pp. 37–58.

involved in outer space related activities have consistently demonstrated a reluctance to engage in adversarial forms of dispute resolution, rules of procedure designed to govern the activities of an arbitration panel must be attractive so as to encourage their adoption and use by States.

Part II

International law of space applications

7

Regulation of telecommunications by satellites

ITU and space services

Yvon Henri, Attila Matas, and Juliana Macedo Scavuzzi dos Santos

Table 7.1 Acronyms and abbreviations

ITU	International Telecommunication Union
CS	Constitution of the ITU
CV	Convention of the ITU
RR	ITU Radio Regulations
Administration	Any governmental department or service responsible for discharging the obligations undertaken in the CS and CV of the ITU and in the Administrative Regulations
Bureau	Radiocommunication Bureau of the ITU
ITU-R	Radiocommunication Sector of the ITU
WRC	World Radiocommunication Conference of the ITU
GSO	Geostationary-Satellite Orbit
Non-GSO	Non-Geostationary-Satellite Orbit
Table	Table of Frequency Allocations as contained in Article 5 of the RR
MIFR	Master International Frequency Register of the Bureau
BR IFIC	International Frequency Information Circular of the Radiocommunication Bureau
PP	ITU Plenipotentiary Conference
RRB	Radio Regulations Board

1 Introduction

Twenty-fifteen marked the hundred and fiftieth anniversary of the creation of the ITU. The ITU is the UN specialized agency in charge of telecommunications and Information Communication Technology (ICT), and is currently comprised of 193 Member States as well as over 800 Sector Members, Associates, and Academia Members from the telecommunication and ICT sectors.[1] Following review by the Member States in 1989, versions of the CS and CV

---

1   ITU, *Message from the Secretary General Houlin Zhao*, compiled in Collection of the Basic Texts of the International Telecommunications Union Adopted by the Plenipotentiary Conference, 2015 Edition (Geneva: International Telecommunications Union, 2015).

were approved in 1992 at the additional PP held in Geneva. Together with the Radio Regulations, and amended by subsequent plenipotentiary conferences, these three instruments currently comprise the entire ITU regulatory regime.[2] The RR are also a binding international treaty according to Article 31 of the CS. The primary purposes of the ITU are to promote cooperation and participation in the development of telecommunication services and associated technologies to bring their benefits to people worldwide.[3] Along with allocation of spectrum and allotment of frequencies and orbital postions, the objectives of the organization are to harmonize and standardize telecommunications practices and eliminate harmful interference with those activities.[4]

The CS, CV, and RR contain the main principles and lay down the specific regulations governing the following major elements:

- frequency spectrum allocations to different categories of radiocommunication services;
- rights and obligations of Member administrations in obtaining access to the spectrum/orbit resources;
- international recognition of these rights by recording frequency assignments and, as appropriate, orbital information for a space station onboard a geostationary-satellite or for space station(s) onboard non-geostationary satellite(s), used or intended to be used in the MIFR or by their conformity, where appropriate, with a plan.

The ITU grants international recognition, a level of protection conditioned by the provisions of the RR and procedures to detect and to eliminate harmful interference for registered assignments in the MIFR.[5] The ITU also promotes the rational, efficient, economic, and equitable use of the radio frequency and orbital positions, which are limited natural resources and, as such, must be available for use by all Member States. In this regard, the ITU gives special consideration to the future use of these resources by developing countries.[6]

The fact that the ITU Constitution and Convention and the Radio Regulations that complement them are *intergovernmental treaties ratified by governments* – means that those governments undertake:[7]

- to apply the provisions in their countries; and
- to adopt adequate national legislation that includes, as the basic minimum, the essential provisions of this international treaty.

The RR are nevertheless oriented mainly towards matters of a global or regional character, and in many areas offer scope for making special arrangements on a bilateral or multilateral basis.

---

2   ITU, *Constitution and Convention*, online: International Telecommunications Union www.itu.int/en/history/Pages/ConstitutionAndConvention.aspx.
3   *ITU Constitution, supra* note 3, art 1.
4   Ibid., art 2.
5   ITU, *Radio Regulations of the Radio Regulations Board*, compiled in The Radio Regulations, Edition of 2012 (Geneva: International Communications Union, 2012) [*RR*], art 8.1.
6   ITU, *Constitution of the International Telecommunications Union*, compiled in Collection of the Basic Texts of the International Telecommunications Union Adopted by the Plenipotentiary Conference, 2011 Edition (Geneva: International Telecommunications Union, 2011) [*ITU Constitution*], arts 44, 45.
7   Ibid., art 6.

2 Major principles

In the process of establishing the ITU's space-related regulations, emphasis was laid from the outset on efficient, rational and cost-effective utilization of limited resources. This concept was implemented through a "first-come, first-served" procedure. This procedure ("coordination before use") is based on the principle that the right to use orbital and spectrum resources for a satellite network or system is acquired through negotiations with the administrations concerned by actual usage of the same portion of the spectrum and orbital resource. If applied correctly (i.e. To cover genuine requirements), the procedure offers a means of achieving efficient spectrum/orbit management; it serves to fill the gaps in the orbit(s) as needs arise. On the basis of the RR, and in the frequency bands where this concept is applied, Member administrations designate the volume of orbit/spectrum resources that are actually required to satisfy their actual requirements. It then falls to the national administrations to assign frequencies and orbital requirements, to apply the appropriate procedures (international coordination and recording) for the space segment and Earth stations of their (governmental, scientific, public and private) networks, and to assume continuing responsibility for the networks. The progressive exploitation of the orbit/frequency resources and the resulting likelihood of congestion of the geostationary-satellite orbit prompted ITU Member countries to consider more and more seriously the question of equitable access in respect of the orbit/spectrum resources. This resulted in the establishment (and introduction into the ITU regulatory regime) of frequency/orbital position plans in which a certain amount of frequency spectrum is set aside for future use by all countries, particularly those which are not in a position, at present, to make use of these resources. Such plans govern a considerable part of the frequency bands available for the space communication services.

During the last 60 years, the regulatory framework has been constantly adapted to changing circumstances and has achieved the necessary flexibility in satisfying the two major, but not always compatible, requirements of efficiency and equity. With the dramatic development in telecommunication services, increasing demand for spectrum/orbit usage for practically all space communication services has been observed. This led the PP held in Kyoto in 1994 to call in its Resolution 18 for a new in-depth review of the ITU spectrum/orbit resource allocation procedures, the results of which were considered and reviewed by WRCs.

3 The Structure and Regulatory Regime of the ITU

3.1 ITU overview

The Membership of the ITU is based on the principle of universality. Sector, Associate, and Academia Members may comprise different representatives from recognized operating agencies such as scientific or industrial organizations and financial or development institutions, which are approved by the Member State concerned. Additionally, other entities dealing with telecommunication matters which are approved by the relevant Member State may also become Sector-Associate-Academia Members. Finally, regional and other international telecommunication, standardization, financial or development organizations can apply for this type of ITU Membership as well.[8] Although Sector Members cannot vote at ITU meetings,

---

8   ITU, *Convention of the International Telecommunications Union,* compiled in Collection of the Basic Texts of the International Telecommunications Union Adopted by the Plenipotentiary Conference, 2011 Edition (Geneva: International Telecommunications Union, 2011) [*Convention*], art 19.

they have been granted the right to fully participate in the activities of the Sector of which they are members subject to specific provisions of the Constitution and the Convention.[9]

Membership in the ITU is not free, and Member States must contribute funds to pay the Union's expenses. Both Member States and Sector Members can, however, choose their class of contribution. The scale of contributions is determined by Article 28 of the Constitution.

Both the Constitution and the Convention may be amended by a proposal by any Member State. The decision to amend them is then taken at the PP. RR can only be amended by a WRC, which must respect the CS and the CV.

The RR aim to fulfill the purposes of the Union, and specifically have the following objectives:[10]

- to facilitate equitable access to and rational use of the natural resources of the radio-frequency spectrum and the geostationary-satellite orbits;
- to ensure the availability and protection from harmful interference of the frequencies provided for distress and safety purposes;
- to assist in the prevention and resolution of cases of harmful interference between the radio services of different administrations;
- to facilitate the efficient and effective operation of all radiocommunication services; and
- to provide for and, when necessary regulate new applications of radiocommunication technology.

3.2 Dispute resolution

In cases involving a dispute arising from the interpretation or application of the CS, CV, or RR, Member States may resort to diplomatic channels or may use arbitration pursuant to the rules as expressed in the CV.[11] In case of an arbitration, the arbitration decision is binding upon the parties. The ITU should assist the procedure by providing to the arbitrator(s) all information necessary to render a decision.[12] The ITU also has an Optional Protocol on the Compulsory Settlement of Disputes Relating to the Constitution and Administrative Regulations which is valid between Parties who have ratified the Protocol, and which may be ratified by any Member State.[13] If none of the afore-mentioned methods for settlement of disputes is chosen by common agreement between the parties to the dispute concerning the interpretation or application of any ITU instrument, the Optional Protocol may be requested as a solution, provided that the parties have previously adhered to the Protocol. In such cases, the Protocol will then initiate compulsory settlement by arbitration pursuant to the procedures as outlined in Article 41.5 of the Convention.[14]

Most disputes at the ITU concern cases involving harmful interference. Whenever dealing with harmful interference, Member States should act with good faith and good will to avoid

---

9   Ibid., art 3, number 3.
10   RR, *supra* note 6, Preamble.
11   *ITU Constitution, supra* note 7, art 56.
12   Ibid., art 41.
13   *ITU Constitution, supra* note 7, Explanatory Notes.
14   ITU, *Optional Protocol on the Compulsory Settlement of Disputes Relating to the Constitution of the International Telecommunication Union, to the Convention of the International Telecommunication Union and to the Administrative Regulations*, compiled in Collection of the Basic Texts of the International Telecommunications Union Adopted by the Plenipotentiary Conference, 2011 Edition (Geneva: International Telecommunications Union, 2011) [*Protocol*], art 1, 175.

harmful interference and resolve the situation. Mutual assistance is also required in order to promote a safe operating environment free of interference and used in accordance with the provisions of the Constitution, Article 45.[15] In this regard, administrations should cooperate in both the detection and elimination of harmful interference.[16]

There are some harmful interference cases that are particularly difficult to resolve through diplomatic channels because they generally involve issues of a complex political nature. As noted by Ram S. Jakhu, because the ITU does not possess any mechanism or power of enforcement or imposition of sanctions against the violators of its rules, regulations and processes (and even though the voluntary compliance approach has worked well in the past), it is doubtful whether this approach will work well in the future, as the number of State and non-State players is increasing, and the competition for scarce resources is becoming severe.[17] Although this constitutes a clear gap in the ITU treaties, none of the Member States has proposed any amendment to rectify this problem.

The recent promulgation of the Permanent Court of Arbitration Optional Rules of Arbitration of Disputes Related to Outer Space Activities could provide both an adequate and desirable mechanism for the resolution of ITU-related disputes, especially to cases involving only private operators. Their broad scope of application, including the fact that they are not limited to outer space disputes, means that they can be used by any party; moreover, the extended confidentiality protections they provide make the Rules a particularly suitable mechanism for settling disputes within the ITU.[18]

3.3 Organizational Structure of the ITU

The organizational structure of the ITU is rather complex, as it is comprised of several different bodies with different missions, but which also share common goals.

3.3.1   The supreme organ of the ITU is the PP, which is formed by a delegation of Member States and convenes every four years unless it decides to assemble an extraordinary one in between. The PP determines the general policies of the Union in order to accomplish its purposes in accordance with Article 1 of the CS. The PP also elects Member States to serve on the Council as well appointing the Secretary-General, Deputy-Director, the Directors of the Bureaux of the Sectors, and the Members of the Radiocommunication Board. Finally, the PP addresses proposals to amend the CS and CV, and conclude or revise agreements between the Union and international organizations that may have been initiated by the Council since the previous conference.[19]

3.3.2   The Council is the organ that acts on behalf of the PP, and therefore governs the Union in between conferences, limited only by the delegated powers given to it by the PP. The Council members are elected by the PP, and must respect an equitable geographical distribution among all regions of the world. The Council facilitates the implementation of the ITU instruments, the

---

15 *RR, supra* note 6, art 15, para 14.
16 *Ibid.*, art 15, para 17.
17 Ram Jakhu, *International Regulatory Process for Communication Satellite Radio Frequencies*, compiled in *Space Law: General Principles, Volume I*, Coursepack (Faculty of Law, McGill University, 2011) at 16.
18 See Juliana Macedo Scavuzzi dos Santos, *The Permanent Court of Arbitration's Optional Rules for the Arbitration of Disputes Relating to Outer Space Activities and Dispute Resolution in the ITU Regulatory System*, presented at the International Astronautical Congress (IAC 2013) (Beijing, September 2013), online: http://swfound.org/media/121731/2013_IAC_Manuscript_Juliana_Macedo_Scavuzzi_dos_Santos_4.pdf.
19 *ITU Constitution, supra* note 7, at arts 7, 8.

decisions of the PP, and any other ITU conferences and meetings. Among other duties, the Council shall respond to changes in the telecommunication sector, and therefore must consider broadening some policies in accordance with the guidelines provided by the PP. Finally, the Council shall contribute to the development of telecommunications in developing countries in accordance with the objectives of the Union. Currently, the elected Council to the 2014–2018 period is formed by 48 Member States divided among all geographic regions:[20]

- Region A (the Americas): 9 seats
  Argentina, Brazil, Canada, Costa Rica, Cuba, Mexico, the United States, Paraguay, Venezuela
- Region B (Western Europe): 8 seats
  France, Italy, Germany, Greece, Lithuania, Spain, Switzerland, Turkey
- Region C (Eastern Europe and Northern Asia): 5 seats
  Azerbaijan, Bulgaria, Poland, Romania, Russian Federation
- Region D (Africa): 13 seats
  Algeria, Burkina Faso, Egypt, Ghana, Kenya, Mali, Morocco, Nigeria, Rwanda, Senegal, Tanzania, Tunisia, Uganda
- Region E (Asia and Australasia): 13 seats
  Australia, Bangladesh, China, India, Indonesia, Japan, Korea (Republic of), Kuwait, Pakistan, Philippines, Saudi Arabia, Thailand, United Arab Emirates

3.3.3 The ITU also holds World Conferences on International Telecommunications, which are normally convened between two PPs. They include World Radiocommunication Conferences (WRC), the World Telecommunication Standardization Assembly (WTSA), the World Telecommunication Development Conference (WTDC), and Radiocommunication Assemblies (RA). The WRC and RA may convene one or two meetings between two PPs, while an additional WTSA could be exceptionally held in accordance with the specific provisions of the Convention.[21]

3.3.4 The ITU-R is the most important part of the ITU in terms of issues involving space. The ITU-R is required to always consider the particular needs of developing countries in fulfilling the objectives of the ITU by ensuring the rational, equitable, efficient, and economical use of the radio-frequency spectrum by all radiocommunication services, including those countries using the GSO or other satellite orbits, subject to the provisions of Article 44 of the Constitution. The ITU-R also conducts studies, without limit, of frequency range, and also adopts recommendations involving radiocommunication matters.[22] The ITU-R works in close coordination with the Telecommunication Standardization and Telecommunication Development Sectors.[23]

The ITU-R is formed by Member States and Sector Members, and it performs its work through the following bodies:[24]

- World and Regional Radiocommunication Conferences;
- the Radio Regulations Board;
- Radiocommunication Assemblies;
- Radiocommunication Study Groups;

20 ITU, *Council Membership*, online: www.itu.int/en/council/Pages/members.aspx.
21 *ITU Constitution, supra* note 7, art 7 and *Convention, supra* note 8, art 3.
22 *ITU Constitution, supra* note 7, art 12, n 1.
23 Ibid., art 12, n 2.
24 Ibid., art 12, n 2.

- the Radiocommunication Advisory Group; and
- the Radiocommunication Bureau.

3.3.5   WRCs are generally convened every four years, and they can revise the Radio Regulations or deal with any specific radiocommunication matters and/or any question of a worldwide character within their competence and associated with their agenda.[25] While the decisions taken by a WRC may change the Radio Regulations, they also must be in conformity with the provisions of both the Constitution and the Convention.[26]

3.3.6   The RRCs are conferences of regional character and are therefore limited to discussions involving regional matters. For instance, their agenda can only contain specific radiocommunication questions of a regional nature, including their instructions to the RRB and the BR, which must be restricted to their work within a specific region. Additionally, a particular RRC must take into consideration the actions of other RRCs, particularly when such actions involve regions over which the RRC has no jurisdiction. Hence, in other words, a particular RCC's instructions may not conflict with the interests of other regions over which it has no jurisdiction.[27] RCC decisions also must be in conformity with the Constitution, the Convention, and the Radio Regulations.[28]

3.3.7   The RRB is comprised of elected members[29] who are recognized by their qualifications in the field of radiocommunications and their practical experience in the assignment and utilization of radio frequencies. Members of the RRB shall consist of no more than 12, or 6 percent, of the total number of Member States, whichever number is greater. Although each Board shall be familiar with particular related conditions of a specific area of the world, they shall not represent specific countries or a region, and should refrain from interfering in decisions involving their own administrations. Therefore, RRBs are precluded from receiving or requesting any instructions from administrations, public or private organizations, or even from the Union itself. Conversely, Member States and Sector Members are required to respect their particular category of operations, and not influence RBB decisions.[30]

The duties of the RRB are defined in Article 14 of the Constitution and include, *inter alia*:[31]

- approval of the Rules of Procedure in conformity with the Radio Regulations and with decisions by radiocommunication conferences.
- examination of any other issue that cannot be resolved through the application of the Rules of Procedure.

Additionally, the Convention also defines that the RRB shall:[32]

- consider reports from the Director of the BR on investigations of harmful interference and propose recommendations;

---

25   Ibid., art 13, n 1–2.
26   *ITU Constitution, supra* note 7, art 13, n 4.
27   *Convention, supra* note 9, art 9.
28   *ITU Constitution, supra* note 7, art 13, n 4.
29   The current composition of the RRB is the following: Japan (Chairman), Netherlands (Vice-Chairman), Morocco, United Arab Emirates, Vietnam, Ukraine, Kenya, Côte d'Ivoire, Italy, Russia Federation, Argentina and United States, ITU, *Twelve Members*, online: www.itu.int/en/ITU-R/conferences/RRB/Pages/Twelve-Members.aspx.
30   *ITU Constitution, supra* note 7, art 14.
31   Ibid., art 14.
32   *Convention, supra* note 9, art 10.

- consider appeals against decisions made by the BR regarding frequency assignments; and
- participate in an advisory capacity at radiocommunication conferences through its Board members, with the caveat that when Board members are advising in conferences and assemblies, they cannot simultaneously be members of their national delegations.

The Board generally convene four times during a year, and must be attended by a minimum of two-thirds of its members. The decisions of the RRB shall attempt to reach consensus, but if this is not possible, a majority of votes of at least two-thirds of the members shall be binding.[33]

3.3.8 The purpose of the Radiocommunication Assembly is to consider the reports of study groups and of the radiocommunication advisory group, and whether to modify, reject or approve their recommendations. According to their approved program of work, the Assembly decides both the fate of existing study groups and whether new groups should be created and, if so, the questions they should attempt to answer. Additionally, the RA also reports to the next WRC on the items that are related to their mandate and that are included in the agenda.[34] Their decisions must be in accord with the provisions of the Constitution, Convention, and the Radio Regulations.[35]

In addition to the questions adopted by radiocommunications assemblies, the radiocommunication study groups investigate matters identified in resolutions and recommendations of the world radiocommunication conferences, and prepare reports of their results for presentation at these conferences. Although these studies should not discuss economic issues, they may consider economic factors when comparing technical and operational choices. Furthermore, they must give due regard to the study and formulation of proposals which are directly related to the establishment, development, and improvement of telecommunications in developing countries at both the regional and international levels. Finally, the Groups must also consider and cooperate with the work performed at the national, regional, and international level by other organizations dealing with radiocommunications while maintaining the superior, international role of the Union in the field of telecommunications.[36] As provided in the Convention, the focus of the study groups are limited to the following topics:[37]

- use of the radio-frequency spectrum in terrestrial and space radiocommunication and of the GSO and other satellite orbits;
- characteristics and performance of radio systems;
- operation of radio stations; and
- radiocommunication aspects of distress and safety matters.

3.3.9 The Radiocommunication Advisory Group acts through the Director, and is open to participants from Member States, Sector Members, and chairs of study and other groups.[38] The Group's duties are established in Article 11 bis of the Convention, which provides that the Group shall:[39]

---

33 Ibid., art 10.
34 Ibid., art 8.
35 *ITU Constitution, supra* note 7, art 13, n 4.
36 *Convention, supra* note 9, art 11.
37 Ibid.
38 Ibid., art 11 A.
39 Ibid.

ITU and space services

- Examine priorities, programs, operations, financial matters, and strategies concerning radiocommunication assemblies, study and other groups, and the preparation of radiocommunication conferences, and any specific issue determined by a conference, a radiocommunication assembly or the Council;
- Recognize areas in which the Bureau has not accomplished its objectives in order to advise the Director on the necessary remedial solutions;
- Offer guidance for the study groups; and
- Suggest actions to promote cooperation and coordination with the Telecommunication Standardization Sector, the Telecommunication Development Sector, and the General Secretariat.

3.3.10 The Radiocommunication Bureau (Bureau) is the executive portion of the Radiocommunication Sector (ITU-R).[40] The work of the Sector is organized and coordinated by the Director of the Bureau. The Director must harmonize the work of study groups, participate in an advisory capacity in radiocommunication conferences, assemblies, and study groups, and also facilitate the participation of developing countries in conferences and study groups. The Director acts as executive secretary to the RRB, and also provides support to the Telecommunication Development Sector.[41] The Bureau is formed by its Director, Chiefs of Departments, engineers, computer specialists, managers, and administrative staff.

The Bureau provides several essential services including:[42]

- administrative and technical assistance to Radiocommunication Conferences, Assemblies, Study Groups, and Advisory Groups;
- application of the Radio Regulations and Regional Agreements;
- registration of frequency assignments and orbital positions in the Master International Frequency Register (MIFR) and updating the Master Register regularly;
- advice to Member States on the equitable, effective and economical use of the radio-frequency spectrum and satellite orbits, particularly at the GSO;
- investigation and support for Member States to resolve cases of harmful interference when requested, including the preparation of a Report to the RRB;
- assistance to developing countries and other Member States with technical information, seminars, and workshops on national frequency management to facilitate the implementation of the Radio Regulations and Member States' obligations under the ITU instruments;
- cooperation with the ITU Telecommunication Development Bureau in providing assistance to developing countries;
- preparation and dispatch of circulars, documents, and publications developed within the Sector;
- promulgation of the Rules of Procedure by the Director to be approved by the Radio Regulations Board (RRB) and, after approval, collection of comments from Member States about the Rules, application of the Rules, the preparation and publishing of findings regarding such Rules, and submission to the RRB when there is request by an administration which cannot be resolved by the Rules itself;

---

40 ITU, *Radiocommunication Sector (ITU-R), Radiocommunication Bureau*, online: www.itu.int/ITU-R/index.asp?category=information&rlink=br&lang=en [*Radiocommunication*].
41 *Convention, supra* note 9, art 12.
42 Ibid. and *Radiocommunication, supra* note 40.

117

- execution of studies regarding the operation of the maximum practicable number of radio channels in those portions of the spectrum where harmful interference may occur, with the objective of promoting the equitable, effective, and economical use of the GSO and other satellite orbits while considering the special needs of developing countries, the specific geographic situation of some particular countries, and requests for assistance from any Member State;
- preparation of a Report on the activities of the sector to the next WRC or to the Council if there is no WRC planned;
- preparation of an estimated Budget of the sector and its submission to the Secretary-General; and
- creation of an annual operation plan covering the forthcoming four years including financial aspects of the activities of the Bureau in support of the entire Sector.

3.3.11 The Telecommunication Standardization Sector studies technical, operational, and tariff-related questions, and adopts recommendations with the aim of standardizing telecommunication procedures worldwide in accordance with the objectives and purposes of the Union. The Sector also considers the special concerns of developing countries.[43]

Standards are essential to the interoperability of Information and Communication Technologies (ICTs) because they enable global communications among the ICT networks and devices of different countries. All Member States and Sector Members are welcome to participate in the creation and development of ITU Recommendations in order to avoid costly market conflict regarding preferred technologies. The Sector also works closely with developing countries to balance the involvement of various levels of companies whether they be located in emerging or more advanced markets, and also focuses on the promotion of access to new markets. The Sector assists countries in building their telecommunications infrastructure, and encourages their economic development, through economies of scale, in order for them to reduce costs for manufacturers, operators, and consumers.[44]

Close coordination is generally performed among all three Sectors: Radiocommunication, Standardization, and Development. Finally, any Member States and Sector Members can participate in the Sector in accordance with the provisions established by the Convention.[45]

3.3.12 The main objective of the Development Sector is to foster international cooperation regarding telecommunication and ICT development issues. This includes[46]

- the promotion of an environment for ICT development,
- the enhancement of confidence and security in the use of telecommunication and ICTs,
- promoting capacity building, digital inclusion and assistance to countries with special needs, and
- improving environmental protection, climate change adaptation, mitigation, and disaster management support through telecommunication and ICTs.

The Sector facilitates and enhances telecommunications development through technical cooperation and support activities, and must cooperate with the other Sectors in matters

---

43 *ITU Constitution, supra* note 7, art 17.
44 ITU, *ITU in Brief*, online: www.itu.int/en/ITU-T/about/Pages/default.aspx.
45 ITU, *ITU in Brief*, online: www.itu.int/en/ITU-D/Pages/About.aspx.
46 *ITU Constitution, supra* note 7, art 17.
47 Ibid. at Article 21.

ITU and space services

relating to the development of telecommunications.[47] In particular, the Development Sector focuses on the following actions:[48]

- raising awareness of decision-makers concerning the important role of telecommunications in the national economic and social development program;
- providing information and advice on possible policy and structural options;
- encouraging the development, expansion, and operation of telecommunication networks and services, particularly in developing countries;
- promoting capacity building, planning, management, resource mobilization, and research and development;
- enhancing the growth of telecommunications through cooperation with regional telecommunications organizations and with global and regional development financing institutions;
- ensuring the execution of projects included in its development program;
- providing financial assistance in the field of telecommunications to developing countries through the promotion of cooperation and lines of credit with international and regional financial and development institutions;
- promoting programs to accelerate the transfer of technologies from developed to developing countries;
- encouraging participation by industry in telecommunication development in developing countries;
- offering advice on the choice and transfer of appropriate technology; and
- executing studies on technical, economic, financial, managerial, regulatory, and policy issues in order to offer appropriate advice as needed.

The Telecommunication Development Sector shall have as members either Member States or Sector Members.[49]

3.3.13 The General Secretariat provides services to the members of the Union, and controls the administrative and financial aspects of the Union's activities. The Secretariat also provides conference services, planning and organization of major meetings, information services, security, strategic planning, and corporate functions such as communications, legal advice, finance, personnel, procurement, internal audit, etc.[50]

4 Allocation structure

4.1 Allocation structure and principles

The allocation structure (Article 5 of the RR) and associated principles represent a basis for the planning and implementation of radiocommunication services. The current approach is based on a block allocation methodology with footnotes. The regulated frequency band (8.3 kHz–3 000 GHz) is segmented into smaller bands and allocated to over 40 defined radiocommunication services.[51] The radio services are identified as primary or secondary (the latter shall cause no harmful interference to, or claim protection from, the former) and footnotes are used to further specify how the frequencies are to be assigned or used. The Table

---

48 Ibid. at Article 21.
49 Ibid.
50 ITU, *General Secretariat*, online: www.itu.int/en/general-secretariat/Pages/default.aspx.
51 *RR, supra* note 6, art 1.

is organized into three Regions of the world (see Figure 7.1) and is supplemented by assignment and allotment Plans for some bands and services, and/or by mandatory coordination procedures.

4.2 Basic principles related to use of the Table

Using the Table as a starting point, the frequency spectrum management authority of each country selects appropriate frequencies with a view to assigning them to stations of a given service. Before taking the final decision to assign a frequency to a station in a given radiocommunication service in a given frequency band and to issue an appropriate license, the authority concerned should be aware of all other conditions regulating the use of frequencies in the band concerned, e.g.:

- Are there other mandatory RR provisions governing the use of the frequencies?
- Is the band concerned subject to a pre-established international assignment or allotment Plan? Are the characteristics of the assignment in accordance with the appropriate entry in the Plan? Is there a need to apply the Plan modification procedure prior to issuing a license?
- Is there a need for effecting the coordination procedure prior to notification of the concerned assignment to the Radiocommunication Bureau (Bureau) or prior to its bringing into use?
- Is the procedure mandatory or voluntary? Is the procedure specified in the RR or in a special agreement?

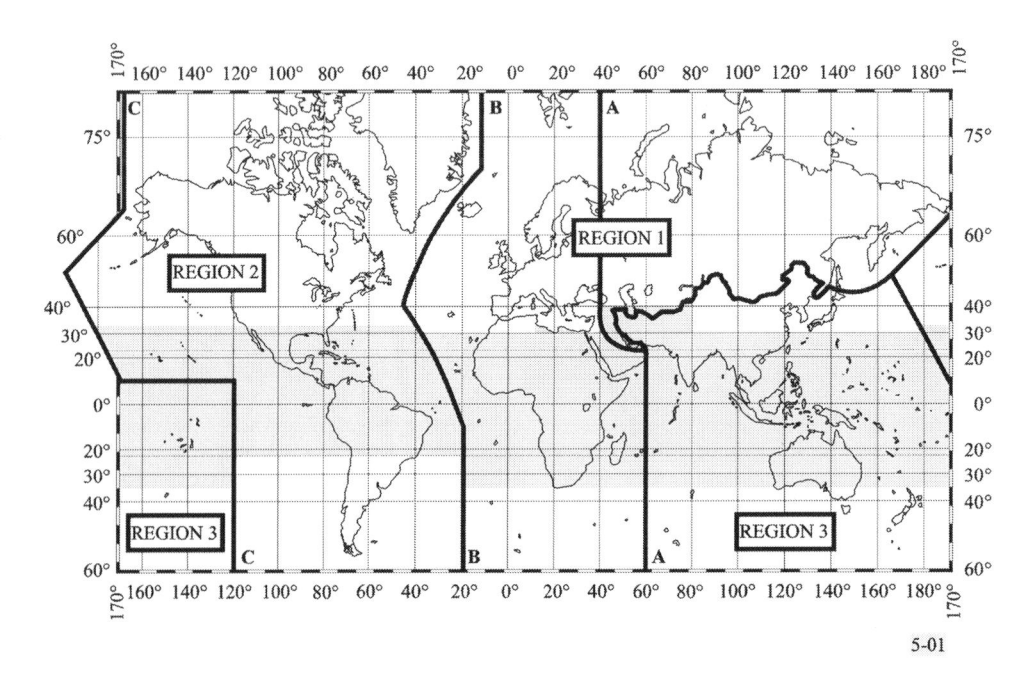

Figure 7.1 Regions for purposes of frequency allocation of the RR

Note: The shaded part represents the Tropical Zones as defined in Nos. 5.16 to 5.20 and 5.21 of the RR.

- Is there a need to notify the frequency assignment to the Bureau? When should such notification be effected? Which characteristics are to be notified? What action should be foreseen after the recording or otherwise of the frequency assignment concerned?

5 Regulations applying to the use of frequencies and orbits by satellite networks or systems

The specific procedures setting out the rights and obligations of the administrations in the domain of orbit/spectrum management and providing means to achieve interference-free radiocommunications have been laid down by successive WRCs on the basis of the two main principles referred to above: efficient use and equitable access. In order to put these principles into effect, two major mechanisms have been developed and implemented:

- *A priori* planning procedures (guaranteeing *equitable access* to orbit/spectrum resources for *future use*), which include:
    - the Allotment Plan for the fixed-satellite service using part of the 4/6 and 10–11/12–13 GHz frequency bands;[52]
    - the Plan for the broadcasting-satellite service in the frequency band 11.7–12.7 GHz[53] and the associated Plan for feeder links in the 14 GHz and 17 GHz frequency bands;[54]
- Coordination procedures (with the aim of *efficiency* of orbit/spectrum use and interference-free operation satisfying *actual requirements*), which include:
    - geostationary-satellite networks (in all services and frequency bands) and non-geostationary-satellite networks in certain frequency bands governed by the No. 9.11A procedure, which are subject to advance publication and coordination procedures;
    - other non-GSO networks (all pertinent services and certain frequency bands), for which only the advance publication procedure is required before notification.

6 Procedures applying to non-planned services

Coordination procedures are contained in Article 9 "Procedure for effecting coordination with or obtaining agreement of other administrations". This article contains all elements of the procedures as well as referring to the provisions of Article 7 of Appendix 30 for the coordination of the fixed-satellite service (FSS) and the broadcasting-satellite service (BSS) in the 11.7–12.7 GHz band and the application of Article 7 of Appendix 30A for the coordination of the fixed-satellite service (space-to-Earth and Earth-to-space) and broadcasting-satellite service with frequency assignments to feeder links for broadcasting-satellite stations. Associated with Article 9 are also Appendix 4, which specifies the various data that must be furnished in any advance publication or coordination request and Appendix 5, that contains criteria for identification of administrations with which coordination is to be effected or agreement sought.

The coordination procedure is based on the principle of "first-come-first served". Successful coordination of space networks or Earth stations gives an international recognition to the use of frequencies by these networks/stations. For such frequency assignments, this right means that other administrations shall take them into account when making their own assignments in order to avoid harmful interference. In addition, frequency assignments in frequency bands

---

52   Ibid., Appendix 30B.
53   Ibid., Appendix 30.
54   Ibid., Appendix 30A.

subject to coordination or to a plan shall have a status derived from the application of the procedures relating to the coordination or associated with the plan. The relevant provisions involve three basic steps:

- advance publication;[55]
- coordination;[56]
- notification.[57]

6.1 Advance publication information (API) procedure

6.1.1   The aim of the advance publication information (API) procedure is to inform all administrations of any planned satellite system and of its general description.[58] This procedure provides a formal mechanism whereby any administration can make a preliminary assessment of the effect that a planned satellite network is likely to have on the stations of existing or planned satellite systems as well as its terrestrial stations in certain frequency bands[59] and comment accordingly.

6.1.2   To this end, the administration responsible for the satellite network has to submit to the Bureau, for publication, the information stipulated in Appendix 4 to the RR. Advance publication information is simplified and streamlined except in those cases where no coordination procedure is applicable. Section I of Article 9 contains two Sub-Sections:

- Sub-Section IA, which applies to non-GSO satellite systems not subject to coordination under Section II of Article 9, for which Appendix 4 information needed to be provided is similar to that of coordination request; and
- Sub-Section IB, which applies either to GSO or non-GSO satellite systems subject to coordination under Section II of Article 9, for which the Appendix 4 information to be provided is quite simple. WRC-15 decision enters into force on 1 January 2017.

6.1.3   The advance information should reach the Bureau not earlier than seven years and preferably not later than two years prior to the planned date of bringing the network into use.[60] This information, when complete, is published by the Bureau in an API/A special section annexed to its BR IFIC Circular, a copy of which is sent to all administrations.[61]

6.1.4   The procedure specifies also the cases in which amendments to the previously published characteristics of a satellite network require re-application of the advance publication procedure; only the use of an additional frequency band or change in the orbital location by more than +/-6 degrees for a space station in the GSO will require the application of the advance publication procedure.[62]

---

55   *RR, supra* note 6, art 9 sec I.
56   Ibid., art 9 sec II.
57   Ibid., art 11.
58   Ibid., art 9, sec I.
59   Bands subject to *RR, supra* note 6, no. 9.21 and no. 9.11 (broadcasting-satellite service (BSS) not subject to plan and No. 9.11A).
60   Ibid., no. 9.1.
61   See, ITU, "Preface to the BR IFIC (Space services)" online: www.itu.int/ITU-R/go/space-preface/en.
62   *RR, supra* note 6, no. 9.2.

6.1.5   Upon receipt of the advance publication, administrations should check whether the planned system is likely to affect their existing or planned systems or stations. Administrations which have any comments should send them to the administration responsible for the planned system, with a copy to the Bureau.[63]

6.1.6   When it receives such comments under Sub-Section IA of Article 9, the administration responsible for the planned satellite network and the requesting administration shall endeavor to cooperate in joint efforts to solve any difficulties, with the assistance of the Bureau if so requested. The publishing administration may take those comments into consideration when initiating the coordination procedure.[64]

6.1.7   The advance publication process is the obligatory first phase of the regulatory registration procedure. It does not give the notifying administration any rights or priority; its main purpose is to inform all administrations of developments in the use of space radiocommunications[65] and to establish a regulatory time-limit to bring into use and notify the assignments in the MIFR.

6.2 Procedure for effecting coordination of frequency assignments

6.2.1   Coordination is a further step in the process leading up to notification of the frequency assignments for recording in the Master Register. WRC-15 removed, as of 1.1.2017, the six-months' time-limit between the advance publication (API) and coordination request (CR).[66]

The coordination procedure is a formal regulatory obligation both for an administration seeking to assign a frequency assignment in its network and for an administration whose existing or planned services may be affected by that assignment. An agreement arising from this coordination confers certain rights and imposes certain obligations on the administrations concerned; as such, coordination must be effected in accordance with the relevant regulatory procedures laid down in the RR and on the basis of technical criteria either contained therein[67] or otherwise agreed to by the administrations concerned.

6.2.2   The coordination procedure in Section II to Article 9 contains two approaches, according to whether the request for coordination is sent by the requesting administration directly to the identified administrations (Earth station/terrestrial station or Earth station/Earth station (operating in opposite direction of transmission) coordination),[68] or to the Bureau (space network/space network or space station/terrestrial station coordination[69] and the procedure for seeking agreement[70]). In the latter case, the publication of the complete information in the BR IFIC by the Bureau is considered as the formal request for coordination whereas, in the former case, the formal coordination request is the one sent directly to the identified administrations and then processed on a bilateral basis by the administrations.

---

63   Ibid., no. 9.3 and 9.5B.
64   Ibid., art 9, sub-sec IB.
65   Ibid., nos.9.5A and 9.5C.
66   Ibid., No. 9.5D.
67   Ibid., Appendix 5.
68   RR, supra note 6, nos 9.15 to 9.19.
69   Ibid., nos 9.7 to 9.14.
70   Ibid., no. 9.21.

6.3 Requirement and request for coordination

6.3.1   Before an administration notifies to the Bureau under Article 11 or brings into use a frequency assignment to a space station, an Earth station intended for communication with a space station, or a terrestrial station within the coordination area of an Earth station, it must effect coordination of the assignment, as required, with any other administration whose space, Earth or terrestrial station frequency assignments are likely to be affected.[71] The frequency assignments to be taken into account in effecting coordination or seeking an agreement are identified using the criteria in Appendix 5. The coordination may be undertaken on a "network basis" using the information relating to the space station, including its service area, and the parameters of one or more typical Earth stations located in all or part of the service area; or on the basis of individual frequency assignments to a space station or an Earth station.

6.3.2   For coordination cases listed under Nos. 9.7 to 9.14 and No. 9.21, the responsible administration shall send to the Bureau the request for coordination together with the appropriate information listed in Appendix 4. On receipt of the request for coordination, the Bureau will promptly examine the information in terms of completeness and conformity with the Convention, the Table of Frequency Allocations and other provisions of the RR.[72]

The Bureau will then examine the information received with a view to identifying any administration with which coordination under Nos. 9.7 to 9.14 and No. 9.21 may need to be effected.

6.3.3   In the above cases, the procedure of Article 9 (except for the case of No. 9.21) requires such coordination with any administration responsible for a frequency assignment to a space station, to an Earth station that communicates with such a space station, or to a terrestrial station, situated in the same frequency band as the planned assignment, pertaining to the same service or another service to which the band is allocated with equal rights or a higher category of allocation, which:

- is in conformity with the Convention, the Table of Frequency Allocations and other provisions of the RR; and
- is recorded in the Master Register with a favorable finding (including registration under No. 11.41); or
- coordinated under the provision of Article 9; or
- included in the coordination procedure with effect from the date of receipt by the Bureau of the characteristics specified in Appendix 4; or
- where appropriate, in conformity with a world or regional allotment or assignment plan and the associated provisions; or
- for terrestrial stations, operating in accordance with the RR, or to be so operated within the next three years from the date of publication of the coordination request, and:
- is considered to affect or be affected, as appropriate, having regard to the threshold levels and conditions given in Tables 5.1 and 5.2 to Appendix 5.

6.3.4   The threshold levels and conditions given in Tables 5.1 and 5.2 to Appendix 5 differ according to the specific cases of coordination. For example:

---

71   Ibid., no. 9.6.
72   Ibid., no. 11.31, Rules of Procedure.

- for GSO/GSO, coordination is criteria based on coordination arc and/or DT/T or pfd depending on the band;[73]
- for GSO FSS/GSO BSS involving Appendix 30 coordination is required when the power flux-density (pfd) of the GSO FSS network on the territory of the BSS administration exceeds specific values given in Appendix 4 to Appendix 30;
- for GSO/non-GSO, coordination is based on frequency overlap;[74]
- for GSO BSS/terrestrial stations[75] and GSO or non-GSO/terrestrial stations for the frequency bands covered by No. 9.11A, coordination is based on frequency overlap and visibility, if there exists no pfd hard or trigger limit for the particular band.

For frequency bands below 3 GHz (space-to-Earth), in addition to the overlap condition, coordination of GSO or non-GSO systems is required with respect to terrestrial stations if the pfd produced at the Earth's surface (GSO or non-GSO system) exceeds threshold values shown in Annex 1 to Appendix 5.

6.3.5 Appendix 5 also defines the conditions under which the agreement of an administration may be required under No. 9.21, and the cases for which no Article 9 coordination is required.

6.3.6 Finally, the Bureau will publish the complete information (Appendix 4 information and, as appropriate, the names of identified administrations with which coordination may need to be effected), in a special section of its BR IFIC. The list of administrations identified by the Bureau under Nos. 9.11 to 9.14 and No. 9.21 is only for information purposes, to help administrations comply with the procedure. Actual administration with which coordination is required is decided based on comments received from administrations within four months and are published in CR/D special section. The list of administrations identified under Nos. 9.7 to 9.7B is the formal list of administrations with which coordination is required, subject to provisions of Nos.9.41 and 9.42. In addition to the administrations, for satellite networks are also identified under No. 9.7 except the band 21.4–22 GHz, the procedures of Nos. 9.41 and 9.42 would apply in establishing the final list of administrations and satellite networks that are included in the coordination procedures and published in CR/E special section.

6.3.7 For cases listed in Nos. 9.15 to 9.19 (Earth station/terrestrial station coordination or Earth station/Earth station (operating in opposite direction of transmission) coordination), for which the coordination request is sent directly by the initiating administration to the identified administrations, the administration receiving the request has 30 days from the date of the request to acknowledge receipt of the information. Should the administration fail to respond to the administration within 15 days of reminder of the request sent then it is possible to seek the assistance of the Bureau. Further, if administration does not respond to a request from the Bureau to acknowledge receipt, then it shall be regarded as unaffected and provisions of Nos. 9.48 and/or 9.48 would be applied by the Bureau on relevant frequency assignments. The coordination condition in these cases is generally based on the coordination area of an Earth station covering the territory of another administration.[76]

---

73 *RR, supra* note 6, no. 9.7.
74 Ibid., nos 9.12 and 9.13.
75 Ibid., no. 9.11.
76 *RR, supra* note 6, Appendix 5.

6.4 Action upon a request for coordination

6.4.1   Having received a coordination request, an administration studies the matter with a view to determining the level of interference likely to be caused to frequency assignments of its networks or stations or caused to assignments of the proposed network or station by its own assignments.[77] Within a total period of four months from the date of the publication of the request for coordination in the relevant special section or the date of dispatch of the coordination data, as appropriate, it shall:

- communicate its agreement to the proposed coordination;[78] or
- provide to the notifying administration (with a copy to the Bureau) the technical data upon which its disagreement is based, along with its suggestions for resolving the problem (No. 9.52).

6.4.2   If an administration with which coordination is sought under Nos. 9.11, 9.12 to 9.14 or No. 9.21 fails to respond within the four-month period after the publication, *this administration shall be regarded as unaffected*.[79]

6.4.3   The Bureau's assistance can be requested at the coordination stage of the procedure, by either the notifying or an objecting administration with a view to resolving any difficulties which may arise. In the particular case of coordination requested under No. 9.14, and within the four-month period from the publication, an administration in need of assistance may inform the Bureau that it has existing or planned terrestrial stations which might be affected and request the Bureau to determine the need for coordination. This request shall be considered as a disagreement, pending the results of the analysis by the Bureau of the need for coordination.[80]

6.4.4   As indicated above, there is an obligation for the notifying administration to coordinate with any administration which has initiated the coordination process at an earlier stage. However, there is also a provision stipulating that both the notifying administration and the objecting administration shall make every possible mutual effort to overcome any difficulties which may arise in a manner acceptable to the parties concerned.[81] The intent of this provision is to facilitate the entry of the newcomer and, even though an administration was first in line, encourage concessions on the basis of mutual cooperation.

6.5 Procedure under Nos. 9.7 and 9.11

The procedure described in Nos. 9.7 and 9.11 is to be used for coordination of frequency assignments to stations in the broadcasting-satellite service (BSS) which are to operate in frequency bands not governed by any plan.

6.6 Procedure under No. 9.21

The use of space services operating in certain frequency bands is governed by the procedure under No. 9.21, in addition to coordination under other Article 9 provisions. This

---

77   Ibid., no. 9.50.
78   Ibid., 9.51 and 9.51A.
79   Ibid., no. 9.52C.
80   Ibid., no. 9.52A.
81   Ibid., no. 9.53.

supplementary procedure is to be applied in cases where a footnote to the Table of Frequency Allocations requires an agreement with an administration. The proposed assignment may only be deemed to be in conformity with the Table in the context of the footnote concerned after such agreement has been reached. The procedure to be followed is the same as the one described in above. In case the required agreement could not be reached, it is possible to notify the assignments under the provisions of No. 11.31.1 with respect to the relevant frequency assignments of those administrations with which agreement could not be obtained.

7 Notification and recording (Article 11)

7.1 The Master International Frequency Register

The procedure for notification and recording of space network frequency assignments in the MIFR is described in Article 11 of the RR. The MIFR represents one of the pillars of the international radio regulatory set-up as it contains *all frequency usage notified to ITU*. It should be consulted before selecting a frequency for any new user. For these reasons, *notification of frequency assignments to the Bureau, with a view to their recording in the MIFR, represents an important obligation for administrations, especially in respect to those frequency assignments that have international implications.*

7.2 Notification procedures

The process of notification of frequency assignments has been streamlined by the revisions of the RR by all recent WRCs, and the relevant provisions are contained in Article 11. In order to keep the process workable, the RR specify quite precisely what should be notified, when the notification information is to be submitted to the Bureau and what information has to be submitted.

According to these provisions, any frequency assignment liable to have an international implication has to be notified to the Bureau (*notice shall reach the Bureau not earlier than three years before the assignments are brought into use*). In other words,

- if an assignment is liable to cause interference to existing or future stations in another country or to suffer interference from such stations; or
- if that assignment is to be used for international radiocommunication; or
- if that assignment is subject to the Article 9 coordination procedure or is involved in such a case; or
- if it is desired to obtain international recognition for that assignment; or
- if it is a non-conforming assignment and if the administration wishes to have it recorded for information,
- it should normally be notified to the Bureau.[82] The Bureau shall publish the notice in PART I-S of the BR IFIC, thereby ensuring that all administrations are informed of the use of the assignments and that they are taken into account in any future planning conducted at the national, regional or international level.

---

82   *RR, supra* note 6, Appendix 4.

7.3 Notification examination by the Bureau and recording in the MIFR

The subsequent processing of a notice varies according to the frequency band and service concerned. Each notice is first examined with respect to its conformity with the Table and the other provisions of the RR (regulatory examination); this examination consists in checking that the assignment (frequency, class of station, notified bandwidth) does indeed correspond to an allocation in the Table or the footnotes thereto and, where appropriate, that it complies with other technical or operating conditions laid down in other articles or appendices of the RR (power limits, authorized classes of emission, minimum elevation angle, etc.). If the result of this examination is *unfavorable* and the administration concerned has not explicitly undertaken that the assignment shall be operated subject to not causing interference to assignments operating in conformity with the RR, making reference to No. 4.4 of the RR, the examination stops there and the notice is returned to the notifying administration after publication of the finding in *PART III-S of the BR IFIC*.

When the result of the first examination[83] is *favorable*, the assignment is *recorded in the MIFR*, or examined further, if appropriate, from the viewpoint of its conformity with the coordination procedures[84] or with a world or regional allotment or assignment Plan.[85]

Following such examinations, the assignment is either recorded in the MIFR and published in *PART II-S of the BR IFIC* (if the finding is *favorable*) or is published in PART III-S of the BR IFIC and returned to the administration (if the finding is unfavorable). The administrations are normally advised to complete the coordination procedure with the identified administrations, or to apply the relevant Plan modification procedure. However, in some specific cases an administration may resubmit the notice without completing the coordination or Plan modification procedure and the concerned assignment may be recorded in the MIFR under specific conditions.

7.4 Time limits

The most important thing to keep in mind is the regulatory time-limit for bringing a satellite network into use and submitting notices for recording in the MIFR. The notified date of bringing into use of any assignment to a space station of a satellite network shall be no later than seven years following the receipt of the advance publication information.[86] WRC-12 introduced further precision and defined bringing into use a satellite network in GSO as contained in No. 11.44B which requires that the

> frequency assignment to a space station in the geostationary-satellite orbit shall be considered as having been brought into use when a space station in the geostationary-satellite orbit with the capability of transmitting or receiving that frequency assignment has been deployed and maintained at the notified orbital position for a continuous period of ninety days. The notifying administration shall so inform the Bureau within thirty days from the end of the ninety-day period.

---

83   *RR, supra* note 6, no. 11.31.
84   Ibid., no. 11.32.
85   Ibid., no. 11.34.
86   Ibid., no. 11.44.

7.5 Responsibilities of the notifying administration after recording in the MIFR

Recording in the MIFR does not mean the end of activities for the notifying administration as regards the concerned frequency assignment. The notifying administration should remain in close cooperation with the licensing authority and satellite operator and any change in the characteristics of the concerned assignment has to be notified to the Bureau so as to be reflected in the MIFR, if necessary following additional coordination with the administrations of other countries concerned.

The notifying administration has also to respond to coordination requests of any administration which has initiated the coordination process at a later stage with the objective, on the basis of mutual cooperation, to overcome any difficulties which may arise in a manner acceptable to the parties concerned.[87]

Furthermore, the notifying administration should remain in close contact with the monitoring authority so as to check whether the concerned frequency assignment is operated in compliance with the notified characteristics and whether other elements (e.g. frequency tolerance) are kept within the limits prescribed by the RR. The notifying administration should also initiate appropriate monitoring programs with a view to detecting any operational or technical irregularities in the operation of frequency assignments pertaining to other administrations, and to initiate appropriate actions in this regard, so as *to ensure interference-free operation* for stations under its jurisdiction.

8 The BSS plans and their associated procedures (Appendices 30/30A)

8.1 The BSS and associated feeder-link Plans and Lists

8.1.1   Appendices 30 and 30A to the Radio Regulations contain Plans for the broadcasting-satellite service (BSS) in the 12 GHz band and the associated feeder-link Plans in the fixed-satellite service (FSS) in the 14 and 17 GHz bands. These Plans are occasionally referred to as the "BSS and the associated feeder-link Plans" and were established with a view to facilitating equitable access to the geostationary-satellite orbit (GSO) for all countries. In Regions 1 and 3 there are also the Lists of additional uses, which are separated from the Plans and annexed to the Master International Frequency Register (MIFR).

8.1.2   The BSS and associated feeder-link Plans and Lists cover the following frequency bands:

    Region 1:   11.7–12.5 GHz (space-to-Earth);
                   14.5–14.8 GHz (Earth-to-space);[88]
                   17.3–18.1 GHz (Earth-to-space);
    Region 2:   12.2–12.7 GHz (space-to-Earth);
                   17.3–17.8 GHz (Earth-to-space);
    Region 3:   11.7–12.2 GHz (space-to-Earth);
                   14.5–14.8 GHz (Earth-to-space);
                   17.3–18.1 GHz (Earth-to-space).

BSS and associated feeder-link assignments in these bands have primary status.

---

87   *RR, supra* note 6, no. 9.53.
88   For countries outside Europe.

8.1.3   The BSS and associated feeder-link Plans are presented in a tabular form in Articles 10 and 11 of Appendix 30 (hereafter referred to as AP30) and Articles 9 and 9A of Appendix 30A (hereafter referred to as AP30A) respectively. The regulatory procedures associated with the Plans are contained in the Articles of those Appendices. They apply to Plan implementation and modification as well as sharing with respect to terrestrial and other space services in the frequency bands of AP30/30A. Several technical annexes exist containing sharing criteria, calculation methods, and technical data relating to the Plans.

8.1.4   The BSS and associated feeder-link Plans are assignment plans. The Plans for Regions 1 and 3 are for national assignments only. In general each country in Region 1 has 10 assignments (channels) and that in Region 3 has 12 assignments (channels) at a single orbital location. Generally, it cannot be changed except under very limited conditions. All other changes such as modifications to assignments to add more channels, change of beam parameters, and so on. Will be permitted subject to successful application of the coordination procedure of Article 4 of AP30/30A, and once completed will be included in a "List", called the "Regions 1 and 3 List of additional uses". Assignments in the List must be compatible with assignments in the Plans.

8.1.5   Proposed modifications to the Region 2 Plan are possible and can only enter the evolving Region 2 Plan after they have satisfied all coordination requirements in accordance with Article 4 of AP30/30A. The Region 2 Plan has direct strappings between feeder-link and downlink assignments.

8.1.6   Characteristics of the national assignments, such as nominal orbital position, ellipse parameters and e.i.r.p. Values, are contained in Articles 10 and 11 of AP30 and Articles 9 and 9A of AP30A. More details, like the test points associated to each beam, are included in the SPS database,[89] which is distributed in the BR IFIC (space service).[90]

The parameters used in characterizing the Plan can be found in Annex 5 of AP30 and Annex 3 of AP30A. Each assignment in the Plan is based on overall C/N values of 14 dB 99 percent of the worst month.

8.1.7   The Regions 1 and 3 List of additional uses was created at WRC-2000. The initial List consisted of satellite networks with:

- notified assignments in conformity with AP30/30A, which had been brought into use and for which the date of bringing into use was confirmed to the Bureau before 1700 hours (Istanbul time) on 12 May 2000; and
- assignments for which the procedures of Article 4 of AP30/30A were successfully completed and for which due diligence information was provided before 1700 hours (Istanbul time) on 12 May 2000, but which had not been brought into use and/or the date of bringing into use had not been confirmed to the Bureau.

There are individual Lists for the downlink and for the feeder-link (14 GHz and 17 GHz). The Lists are separated from the Plans and annexed to the MIFR. Assignments in the Lists must be compatible with assignments in the Plans. The Lists are evolving and are updated and published periodically by the Bureau, for example when a new network is added to a List. The detailed characteristics of all the assignments in the List are included in the above-mentioned SPS database.

---

89   ITU, "Space Network Systems Online" online: www.itu.int/sns/.
90   ITU, "Appendices 30 and 30A BSS Plan (including associated MSPACEg software)" online: www.itu.int/en/ITU-R/space/plans/Pages/AP30-30A.aspx.

8.2 Procedure for implementation of Plan or List assignments (Article 5)

8.2.1   The procedure of Article 5 of AP30/30A is applied when an administration notifies to the Bureau the use of its assignments in the appropriate Regional Plans or the Region 1 and 3 Lists using Appendix 4 format.

8.2.2   The Bureau then examines the submission to assure that the information received is complete, that the data elements are in conformity with Appendix 4, that the notified characteristics comply with those of the entries in the Plans or Lists, and the coordination requirements specified in the Remarks column of Article 10 or 11 of AP30 or Article 9 or 9A of AP30A, if any, are satisfied.

8.2.3   If the administration responsible for the Plan or List assignments wants them entered in the Master Register, the notified technical characteristics will have to comply with those listed in the Plans or Lists.[91] The only exception is in limited cases of AP30/30A where it is evident that the deviation in its characteristics will not increase its interference potential to other assignments in the Plans or Lists or other services nor claim protection from other assignments in the Plan and/or the Lists.[92]

8.3 Procedures for modifications to the Region 2 Plan or Regions 1 and 3 List (Article 4)

8.3.1   Although these Plans are based on *a priori* frequency assignments, nevertheless there is a possibility to make modifications (changes, additions and cancellations) to the Plans. Modified characteristics can be included in the Region 2 Plan or Region 1 and 3 List after successful application of the relevant procedures of Article 4 of AP30/30A.

8.3.2   The whole process for an assignment entering into the Region 2 Plan or Region 1 and 3 List through the application of Article 4 of AP30/30A can be divided into two stages:

- Stage A: for agreement seeking, relating to a submission under § 4.1.3 and 4.2.6 of AP30/30A and a publication in Part A of Special Section AP30/E/, AP30A/E or AP30-30A/E/ under § 4.1.5 and 4.2.8 of AP30/30A;
- Stage B: for inclusion into Region 2 Plan or Regions 1 and 3 List of AP30/30A, relating to a submission under § 4.1.12 and 4.2.16 of AP30/30A and a publication in Part B of Special Section AP30/E/, AP30A/E or AP30-30A/E/ under § 4.1.15 and 4.2.19 of AP30/30A.

8.3.3   Procedures for modifications to Region 2 Plan

8.3.3.1   The modification procedures for the Region 2 Plan are stipulated in Section 4.2 of Article 4 of AP30/30A. The submission in Appendix 4 format shall be sent not earlier than eight years and not later than two years before the planned date of bringing into use the assignments of the proposed network. The Bureau examines the submission to assure that the information received is complete. The notifying administration has to provide missing information and clarification if requested by the Bureau. When the submission is considered as complete, its formal date of receipt is established. The Bureau treats the submissions in sequence of receipt.

---

91   See, for examples, ITU, "Space Network List (SNL)" online: www.itu.int/ITU-R/go/space/snl/en.
92   Ibid., prov 5.2.1 d.

8.3.3.2 In order to assess whether or not a proposed modification would affect other assignments in the Region 2 Plan, the Bureau has to evaluate the impact on the reference situation of all assignments in the Region 2 Plan using the criteria in § 2 and 3 of Annex 1 of AP30 and AP30A respectively. Additional technical examinations are necessary to determine whether other services (terrestrial, non-planned BSS and fixed-satellite services) and the appropriate Regions 1 and 3 Plan and List assignments that share the same frequency band are affected using the criteria in § 3, 4, 6 and 7 of Annex 1 of AP30 and § 5 of Annex 1 of AP30A. These examinations identify administrations whose services are considered to be affected. This information is published in Part A of Special Section AP30-30A/E/ of the International Frequency Information Circular (BR IFIC).

8.3.3.3 The administration proposing to include the modified assignment in the Plan then has to seek the agreement of those administrations whose services/assignments are considered to be affected and who have commented within the four-month period. When no comment is received within the four-month period, it is considered that the administration has agreed to the assignments of the proposed network. After the four-month period, the Bureau will publish the list of administrations whose agreements are required in Part D of Special Section AP30-30A/E/.

8.3.3.4 If agreements have been reached with all objecting administrations or the characteristics are modified to ensure that the identified networks of other administrations are no longer affected, the administration proposing the new or modified assignment can submit the final characteristics of the assignments in Appendix 4 format in order to include them in Region 2 Plan and may continue with the appropriate procedure under Article 5. In cases where an agreement cannot be reached between administrations, there are provisions in paragraphs 4.2.20 to 4.2.21D of Article 4 to enable the matter to proceed further by allowing the assignment to be provisionally included in the Region 2 Plan on a non-interference basis. In order to verify whether the coordination requirements have been fulfilled for successful completion of the Article 4 procedure, the Bureau performs a series of examinations.[93] The technical examinations verify whether objecting administrations are excluded from the list of affected administrations and that no additional interference is imposed on an administration that has not objected or has previously agreed after an objection. Once the Article 4 procedure is completed, the modification is added to the Plan. If the proposed assignments are not included in the Region 2 Plan or not brought into use within eight years from the date of receipt of a submission under § 4.1.3 and 4.2.6 of AP30/30A, they will be cancelled.

8.3.4 Procedures for modifications to Regions 1 and 3 List

8.3.4.1 The Regions 1 and 3 Plan, however, cannot be changed except under very limited conditions. All other changes such as modifications to assignments, additional channels, change of beam parameters, and so on, are permitted subject to the procedures in Section 4.1 of Article 4 and, if successful, are included in the Regions 1 and 3 List of additional uses.

8.3.4.2 Similarly to modification to Region 2 Plan the submission in Appendix 4 format shall be sent not earlier than eight years and not later than two years before the planned date of bringing into use the assignments of the proposed network. When the submission is considered as complete, its formal date of receipt is established.

8.3.4.3 In order to assess whether or not a proposed modification would affect other assignments, the Bureau has to apply the criteria in § 1 of Annex 1 of AP30 and § 4 of Annex 1 of AP30A (EPM and power flux-density limits) to all entries in the Regions 1 and 3 Plan

---

93 *AP30/30A, supra* note 88, art 4 § 4.2.15.

and List. Additional technical examinations are necessary to determine whether other services (terrestrial, non-planned BSS and fixed-satellite services) and the Region 2 Plan that share the same frequency band are affected. These examinations identify administrations whose services are considered to be affected using the criteria in § 3, 4 and 6 of Annex 1 of AP30 and § 5 and 6 of Annex 1 of AP30A. This information is published in Part A of Special Section AP30/E/ and/or AP30A/E/ of the BR IFIC.

8.3.4.4 Similarly to modification to Region 2 Plan, the administration proposing to include a new or modified assignment in the List then has to seek the agreement of those administrations whose services/assignments are considered to be affected and who have commented within the four-month period. As agreed by WRC-15, an administration that has not notified its agreement either to the administration seeking agreement or to the Bureau within a period of four months shall be deemed to have not agreed to the proposed assignment unless assistance from the Bureau is requested by the notifying administration. The notifying administration may request the above-mentioned assistance in respect of an administration that is considered to be affected but has not commented within the above-mentioned four-month period. If the identified administration fails to reply within 30 days after the Bureau's reminder, it shall be deemed to have agreed to the proposed assignments.

8.3.4.5 If agreements have been reached with all objecting administrations or the characteristics are modified to ensure that the identified networks of other administrations are no longer affected, the administration proposing the new or modified assignment can submit the final characteristics of the assignments in Appendix 4 format in order to include them in Regions 1 and 3 List and may continue with the appropriate procedure under Article 5. In cases where an agreement cannot be reached between administrations, the matter can proceed further by allowing the assignment to be provisionally included in the List on a non-interference basis.[94] In order to verify whether the coordination requirements have been fulfilled for successful completion of the Article 4 procedure, the Bureau performs a series of examinations.[95] The technical examinations verify whether objecting administrations are excluded from the list of affected administrations and that no additional interference is imposed on an administration that has not objected or has previously agreed after an objection.

8.3.4.6 Once the Article 4 procedure is completed, the assignment is added to the List. Assignments in the List have a maximum period of operation of 15 years. However, this may be extended for another 15 years if all the characteristics of the assignment remain unchanged. If the proposed assignments are not included in the Regions 1 and 3 List or not brought into use within eight years, they will be cancelled.

8.3.5 Space Operation Functions (SOF) in support of the operation of planned BSS networks

Article 2A of AP30/30A stipulates a coordination mechanism for the use of the guard bands of AP30/30A to provide Space Operation Functions (SOF) in support of the operation of planned BSS networks. To use the guard bands, advance publication information (API) is not required to be submitted. SOF assignments are to be coordinated with other assignments using the provisions of Nos. 9.7, 9.17, 9.17A, 9.18 and the associated provisions of Section II of Article 9, the provisions of § 4.1.1 d) 4.1.1 e) 4.2.3 d) or 4.2.3 e) of Article 4 of AP30 and § 4.1.1 d) of Article 4 of AP30A or the provisions of Article 7 of AP30/30A, as appropriate. SOF assignments are notified under Article 11.

---

94 Ibid., art 4 paras 4.1.17 to 4.1.20.
95 Ibid., art 4v§ 4.1.11.

9 The FSS Plan and its associated procedures (Appendix 30B)

9.1 The FSS Plan and the associated List of assignments

9.1.1 Appendix 30B of the Radio Regulations contains the Plan for the fixed-satellite service (FSS) in the 6/4 GHz frequency bands and in the 13/10-11 GHz frequency bands. This Plan is also referred to as the "FSS Plan" and was established with a view to facilitating equitable access to the geostationary-satellite orbit (GSO) for all countries.

The FSS Plan covers the following frequency bands:

- 4 500–4 800 MHz (space-to-Earth);
- 6 725–7 025 MHz (Earth-to-space);
- 10.70–10.95 GHz (space-to-Earth);
- 11.20–11.45 GHz (space-to-Earth);
- 12.75–13.25 GHz (Earth-to-space),
- resulting in a total bandwidth of 800 MHz in each direction.

FSS assignments in these bands have primary status.

9.1.2 The FSS Plan is contained in Appendix 30B (hereafter referred to as AP30B) together with its associated regulatory procedures. Several annexes exist containing criteria, calculation methods, and technical data relating to the Plan. The FSS Plan is an allotment plan. Each allotment in the Plan comprises:

- a nominal orbital position;
- a bandwidth of 800 MHz (uplink and downlink) as listed in paragraph 1 above;
- a service area for a national coverage.

Characteristics of the national allotments, such as nominal orbital position, ellipse parameters and power-density values, are contained in Article 10 of AP30B. More details, like the test points associated to each beam, are included in the AP30B database, which is distributed in the BR IFIC (space service).[96]

The parameters used in characterizing the Plan can be found in Annex 1 of AP30B. Each allotment in the Plan is based on C/N values of 21 dB and 15 dB for uplink and downlink respectively under rain-faded conditions and availability of 99.95 percent for the 6/4 GHz frequency bands and 99.9 percent for the 13/10–11 GHz frequency bands. In addition, the Plan has been prepared with a view to ensuring for each allotment an overall aggregate C/I value of 21 dB and a single-entry C/I value of 25 dB under free space path loss conditions.

9.2 Procedure for implementation of allotment in the Plan or introduction of an additional system

9.2.1 Before the orbital position and frequency resources of an allotment can be utilized by a satellite system, the national allotment has to be converted into an assignment through the application of the procedures of Article 6 of AP30B. The assignments are then recorded in the AP30B List (hereafter referred to as List), and they are entitled to protection against systems received by the Bureau at a later date.

---

96 ITU, online www.itu.int/en/ITU-R/space/plans/Pages/AP30B.aspx.

9.2.2 Additional systems can also be included in the List after successful application of the relevant procedures of Article 6 of AP30B. In the context of this Appendix, an additional system is a system for which the assignments are not the result of conversion of an allotment into assignments. When an administration submits an additional system, the allotment of that administration in the Plan is retained.

9.2.3 The whole process for an assignment entering into the List through the application of Article 6 of AP30B can be divided into two stages:

- Stage A: for coordination/agreement seeking, relating to a submission under § 6.1 of AP30B and a publication in Special Section AP30B/A6A/ under § 6.8 of AP30B;
- Stage B: for inclusion into the List of AP30B, relating to a submission under § 6.17 of AP30B and a publication in Special Section AP30B/A6B/ under § 6.23 of AP30B.

The detailed characteristics of all the assignments in the List are included in the above-mentioned AP30B database.

9.2.4 After being entered in the List of AP30B, an assignment can be notified for its inclusion into the Master Register.[97]

9.3 Procedure for inclusion of assignment in the List (Article 6)

9.3.1 The procedure of Article 6 of AP30B is applied when an administration submits to the Bureau either: the conversion of an allotment into an assignment, the introduction of an additional system or the modification of an assignment in the List that has already been brought into use. The submission shall be sent not earlier than eight years and not later than two years before the planned date of bringing into use the assignments of the proposed network. The Bureau examines the submission to assure that the information received is complete and the data elements are in conformity with the requirements of Appendix 4 and the Table of Frequency Allocations. The notifying administration has to provide missing information and clarification if requested by the Bureau. When the submission is considered as complete, its formal date of receipt is established. The Bureau treats the submissions in sequence of receipt.

9.3.2 The Bureau first examines the submission against the limits in Annex 3 of AP30B as well as other limits contained in Articles 21 and 22 of the RR. Following a favorable finding, the Bureau further evaluates the impact of the proposed assignments on the reference situation of allotments in the Plan, the assignments in the List and the assignments that the Bureau has previously examined, using the method and criteria of Annex 4 of AP30B. This examination under § 6.5 of AP30B identifies administrations whose networks are considered to be affected. The Bureau also identifies the administrations whose territories have been partially or wholly included in the service area of the assignments under examination in accordance with § 6.6 of AP30B. The submitted information and the names of the identified administrations are published in a Special Section AP30B/A6A/ of the BR IFIC together with the relevant AP30B database.

9.3.3 The administration whose networks are identified as being potentially affected (under § 6.5 of AP30B) should send its comments to the Bureau and to the notifying administration (directly or through the Bureau) within four months following the publication of the AP30B/A6A/ Special Section. When no comment is received within the four-month period,

---

97 AP30/30A, *supra* note 88, art 8.

it is considered that the administration has not agreed to the assignments of the proposed network unless an assistance under § 6.13 to § 6.15 of AP30B is requested by the notifying administration.

9.3.4   The notifying administration may request the above-mentioned assistance in respect of an administration that is considered to be affected but has not commented within the above-mentioned four-month period. If the identified administration fails to reply within 30 days after the Bureau's reminder, it shall be deemed to have agreed to the proposed assignments.

9.3.5   The comments from the administrations whose territories are included in the service areas of the published assignments can be sent at any time during or after the above-mentioned four-month period. The notifying administration must obtain explicit agreement from those administrations before the assignments are included in the List.

9.3.6   For the purpose of entering into the List, the administration proposing the new or modified assignments has to either reach agreement with affected administrations or modify the characteristics of its assignments to ensure that the identified networks of other administrations are no longer affected. The final characteristics of the proposed assignments should be submitted to the Bureau in accordance with § 6.17 of AP30B together with the names of administrations with which agreements have been reached. The Bureau checks if required agreements from the identified administrations are obtained.[98] If not, an unfavorable finding is given to the assignments and the whole notice is returned to the administration. In the examination under § 6.22 of AP30B the Bureau uses the method and criteria in Annex 4 of AP30B to identify the newly affected networks due to the changes of characteristics. If all the examinations lead to favorable findings, the submitted assignment is entered in the List and is published in a Special Section AP30B/A6B/ of the BR IFIC. If the examination leads to unfavorable findings, the submitted notice is returned. However, if a notice is returned due to unfavorable findings under Annex 4 of AP30B examination with respect to assignments, but the findings with respect to the allotments in the Plan are favorable, the submitted assignments can be provisionally entered in the List after resubmission of the notice by the notifying administration, together with a commitment indicating that its assignments shall not cause unacceptable interference to nor claim protection from the assignments for which agreement still needs to be obtained.[99]

9.3.7   If the proposed assignments are not included in the List within eight years from the date of receipt of a submission under § 6.1 of AP30B, they will be cancelled.

9.4 Procedure for inclusion of assignment in the MIFR (Article 8)

9.4.1   Any assignment for which the relevant procedure of Article 6 of AP30B has been successfully applied shall be notified to the Bureau in accordance with Article 8 of AP30B not earlier than three years before the assignment is brought into use.

9.4.2   The Bureau first examines the notification to verify its compatibility with the Table of Frequency Allocations, the Plan, and other relevant provisions of the Radio Regulations and then examines its conformity with the characteristics of the corresponding assignment in the List. A new assignment is included in the Master Register and published in Parts I-S and II-S of the BR IFIC if the examinations lead to favorable findings. If the examinations lead to unfavorable findings, the assignment is published in Part III-S, and returned.

---

98   Ibid., § 6.19 & § 6.21.
99   *AP30/30A, supra* note 88, Appendix 4, A.19a.

9.4.3   If an assignment is not notified and brought into use within the eight-year regulatory period, the assignment in the List will be cancelled. If the cancelled assignment is the result of a conversion from an allotment, this allotment shall be reinstated with the same characteristics as the cancelled assignment, except for its service area, which should be the national territory.

9.5 Procedure for the addition of a new allotment for a new Member (Article 7)

9.5.1   An administration that has joined the Union as a new Member State and does not have a national allotment in the Plan or an assignment stemming from the conversion of an allotment can obtain a national allotment in application of Article 7 of AP30B. That administration shall submit its request for an allotment to the Bureau, with the following information:

- the geographical coordinates of not more than 20 test points for determining a minimum ellipse to cover its national territory;
- the height above sea level of each of its test points;
- any special requirement which is to be taken into account to the extent practicable.

9.5.2   The request for a new allotment is processed ahead of submissions received under Article 6 of AP30B which have not yet been examined. The Bureau proposes appropriate technical characteristics and associated orbital positions for the new allotment and informs the requesting administration, who should respond to the Bureau's proposal within 30 days.

9.5.3   Upon receipt of a reply on the selection of an orbital position and technical parameters from the requesting administration, the Bureau verifies its compatibility with allotments, assignments in the List and the assignments which have been examined as well as the conformity with the Table of Frequency Allocations and other provisions of the Radio Regulations.

9.5.4   The new allotment is then included in the Plan and published in a Special Section of BR IFIC if the above-mentioned examinations lead to favorable findings.[100]

9.5.5   If affected administrations are identified in this process, the corresponding agreements are required. If the calculated C/I values of the new allotment are below the required criteria, the requesting administration has to accept the excess degradation. Otherwise, the request for a new allotment in the Plan will be treated as a submission and processed ahead of other Article 6 submissions which have not yet been examined by the Bureau.[101]

10 Administrative due diligence (Resolution 49 (WRC-12) and Resolution 552 (WRC-12))

10.1   Following one of the recommendations in the report by the Director of the BR on Resolution 18 (Kyoto, 1994), WRC-97 adopted Resolution 49, which has been modified by subsequent WRCs, on the administrative due diligence applicable to some satellite communication services as a means of addressing the problem of reservation of orbit and spectrum capacity without actual use. This resolution will apply to any satellite network of the fixed-satellite service, mobile-satellite service or broadcasting-satellite (except in 21.4–22 GHz band) service in frequency bands subject to coordination under Section II of Article 9, as well as

---

100   Ibid., AP30B/A7/.
101   *AP30/30A, supra* note 88, art 6.

modifications of the Appendices 30 and 30A Plans and additional uses in the Appendix 30B planned services.

10.2   For the above cases, an administration shall send to the Bureau due diligence information relating to the identity of the satellite network (name of the satellite, notifying administration, reference to the special section publication, frequency range, name of the operator, orbital characteristics) and the spacecraft manufacturer (name of the manufacturer, date of execution of the contract, delivery window, number of satellites procured); this information is to be submitted as early as possible before bringing into use, but must in any case be received before the end of the seven-year period established as a time-limit for bringing into use a satellite network. Before notifying its satellite network for recording in the MIFR, the administration shall also send to the Bureau information relating to the launch services provider (name of the launch provider, date of execution of the contract, anticipated launch or in-orbit delivery window, name of the launch vehicle, name and location of the launch facility).

10.3   After verifying its completeness, the Bureau will publish the information in a special section of the BR IFIC. Should an administration fail to supply the complete required due diligence information in time, the networks concerned shall be cancelled (cancellation of the coordination request or modification to the Plan or entry in the MIFR) and shall not be recorded in the MIFR.

10.4   Resolution 552 (WRC-12) contains due diligence procedure for BSS in the band 21.4–22 GHz. The Resolution is entitled "Long term access to and development in the band 21.4–22 GHz in Region 1 and 3". The content of this resolution is somewhat similar to Resolution 49 and new data elements are required to be submitted by administrations under this Resolution, which are listed in Annex 2 to the resolution. Under this resolution administrations have to submit due diligence information not only when the space station is brought into use for the first time but also submit information about any further change, like deorbiting of the satellite or moving of the satellite to another orbital location. Further, this Resolution requires ITU to provide an ITU-ID for each physical satellite network brought into use in this band and this satellite ID remains same for the life time of the satellite irrespective of the orbital location of the satellite or its responsible administration until it is deorbited.

11 Cost recovery

11.1   Cost recovery is to apply to satellite network filings received by the Bureau after 7 November 1998.[102] Additionally the WRC-03 and WRC-07 adopted provisions referring to Decision 482, as amended, *under which a satellite network filing is cancelled if payment is not received in accordance with the provisions of this decision.*

11.2   The cost recovery for satellite network filings is consistent with the general principles for cost recovery adopted in Resolution 91 (Minneapolis, 1998), in particular *resolves* 4 and the need to ensure that no more than the actual costs of providing products and services are recovered.[103]

---

102 ITU, Resolution 88 (rev Marrakech, 2002) online: www.itu.int/council/groups/Res88-e.doc . ITU, Council Decision 482 online: www.itu.int/en/ITU-R/space/Documents/Decision%20 482(C2013)-E.pdf.
103 ITU, "Cost recovery for satellite network filings" online: www.itu.int/ITU-R/go/space-cost-recovery/en.

11.3 It is applicable for the production of the special sections of the BR IFIC (space services) concerning advance publication (API), and their associated requests for coordination[104] and requests for modification of the space service plans and lists contained in Appendices 30, 30A and 30B to the RR, received by the Bureau after 7 November 1998. It is also applicable to all satellite network filings concerning notification for recording of frequency assignments in the MIFR[105] received by the Bureau on or after 1 January 2006 if, they refer to advance publication or modification of the space service plans or lists, as appropriate, received on or after 19 October 2002 and for all requests for the implementation of the fixed-satellite service plan (former Sections IA and III of Article 6 of Appendix 30B to the RR) if, they have been received by the Bureau on or after 1 January 2006.

11.4 Each Member State shall be entitled to the publication of special sections or parts of the BR IFIC (space services) for one satellite network filing each year without the charges referred to above. Each Member State in its role as the notifying administration may determine which network shall benefit from the free entitlement.

11.5 Publication of special sections for the amateur-satellite service, the notification for recording of frequency assignments for Earth stations, for the conversion of an allotment into an assignment in accordance with the procedure of former Section I of Article 6 of Appendix 30B, the addition of a new allotment to the plan for a new Member State of the Union in accordance with the procedure of Article 7 of Appendix 30B and submissions under *resolves 3 and 4* of Resolution 555 (WRC-12) shall be exempt from any charges.

12 Pico, nano and small satellites

There is no regulatory definition for small satellites. The RR recognize only GSO and non-GSO satellites. During WRC-12, the conference considered that nanosatellites and picosatellites might require regulatory procedures which take account of the short development cycle, the short lifetimes and the typical missions of such satellites. The conference requested the ITU-R to examine the procedures for notifying space networks and consider possible modifications to enable the deployment and operation of nanosatellites and picosatellites, taking into account the short development time, short mission time and unique orbital characteristics.[106]

12.1 ITU-R study related to satellite systems using nano and picosatellites

The ITU-R WP 7B is currently studying a Question ITU-R 254/7 "Characteristics and spectrum requirements of satellite systems using nano and picosatellites":

a) What are the distinctive characteristics of nano and picosatellites and satellite systems in terms of their use of the radio spectrum as defined by data rates, transmissions time and bandwidths?

b) Taking into account such distinctive characteristics, what are the spectrum requirements for nano and picosatellite systems?

c) Under which radiocommunication services can satellite systems using nano and picosatellites operate?

---

104 *RR, supra* note 6, art 9.
105 Ibid., art 11, Appendices 30/30A art 5 and Appendix 30B, art 8.
106 ITU, Resolution 757 (WRC-2012) "Regulatory aspects for nanosatellites and picosatellites", online: www.itu.int/dms_pub/itu-r/oth/0c/0a/R0C0A00000A0025PDFE.pdf.

The space research, Earth exploration, amateur, and educational communities, like other communities focused on leveraging space-based radiocommunication technologies, have an interest in utilizing the potential benefits offered by *small satellites, including those referred to as nanosatellites or picosatellites*. These technologies allow many projects to be developed quickly and deployed with lower cost than with traditional, larger satellites. While even the most advanced nanosatellites are typically no more than a few million United States Dollars (USD), the smallest missions may have a total developmental and operational budget (excluding launch and ground infrastructure) of only a few tens of thousands of USD. Small satellites also provide a means for testing emerging technologies and economical commercial off-the-shelf (COTS) components that may be useful in future space missions, including those utilizing larger satellite platforms. They offer new opportunities for existing and new satellite operators, such as universities, educational institutes, governments, and private industry that might not otherwise have considered or been able to afford the use of satellite technologies. They have been demonstrated in a variety of practical applications, including Earth observation, space astronomy, space physics, and maritime communications. Recent proposals for the use of small satellites include solar system exploration, interplanetary and even outer solar system missions.

12.2 Characteristics of small satellites

Small satellites are commonly described as:

- ranging in mass from 0.1 to 10 kg and measuring less than 0.5 m in any linear dimension, with physical characteristics that differ from those of larger satellites;
- typically taking a short (1–2 years) development time and low cost, often using off-the-shelf components;
- having an operational lifetime ranging from several weeks up to a few (< 5) years depending on their mission;
- being used for a wide variety of missions and applications, including remote sensing, space weather research, upper atmosphere research, astronomy, communications, technology demonstration and education, as well as commercial applications, and therefore may operate under various radiocommunication services;
- typically launched as secondary payloads;
- requiring simultaneous launches and operation of several such satellites in formation or as a constellation for some missions;
- limited orbit control capabilities.

To carry out the studies related to the question the class of objects to which the studies apply, as opposed to all satellites, needs to be established. A convenient way to classify satellites is by their mass. Satellites that weigh less than ~500 kg are often referred to as small satellites; they can be further classified as shown in Table 7.2 and challenge matrix in Table 7.3.

The Bureau recently organized a global Symposium to addresses regulatory requirements for small satellite communication systems with aim to ensure sustainable deployment of new generation of small satellites in outer space.[107]

---

107 See, ITU, "ITU Symposium and Workshop on small satellite regulation and communication systems, Prague, Czech Republic, 2–4 March 2015" online: www.itu.int/GO/ITU-R/Prague-2015.

Table 7.2 Typical characteristics of small satellites

Denomination	Mass (kg)	Max. bus power (W)	Typical cost (US$)	Max. dimensions (m)	Development time (years)	Orbit	Mission duration (years)
Minisatellite	100–500	1,000	30–200 M	3–10	3–10	GEO MEO LEO HEO	5–10
Microsatellite	10–100	150	10–150 M	1–5	2–5	LEO (HEO)	2–6
Nanosatellite	1–10	20	100 k–10 M	0.1–1	1–3		1–3
Picosatellite	0.1–1	5	50 k–2 M	0.05–0.1			
Femtosatellite	< 0.1	1	< 50 k	0.01–0.1	1		< 1

Table 7.3 Small satellites challenge matrix

Source	Effect	Concern
Launch as piggyback	Orbital elements are not known until late in the satellite system design	More specific orbital elements may be needed for frequency coordination
No thrusters	Uncontrolled orbital changes during satellite operation, inability to hold exact orbital position	Movement of radiation pattern with time (most of satellite uses omni-directional antennas)
Short development process	Specific spectral parameters desirable at the beginning of design process that could be difficult to change later on	Too lengthy coordination
Low onboard power	Low RF transmission power	Still has potential for interference due to narrow bandwidth and resulting power spectral density
No or ineffective attitude control	Omni-directional antennas commonly used	Potential interference to other satellites in orbit and terrestrial systems

13 Space protocol

The Space Protocol is part of a family of international treaties beginning with the *Convention on International Interests in Mobile Equipment*[108] and the *Protocol on Matters specific to Aircraft Equipment*.[109] The Space Protocol is an instrument designed to facilitate asset-based financing for the acquisition and use of space assets, such as satellites and transponders that move beyond frontiers.

---

108 *Convention on International Interests in Mobile Equipment*, 16 November 2001, 2307 UNTS 285.
109 *Protocol on Matters specific to Aircraft Equipment*, 16 November 2001, OJ L121 of 15/05/2009.

Under an international legal framework of asset-based financing, a creditor could enforce its rights against the equipment in the event of default by the debtor. Under the current legal regime, it is the law governing the location of the equipment that will normally decide questions regarding the validity, priority ranking and enforcement of security and leasing rights in such equipment. However, there is currently no applicable law governing the location of equipment in space. From the viewpoint of a lender, this situation makes the risks of asset-based financing less acceptable.

The Space Protocol is establishing the legal foundation for the creation, priority ranking and enforcement of security and leasing rights in space-based equipment. One of the key features of the Space Protocol is the creation of an international registry for space assets in which those rights may be registered. The Registry would determine priority among rights on the basis of the first-come, first-served principle to give lenders a degree of legal certainty relating to asset-based financing. The Registry would be operated and administered by the Registrar on a 24 hour / seven day a week basis.

The Supervisory Authority would oversee the operation of the Registry by the Registrar. In particular, it would nominate and dismiss the Registrar, monitor its activities, establish regulations in relation to the functioning of the Registry after approval by Contracting States and would be assisted by a commission of experts nominated by Signatory and Contracting States. It would determine and periodically review the structure of fees for the Registry's services.

13.1 The Space Protocol: progress and outcomes

Pursuant to Resolution 1 of the diplomatic Conference for the adoption of the draft *Protocol to the Convention on International Interests in Mobile Equipment on Matters specific to Space Assets* (Berlin, 27 February–9 March 2012), a Preparatory Commission (1st Session, UNIDROIT Rome, 6–7 May 2013, 2nd Session, UNIDROIT Rome, 27–28 January 2014, 3rd Session, UNIDROIT Rome, 11–12 September 2014 and 4th Session, UNIDROIT Rome, 10–11 December 2015) was set up to act as Provisional Supervisory Authority for the establishment of the International Registry for Space Assets under the guidance of the UNIDROIT General Assembly.[110]

Draft implementation schedule:
- 2015: Completion of the Regulations for the International Registry for Space Assets/ Selection of the Registrar (Rome, 10–11 December 2015);
- 2016: Proposal for the selection of a Registrar, determination of the fees for use of the Registry facilities, establishment of a Commission of experts to assist the Commission in the discharge of its function;
- 2017: Taking the above achievement into account, the Preparatory Commission would act with full authority as Provisional Supervisory Authority for the establishment of the International Registry for Space Assets and would possibly be in a position to hand over responsibility to ITU in the 2017 timeframe subject to the entry into force of the Protocol (three months after the deposit of the tenth instrument of ratification, approval, accession) and provided that ITU officially notifies its decision to assume the role of Supervisory Authority.

---

110 UNIDROIT, "Space Preparatory Commission" (11 November 2015) online: www.unidroit.org/ work-in-progress-studies/current-studies/space-prepcom.

The ITU's role as Supervisory Authority of the future international registration system for Space Assets under the Space Protocol has been discussed since 2011 within the organization. In that regard, the 2014 session of the ITU PP agreed that "[the ITU] Council continue to monitor any further development on this matter, and that the Secretariat continue to express interest in ITU becoming the Supervisory Authority and respond to any questions raised by the Member States between now and the next Plenipotentiary Conference" noting that the matter of whether or not ITU could become the Supervisory Authority should not be prejudged at the current stage.[111]

14 Concluding thought

As has been previously articulated by one of this chapter's authors, "With a concerted effort, we can reduce, and to the extent possible remove, all obstacles impeding the development and bringing into operation of new satellite networks; we have to think carefully about how we can continue to use and improve satellite access to help connect the unconnected, and make the world a better and a fairer place for all."[112] This should be kept in mind as an objective for the ITU, lest the spirit of the endeavor be lost in highly technical regulations and procedures.

---

111 ITU, "Supervisory Authority of the future international registration system for Space Assets" online: www.itu.int/en/ITU-R/space/Pages/spaceAssets.aspx.
112 ITU, "Orbit/Spectrum International Regulatory Framework" online: www.itu.int/en/ITU-D/Regional-Presence/AsiaPacific/Documents/Events/2015/October-IISS-2015/Presentations/S1_Yvon_Henri.pdf.

8

Regulation of remote sensing by satellites

Sa'id Mosteshar

Preface

Two sets of rules apply to remote sensing for the management of disasters. They are the UN Remote Sensing Principles,[1] and the Disaster Charter.[2] The Remote Sensing Principles apply to all non-security related remote sensing of Earth from space. The Disaster Charter covers not only remote sensing but also other space-based services of use in disaster situations.

The Remote Sensing Principles were a culmination of many years of discussion and negotiation, finally coming to fruition in 1986. They aim to strike a balance between the interests of sensing States and those of sensed States. In its 2011 report,[3] UN COPUOS recognized the value of remote sensing in disaster management.

The Disaster Charter was founded by ESA and the French space agency, CNES, and formally began operating in November 2000. The Charter supports relief efforts and allows registered users to request and access free satellite data over stricken regions. In its first ten years, the Disaster Charter provided satellite data of more than 300 disaster events such as earthquakes, hurricanes, cyclones, floods and fires, spanning nearly 100 countries.[4]

There is a significant distinction between the Remote Sensing Principles and the Disaster Charter: States are parties to the Remote Sensing Principles, while members of the Disaster Charter are not States, but their space agencies and space system operators, including private entities.

---

1 *The Principles Relating to Remote Sensing of the Earth from Outer Space,* UN Doc A/RES/41/65 (1986) [Remote Sensing Principles].
2 *International Charter on Cooperation to Achieve the Coordinated Use of Space Facilities in the Event of Natural or Technological Disasters,* Rev. 3 (25/04/2000).2, online: Disaster Charter, www.disasterscharter.org/web/guest/text-of-the-charter;jsessionid=70D7B107F1EE93127D61DE129E41DA87.intlcharter-prod4040 [Disasters Charter].
3 *Contribution of the Committee on the Peaceful Uses of Outer Space to the United Nations Conference on Sustainable Development: harnessing space-derived geospatial data for sustainable development,* UN Doc A/AC.105/993 (2011).
4 "International Disaster Charter Celebrates 10th Anniversary" (20 October 2010) online: ESA, www.esa.int/About_Us/ESRIN/International_disaster_charter_celebrates_10th_anniversary.

The Remote Sensing Principles are contained in a UN General Assembly resolution passed and adopted by unanimous consent. They are effectively non-binding, but in practice are adhered to by all States. Indeed, in their remote sensing activities States can and often do exceed the requirements of the Principles. The Disaster Charter is one example of this.

The Disaster Charter is by contrast a cooperation agreement between its members. There are no dispute resolution provisions in the Disaster Charter, although its members are free to withdraw. This would not remove obligations on the States: requirements on States to cooperate also exist under the Outer Space Treaty (OST), particularly to address the interests of developing countries.

Although they are of different application and scope, both the Remote Sensing Principles and the Disaster Charter provide for access to remote sensing information in order to assist countries and communities in distress. This commonality raises the question of whether there is an obligation under international law to assist in such circumstances. Many countries have laws dealing with this type of obligation, commonly referred to as "good Samaritan" laws,[5] although generally they exclude man-made disasters created by wars, persecution and forms of violence. The Remote Sensing Principles and the Disaster Charter do not create obligations, but create mechanisms to provide information and other assistance.[6]

A potential impediment to making remote sensing data and information available under both the Remote Sensing Principles and the Disaster Charter may arise under other international obligations that need to be observed. An important one is the intellectual property right that may exist in the relevant data and information. At the international level, there is an international copyright convention[7] that invokes protection in each relevant jurisdiction. Within Europe there is a broader *sui generis* right in databases that may not qualify for copyright protection. This protection was created under a Commission Directive.[8] A further discussion of intellectual property rights in space may be found in Chapter 16.

Private operators of remote sensing systems may assert their copyright or database rights to control access to the relevant data. However, in practice these potential impediments may be over-ridden in the case of disaster. In addition, there is also a European Directive[9] that obliges public authorities to make environmental information systematically available for dissemination to the public, at a reasonable cost in all circumstances, not just disasters. The information that must be made available includes data on activities affecting the environment, environment impact studies and risk assessments, reports on the state of the environment and environmental authorizations and agreements. Although under the Directive the information needs to be made available within a month of a request, any information relating to imminent threats to

---

5   General obligations to assist are not addressed in this chapter.
6   Mere practice by States does not create international law. As noted in Article 38 (1)(b) of the Statute of the ICJ, practice *and* acceptance as law provide the basis for the formation of general international law.
7   Berne Convention for the Protection of Industrial Property, 9 September 1886, 828 UNTS 221. Since the ratification of the Berne Convention by the USA on 1 March 1989 following passage of Berne Convention Implementation Act of 1988, the Universal Copyright Convention was rendered virtually obsolete.
8   EC, European Parliament and the Council Directive 96/9/EC of 11 March 1996 on the legal protection of databases [1996] O.J. L 77/20. This followed a 1993 report from the author and others under the chairmanship of Professor Philippe Gaudrat.
9   EC, Council Directive 2003/4/EC of 28 January 2003 [2003] OJ, L 41/26, repealing EC, Council Directive 90/313/EEC of 7 June 1990 [1990] OJ, L 158.

human health or the environment must be immediately disseminated to the public likely to be affected.[10]

The following is a discussion of the legal regime and framework of the Remote Sensing Principles and the Disaster Charter.

UN Principles relating to remote sensing from outer space

Introduction

Remote sensing of the Earth from space[11] has been practiced since the 1960s, and differing views of the activity have developed among States.[12] Those States engaged in remote sensing held the view that acquisition and dissemination of information is consistent with and advances the achievement of significant international benefits. Others, particularly developing countries, took the view that the acquisition and dissemination of information about the territory and natural resources of a State constituted a violation of sovereignty, and that such activities should require prior consent of the sensed State.

It was in this context that the United Nations began to consider the international norms for the practice of remote sensing. A combination of the discussions and reports led to the *UN General Assembly Resolution on Remote Sensing Principles*.[13] The adoption of the Remote Sensing Principles by the General Assembly was a compromise between the two positions. It removed the restriction on the dissemination of data and information and it gave an advantage to developing countries.

As with other UN resolutions, the Remote Sensing Principles were adopted by consensus, recognizing the long established practice of remote sensing by States and international organizations. Adoption of the Remote Sensing Principles also amounts to acknowledgment that sensing does not violate the territorial sovereignty of the sensed State.[14] The disagreement between those advocating prior consent by the sensed State and those asserting the freedom of the use of outer space for remote sensing in accordance with Article I of the OST[15] seems definitively resolved in favor of the latter.[16] However, as noted below, the Principles recognize the sovereignty of States over their resources.[17] It should also be noted generally that many of the Remote Sensing Principles restate or elaborate existing international law articulated in the OST.[18]

---

10 Ray Harris; "Remote Sensing Policy" (2009), in Timothy A. Warner, Giles M. Foody and M. Duane Nellis,, eds, *The SAGE Handbook of Remote Sensing* (New York: SAGE Publications Ltd, 2009) at 18–29.
11 Hereinafter "Remote Sensing".
12 Carl Q. Christol, *The Modern International Law of Outer Space* (Oxford, Pergamon Press, 1982) at 720.
13 Remote Sensing Principles, *supra* note 1.
14 Christol, Carl Q., *Space Law: Past, Present, and Future* (Deventer: Kluwer Law and Taxation Publishers, 1991) at 297.
15 *Treaty on Principles Governing the Activities of States in the Exploration and Use of Outer Space, including the Moon and Other Celestial Bodies*, 27 January 1967, 610 UNTS 205 [OST].
16 Sergio Marchisio, "Remote Sensing for Sustainable Development in International Law" in: Gabriel Lafferranderie, and Daphné Crowther, eds, *Outlook on Space Law over the Next 30 Years* (The Hague: Kluwer International, 1997) p. 340.
17 Remote Sensing Principles, *supra* note 1, IV.
18 Alexander Soucek, "International Law" in Christian Brünner and Alexander Soucek, eds, *Outer Space in Society, Politics and Law: Studies in Space Policy* (Vienna: Springer-Verlag, 2011) at 369.

Those participating in remote sensing activities will in general observe best practices and international guidelines.[19] In relation to natural disasters, a separate international document has been established dealing specifically with cooperation and assistance in cases of natural disasters. This is the Disaster Charter, which refers directly to the Remote Sensing Principles and the provisions of Principle XI, which could be argued to support the recognition of the applicability of the Principles to natural disasters, at least by Charter Members.

Definitions

The Remote Sensing Principles define several relevant terms, and sets out regulations that arise in relation to different types of data and circumstances. The "remote sensing activities"[20] covered by the Remote Sensing Principles are not confined to the sensing of the Earth, but also include the "primary" and "processed" data and information obtained through remote sensing, their acquisition, storage and processing activities.

The purpose for which remote sensing is conducted further refines the application of the Remote Sensing Principles. To apply, the *"remote sensing"*[21] needs to be for the purpose of improving *natural resources management, land use* and the *protection of the environment*. It is arguable that the detection of resources, including minerals or water, is not subject to the Remote Sensing Principles. The limitation on purposes for which remote sensing is conducted are further elaborated below.

Further definitions relate to the distinction between primary, processed and analyzed information. Primary data gathered by remote sensing is not immediately useful or easily intelligible. It is raw data acquired by Remote Sensors borne by a space object, transmitted or delivered to the ground by telemetry in the form of electromagnetic signals, photographic film, magnetic tape or any other means.[22] It usually consists of a binary representation of the received radiation. As such, it needs to be made usable by processing, analysis and interpretation.

These definitions determine what can be done with the remote sensing product in various circumstances dealt with in the Remote Sensing Principles. For example, Principle XI deals with protection of mankind from natural disasters. It specifies an obligation arising for a State that identifies processed data and analyzed information in its possession, relating in specific ways to a State that might be affected by a disaster.

The term 'Earth Observation' is often used interchangeably with "remote sensing" to mean *observation by remote sensing techniques from satellites*. These activities provide detailed information for military and for civilian purposes.[23] Information arising from military remote sensing is not covered by the Principles, which effectively exclude military remote sensing.

The definition of remote sensing in the Principles is confined to that which uses sensors from space to detect electromagnetic radiation[24] only from the surface of the Earth. Thus, it does not cover other means of detecting Earth characteristics or resources. An example of a system not within this definition is NASA's Gravity Recovery and Climate Experiment

---

19 The guidelines of the World Metrological Organisation will be particularly relevant; Nicolas M. Matte, *Aerospace Law* (Toronto: Carswell, 1977), at 47–51.
20 Remote Sensing Principles, Principle I(e).
21 All emphasis in this Chapter has been added.
22 Defined in Remote Sensing Principles, Principle I(b).
23 Science Dictionary, *What is Earth Observation? Definition of Earth Observation*, online: Science Dictionary http://thesciencedictionary.org/earth-observation/. See also Sa'id Mosteshar *et al.*, *Evidence from Space* (London: London Institute of Space Policy and Law, 2012) at 295.
24 Remote Sensing Principles, *supra* note 1, I(a).

(GRACE)[25] that detects aquifers and other features. The system does use electromagnetic radiation to measure the distance between two satellites, but it does not carry out any sensing of the Earth's surface. Furthermore, the definition does not include sensing of planets other than the Earth.[26] Therefore, it does not apply to astronomical observation satellites like the Hubble Space Telescope or the Voyager missions.

The Principles were initially considered to apply only to remote sensing of the land surface. Since then "protection of the environment" has assumed a much wider meaning because of concerns about climate change.[27] The Remote Sensing Principles might therefore cover monitoring of climate change. However, the information needed for protection of the environment would not require Very High Resolution (VHR) data (better than about 10 m), so such data may fall outside the scope of the Principles.[28] The Remote Sensing Principles only relate to information sufficient to address protection of the environment, although States can create obligations that go beyond the Principles.

The definitions enunciated in Principle I further limit the application of the Remote Sensing Principles to three specific purposes. These are management of natural resources, land use and the protection of the environment. Reflecting security considerations and related concerns of States, the definitions operate to exclude their application to security-related remote sensing.[29] The application of the requirements of common benefit and interest and access to data[30] to security-sensitive data and information would be a difficult, if not impossible, task. It is also noteworthy that in relation to disasters, the UN requested Charter participants not to use VHR data in order to preserve the security and other crucial interests of the sensed States.

A further question arises in relation to *commercial* remote sensing. It may be argued that the Remote Sensing Principles apply only in cases where the commercial provider supplies the data or information for one of the three specified uses. On a strict interpretation of Principle I(a), commercial uses are not covered.[31]

Modern sensors record and transmit un-interpreted *primary data* (also known as *raw data*) in digital form that must be *processed* to become intelligible and capable of interpretation by experts. The data is then *analyzed* to provide usable *information*. To arrive at useful information, the analysis will often need to be combined with other knowledge in addition to the product of *processed data*. At each stage of the process the sensed data is further refined before it becomes information that is a useful product. As will be seen, different rules and obligations arise in relation to data at each of these stages. At each stage of the process, the question arises whether the data or information is covered by the Remote Sensing Principles.

---

25 *Gravity Recovery and Climate Experiment (GRACE)*, online: University of Texas www.csr.utexas.edu/grace/.
26 Soucek, *supra* note 17 at 367.
27 Harris, *supra* note 9 at 19.
28 Frans von der Dunk, "Legal aspects of using space-derived geospatial information for emergency response, with particular reference to the Charter on Space and Major Disasters" in *Geospatial Information Technology for Emergency Response* (2008), edited by Sisi Zlatanova and Jonathan Li. (London: Taylor & Francis, 2008) at 21–40 (also in *Space and Telecommunications Law Program Faculty Publications*, Paper 14, online: Digital Commons, http://digitalcommons.unl.edu/spacelaw/14 at 26.
29 Soucek, *supra* note 17 at 368.
30 Remote Sensing Principles, *supra* note 1, IV and XII.
31 Soucek, *supra* note 17 at 368.

The Principles

Principles II and III

Principles II and III align the conduct of remote sensing with other space activities, providing for the sharing of the benefits of remote sensing among States.[32] In particular, the Principles repeat the obligation stated in Article I of the OST to conduct space remote sensing activities "for the *benefit* and in the *interests* of all countries, irrespective of their degree of economic, social or scientific and technological development, and taking into particular consideration the needs of the developing countries", in relation to remote sensing activities.

Whether there is a distinction between *benefit* and *interests* may not have any practical impact. However, it may be that a *benefit* is more general and indirect, and that *interest* has a direct and more immediate impact on the subject country.[33]

The OST's Article I is also incorporated in Principle III, which uses the same terms as Article III of the OST. Therefore, for OST Parties, no additional requirement is imposed. Principle XII is also relevant to Article I of the OST, because remote sensing is a space activity and a use of space.

Principle IV

This Principle reiterates the application of international law to remote sensing activities.

Article I of the OST stipulates the free use of outer space "by all States without discrimination of any kind, on a basis of equality and in accordance with international law." To articulate the scope of the freedom of each State concerned in relation to remote sensing, Principle IV incorporates and determines the interests of all States,[34] and specifically refers to the sovereignty of each State over its wealth and natural resources.

Thus, the Principle both stipulates the *principle of freedom of exploration and use of outer space,* and respects the *sovereignty of all States and peoples over their own wealth and natural resources* by requiring remote sensing activities *not be conducted in a manner detrimental to the legitimate rights and interests of the sensed State*. This last provision can be argued to impose an obligation on a sensing State to disclose detection of mineral and other resources that may be exploited by the sensed State, preventing unfair advantage to be taken of the sensed State in any negotiation for rights to the resources.

Principles V and VI

These Principles address international cooperation and the manner in which they may take place.

The Remote Sensing Principles provide for equitable participation in remote sensing by other States. Data collection and storage facilities are to be shared under agreements between the parties involved. There are standards developed for the collection and storage of data, which ease the exchange and access to the data. A number of these are International Organization for

---

32   Michael S. Dodge, "Earth Observation and the Needs of the Many: the Future Structure of International Disaster Relief Law and Disaster Management" (2014) XXXIX Annals of Air and Space Law 355.
33   Brief private conversation between the author and Professor Bin Cheng, 20 May 2015.
34   See OST, *supra* note 14, Art I.

Standardization (ISO) standards dealing with collection, storage and dissemination of remote sensing data and information, introducing a level of uniformity and ease of access to remote sensing products.[35]

Principles VII and VIII

These Principles deal with cooperation and the assistance that may be given to other, particularly less advanced, States. The United Nations has played an active role in training personnel and providing assistance for the development of remote sensing technology.

Principle IX

This provision deals with the registration of remote sensing space objects, in accordance with Article IV of the Convention on Registration of Objects Launched into Outer Space[36] and Article XI of the OST, and to inform the Secretary-General of the United Nations State when carrying out a program of remote sensing. Additional information is to be given to the affected States.

Registration of space objects is the obligation of a Launching State.[37] This, together with the OST provisions[38] on supplying information to the Secretary-General and to the international scientific community and the public, are reiterated and incorporated in Principle IX. However, this Principle goes further than the previously existing obligations, by its extension providing States affected by the remote sensing program[39] *any other information* to the greatest extent feasible and practicable. For the latter obligation to arise there needs to be a request by the affected State.

A missing element here is any obligation to give prior notice to potentially affected States. This is not met by the provision to give information "*to the greatest extent feasible and practicable*". Even information that is to be given requires a request by the affected State. Article IX of the OST also does not create such an obligation, dealing as it does only with harmful interference that is not the subject of this Principle. The only obligation to give notification without the request of the sensed State arises in the case of averting harm to the Earth's natural environment or protecting mankind from a natural disaster.[40] Furthermore, there is no time specified within which the Secretary-General should be informed.

Principles X and XI

These Principles deal with disclosure of processed data and information useful to the protection both of the natural environment and to dealing with the consequences of changes

---

35   Wolfgang Kresse, "*Status of ISO Standards for Photogrammetry and Remote Sensing*" (2010) online: ISPRS www.isprs.org/proceedings/XXXVIII/Eurocow2010/euroCOW2010_files/papers/24.pdf. See generally "International Organization for Standardization" online: ISO, www.iso.org; and "International Society of Photogrammetry and Remote Sensing" online: ISPRS www.isprs.org.
36   *Convention on Registration of Objects Launched into Outer Space,* 14 January 1975, 1023 UNTS 15 [Registration Convention].
37   Ibid., arts II to IV.
38   OST, *supra* note 14, Art XI.
39   There is no definition of "*programme of remote sensing*", creating some uncertainty about the actions that trigger reporting under this Principle. It will be noted that *remote sensing activity* covers not only the operation of the relevant space system, but actions taken in relation to the data (Principle I(e)). It may therefore be assumed that a programme encompasses all remote sensing activities.
40   Remote Sensing Principles, *supra* note 1, X and XI.

in the environment. Data and information must be disclosed to States affected, or likely to be affected, by a natural disaster.

Principles X and XI are two sides of the same coin in the sense that Principle X protects the natural environment of the Earth through disclosure of information about possible harm to the environment, while Principle XI is aimed at protecting mankind from environmental events. Principle X, taken together with the requirement for international cooperation and the obligation to use outer space for the benefit and in the interests of all countries, makes it difficult for States and their private entities not to observe its provisions.[41]

It should be noted that while Principle X applies only to *information*, Principle XI extends to *processed data* and *analyzed information*. As a consequence the protection of mankind is given greater priority, requiring more and earlier information to be given to avert the effects of events potentially harmful to people. As will be seen later in this chapter, the Charter provides the institutional and structural framework to give effect to Principle XI.

On a literal interpretation of the purposes to be served by remote sensing, natural disasters do not fall within the definition of *remote sensing* in Principle I(a). The acquisition of data and information about natural disasters, and the act of saving lives, do not fall within the remit of improving the management of natural resources, nor do they improve land use as they do not relate to the utilization of land; furthermore they do not protect the environment.

The Principles make a distinction between the protection of the environment (Principle X) and the protection of mankind from natural disasters (Principle XI). Were one to interpret avoidance of the consequences of natural disasters as the protection of the environment, Principle XI may be argued to be redundant.

The inclusion of Principle XI also points to the need to interpret these Remote Sensing Principles more broadly than merely focusing on the literal definition of remote sensing in Principle I(a), but so as to give effect to the general intent of the Principles. This interpretation includes the totality of the Remote Sensing Principles, as well as the purpose disclosed in the Preamble.

Principle XII

This Principle is central to establishing the right to conduct remote sensing of other States without their consent. The requirement to provide access to data to the sensed State presupposes the right to obtain such data.

The policy underlying Principle XII is not that data would necessarily be available or free. Rather, it should be provided on a non-discriminatory basis. If data is not shared, the sensed State has no preferential right to it compared to others.[42] The sensed State does not have an automatic or greater right than other States to the data and information about its territory, but only a right to obtain the data and information *on the same terms as others* and at *reasonable cost*. It is, however notable that in determining the terms and costs at which data is provided, the sensing State is to take into account the needs and interests of developing countries.

In addition, in relation to analyzed information, it would appear that the sensed State may only claim such information in the hands of a sensing State, and not of a private entity for which the sensing State is internationally responsible.[43]

---

41   von der Dunk, *supra* note 27 at 21–40.
42   See for example Soucek, *supra* note 17 at 371.
43   von der Dunk, *supra* note 27 at 21–40.

Finally, it should be noted that many providers of remote sensing data and information distinguish between different types of users in their pricing structure. For example, they may charge a lower fee for those using the data for scientific or non-commercial purposes, as opposed to commercial users. Such pricing structures are not considered discriminatory.

Principles XIII and XIV

The promotion of cooperation and harmony among States and the observation of international law in the conduct of space activities are fundamental objectives of all space-related rules. Cooperation under Principle XIII would take place only at the request of the sensed State. There is no corresponding need to notify the sensed State. Although Principle IX provides for extensive information to be given to the sensed State, it too is dependent on a request from the sensed State, save in the two cases under Principles X and XI. Without prior notice that sensing is to take place, any participation by the sensed State may therefore only occur after the program has been launched.

Nevertheless, in the right circumstances, sensed States can and do request consultation on the terms under which they can participate in the remote sensing activities. This often occurs through the establishment of data receiving and processing capabilities in the sensed State.[44] Note also that bodies such as the Group on Earth Observation (GEO) assist in the development of policies and means for data sharing.[45]

In its essential provisions, Principle XIV paraphrases the OST Article VI to apply to remote sensing activities. It extends State responsibility to remote sensing activities conducted by the State, its private entities or international organizations in which it participates. The thrust of this Principle is to extend responsibility for compliance with the Principles, and for remote sensing activities such as data processing that may not be regarded as space activities, to the State.

Principle XV

The aim of Principle XV is to provide for peaceful resolution of disputes relating to compliance with the Remote Sensing Principles in conducting remote sensing activities.

Its scope extends not only to the interpretation and implementation of the Principles, but to disputes relating to any remote sensing activity as defined by the Principles.

International Disasters Charter[46]

Introduction

Growing appreciation of the usefulness and availability of Earth observation information in early warnings and managing the impact of disasters brought about the establishment of the International Disaster Charter ("Disaster Charter").

44　See, for example, Group on Earth Observation (GEO) and its system of systems (GEOSS), online: Earth Observations, www.earthobservations.org.

45　Group on Earth Observations, "Report on Data Sharing Principles Post-2015 and Mechanisms to Ensure Legal Interoperability of Data Shared Through GEOSS"; online: Earth Observations, www.earthobservations.org/documents/geo_xi/GEO-XI_08_Report%20on%20Data%20Sharing%20Principles%20Post-2015%20and%20Mechanisms%20to%20Ensure%20Legal%20Interoperability%20of%20Shared%20Data.pdf.

46　Disasters Charter, *supra* note 2.

The Disaster Charter, which currently has 16 members,[47] has two main objectives:[48]

- Supply during periods of crisis,[49] to States and communities whose population, activities or property are exposed to an imminent risk, or are already victims, of natural or technological disasters, data providing a basis for critical information for the anticipation and management of potential crises; and
- Participation, by means of this data and of the information and services resulting from the exploitation of space facilities, in the organization of emergency assistance or reconstruction and subsequent operations.

The development of the Disaster Charter followed UNISPACE III,[50] at which Earth observation was a major topic of discussion. Its Report of Resolutions[51] of the meeting includes:

1. *Declare* the following as the nucleus of a strategy to address global challenges in the future:
   (a) ….
   (b) Using space applications for human security, development and welfare: action should be taken:
      (i) ….
      (ii) To implement an integrated, global system, especially through international cooperation, to manage natural disaster mitigation, relief and prevention efforts, especially of an international nature, through Earth observation, communications and other space-based services, making maximum use of existing capabilities and filling gaps in worldwide satellite coverage.

The Disaster Charter is a tangible and practical implementation of the aspirations and strategy embodied in this declaration. It promotes the cooperative use of facilities by space agencies and system operators to provide data and other services during emergency operations.[52] To achieve

---

47   The Membership of the Charter comprises the following space agencies and their associated operators: ESA, CNES (France), Agencia Bolivariana para Actividades Espaciales (ABAE), Airbus Defense and Space GEO-Information Services (France), National Space Organization (NSPO, Taiwan), Canadian Space Agency (CSA), Indian Space Research Organization (ISRO), National Oceanic and Atmospheric Administration (NOAA, USA), Argentina's Comisión Nacional de Actividades Espaciales (CONAE), Japan Aerospace Exploration Agency (JAXA), United States Geological Survey (USGS), Digital Globe, GeoEye, UK Space Agency (UK), DMC International Imaging (DMCii), Centre National des Techniques Spatiales (Algeria), National Space Research and Development (Nigeria), Tübitak-BILTEN (Turkey), China National Space Administration (CNSA), German Aerospace Center (DLR), Korea Aerospace Research Institute (KARI), National Institute For Space Research (INPE, Brazil), European Organization for the Exploitation of Meteorological Satellites (EUMETSAT), The Russian Federal Space Agency (Roscosmos).
48   Harris, *supra* note 9 at 20.
49   The term "*crisis*" means the period immediately before, during or immediately after a natural or technological disaster, in the course of which warning, emergency or rescue operations take place.
50   UNISPACE III, held in Vienna, 19–30 July 1999.
51   *Report of the Third United Nations Conference on the Exploration and Peaceful Uses of Outer Space*, Resolution 1, UN Doc A/CONF.184/6 (18 October 1999); online: UNOOSA, www.unoosa.org/pdf/sap/hsti/UNISPACE_report.pdf.
52   Joanne Irene Gabrynowicz, "*Charter on Cooperation to Achieve the Coordinated Use of Space Facilities in the Event of Natural or Technological Disasters*" (Presentation delivered at the Woodrow Wilson International Center, Washington DC, 30 November 2012).

its aims, it provides the mechanism for requests to Charter Members for the supply of relevant data, information and other services to States or communities influenced or threatened by natural or technological disasters, as well as a unified system for the acquisition and delivery of the data.

Its focus is clearly that of enhancing the protection and betterment of the life of mankind. The intent of the Disaster Charter is to provide a combination of services that include remote sensing, but it is not confined to that service alone. The organizational structure for data requests and delivery provides a means of ensuring that any data and information supplied will be used for an appropriate purpose.[53]

Its Preamble includes a reference to the Remote Sensing Principles, with the implication that they are to be observed in the activities under the Disaster Charter.[54]

As has been noted, on a strict reading, the Remote Sensing Principles do not apply to their use for the protection of mankind.[55] It may, however, be relevant that since the adoption of the Principles, remote sensing activities are regarded as having "become a universe of their own. The Principles are the common political understanding that such activities shall be for the benefit of all, to the greatest extent possible."[56]

Purpose and terms of the Charter

It is important to remember that members of the Charter are not States – they are space agencies, or national or international space system operators with access to space facilities [Art VI], whereas States are the subjects of the UN Principles. It should be noted that the space facilities to be accessed are not confined to remote sensing, but also include other space systems providing meteorology, positioning, telecommunications and TV broadcasting, receiving equipment including VSATs and archives [Art I].

Charter Members are of course bound by any other international agreements to which they are party, including those relating to intellectual property and liability. However, the Disaster Charter provides for waiver of the liability of satellite operators who provide data under the Disaster Charter.

The disasters covered by the Charter are any natural or unintended man-made events that

---

53 von der Dunk, *supra* note 27 at 21–40.
54 RECOGNISING the potential applications of space technologies in the management of disasters caused by natural phenomena or technological accidents, and in particular Earth observation, telecommunications, meteorology and positioning technologies;
RECOGNISING the development of initiatives concerning the use of space facilities for managing natural or technological disasters;
RECOGNISING the interest shown by rescue and civil protection, defence and security bodies and the need to respond to that interest by making space facilities more easily accessible;
DESIROUS to strengthen international cooperation in this humanitarian undertaking;
HAVING REGARD to United Nations Resolution 41/65 of 1986 on remote sensing of the Earth from space;
BELIEVING that by combining their resources and efforts, they can improve the use of available space facilities and increase the efficiency of services that may be provided to crisis victims and to the bodies called upon to help them.
55 Remote Sensing Principles, *supra* note 1, Section 2 Definitions.
56 Soucek, *supra* note 17 at 373.

cause loss of life or widespread property damage.[57] The period during which the relevant services are to be provided spans from immediately before the event occurs to immediately after the event, although *immediately* is undefined in the Charter.

The space data provided is the data detected by a space system to which a Charter party has access, including the processed information that has been prepared for the management of crises. At the time of writing, the Disaster Charter had been activated to respond to hundreds of crises.[58]

Mechanisms to activate the Charter

There are several mechanisms for a user organization to submit a request to activate the Charter.[59] They include direct activation by a pre-defined list of appointed users, known as 'Authorized Users' (AUs), that can submit a request for a disaster occurring in their country. These are the only bodies that can directly request the Disaster Charter activation (typically civil protection agencies, governmental relief organizations, or other authorities with a mandate related to disaster management).

Activation can also be requested by an Authorized User on behalf of a user from a non-member country ('sponsor Authorized User') to request support for a disaster in a country with which they cooperate for relief purposes.

The Charter has an agreement with UN OOSA[60] (Vienna) and UNITAR/UNOSAT[61] (Geneva) to provide support to UN agencies. UN OOSA and UNITAR/UNOSAT may submit requests on behalf of users from the UN.

The move to expand access to the Charter continues, particularly under the measures to provide universal access, adopted by Charter Members. This would benefit disaster management agencies in countries not previously able to access the Charter, subject to the appropriate procedures that are clearly articulated by the Charter.[62] Activation for Asia Pacific users is via Sentinel Asia's partner, the Asian Disaster Reduction Centre. Sentinel Asia is a regional collaboration for Earth observation based emergency response in 31 Asia Pacific countries. The arrangement with Sentinel Asia is limited to Earth observation and does not extend to all *space facilities* of Disaster Charter Members.

---

57   The term "natural or technological disaster" means a situation of great distress involving loss of human life or large-scale damage to property, caused by a natural phenomenon, such as a cyclone, tornado, earthquake, volcanic eruption, flood or forest fire, or by a technological accident, such as pollution by hydrocarbons, toxic or radioactive substances. A disaster has also been defined as "a sudden, calamitous event that seriously disrupts the functioning of a community or society and causes human, material and economic or environmental losses that exceed the community's or society's ability to cope using its own resources"; "International Federation of Red Cross and Red Crescent Societies" online: IFRC, www.ifrc.org/en/what-we-do/disaster-management/about-disasters/what-is-a-disaster/. Article I.
58   "Charter Activations" online: Disasters Charter, www.disasterscharter.org/web/guest/activations/charter-activations.
59   For the procedures and a full account of the manner in which the Charter can be activated see, "Activating the Charter" online: Disasters Charter, www.disasterscharter.org/web/guest/activating-the-charter#mechanisms.
60   UN Office of Outer Space Affairs, located in Vienna.
61   UNOSAT is the United Nations Institute for Training and Research (UNITAR) Operational Satellite Applications Programme.
62   "The International Charter "Space and Major Disasters' Implementing Universal Access" online: Disasters Charter, www.disasterscharter.org/documents/10180/13699/CharterUniversalAccess BrochureEnglish.pdf/59f36812-1f3f-47b1-982e-5972f6dce352?version=1.0.

The scope of the Disaster Charter is being expanded, with the first move being to improve access to the Disaster Charter during emergencies, to the Group on Earth Observation (GEO). In 2009, the Charter initiated a formal user consultation to address the improvement of Charter access in African countries.

The terms used in the Disaster Charter are defined in Article 1, some by reference to other Articles.

> The term "*space data*" means raw data gathered by a space system controlled by one of the parties, or to which that party has access, and transmitted or conveyed to a ground receiving station;
> The term "*information*" means data that have been corrected and processed by the parties using an analysis program, in preparation for use in crisis management by one or more associated bodies in aid of the beneficiaries; it forms the basis for the extraction of specific products for use on location;
> The term "*space facilities*" means space systems for observation, meteorology, positioning, telecommunications and TV broadcasting or elements thereof such as on-board instruments, terminals, beacons, receivers, VSATs and archives;
> The term "*parties*" means the agencies and space system operators that are signatories to the Charter;
> The term "*associated bodies*" means the rescue and civil protection, defense and security bodies or other services referred to in Articles 5.2 and 5.3;
> The term "*cooperating bodies*" refers collectively to the various bodies and institutions, referred to in Article 3.5 of the Charter, with which the parties cooperate;
> The term "*crisis victims*" means any State or community for whose benefit the intervention of the parties is sought by the associated bodies;
> The term "*beneficiary bodies*" means all the bodies benefiting from information intended for crisis management; for example, the authorities and bodies concerned in countries affected by a disaster. Certain associated bodies may also be beneficiaries at the time of a disaster.

Purpose and operation of the Charter

The Disaster Charter provides the framework for cooperation among space agencies and space system operators for the use of space capabilities, to assist States and communities to avoid, minimize or manage the consequences of disasters. However, the Disaster Charter cannot be activated for slow-onset disasters like droughts.[63]

There is a well-defined process by which countries affected by disaster can request the assistance of the Charter's members. A Board, with an executive Secretariat that is responsible for its implementation, administers the Charter. A request for assistance can be made directly to the Secretariat, or through a number of other channels.[64] Once a request is made, the providing entity will obtain the relevant information and analyze it, then disseminate it free of charge via an "associated body".[65]

---

63 "UN-SPIDER International Charter on Space and Major Disasters" online: UNSPIDER http://UN-SPIDER.org/space-application/emergency-mechanisms/international-charter-space-and-major-disasters. See also Dodge, *supra* note 31.
64 Disasters Charter, *supra* note 2, Art III.
65 Disasters Charter, *supra* note 2, Art V(2).

It is possible, and is often the case that the information provided is not directly used by the agency requesting it, but may be used by others providing assistance such as relief organizations. A strength of the Charter is its mechanism to provide coordination among those who respond to a call for assistance.[66] There is also the option for an Authorized User to gain access to the Charter under expanding universal access arrangements.

Purpose of the Charter and organization of cooperation

The Disaster Charter is intended to advance cooperation between space agencies to share their space facilities for the management of crises arising from natural or technological causes during periods of crisis, to States or communities whose population, activities or property are exposed to an imminent risk, or are already victims, of natural or technological disasters, data providing a basis for critical information for the anticipation and management of potential crises.

Whereas the Remote Sensing Principles deal only with Earth observation, the Disaster Charter extends to all "space facilities" of cooperating parties to the Disaster Charter, including Earth observation, communication and other space systems.[67]

Overall organization of cooperation

The parties to the Disaster Charter cooperate voluntarily, without any funds being exchanged between them.[68] Its membership is open to space agencies and national or international space system operators wishing to cooperate in it.[69]

Article IV – contributions by the parties

For the Disaster Charter to be of effective assistance to countries in crisis and to the Secretariat responsible for its implementation, there must be clear description of space assets and the areas and extent of the coverage they can provide. Article IV provides not only for this to occur, but also for the participating parties to learn from experience, as well as to anticipate circumstances in which their capabilities can be deployed, and the manner in which this should occur.

Once the Secretariat has been notified of a crisis, it will be in a position to plan the appropriate responses and to identify the parties that can assist, based on the capabilities of the parties and the scenarios developed in anticipation of future crises.

Scenario-writing [Article 4.2] is an important aspect of the operation of the Disaster Charter. It allows Charter Members to examine situations that may arise and to develop optimum responses to meet the circumstances. The writing of the scenario is intended to help shorten the time within which a response can be made, and to ensure the deployment of the most appropriate systems.

The remainder of Article IV addresses identification of a crisis situation, planning space facility availability and providing assistance with regard to planning and organizational arrangements.

---

66   Jenny R. Hernandez and Anne D. Johnson, "A Call to Respond: the International Community's Obligation to Mitigate the Impact of Natural Disasters" (2001) 25 Emory International Law Review 1087 at 1092.
67   Disaster Charter, Art II.
68   Disaster Charter, Art 3.1.
69   Ibid., Art 3.2 and IV.

Article V – associated bodies

Assistance under the Disaster Charter can be requested by a host of public authorities of the State affected by a disaster. The request can be addressed to the Charter Member space agency, or to any body with responsibility for rescue and civil protection of the State whose space agency is a Charter Member. The request may also be addressed to such bodies of a State that is a member of an international organization, such as ESA, where that organization is a Charter Member.

Article V also gives effect to an underlying principle of the cooperation arrangement, namely that there is to be no payment made by any party to another. It also requires that there be an undertaking by any associated body to take no legal action against the parties in the event of injury, damage or financial loss.

The waiver of liability provided under the Charter [Article 5.4] is further strengthened by the fact that Charter Members are only required to use their "best efforts" to provide information,[70] and are not responsible for ensuring a successful outcome.

Article VI – accession

The Disaster Charter recognizes the advantage of bringing to bear the widest range of services and capabilities when dealing with disasters. This philosophy is embodied in the Disaster Charter's provision encouraging and providing the mechanism for participation by all space agencies and space system operators. In permitting applicants to attain member status, it is important that they make a positive contribution to the capacity and capabilities for intervening in crisis situations, and that they should be prepared to make the voluntary commitments central to the Disaster Charter as articulated in Article 6.2.

Article VII – entry into force, expiry and withdrawal

The Disaster Charter runs for automatically renewable periods of five years, although Members can withdraw by notice to the other parties. This allows for periodic consideration of the Disaster Charter's terms, and encourages greater membership.

Article VIII – implementation

The implementation of the Charter includes arrangements for receiving and responding to calls for assistance. Delegating this task to the Board ensures that the workings of the Charter remain flexible, and that they can be adjusted to accommodate changing circumstances and technology development.

National implementation

There are considerable differences among States' approaches to remote sensing regulation, depending on their perceived needs for security, access to information and other factors.

---

70   Disasters Charter, *supra* note 2, Art 4.1. The phrase used is "best endeavours".

Previous research on the topic has identified data resolution and user identity as important concerns.[71]

Growing availability and awareness of the utility of remote sensing information, as well as a general desire to regulate information and its flow has resulted in an increasing number of States introducing and reviewing their relevant laws.

Given the excellent work already done on this topic,[72] it suffices to say here that in legislating remote sensing and its use, States need to consider carefully how they define the relevant concepts and the scope of the activities covered, to ensure proper effect is given to their policies.

Conclusion

More than half of the Remote Sensing Principles[73] repeat or elaborate the rules contained in the OST, or are reminders of general principles of international conduct.[74] However, the application of the Remote Sensing Principles to the protection of the environment and of mankind clearly recognizes long practice, and is one of the most valuable contributions of space activities to the well-being of the Earth and its inhabitants.

Although the UN Remote Sensing Principles and the Disaster Charter are of different origin, and their binding effects are distinct, they do have an important relationship. Much of the civilian remote sensing activity worldwide is focused on the growing concern about climate change and amelioration of the impact of disasters on communities around the world. On a strict view, these are not covered by the Remote Sensing Principles. Nevertheless, participants in remote sensing increasingly tend to share data and information, and this sharing may be crucial in dealing with disasters and climate change.

National policies and laws increasingly encourage private commercial application of space activities, with remote sensing receiving particular attention. These laws tend to regulate the acquisition and dissemination of security-sensitive data and information. New and improving sensors and data analysis techniques are increasing the number of remote sensing operators and cooperation among them. National regulation of remote sensing should enable full advantage to be taken of the potential benefits, while permitting the widest scope for cooperation and sharing of information.

---

71 Joanne I. Gabrynowicz, "The Land Remote Sensing Laws and Policies of National Governments: A Global Survey" (2007) Report Prepared for the US Department of Commerce and National Oceanic and Atmospheric Administration, online: The National Center for Remote Sensing, Air and Space Law; www.spacelaw.olemiss.edu/resources/pdfs/noaa.pdf. See also International Law Association, "Legal Aspects of the Privatisation and Commercialisation of Space Activities: Remote Sensing and National Space Legislation" (2006) online: ILA, https:// www.ila-hq.org.
72 Ibid.
73 Remote Sensing Principles, *supra* note 1.
74 Soucek, *supra* note 17 at 369.

9

Regulation of global navigation satellite systems

Michael Chatzipanagiotis and Konstantina Liperi

9 Introduction

Global Navigation Satellite Systems (GNSS) and their applications become increasingly important for a wide range of everyday activities. Satellite navigation infrastructure is constantly being developed and anticipated to increase considerably in the near future. This chapter provides an overview of the relevant regulatory issues.

9.1 Technical overview

9.1.1 Definition and applications

GNSS can be defined as space-based systems designed to transmit signals in order to provide three main services: Position, Navigation, and Timing (PNT).[1] GNSS consist of three main segments: the space, the ground and the user segment.

The space segment is comprised of a group of satellites (constellation) placed in Medium Earth Orbits (MEO). The satellites constantly emit positioning information, *ephemeris*,[2] in a rigorously synchronous time. Satellites are equipped with identical atomic clocks, which are extremely precise and provide Coordinated Universal Time (UTC).

Anyone with an appropriate receiver can receive the satellite signals along with a time signal. In order for the user to pinpoint its exact location, the receiver has to simultaneously receive broadcasts from at least four navigation satellites. The receiver can then compute its own location, altitude speed and direction, by calculating the time taken by the signal to travel from the satellites to the receiver.[3]

In order to operate properly, the system needs terrestrial uplink stations and control centers. The ground segment, *inter alia*, monitors and controls the satellites, ensures the health of its

---

1 The Royal Academy of Engineering, *Global Navigation Space Systems: Reliance and Vulnerabilities*, (London: The Royal Academy of Engineering, 2011) at 10, online www.raeng.org.uk/publications/reports/global-navigation-space-systems [all websites last visited on 17 Aug. 2016).
2 See ssd.jpl.nasa.gov/?glossary&term=ephemeris.
3 See gps.about.com/od/glossary/g/trilateration.htm.

components, makes clock corrections, synchronizes time across the constellation and resolves satellites' anomalies. The ground stations' main task is to safeguard the system's accuracy by taking precise measurements of the navigation signals. In order to achieve this, a worldwide network of GNSS ground stations is needed.

The majority of GNSS systems are dual use: military and civil.

As to civil applications, GNSS is used for a wide range of applications. Transport by all means is extensively dependent on GNSS services. GNSS applications are also increasingly used in agriculture and fisheries, energy management, and surveying. Moreover, GNSS can be used to monitor the surface of the Earth, contributing to the prediction of natural disasters. Noteworthy is also the operational CORPAS-SARSAT system[4] for Search and Rescue (SAR). GNSS satellites will host SAR payloads, to improve the performance of CORSPAS-SARSAT by including SAR capability into MEO (MEOSAR).[5]

9.1.2 Core-constellation systems and augmentation systems

A core-constellation system along with the receivers constitutes the basic GNSS. The augmentation systems improve the GNSS performances, by providing higher accuracy, availability, integrity and reliability.

9.1.2.1 Core-constellation systems

Global core-constellation systems are the U.S. NAVSTAR *Global Positioning System* (GPS) and the Russian *GLONASS*, which are currently operational. Under development are the European Union's *Galileo* and the Chinese *Beidou 2 – COMPASS*. Furthermore, there is the *Indian Regional Navigation Satellite System* (IRNSS), a regional system.

GPS was developed initially for military purposes. In 1994, the US sent a letter to the International Civil Aviation Organization (ICAO) and the International Maritime Organization (IMO) offering the GPS signals for the use of international aviation.[6] GPS became fully operational in 1995. It includes at least 24 operational GPS satellites, in six orbital planes, which fly in MEO at an altitude of approximately 20 200 km. GPS PNT services are available to all, continuously and free of charge.[7]

The Russian GLONASS, fully operational since 1995, offers also signals to ICAO free of charge. In May 2007, President Putin announced open access to GLONASS signals for civil, free and unlimited use.[8] GLONASS comprises 24 Glonass – M satellites deployed in three circular orbital planes.[9]

The European GALILEO is an initiative launched by the European Commission (EC) and the European Space Agency (ESA) and will be owned by the European Union (EU). Once

---

4   CORPAS-SARSAT System is a satellite-based search and rescue system in Low Earth Orbit (LEO), which detects and locates distress signals. It is not a GNSS service itself. See www.cospas-sarsat.int/en/system-overview/cospas-sarsat-system.
5   See www.cospas-sarsat.int/en/2-uncategorised/177-meosar-system.
6   See the letter at www.gps.gov/policy/cooperation/icao/1994-service-commitment.pdf.
7   See UNIDROIT Secretariat, An Instrument on Third Party Liability for Global Navigation Satellite System (GNSS) Services: a Preliminary Study, March 2010, p. 4, available at www.unidroit.org/english/documents/2010/study79/s-79-preliminarystudy-e.pdf [UNIDROIT Study].
8   See UNIDROIT Study, *supra* note 7, at p. 5.
9   www.navipedia.net/index.php/GLONASS_General_Introduction.

fully operational, it will comprise 30 satellites in three orbital planes, under civilian control. Five key services will be offered: open, safety of life, commercial, public regulated and SAR service.[10] The open service will be interoperable with the GPS and GLONASS civil signal.[11]

Beidou 2 – COMPASS is China's GNSS. In accordance with Beidou 2 – COMPASS system's construction plan, the initial satellite navigation system will provide coverage in the Asia-Pacific region and global coverage around 2020. It contains five geostationary orbit (GEO) satellites and 30 non-GEO satellites and will offer an open and an authorized service.[12]

The Indian Regional Navigation Satellite System is a regional system consisting of seven satellites, some of which will be placed in GEO. It will provide an open service and an encrypted service, restricted to authorized users.[13]

9.1.2.2 Augmentation systems

Core-constellation systems do not meet the necessary performance requirements for high-performance applications, like precision approaches of aircraft and dock maneuvering of ships.[14] Therefore, augmentation systems have been developed to advance the services provided by the core constellations systems.

The US has developed the Wide Area Augmentation System (WAAS), to permit aircraft to rely on GPS through all phases of flight. WAAS consists of a space segment comprising three GEO satellites and a ground segment.[15]

Russia is developing the *System for Differential Corrections and Monitoring* (SDCM) which will augment both GPS and GLONASS. SDCM space segment will be comprised of three GEO satellites plus one spare satellite.[16]

The European Geostationary Navigation Overlay Service (EGNOS) has been operational since 2009. It augments GPS signals in Europe and will augment Galileo's signals when the latter becomes operational. It consists of three GEO satellites and a number of ground stations.[17]

Japan has created the MTSAT[18] Satellite Based Augmentation System (MSAS), to augment GPS signals and provide coverage for the hemisphere centered on 140°, which includes Japan and Australia.[19] It consists of two GEO satellites and network of ground stations. In addition, Japan is developing the *Quasi Zenith Satellite System* (QZSS), a regional SBAS system consisting of three satellites in periodic Highly Elliptical Orbit (HEO), so that one satellite always appears near the

---

10 See art.2 of the Regulation (EC) No. 876/2002 and Regulation (EC) No. 683/2008.
11 See www.unoosa.org/oosa/en/ourwork/icg/providers-forum/principles.html.
12 See http://en.beidou.gov.cn/introduction.html.
13 See www.isro.gov.in/irnss-programme.
14 These requirements include: *accuracy*, i.e. the difference between estimated and actual GNSS-user position; *integrity*, i.e. the measure of trust that can be placed in the correctness of the information supplied by the total system, including the ability of the system to alert the user when the system should not be used for the intended operation; *continuity*, i.e. the capability of the system to perform its function without unscheduled interruptions during the intended operation; *availability*, i.e. the time during which the system is simultaneously delivering the required accuracy, integrity and continuity. See ICAO, *Global Navigation Satellite System (GNSS) Manual*, 1st ed, ICAO Doc 9849/AN/457 (Montreal: ICAO, 2005), para 4.2 [*ICAO GNSS Manual*].
15 See www.faa.gov/about/office_org/headquarters_offices/ato/service_units/techops/navservices/gnss/waas/.
16 See www.sdcm.ru/index_eng.html.
17 See http://egnos-portal.gsa.europa.eu/discover-egnos/programme-information.
18 = Multi-functional Transport Satellite.
19 See www.navipedia.net/index.php/MSAS_Architecture.

zenith above Japan. It enhances GPS availability and performance over Japan and Oceania.[20]

The Indian *GPS Aided GEO Augmented Navigation system* (GAGAN) has been jointly developed by the Indian Space Research Organization (ISRO) and the Airports Authority of India (AAI). It consists of three Geostationary Navigation Payloads and a network of ground stations. The Indian Directorate General of Civil Aviation has certified GAGAN for use in aviation.[21]

9.1.3 International cooperation on GNSS

The increasing importance and use of GNSS in many domains has necessitated international cooperation, which has taken two forms: the establishment of the International Committee on GNSS, and the conclusion of bilateral agreements on interoperability and compatibility.

9.1.3.1 International Committee on GNSS

The International Committee on GNSS (ICG) was established by the United Nations (UN) General Assembly Resolution 61/111 of 14 December 2006.[22] The ICG is an informal body, founded on a voluntary basis. Its mission is to enhance cooperation in space-based PNT services for the benefit of particularly developing nations. It promotes interoperability, compatibility and transparency between the providers of the different global, regional, and augmentation navigation satellite systems.

All countries or entities that are either GNSS providers or users of GNSS services are eligible to participate. ICG's Providers Forum serves for coordination and cooperation to improve overall service provision between countries operating GNSS systems or with plans to develop one. ICG's work plan addresses, through special working groups, various aspects of GNSS.[23]

9.1.3.2 Bilateral agreements

GNSS constellations are most effective, when they can be used in combination with each other. To that effect, States operating core constellations have concluded bilateral agreements on interoperability and compatibility.

Compatibility is the ability of space-based PNT services to be used either independently or together, without causing any interference to each separate service or signal and without affecting national security.[24] Interoperability is the ability to use combined services from different systems, to benefit from improved capabilities.[25]

To achieve compatibility and interoperability, coordination is crucial. Hence, satellite navigation service-providers conclude bilateral agreements, as this appears to be the optimal way to eliminate disclosure of classified information.[26]

20   See http://qzss.go.jp/en/overview/services/sv01_what.html.
21   See www.navipedia.net/index.php/GAGAN.
22   *International Cooperation in the Peaceful Uses of Outer Space*, GA Res 61/111, UNGAOR, 2006, UN Doc A/RES/61/111.
23   See www.unoosa.org/oosa/en/ourwork/icg/working-groups.html.
24   UNOOSA, *Current and Planned Global and Regional Navigation Satellite Systems and Satellite-based Augmentations Systems of the International Committee on Global Navigation Satellite Systems Provider's Forum* (New York: UN, 2010) at 31, www.unoosa.org/pdf/publications/icg_ebook.pdf.
25   Ibid.
26   Stephan Kaiser, "Satellite Navigation Systems: The Impact of Interoperability" (2012) XXXVII Ann Air &Sp L 1 at 15.

The US has concluded bilateral arrangements ("Joint Statements"), which encourage cooperation and address issues of compatibility and interoperability between GPS and other systems. The US has concluded Joint Statements with Australia, China, Europe, India, Japan, and Russia.[27]

The EU and its Member States have concluded agreements with China, Israel, India, Ukraine, Morocco, Korea, Norway, and Switzerland. These agreements not only address issues of interoperability and compatibility, but also encourage scientific research and trade. In 2004, the EU signed a historic agreement with the US establishing cooperation between GPS and Galileo.[28]

9.2 Cross-sector international rules applicable to GNSS

9.2.1 Space law

GNSS satellites, being objects launched in outer space, trigger the applicability of the international space legislation. However, the rapid technological advances and the massive use of outer space give rise to several legal considerations.

9.2.1.1 Authorization and supervision

The Outer Space Treaty (OST)[29] applies to activities undertaken in the "exploration and use of outer space".[30] Article VI of OST establishes the international responsibility of the States Parties for national activities in outer space, undertaken both by governmental and non-governmental entities, and for authorizing and continuously supervising such activities.[31] The same article applies also to international organizations conducting such activities as well as their Member States, which are Parties to the OST.[32] The latter provision covers Galileo and EGNOS owned by the EU. Therefore, in case of damage occurring as a result of GNSS activities, the OST holds responsible the State or the international organization involved.

9.2.1.2 Liability

As to liability, Article VII OST provides that a State Party is internationally liable for damage *caused by a space object or its components parts, launched into the outer space*.[33] Article VII along with Article VI OST aim to ensure that States are both responsible and liable with respect to damage resulting out of their national activities.[34] Article VII OST can be considered a generic rule (*lex*

---

27 See www.gps.gov/policy/cooperation/. Yet, since April 2014, the US-Russia cooperation is on hold.
28 *Agreement on the Promotion, Provision and Use of GALILEO and GPS Satellite-Based Navigation Systems and Related Applications*, 26 June 2004, www.gps.gov/policy/cooperation/europe/2004/gps-galileo-agreement.pdf.
29 *Treaty on Principles Governing the Activities of States in the Exploration and Use of Outer Space, Including the Moon and other Celestial Bodies*, 27 January 1967, 610 UNTS 205 [OST].
30 Ibid., art XIII.
31 Ibid., art VI.
32 Ibid.
33 See Ibid., art VII.
34 Armel Kerrest & Lesley Jane Smith, in Stephan Hobe *et al.*, eds, *Cologne Commentary on Space Law* (Cologne: Heymanns, 2009) vol 1, Article VII OST, para 2.

generalis), which has been elaborated by the Liability Convention (LC).[35]

The LC provides a twofold liability scheme based on the location and the type of damage. *Strict liability* applies to a launching State for damage caused by its space object on the surface of the Earth or to an aircraft in flight (Art. II). In cases of damage caused by a space object, elsewhere than on the surface of the Earth, to a space object of another launching State or to persons or property on board, the liability is limited to cases of *fault* (Art. III).

In both cases of liability, the damage has to be caused by a space object launched by the State against whom the claim is brought. The question in relation to GNSS is whether the LC applies when damage is caused by a satellite signal.[36] In order to answer this question, "space object" and "damage" should be defined.

The LC does not define "space object". Art. I clarifies that the term "includes component parts of a space object as well as its launch vehicle and parts thereof". It is unclear whether intangible parts of a space object, such as signals, are included. Similarly, there is an ambiguity regarding the definition of damage, which Art. I LC defines as "loss of life, personal injury or other impairment of health; or loss of or damage to property". This definition leaves open the question whether the LC covers damage caused not by physical contact with the space object.[37]

There is no consensus as to what types of damage are covered by the LC. Some authors suggest that the LC refers only to direct physical damage resulting from the fall or collision of space objects.[38] Others support a broader interpretation and suggest that damage resulting from the malfunctioning of a space object is also recoverable under the LC.[39] They invoke the *travaux préparatoires* of the Liability Convention and the victim-oriented character of the Convention as stated in its preamble.[40] Hence, a broad interpretation, which encompasses damage from intangible electromagnetic waves, appears a reasonable one.[41]

Moreover, proving primary causation between the erroneous signal and the damage would be challenging. Since damage may be the result of a chain of events, it should be established that it was caused by the erroneous signals and that the causal link was not broken by another, overriding event.[42] Thus, claimants should prove that damage was due to a defective signal and not a malfunction of the receiver, an atmospheric disturbance that affected the signal or any other cause. Besides, a user may suffer damage after receiving signals from more than one

---

35 *Convention on the International Liability for Damage Caused by Space Objects*, 29 March 1972, 961 UNTS 187 [*Liability Convention*].
36 Armel Kerrest & Lesley Jane Smith, in Stephan Hobe *et al.*, eds, *Cologne Commentary on Space Law* (Cologne: Heymanns, 2013) vol 2, Article II LC, paras 110 et seq.
37 See Kerrest & Smith, Ibid.
38 See e.g. Sergio M Carbone & Maria Elena De Maestri, "The Rationale for an International Convention on Third Party Liability for Satellite Navigation Signals" (2009) 14:1–2 Unif L Rev 35 at 38; Stephen Gorove, "Cosmos 954: Issues of Law and Policy" (1978) 6:2 J Space L 137 at 141; Kaiser, *supra* note 26 at 19–20.
39 See e.g. Carl Q Christol, "International Liability for Damage Caused by Space Objects" (1980) 74:2 AJIL 346 at 362; BD Kofi Henaku, "The International Liability of the GNSS Space Segment Provider" (1996) XXI:I Ann Air & Sp L 170; Lesley Jane Smith, "Legal Aspects of Satellite Navigation" in Frans von der Dunk & Fabio Tronchetti, eds, *Handbook of Space Law* (Cheltenham: Edward Elgar Publishing, 2015) 554 at 585 [Smith, "Legal Aspects"].
40 See *Liability Convention*, *supra* note 35, Preamble.
41 For an extensive analysis, see Elena Campanelli & Brendan Cohen, "The Notion of 'damage' Caused by a Space Object under the 1972 Liability Convention" in Corinne M Jorgenson & International Institute of Space Law, eds, *Proceedings of the International Institute of Space Law 2013* (The Hague: Eleven International, 2014) 29 at 34–44.
42 Kerrest & Smith, *supra* note 34 at paras 57–58.

operators, e.g. GPS and GLONASS, making it difficult to determine which operator, if at all, is at fault.

It should be noted that claims under the Liability Convention concern only international liability between States. A user that wants to sue a GNSS operator will have to refer to national civil liability law.[43] The LC's short limitation period of one year [Art. X (1)] may also constitute an incentive to bring claims before national courts.

9.2.1.3 Registration and return of space objects

According to the Registration Convention,[44] all space objects, thus also GNSS satellites, launched into Earth orbit must be registered by the launching State in an appropriate national registry and in the central Register maintained by the UN Secretary General.[45] Registration indicates the potentially liable launching State of a space object. Furthermore, the State of registry retains jurisdiction and control over the GNSS satellites in accordance with Article VIII of the OST.[46]

The Rescue Agreement[47] is relevant as to the return of GNSS satellites on Earth. It provides that States shall, upon request, assist the launching State in recovering space objects that return to Earth beyond its territorial limits.[48]

9.2.2 Frequency allocation

The International Telecommunication Union (ITU) provides the global regulatory framework for frequency allocation. In particular, ITU is responsible for the allocation and assignment of global radio spectrum and satellite orbits, to avoid harmful interference.[49] ITU's International Radio Regulations are set by decisions of ITU's Member States (MS) during ITU-R World Radiocommunications Conferences (WRC) conducted every four years.[50] The MS ratify the WRC decisions and transfer them into national law.[51]

In order to minimize interference, ITU retains a system of registration and coordination for notified stations and radio systems by MS. In case of harmful spectrum interference, the States or organizations concerned co-ordinate the technical details bilaterally.

---

43 Souichirou Kozuka, "Third Party Liability arising from GNSS-related services" in, *Proceedings of the International Institute of Space Law 2009* (Reston, VA: American Institute of Aeronautics and Astronautics, 2010) 232 at 235.
44 *Convention on Registration of Objects Launched into Outer Space*, 14 January 1975, 1023 UNTS 15 [*Registration Convention*].
45 Ibid., art II.
46 See *Outer Space Treaty, supra* note 29, art VIII.
47 *Agreement on the Rescue of Astronauts, the Return of Astronauts and the Return of Objects Launched into Outer Space*, 22 April 1968, 672 UNTS 119 [*Rescue Agreement*].
48 See Ibid., art 5.
49 See Constitution of the International Telecommunication Union: Final Acts of the Additional Plenipotentiary Conference, done in Geneva, 22 December 1992 and entered into force 1 July 2014, 1825 UNTS,1; UKTS 1996 No. 24; Cm. 2539; ATS 1994 No. 28; Final Acts of the Additional Plenipotentiary Conference, Geneva, 1992 (1993), at art. 1.2 (29) as amended by the Final Acts of the Plenipotentiary Conference in Minneapolis, 1998 (Geneva: ITU 1999).
50 See *Ibid.*, art. 13.2 (90) as amended by the Final Acts of the Plenipotentiary Conference in Minneapolis, 1998 (Geneva: ITU 1999) and in Antalya, 2006 (Geneva, ITU, 2007).
51 See Ibid., art. 4.3(31) amended by the Final Acts of the Plenipotentiary Conference in Minneapolis, 1998 (Geneva: ITU 1999).

In relation to GNSS, ITU has been working on the allocation of the radio-frequency bands used by the Radio Navigation Satellite Services (RNSS), as the use for other purposes of frequencies suitable for GNSS services increases. For example, the WRC held in 2000 in Istanbul approved new frequency allocations to RNSS in the bands 1164–1215MHz, 1260–1300MHz, 1300–1350MHz, and 5000–5150MHz, to support the growth of RNSS taking into consideration the upcoming development of new GNSS systems, like Galileo.[52]

9.2.3 International trade law

9.2.3.1 Market access

The World Trade Organization (WTO) is an intergovernmental organization that establishes global trade rules to facilitate trade and dispute resolution among nations.[53] The core of these rules are the WTO *Multilateral Agreements*, which bind all WTO Member States (MS)[54] and guarantee non-discriminatory trade rights, transparent trade policies and efficient dispute resolution. The most important of them are: the Agreements on trade of goods, especially the 1994 GATT;[55] the GATS on services;[56] the TRIPS on intellectual property;[57] the Trade Policy Review Mechanism;[58] and the Dispute Settlement Understanding.[59]

GATT, GATS and TRIPS contain general principles, additional agreements and annexes on specific sectors, and detailed schedules of commitment of each country regarding access of foreign products and service-providers to its market.[60]

In addition, there are two plurilateral agreements in force: the Agreement on Trade in Civil Aircraft[61] and the Agreement on Government Procurement.[62] WTO MS are not obliged to become parties to these agreements.

9.2.3.1.1 Principles and structure of the WTO framework
The WTO legal framework is characterized by general principles, followed by a common structure of the WTO Treaties.

---

52 José-Ángel Ávila-Rodríguez *et al.*, "A Vision on New Frequencies, Signals and Concepts for Future GNSS Systems" in *20th International Technical Meeting of the Satellite Division of The Institute of Navigation: ION GNSS 2007: September 25–28, 2007, Fort Worth, Texas, USA* (Red Hook, NY: Institute of Navigation, 2007) vol 1, 517 at 524.
53 The WTO is the successor of the General Agreement of Tariffs and Trade, which was signed in 1947. The GATT system was developed through a series of international negotiations, known as *rounds*. The WTO's agreements are often called the Final Act of the 1986–1994 *Uruguay Round* of trade negotiations. The *Doha Round* started in 1994 and has not been completed yet.
54 All WTO Agreements have the form of Annexes to *Final Act Embodying the Results of the Uruguay Round of Multilateral Trade Negotiations*, 15 April 1994, [*Final Act of Marrakesh*].
55 *General Agreement on Tariffs and Trade 1994*, 15 April 1994, 1867 U.N.T.S. 187.
56 *General Agreement on Trade in Services*, 15 April 1994, 1869 U.N.T.S. 183.
57 *Agreement on Trade-Related Aspects of Intellectual Property Rights, including Trade in Counterfeit Goods*, 15 April 1994, 1869 U.N.T.S. 299.
58 1869 U.N.T.S. 480.
59 Understanding of Dispute Settlements and Procedures, 1869 U.N.T.S. 401.
60 For a brief explanation of the structure of the WTO Multilateral Agreements, see www.wto.org/english/thewto_e/whatis_e/tif_e/agrm1_e.htm.
61 15 April 1994, 1869 U.N.T.S. 508.
62 15 April 1994, 1869 U.N.T.S. 508.

The principle of the *Most Favored Nation* (MFN) requires that any preferential treatment granted by a State to another State regarding international commerce is unconditionally and automatically expanded to all other WTO MS. Exceptions are allowed, yet only under strict conditions.[63]

Under the principle of *National Treatment*, WTO MS are obliged not to discriminate between foreign and domestic goods, services or intellectual property rights, but only after these have entered the domestic market – which means that the principle does not apply to custom duties.[64]

Moreover, WTO Treaties contain *Schedules*, which are the specific sectors to which MS accept to apply the Treaty provisions, as well as *Commitments*, which contain concrete measures that each MS agrees irrevocably to adopt in compliance with the Treaty provisions, to facilitate trade liberalization in its territory.

9.2.3.1.2 GNSS and WTO treaties

The General Agreement on Tariffs and Trade (GATT) 1994 incorporates the provisions of the GATT 1947,[65] the predecessor of the WTO, and concerns international trade in products. In general, it provides for fair and transparent trade regulations, including taxation, import duties, subsidies and anti-dumping measures.[66] However, it does not affect national security measures (Art. XXI). Given that GNSS use includes national security applications, this exception may play an important role in the international trade of the related equipment.

The General Agreement on Trade in Services (GATS) is the equivalent of GATT in services. It also provides for fair and transparent trade regulations and practices (Art. III). Governmental services offered outside market conditions are excluded from its scope [Art. I(3)]. GATS is especially important for PNT services based on GNSS signals, which are the majority of GNSS applications.

The Technical Barriers to Trade Agreement (TBT) aims at ensuring that technical regulations, standards, testing and certification procedures are not misused to create artificial trade barriers and give domestic products an unfair advantage (Arts 2 and 3). It obliges States to lay down transparent and fair procedures on quality assessment of products (Art. 10). The TBT plays a significant role in areas where certification is necessary to ensure high quality of safety critical products, for example aviation and maritime safety.

The Agreement on Government Procurement (GPA) aims at ensuring that government procurement rules and procedures are transparent, promote international competition, and do not result in discriminations against foreign suppliers (Arts 6 et seq.). The GPA is important for GNSS signals of increased accuracy designed for public services, like the GALILEO PRS signal.

The Agreement on Civil Aircraft applies to civil aircraft, engines and components (Art. 1). It requires Member States to eliminate any custom duties imposed thereon (Art. 2.1), and to ensure that government-directed procurement and inducements to purchase shall not discriminate in favor of domestic sources (Arts 4 et seq.). The Agreement covers also GNSS avionics [Art. 1.1(c)].

---

63   Art. I GATT 1947; Art. II GATS; Art. IV TRIPS.
64   Art III GATT; Art. XVII GATS; Art. III TRIPS.
65   General Agreement on Tariffs and Trade, 55 UNTS 194 (1947).
66   GATT 1947, Arts VI et seq.

9.2.3.2 Intellectual property rights (IPRs)

IPRs are the legal rights that result from intellectual activity in the industrial, scientific, literary and artistic fields.[67]

Although IPR acquisition and protection are regulated by national legislation, there are global uniform rules on IPRs, which determine a minimum of IPR protection. Additionally, there are regional uniform rules as well as internationally coordinated filing procedures.[68]

International cooperation and coordination on IPR is managed by the World Intellectual Property Organization (WIPO), a specialized agency of the UN.[69] WIPO administers a series of IPR treaties,[70] the most important of which are the Paris Convention on Industrial Property[71] and the Berne Convention on Copyright.[72] Equally important is the TRIPS Agreement, concluded in the framework of the WTO,[73] mainly in order to enhance and modernize the existing conventions.

IPRs are distinguished into *industrial property rights* (which comprise rights like patents, utility models, trademarks and industrial designs, granted in principle through a formal filing procedure) and *copyright*, which protects literary and artistic works, including software and databases, without necessitating any formal registration.[74]

9.2.3.2.1 General principles

The international IPR conventions allow us to deduce some general principles that govern IPRs, which are:

Territoriality: The parameters for the protection of IPRs, such as conditions, extent, content, and duration of protection, are determined by the law of the State from which protection is asked.[75]

National treatment/assimilation: Protection of IPRs is granted to foreigners under the same conditions as to own nationals.[76]

Most favored State: In accordance with the WTO legal framework, Article 4 of TRIPS prescribes that any preferential treatment granted by a Member to the nationals of any other country shall be accorded immediately and unconditionally to the nationals of all other Members.

---

67 WIPO Intellectual Property Handbook, WIPO Geneva 2004, para 1.1, www.wipo.int/export/sites/www/about-ip/en/iprm/pdf/ch1.pdf [WIPO Handbook].
68 See e.g. *Convention on the Grant of European Patents (European Patent Convention)*, 5 October 1973, 1065 UNTS 255.
69 *Convention Establishing the World Intellectual Property Organization*, 14 July 1967, 828 UNTS 5.
70 See www.wipo.int/treaties/en/.
71 *Paris Convention for the Protection of Industrial Property of March 20, 1883, as revised at Brussels on December 14, 1900, at Washington on June 2, 1911, at The Hague on November 6, 1925, at London on June 2, 1934, at Lisbon on October 31, 1958, and at Stockholm on July 14, 1967*, 14 July 1967, 828 UNTS 307 [Paris Convention].
72 *Berne Convention for the Protection of Literary and Artistic Works of September 9, 1886, completed at Paris on May 4, 1896, revised at Berlin on November 13, 1908, completed at Berne on March 20, 1914, revised at Rome on June 2, 1928, revised at Brussels on June 26, 1948, and revised at Stockholm on July 14, 1967*, 14 July 1967, 828 UNTS 223 [Berne Convention].
73 *Supra* note 57.
74 See WIPO Handbook, *supra* note 67, paras 1.4–1.5.
75 See Cristopher Wadlow, *Enforcement of Intellectual Property in European and International Law: the New Private International Law of Intellectual Property in the United Kingdom and the European Community* (London: Sweet & Maxwell, 1998) at paras 1–18.
76 See e.g. *Berne Convention*, art 5(1); *Paris Convention*, art 2; *TRIPS*, arts 3(1), 9.

Procedural rules and priority: IPRs are protected according to the date they are acquired, that is on a priority basis. Although such a date depends on national law, the international conventions on industrial property establish uniform procedural rules and facilitate claims of priority rights based on the date of the first filing.[77]

9.2.3.2.2 IPR aspects of GNSS

The provision of GNSS services and applications incorporates IPRs concerning both the hardware[78] and the software.[79] The most pertinent IPRs are patents, utility models, copyright, and trade secrets.

Patents protect inventions, which are innovative solutions to technical problems.[80] Utility models are also solutions to technical problems, yet the innovation requirements are lower, and they last for a shorter time.[81] Copyright protection is important as to software and databases related to GNSS services.[82] Trade secrets are secret information of commercial value and are protected without any filing requirements.[83]

The serious implications IPRs may have on GNSS were demonstrated in 2012, when it became known that Ploughshare Innovations, an R&D subsidiary of the UK Defense Ministry, had asked royalties from US companies, based on a patent it had obtained by the European Patent Office, regarding aspects of modulation signals that enable the interoperability between the open signal of GPS (L1C) and Galileo (E1).[84] These had been developed by a joint EU-US taskforce on the basis of a 2004 US-EU cooperation agreement,[85] whose members comprised employees of the UK Defense Ministry. The claims caused grave concerns in the US and the EU, among fears that such patents could seriously undermine the use of free GNSS signals.[86] In 2013, the US and the UK settled the issue as to the GPS civil signal, agreeing to ensure that the signal remains "perpetually free and openly available worldwide".[87]

9.2.4 GNSS liability

Liability arising from the provision of GNSS services is connected to the vulnerabilities of satellite signals to disruption and loss of signal. The main vulnerabilities are: ionospheric effects, which affect the propagation of the signal; interference from other electromagnetic emitters

---

77 See e.g. *Paris Convention*, art 4; *TRIPS*, art 2(1).
78 For example, transmitters, receivers, clocks, processors, etc.
79 For example, programs for integrity monitoring, data-user interface, and warning systems.
80 See e.g. *TRIPS*, art 5(1).
81 Usually 7–10 years, against the 20-year protection usually accorded to patents.
82 *TRIPS*, art 10.
83 *TRIPS*, art 39.
84 See "Modulation signals for a satellite navigation system", European Patent No. 1830199 (1 September 2004) (patent granted on 1 February 2012).
85 Agreement on the Promotion, Provision and Use of Galileo and GPS Satellite-Based Navigation Systems and Related Applications, signed at Dublin, on 26 June 2004 available at www.gps.gov/policy/cooperation/europe/2004/gps-galileo-agreement.pdf.
86 Dee Ann Divis, "MBOC Patent Dispute Could Affect U.S. Military, European Civil GNSS Users", *Inside GNSS News* (19 May 2012), online: Inside GNSS www.insidegnss.com/node/3055.
87 *Joint United Kingdom–United States Statement Regarding Global Positioning System (GPS) Intellectual Property*, 17 January 2013, www.gps.gov/policy/cooperation/uk/2013-joint-statement/. So far, the UK is still negotiating with the European Commission on this issue, while similar patents have been obtained also by France. See Peter B de Selding, "Prospective Galileo Receiver Makers Concerned over Patent Issue", *SpaceNews* (30 January 2014), spacenews.com/39331prospective-galileo-receiver-makers-concerned-over-patent-issue/.

(e.g., TV signals); increased solar activity, which may interfere with all electronic systems; jamming, which intentionally prevents receivers from receiving signals; spoofing, which is the intentional emission of legitimate-looking false signals to the receiver; and, degradation or interruption of the GNSS constellation because of lack of funds or national emergencies.[88]

GNSS-related liability may take various forms, depending on the circumstances of the particular case. There are no international uniform rules thereon, despite the efforts undertaken in the past by the International Civil Aviation Organization (ICAO) and the International Institute for the Unification of Private Law (UNIDROIT).[89] The arising issues could be distinguished into procedural and substantive. A separate, yet related, issue is insurance coverage.

The analysis considers only claims presented before national courts. Issues concerning international liability between States are analyzed in the sections on space law.[90]

9.2.4.1 Procedural issues

9.2.4.1.1 Sovereign immunity

Since GNSS are used also for military applications, they are controlled by governmental authorities. Therefore, in the event of an accident, claimants would have to overcome sovereign immunity.

Sovereign immunity prevents national courts from establishing jurisdiction over acts and omissions of another State. There is no universal agreement on the exact content of international law in this regard. However, a generic consensus has been reflected in the *Convention on Jurisdictional Immunities of States and their property*,[91] which reflects significantly current international law. According to Article 10 of the Convention, immunity cannot be invoked for commercial transactions of the State with foreign nationals, unless otherwise agreed.

The existence of a commercial transaction between the signal provider (State) and the user is doubtful, especially concerning the open signal, which is made available for free to everyone. Nevertheless, even if there is a commercial transaction, the free use of the open signal combined with the declaration that the State accepts no related liability, can be interpreted as an agreed recognition of State immunity.

9.2.4.1.2 Competent courts

The courts competent to rule on liability claims will be determined by the national law of the court seized on the case (*lex fori*). In most States, jurisdiction belongs to the courts of the place where the defendant has its principal place of business or registered seat.[92] Contractual claims

---

88 See John A Volpe National Transportation Systems Center, "Vulnerability Assessment of the Transportation Infrastructure Relying on the Global Positioning System", Final Report (29 August 2001), para 3.2, www.navcen.uscg.gov/pdf/vulnerability_assess_2001.pdf; ICAO Secretariat, *Global Navigation Satellite System (GNSS) Implementation issues*, ICAO Air Navigation Conference, Doc AN-Conf/12-WP/21 (26 May 2012) para 2.2, www.icao.int/Meetings/anconf12/WorkingPapers/ANConfWP21.6.1.EN.pdf.
89 On ICAO efforts and the feasibility of a UNIDROIT Convention, see Hans-Georg Bollweg, "Initial Considerations regarding the Feasibility of an International UNIDROIT Instrument to Cover Liability for Damage Caused by Malfunctions in Global (Navigation) Satellite Systems" (2008) 13:4 Unif L Rev 917, 920 ff.
90 *Supra* section 9.2.1.
91 *United Nations Convention on Jurisdictional Immunities of States and Their Property*, 17 January 2005 (adopted on 2 December 2004 by UN GA Resolution 59/38, not yet in force). See also *European Convention on State Immunity*, 16 May 1972, 1495 UNTS 182 (ratified by only five States).
92 E.g. *Regulation (EC) No. 44/2001 of 22 December 2000 on jurisdiction and the recognition and enforcement of judgments in civil and commercial matters*, [2001] OJ, L 12/1, art 2(1) [*Regulation 44/2001*].

will be judged by the courts of the State designated by the parties or, absent that, by the courts of the place of contractual performance.[93] Jurisdiction on tortious claims usually belongs to the courts of the place where the harmful event took place (e.g., aircraft accident) and/or the harm occurred (e.g. the place where the injured person died).[94]

The number of potentially competent courts may encourage claimants to choose the jurisdiction most convenient to their interests (*forum shopping*). Nevertheless, this creates legal uncertainty, increases litigation cost and affects the insurability of claims. Therefore, the designation of a single competent jurisdiction through an international convention has been proposed.[95]

9.2.4.1.3 Applicable law

The law applicable to the case depends also on the nature of the claim. Contractual claims are often governed by the law designated by the parties or by the law of the State closest connected to the dispute, which is highly case-dependent.[96] Extra-contractual claims are usually governed by the law of the State where the harmful event occurred.[97]

9.2.4.1.4 Recognition and enforcement of judgments

Recognition and enforcement of judgments are important for the effective protection of claimants' rights in cases involving multiple jurisdictions. The related requirements are set by national legislation, yet there are also regional instruments. In general, most jurisdictions require that the judgment is final and conclusive, has been rendered by a competent court, the defendant has been given proper notice of the suit and the opportunity to be heard, and the judgment does not offend the public order of the forum. Sometimes reciprocity is also necessary.[98]

9.2.4.2 Substantive issues

Substantive issues concern the requirements for establishing GNSS-related liability.

9.2.4.2.1 Basis and form of liability

The basis of GNSS liability depends on the cause of damage/injury and the relationship(s) of the parties in the case under examination. The damage/injury may be due to:

(a) A hardware malfunction of the space or ground segment, or the receiver of the end-user. In this case, the rules on product liability would apply. This would also be the case, if the

---

93   E.g. *Restatement (Third) of Foreign Relations Law of the United States* § 421 (1987); *Regulation 44/2001*, supra note 92, art 23.
94   Ulrich Magnus, "Civil liability for Satellite-based Services" (2008) 13:4 Unif L Rev 935 at 948–50.
95   See Magnus ibid. at 960, who proposes the courts of the place of the operator's seat; Pietro Manzini & Anna Masutti, "An International Civil Liability Regime for the Galileo Services: A Proposal" (2008) 33:2 Air & Space L 114 at 130–31, who prefer the courts of the place of the accident.
96   E.g. *Restatement (Second) of Conflict of Laws* §§ 187, 188 (1971) [*Restatement of Conflict*]; EC, Regulation (EC) No. 593/2008 of the European Parliament and of the Council of 17 June 2008 on the law applicable to contractual obligations (Rome I), [2008] OJ, L 177/6, arts 3, 4; *Russian Civil Code*, arts 1210, 1211.
97   See e.g. *Restatement of Conflict of Laws*, supra note 96, § 146; Regulation (EC) No. 864/2007 of the European Parliament and of the Council of 11 July 2007 on the law applicable to non-contractual obligations (Rome II), [2007] OJ, L 199/40, art 4; *Russian Civil Code*, art 1219.
98   See Magnus, *supra* note 94 at 956.

hardware malfunction was caused by a software defect and the software can be deemed a component of the end product. However, it has been suggested that product liability claims will be limited in practice. They could be presented regarding GNSS receivers, but their success chances as to Signal in Space errors or malfunctions are very limited.[99]
(b) A software defect, irrespective of its incorporation into another product. In this scenario, we may have a form of liability for negligent misstatement/misrepresentation or for failure to warn, which could be a contractual or a tortious claim, depending on the jurisdiction and the circumstances of the particular case.
(c) A signal defect, for example a signal lacking the required accuracy. Such defect could be due to malicious interference of a third party, which could have been facilitated by the signal provider's failure to adopt appropriate security measures, like encryption. In general, satellite signals are not considered products, but a form of service provision. Thus, there would be a case of improper service provision, which is usually a form of contractual liability, often subject to liability limitations and waivers.[100] However, should the user present an extra-contractual claim against the satellite operator, the legal basis could be product liability, by analogy to liability for aeronautical charts.[101]

In practice, it will be very difficult to identify the exact cause of the damage, namely which segment/device/component malfunctioned. This is exacerbated by the interoperability of the open signal, which enables the end-user to receive signals from more core constellations.

9.2.4.2.2 Liability chain – persons liable

The occurrence of damage/injury may lead to a combination of claims, presented by different persons and on different bases. The persons liable will be determined by the applicable law and the circumstances of the case.

The damaged/injured person could turn against the vendor of the GNSS receiver (usually based on the contract of sale) or the provider of the GNSS service. These could present contractual regress claims against the manufacturer of the malfunctioned receiver or other hardware component. The hardware manufacturer might seek indemnification from the software manufacturer that caused the hardware to malfunction, based on the contract between them.

Notwithstanding issues of sovereign immunity, State liability is also conceivable, e.g. for negligent certification or for negligent supervision of the service provider, if such supervision duty arises from international conventions and has been reflected in domestic legislation.[102]

The uncertainty created in the identification of the persons liable has led to the suggestion that compensating the victims is best served by channeling liability to a single person and allowing for subsequent regress claims.[103]

---

99 Smith, "Legal Aspects", *supra* note 39 at 591.
100 See Lesley Jane Smith, "The Current Challenges of Liability for Loss of Satellite-based Services" in *Proceedings of the International Institute of Space Law 2013* (The Hague: Eleven International, 2014), p. 291.
101 Kozuka, *supra* note 43 at 235–36; Andreas Loukakis, "Product Liability Ramifications for Erroneous GNSS Signals: Is an Alternative Approach Possible?" *Proceedings of the International Institute of Space Law 2013* (The Hague: Eleven International, 2014) 305 at 321.
102 See e.g. *Outer Space Treaty*, *supra* note 29, art VI; *Convention on International Civil Aviation*, 7 December 1944, 15 UNTS 295, art 38 [*Chicago Convention*].
103 Magnus, *supra* note 94 at 963–64, 966; Manzini & Masutti, *supra* note 95 at 123–25.

9.2.4.2.3 Negligence/fault

Negligence of the persons involved in a case plays also an important role. Negligence *on the part of the defendant* may be important, first in establishing a duty to compensate. Depending on the applicable law, liability can be fault-based or strict. However, even in cases of strict liability, the defendant may be exonerated upon proof of *force majeure*, like space weather.[104] Moreover, the existence and the degree of the defendant's negligence may determine the adjudication of mental damages or even punitive damages to the claimant.

Negligence *on the part of the claimant* could reduce the amount of compensation due (comparative negligence) or even exempt the defendant completely (contributory negligence). Such would be the case, if the claimant violated safety provisions that required use of GNSS-based navigation in combination with other navigational aids, or if the claimant ignored warnings of temporary signal degradation, for example owing to maintenance works or adverse space weather.

9.2.4.2.4 Particularities of the open signal

The open signal of the core satellite systems presents additional challenges. The signal is provided "as is", which means that the providers do not accept any responsibility for its quality and warn users that they use it at their own risk.[105] It has also been observed that, largely because of the prior accessibility to GPS, there is a tendency to regard GNSS as a self-understood gratuitous public service.[106]

In practice, this could bar recovery for defective open signals, although claimants could invoke counter-arguments, such as the existence of a commercial transaction.[107] Moreover, it is likely that courts will accept at least comparative negligence of the claimant based on his/her decision to use a signal without any quality guarantees.

9.2.4.3 Relationship with existing international conventions

GNSS-related damage/injury may result in liability of the operator of the affected transportation mode (aircraft, ship, rail, etc.) or installation (nuclear facility, airport, etc.). In such cases, compensation for claimants may be based on special international instruments regulating the operator liability.[108] The operator could subsequently seek regress against other persons or entities liable.[109]

9.2.4.4 Insurance

Standard third-party liability insurance for GNSS failures is not available yet. Insurance contracts are expected to provide limited coverage according to the service offered.[110] *De lege*

---

104 Especially, solar storms could seriously affect electronic devices both in space and on Earth or cause a degradation of the signal quality through interaction with the ionosphere of the Earth.
105 See UNIDROIT Study, *supra* note 7, para 205.
106 Smith, "Legal Aspects", *supra* note 39 at 588, 592–93.
107 See section 9.2.4.1.1, *above*; UNIDROIT Study, *supra* note 7, paras 206–07.
108 See e.g. *Convention for the Unification of Certain Rules for International Carriage by Air*, 28 May 1999, 2242 UNTS 309, ICAO Doc 9740; *Athens Convention relating to the Carriage of Passengers and their Luggage by Sea, 1974*, 13 December 1974, 1463 UNTS 20; *Vienna Convention on Civil Liability for Nuclear Damage*, 21 May 1963, 1063 UNTS 266; UNIDROIT Study, *supra* note 7, paras 84ff.
109 See UNIDROIT Study, *supra* note 7, para 175, which suggests that such right should be recognized even if not explicitly foreseen in the applicable international convention.
110 Smith, "Legal Aspects", *supra* note 39 at 593–94.

ferenda, compulsory third-party liability insurance requirements for GNSS providers are intertwined with the problems of GNSS-related liability issues.[111]

9.2.4.5 Conclusion on GNSS liability

The international community appears reluctant to adopt uniform rules on GNSS liability. Instead, States have opted for an *ad hoc* treatment of liability issues, which is connected to their desire to ensure maximum flexibility and safeguard their national security interests given the dual use of most GNSS constellations. However, such attitude leads to great legal uncertainty. Consensus on at least a model law on such issues, which would include obligatory insurance requirements, could prove very useful.

9.3 Sector-specific rules

9.3.1 Aviation law

GNSS has significant importance in aviation and is expected to become the cornerstone of future Air Navigations Services (ANS). Its advantages include the ability to support all phases of flight by providing seamless global navigation guidance; accurate aircraft guidance in remote and oceanic areas; use of efficient flight paths; improvement of airport usability and noise abatement; and, mitigation or even avoidance of the cost to replace traditional navigation aids.[112] Moreover, GNSS plays an increasingly important role in flight tracking and emergency locating of aircraft as part of the ICAO Global Aeronautical Distress and Safety System.[113]

Due to the GNSS limitations on accuracy and integrity, a variety of augmentation systems are used. Apart from ground-based and space-based augmentation systems, aircraft-based augmentation systems are employed in aviation, which augment and/or integrate GNSS information with information available on board the aircraft.[114]

9.3.1.1 PBN and ATM modernization

GNSS technologies and applications are the key enablers of the concept of Performance Based Navigation (PBN), which is the foundation of the worldwide Air Traffic Management (ATM) modernization efforts.

9.3.1.1.1 PBN
Under PBN, which is the opposite of the traditional sensor-based navigation, the requirements regarding the performance of aircraft navigation systems are identified in navigation specifications. PBN enables more efficient use of airspace and greater harmonization of regulatory requirements across States. Furthermore, operators can evaluate for themselves how to meet the specific requirements, choosing among the systems and technologies available, rather than being

---

111 See Ibid. at 617; Masutti & Manzini, *supra* note 95 at 128; Magnus, *supra* note 94 at 966.
112 For details, see *ICAO GNSS Manual, supra* note 14, para 1.3.
113 For details, see *Conclusions and Recommendations of the Multidisciplinary Meeting on Global Flight Tracking*, 12–13 May 2014, www.icao.int/Meetings/GTM/Documents/Final%20Global%20 Tracking%20Meeting%20Conclusions%20and%20%20Recommendations.pdf.
114 See *ICAO GNSS Manual, supra* note 14 at para 2.2.

obliged to have specific pieces of equipment required by sensor-based navigation.[115] PBN is based on the concepts of Area Navigation (RNAV)[116] and Required Navigation Performance (RNP).[117]

9.3.1.1.2 ATM modernization

The main ATM modernization efforts in place are NextGen in the US and the Single European Sky (SES) in Europe with its technological pillar SES ATM Research (SESAR). Both projects rely on PBN with extensive use of GNSS, to increase airspace capacity and improve efficiency of operations. They also attempt to integrate new technologies and operational concepts, such as ADS-B[118] and 4-D trajectories,[119] which take advantage of the increased GNSS coverage and availability resulting from the compatibility and interoperability of GNSS core constellations.

9.3.1.2 Global regulation of GNSS provision in aviation

From a regulatory view, global regulation of GNSS provisions belongs to the competency of ICAO. Many aspects of GNSS provision fall under the rules of the Chicago Convention. Furthermore, there are principles on GNSS policy as well as technical rules and guidelines on GNSS.

9.3.1.2.1 Chicago Convention

Article 1 of the Chicago Convention (CC) recognizes the exclusive sovereignty of States over their national airspace. Article 12 obliges States to adopt measures on air traffic above their territory. Article 15 prohibits any discrimination between national and foreign aircraft when raising airport and similar charges, which include ANS charges. Article 28 lays down the duty of States to provide ANS in their territory and to publish aeronautical maps and charts. The combination of these Articles reveals that each State regulates the conditions and charges for providing GNSS in its territory and has to inform other States thereon.

Moreover, Article 30 CC permits the use of radio-transmitting devices only upon license from the State of registry, which applies to ADS-B devices.

---

115 ICAO, *Performance-based Navigation (PBN) Manual*, 3rd ed, ICAO Doc 9613/AN/937 (Montreal: ICAO, 2008) at paras 2.2–2.3 [*ICAO PBN Manual*].
116 RNAV is a navigational method that permits the operation of an aircraft on any desired flight path rather than on only a specific airway – see www.skybrary.aero/index.php/Area_Navigation_Systems. RNAV is accompanied by navigation specifications that allow the aircraft to operate safely in a specific route or a specific airspace concept. An airspace concept provides the outline and intended framework of operations within a specific part of airspace. It is developed to satisfy policy objectives, such as improved safety, increased air traffic capacity, etc. By areas of operation, aerospace concepts are distinguished into oceanic and remote continental, continental en-route, terminal and approach see *ICAO PBN Manual*, *supra* note 115, paras 2.2–2.3.
117 RNP is an RNAV specification with the additional requirement of on-board performance monitoring and alert – *ICAO PBN Manual*, *supra* note 115, para 1.2.
118 Automatic Dependent Surveillance – Broadcast (ADS-B) is a surveillance technique that transmits the identity of the aircraft and data derived from GNSS Systems, especially position and velocity, to Air Traffic Control (ADS-B Out) and to other aircraft (ADS-B In) – see www.skybrary.aero/index.php/Automatic_Dependent_Surveillance_Broadcast_%28ADS-B%29.
119 A 4D trajectory integrates time into the 3D aircraft trajectory. It ensures flight on an optimum trajectory, provided that the aircraft meets accurately an arrival time over a designated point – see www.skybrary.aero/index.php/4D_Trajectory_Concept.

9.3.1.2.2 Policy principles

Based on the above provisions and considering the international nature of GNSS, the ICAO Assembly has laid down policy principles regarding the GNSS. These are established mainly in ICAO Assembly Resolution A32-19,[120] the content of which can be summarized as follows.

Aviation safety is recognized as the paramount principle. All States, without any discrimination, should have access to GNSS services. State sovereignty within the national airspace remains unaffected. Every State providing GNSS services or under whose jurisdiction such services are provided shall ensure their continuity, availability, integrity, accuracy and reliability. The highest practicable degree of uniformity in the provision and operation of GNSS services must be ensured, including agreements on regional provision of GNSS services. Any charges for GNSS services shall be made in accordance with Article 15 CC. When providing GNSS services, States should have due regard to the interests of other States, and facilitate global planning and implementation of such services through international cooperation.[121] The above principles have been reiterated with some variations in ICAO Assembly Resolutions A31-20 and A33-15.[122]

9.3.1.2.3 SARPs

Standards and Recommended Practices (SARPs) are technical rules adopted under Article 37 of the Chicago Convention and are designated as Annexes to the Convention for convenience.[123] They are not binding in strict legal sense; however, in practice, they carry tremendous weight.[124]

Rules related to GNSS are foreseen mainly in Annex 10, volume I (*Radio Navigation Aids*). There are also relevant provisions in Annexes 2 (*Rules of the Air*), 4 (*Aeronautical Charts*), 6 Part I (*International Commercial Air Transport – Aeroplanes*) and Part II (*International General Aviation – Aeroplanes*), 11 (*Air Traffic Services*), 14 Vol I (*Aerodrome Design and Operations*), and 15 (*Aeronautical Information Services*). More details on these rules coupled with guidance on their implementation are contained in the ICAO *GNSS Manual*, and ICAO Circulars 257 and 278.[125]

9.3.2 Maritime law

9.3.2.1 IMO policy

The International Maritime Organization (IMO) has laid down its GNSS policy in IMO

---

120 *Charter on the Rights and Obligations of States Relating to GNSS Services*, ICAO Assembly Res A32-19, 32nd Sess, ICAO Doc 9790, V-3, available at www.icao.int/publications/Documents/9790_en.pdf.
121 See Ibid.
122 See *Apportionment of expenses of ICAO among Contracting States*, ICAO Assembly Res A31-20, 31st Sess, ICAO Doc 9790, X-6, online: ICAO www.icao.int/publications/Documents/9790_en.pdf; *Consolidated statement of continuing ICAO policies and practices related to communications, navigation and surveillance/air traffic management (CNS/ATM) systems*, ICAO Assembly Res A33-15, 33rd Sess, ICAO Doc 9790, I–50, www.icao.int/publications/Documents/9790_en.pdf.
123 See arts 38, 54(l), 90 CC.
124 See also Michael Milde *Enforcement of aviation safety standards – Problems of safety oversight*, ZLW 1996, 3 (5–6), who states that SARPs have practically "a persuasive objective force comparable to the law of gravity".
125 *ICAO GNSS Manual*, supra note 14; ICAO, *Economics of Satellite-based Air Navigation Services: Guidelines for Cost/Benefit Analysis of Communications, Navigation and Surveillance/Air Traffic Management (CNS/ATM) Systems*, Circular 257-AT/106 (1995); ICAO, *National Plan for CNS/ATM Systems Guidance Material*, Circular 278 (2000).

Assembly Resolution A.915(22).[126] GNSS should serve mainly general navigation purposes (para. 3.1.1). However, precision applications are also envisaged and are currently employed using local augmentation systems, such as the EGNOS in Europe and the Maritime Differential GPS System or the WAAS in the US. The Resolution recommends that augmentation provisions should be harmonized worldwide, to enable ships to carry only one shipborne receiver (para. 3.1.3). Besides, GNSS should be reliable and of low user cost. Cost recovery and allocation methods should distinguish between maritime users that rely on the system for safety reasons and those that additionally benefit from the system in commercial or economic terms, taking into account also the interests of both shipping and coastal States (para. 3.1.5).

9.3.2.2 Operational requirements

IMO requires all ships constructed after July 1, 2002 and all passenger ships to have a GNSS receiver on board.[127] There are also performance standards for such equipment regarding mainly accuracy, continuity and integrity monitoring.[128] Furthermore, Appendixes II and III of the IMO Resolution A.915(22) provide for minimum maritime user requirements for general navigation and positioning respectively.

9.3.2.3 Institutional requirements

IMO Assembly Resolution A.915(22) clarifies that IMO cannot provide and operate a GNSS. However, IMO should be able to assess and recognize that GNSS meets maritime user requirements, that internationally established principles on cost allocation and recovery as well as on liability are applied, and that GNSS services are provided to users on a non-discriminatory basis (para. 3.1.18).

9.4 From global navigation to cosmic navigation systems

The high effectiveness of GNSS for navigation on Earth has led scientists to search for similar navigation methods for exploration missions in deep space or on the surface of celestial bodies. The most promising method seems to be using radiation emitted by fast spinning and strongly magnetized neutron stars, called pulsars.[129] Pulsars that emit X-rays are most suitable for this purpose, because their beamed periodic signals are so stable that have timing characteristics

---

126 *Revised Maritime Policy and Requirements for A Future Global Navigation Satellite System (GNSS)*, IMO Publication Product No. 1022E (2002) 66.
127 *International Convention for the Safety of Life at Sea, 1974*, 1 November 1974, 1184 UNTS 278, c V, reg 19, para 2.1.6.
128 See e.g. *Adoption of the Revised Performance Standards for Shipborne Global Positioning System (GPS) Receiver Equipment*, IMO Resolution MSC.112(73), Doc MSC 73/21/Add.3 (2000), Annex 25; *Adoption of the Revised Performance Standards for Shipborne GLONASS Receiver Equipment*, IMO Resolution MSC.113(73), Doc MSC 73/21/Add.3 (2000), Annex 26; *Adoption of the Performance Standards for Shipborne GALILEO Receiver Equipment*, IMO Resolution MSC.233 (82), Doc MSC 82/24/Add.2 (2006), Annex 25; *Adoption of the Revised Performance Standards for Shipborne DGPS and DGLONASS Maritime Radio Beacon Receiver Equipment*, IMO Resolution MSC.114(73), Doc MSC 73/21/Add.3 (2000), Annex 27.
129 Neutron stars are the compact remnants of stars which had a mass about 8–30 times the mass of the Sun, expelled their matter in a super-nova explosion and their cores collapsed, with the protons and electrons essentially melting into each other to form neutrons. See Nola Taylor Redd, "Neutron Stars: Definition and Facts", *Space.com* (31 July 2013) at www.space.com/22180-neutron-stars.html.

comparable to atomic clocks. Thus, they can be used as natural navigation beacons, quite similar to the use of GNSS satellites for navigation on Earth. By comparing pulse arrival times measured on board a spacecraft with predicted pulse arrivals at a reference location, the spacecraft position can be determined autonomously and with high accuracy everywhere in the solar system and beyond.[130]

X-ray pulsar navigation could replace the current standard method of deep-space navigation, which consists of combining radio data (obtained by tracking stations on Earth) with optical data from an on-board camera during encounters with solar system bodies. Nonetheless, the effectiveness of the current method decreases as the distance from Earth increases.[131]

Conclusion

The importance of GNSS and its applications are rapidly increasing. Core constellation and augmentation systems expand and improve their performance, which is further enhanced through bilateral agreements on compatibility and interoperability. Nevertheless, the dual use of GNSS induces several restrictions in terms of international cooperation. States prefer to conduct bilateral, instead of multilateral, cooperation agreements on GNSS issues. At the same time, they are reluctant to agree on international uniform rules governing liability, despite the regulatory fragmentation and legal uncertainty created by the applicability of traditional choice-of-laws rules combined with sovereign immunity.

With respect to international space law, the main question is its ability to adequately address modern GNSS legal issues. To the extent feasible, we should interpret current space rules taking into account contemporary and future needs.

The increasing commercial importance of GNSS applications is also reflected in the efforts to protect IPRs, yet without affecting the availability of the Open Service, which has become a kind of a common good. At the same time, GNSS-related services and products have become part of the international discussion on unrestricted market access.

Satellite-based navigation becomes gradually the cornerstone of navigation systems in aviation and shipping. Technical standards are constantly developed, to meet current and anticipated needs, and ensure safe operations. Besides, the principles applied in GNSS are so successful that scientists study their employment for navigation in deep space.

In sum, GNSS are multi-faceted systems with numerous applications. There are no uniform rules, apart from some general sector-specific policy guidelines. This creates a complicated regulatory situation and legal uncertainty. However, the dual use of GNSS for both civil and national security applications, as well as vested national interests concerning international trade, do not allow for uniform rules to be developed and, even more, adopted to a global scale. Therefore, it would be more realistic to pursue unification mainly at regional level combined with non-binding international recommendations on regulatory best practices.

---

130 See Werner Becker, Mike G Bernhardt & Axel Jessner, "Autonomous Spacecraft Navigation With Pulsars" (2013) 7 Acta Futura 11.
131 The disadvantages of the current method relate to the dependency on ground-based control and maintenance, the increasing position and velocity uncertainty with increasing distance from Earth as well as the large propagation delay and weakening of the signals at large distances.

10

Space traffic management and space situational awareness

Rafael Moro-Aguilar and Steven A. Mirmina

Introduction

In recent years, a growing number of spacefaring nations and commercial companies has launched objects into orbit. Simultaneously, there has been an increase of space debris in orbit around the Earth. As a result, the risk of interference between objects in space is growing.

Article IX of the 1967 Outer Space Treaty requires that States maintain cooperation, mutual assistance, and due regard to the interests of others in outer space.[1] Moreover, States are required to undertake consultations in case of potential interference.[2] Significant growth in the volume of near-Earth outer space traffic implies that the principles embodied in this provision of the Treaty have become more essential than ever.

At present, the International Telecommunication Union is the only international organization performing any kind of "space traffic management" (STM). However, the ITU currently lacks legal authority to regulate several aspects of a space traffic management system. Of increasing importance is a global space situational awareness coordination system, which would provide timely information to operators to avoid collisions in orbit.

There are proposals for establishing some universal "rules of the road," and even for establishing a system of STM, to protect the long-term sustainability of space activities. Establishing a global STM system, however, poses significant challenges, and its implementation would require international consensus based on the perceived benefits of all space actors.

Definition of space traffic management (STM)

The concept of STM is relatively recent, having been introduced in 1982.[3]

---

1 Treaty on Principles Governing the Activities of States in the Exploration and Use of Outer Space, Including the Moon and Other Celestial Bodies, located at www.state.gov/t/isn/5181.htm. [All websites last visited 22 February 2016].
2 Id.
3 Czech academic Lubos Perek is credited with first stating the possible need for some kind of traffic control in outer space, similar to existing air traffic control for aviation. See Lubos Perek, "Traffic Rules for Outer Space," *25 IISL Proceedings* (1982), p. 37.

The International Academy of Astronautics (IAA) published in 2006 a study on STM, the first major academic contribution to this emerging field.[4] The IAA defined STM as "the set of technical and regulatory provisions for promoting safe access into outer space, operations in outer space, and return from outer space to Earth free from physical or radio-frequency interference."[5]

Indeed, STM may be viewed as an evolutionary step away from the "fragmented" system of current space law towards a more comprehensive system of traffic rules, which would cover various aspects of spaceflight. It could include safety rules, priority rules, sustainability rules, environmental protection, and generally the coordination of applicable international law (including international air law, space law, and telecommunications law). The main purpose of STM is to conduct space activities without suffering any harmful interference.[6]

There is arguably an increasing need for STM, given the sharp rise in the volume of traffic in outer space. Space activities have multiplied: as of 2015, almost 5,000 launches had placed some 6,600 satellites into Earth orbit, of which about 3,600 remain still in space. There are also more than 9,000 large-size pieces of debris, and experts estimate the population of non-functional objects and fragments larger than 1 cm to be in the order of 750,000.[7]

The number of space actors is also growing: not only more launching States, but also more non-governmental entities are making use of outer space. In addition, new technologies are being developed, including suborbital vehicles, SmallSats, and LEO and MEO constellations. A proliferation of orbital launches and possibly also suborbital flights could happen in the next decade.

An eventual STM system could include several elements:

- First, "the transit of space objects through other States' airspace on launch or re-entry would require coordination with relevant air traffic control."[8]
- Second, a set of "rules of the road" and guidelines, particularly concerning space traffic and the reduction of space debris, are needed in near-Earth orbits to ensure the safe operation of functional satellites and spacecraft. Such rules could be applied either internationally or through national means.
- Third, a global coordination platform for space situational awareness could be established, including international notification standards and universal, exhaustive databases to be freely accessed by all interested parties. This way, all space actors would share information on what they are doing at each moment.
- Fourth, "there is the question of the use of orbits."[9] It would make sense to use rationally these natural resources, following the model of the GEO radio frequencies and associated orbital positions as currently managed by the ITU. This matter is not crucial yet, but in the longer term some kind of operational infrastructure similar to the currently existing international centers for air traffic management (e.g. Eurocontrol) might be given the task of orbital oversight.

---

4   Corinne Contant-Jorgenson, Petr Lala & Kai-Uwe Schrögl, eds, "Space Traffic Management," IAA Cosmic Study, 2006, available at https://iaaweb.org/iaa/Studies/spacetraffic.pdf. (Hereinafter, "IAA 2006 Study").
5   IAA 2006 Study, pp. 10, 17.
6   Alexander Soucek, "Space Law Essentials", 2015, p. 135.
7   European Space Agency (ESA), 2015, quoted in A. Soucek, ibid.
8   Francis Lyall & Paul B. Larsen, "Space Law – A Treatise, 2009," p. 300.
9   F. Lyall & P. B. Larsen, ibid.

- Fifth, proposals have also emerged for a unified control system of aviation and space. In the longer term, the fusion of terrestrial air traffic, and space launch and re-entry traffic control has a certain attraction, and could well be combined with a more general system of STM.[10]
- Finally, it has also been noted that, since information on space weather is very important for the operation of space objects, the constant monitoring and prediction of space weather conditions could be an additional tool in implementing a global STM system.[11]

The IAA is revising its 2006 study on STM, to take into account new academic, technical, legal and diplomatic developments. The new study is expected to include a concrete roadmap for implementation of a STM regime and a set-out of potential traffic rules.[12]

The current international legal framework

Public international law

The current international legal framework for space activities comprises the five United Nations space law treaties, the eight UN General Assembly Resolutions, and a number of other soft-law texts. There are also the Radio Regulations approved by the ITU concerning allocation of radio frequencies to services and management of the associated orbits. Finally, international air law has also to be taken into account when discussing STM.

In addition, the regulation of international common spaces, that is high seas, deep sea-bed, Antarctica, and outer space, could provide some guidance for a future STM system. The corresponding treaties provide the basic rules, rights and obligations.

In particular, the law of the sea has been quoted as a possible inspiration for STM.[13] In this area, the tendency is to recognize increasing powers and jurisdiction to the coastal States and port States over vessels crossing their territorial waters or sailing into their harbors. However, the extension of "coastal" jurisdiction into outer space is an impossible solution for obvious technical reasons. The solution of the port State is also not usable, since most space objects do not fly back to Earth.[14] Nevertheless, there are some interesting elements from the UNCLOS[15] set of ship traffic rules, distinction of maritime zones, and associated rights and obligations which could serve as a model for a future STM regime.

Given the comparable legal status of outer space with the airspace over the high seas, ICAO's regulation of the latter may provide an interesting reference for drafting STM rules. Above the high seas the rules in force (*rules of the air*) are established under Art. 12 Chicago Convention[16] and specified in Annex 2 to the Convention.

Also, by virtue of regional air navigation agreements, some States provide air traffic services in

---

10   F. Lyall & P.B. Larsen, ibid., p. 173.
11   IAA 2006 Study, p. 11. We will not however include space weather considerations in the present chapter.
12   Corinne Jorgenson, "STM Studies of the IAA," 2015 IISL/ECSL Symposium on STM, www.unoosa.org/pdf/pres/lsc2015/symp-01.pdf.
13   Stephan Hobe, "Rights and obligations in the International Commons – The case of outer space," 2015 IISL/ECSL Symposium on STM, www.unoosa.org/pdf/pres/lsc2015/symp-02.pdf.
14   IAA 2006 Study, pp. 56–58.
15   UN Convention on the Law of the Sea (UNCLOS, or UNCLOS II), adopted in Montego Bay (Jamaica) on 10 December 1982, in force on 16 November 1994.
16   Convention on International Civil Aviation (CICA), signed in Chicago on 7 December 1944, in force since 4 April 1947.

portions of the airspace over the high seas.[17] In practice, coastal States control the air routes over high seas as well. The state of destination of the international route is in charge of managing flights moving towards its territory. Therefore, the experience gained with air traffic management above the high seas might provide a useful starting point for STM of in-orbit operations.[18] However, these rules may not translate easily in such a different environment as outer space.[19]

Another important problem is determining the authority in charge of imposing the STM rules on the space actors. Outer space is free of any State jurisdiction. No one State can regulate navigation – or traffic – in outer space. In the law of the sea there is the International Maritime Organization (IMO), which is in charge of managing maritime traffic and safeguarding the principle of free navigation in the high seas. In air law, we have ICAO tasked with similar functions.

Following the successful flights of *SpaceShipOne*, the President of the ICAO Council, – the permanent legislative organ of ICAO – suggested that ICAO would be the most appropriate organization to regulate the safety of suborbital flights. The debate following this statement also brought up the idea of establishing ICAO as the STM organization in the future.[20]

International space law

Focusing on international space law, there are several provisions relevant to STM. The freedom to use outer space, the duty for States to cooperate in outer space, and other principles embodied in the 1967 Outer Space Treaty (OST) seem to call for more precise regulation to ensure overall safety.

A legal duty to use space for the benefit of all is enshrined in Art. I of the OST, which declares outer space as the "province of all mankind." A universal freedom to use outer space is also present in Art. I: entities are entitled to operate in outer space free from any interference.

Furthermore, Art. VI of the OST requires domestic licensing of national space activities. A number of national standards and procedures are already being implemented. These rules will be examined in more detail below.

Notwithstanding that, the most significant international rule for STM purposes is the "due regard" principle (Art. IX OST). There is a general obligation for all States Parties to the OST to pay due regard to the corresponding interests of other States, and avoiding any harmful interference to the activities carried out by other States in outer space. This principle has been invoked to address the problem of space debris. It could also serve as a basis for an eventual international STM regime.[21]

---

17 Annex 11 to the Chicago Convention.
18 IAA 2006 Study, p. 55.
19 As noted by the IAA study, p. 28, space traffic has some fundamental characteristics, which distinguish it from human activities in other environments. In the air or on the land, an object may speed up or slow down, or it may change direction; however, in space, it is more atypical to change direction and velocity. Similarly, on Earth, an object may rest indefinitely, while a similar object in space may stay in space only if in "orbital motion."
20 Peter van Fenema, "Suborbital Flights and ICAO," *30 Air and Space Law 6* (2005). The Air Navigation Commission – which is the main "technical" organ within ICAO, charged with the task to propose or amend traffic management rules – could be the most appropriate body for this purpose. However, so far neither the topic of STM nor the use of airspace by reusable aerospace vehicles has entered the official ICAO deliberations. IAA 2006 Study, pp. 49, 51–52.
21 On "due regard," see Sergio Marchisio, "Article IX," in Stephan Hobe, Bernhard Schmidt-Tedd & Kai-Uwe Schrögl (eds.), "Cologne Commentary on Space Law," Vol. 1 (Outer Space Treaty), 2009, pp. 175–6.

Art. IX also binds States Parties to undertake "appropriate international consultations" before proceeding with any "activity or experiment planned by it or its nationals in outer space" that the State "has reason to believe …would cause potentially harmful interference." Art. IX further provides States with a right to request consultation concerning "an activity or experiment planned by another State in outer space" for which the State requesting consultation has a "reason to believe … [it] would cause potentially harmful interference with activities in the peaceful exploration and use of outer space …."

Art. IX does not specify the procedures needed to conduct "appropriate international consultations" or secure such non-interference. One might expect, however, that a State is obligated by the Treaty to contact the potentially affected parties and provide them with information sufficient to prevent any possible harmful interference, or mitigate its effects.[22]

In terms of information and notification, there are several pertinent rules and principles in space law. OST Art. XI obliges States Parties "to the greatest extent feasible and practicable" to exchange information on the nature, conduct and locations of their activities in outer space. However, such formulation renders the provision relatively vague in its obligatory content.

The 1975 Registration Convention obliges launching States to register space objects and internationally notify on such registration.[23] However, such registration takes place after the launch into outer space, and it is binding only on those States and organizations that are parties to the Registration Convention.[24] Registration of space objects has been enhanced under the UNGA Resolution 62/101 adopted in 2007.[25] Even so, it is not enough: a pre-launch notification system would be needed for establishing a meaningful STM system. Moreover, a current, official list of active satellites orbiting the Earth does not exist.

Concerning non-binding law, the guidelines on space debris reduction are particularly relevant. On the basis of the guidelines previously adopted by the IADC,[26] the Scientific and Technical Subcommittee of COPUOS adopted in 2007 its own set of guidelines, intended to be applicable, on a voluntary basis, to all UN Member States conducting space activities.[27]

Some of these guidelines, such as the prevention of in-orbit break-ups and the limitation of objects released during normal operations, have an indirect impact on STM, as they help in keeping the space environment safe. Other guidelines go to the core of STM, in particular the provisions on removing non-operational spacecraft from the most useful and densely populated

---

22 Michael Mineiro, "Principles of Peaceful Purpose and the Obligation to Undertake Appropriate International Consultations in Accordance with Article IX of the Outer Space Treaty," 5th Eilene Galloway Symposium on Critical Issues in Space Law, Washington, DC, 2 December 2010, p. 2.
23 IAA 2006 Study, p. 63.
24 All other States may still register their space objects with the UN as per the 1961 UNGA Resolution 1721 (XVIII).
25 Recommendations on enhancing the practice of States and international intergovernmental organizations in registering space objects, UNGA Resolution 62/101(2007).
26 Inter-Agency Debris Coordination Committee (IADC): www.iadc-online.org/.
27 Space Debris Mitigation Guidelines of the United Nations Committee on the Peaceful Uses Of Outer Space, UNGA Resolution 62/217 (2007). The Guidelines reflect existing practices of national and international organizations. They are applicable mainly to mission planning and the operation of newly designed spacecraft and orbital stages. There are seven guidelines: a) to limit debris released during nominal operations, b) to minimize the potential for break-ups during operational phases, c) to limit the probability of accidental collision in orbit, d) to avoid intentional destruction and other harmful activities, e) to minimize the potential for post-mission break-ups resulting from stored energy, and f) to limit the long-term presence of spacecraft and launch vehicle orbital stages in the low-Earth orbit (LEO) region and g) in the geostationary Earth orbit (GEO) region after the end of their mission.

regions (i.e. LEO and GEO). The guidelines also set requirements for information and notification, e.g. for controlled re-entry.[28]

In brief, both sets of guidelines (IADC and COPUOS), despite their soft-law status, constitute a potential basis for specific elements of an STM system.[29]

In any case, current international space law lacks numerous provisions necessary for a comprehensive STM regime:[30]

- The Registration Convention does not require pre-launch notification. Provisions for such notifications only exist in the non-binding Hague Code of Conduct against Ballistic Missile Proliferation (HCOC), regarding arms control/disarmament.[31]
- There is no prioritization of certain space activities, no "right-of-way-rules," nor is any kind of utilization of space ruled out (except when it is against the peaceful uses).
- There is no prioritization of maneuvers, no traffic separation ("one-way-traffic").
- There are no "zoning" rules (restriction of certain activities in certain areas).
- There are no communication rules (advance notification and communication if orbits of other operators are passed).
- There is no legal distinction between active spacecraft and space debris.
- There are no binding rules for the mitigation of space debris, the disposal of non-functional space objects, and the prevention of pollution of the atmosphere.
- Space law lacks enforcement mechanisms.
- Private space activities could in some cases "escape" international space law, which is still largely State-centric.
- There is no delimitation between airspace and outer space.

As a new system of STM is formulated, the international community may address some of the above shortcomings.

National space law

Some rules intending to achieve safe access and re-entry to and from outer space, safe operations of space activities, and prevention of pollution in Earth orbit, can be found within national space acts, regulations, and licensing regimes. However, one has to take into account that these rules are not meant for dealing with STM, but rather with overall safety of space activities.[32]

The IAA Study provided an overview of existing national space rules applying to safe operations, preservation of the space environment, safe launches, and other aspects related to STM. For instance, the UK Outer Space Act provides that the holder of a license may be required to avoid any interference with the activities of others in the peaceful exploration and use of outer space.[33] As in international law however, there are generally no norms in national

---

28 "In the case of a controlled re-entry of a space system, the operator of the system should inform the relevant air traffic and maritime traffic authorities of the re-entry time and trajectory and the associated ground area" (IADC Guidelines, par. 5.3.2). Interestingly, this requirement has not been reproduced in Guideline 6 of the Space Debris Mitigation Guidelines of COPUOS.
29 IAA 2006 Study, p. 53.
30 IAA 2006 Study, pp. 39–40.
31 The Hague CoC of November 2002 provides for the exchange of pre-launch notifications on national Ballistic Missile and Space Launch Vehicle launches and test flights. IAA 2006 Study, pp. 45–46.
32 IAA 2006 Study, p. 40.
33 UK Outer Space Act 1986, Sec. 5(2)(e). Available at: www.legislation.gov.uk/ukpga/1986/38/introduction.

legal systems dealing with such important STM issues as "right of way" rules, collision avoidance, observation of space objects, or the in-orbit phase of space operations.[34]

In 2003, NASA revised its Policy Directive 8710.3A on limitation of space debris generation.[35] According to this policy, the program or project manager has to coordinate with the Department of Defense before any maneuver that changes the altitude of the orbit by 1 kilometer.

In 2004, the US FAA/AST developed a project for accommodation of new commercial space transportation operations into the national airspace system. The goal was to establish a Space and Air Traffic Management System (SATMS) in which space and aviation operations would be fully integrated in a modernized national airspace system.[36] Against the background of the increasing number of launch activities, as well as the upcoming use of RLVs and aerospace vehicles using the same airspace as aviation traffic, the integration of space and aviation operations was viewed as essential. FAA recommended that, regarding the re-entry of space objects, notification of and coordination with local and downrange air traffic, maritime authorities and local government officials be conducted.[37]

Launch and re-entry operations of lifting-body vehicles raise specific safety issues that might not be addressed by using "segregated" airspace as for traditional launch operations. Such issues concern different phases of flight, including the abort mode (i.e. failure to achieve orbit during the ascent phase; the vehicle then has to use an emergency landing site – as with the US Space Shuttle abort landing sites in France, Spain, and other countries) and accident during return (as happened to the Shuttle *Columbia*, if a vehicle were to disintegrate while overflying the controlled airspace).[38]

The FAA also contemplated the possibility of having to add a growing number of suborbital flights in the next few years, particularly those performed by commercial manned vehicles for both scientific and touristic purposes. These flights are more likely to be regulated initially under national air or space law.[39]

International telecommunications law

Every new satellite or spacecraft must additionally follow the international telecommunications procedures, as it will use certain frequencies of the radio spectrum. International telecommunications law already contains certain features of a rudimentary STM regime, to avoid primarily radio frequency interferences, but also in some cases physical interferences.

The International Telecommunication Union (ITU), a UN system agency, is in charge of coordinating radio communications with any object which is beyond the Earth's atmosphere. Radio frequencies are a limited natural resource to be used "rationally, efficiently and economically."[40] According to the ITU Radio Regulations, certain bands are specifically allocated to space operation services.[41]

34 IAA 2006 Study, pp. 40–43.
35 As it is an internal directive solely within NASA, it does not have the status of legislation.
36 IAA 2006 Study, pp. 44, 48.
37 IAA 2006 Study, p. 13.
38 Isabelle Rongier, "Space safety and STM," IISL/ECSL 2015 Symposium on STM, www.unoosa.org/ pdf/pres/lsc2015/symp-03.pdf.
39 On this particular topic, see e.g. Tanja Masson-Zwaan & Rafael Moro-Aguilar "Regulating private human suborbital flight at the international and European level: Tendencies and suggestions," *92 Acta Astronautica* (2012), pp. 243–54.
40 ITU Constitution Arts. 44.1 and 44.2.
41 ITU Radio Regulations Art. 5.

Not only telecommunications satellites must follow the ITU procedures. Normally, functional space objects require radio for tracking, telemetry and command, which are critical functions for satellites, as well as frequencies for the data and other communications which they receive and transmit.[42]

The listing by ITU in its Master International Frequency Register constitutes a statement that a satellite or spacecraft operating at the assigned location and complying with certain stated parameters, will neither generate nor suffer from harmful interference with other communication systems.[43]

Satellites placed in the Geostationary Earth's Orbit (GEO) in particular suffer from significant electromagnetic interferences between stations, in addition to being in one of the most physically congested regions of outer space.[44]

Around 465 GEO satellites are currently operating, and the ITU is unofficially the body that manages space traffic in the GEO belt. It utilizes coordination procedures between ITU member States, allocation of radio frequencies to telecom satellites and other communications services, and allotment of associated orbital positions (or "slots") to user States.

Sometimes the ITU tackles additional STM-related aspects which simply derive from a proper management of the radio frequencies. For example, the ITU's Radiocommunication Sector issued in 1993 a Recommendation to all member States that at the end of their active lifetime, geostationary satellites should be removed out of the GEO belt.[45]

The ITU however does not deal with launch activities, and it has no specific rules for movement in outer space; it only deals with the static question of positioning satellites in a specific orbital position. In-orbit operations of spacecraft, as well as the choice of radio frequencies and particular orbits used to provide satellite telecommunications, is left to the operators of the systems, since the ITU has powers only over frequencies but not over all other aspects of managing the orbits.[46]

In brief, through the coordination of frequencies and associated orbital positions in GEO, the ITU is in practice regulating this segment of outer space, thus providing a basis for a comprehensive traffic management regime in this specific area. It includes a pre-launch notification system, the separation or spacing of the satellites (to avoid radio and physical interference), and even elements of a dispute settlement mechanism.

The basic legal foundation is the principle that GEO is a limited natural resource. Most recently, the status of limited natural resource has been enlarged to include all satellite orbits.[47] This could enable further actions by the ITU to establish elements of an STM system in other orbits, especially in LEO and MEO, which will be increasingly populated by SmallSats and satellite constellations. According to the ITU Constitution, all orbits must be used rationally, efficiently and economically, while guaranteeing equitable access by all countries to those orbits.[48]

---

42   Yvon Henri, "Frequency Management and STM," 2015 IISL/ECSL Symposium on STM, www.unoosa.org/pdf/pres/lsc2015/symp-04.pdf.
43   IAA 2006 Study, p. 22.
44   www.spacedaily.com/reports/Battling_Satellite_Interference_999.html.
45   Recommendation first adopted in 1993 as ITU-R.S.1003 (04/93), and reissued in 2004 as S.1003 (04/93), "Environmental Protection of the Geostationary-satellite Orbit." The recommendation asks to send inactive satellites into a "graveyard" orbit, i.e. an orbit located at least 300 km higher than GEO.
46   IAA 2006 Study, pp. 44–45.
47   Art. 44.2 of the ITU Constitution.
48   IAA 2006 Study, p. 45.

To conclude: a number of rules exist in international telecommunications law, especially through the ITU Radio Regulations, which can be considered as potential elements of an eventual STM system. These rules, however, are neither complete nor harmonized. ITU rules aiming at the avoidance of radio frequency interference are far more advanced than rules aiming at the avoidance of physical interference.[49]

STM from the perspective of space safety

Congestion in space

As of 31 January 2015, there were 1,265 operating satellites, including 465 in GEO. But hundreds of new satellites could be launched in the next few years, due to the current expansion in the use of small satellites, and to prospective constellations for internet connection, broadcasting, Earth observation, and other purposes. Many of these satellites are not maneuverable, particularly SmallSats.[50]

Innovations in terms of miniaturization and other capabilities have attracted considerable excitement in the space community in recent years. This has fostered rapid increases in the numbers of satellites deployed in LEO, including hundreds of new, simple CubeSats. In February 2014 alone, the ISS deployed 33 CubeSats.[51] The increasing number of satellites in LEO has brought about concerns about growing domain congestion.

Disposal of spacecraft and orbital stages at the end of their useful lives is now recognized as an important aspect of mission design and planning. Operators are increasingly working to comply with current end-of-mission guidelines for disposing of spacecraft. The two principal objectives are to avoid risks to operational spacecraft and to mitigate the accumulation of debris in orbit.[52]

The techniques of satellite disposal in LEO and GEO are different. In LEO, spacecraft are normally de-orbited directly into the atmosphere over a broad ocean area, or are transferred into a lower orbit with a natural decay time of less than 25 years.[53] In GEO, spacecraft have to be moved to a higher orbit to prevent collisions or close encounters with active satellites.[54]

By contrast, the removal of non-functional spacecraft that were sent to orbit before the guidelines were approved remains a considerable challenge technically, economically, and legally.

Space debris

According to NASA estimates, there are currently more than 21,000 pieces of space debris larger than 10 centimeters (4 inches) orbiting the Earth. Material in lower orbits travels at least

---

49   IAA 2006 Study, p. 11.
50   I. Rongier, ibid., note 38 *(supra)*.
51   A CubeSat has a volume of exactly one liter (10 cm cube), or some multiple of that volume. Most employ commercial off-the-shelf components for the electronics. James D. Rendleman, "Space Traffic Management Options," in *57 IISL Proceedings* (2014), note 5, pp. 109–110.
52   IAA 2006 Study, pp. 33, 68–69. See also the IADC and COPUOS Space Debris Guidelines.
53   Not all satellites in LEO, particularly smallsats, are being de-orbited according to the international guidelines. See http://spacenews.com/1-in-5-cubesats-violate-international-orbit-disposal-guidelines/?utm_content=buffer0d598&utm_medium=social&utm_source=linkedin.com&utm_campaign=buffer.
54   IAA 2006 Study, p. 34. Not all satellites in GEO are following the rule; neither the ITU Recommendation nor the IADC or COPUOS guidelines are obligatory.

at 7 km per second, so the kinetic energy of a collision can be considerable. Also, one collision risks producing many fragments that then could collide with others, with the resulting creation of a belt of debris in a particular orbit which could imperil any space object crossing that orbit.[55]

If debris could be removed from key orbits, the hazard to space operations would decrease. Several projects have been proposed for "active debris removal." However, no scheme to remove existing debris from orbit has yet been implemented, and the technical consensus is that none of the proposed approaches is likely to be feasible in the near future.[56]

Satellites, spacecraft, and even astronauts are therefore at risk due to the presence of space debris. A growing number of close approaches (i.e. passes within less than one kilometer) between catalogued objects is taking place on a daily basis.

As a result, collision avoidance maneuvers are increasingly numerous, to avoid collisions that would be catastrophic for astronauts or operational satellites. Maximum predictability is needed for all space objects as the orbits become more and more crowded.[57]

The challenge for accurate predictions of close approach situations is availability of accurate data on the approaching vehicles, accurate orbit propagators, and models that provide useful information to satellite operators. Given that location is not precisely known, predicting collisions or even close approaches can be very difficult. An alternative is to use a probabilistic approach that accounts for the uncertainties in the locations of both objects. This procedure was used for the Space Shuttle and is one of the procedures still in use for the ISS. In general, space catalogues must be improved in order to provide meaningful collision avoidance services. In addition, a predicted close approach could be significantly in error, if the approaching object maneuvers or does a small station-keeping burn. Collision avoidance services must know a satellite's planned trajectory, with maneuvers included, to provide accurate predictions.[58]

With the growing numbers of on-orbit close approaches and the consequent growth in collision risks, it seems reasonable to improve existing surveillance systems and promote international collaboration, to mitigate the risks.

The importance of Space Situational Awareness (SSA)

Definition

The term "space situational awareness" (SSA) refers to monitoring the outer space environment for the purpose of identifying and assessing spaceflight hazards and risks to space assets. One essential part of SSA is space surveillance: the detection and monitoring of space objects in orbit. Another important subset of SSA is collision warning.

STM is completely dependent on space situational awareness: "managing" traffic in space requires knowing where and what the "traffic" is. Operational satellites in orbit must take care to avoid not only other operational satellites, but also more than 21,000 trackable man-made objects in space, in addition to the approximately 100,000 objects too small to be tracked with current capabilities, all of which pose a threat to operators in space.

---

55   www.spacedaily.com/reports/ISS_Adjusts_Orbit_to_Evade_Space_Junk_999.html.
56   IAA 2006 Study, pp. 70–71.
57   For a discussion of measures that States may take to reduce the proliferation of orbital debris, see Steven Mirmina, "Reducing the Proliferation of Orbital Debris: Alternatives to a Legally Binding Instrument," 99 Am. J. Int'l L. 649 (2005).
58   IAA 2006 Study, p. 67.

International measures to increase SSA

No country can, on its own, have sufficient accurate and timely information necessary to protect human spaceflight or the multitude of satellites on which countries across the globe have all grown to depend.

Therefore, over the last several years, the US has initiated a multi-tiered approach of pursuing bilateral and multilateral agreements to encourage greater responsibility in space. Some of these initiatives are known as "Transparency and Confidence Building Measures" (TCBMs), and other approaches involve participating in multilateral cooperation activities such as the International Code of Conduct for Outer Space Activities proposed by the EU, or the guidelines drafted by COPUOS and its Working Group on Long Term Sustainability of Outer Space Activities.

What is an SSA agreement?

Essentially, SSA agreements involve sharing technical information among operators in space, in an agreed format. At least six international bilateral agreements regarding sharing SSA information exist: One is between the US and the European Space Agency (ESA), and the other five are between the US and the governments of Australia, France, Canada, Japan, and the UK. In the US, the Departments of Defense and State collaborate with their counterparts around the world to conclude these agreements. In addition, the US has also entered SSA data sharing agreements with more than 40 commercial entities.

Legal authority of the US to provide information to foreign entities

The legal authority for the US Department of Defense (DOD) to provide SSA services and information to non-US Government (USG) entities comes from a specific law passed by the US Congress in 2003 and most recently amended in 2009. 10 USC § 2274 authorizes the Secretary of Defense to provide SSA services and information to, and obtain SSA data and information from, non-USG entities, when such action is "consistent with the national security interests of the United States."[59] This law enables the DOD to conclude SSA agreements with foreign governments and foreign commercial entities, subject to certain restrictions. The foreign entity must: (1) agree to pay what the DOD charges (if anything; currently there is no charge for these data); (2) agree not to transfer data or information received under the agreement to other entities (without express approval of DOD); (3) agree to whatever terms and conditions the Secretary of Defense deems necessary. One key provision is found in section (g) concerning immunity: the law explicitly protects the US and any agency thereof, and any contractors working on behalf of the US from "any suit in any court for any cause of action arising from the provision or receipt of space situational awareness services or information," whether or not provided in accordance with this law. The reason for this immunity is because the information provided is only as good as the data are, and there could be faults in the data or in their analysis. If the US were liable for damages as a result of the service, then there could be a reluctance of the DOD to share the data.

---

59   www.law.cornell.edu/uscode/text/10/2274.

Contents of SSA Agreements

The content of the SSA agreements between the US and other countries does not vary widely. They contain many of the same provisions as the law referenced above. Generally speaking, the SSA agreements provide that, upon request by the foreign government, the US will provide SSA "services and information on the orbit of space objects including their launch vehicles." The information provided remains the property of the "originating Government," and the "receiving Government has an obligation to protect the data from "unauthorized disclosure." Any disputes between the parties concerning the SSA cooperation will be resolved through amicable consultations. For the US, the actual implementing agency for the agreement is the US Strategic Command (or "Stratcom").[60] Generally speaking, it would be Stratcom's responsibility to plan maneuver support for collision avoidance, and it is the satellite owner/operator's responsibility to report to Stratcom any anomaly affecting the spacecraft bus, telemetry subsystem or other payload or subsystems aboard the spacecraft.[61]

SSA as a public-private partnership

Cooperation between industry and government is essential for successful SSA, because in the event of a conjunction, the possessor of the information must be able to rapidly inform the potentially affected satellite owners and operators. Thus, the US State Department works very closely with Stratcom to identify contact information for commercial satellite operators. As SSA information continues to improve, having the ability to notify the operators of spacecraft as early and accurately as possible is critical to enable affected operators to make the most well-informed decisions to execute evasive maneuvers. Stratcom is also concluding SSA agreements with both commercial partners and foreign governments.[62]

Notification of operators of possible conjunctions

In practice, the US has a well-entrenched practice of issuing notifications of close approaches. First, Stratcom's Joint Functional Component Command for Space (JFCC Space) provides the notification through its Joint Space Operations Center (JSPOC) to both US and international satellite operators. The JSPOC issues an average of 70–100 notifications per week via email and other means. The operators are encouraged to provide back to Stratcom the satellite ephemeris data; this helps to increase the accuracy of assessing the risk of collisions, especially if the satellite has recently maneuvered. In this case, the "ephemeris data" means not only the health of the satellite, but also the location of the satellite relative to the Earth and other satellites. This helps everyone know the precise location of the satellite. Satellite operators need not only time to decide what is the best evasive maneuver knowing a conjunction with an oncoming satellite or piece of debris is imminent, but also on-board propellant and the ability to maneuver. Maneuvers must be coordinated with other operators. Otherwise, an attempted evasive maneuver can cause satellites to move into each other's paths actually causing a collision, if not merely wasting valuable propellant.

---

60   Stratcom is one of nine unified commands under the US Department of Defense, and it has overall responsibility for US military space operations.
61   See e.g. the SSA Agreement between the US and Japan at: www.state.gov/documents/organization/219765.pdf.
62   As of April 2015, Stratcom had concluded SSA agreements with 47 commercial entities and with 11 governments and intergovernmental organizations.

Private efforts to increase SSA information sharing

Apart from the governmental SSA arrangements, there is also at least one private association of satellite operators that has as its purpose the sharing of SSA data. The Space Data Association (SDA) was formed in 2009 by several of the world's largest commercial satellite companies: Intelsat, Inmarsat, and SES. SDA's charter says that it will "seek and facilitate improvements in the safety and integrity of satellite operations through wider and improved coordination among satellite operators and to facilitate improved management of the shared resources of the space environment and the RF spectrum."[63] Its members also include Airbus, Arabsat, Echostar, NASA, NOAA, Loral, Orbcomm, Embratel, Turksat, and several others. SDA collects and shares orbital data with its members, to reduce the risks of on-orbit collisions and radio frequency interferences. It is noteworthy that neither the US Stratcom nor the SDA alone (nor any other entity) can know where all orbiting satellites and debris are at all times. For this reason, international cooperation and collaboration are strongly encouraged.

Other countries' efforts regarding SSA

In order to systematically monitor space traffic, a global network of observational points and considerable computational capacity must be functioning. At present, there are only two global networks that perform this task: the US Space Surveillance Network (SSN) and the Russian Space Surveillance System (SSS), both of which operate numerous, high-powered radars and several sophisticated optical systems around the world to monitor near-Earth space. This involves detecting, tracking and cataloguing orbiting space objects. Other countries maintain tracking and telemetry stations for control of their space assets, but lack the capability to monitor space traffic as a whole.[64]

A Space Surveillance and Tracking (SST) system is currently under development by the European Union. Through their Decision of 16 April 2014,[65] the European Parliament and Council jointly established a technical SST support framework aimed to "protect European citizens and space and terrestrial infrastructure." Its implementation was approved by the space agencies of France, Germany, Italy, Spain, and the United Kingdom in June 2015. The system was expected to start rendering services in 2016. It will provide European users with different types of warnings with respect to possible collisions of objects in Earth orbit or possible re-entries of space objects into the atmosphere.[66]

Summary

As stated at the outset, any STM system depends upon knowing where the traffic is. For this reason, there is increasing international cooperation in the sharing of information concerning the space environment and the activities in space that affect all space operators. These activities involve detecting and characterizing threats, as well as taking steps to warn about potential collisions between objects in space.

In the most recent US National Space Policy (2010), SSA is called out specifically. This Presidential policy provides that the US shall: "Develop, maintain, and use space situational awareness information from commercial, civil, and national security sources to detect, identify,

---

63   www.space-data.org/sda/about/sda-overview/.
64   IAA 2006 Study, pp. 35–36.
65   Based on Art. 182 (2) of the 2009 Treaty on the Functioning of the European Union.
66   http://spacenews.com/a-european-space-surveillance-network-inches-forward/.

and attribute actions in space that are contrary to responsible use and the long-term sustainability of the space environment."[67] Without SSA, misperceptions and mistrust could feed the flames of conflict between countries. As the number of countries that rely on space for economic and national security continues to increase, SSA provides an increasing role in promoting peace, security and stability.

The way forward on STM

The need for international collaboration

Near-Earth space is becoming increasingly congested. In the future, space actors must coordinate and cooperate with each other. However, as of today, operators often keep their plans confidential and do not make them public until shortly before launch, or even after launch, if ever. This makes it very difficult to undertake a global effort of coordination and planning by other actors.

For the purpose of achieving a common good, which also should be in their self-interest, spacefaring States and operators must follow specific rules. In particular, developing an STM system capable of managing launches, certain on-orbit operations, and re-entries would put into practice the important principles of cooperation, mutual assistance, due regard, and the affirmative duty to consult, as established in Art. IX of the OST.[68]

Most importantly, any SSA system needs to work in an international context, much like aviation does. A system where commercial entities and States voluntarily pool their SSA data – with information then made available to all participants – can be envisioned. Eventually, such an international, civil SSA system might form the foundation for a global STM system.[69]

An additional issue involves international technical coordination requirements with the existing rules and standard procedures on air and maritime traffic control. Notification of and coordination with local and downrange air traffic, maritime authorities, and local government officials is already considered a best practice in coordinating launch activities.

A promising approach for developing rules of the road for STM (in particular for private space activities) is to incorporate rules into national space regulations and licensing regimes.[70] The responsibility of national space authorities that license launch and re-entry operations (e.g. FAA/AST) could, in time, be extended to include civil and commercial STM services.[71]

Ways to implement a global STM system

A global effort of STM requires international cooperation. Here are some options to consider:

1. All operators publicize their plans in terms of orbits and frequencies and make them accessible to everybody (e.g. by posting them in their website). One problem that arises here is how to maintain the confidentiality of those data.
2. All space operators deliver their plans to a new governmental agency, a private company working on a commercial basis, or a private entity working on a non-profit basis. This

---

67 www.whitehouse.gov/sites/default/files/national_space_policy_6-28-10.pdf.
68 See J.D. Rendleman, ibid., note 51 (supra), p. 115.
69 www.space.com/6080-space-traffic-control-system-needed.html.
70 IAA 2006 Study, pp. 85–86.
71 I. Rongier, ibid.

agency, company or entity will keep the plans confidential except insofar as necessary to share them with other operators to maintain spacecraft safety.
3. An international effort of cooperation is launched for creating universal voluntary STM guidelines, following the model for cooperation of the IADC. These guidelines could be later implemented on a national basis.
4. An intergovernmental organization is put in charge of STM by means of an international treaty. Such an international organization could fill similar functions as the FAA/AST does in the United States.

The IAA Study defended a different path, i.e. An international agreement on STM that would be structured in two levels, as per the ITU or ICAO models: 1) a core international agreement that would be difficult to change, and 2) a set of technical annexes that would be easier to change and thus could be adapted more easily. Implementation of the provisions could be monitored by ICAO, for example, which would receive the mandate and evolve into a body shaped for that purpose.[72]

Some authors argue however that a hard-law treaty-based STM regime is not necessary at this stage. Alternative ways to develop an STM regime are suggested instead, such as taking full use of COPUOS or other international fora, clarifying the basic issues in space treaties and principles, promoting guidelines as a useful supplement, developing technical standards, and facilitating international cooperation.[73]

A role for existing organizations?

The International Civil Aviation Organization (ICAO) is a specialized agency of the United Nations charged with coordinating and regulating international air travel. It has responsibility for establishing standards (SARPs) aimed to ensure civil aviation and airport safety. The Chicago Convention under which ICAO operates creates a broad mandate in this regard, and some have argued that ICAO, under the existing convention, already has the authority to establish a coordinated approach to space and aviation safety standards not only for airspace but for the region extending all the way to low Earth orbit.

As suggested by Professor Paul Dempsey and Dr. Michael Mineiro, creating a new international organization tasked with STM would require significant political effort and economic expense. The exercise by ICAO, or by another international organization currently in existence, of authority to coordinate suborbital and orbital traffic, or at least standardize navigation for space vehicles traversing airspace, may indeed be a better approach.[74]

Other observers, however, have noted that ICAO's exercise of legal authority over space activities would require either amending the Convention, or a very broad interpretation by ICAO of its existing jurisdiction under the Convention over suborbital and orbital vehicles to the extent they impact the safety, regularity, and efficiency of commercial air navigation.

There may also be a role for COPUOS. STM is related to long-term sustainability of space activities, an item that is already on the agenda of COPUOS. In addition, during the 2015 session of the Legal Subcommittee of COPUOS, "Exchange of views on the concept of Space

---

72 IAA 2006 Study, pp. 14–15.
73 Guoyu Wang, "Space Traffic Management (STM) and the Governance of Space Activities (GSA)," IISL/ECSL 2015 Symposium, www.unoosa.org/pdf/pres/lsc2015/symp-05.pdf.
74 Paul S. Dempsey & Michael C. Mineiro, "Space Traffic Management: A Vacuum in Need of Law," 48th IISL Colloquium, Glasgow, 2008, IAC-08-E3.2.3, p. 3.

Traffic Management" was adopted as a new item for discussion. The purpose was "to reflect on the concept of STM, on what it entails and on what consequences it would have for the organization and governance of space activities. In particular the contribution of STM to the safety of space operations benefiting all users of outer space (…) could be investigated."[75]

A private STM system?

The general principles of space law provide a basis and rationale to establish a STM regime. However, STM will require additional regulation (with regard to information about space missions), which could be perceived as limiting the freedom of use of outer space guaranteed by the OST. An international consensus on binding regulations will only be achieved if States and operators expect a specific and collective advantage from a comprehensive STM system, including an economic benefit.[76]

A privately performed STM system that would work for instance by setting standards might provide a more flexible, responsive and evolutionary process, thus reducing drastically in turn the space operator compliance costs.[77] Indeed, recent activities of the SDA point to the possibility of an independent, private self-regulation scheme, at least for the commercial satellite industry.[78]

Conclusion

Until now, STM has been more of a theoretical rather than a practical problem. Outer space is large and the probabilities of collision remain small. And though the radio spectrum and the GEO belt are limited natural resources, the coordination of States through the ITU has been largely sufficient up till now to prevent collisions and significant electromagnetic interference.

However, in the next few decades a proper system of STM may become necessary, in view of the growing number of space actors and the increasing use of radio frequencies and orbits. Same as the growth in air travel led to air traffic management and the creation of ICAO and the SARPs, assuring that functional space assets will have minimal interference to their future operations may require a set of traffic rules and an international management system to warn operators of the presence of space debris, potential collisions, and other hazards. Moreover, States establishing or agreeing to be coordinated by an STM system seems consistent with the obligations imposed upon them by the OST, most notably the duties of cooperation, mutual assistance, due regard, and consultations.

Fortunately, we are not yet at the stage where this matter is crucial. The international community may well adopt a reactive approach, namely waiting till an accident happens. Until then, there remains some time to decide upon the best solution.[79] Negotiating an international agreement on STM (i.e., a "Space Traffic Treaty" complementing the current legal framework),

---

75   See COPUOS document: www.unoosa.org/pdf/limited/c2/AC105_C2_2015_CRP13E.pdf.
76   IAA 2006 Study, pp. 10–12, 54.
77   J.D. Rendleman, ibid., pp. 107, 131.
78   J.D. Rendleman, ibid., pp. 107, 132.
79   In this regard, the new space law passed by the US Congress in November, 2015 contains an important Section 109 on Orbital Traffic Management. It requires the NASA Administrator to consult with other Agencies and report to Congress on the current roles and responsibilities within the government, private sector, and international community related to SSA, orbital traffic management, and orbital debris mitigation measures. The law itself states that it was the sense of the US Congress that "an improved framework may be necessary for space traffic management…."

or empowering ICAO or some other new international organization with STM tasks, does not seem critical or necessary at the moment. For the time being, international technical coordination among States and private operators, through initiatives such as SDA and US Stratcom, seems to be a functional approach.

In the medium term, other ways for the development of STM and SSA rules exist, including the elaboration of non-binding guidelines and standards by a space-agency coordination forum (akin to what IADC has done for space debris mitigation) or by non-governmental technical organizations (such as the IAASS).[80] At the moment, those approaches seem to be the most palatable politically to most space faring entities.

---

80 International Association for the Advancement of Space Safety: http://iaass.space-safety.org/.

11

Law and military uses of outer space

Setsuko Aoki

1 Introduction: the past and present situation of the military uses of outer space

It is now widely known that no sooner had World War II ended than the race to launch a military satellite into outer space by the United States (US) and the former Soviet Union (USSR) began.[1] It is estimated that approximately 75 percent of the satellites launched during the Cold War era were exclusively for military purposes.[2] Although the ratio has since decreased to about 20 percent as of 2015,[3] it does not mean that military uses of outer space have also decreased. Surveys on this issue indicate that military operations have been using commercial space systems extensively for more than two decades. Early examples include the fact that about 60 percent of satellite communications services in air operations against the Federal Republic of Yugoslavia in 1999 were provided from the commercial sectors[4] and that both the US National Reconnaissance Office (NRO) and National Imagery and Mapping Agency (NIMA) extensively purchased commercially-based images such as IKONOS and SPOT in the 2001 Afghanistan War.[5]

Further, a wide range of offensive space capabilities for possible armed conflicts in space have been pursued at least by the three space powers; the US, the USSR/Russia and China. One study shows that more than 4,500 pieces of space debris have been generated in the low earth orbit (LEO) as a result of more than 50 anti-satellite (ASAT) tests conducted from 1959 to

---

1   See, e.g., Paul Stares, *The Militarization of Space: U.S. Policy 1945–1984* (Ithaca, NY: Cornell University Press, 1985) at 22–29.
2   This is calculated from various documents including the annual publication of Stockholm International Peace Research Institute (SIPRI) ed., *World Armaments and Disarmament: SIPRI Yearbook* series from 1973 to 1990.
3   See, e.g., "UCS Satellite Database" online: Union of Concerned Scientists www.ucsusa.org/nuclear_weapons_and_global_security/solutions/space-weapons/ucs-satellite-database.html#.VWGzj1Jg9dw.
4   Michael N. Schmitt, "International Law and Military Operations in Space" (2006) 10 *Max Planck UNYB* 89 at 98.
5   Loring Wirbel, *Star Wars: US Tools of Space Supremacy* (London: Pluto Press, 2004) at 114–115.

2014.[6] While the US (29 tests, 459 trackable pieces)[7] and the USSR (23 tests, 842 trackable pieces)[8] conducted more tests than China (six tests, 3,280 trackable pieces),[9] more attention tends to be paid to the 2007 Chinese ASAT test. This seems motivated by the fact that more than 70 percent of trackable debris was produced by its 2007 test and that it was the first test after a two-decade moratorium on ASAT tests producing physical space debris.[10]

Today, while military use of outer space is recognized as a legitimate activity so long as it is conducted in accordance with international law, the permissible scope thereof seems somewhat vague compared with that on the Earth. This may be because of the non-occurrence of armed conflicts in outer space until today. In addition, the inherently dual-use nature of space technology, more conspicuous than that of other advanced technologies such as nuclear power generation, may well have acted as an obstacle to creating a clear picture of lawful military uses of space.

This chapter, therefore, describes legal regulations on the military uses of outer space in a variety of aspects, both *jus ad bellum* and *jus in bello*.[11] Needless to say, the *Charter of the United Nations* (UN Charter) is of utmost importance in determining legality and illegality of any space activities analyzed below.[12]

2 International law and military activities in outer space

(1) Early years efforts: 1957–1963

The first United Nations General Assembly (UNGA) resolution referring to outer space[13] was adopted within two months of the successful launch of the first artificial satellite, Sputnik I, on 4 October 1957. It was not, however, the prompt and direct reaction to the start of the space age, but a result of disarmament discussions in the first Committee of the UNGA, where views were divided between the "general and complete disarmament" (GCD) advocated by the USSR and Eastern bloc countries and the partial disarmament supported by the US and its Western allies.[14] That resolution, UNGA Res. 1148 (XII), within the context of the recommendation to negotiate an agreement for nuclear reduction schemes, urges consideration of an inspection system to ensure that "the sending of objects through outer space shall be exclusively

---

6   Brian Weeden, *Through a Glass, Darkly: Chinese, American and Russian Anti-Satellite Testing in Space* (17 March 2014) at 17, 21–27, 29–30; online: The Space Review www.thespacereview.com/article/2473/1.
7   Ibid., at 21–27.
8   Ibid., at 29–30.
9   Ibid., at 17. At least one more ASAT test which did not generate space debris was confirmed after the publication of Dr. Weeden, thus making six tests in total as of June 2015.
10 Ibid., at 25.
11 See, e.g., Steven Freeland, "The Laws of War in Outer Space" in Kai-Uwe Schrogl *et al.*, eds., *Handbook of Space Security, vol.1* (New York: Springer, 2015) 81 at 81–112; Fabio Tronchetti, "Legal Aspects of the Military Uses of Outer Space" in Frans von der Dunk, ed., *Handbook of Space Law* (Cheltenham: Edward Elgar, 2015) 331 at 331–381.
12 Ricky J. Lee, "*The Jus ad Bellum in Spatialis*: The Exact Content and Practical Implications of the Law on the Use of Force in Outer Space" (2003) 29 *J. Space L.* 93 at 93–119.
13 UN Doc. A/RES/1148 (XII) (14 November 1957).
14 Both Satellites and ICBMs were included as the subjects for the international inspection in the US proposal, for early proposals did not distinguish missiles from spacecraft. UN GAOR IX A/C.1/738 (12 January 1957); UN Doc. DC/SC/166 (29 August 1957). See, also, Joseph R. Soraghan, "Reconnaissance Satellites: Legal Characterization and Possible Utilization for Peacekeeping" (1964) 13 *McGill L. J.* 458 at 460.

for peaceful and scientific purposes" so that the launch of nuclear-tipped ballistic missiles would be avoided.[15] Further progress on the discussions of space disarmament was rendered impossible in this Committee due to the USSR's desire to eliminate all US military bases outside its territory in exchange for the total ban on military use of space.[16]

As it was evident that emerging space activities had much wider goals than disarmament, the US and USSR agreed in 1958 to consider the "Question of the Peaceful Use of Outer Space"[17] independently from disarmament issues in the first Committee of the UNGA. That resulted in UNGA Res. 1348 (XIII) and UNGA Res. 1472 (XIV) which established an *ad hoc* and permanent Committee on the Peaceful Uses of Outer Space (COPUOS) in which the study of the "peaceful uses of outer space" was included in the mandates.[18] Therefore, "peaceful uses" was the prerequisite for space activities pursued in COPUOS while the meaning of "peaceful" was not defined.[19] Subsequently, landmark instruments UNGA Res. 1721A (XVI)[20] and UNGA Res. 1962 (XVIII)[21] were adopted in 1961 and 1963 respectively: the former defined the legal status of outer space as *res communis omnium*[22] and the latter was incorporated virtually *in toto* in the 1967 *Outer Space Treaty* (OST)[23] as the Magna Carta of outer space.

The important issue that surfaced in this period was if "peaceful" should equate with "non-military" or "non-aggressive". Except in the very early period through 1958, the US position was "peaceful" being "non-aggressive" and as such, military activities are permitted except in so far as they are expressly forbidden by international law.[24] Only "aggressive activities" in outer space can be considered as "non-peaceful".[25] On the other hand, the USSR interpreted "peaceful" to mean "non-military", and therefore declared all military activities in outer space as "non-peaceful".[26] Which of the two interpretations should be taken is critical, for example, in determining as to whether collecting intelligence data from space is lawful under international law. The US and most Western writers regarded the non-aggressive operation of reconnaissance satellites as in conformity with international law, for outer space had been recognized as *res communis omnium*[27] similarly to the high seas where States may carry out activities of military nature such as naval maneuvers and testing of weapons in accordance with

---

15 UN Doc. A/RES/1148 (XII), *supra* note 13, para. 1 (f).
16 See, e.g., J.F. McMahon, "Legal Aspects of Outer Space" (1962) 38 *BYIL* 339 at 360–364.
17 This is a combined agenda proposed by the USSR on 15 March 1958 and US on 2 September 1958 respectively.
18 UN Doc. A/RES/1348 (XIII) (13 December 1958), preface, para. 1 (a) (b) & para. 2; UN Doc. A/RES/1472 (XIV) (12 December 1959), preface, para. 1 (a).
19 See, e.g. Howard J. Taubenfeld, "Consideration at the United Nations of the Status of Outer Space" (1959) 53 *AJIL* 400 at 400–405.
20 UN Doc. A/RES/1721A (XVI) (20 December 1961).
21 UN Doc. A/RES/1962 (XVIII) (13 December 1963).
22 UN Doc. A/RES/1721A, *supra* note 20, preface & para. 1 (b).
23 *Treaty on Principles Governing the Activities of States in the Exploration and Use of Outer Space, including the Moon and Other Celestial Bodies*, 27 January 1967, 610 UNTS 205 [Outer Space Treaty or OST].
24 See, e.g., Ivan A. Vlasic, "The Legal Aspects of Peaceful and Non-Peaceful Uses of Outer Space" in Bhupendra Jasani, ed., *Peaceful and Non-Peaceful Uses of Space: Problems of Definition for the Prevention of an Arms Race* (London: Taylor & Francis, 1991) 37 at 38–39.
25 See, e.g., American Bar Foundation, *Committee on the Law of Space, Report to NASA* (1961) at 25–26; Edward R. Finch, Jr., "Outer Space for 'Peaceful Purposes'" (1968) 54 *ABA Journal* 365 at 365–367.
26 See, e.g., G. Zhukov, "Practical Problems of Space Law" (May 1963) *International Affairs (Moscow)* 27 at 27–28.
27 See, e.g., UN Doc. A/RES/1721A, *supra* note 20, para. 1 (b).

relevant international law.[28] Eastern bloc writers tended to be opposed to that interpretation from its "non-military" doctrine,[29] and the Soviet position was explicitly stated at the Legal Subcommittee (LSC) of the COPUOS in 1962 when it proposed the prohibition on "the use of artificial satellites for the collection of intelligence information in the territory of foreign States".[30] The Soviet objections had subsided by the time the OST was negotiated in the COPUOS/LSC as its reconnaissance satellites had been successfully operated.[31]

(2) PTBT and UNGA Resolution 1884 (XVIII) (1963)

The breakthrough in space disarmament was made in 1963 by the introduction of two important instruments. First, eight years of discussion led to the conclusion and entering into force of the *Partial Test Ban Treaty* (PTBT) in 1963,[32] which obligates States Parties not to carry out any nuclear weapon test explosion, or any other nuclear explosion, in the atmosphere, under water, or in outer space.[33] The PTBT was motivated, in part, by the fact that EMP radiation generated by the US and Soviet nuclear tests in outer space disabled at least six satellites of these two countries and the United Kingdom,[34] and that nuclear explosion detection satellites proved to be able to adequately verify compliance with the PTBT.[35] While this treaty prohibits nuclear explosions in outer space either as a weapon test or otherwise, the possibility of the use of nuclear weapons in case of, for example, self-defense, would be determined by the UN Charter, thereby beyond the scope of the PTBT.[36]

Second, UNGA Res. 1884 (XVIII) was adopted which calls on all States "[t]o refrain from placing in orbit around the earth any objects carrying nuclear weapons or any other kinds of weapons of mass destruction, installing such weapons on celestial bodies, or stationing such weapons in outer space in any other manner".[37] It is noteworthy that UNGA Res. 1884 originated not in COPUOS, but in the 1962 proposals by the USSR and the US in the

---

28 Legal status of espionage also has to be considered in determining the legality of the reconnaissance satellites. See, e.g., Spencer M. Beresford, "Surveillance Aircraft and Satellites: A Problem of International Law" (1960) 27 *J. Air L. & Com.* 107 esp. at 115–116; Soraghan, *supra* note 14 at 469–470; McMahon, *supra* note 16 at 365–380. In addition, lack of the effective control means for the reconnaissance satellites was explained as the reason to support its legitimacy. M.S. Vazques, *Cosmic International Law* (Detroit: Wayne State University Press, 1965) at 170.
29 See, e.g., G. Zhukov, "Space Espionage Plans and International Law" (October 1960) *International Affairs (Moscow)* 53 at 53–57. Gyula Gál, *Space Law* (English Translation) (Leiden: A.W. Sijthoff & Oceana, 1969) at 175–181. Note has to be taken, however, that scholars of the Socialist countries did not necessarily interpret satellite monitoring against international law. See, e.g., E. Korovin, "International Status of Cosmic Space" (January 1959) *International Affairs (Moscow)* 53 at 53–59.
30 A/AC.105/L.2 (10 September 1962), para. 8.
31 D. Brennan, "Arms and Arms Control in Outer Space" in L.P. Bloomfield ed., *Outer Space- Prospects for Man and Society* (Eaglefield Cliffs, NJ: Prentice-Hall, 1962) at 161; G.A. Steinberg, *Satellite Reconnaissance: the Role of Informal Bargaining* (New York: Praeger Publishing, 1983) at 59–63.
32 *Treaty Banning Nuclear Weapon Tests in the Atmosphere, in Outer Space and Under Water*, 5 August 1963, 480 UNTS 43 [PTBT].
33 Ibid., Art. 1 (1) (a) (b) & (2).
34 James Clay Molts, *The Politics of Space Security: Strategic Restraint and the Pursuit of National Interests* (Stanford, CA: Stanford University Press, 2008) at 119.
35 C.W. Jenks, *Space Law* (London: Stevens & Sons, 1965) at 51–52, 305–308.
36 See, e.g., Steven Freeland, "In Heaven as on Earth? The International Legal Regulation of the Military Use of Outer Space" (2011) 8 *US-China L. Rev.* 272 at 277.
37 UN Doc. A/RES/1884 (XVIII) (17 October 1963), para. 2 (a).

Eighteen Nation Committee on Disarmament (ENDC),[38] which was followed by the adoption in the first Committee of the UNGA in October 1963.[39] The text of UNGA Res. 1884, para. 2. (a) is almost identical to Art. IV (1) of the 1967 Outer Space Treaty.

(3) The Outer Space Treaty (1967)

A. Brief drafting process of the outer space treaty

UNGA Res. 1962 was eventually followed by intensive discussions in COPUOS/LSC and the first Committee in the UNGA in the latter half of 1966, which led to the adoption of the Outer Space Treaty. In comparison with other important international treaties adopted in the twentieth century, the drafting process of the OST was swift. After the submission of the draft treaty by both the USSR and the US on 16 June 1966,[40] it took only about six months before the OST was adopted in the UNGA.[41]

There is no doubt that Art. IV of the OST remains by far the most important accomplishment in space disarmament, just as it was in 1967.

Art. IV reads:

> States Parties to the Treaty undertake not to place in orbit around the Earth any objects carrying nuclear weapons or any other kinds of weapons of mass destruction, install such weapons on celestial bodies, or station such weapons in outer space in any other manner.
>
> The Moon and other celestial bodies shall be used by all States Parties to the Treaty *exclusively for peaceful purposes*. The establishment of military bases, installations and fortifications, the testing of any type of weapons and the conduct of military maneuvers on celestial bodies shall be forbidden. The use of military personnel for scientific research or for any other peaceful purposes shall not be prohibited. The use of any equipment or facility necessary for peaceful exploration of the Moon and other celestial bodies shall also not be prohibited. (emphasis added)

Views differed concerning what kinds of activities were precisely prohibited by Art. IV for reasons including the absence of a definition of "exclusively peaceful purposes" and the dominance of the US-Soviet role determining the text outside the UN before its final adoption in the UNGA. The present author finds that scholars and governmental officials presented at least four categories of interpretations at that time and five interpretations are theoretically possible.

Before illustrating those interpretations, however, points of importance both clarified and remaining vague during the drafting phase are touched upon below. First, it was agreed that an intercontinental ballistic missile (ICBM) was not banned as it does not orbit around the Earth or would otherwise be stationed in outer space.[42] Likewise, Fractional Orbital Bombardment

---

38 UN Doc. ENDC/2 (15 March 1962); UN Doc. ENDC/30 (18 April 1962).
39 UN Doc. A/C.1/PV.1311 (18 October 1963).
40 See, e.g., Bin Cheng, "The 1967 Space Treaty" in idem, *Studies in International Law* (Oxford: Clarendon Press, 1997) 215 at 220.
41 As for the drafting history, ibid., at 215–226; Stephan Hobe, Bernhard Schmidt-Tedd & Kai-Uwe Schrogl, eds. [Hobe *et al.*], *Cologne Commentary on Space Law, vol. 1* (Cologne: Carl Heymanns Verlag, 2009) at 72–75.
42 See, e.g., US Senate Committee on Aeronautical and Space Sciences [US Senate], *Outer Space Treaty Analysis and Background Data Staff Report* (1967) at 26.

Systems (FOBS) being developed by the USSR around that time were not probably banned by the OST because such systems would de-orbit before orbiting the Earth once.[43] Second, the Indian proposal to add the phrase "exclusively for peaceful purposes" also in Art. IV (1) was not adopted,[44] which did not however resolve the interpretative differences as to whether the outer void space[45] was free from the obligation to be utilized for "exclusively peaceful purposes". Third, a certain ambiguity remained if the expressly prohibited actions on the Moon and other celestial bodies specified in Art. IV (2) represented a definitive list or just an exemplified list. While the original US proposal traceable to Art. I of the *Antarctic Treaty*[46] suggested such were exemplified, thus aiming at the demilitarization of the Moon and other celestial bodies,[47] the Soviet text eventually taken as the final product seemed rather definitive, and as such, the wording of Art. IV (2) left room for interpretation. Taking this in mind as a prerequisite, then, several interpretations regarding what is prohibited are described below.

B. Five possible interpretations for "peaceful" purposes

(i) "Peaceful" shall be interpreted as "non-military" and the obligation of non-military use is extended not only to the Moon and other celestial bodies but also to outer void space. The main reason that outer void space shall be used for "non-military" purposes is explained by the commentators supporting this interpretation that any military activity could serve only one State or a group of States and never "for the benefit and in the interests of all countries"(Art. I), thus contradicting the legally-binding obligation of the OST if a "non-military" interpretation is not applied.[48] It follows from this interpretation that not only conventional weapons and reconnaissance satellites to be placed in orbit around the Earth but also ballistic missiles maneuvered through outer space shall be prohibited. Such interpretation contradicts the US-Soviet agreement that the treaty would not change the earthly situation on ICBMs,[49] State practice of these two countries and, above all, the text provided for in Art. IV (1). According to the commentators who advocate this interpretation, such contradiction would be addressed by a future GCD agreement.[50]

(ii) "Peaceful" shall be interpreted as "non-aggressive" for both outer void space and the Moon and other celestial bodies. Hence, while the possibility of military use on celestial

---

43 Statement by Mr. McNamara on 3 November 1967. Stares, *supra* note 1 at 99; Eric Stein, "Legal Restraints in Modern Arms Control Agreements" (1972) 66 *AJIL* 255 at 264. Opposing view was presented by Italy in A/7221 (10 September 1968).
44 A/AC.105/35 Annex WP. No.15 (25 July 1966); A/AC.105/C.2/SR/66 (21 October 1966) at 5–6. Argentina, Iran, Brazil, United Arab Republic, Canada, Austria and Japan supported India.
45 "[O]uter void space" is a term made by Prof. Bin Cheng, meaning the vast empty void space between celestial bodies beyond terrestrial national space. Bin Cheng, "The Military Use of Outer Space and International Law" in Cheng, *supra* note 40, 523 at 529.
46 The Antarctic Treaty, 1 December 1959, 402 UNTS 71.
47 See, e.g., US Senate, *supra* note 42 at 24–25; Cheng, *supra* note 40 at 247–248.
48 See, e.g., Marko G. Markoff, "Disarmament and 'Peaceful Purposes' Provisions in the 1967 Outer Space Treaty" (1976) 4 *J. Space L.* 3 at 11–12; G.P. Zhukov, "On the Question of Interpretation of the Term 'Peaceful Use of Outer Space' Contained in the Space Treaty" in *Proceedings of the 11th (1968) Colloquium on the Law of Outer Space* (1969) 36 at 36–38 [*11th IISL Proceedings*]; Marko G. Markov, "The Juridical Meaning of the Term 'Peaceful' in the 1967 Space Treaty" in ibid., 30 at 30–35.
49 US Senate, *supra* note 42 at 26.
50 See, e.g., Marko G. Markov, "Against the So-Called 'Broader' Interpretation of the Term 'Peaceful'" in *11th IISL Proceedings*, *supra* note 48, 73 at 80–81.

bodies is currently slim due to the comprehensiveness of enumerated banned actions which are almost tantamount to demilitarization, it is yet permissible to carry out military activities not specifically prohibited in Art. IV (2).[51] This interpretation is supported by a number of Western experts.[52]

(iii) Outer void space is under the obligation of "non-aggressive" use while the Moon and other celestial bodies are subject to "non-military" use of space. The fact that Art. IV (2) is modeled on its predecessor, the *Antarctic Treaty* (Art. I), which demilitarized Antarctica,[53] is often used as evidence for the obligation of the non-military use of the Moon and other celestial bodies, in addition to the fact that the word "exclusively" is added to "peaceful purposes".[54]

(iv) The obligation of "peaceful" as "non-aggressive" uses of space is imposed only on the Moon and other celestial bodies, and "exclusively for peaceful purposes" is not imposed on outer void space, where only the banning of weapons of mass destruction (WMD) and the threat or use of force (Art. 2 (4) of the UN Charter) is obligatory.[55]

(v) Irrespective of the fact that it is possible from the theoretical point of view, no commentators seem to specifically advocate that the Moon and other celestial bodies are for non-military use whereas no obligation of peaceful use is imposed on outer void space.

There are yet some commentators who are of the opinion that the dichotomy between "non-aggressive" and "non-military" is not a useful test and what is prohibited should be determined under the expressly stated text of the OST and the relevant provisions of the UN Charter.[56]

C. Assessment of the different interpretations

Among the different interpretations on the obligation of peaceful uses of outer void space, virtually no difference can be found between the peaceful=non-aggressive interpretation and

---

51 See, e.g., Robert L. Bridge, "International Law and Military Activities in Outer Space" (1980)13 *Akron L. Rev.* 649 at 659; Alex Meyer, "Interpretation of the Term 'Peaceful' in the Light of the Space Treaty" in *11th IISL Proceedings, supra* note 48, 24 at 29.

52 Martin Menter, "Peaceful Uses of Outer Space and National Security" (1983) 17 *International Lawyer* 581 at 584–585; Bin Cheng, "Definitional Issues in Space Law: the 'Peaceful Use' of Outer Space, including the Moon and other Celestial Bodies" in Cheng, *supra* note 40, 513 at 515–522. Canadian Working Paper submitted to the Conference on Disarmament (CD) also takes this position while it does not purport to provide Canadian government position. CD/618, CD/OS/WP.6 (23 July 1985) at 11. Note has to be taken, however, that there are a number of Western lawyers who are of the view that the Moon and other celestial bodies are restricted to only for the non-military uses. See, e.g., Cheng, ibid., at 521; Hobe, et al., *supra* note 41 at 82–84; Lee, *supra* note 12 at 95–98.

53 Art. IV (2) of the OST, however, does not contain the phrase "*inter alia,* any measures of a military nature" found in the Antarctic Treaty (Art. I (1)) which suggests the exemplified nature of the expressly prohibited actions.

54 See, e.g., Professor V. Kopal's statement in "Summary of Discussions" in *Proceedings of the 10th (1967) Colloqium on the Law of Outer Space* (1968) 114 at 114 [*10th IISL Proceedings*]; Cheng, *supra* note 52 at 518–519; Meyer, *supra* note 51 at 24–29.

55 See, e.g., Istvan Herczeg, "Problems of Interpretation of the Space Treaty of 27 January 1967" (as a view of Mrs. Eileen Galloway) in *10th IISL Proceedings, supra* note 54, 105 at 106–107. While Professor Carl Q. Christol seemed to think this "non-military- or- non-aggressive" dichotomy was not useful, his view is nearer to this school of thought. Carl. Q. Christol, *The Modern International Law of Outer Space* (New York: Pergamon Press, 1982) at 20–30.

56 See, e.g., Christol, *supra* note 55 at 28–29; Stephen Gorove, "Arms Control Provisions in the Outer Space Treaty: A Scrutinizing Reappraisal" (1973) 3 *Ga J. Int'l & Comp. L.* 114 at 117–122.

the interpretation that the obligation of "exclusively peaceful purposes" is not incurred. As outer space activities shall be in any case conducted in accordance with international law including the UN Charter (Art. III of the OST), permissible action in the outer void space shall be within the prohibition of "threat or use of force" (Art. 2 (4) of the UN Charter), which equates with or is almost identical to "non-aggressive" use. In other words, in both interpretations, the prohibition of a) "threat or use of force", plus ii) stationing WMD in outer void space is the dividing line of permissible and impermissible use. Further, it can be safely said that non-military use of outer void space could not be corroborated by either consistency in interpretation in the wording of Art. IV (1) or subsequent State practice. If State practices are taken into account, it seems appropriate to conclude that both the US and USSR shared benefits in using outer space as freely as possible within the restrictions of the UN Charter which prohibits "threat or use of force" (Art. 2 (4)). As a result, scant media attention was paid in 1978 when US President Carter finally officially admitted to the use of military satellites.[57] As for on the Moon and other celestial bodies, it seems that "peaceful" may be interpreted as either non-military or non-aggressive, and depending on the interpretation taken, the scope of the permissible activity could theoretically differ, though virtually no difference will arise under today's technological development.

Arts. I, III, IX, X and XII of the OST are indirectly related to space arms control although these Articles would not influence the interpretation of Art. IV.

D. The definition of WMD

With respect to the scope of weapons prohibited in outer void space, the definition of WMD matters, for it would directly affect the scope of the prohibition. At the time of drafting the OST, WMD was understood as defined by the UN Commission for Conventional Armaments: "atomic explosive weapons, radio-active material weapons, lethal chemical and biological weapons, and any weapons developed in the future" which have comparable in destructive effect to such existent weapons.[58] Today, new types of possible WMD have been discussed including radiological weapons in the Conference on Disarmament (CD)[59] and UN Disarmament Commission.[60]

(4) The ENMOD Convention (1977)

The *Convention on the Prohibition of Military or Any Other Hostile Use of Environmental Modification Techniques* (ENMOD Convention)[61] bans States Parties from engaging in military or any other hostile use of "environmental modification techniques" (defined in Art. II) having widespread, long-lasting or severe effects (Art. I) in areas including outer space (Art. II).[62] The hostile use of

---

57   Stares, *supra* note 1 at 186.
58   UN Doc. S/C.3/32/Rev.1 (18 August 1948).
59   See, e.g., CD/2004 (10 September 2014), agenda item 5.
60   See, e.g., Francis Lyall and Paul B. Larsen, *Space Law: A Treatise* (Burlington: Ashgate, 2009) at 515–516.
61   18 May 1977, 1108 UNTS 151.
62   "Understandings Regarding the Convention" defines "widespread" (several hundred square kilometers), "long-lasting" (a period of months, or approximately a season) and "severe" (serious or significant disruption or harm to human life, natural and economic resources or other assets) relating to Art. I. In contrast, the term "long-term" found in Art. 35 (3) of the AP I is interpreted as a period of decades. See, *infra* note 219.

ASAT weapons generating significant amounts of space debris will not be considered the violation of the ENMOD Convention because such action would not be interpreted as the deliberate manipulation of natural processes bringing the change of dynamics, composition, or structure of outer space (Art. II).[63] However, this Convention is important as a precautious measures for future weapons. (See, 5 (2) B. of this chapter.)

(5) The Moon Agreement (1979)

At first glance, the last of the legally-binding instruments made in COPUOS, the *Moon Agreement* (MA)[64] only reiterates the Art. IV (2) of the OST irrespective of the additional limitations found in Art. 3(2) thereof, which prohibits "[a]ny threat or use of force or any other hostile act or threat of hostile act on the Moon". However, considering the unique definition in the MA that the reference to the Moon shall include "orbits around or other trajectories to or around it" (Art. 1 (2)), it may be said that this Agreement virtually de-militarizes some part of outer void space. If so, this clearly marks a milestone in disarmament in outer space.

The clarification process of Art. 1(2) of the MA in the COPUOS/LSC in 1979 seems to provide a key to evaluate if this assumption is applied. It confirmed "that the trajectories and orbits mentioned in Art. 1 para. 2 do not include trajectories and orbits of space objects in Earth orbits only and trajectories of space objects between the Earth and such orbits."[65] As a result, it may follow that establishing military bases, installations and fortifications, the testing of any type of weapons or any conduct of military maneuvers would be prohibited in the residual orbits and trajectories within the solar system.[66] Canada supported this interpretation,[67] but the views of Russia and China expressed in the twenty-first century are that arms control "on the Moon" does not cover activities in any outer void space.[68] Either way, it has been said that small number of States Parties lessens the importance of the MA.[69]

(6) ABM Treaty (1992)

The 1972 *Treaty between the US and the USSR on the Limitation of Anti-Ballistic Missile Systems* (ABM Treaty)[70] had been the most stringent space arms control treaty as it prohibited conventional weapons deployed in outer space. Both counties undertook not to "develop, test, or deploy ABM systems or components which are sea-based, air-based, space-based, or mobile land-based" (Art. V (1)). This Treaty, however, was terminated in 2002.[71]

---

63   The test of "severe" effect also seems difficult to meet. See, *supra* note 62.
64   *Agreement Concerning the Activities of States on the Moon and Other Celestial Bodies*, 18 December 1979, 1363 UNTS 3 [MA].
65   UN Doc. A/34/20 (1979), para. 63.
66   The scope of the MA is within the solar system. MA, *supra* note 64, Art. 1(1).
67   CD/618, CD/OS/WP.6, *supra* note 52 at 32.
68   CD/1780 (22 May 2006), para. 11.
69   As of 2015, only 16 States are parties to the MA among which no major space faring nations are included.
70   *Treaty Between the United States of America and the Union of Soviet Socialist Republics on the Limitation of Anti-Ballistic Missile Systems,* 26 May 1972, 944 UNTS 13 [ABM Treaty].
71   Six months prior to withdrawal, the US gave notice its decision to Russia based on Art. XV (2) of the ABM Treaty.

(7) Treaties to provide for satellite-based mutual monitoring mechanisms

A. A series of US-USSR/Russia Nuclear arms control agreements

A series of US-USSR/Russia nuclear arms control agreements since the 1972 *Interim Strategic Arms Limitation Treaty* (SALT I)[72] (Art. V) and the ABM Treaty (Art. XII) specify almost identical provisions for verifying treaty obligations. That is: (i) allow each other to monitor compliance with the treaty provisions using its "national technical means of verification" (NTMs) at its disposal in a manner consistent with generally recognized principles of international law (para. 1); (ii) prohibit interfering with the NTMs of the other Party (para. 2); and (iii) prohibit using deliberate concealment measures which impede verification by NTMs (para. 3). While NTMs comprised extensive networks of technological instrumentality, the most important were satellite-based verification mechanisms.[73] It may be said that such provisions therefore play a role as bilateral ASAT ban agreements, for interference with military satellites is prohibited.

US-USSR/Russia bilateral treaties in this category include: the 1974 *Limitation of Underground Nuclear Weapon Tests Treaty* (TTBT) (Art. II), the 1976 *Peaceful Nuclear Explosions Treaty* (PNET) (Art. IV), the 1979 *SALT II* (Art. XV), the 1987 *Intermediate-Range Nuclear Forces Treaty* (INF Treaty) (Art. XII), the 1991 *Strategic Arms Reduction Treaty* (START I) (Art. IX), the 1993 *START II* (Art. IV) and the 2010 *New START* (Art. X).[74]

B. Multilateral treaty for this kind

Attention has to be paid to the 1990 *Treaty on Conventional Armed Forces in Europe* (CFE Treaty)[75] to which European countries, the US, Canada and Russia[76] are States Parties. Similar verification clauses to the above-mentioned US-USSR/Russia bilateral treaties are also found in the CFE Treaty with necessary modifications. Instead of just NTMs, this Treaty provides for "national or multinational technical means of verification" (Art. XV). Therefore, the CFE Treaty may also be thought of as a proxy to a multilateral ASAT ban treaty in that interfering with satellites is banned, even if it is only implicitly agreed.

3 Three decades of arms control efforts in the CD

(1) Summary of the discussions in the CD

A. Program of work

Multilateral efforts to strengthen arms control in outer space have been pursued in the CD since its establishment in 1979 as the only formal multilateral disarmament negotiation forum.[77]

---

72 SALT I was terminated in 1977.
73 R.A. Schribner, T.J. Ralston & W.D. Metz, *The Verification Challenge: Problems and Promise of Strategic Nuclear Arms Control Verification* (Zurich: Birkhauser, 1985) at Chapter 3.
74 Only the 2002 *Strategic Offensive Reductions Treaty* (SORT) replaced by the New START did not provide for NTMs.
75 *Treaty on Conventional Armed Forces in Europe*, 19 November 1990, See, e.g., (1991) 30 *ILM* 1.
76 Russia suspended the implementation of the Treaty in December 2007 and announced its withdrawal in March 2015.
77 Committee on Disarmament (CD) established in 1979 was renamed as Conference on Disarmament (CD) in 1984.

An *ad hoc* Committee on Prevention of an Arms Race in Outer Space (PAROS) was established in 1985 in the CD with a view to undertaking negotiations for the conclusion of an agreement or agreements to prevent an arms race in all its aspects in outer space.[78] The program of work of this *ad hoc* Committee was formally accepted at the second session in 1986[79] and maintained until 1994, the last year this *ad hoc* Committee was successfully re-established.[80] Subsequently, discussions have been conducted in the plenary and informal plenary meetings under the agenda item "Prevention of an Arms Race in Outer Space".[81] The program of work of this Committee is as follows:

1   Examination and identification of issues relevant to the prevention of an arms race in outer space;
2   Existing agreements relevant to the prevention of an arms race in outer space; and
3   Existing proposals and future initiatives on the prevention of an arms race in outer space.[82]

On each of the three items, there was a tendency for member States to reconfirm and elaborate their respective positions and differing perspectives. Therefore, little tangible progress was made to converge views into negotiating a concrete proposal.

B. Examination and identification of the issues

(i) "Weaponization of space" v. "military use of space"

As for the first item, issues identified by member States include: i) the pursuit of precision in terminology and definitions as the basis of considering future legal regime, ii) the existence or non-existence of an arms race in outer space, iii) the recognition of ASAT as the most imminent threat, iv) the identification of the role of multilateral agreements and bilateral agreements to address the ASAT issue and v) the importance of verification as the prerequisite for negotiating a space arms control agreement.[83]

Differences remain to be solved on the basic terminology such as "peaceful purposes" in the

---

78   UNGA adopted, for the first time in 1982, a resolution to request the CD to establish an *ad hoc* working group on PAROS in its 1983 session by an overwhelming majority in favor with only the US against it. UN Doc. A/RES/37/83 (9 December 1982). Two more UNGA resolutions were needed to set up an *ad hoc* PAROS Committee. UN Doc. A/RES/38/70 (5 December 1983); UN Doc. A/RES/39/59 (12 December 1984).
79   CD/OS/WP.11 (24 June 1986).
80   Having failed to re-establish the *ad hoc* Committee for the consecutive three sessions since 1995, UN Doc. A/RES/52/37 (23 December 1997) removed the paragraph to request the re-establishment of an *ad hoc* Committee for the next session. That resolution instead invited the CD to re-examine the mandate so as to agree on the re-establishment of the *ad hoc* Committee again (para. 6). Such an invitation has been sent to the CD 11 consecutive times without any success. Since 2009, the setting-up of a working group under the agenda item "PAROS" is required. See, e.g., UN Doc. A/RES/53/76 (4 January 1999); UN Doc. A/RES/63/40 (12 January 2009); UN Doc. A/RES/64/28 (12 January 2010); UN Doc. A/RES/69/31 (11 December 2014).
81   See, e.g., CD/1963 (12 September 2013), paras. 43–45; CD/2004, supra note 59, paras. 41–43.
82   Substantially the same issues were discussed in the CD before the program of work was agreed upon in the *ad hoc* Committee. See, e.g., CD/641 (26 August 1985), para. 6.
83   See, e.g., CD/726 (19 August 1986) at 3–5; CD/787 (28 August 1987) at 162–165; CD/833 (25 April 1988) at 3–7; CD/954 (24 August 1989) at 4–9; CD/1034 (16 August 1990) at 3–9; CD/1105 (23 August 1991) at 5–8.

1980s[84] as well as in the twenty-first century.[85] However, such ideological difference has long lost significance. The truly important issue in this regard after the adoption of the OST is to extract destabilizing actions which are not banned under current international law to make them prohibited.[86] Such category of actions is termed "weaponization of space" in contrast to "military use of space" which is believed to remain permissible. The structure seems, at first glance, a dichotomy: the whole of military activities in space minus activities corresponding to "weaponization of space" are permissible "military use of space".[87] However, yet another term "militarization of space" is also used. "Military use of space" is sometimes used interchangeably with "militarization of space" in the CD and more often so in the national security community,[88] but precisely speaking, these two terms could be conceptually different as "militarization of space" implies more military connotation, such as using satellites to enhance offensive military capabilities on the Earth while "military use of space" means less, shown as in the example of using surveillance satellites for the verification of the multilateral arms control agreements. As a result, "militarization of space" might be placed somewhere between "weaponization of space" and "military use of space".[89] However, for the purposes of this chapter, "military use" and "militarization" will be used interchangeably as drawing a precise distinction between the two terms is difficult and, more essentially, the most critical issue is to identify the actions to be banned as "weaponization of space".

(ii) Difficulty to define "weaponization of space"

"Weaponization of space" has seldom been defined, but is generally thought to refer to deploy weapons in outer space to attack, destroy and otherwise damage objects in outer space, as well as human beings and objects on the Earth.

A number of reasons exist for the difficulty in defining this term. First, it is difficult to define "space weapons" or "weapons in space" and such definition is often thought to be necessary to define "weaponization of space". It is pointed out that there are a variety of "space weapons" including space-mine type satellites, kinetic weapons to be launched by ballistic missiles or fighters into the target orbit, and from-space-to-hit-the-target satellites. The scientific concept of "space weapons" includes kinetic, electronic, thermodynamic, laser, and so on.[90] Second, as "space weapons" are defined by specifying the stationed place (ground, water, air, outer space, etc.) and the targeting area (ground, water, air, outer space, etc.), questions arise which will lead to the essential difficulty in distinguishing missile defense systems from ASAT systems. Questions asked, for example, are whether ground-based ballistic missiles should be included

---

84 See, e.g., CD/641, *supra* note 82 at 6–7; CD/716, CD/OS/WP.15 (16 July 1986) at 9–14; CD/726, *supra* note 83 at 5; CD/786 (24 August 1987) at 8–9.
85 CD/1779 (22 May 2006) at 3; CD/1818 (14 March 2007) at 7.
86 CD/607, CD/OS/WP.3 (5 July 1985) at 1–3; CD/641, *supra* note 82 at 6–9; CD/716, CD/OS/WP.15, *supra* note 84 at 4–5; CD/786, *supra* note 84 at 5; CD/1753 (8 July 2005) at 4–6; CD/1784 (14 June 2006).
87 See, e.g., CD/716, CD/OS/WP.15, *supra* note 84 at 4–5.
88 See, e.g., Matthew Mowthorpe, *The Militarization and Weaponization of Space* (Lanham, MD: Lexington Books, 2004) at 1–9.
89 See, e.g., CD/716, CD/OS/WP.15, *supra* note 84 at 5. Militarization has also been interpreted to mean "weaponization" by some Sates. Péricles Gasparini Alves, *Prevention of an Arms Race in Outer Space: A Guide to the Discussions in the Conference on Disarmament* (UNIDIR/91/79) (New York: UN Publication, 1991) Part I at 14.
90 See, e.g., Robert Preston, Dana J. Johnson *et al.*, *Space Weapons Earth Wars* (Santa Monica, CA: Rand Corporation, 2002); Tronchetti, *supra* note 11 at 333–334.

in space weapons in case they attack, destroy or otherwise damage satellites in outer space.[91] In connection with this, it can be claimed that a ballistic missile flying in outer space – while there is no established demarcation line between air space and outer space – is regarded as a space object, then ground-based missile defense components hitting a target in the exoatmosphere may be considered a space weapon. Such discussions complicate the definition issue as missile defense systems are firmly embedded in national defense strategies. Third, any distinction between the dedicated space weapons systems, and ancillary systems is difficult. For example, a modified ballistic missile is easily used for destroying a satellite. On this point, some proposals in the CD claimed that to be a space weapon, it did not have to be specifically designed and manufactured for that purpose, although this view did not prevail.[92]

Among a small number of definitions in the twentieth century, those by China (1985)[93] and Venezuela (1988)[94] are rather comprehensive in that both definitions include ASAT weapons stationed elsewhere than in outer space. The Venezuelan definition is even broader in that it expressly includes missile defense systems deployed on the Earth.[95]

C. Existing agreements relevant to PAROS

As for the existing legal regime, a considerable amount of discussion was held as to whether the present set of space arms control agreements in addition to the UN Charter are sufficient. While the majority of delegations were of the opinion that the present regime was not adequate for the purpose of PAROS, a few States such as the US stated that the UN Charter, especially the combination of Art. 2 (4) and Art. 51, coupled with the OST, etc. provide equitable, balanced and extensive guarantees for the strict prohibition of the use of force in outer space.[96]

D. Existing proposals and future initiatives

A number of draft treaties proposed in the *ad hoc* Committee on PAROS and plenary of the CD seem to be divided into two types: the first type is aimed at the de-weaponization of space, and the second type pursues an ASAT weapon ban treaty. The former could be named "comprehensive approach" while the latter, "partial approach". Defining "ASAT weapons", however, encountered the same difficulty as "comprehensive space weapons",[97] and therefore, neither approach has been successful. In the 1990s, as a result, the immediate goals seemed to have shifted from negotiating a new treaty to constructing "confidence building measures" (CBM). Since the beginning of the twenty-first century, enthusiasm for pursuing a de-weaponization treaty resurrected; this time Russia and China jointly took the initiative.

---

91 Venezuela and Peru included it in weaponization of space. See, *infra* notes 101–102.
92 The 1982 Soviet proposal (Art. 1 (1)) and Venezuelan proposal applied a capability-based definition for a weapon. Other de-weaponization proposals (the list is shown 3(2) A of this chapter) restrict space weapons only to those deliberately designed and manufactured to be a weapon. See, *infra* notes 98–106.
93 CD/579 (19 March 1985) at 1. See, also, CD/1606 (9 February 2000) at 4.
94 CD/851, CD/OS/WP.24 (2 August 1988) at 1.
95 Ibid.; CD/579, *supra* note 93 at 1; see, also, CD/709/Rev.1, CD/OS/WP.13/Rev.1 (22 July 1986) at 2; CD/709, CD/OS/WP.13 (8 July 1986) at 1–2.
96 See, e.g., CD/787, *supra* note 83 at 165–169; CD/954, *supra* note 83 at 9–15; CD/1105, *supra* note 83 at 9–10; CD/1271 (24 August 1994) at 6–7.
97 See, 3 (3) of this chapter.

(2) Comprehensive approach

A. List of proposals

The list of the comprehensive de-weaponization proposals made in the CD is as follows:

(i) Italian Proposal (1979) Additional Protocol to the 1967 Outer Space Treaty with a View to Preventing Arms Races in Outer Space;[98]
(ii) Soviet Proposal (1982) Draft Treaty on the Prohibition of the Stationing of Weapons of Any Kind in Outer Space;[99]
(iii) Soviet Proposal (1984) Draft Treaty on the Prohibition of the Use of Force in Outer Space and From Space against the Earth;[100]
(iv) Venezuelan Proposal (1988) Proposed Amendment to the Outer Space Treaty;[101]
(v) Peruvian Proposal (1989) Proposal for Amendment of the Outer Space Treaty (1989);[102]
(vi) Chinese Proposal (2001) Treaty on the Prevention of the Weaponization of Outer Space;[103]
(vii) Russian/Chinese Joint Proposal (2002) Treaty on the Prevention of the Deployment of Weapons in Outer Space, the Threat or Use of Force against Outer Space Objects ("first PPWT");[104]
(viii) Russian/Chinese Joint Proposal (2008) Draft Treaty on Prevention of the Placement of Weapons in Outer Space and of the Threat or Use of Force against Outer Space Objects ("second PPWT");[105] and
(ix) Russian/Chinese Joint Proposal (2014) Draft Treaty on Prevention of the Placement of Weapons in Outer Space, the Threat or Use of Force against Outer Space Objects ("third PPWT").[106]

B. General contents of the nine proposals

(i) Form of a treaty: amendment to the OST or a new treaty

Two methodologies were found in these nine proposals: the first was aimed at the amendment of the Art. IV (1) of the OST from the prohibition of WMD to any kind of weapons in outer space (Italian, Venezuelan and Peruvian proposals). The second was to adopt a new independent treaty (Soviet/Russia, China, Russia and China proposals).

---

98   CD/9 (26 March 1979). Italian proposal is similar in content to its previous two proposals submitted to the UNGA as early as 1968 and at the Special Session on Disarmament (SSOD)-1 in 1978. A/7221 (9 September 1968); A/AC.187/97 (1 February 1978).
99   CD/274 (7 April 1982). The same proposal was submitted to the UNGA in 1981 as UN Doc. A/36/192 (20 August 1981). This proposal was unpopular, because it prohibited destroying, damaging and disturbing space objects of other States Parties only if such space objects were "placed in orbit in strict accordance with" Art. 1 (1) of this proposal. Such wording induced suspicions if otherwise the space object in question could be lawfully disturbed, damaged or destroyed.
100 CD/476 (20 March 1984). The same proposal was submitted to the UNGA in 1983 as UN Doc. A/38/194 (23 August 1983).
101 CD/851, CD/OS/WP.24, *supra* note 94.
102 CD/939, CD/OS/WP.37 (28 July 1989).
103 CD/1645 (6 June 2001).
104 CD/1679 (28 June 2002). The working paper containing this draft treaty is supported and co-presented by Vietnam, Indonesia, Belarus, Zimbabwe and Syria let alone Russia and China.
105 CD/1839 (29 February 2008).
106 CD/1985 (12 June 2014).

(ii) Prohibited actions[107]

Commonly prohibited in all nine proposals are: testing, deployment or use in outer space of any weapons against objects in outer space or on the Earth.[108] "Outer space" is defined only by the Chinese proposal (2001) and second PPWT (2008), in which outer space means the space above the Earth in excess of 100 kilometers above sea level.[109] In addition, the Venezuelan proposal clearly banned the use of weapons against space objects in outer space from the Earth,[110] and the Peruvian proposal suggested similar regulation.[111] The Soviet proposal (1984) and first to third PPWT (2002, 2008, 2014) prohibit resorting to the threat or use of force against space objects (Soviet proposal), or "outer space objects" (PPWTs).[112]

The latest proposal, or third PPWT in 2014 forbids States Parties from: i) placing any weapons in outer space; ii) resorting to the threat or use of force against "outer space objects" of States Parties to the PPWT, iii) engaging in outer space activities inconsistent with the objects and purposes of the PPWT; and iv) assisting or inducing other States and international governmental organizations as well as non-governmental organizations and entities to participate in activities inconsistent with the objects and purposes of the PPWT.[113] Taking note of the definition of "weapon in outer space" as "any outer space object or component thereof" (Art. I (b)) which are "placed in outer space" (Art. I (c)), terrestrially-based ballistic missiles are excluded from prohibited weapons, although a space-based ASAT system or missile defense system will be included as long as it "orbits the Earth at least once, or follows a section of such an orbit before leaving that orbit, or is permanently located in outer space" (Art. I (c)). Concerning the definition of the "use of force", the phrase "temporarily or permanently disrupting their normal functioning" expressly contained in the second PPWT (Art. I (e)) was removed in the third PPWT. This may be because such disruptions have been a part of everyday conduct for military powers.[114]

---

107 On the detailed explanation of the draft proposals, especially the second PPWT, see, e.g., Setsuko Aoki, "Space Arms Control: The Challenges and Alternatives" (2009) 52 *Japanese Yearbook of Int'l L.* 191 at 202–209.
108 Italian proposal, Art. 1; Soviet Proposal (1982), Arts. 1 (1) & 3; Soviet Proposal (1984), Arts. 1 & 2 (1) (2); Venezuelan and Peruvian proposal; Chinese proposal (2001) Point III, Russia-China proposal (2002), Point III; Russia-China proposals (2008 and 2014), Art. II.
109 Chinese proposal (2001), Point IV; Russia-China proposal (2008), Art. I (a).
110 The Venezuelan proposal is the most comprehensive among the all proposals in the CD as it explicitly banned both ASAT and ABM weapons by including any offensive or defensive device that is "(a) capable of destroying or damaging from its place of deployment in outer space an object situated in outer space, in the air, in water or on land, (b) capable of destroying or damaging from its place of deployment in the air, in water or on land an object situated in outer space" as well as "capable of intercepting, from outer space or from land, water or the atmosphere, ballistic projectiles during their flight" in its definition of space weapons. CD/851, CD/OS/WP.24, *supra* note 94 at 1.
111 Peru suggested that the first additional protocol to be supplemented in the future will prohibit the development, production, storage and deployment of ASAT weapons that are not stationed in outer space, as well as limit ABM systems irrespective of their nature. Peruvian Proposal, explanation of Art. IV, CD/939, CD/OS/WP.37, *supra* note 102 at 2; CD/954, *supra* note 83 at 16.
112 USSR (1984), Art. 1 (2); Russia/China (2002), Art. III; Russia/China (2008), Art. II; Russia/China (2014), Art. II. A new term "outer space object" is used in the three Russia/China joint proposals in the twenty-first century, which is defined in the 2008 and 2014 proposals but in a different way. Russia/China (2008), Art. I (b); Russia/China (2014), Art. I (a). Further, Art. 1 of the Italian proposal, while indirectly, forbade threat or use of force against space objects.
113 Third PPWT, Art. II. The first sentence is an Italian-Venezuelan-Peruvian line and the second and third sentences have been traditional Russian proposals since 1984. "[T]hreat or use of force" was defined in the second and third PPWT (Art. I (e) and Art. I (d) respectively), but its definition was largely changed.
114 See, e.g., CD/1847 (26 August 2008) at 3.

As in the second PPWT, the third PPWT also expressly provides for "the States Parties' inherent right to individual or collective self-defense, as recognized in Article 51 of the Charter of the United Nations" (Art. IV).[115] Thus, a question emerges if the use of a forbidden "weapon in outer space" could become permissible if it is declared as the exercise of the self-defense subject to Art. 51 of the UN Charter.[116]

The US criticized the third PPWT as in the case of the second PPWT[117] concerning the scope of the prohibition which does not include the research, development, testing, production, storage or deployment of terrestrially-based anti-satellite weapons[118] and the lack of verification system.[119]

The experiences in the CD appear to show that defining space weapons as a prerequisite for de-weaponization has been failed. Instead, an agreement to prohibit destroying or otherwise physically damaging space objects should be pursued. Such an agreement would indirectly but automatically prohibit attacks by terrestrially-based weapons without a definition of "space weapons". In that case, however, because a strict inspection system for "space weapons" has to be sacrificed, the issue is whether consensus could be reached on negotiating a non-verifiable arms control agreement. US national space policy expressly rejects this idea.[120]

(3) Partial approach

Second is the partial approach, which pursues an ASAT weapons ban among "space weapons" as an imminent concern. The ASAT ban proposals seem to be grouped into two; a total ASAT ban and a partial ASAT ban. Similar difficulties experienced in defining "space weapons" and their verifiability also failed the pursuit of the total ASAT ban.[121] Then, the partial ban of ASAT weapons was pursued: one proposal was to prohibit only high-altitude ASAT weapons because low-altitude ones had been already tested;[122] and another was to prohibit only "dedicated" ASAT weapons excluding "ancillary" ones.[123] Even this approach did not narrow the differences among the delegations concerning definition and verification issues.

(4) CBM/TCBM ideas

While the concept of CBM already existed at the time of the setting up of the CD, increasing attention was paid to the CBM initiatives since around 1990 when both de-weponization and ASAT weapons ban proposals seemed to hit a stalemate.[124] That trend became decisive from the

---

115 Second PPWT, Art. V. The first PPWT did not contain such provision.
116 Although the OST may induce a similar question concerning the use of WMD as an exercise of self-defense, the difference is that the OST does not explicitly provide for the right of self-defense.
117 CD/1847, *supra* note 114.
118 CD/1998 (3 September 2014) at 4.
119 Ibid., at 3.
120 The latest US National Space Policy specifies that "[t]he United States will consider proposals and concepts for arms control measures if they are equitable, effectively verifiable, and enhance the national security" of the US and its allies. *The US National Space Policy* (28 June 2010) at 7; online: White House www.whitehouse.gov/sites/default/files/national_space_policy_6-28-10.pdf.
121 Total ban of the ASAT weapons is supported: CD/726, *supra* note 83, para. 26; CD/905, CD/OS/WP.28 (21 March 1989) at 15–16.
122 CD/642 (4 September 1985) at 123; CD/905, CD/OS/WP.28, *supra* note 121 at 13; CD/PV.263 (12 June 1984).
123 CD/870 (12 September 1988), para. 30.
124 See, e.g., CD/1105, *supra* note 83, para. 25.

mid-1990s.[125] Since around 2005, the term "transparency and confidence building measures" (TCBM) has been more prevalent.[126]

Prevalent CBM/TCBM ideas include:

(i) Declaration of the non-deployment of weapons in outer space[127]

In 1985, the USSR stated that it had started the moratorium on stationing of ASAT weapons in outer space in 1983 and would keep that moratorium as long as other States would act the same way.[128] The USSR also stated that it would not be the first to place weapons in outer space since the late 1980s.[129] Gradually such unilateral declarations developed into a joint statement of "no first placement of weapons in outer space". The latest examples include joint statements of Russia and Cuba as well as Russia and Argentina which declared that "they will not in any way be the first to place weapons of any kind in outer space" and called upon States with space capabilities to follow their example.[130] As of June 2015, Argentina, Armenia, Belarus, Brazil, Cuba, Indonesia, Kazakhstan, Kyrgyzstan, Russia, Sri Lanka and Tajikistan made "no first placement" statements.[131]

(ii) Strengthening the *Convention on Registration of Objects Launched into Outer Space* (the Registration Convention)[132]

One of the most frequently proposed ideas is to amend or make an additional protocol to the *Registration Convention* to improve transparency. The main idea is to add provisions to collect more detailed information on the functions of space objects, and to verify the accuracy of the notified information.[133]

(iii) International space inspectorate (ISI) for the pre-launch inspection

There are certain changes in ISI proposals made over the past three decades, but the core of the ISI idea is to temporarily or permanently dispatch an international expert team to national

---

125   See, e.g., CD/1165 (12 August 1992) at 8. From 1989 to 2001, no proposal was submitted on the de-weaponization treaty in the CD.
126   Russia introduced the concept of TCBM in the First Committee of the UNGA since 2005. UN Doc. A/RES/60/66 (6 January 2006); UN Doc. A/RES/61/75 (18 December 2006); UN Doc. A/RES/62/43 (8 January 2008).
127   See, e.g., CD/786, *supra* note 84, para. 27; CD/833, *supra* note 83, paras. 24 & 26; CD/905, CD/OS/WP.28, *supra* note 121 at 3; CD/927, CD/OS/WP.33 (26 June 1989) at 1–7.
128   CD/611 (10 July 1985), para. 3.
129   CD/870, *supra* note 123, para. 39; CD/956 (4 September 1989), para. 59.
130   CD/2001 (4 September 2014) at 2; CD/1991 (24 June 2014) at 2. See, also, CD/1996 (25 August 2014), para. 3. In 2013, Russia and Indonesia submitted a joint statement. CD/1954 (31 July 2013) at 2.
131   UN Doc. A/RES/69/32 (11 December 2014) at 2.
132   14 January 1975, 1023 UNTS 15.
133   CD/642, *supra* note 122, para. 42; CD/726, *supra* note 83, para. 35; CD/786, *supra* note 84, paras. 27 & 34; CD/833 (25 April 1988), para. 24. CD/870, *supra* note 123, para. 38; CD/905, CD/OS/WP.28, *supra* note 121 at 24–25; CD/937, CD/OS/WP.35 (21 July 1989) at 7–8; CD/954(24 August 1989), para. 56; CD/1015, CD/OS/WP.42 (18 July 1990) at 1–7; CD/1092, CD/OS/WP.46 (1 August 1991) at 2–3; CD/1111 (4 September 1991), paras. 45 & 47; CD/1165, *supra* note 125, para. 23; CD/1217 (19 August 1993), paras. 10–11.

launch sites worldwide to verify that no weapons are on board launch vehicles before such vehicles are launched into outer space.[134]

(iv) Keep-out zones (KOZ) to ensure non-interference with other States' space objects

While the precise content has been amended over the years, simply put, KOZ is an idea to require on-orbit space objects to keep a certain distance from each other to avoid the misconception of potential attacks, and so on.[135] Likewise, "immunity of satellites", either for all satellites or only non-military satellites, has been proposed with a view to ensuring non-interference.[136]

(v) Satellite monitoring systems[137]

A number of international verification systems using satellites have been proposed, often with a phased development process. One of the most interesting ideas is the 1987 Canadian "PAXSAT A" proposal as a space-to-space monitoring system to verify non-weaponization of outer space.[138] This was proposed again in 2006.[139]

(vi) Elaboration of a code of conduct, rules-of-the-road instruments, etc.

In addition, the elaboration of legally non-binding instruments such as a code of conduct, rules-of-the-road, and "open outer space concept guidelines" were proposed containing a variety of CBM ideas described above.[140] While many countries were supportive of such instruments, countries which proposed a treaty made it clear that CBM could not be a substitute for a treaty.[141]

---

134 In early years it was named "International Inspectorate". CD/786, *supra* note 84, para.44; CD/817, CD/OS/WP.19 (17 March 1988), paras. 10 & 37; CD/905, CD/OS/WP.28, *supra* note121 at 16–17 & 21–22.

135 CD/786, *supra* note 84; CD/905, CD/OS/WP.28, *supra* note 121 at 21–22; CD/956, *supra* note 129, paras. 44 & 55; CD/1039 (30 August 1990), para. 47; CD/1111, *supra* note 133, para. 54 (a new KOZ concept was introduced.); CD/1165, *supra* note 125, para. 24; CD/1092, CD/OS/WP.46, *supra* note 133 at 4; CD/1105, *supra* note 83, para. 54. This is one of a variety of CBMs, which could lead to a concrete rule of the space traffic management regulations in the future. See, e.g., IAA, *Cosmic Study on Space Traffic Management* (2006) at 65–70.

136 See, e.g., CD/726, *supra* note 83, para. 28; CD/833, *supra* note 83, paras. 25–26; CD/956, *supra* note 129, para. 52; CD/905, CD/OS/WP.28, *supra* note121 at 8–11. Note has to be taken, however, immunity of satellites is often included in an ASAT ban draft treaty as a supplementary method to ensure ASAT ban. See, e.g., CD/777 (31 July 1987).

137 Various types of satellite monitoring systems and their precursor entities were proposed. See, e.g., CD/642, *supra* note 122, para. 44; CD/786, *supra* note 84, para. 44; CD/817, CD/OS/WP.19, *supra* note 134 at 16–17 & 21–22; CD/875 (20 September 1988), para. 42 (PAXSAT); CD/956, *supra* note 129, paras. 50 & 65–67.

138 CD/905, CD/OS/WP.28, *supra* note 121 at 20; see, also CD/875, *supra* note 137, para. 42.

139 CD/1785 (21 June 2006).

140 See, e.g., CD/1039, *supra* note 135, para. 34; CD/1111, *supra* note 133, para. 45.

141 See, e.g., CD/1217, *supra* note 133, para. 15.

(5) TCBM efforts in the twenty-first century

A. HCOC

The *International Code of Conduct against the Proliferation of Ballistic Missiles* (widely known as "Hague Code of Conduct" (HCOC)), opened for signature on 25 November 2002,[142] has been one of the most important results of the CBM/TCBM efforts outside the CD. As a non-legally binding instrument, HCOC urges Subscribing States to commit themselves to pre-launch notifications of launches and test flights of not only their ballistic missiles but also space launch vehicles (SLVs),[143] and also to provide annual declaration of their SLV policies as well as information on the SLV launches and test flights of the preceding year.[144] It also recommends that Subscribing States invite international observers to their launch sites.[145] The UNGA adopted a resolution to welcome the HCOC in 2004[146] and its importance has been reaffirmed in subsequent UNGA resolutions.[147] Subscribing States have been increased from the original 93 States in 2002 to 137 as of December 2014, while some of the major space faring nations such as China and India are not members.[148]

B. UN GGE

Following the request by the UNGA resolution adopted on 8 December 2010,[149] the UN Secretary General (UNSG) established in 2011 a second group of governmental experts (GGE) on outer space CBM/TCBM[150] to conduct a study thereon and submit a report containing concrete TCBM proposals to the 2013 UNGA. In addition to the views of the 15 States which provided their experts,[151] inputs from a wide range of States and other entities were encouraged to compliment the work of the GGE.[152] The GGE Report seems characterized by the clear description of the nature, purpose and criteria of outer space TCBM as a prerequisite so that basic principles and concrete transparency measures recommended may be translated into actions.[153]

Important transparency measures recommended include: i) information exchange on national space security matters such as space security policies, major military space expenditures and other related national activities;[154] ii) information exchange of basic orbital parameters of

---

142 "Text of the HCoC" (last updated November 2012) online: HCOC www.hcoc.at/?tab=what_is_hcoc&page=text_of_the_hcoc.
143 Ibid., 4 a) iii).
144 Ibid., 4 a) ii).
145 Ibid.
146 UN Doc. A/RES/59/91 (3 December 2004).
147 Recent examples include UN Doc. A/RES/67/42 (4 January 2013) and UN Doc. A/RES/69/44 (11 December 2014).
148 UN Doc. A/RES/69/44, *supra* note 147, para. 1 of the operative part.
149 UN Doc. A/RES/65/68 (13 January 2011), para. 2.
150 First GGE, established in 1991 to study CBM in outer space, completed its report in 1993. UN Doc. A/45/55B (4 December 1990), para. 3; UN Doc. A/48/305 (15 October 1993); UN Doc. A/RES/48/74 (7 January 1994).
151 Five permanent members of the SC plus Brazil, Chile, Italy, Kazakhstan, Nigeria, Republic of Korea, Romania, South Africa, Sri Lanka and Ukraine.
152 UN Doc. A/CONF.220/1 (27 July 2012), para. 6.
153 UN Doc. A/68/189 (29 July 2013).
154 Ibid., paras. 37–38.

space objects, other spaceflight activities and notification of planned spacecraft launches, thus enabling the avoidance of mishaps, misperceptions and mistrust;[155] iii) notifications of high-risk re-entry events, controlled or uncontrolled, emergency situations and intentional orbital break-ups[156] and iv) voluntary familiarization visits of launching sites.[157]

Few of recommended measures for enhancing transparency were novel ideas. Rather, those have been repeatedly proposed for the last three decades. This may be because while actions should be taken for promoting TCBM is clear, concrete steps and procedures to adequately implement them remain ambiguous. Thus, it may be said that the proposals on international cooperation, consultative mechanisms, outreach and coordination of the GGE Report indicate realistic and reasonable steps for enhanced TCBMs.[158]

C. Efforts for international code of conduct (ICOC)

Responding to the UNGA Res. 61/75 requested by the UNSG to submit concrete proposals on TCBM in outer space activities,[159] in September 2007, Portugal, on behalf of the EU, submitted a proposal to the first Committee of the UNGA on the elaboration of the EU non-legally binding code of conduct on TCBM.[160] Portugal stated that such a code of conduct may be supplemented by the COPUOS best practices guidelines under the agenda item on the preservation of the space environment.[161]

The EU subsequently adopted a draft code of conduct (CoC) for Space Activities in December 2008[162] and revised it twice[163] before the efforts started in June 2012 to develop the EU CoC into an international one. This development was largely triggered by the declaration of the US Secretary of State that the US would make an international CoC (ICOC) on this subject with the EU and other countries in January 2012.[164] Since then, the draft ICoC has been further revised twice[165] based on the multilateral exchange of views including open-ended consultations.[166] As of June 2015, the draft ICoC remains to be finalized, partly because of the differing views on the forum in which the ICoC should be negotiated. While ICoC was first planned to be adopted outside the UN, like the HCOC precedent, more than a few countries believe that it should be negotiated within the UN framework.

---

155 Ibid., paras. 39–41.
156 Ibid., paras. 42–45.
157 Ibid., paras. 46–47.
158 Ibid., paras. 49–67.
159 UN Doc. A/RES/61/75, *supra* note 126, para. 1.
160 UN Doc. A/62/114/ Add.1 (17 September 2007) at 5–8.
161 As an early proposal in the COPUOS to make a best practice guidelines, see, e.g., A/AC.105/L.268 (10 May 2010), paras. 2–6 & 26–29. This seems to have been developed into a long-term sustainability guidelines being made in the Scientific and Technical Subcommittee (STSC) of the COPUOS.
162 Council of the EU, 17175/08, PESC 1697, CODUN 61 (17 December 2008).
163 It was 11 October 2010 and 5 June 2012. See, Council of the EU, 14455/10, PESC 1234, CODUN 34, ESPACE 2, COMPET 284 (11 October 2010); (EU News 235/2012, published on 6 June 2012, A/252/12).
164 Hillary Rodham Clinton, "International Code of Conduct for Outer Space Activities" (17 January 2012) online: US Department of State www.state.gov/secretary/20092013clinton/rm/2012/01/180969.htm.
165 It was 16 September 2013 and 31 March 2014.
166 The Open-ended consultation meeting was held in May and November 2013, and May in 2014 with the participation of about 65 countries.

The substantive aspect of the future ICoC is relatively more settled. The purpose of the ICoC is to establish the non-legally binding TCBM norms "of all outer space activities"[167] (para. 1.1), either military or civil/commercial as with the UN GGE Report. Transparency measures recommended in the prospective ICoC include concrete notification, information exchange and consultation mechanisms. Suggested actions to notify are scheduled maneuvers which could pose a risk to the space objects of other States, predicted conjunctions posing an on-orbit collision risk, launch of space objects (pre-notification), any break-ups in orbit, and malfunctions of space objects (para. 5.1). As for information exchange, annual exchange of information on national space policies and programs (para. 6.1) and timely information exchange of space environmental conditions and forecasts collected through national space situational awareness (SSA) are recommended (para. 6.2). Further, familiarization visits and expert visits to space launch sites as well as observations of launches of space objects are recommended (para. 6.4).

Similar to the Russia-China draft PPWT, this draft ICoC refers to the "inherent right of states to individual or collective self-defense" as recognized in the UN Charter, and the responsibility of States to refrain from the threat or use of force (para. 2). That the future ICoC contains such provisions may also be a strong indicator that military use of space has been well established under existing international law.

4 Legal controls of international transfer of space technology

State-of-the-art science and technology is involved in all aspects of space activities from designing and manufacturing rockets and satellites, to launching, maneuvering and operating them and to intentionally returning them to Earth. Dissemination of space-based data and information can also be included depending on the definition of space activities. The limited number of countries equipped with launch capabilities,[168] the critical importance of space assets to support military operations in space and increased dual-use of space technology necessitate pertinent control of space technology for international and national security reasons. The close similarity in technology between the rocket and missile as the means of delivery of WMD only reinforces the necessity of the legal controls of space technology. This section, therefore, briefly touches upon the legal controls of international transfer of space technology.[169]

(1) Missile technology control regime

As opposed to WMD themselves, there are no legally-binding instruments to regulate the manufacturing, testing, possessing, stockpiling and transferring their means of delivery, namely missiles. Thus, the like-minded States' voluntary association, the Missile Technology Control Regime (MTCR) was established in 1987 to prevent the proliferation of unmanned delivery means of WMD through the coordination of national export control systems of the participating States.[170] The MTCR created common export policy guidelines, or the "MTCR

---

167 "Draft International Code of Conduct for Outer Space Activities" (31 March 2014) online: EU www.eeas.europa.eu/non-proliferation-and-disarmament/pdf/space_code_conduct_draft_vers_31-march-2014_en.pdf.
168 The USSR (1957), the US (1958), France (1965), Japan (February 1970), China (April 1970), India (1980), Israel (1988), Iran (2009), DPRK (2012) and the ROK (2013) have autonomous launch capability. The UK launched its rocket from Australia.
169 On the international control of space technology, see. e.g., Ulrike M. Bohlmann, "Space Technology Export Controls" in Schrogl *et al.*, eds., *supra* note 11, 273 at 273–289.
170 As of August 2015, 34 countries belong to the MTCR.

Guidelines" providing the overall structure and rules, as well as the list of controlled items, called the "MTCR Equipment, Software and Technology Annex" ("MTCR Annex"), pursuant to which each member State adopts and implements its national export controls of missiles and SLVs.[171]

The MTCR Annex consists of two categories of items: Category I items and Category II items. It has to be noted that "items" include equipment and technology.[172] Member States are invited to implement more stringent export control for the Category I items on which "a strong presumption to deny"[173] is required in the consideration of export. Category I items consist of complete rocket systems (including ballistic missile systems, SLVs and sounding rockets) as well as unmanned aerial vehicle systems (UAVs) (including cruise missile systems, target and reconnaissance drones) capable of delivering at least a 500 kilogram payload to a range of at least 300 kilometers.[174] Category I items also include production facilities for such systems,[175] and major sub-systems including rocket stages, re-entry vehicles, rocket engines, guidance systems and warhead mechanisms.[176] Currently, the export of the production systems for Category I items is not authorized.[177] The export of the other Category I items could only rarely be admitted when: i) the government-to-government legally-binding guarantee agreement is adopted which pledges the assured use in accordance with the MTCR Guidelines; and ii) the recipient government assumes responsibility that exported items will be used only for its stated end-use.[178]

Category II items contain complete rocket systems and UAVs capable of delivering a payload of less than 500 kilograms to a range equal to or greater than 300 kilometers, as well as a wide range of both military and dual-use equipment, material, and technologies related to such systems.[179] MTCR member States have greater flexibility in licensing export for Category II items on a case-by-case basis.[180]

Further, the MTCR Guidelines specify that the transfer of the non-listed items is also subject to the authorization process when i) an exporter is informed by the competent authority of the government that the items concerned may be used, if exported, with a view to making delivery systems for WMD, or ii) the exporter is aware that the items concerned are intended to contribute to such activities.[181] These so-called "catch-all controls" have been implemented pursuant to the individual national export control legislation not only relating to the MTCR, but also other export control regimes against the proliferation of WMD, such as the Nuclear Suppliers Group (NSG)[182] and Australia Group (AG).[183]

---

171 "The Missile Technology Control Regime" online: MTCR www.mtcr.info/english/.
172 MTCR Guidelines, para. 2; online: MTCR www.mtcr.info/english/guidetext.html.
173 Ibid.
174 MTCR Annex, MTCR/TEM/2014/Annex (2 October 2014), 1.A.1 & 1.A.2; online: MTCR www.mtcr.info/english/annex.html.
175 Ibid., 1.B.1.
176 Ibid., 2.A.1– 2.E.1.
177 MTCR Guidelines, *supra* note 172, para 2.
178 Ibid., paras. 2 & 5.
179 MTCR Annex, *supra* note 174, Category II, Item 3–Item 20.
180 MTCR Guidelines, *supra* note 172, esp. paras. 3 & 4.
181 Ibid., para. 7.
182 Established in 1974 and consisted of 48 member States as of August 2015.
183 Established in 1985 and consisted of 41 member States and EU as of August 2015.

(2) Wassenaar Arrangement

The Wassenaar Arrangement on Export Controls for Conventional Arms and Dual-Use Goods and Technologies (WA) was established in 1996 to prevent destabilizing accumulations of conventional weapons though enhancing transparency and greater responsibility in transfers of conventional arms and dual-use goods and technologies.[184] Similar to the MTCR, participating States implement the purposes of the WA through their own national laws and policies based on a series of guidelines, elements and procedures made in the WA.[185] The decision to transfer or deny transfer of any item is the sole responsibility and national discretion of an each State, but its transfers and denials are appropriately notified in accordance with the provisions of the WA rule.[186]

Controlled goods, equipment, software and technologies in relation to space activities are set forth in the List of Dual-Use Goods and Technologies, consisting of Category 1 to Category 9 items, the Sensitive List, and the Very Sensitive List as well as the Munitions List. Examples specified in the Dual-Use Goods and Technology List include: space-qualified optical sensors, optics, and radars in Category 6 (Sensors and "Lasers");[187] Global Navigation Satellite Systems (GNSS) related items and technology in Category 7 (Navigation and Avionics);[188] and liquid, solid and hybrid rocket propulsion systems in Category 9 (Aerospace and Propulsion).[189] Rapid progress of technology causes additional regulation and lifting or relaxation with regard to various goods and technologies on a regular basis. For instance, changes on launch vehicles, spacecraft, spacecraft buses, spacecraft payloads, terrestrial equipment for spacecraft, and so on have been newly introduced in Category 9 in the 2014 Plenary.[190] In addition to the controlled items shown in the Sensitive List[191] and Very Sensitive List,[192] both are under the Dual-Use Goods and Technology List, the Munitions List contains GNSS jamming equipment and specially designed components thereof as well as spacecraft specially designed or modified for military use and the components thereof as of 2015.[193]

Participating States of the WA agreed in the 2003 Plenary to take appropriate measures to ensure that non-listed dual-use items to destinations subject to UN Security Council (SC) arms embargoes, and so on, would also be subject to authorization when the authorities of the government inform the exporter that the items in question are likely to be intended for a military end-use.[194] WA members, therefore, implement such so-called "catch-all controls" through their national export control legislation. Note has to be taken, however, that the WA is not related to the non-proliferation of WMD, and as such, *bona fide* transactions between any

---

184 See, "Guidelines & Procedures, including the Initial Elements" (12 July 1996 as amended), Initial Elements, I. Purposes; online: WA www.wassenaar.org/wp-content/uploads/2015/07/5-Initial-Elements.pdf [Initial Elements].
185 Ibid., II. Scope, para. 7.
186 Ibid., paras. 3–4.
187 List of Dual-Use Goods and Technologies and Munitions List, WA-LIST (14) 2 (25 March 2015) see, e.g., 6.A.2.a.1.a-d, 6.A.2.b, 6.A.2.d, 6.A.4.c, 6.A.8.d & 6.A.8.j; online: WA www.wassenaar.org/wp-content/uploads/2015/07/WA-LIST-14-2.pdf.
188 Ibid., e.g., 7.A.3. Technical Notes 1, 7.A.5 & 7.D.5.
189 Ibid., 9. A. 5- 9.A.9 concerning propulsion.
190 Ibid., 9.A.4.a–9.A.4.f. & 9.A.10 concerning spacecraft, etc.
191 Ibid., see, e.g., 3.A.2.g.1, 6.A.2.a.1.d & 6. A. 4.c. (at 159–165).
192 Ibid., at 167–168.
193 Ibid., ML.11.a–c, at 191.
194 "Public Statement – 12 December 2003" (12 December 2003); online: WA www.wassenaar.org/public-statement-12-december-2003/.

countries have to be duly respected concerning state-of-the-art dual-use items and arms to defend themselves pursuant to Art. 51 of the UN Charter unless those countries are under UNSC sanctions, and so on.[195] Thus, the scope of the catch-all controls is narrower than that of the MTCR, NSG or AG.

(3) Other important export control measures, etc.

Note has to be taken to the role of the legally-binding UNSC resolutions under Chapter VII of the UN Charter in controlling the transnational transfer of space-related materials and technologies. One example is a series of UNSC resolutions starting with UNSC Res. 1718 (2006), which "demands that the DPRK not conduct any further nuclear test or launch of a ballistic missile".[196] Responding to that, under the oversight of the UNSC Committee established by UNSC Res. 1718,[197] UN member States have to adopt and implement appropriate embargoes, export controls, border controls, financial sanctions and cargo inspections, and so on, in which space-related items and technologies are included.[198]

Another example is a legally-binding UNSC Res.1540 by which UN member States are tasked with preventing proliferation of WMD and their means of delivery to non-State actors.[199] UN member States have to maintain appropriate effective border controls and law enforcement efforts, as well as establish and maintain effective national export and trans-shipment controls.[200] The 1540 Committee established pursuant to UNSC Res.1540 guide member States to observe such obligations using reporting systems.[201] This may be said to be a kind of export control framework though not as effective as MTCR concerning SLVs and components thereof.

Finally, it has to be reconfirmed that it is the national export control measures which play the most important role as transfer of space goods and technology. In this regard, US export control systems and that of the EU are most relevant.[202]

---

195 Initial Elements, *supra* note 184, I. Purposes, para. 4.
196 S/RES/1718 (14 October 2006), para. 2; S/RES/1874 (12 June 2009), paras. 2 & 3; S/RES/2094 (7 March 2013), paras. 2 & 6. Since UNSC Res. 1874 (2009), a series of UNSC resolutions against the DPRK demand "that the DPRK not conduct any further nuclear test or *any launch using ballistic missile technology*" (emphasis added). Therefore, the scope of the prohibition is clearer than UNSC Res. 1718.
197 S/RES/1718, *supra* note 196, para. 12.
198 Ibid., para. 8; S/RES/1874, *supra* note 196, paras. 7, 9 & 12–26; S/RES/2087 (22 January 2013), para. 6 et seq. S/RES/2094, *supra* note 196, para. 7 et seq.
199 S/RES/1540 (28 April 2004).
200 Ibid., paras. 3, 6, 8 & 10.
201 Ibid., para. 4. The mandate of the 1540 Committee has been extended until 25 April 2021. S/RES/1673 (27 April 2006), para. 4; S/RES/1810 (25 April 2008), para. 6; S/RES/1977 (20 April 2011), para. 2.
202 Legal controls on the international transfer of space technology in general, see, e.g., Michael C. Mineiro, *Space Technology Export Controls and International Cooperation in Outer Space* (New York: Springer, 2012). For the US legislation, see, e.g., Henry R. Hertzfeld & Raymond L. Jones, "International Aspects of Technology Controls" in Christian Brünner & Alexander Soucek, eds., *Outer Space in Society, Politics and Law* (New York: Springer, 2011) 638 at 638–663.

5 Law and armed conflicts and rules of engagement (re military space operations)

(1) The scope of the applicability of the LOAC to armed conflicts in space

When the use of force in outer space occurs, the *jus in bello*, currently called the law of armed conflict (LOAC) or international humanitarian law (IHL) applies.

For the purposes of this chapter, the term LOAC is used and it includes the law of neutrality.[203] The problem is that vagueness prevails concerning the direct applicability of the LOAC in armed conflicts in space for two primary reasons. First, the LOAC had been developed under the circumstances where warfare was not banned as the means for the settlement of interstate disputes. That means some parts of the LOAC were deemed obsolete after the World War II. In addition, as the general participation clause found in LOAC treaties before the World War I restricts applicability unless all the belligerents are parties thereto,[204] this will also affect the applicability of the LOAC in outer space unless relevant rules have been established as customary international law.

Second, the LOAC had been developed for land, sea and air space as the scope of the individual instruments as demonstrated by the title of the many LOAC treaties.[205] This situation has not been changed decades after the space age, as exemplified by one of the latest LOAC treaties, the 1977 *Additional Protocol I to the 1949 Geneva Convention* (AP I),[206] which referred only to "on land, at sea or in the air".[207] Does this indicate that outer space is excluded from the scope of the AP I? Probably not, given that no indications existed from the drafting history of the AP I that it intentionally excluded armed conflicts in outer space from its scope.[208] It is said that the scope of the AP I would include space-based attacks against the Earth as well as attacks against space object from outer space and from the Earth provided that such attacks will affect the civilian population by, for example, the loss of emergency communications in the event of a disaster.[209]

Hence, determining the pertinent scope of the applicability of the LOAC seems critical. This requires efforts to narrow the gap between old terminology in legal instruments and current technology development, including the consideration of, for instance, whether warships can be read as military satellites and "wireless telegraphy apparatus"[210] may be replaced with military communications satellites in the specific LOAC treaties.

Further, the uniqueness of the space law regime must be considered. As opposed to the space law system where States shall bear international responsibility for the non-governmental

---

203 The scope of LOAC for the purpose of this chapter is found in e.g., Dietrich Schindler & Jiri Toman eds., *The Laws of Armed Conflicts: A Collection of Conventions, Resolutions and Other Documents* (Leiden: Martinus Nijhoff, 2004).
204 See, e.g., Art. 2 of the *Convention (IV) respecting the Laws and Customs of War on Land*, 18 October 1907, 205 Consol. TS 277 [Hague IV Convention]; Art. 20 of the *Convention (V) respecting the Rights and Duties of Neutral Powers and Persons in Case of War on Land*, 18 October 1907, 205 Consol. TS 299 [Hague V Convention]; Art. 8 of the *Convention concerning Bombardment by Naval Forces in Time of War*, 18 October 1907, 205 Consol. TS 345 [Hague IX Convention].
205 Examples are Hague IV Convention and Hague IX Convention.
206 *Protocol Additional to the Geneva Convention of 12 August 1949, and relating to the Protection of Victims of International Armed Conflicts*, 12 December 1977, 1125 UNTS 3 [AP I].
207 See. e.g., ibid., Art. 49 (4).
208 Schmitt, *supra* note 4 at 115–116.
209 Ibid.
210 Hague V Convention, *supra* note 204, Art. 8.

activities in outer space (OST, Art. VI), the law of neutrality is characterized by the clear demarcation of the status between States and private persons. One example is the 1907 *Hague Convention (V) Respecting the Rights and Duties of Neutral Powers and Persons in Case of War on Land* (the Hague V Convention), which provides that a neutral State is not called upon to prevent its private persons from exporting or transporting arms and munitions of war to the belligerents.[211] As the concept of the dichotomy between the law of war and law of peace has been obsolete since World War II, the UN treaties on outer space are applicable in times of armed conflict. Thus, it would be safer for a neutral State to apply more stringent space law rules in case of an armed conflict.

Taking such limitations into account, possible LOAC governing armed conflicts from, to and within outer space will be briefly studied below with emphasis placed on ASAT attacks.

(2) LOAC surrounding ASAT attacks

A. Satellites as military objectives

One of the most important principles in the LOAC is that the "attacks", namely "acts of violence against the adversary" (AP I, Art. 49 (1)), shall be limited strictly to military objectives. Military objectives are "those objects which by their *nature, location, purpose or use* make an effective contribution to military action and whose total and partial destruction, capture or neutralization, in the circumstances ruling at the time, offers a definite military advantage" (AP I, Art. 52 (2)) (emphasis added). Military satellites are military objectives based on the "nature" criterion even if they are also used for civilian purposes like the US GPS constellations. So are civilian satellites which serve for military operations by virtue of "use".[212] Such "dual-use" satellites are often owned by a private person of the State outside the armed conflict concerned. Thus, the law of neutrality in the space context has to be studied concerning the use of dual-use satellites, which is discussed below (5 (2) C of this chapter). The remaining "location" and "purpose" criteria are more difficult to apply with certainty.[213]

In attacking military objectives, AP I provides that all feasible precautions in the choice of means and methods of attack shall be taken to avoid and minimize collateral damage.[214] In addition, any attack has to be avoided if it may cause excessive incidental loss of civilian life or damage to civilian objects in relation to the concrete and direct military advantage anticipated (proportionality principle).[215] Hence, in order to avoid the incidental damage caused by space debris to a civilian satellite that serves, for example, telemedicine, it can be said that ground-based cyber attacks against military satellites should be chosen.[216]

As precautionary measures not to attack civilian satellites, the State intending to attack may be recommended to refer to the relevant information specified in the Register maintained by the UNSG pursuant to the Registration Convention (Art. III) such as "[g]eneral function of the space object" (Art. IV 1(e)). If so, however, more precise and detailed information is

---

211 Ibid., Art 7. See, also, David L. Willson, "An Army View of Neutrality in Space: Legal Options for Space Negation" (2001) 50 *A.F.L. Rev.* 175 at 193–195.
212 Schmitt, *supra* note 4 at 116.
213 Ibid., at 117. See also, Michel Bourbonnière, "Law of Armed Conflict (LOAC) and the Neutralisation of Satellites or *IUS in Bello Satellitis*", (2004) 9 *J. Conflict & Sec. L.* 43 at 59–61.
214 API, *supra* note 206, Art. 57 (2) (a) (ii).
215 Ibid., Arts. 51 (5) (b), 57 (2) (a) (iii) & 57 (2) (b). See, also, Robert A. Ramey, "Armed Conflict on the Final Frontier: the Law of War in Space" (2000) 48 *A.F.L.Rev.* 1 at 39–40.
216 See, e.g., Schmitt, *supra* note 4 at 117 & 120–121.

necessary, because the present practice is insufficient and sometimes misleading.[217] At the same time, registering a military satellite as a civilian satellite may be tantamount to feigning civilian status, thus interpreted as "perfidy" prohibited under the customary international law reflected in AP I (Art. 37 (1)).[218]

B. Prohibited methods or means of warfare

ASAT attacks producing significant amounts of space debris that may affect the orbital environment for decades could be classified as a prohibited method or means of armed conflict under Art. 35 (3) of AP I depending on the definition of the "natural environment."[219] Moreover, it seems that such attacks violate the obligation of due regard for the interests of other States required in the OST (Art. IX).

It is worth noting that AP I provides that a State which develops, acquires or adopts a new weapon, means or method of warfare is under the obligation to determine whether its employment would be prohibited by international law (Art. 36). This means that the burden of proof is incumbent on the State that tries to employ a new weapon, means or method of armed conflict. This rule will be a mighty tool as much in the realm of the LOAC as effective space arms control and disarmament.[220]

C. Importance of the study of the law of neutrality in space armed conflicts

As already mentioned, among the ambiguity of the LOAC applications to space warfare, the law of neutrality is the least predictable area. Consider one hypothetical case. Granting that State A and State B engage in armed conflict, and A plans to attack a dual-use satellite operated by a company X of the non-belligerent (neutral) State C because that satellite assists B's military operations, what are the rights and obligations between State A and State C? It is true that a neutral State shall maintain impartiality towards all belligerents, but within those restrictions, it is under no obligation "to forbid or restrict the use on behalf of the belligerents of *telegraph or telephone cables or of wireless telegraphy apparatus* belonging to it or to companies or private individuals" (Hague V Convention, Art. 8) (emphasis added). Granting that "wireless telegraphy apparatus" can be replaced in today's technological development by civilian communications, navigation and weather satellites in view of the similarity of the nature as public utilities service, granting also that communication services by company X are provided in a nondiscriminatory fashion. In that case, can it be construed that State C does not violate the law of neutrality and State A would violate the LOAC in this regard? The answer could be yes.[221] (Of course as also already mentioned, it is safer in practice that State C prohibits company X from providing communication services to any of the belligerents noting the unique space law regime.)

---

217 For instance, the function of the US satellites are, in most cases, explained as "[s]pacecraft engaged in practical applications and uses of space technology such as weather or communications". See, e.g., ST/SG/SER.E/725 (12 August 2014) at 2.
218 See, e.g., Michel Bourbonnière, "National Security Law in Outer Space: The Interface of Exploration and Security" (2005) 70 *J. Air L. & Com.* 3 at 49.
219 The threshold of "long-term" in Art. 35 (3) of the AP I is a period of decades, thus higher than the ENMOD Convention. See, 2 (4) of this chapter. Note has to be taken that Art. 55 (1) of AP I prohibits the use of such methods or means of warfare only when the health or survival of the population is affected.
220 Lyall & Larsen, *supra* note 60 at 527.
221 Willson, *supra* note 211 at 193–199.

The essence of Art.8 is that the neutral State must not become an intelligence bureau transmitting messages from State C to State A or State B.[222] In this regard, remote sensing satellite imagery is thought to be a different kind of product as it is essentially intelligence information. Then, in this hypothetical example, in case X provides high-resolution imagery of State A to State B, State C might lose its status of neutrality. In light of the precautionary measures and proportionality principles, State A seems to be required to warn C before resorting to the right of self-defense on X's remote sensing satellite. (OST, Art. IX; AP I, Art. 57 (2) (c), etc.)

LOAC, especially the law of neutrality is vague in applicability in case of armed conflicts in space. Therefore, it seems desirable to make an international effort to find a contemporary restatement of international law applicable to armed conflicts in outer space.

---

222   Ibid., at 193–194.

12
The intersection between space law and international human rights law*

Steven Freeland and Ram S. Jakhu

Introduction – same era, different legal regimes?

The international legal regulation of outer space represents an ongoing challenge in terms of establishing and implementing frameworks that are appropriate means of global governance. Those of us who are concerned with the legal regulation of outer space have come to realize that there are myriad factors associated with this regime. These are both of a 'law' (hard and 'soft') nature, as well as stemming from a range of other non-legal areas such as history, technology, science, economics, sociology etc. Dealing with the traditional legal aspects, the United Nations Space Treaties and specific space-related General Assembly Resolutions undoubtedly form an important corpus of rules and guidelines which serve to fashion our conduct in the exploration and use of outer space. The fundamental principles that these instruments set out represent important foundations upon which humankind's endeavours in outer space have traditionally been based, at least in the public debate. They have also been largely successful in – thus far – steering us away from cataclysmic errors of judgment in the way that we have utilized outer space.

However, it would be far too simplistic and plainly inaccurate to assume that the applicable legal regime begins and ends with these instruments. Notwithstanding their importance, there is much more to consider. The wide ranging and ever increasing number of space activities clearly demonstrates that many issues impact on this legal regime, at the same time that the regime itself impacts on a broad facet of human interactions. In this sense, outer space asserts a far greater influence upon the directions taken by humankind than one might at first instance imagine – yes, the exploration and use of outer space has been designated as the 'province of mankind',[1] but it is not only a place for us to venture to in order to explore and exploit, but is also a phenomena that has real impacts upon all on Earth every day of our lives.

---

*   This chapter is an updated (December 2015) version of a paper presented by the authors at the 2013 Colloquium on the Law of Outer Space and printed in *Proceedings of the International Institute of Space Law* (2014), 365.
1   See Treaty on Principles governing the Activities of States in the Exploration and Use of Outer Space, including the Moon and Other Celestial Bodies, 610 UNTS 205 (1967) (Outer Space Treaty), article I.

This is, in fact, expressly recognized in the preamble of the Outer Space Treaty. Paragraphs 2 and 3 respectively confirm that, at the time these principles had been codified, the international community had:

> Recogniz[ed] the common interest of all mankind in the progress of the exploration and use of outer space for peaceful purposes,

and

> Believ[ed] that the exploration and use of outer space should be carried on for the benefit of all peoples irrespective of the degree of their economic or scientific development

In essence, the Outer Space Treaty makes clear from the outset that the international legal regulation of outer space is founded on an assumption that this (at the time) new frontier raised important issues about humanity. We hold the firm view that this is still the case, despite the realities associated with the rapid diversification of space activities to incorporate, for example, military uses, and the increasing involvement in outer space of commercial (private) enterprise, whose agendas may not match up with a spirit of sharing and community.

Given this obvious 'human' face to space activities both as to cause and effect, it is therefore quite surprising that the interaction and intersection between the specific international legal regime of outer space and the international legal regulation of human rights has not been the subject of greater considered scholarship in the past. Apart from a small number of interesting commentaries,[2] these two legal paradigms have largely been considered in isolation, even though their formal codification coincided from a temporal viewpoint, and despite the fact that the same actors were involved in the detailed conversations and negotiations that led to their finalization.

The two legal regimes are largely products of the post-Second World War period. From the perspective of outer space, the late 1940s saw a ratcheting up of distrust between the 'west' and 'east', giving rise to diplomatic tensions and, ultimately, the onset of the 'Cold War'. This geopolitical rivalry saw the two main protagonists, the Soviet Union and the United States, intensify their efforts to build upon the weapons-related technology that had been developed during the war period, including in the area of rocket technology. Both of these superpowers made significant strides towards developing space capabilities, and devoted significant resources towards that end. In the end, on 4 October 1957, a Soviet space object, Sputnik I, was launched and subsequently orbited the Earth over 1,400 times during the following three month period. This milestone heralded the dawn of the space age, the space race, and the legal regulation of the use and exploration of outer space. There then followed an intense period of international discussion and consideration of how best to provide for a framework of legal principles to regulate human activities in outer space, culminating in the first instance in the Outer Space Treaty.

The Second World War had also starkly illustrated the horrors that flow from a gross and systematic violation of human rights and human dignity. Up until that time, there were barely any international instruments that addressed the concept or content of the fundamental rights

---

2   See Irmgard Marboe, 'Human Rights Considerations for Space Activities' in Stephan Hobe and Steven Freeland, *In Heaven as on Earth? The Interaction of Public International Law on the Legal Regulation of Outer Space* (2013), 135, and the references at footnote 1 of that chapter.

of the individual. Indeed, the reference in the United Nations Charter to the international community's determination:[3]

> to reaffirm faith in fundamental human rights, in the dignity and worth of the human person, in the equal rights of men and women and of nations large and small

was in more practical terms recognition of the need to codify these rights as a first step towards the promotion and protection of those ideals, in order to have any chance of avoiding such catastrophes again (sadly, subsequent history suggests that we have thus far failed in this regard). The first stages of this human rights 'movement' saw the conclusion of a number of very significant legal instruments that set out to codify the fundamental rights and freedoms that underpin international human rights law. The 'twin covenants' of 1966,[4] which incorporate into treaty form the principles set out in the 1948 Universal Declaration of Human Rights,[5] were being negotiated – sometimes quite fiercely – at the same time that the space race had begun, and the most important ground-rules of space law were being developed. In both instances, the same geopolitical rivalries and ideological differences shaped the final structure of each regime. A fact not often acknowledged is that the ICCPR and ICESCR were finalized by the United Nations General Assembly and opened for signature on 16 December 1966, just a matter of a few weeks before the Outer Space Treaty (27 January 1967).

The development of these two legal regimes also coincided with a process of decolonization, largely under the stewardship of the United Nations system. Both the UN Charter and the twin covenants make express reference to the right of self-determination of 'peoples',[6] and this galvanized a momentum that ultimately led to the establishment of a significant number of new States in the period between the 1950s and 1970s, many of these in Asia and Africa.[7] Most of these new States were established as a result of decolonization, and with this newly-won independence came the clear resolve of those States to be fiercely independent and to reject as much as possible the geopolitics and single-minded resource exploitation that had existed during the time of colonialism. This stance is reflected, for example, by the opening paragraph of the Outer Space Treaty, which demands that the exploration and use of outer space be 'for the benefit and in the interests of all countries, irrespective of their degree of economic or scientific development'.

Nonetheless, this period was also characterized by an increasing divide, both in actual but also ideological terms, between what became known as 'developed' and 'developing' States – a division that formed an important, and sometimes controversial[8] element in the formulation of

---

3 Charter of the United Nations, 1 UNTS 16 (1945) (UN Charter).
4 International Covenant on Civil and Political Rights, 999 UNTS 171 (1966) (ICCPR); International Covenant on Economic, Social and Cultural Rights, 993 UNTS 3 (1966) (IESCR). Collectively these two instruments are often referred to as the 'Twin Covenants'.
5 United Nations General Assembly Resolution 217A (III) (10 December 1948) on the Universal Declaration of Human Rights (UDHR). Reference should also be made to other very significant treaties finalized at that time, including the Convention on the Prevention and Punishment of the Crime of Genocide, 78 UNTS 277 (1948); the four 'Geneva Conventions' of 1949; the European Convention for the Protection of Human Rights and Fundamental Freedoms, 213 UNTS 221 (1950) (ECHR).
6 See UN Charter, article 1(2); ICCPR, article 1(1); ICESCR, article 1(1).
7 For example, at the time of the adoption of the UDHR in 1948, the membership of the United Nations stood at 56. By 1967, when the twin covenants and the Outer Space Treaty had been finalized, this number had more than doubled.
8 See Agreement Governing the Activities of States on the Moon and other Celestial Bodies, 1363 UNTS 3 (1979) (Moon Agreement), article 11(7)(d).

various of the space law source documents.[9]

Moreover, the overall trusteeship of the two international legal regimes remains to a large degree (although not exclusively) within the United Nations; space law through the United Nations Committee on the Peaceful Uses of Outer Space (UNCOPUOS) and the United Nations Office of Outer Space Affairs (UNOOSA), and human rights law through a series of Charter Bodies, including the Office of the High Commissioner for Human Rights (OHCHR), the Human Rights Council (which replaced the United Nations Commission on Human Rights in 2006) and the Economic and Social Council (ECOSOC), as well as various United Nations Treaty Bodies such as the Human Rights Committee, which was established to monitor compliance with the ICCPR.

In addition to their shared historical antecedents, the lack of a coordinated analysis of these coinciding regimes is also at odds with the structure of outer space regulation itself. It is undisputed that, from a 'legal rules' perspective, the international regulation of outer space – past, present and future – is 'embedded' in international law. It is not an esoteric and separate paradigm limited solely to the *lex specialis* of space law with which we are all familiar. In a sense, this is an obvious point, particularly given the complexity of human activities in space and their impacts on all of us, but one that is worthwhile emphasizing. The space-related instruments cannot and do not purport to provide a comprehensive legal framework for every activity, nor for every contingency that may arise. It has often been noted that there are *lacunae* within these instruments with respect to the specifics of many space activities, a trend that continues to increasingly show itself as new uses of space are undertaken that would almost certainly have been outside of the contemplation of the drafters of those documents in the 1960s and 1970s. Notwithstanding the continuing applicability of the fundamental framework of space principles, in such cases, were the need to arise, it will often become necessary to draw upon other areas of (international) law to resolve a particular dispute.

This is also a logical consequence of the wording of article III of the Outer Space Treaty, which requires that activities in the exploration and use of outer space are to be carried out 'in accordance with international law, including the Charter of the United Nations'. We have previously sought to highlight this point in relation to other international law contexts,[10] and it remains no less relevant when it comes to the relationship between the regulation and conduct of outer space activities and the fundamental human rights of individuals on Earth.

This chapter, therefore, seeks to briefly highlight some of the ways in which the use and exploration of outer space overlaps with principles viewed from a core human rights perspective. We will illustrate this intersection with a number of examples, drawing upon

---

9   See, for example, Principles Governing the Use by States of Artificial Earth Satellites for International Direct Television Broadcasting, United Nations General Assembly Resolution 37/92 (10 December 1982) (Direct Broadcasting Principles), principles 2, 6, 11; Principles Relating to Remote Sensing of the Earth from Outer Space, United Nations General Assembly Resolution 41/65 (3 December 1986) (Remote Sensing Principles), principles II, IX, XII, XIII; Principles Relevant to the Use of Nuclear Power Sources in Outer Space, United Nations General Assembly Resolution 47/68 (14 December 1992), principle 7(2)(b); Declaration on International Cooperation in the Exploration and Use of Outer Space for the Benefit and in the Interest of All States, Taking into Particular Account the Needs of Developing Countries, United Nations General Assembly Resolution 51/122 (13 December 1996).

10 See, for example, Ram S. Jakhu and Steven Freeland, 'The Relationship between the United Nations Space Treaties and the Vienna Convention on the Law of Treaties' in *Proceedings of the International Institute of Space Law* (2012), 375; Ram S. Jakhu and Steven Freeland, 'The Sources of International Space Law' in *Proceedings of the International Institute of Space Law* (2013), 461.

references from both the *lex specialis* of space law and the 'International Bill of Rights'.[11] In doing this, it is not our intention to describe in detail every aspect of those human rights principles that are relevant in the context of outer space activities; rather we seek to highlight these issues of convergence in the hope that it can stimulate further careful consideration and research, as well as encouraging a more 'holistic' approach to the future direction of the legal regulation of outer space. In our view, this represents an integral foundational approach to a proper consideration of the main features and requirements relevant for the design and implementation of a structure appropriate for the future global governance of outer space.

In essence, therefore, the purpose of this chapter is to emphasize that the fundamental concepts of space law are invariably linked with the fundamental concepts of rights and freedoms that we all (in theory) enjoy. In this regard, accepted principles of human rights law are highly relevant for our activities in space. We recognize that this pronouncement on our part is not a 'eureka' moment – instead we believe that we are, to a certain degree, stating the obvious. However, it is also an 'obvious' that has perhaps been overlooked or cast aside, particularly as the use and exploration of outer space becomes ever more complex, and increasing emphasis is placed upon the 'congested, contested and competitive' nature of outer space,[12] rather than its underpinning elements of humanity. This has, in our view, led to a largely skewed view of the relevance of human rights in relation to activities involving outer space.

We also wish to emphasize that, of course, other areas of international law – for example international humanitarian law[13] and international environmental law[14] – are also highly relevant in this regard, and that they, too, incorporate concepts relating to the fundamental rights of individuals and communities into a consideration of the broad legal framework of outer space activities. However, for the purposes of this chapter, we limit ourselves to indicating areas of cross-over with principles elaborated in the major human rights instruments.

We also assume in this chapter an expansive viewpoint of human rights principles. Whilst there is still debate among human rights scholars about the various 'levels' and 'types' of human rights, we prefer for the purposes of this discussion to accept the principles as they are codified in the twin covenants, as well as incorporating the developing 'generations' of human rights, encompassing both *individual* rights (civil, political, economic, social and cultural) as well as *collective* and/or *community* rights. The traditional and restrictive view has been that human rights principles by definition extend only to individual members of a group, but *not* to the group itself.[15] Some may still assert that such a hierarchical approach should be applied to a study of human rights *per se* but, at least in the context of this chapter, which seeks to highlight the intersection between outer space and human rights in broader terms, we believe that all such rights should be considered as potentially applicable to the exploration and use of outer space. This is particularly so given the very broad impact that outer space activities can have upon the lives and livelihoods of large sectors of a population.

11 The three instruments, the UDHR, ICCPR and ICESCR are often referred to as the 'International Bills of Rights'.
12 See, for example, United Nations General Assembly, 'Outer Space Increasingly "Congested, Contested and Competitive"', First Committee told, as Speakers urge Legally Binding Document to prevent its Militarization', Press Release 25 October 2013, UN Doc GA/DIS/3487.
13 See, for example, Steven Freeland, 'The Applicability of the *Jus in Bello* Rules of International Humanitarian Law to the Use of Outer Space' in *Proceedings of the Colloquium on the Law of Outer Space* (2006), 338.
14 See, for example, Ulrike M. Bohlmann and Steven Freeland, 'The Regulation of Space Activities and the Space Environment' in Shawkat Alam, Md Jahid Hossain Bhuiyan, Tareq M.R. Chowdhury and Erika J. Techera (ed), *Routledge Handbook of International Environmental Law* (2013), 375.
15 Peter Bailey, *Human Rights Law* (2012), 9.

With these caveats in mind, we will now touch on a number of areas of convergence stemming from the rights codified in the International Bill of Rights, which we use as our reference point:

The right to peace

The first paragraph of the preamble of the UDHR provides as follows (emphasis added):[16]

> Whereas recognition of the inherent dignity and of the equal and inalienable rights of all members of the human family is the foundation of freedom, justice and *peace in the world*.

From the outset, therefore, the UDHR emphasizes the importance of peace as a 'right' of everyone on Earth. This is not particularly surprising given that the instrument was a direct response to the war that, at the time that it was finalized, had only very recently ended. This form of apparent collective right, as noted above, raises specific issues with human rights scholars as to whether it is truly a fundamental 'human' right. Interesting questions, which are beyond the scope of this chapter, arise as to whether each person *individually* does, in fact, have a right to peace in the world, despite the broad terms of the preamble. These discussions have led to the evolution of so-called 'second' and 'third' generation rights, the latter of which encompass such collective concepts of rights.

Irrespective of the niceties of rights classification, it is undoubted that an underlying motivation of the International Bill of Rights is one of peace. The same can be said about the international space law *lex specialis*. Indeed, the immediate acceptance by community of States, including both the major space faring States of the time, that outer space was to be regarded as being similar to a *res communis omnium*[17] and the subsequent codification of the so-called non-appropriation principle in the Outer Space Treaty[18] were important proactive steps that were intended to cement and protect the peaceful nature of outer space.

Indeed, it is, of course, no coincidence that UNCOPUOS contains the important descriptor 'peaceful'. The 'peaceful purposes' doctrine is an important element of the international regulation of outer space[19] although, as is well known, there have been conflicting views as to its interpretation and subsequent practical application.[20] Yet there is no doubt that the concept of peaceful for the purposes of outer space encompasses an absence of fully-blown 'armed conflict', and is therefore symmetrical with the fundamental element of the right to peace as referred to above. The possibility of a space arms race has continuously been recognized by the international community. Since the early 1980s, the United Nations General Assembly has each year adopted overwhelmingly resolutions regarding the Prevention of an Arms Race in Outer Space (PAROS).[21] More importantly, several newspaper headlines during the second half of

---

16 See also ICCPR, preamble para. 1; ICESCR, preamble para. 1.
17 Antonio Cassese, *International Law* (2005), 95.
18 See Outer Space Treaty, article II. For a detailed analysis of this provision, see Steven Freeland and Ram Jakhu, 'Article II' in Stephan Hobe, Bernhard Schmidt-Tedd and Kai-Uwe Schrogl (eds), *Cologne Commentary on Space Law, Volume I – Outer Space Treaty* (2009), 44.
19 See Outer Space Treaty, article IV; Moon Agreement, article 3(1).
20 See Steven Freeland, 'Outer Space, Technology and Warfare' (2014) 13:1 *The Aviation & Space Journal* 35, 36.
21 *Prevention of an arms race in outer space*, GA Res 69/31, UNGAOR, 69th Sess, UN Doc A/RES/69/31 (2014).

2015 have indicated that the possibility of a conflict in space is increasing.[22] The obvious implication of these developments is threat to the right to peace.

The right to privacy

Article 12 of the UDHR provides as follows:

> No one shall be subjected to arbitrary interference with his privacy, family, home or correspondence, nor to attacks upon his honour and reputation. Everyone has the right to the protection of the law against such interference or attacks.

As the resolution capabilities of remote sensing satellites increase and their use by private companies grows, there arise inevitable concerns about an individual's right to privacy. Threats to privacy through the use of satellites are much more pervasive than those posed by terrestrial based systems. There is no specific hard or soft space law instrument that protects such interference with privacy via extra-terrestrial means. Article 12 of the UDHR is considered to be applicable to space activities, but its implementation is to be carried out through appropriate national laws and regulations. On the contrary, the States with strong traditions and legal regimes governing freedom of information are more inclined to allow freer circulation of information obtained through the use of satellites, with a consequent diminishment of the right to privacy. For example, it has been reported that the United States Government allowed a private company, Digital Globe, to 'sell images that showed features as small as 31cm', as opposed to earlier limit of 50 cm.[23]

The right to honour and reputation is protected under international law that has been summed up as follows:[24]

> International law clearly forbids the higher officials of a state to indulge in uncomplimentary or insulting comments upon the personality of another state or its rulers.

This rule of law still applies today to space operations.

The right to privacy of correspondence by electronic means is protected under the Constitution of the International Telecommunication Union (ITU). Member States of the ITU are obliged to ensure the secrecy of international correspondence by all means, including through the use of satellites. Nevertheless, in order to ensure compliance with their national laws or their international obligations, they may communicate such correspondence to the competent authorities.[25]

---

22 See Lee Billings, 'War in Space May Be Closer Than Ever', *Scientific American* (10 August 2015), online: Scientific American www.scientificamerican.com/article/war-in- space-may-be-closer-than-ever/; Ari Yashar, 'US and China Gear Up for Space Combat', *Cosmos* (26 April 2015), online: Cosmos http://cosmoso.net/us-andchina-gear-up-for-space-combat/; Brendan McGarry, 'A Coming War in Space?', *Defense Tech* (3 August 2015), online: Defense Tech http://defensetech.org/2015/08/03/a-coming-war-in-space/.
23 'US lifts restrictions on more detailed satellite images', *BBCNEWS*, 16 June 2014 www.bbc.com/news/technology-27868703 (last accessed 10 December 2015).
24 Charles Hyde, *International Law, Chiefly as Interpreted and Applied by the United States* (1945), 709, cited in Arthur Larson, 'The Present Status of Propaganda in International law' (1966) 31 *Journal of Law and Contemporary Problems* 439, 447.
25 ITU Constitution (2010), article 37.

The right to freedom of expression/right to receive and impart information

Article 19 of the UDHR provides as follows:[26]

> Everyone has the right to freedom of opinion and expression; this right includes freedom to hold opinions without interference and to seek, receive and impart information and ideas through any media and regardless of frontiers.

The right of freedom of information is also codified in article 19 of the ICCPR, and in other regional treaties on human rights.[27] More importantly, this right is incorporated in Principle 1 of the Direct Broadcasting Principles, thus making it specifically applicable to satellite broadcasting. However, this right has not been fully complied with in the use of satellite communications.[28] The international community has adopted several soft law and hard law instruments that deny or restrict the application of the right to freedom of expression 'regardless of frontiers.' For example, the 1972 UNESCO Declaration of Guiding Principles on the Use of Direct Broadcasting by Satellite recognizes both the right of freedom of information and the prohibition of propaganda.[29] However, it specifies that it is necessary for States to:[30]

> reach or promote prior agreements concerning direct satellite broadcasting to the population of countries other than the country of origin of the transmission.

Similarly, according to the Direct Broadcasting Principles, international direct television broadcasting satellite services must only be established after consultation between the transmitting and receiving States, on the basis of agreements and/or arrangements between the two and in conformity with the relevant instruments of the ITU.[31]

These two soft law instruments attempt to incorporate both the freedom of, and restriction on information. On the contrary, the hard law international rules impose constraints on the freedom of international satellite broadcasting. These limitations are in the form of regulations adopted through the ITU. For example, of the ITU Radio Regulations oblige States to design and build their broadcasting satellites in such a way that they must:[32]

> reduce, to the maximum, the radiation over the territory of other countries unless an agreement has been previously reached with such countries.

---

26 See also ICCPR, article 19(2).
27 For example, ECHR, article 10; American Convention on Human Rights 'Pact of San José, Costa Rica' (1978), article 13; African Charter on Human and Peoples Rights (1986), article 9.
28 See Ram S. Jakhu, 'Direct Broadcasting Via Satellite And A New Information Order' (1980) 8:2 *Syracuse Journal of International Law and Commerce* 375.
29 See United Nations General Assembly Resolution 110(II) (3 November 1947) on Measures to be Taken against Propaganda and the Inciters of a New War.
30 UNESCO Declaration of Guiding Principles on the Use of Satellite Broadcasting for the Free Flow of Information, the Spread of Education and Greater Cultural Exchange (15 November 1972), principle IX.
31 Direct Broadcasting Principles, principles 13 and 14. United Nations General Assembly resolution 37/92, adopted on 10 December 1982.
32 ITU Radio Regulations (2012), article 23.13 (4).

In other words, it is illegal to operate a broadcasting satellite that broadcasts its programmes into the territory of foreign States unless there is an appropriate agreement between the transmitting and receiving States, or such spill-over of satellite signals cannot be technically feasible to avoid. It is interesting to note that some States are by-passing this requirement by using radio frequencies that are allocated for Fixed Satellite Service (FSS), in order to provide satellite direct broadcasting service (DBS, also known as Broadcasting Satellite Services, BSS under the ITU Radio Regulations). They are avoiding compliance with the requirement of seeking prior consent from the receiving State, but are in violation of the ITU Radio Regulations that oblige ITU Member States not assign to their radio stations (including satellites) any radio frequency in derogation of provisions of the Regulations.[33] Since satellites that use FSS radio frequencies to carry on broadcasting services are not in compliance with the ITU Radio Regulations, they may not be entitled to a right of protection against harmful interference.[34]

The ITU Radio Regulations allow the use of the 12 GHz band of radio frequencies for direct satellite broadcasting service for national coverage only.[35] Such frequencies can be legally used for international services only on the basis of prior agreement between the transmitting and receiving States, and only after following procedures for the modification of relevant ITU Frequency Allotment Plans for this service. Therefore, the receiving State is legally entitled, if it chooses, to object to any unwanted DBS transmissions from other States, and may impose restrictions on the right of freedom of information.

The right of freedom of information has also played an important role in the development of principles and guidelines with respect to the use of remote sensing satellites. In the 1970s and 1980s, UNCOPUOS discussed the adoption of a specific legal regime governing the acquisition and distribution of satellite remote sensing imagery.[36] Based on the right of freedom of information, some States advocated the freedom of acquisition and distribution of satellite remote sensing imagery without seeking the consent of the sensed States. Other States insisted on the requirement of prior consent, based on the right of sovereignty over their natural resources.[37]

Finally, a compromise was adopted in the form of the Remote Sensing Principles. In the conduct of remote sensing activities, these principles require 'respect for the principle of full and permanent sovereignty of all States and peoples over their own wealth and natural resources' (Principle IV). They also entitle the sensed States to have access to the satellite imagery (basic data and analysed information) concerning their territories 'on a non-discriminatory basis and on reasonable cost terms' (Principle XII). This is in accordance with the right to seek information. However, contrary to these principles, 'several States have started making such access subject to their national security concerns, foreign policy interests or international obligations.'[38]

Thus, even though the right to freedom of information is applicable to space activities, its proper implementation has not been fully respected. This failure becomes ever more significant

---

33   Ibid., article 4.4.
34   See Ram S. Jakhu, 'Regulatory Process for Communications Satellite Frequency Allocations' in J. Pelton, S. Madry and Lara S. Camacho (eds), *Handbook of Satellite Applications* (2013), 272, 279.
35   ITU Radio Regulations (2012), Appendixes 30, 30A.
36   See Ram S. Jakhu, 'International Law Governing the Acquisition and Dissemination of Satellite Imagery' (2003) 29 *Journal of Space Law* 65 *et seq*.
37   United Nations General Assembly Resolution 1803 (XVII) (14 December 1962) on the Declaration on Permanent Sovereignty over Natural Resources.
38   See Jakhu, *supra* note 36, 90.

in the current geopolitical climate of many countries, where attempts are still being made to deny large sways of the population from accessing (sensitive) information, as well as the increasing resort by various Government agencies to a strategy of 'misinformation'.

Sovereign right to natural resources

Article 1(2) of both the ICCPR and ICESCR provides in part as follows:

> All peoples may, for their own ends, freely dispose of their natural wealth and resources without prejudice to any obligations arising out of international economic co-operation, based upon the principle of mutual benefit, and international law. In no case may a people be deprived of its own means of subsistence.

This legal principle confirming the sovereign right to natural resources has also been included in a landmark United Nations General Assembly Resolution.[39] This principle, which is considered to have become a part of those *jus cogens* rules of law applicable to all States,[40] played an important role, as noted above, during the negotiations of the Remote Sensing Principles and has been included in those Principles. However, it should be recognized that this right is limited to the natural resources of the Earth and would have limited, if any, application to the natural resources of outer space and celestial bodies.[41] That said, we have previously pointed to some analogous symmetry between this terrestrial right and the non-appropriation principle encapsulated in article II of the Outer Space Treaty.[42]

Prohibition of propaganda for war/hate speech/incitement

Article 20 of the ICCPR provides as follows:

1. Any propaganda for war shall be prohibited by law.
2. Any advocacy of national, racial or religious hatred that constitutes incitement to discrimination, hostility or violence shall be prohibited by law.

This prohibition is based on the UN General Assembly Resolution 110 (II) referred to above, which is applicable to outer space activities. The second last paragraph of the preamble to the Outer Space Treaty states that:

> United Nations General Assembly resolution 110 (II) of 3 November 1947 ... condemned propaganda designed or likely to provoke or encourage any threat to the peace, breach of the peace or act of aggression, and ... that the aforementioned resolution is applicable to outer space.

Although, as a United Nations General Assembly Resolution,[43] Resolution 110 (II) is not legally binding, its inclusion in the preamble to the Outer Space Treaty enhances its value as a

---

39   United Nations General Assembly Resolution 1803 (XVII) (14 December 1962) on the Declaration on Permanent Sovereignty over Natural Resources.
40   See Ian Brownie, *Principles of Public International Law* (1998), 515.
41   See, for example, Moon Agreement, article 11(1).
42   See Freeland and Jakhu, *supra* note 18, 60.
43   See also Jakhu and Freeland, 'Sources', *supra* note 10.

tool for the proper interpretation of the provisions of that instrument.[44] Since article III of the Treaty obligates States Parties to carry on space activities

> in the interest of maintaining international peace and security and promoting international co-operation and understanding

they must not use communication satellites for broadcasting the prohibited propaganda. Moreover, the Direct Broadcasting Principles make the prohibition of propaganda specifically applicable to international direct broadcasting via satellites.

In addition, the 1936 Convention on Broadcasting[45]

> prohibits broadcasting which constitutes, or is likely to lead to, an incitement to war against another Contracting State

and the States Parties to the Convention are obliged to

> undertake to prohibit and, if occasion arises, to stop without delay the broadcasting within their respective territories of any transmission which to the detriment of good international understanding is of such a character as to incite the population of any territory to acts incompatible with the internal order or the security of a territory of a High Contracting Party.

Although the 1936 Convention predates both the ICCPR and the Outer Space Treaty, it is regarded as applicable to the outer space activities of the States Parties to the Convention, because its scope and objective are broad enough to cover the prohibition of propaganda by satellites. However, the Convention is applicable to only about 60 States; the United States never became party and the United Kingdom denounced it on 24 July 1985.

States Parties to the ICCPR are under an obligation to prohibit, through their respective national laws and regulations, the following propaganda-like activities arising from their satellite communications:[46]

> [a]ny advocacy of national, racial or religious hatred that constitutes incitement to discrimination, hostility or violence.

In addition, a EU Council Directive on 'Television without Frontiers' and the European Convention on Transfrontier Television, which are both applicable to satellite broadcasting, impose an obligation not to broadcast anything that is indecent and in particular contain pornography and/or 'give undue prominence to violence or [is] likely to incite to racial hatred.'[47]

44   1969 Vienna Convention on the Law of Treaties, 1155 UNTS 331, article 31. See also Jakhu and Freeland, 'Relationship', *supra* note 10.
45   1936 International Convention Concerning the Use of Broadcasting in the Cause of Peace, 186 LNTS 301, articles 1 and 2.
46   ICCPR, article 20.
47   European Union Council Directive of 3 October 1989 (as amended in 1997) on the coordination of certain provisions laid down by law, regulation or administrative action in Member States concerning the pursuit of television broadcasting activities (89/552/EEC), article 22a; European Convention on Transfrontier Television, 5 May 1989 (as amended in 2002), article 7. The text of the Convention can be found at http://conventions.coe. int/Treaty/en/Treaties/Html/132.htm (last accessed 10 December 2015).

The human right of freedom of information and the related prohibition of propaganda are therefore both applicable to space activities such as satellite communications. However their role/value in space law appears to have been limited because they are inconsistent with one another. This may raise the issue of hierarchy of legal norms and the challenge in their application in practice when a State uses satellites for imparting information through satellite broadcasting programmes that, at the same time, also constitute propaganda as prohibited by article 20 of the ICCPR.

International co-operation

Article 11(1) of the ICESCR provides that:

> The States Parties to the present Covenant recognize the right of everyone to an adequate standard of living for himself and his family, including adequate food, clothing and housing, and to the continuous improvement of living conditions. The States Parties will take appropriate steps to ensure the realization of this right, recognizing to this effect the essential importance of international co-operation based on free consent.

This very general and broad right seems to have influenced the formation of the foundation of space law, particularly as specified in the preamble and article I(1) of the Outer Space Treaty, as well as other United Nations space treaties and resolutions. The necessity and importance of international co-operation have resulted in various agreements and soft law mechanisms that attempt to facilitate many types of space activities giving effect to the right of everyone to have better quality of life.

Pursuant to the United Nations General Assembly Resolution 1721 (D) of 1961, which specified that satellite telecommunication services should be made available on a global and non-discriminatory basis, INTELSAT was created in 1971 as a permanent intergovernmental organization to provide international public telecommunications services of high quality and reliability, to be available on a non-discriminatory basis to all areas of the world and all users paying non-discriminatory charges for its services.[48] This organization, although now a privatized company, for the first time in the history of humankind revolutionized global communications connecting people in all corners and remote areas of the world.

There are also several other institutions and/or arrangements that provide humanitarian services through the use of satellites; for example, COSPAS-SARSAT for search and rescue services,[49] and international arrangement for disaster management,[50] which is a unique international co-operative effort for global humanitarian purposes to use space facilities for the management of natural and technological disasters. Currently there are hundreds of such multilateral/bilateral co-operative agreements/arrangements among numerous countries, their space agencies and private companies. These seek to develop space technologies and applications in various forms, in order to improve the living conditions of individuals.

---

48 1971 Agreement Relating to the International Telecommunications Satellite Organization (INTELSAT), 10 ILM 1909.
49 For a text of the Agreement and International Cospas-Sarsat Programme Privileges and Immunities Order, see Canada, SOR/2005-112, 5 August 2014.
50 International Charter on Cooperation to Achieve the Coordinated Use of Space Facilities in the Event of Natural or Technological Disasters www.disasterscharter.org/web/charter/charter (last accessed 10 December 2015).

Space co-operation has thus become indispensable for practical uses of space applications. However, it must be kept in mind that space co-operation has been pursued not as an international obligation, but rather as a political expediency and economic necessity among the co-operating countries. This reflects the undeniable strategic value associated with co-operative space activities between States that, by contrast, may perhaps be less inclined to work together in their terrestrial inter-relationships in relation to sensitive areas.[51]

Concluding remarks

The use, exploration and exploitation of outer space have developed exponentially since Sputnik I took that fateful journey in October 1957. No-one could imagine then how space technology has changed and shaped the lives of everyone on Earth. The same remains the case today – it is impossible for us to contemplate what might/will be possible over the next 50 years, particularly given the diversity of actors engaged in outer space activities, each with their differing agendas.

One constant, however, remains – the 'humanity' of outer space and its unerring relationship with the possibilities open to individuals, groups and communities to freely 'express' themselves (in a broad sense of that word) and conduct their activities in a dignified and peaceful manner. In this regard, we believe that it is only by recognizing that the legal regimes of outer space and human rights are inextricably linked, and that space activities must be developed only after careful consideration of imperative to maintain and respect those rights, that humankind will be in a position to utilize the full positive potential that outer space offers.

In this regard, some important steps are now beginning to be taken. For example, it is welcome to note the initiatives of the UNOOSA to highlight the interconnections between the exploration and use of outer space and the post 2015 United Nations Development Agenda.[52] This is an excellent example of the way forward for the development of space regulatory frameworks – through a coordinated and comprehensive approach that recognizes the crucial role that space does and will play in the future sustainability of humankind.

Our fundamental rights and freedoms already do and should therefore continue to represent very important factors in shaping the framework for future international legal regulation of outer space through both 'hard' and 'soft' law instruments. We therefore hope that this brief overview will stimulate further discussion of ways in which humanity's interests will be at the forefront of our future adventures in outer space. The risks associated with not doing so are too grave to contemplate.

---

51   See, for example, Steven Freeland, 'The US-Russian Space Station Mission is a Study in Co-operation', The Conversation, 1 May 2015 https://theconversation.com/the-us-russian-space-station-mission-is-a-study-in-cooperation-41077 (last accessed 10 December 2015).
52   See UNOOSA Press Release, 'Space for the post-2015 development agenda – UN Outer Space Committee opens today' UNIS/OS/455, 10 June 2015, available at www.unoosa.org/oosa/en/informationfor/media/ 2015-unis-os-455.html and the references made therein.

Part III
National regulation of space activities

13

Law relating to remote sensing – Earth observation

Lesley Jane Smith and Catherine Doldirina

1 Introduction

This chapter discusses how the activities undertaken in outer space known as Earth observation, remote sensing, or the gathering of information through the use of satellite technology, are governed, with a focus on regulation at national level. In Chapter 7 of this same volume, Sa'id Mosteshar discusses the international aspects of remote sensing, notably the UN Principles Relating to Remote Sensing of the Earth from Outer Space[1] and other space-based international humanitarian arrangements under the Disaster Charter,[2] as well as data-sharing initiatives for aid-relief, such as UN Spider.[3]

Remote sensing is a category of space operations that enables raw observational data to be collected, processed and developed into Earth observation applications and services, from mapping to weather forecasting. With historical roots closely linked to reconnaissance activities, this activity constitutes a legitimate use of outer space in terms of UN treaty law on outer space.[4] Traditionally government-driven, and dominated in the twentieth century by Cold War considerations, developments in Earth observation in the twenty-first century owe much to

---

1   United Nations Principles Relating to Remote Sensing of the Earth from Outer Space. G.A. Res. 41/65, U.N. Doc. AIRES/41/65, December 3, 1986, available at www.unoosa.org/oosa/en/ourwork/spacelaw/principles/remote-sensing-principles.html (last accessed 15 December 2015).
2   The International Charter "Space and Major Disasters", known as the Disaster Charter, was created in November 2000 and has 15 member organizations. Further information on how the Charter is activated and the related data sharing mechanisms are available at www.disasterscharter.org/web/guest/home (last accessed 15 December 2015).
3   See Chapter 7, pp. 109–143, above; the UN Spider is a UN space-based information exchange system for disaster management and relief established by UN GA Resolution 61/110 on 14 December 2006, and based in Bonn; further information is available at www.un-spider.org/ (last accessed 15 December 2015).
4   Spying by satellite does not per se constitute an illegal activity, see Purdy and Ray, "Legal and Privacy Implications of *Spy in the Sky* satellites", Mountbatten. Journal of Legal Studies, 1999, 3 (1), 63–79; for a commentary and analysis of UN Principles Relating to Remote Sensing of the Earth from Outer Space, see Hobe, Schrogl, Schmidt-Tedd (eds), Remote Sensing Principles, Cologne Commentary on Space Law, CoCoSL, Volume III, Heymann, 2015, Cologne.

more recent developments under the US American Landsat legislation.[5] The Landsat program, which authorized commercial satellite observation in land use management as from the 1980s, remains a core policy-driven move that enabled land observation to develop into what is now a major service industry for governments in supporting a growing global, digital geo-information market. Almost 30 years on from Landsat, the trend towards commercially dominated Earth observation continues.[6] Despite the presence of the commercial sector, overriding policy considerations continue to shape the approach adopted by individual states in legislating for their space activities. In the field of Earth observation, these are notably national interest, security and defense, as well as title to satellite programs, economic investment, and restricting access to data.

This chapter first looks at the technical capabilities required for remote sensing and Earth observation, and thereafter its legal regulation at national level. It subsequently examines whether current developments in the commercial remote sensing and space data market can maintain the traditional balance between the interests of the economic and legal title holder to the satellite programs as well as access to and use of the remote sensing data. Finally it offers some reflections about the legal and contractual basis on which remote sensing data are made available.

1.1 Remote sensing: parties, responsibilities, and interests

Remote sensing and Earth observation activities are traditionally undertaken by states (civilian observation, notably by space agencies, alongside military),[7] as well as by international satellite organizations[8] and commercial operators, some on behalf of governments, others for purely private commercial purposes.[9] In response to states' and international organizations' needs to comply with their international obligations, notably under Article VI Outer Space Treaty (OST), the gathering and collection of remote sensing data are subject to approval and

---

5   For a history of the development of US leadership and liberalization policy in the field of commercial remote sensing, see J. Gabrynowicz, cited in F. Lyall. P. Larsen, *Space Law: A Treatise* (2009) 414; further Fabio Tronchetti, i: von der Dunk, Tronchetti (eds), *Handbook of Space Law*, Edgar Elgar, 2015, 507ff.

6   See Ram S. Jakhu, "Regulation of Space Activities in Canada", in Jakhu (ed), National Regulation of Space Activities, 2010, Springer, for a discussion on the main regulatory aspects contained in national space legislation; further, 2003 US Commercial Remote Sensing Policy, April 25, full text available at www.space.commerce.gov/policy/u-s-commercial-remote-sensing-space-policy (last accessed 15 December 2015).

7   On the development of Spot satellites by CNES, the French space agency from the early 1980s, and its continuation as a private cooperation with Airbus, see https://spot.cnes.fr/en/SPOT/index.htm. Germany's aeronautics and space research center, DLR, was instrumental in supporting the development of the SAR synthetic aperture radar satellites; for registration of scientific interests, see http://sss.terrasar-x.dlr.de ((last accessed 15 December 2015).

8   See further, information about the operations and data distribution by the Convention for the Establishment of a European Organization for the Exploitation of Meteorological Satellites (EUMETSAT), June 19, 1986. At www.eumetsat.int/website/home/Data/DataDelivery/DataRegistration/index.html; for satellite based telecommunication services, set up by the International Maritime Organisation, IMO, and thereafter semi-privatized, INMARSAT, www.inmarsat.com/ (both last accessed 15 December 2015).

9   Airbus is a major satellite operator and sole authorized licensee for distribution of high resolution data in Germany; Planet Labs, based in San Francisco, is developing flocks of small sats. designed to deliver real time images of planet Earth; e-Geos is an Italian company with sole license to distribute imagery of Cosmo Skymed mission.

supervision by the responsible state, as are all other space operations, such as communication or navigation.[10] As a core provision of international space law, Article VI OST requires states and international organizations to ensure the ongoing supervision and monitoring of their national space activities.[11] This provision, in conjunction with Art VII and Art VIII OST, means that states hosting companies, as well as international organizations with their own satellite remote sensing capabilities, are required to ensure that all their space operations, including remote sensing, are authorized and controlled.[12] Collecting space data, as an integral part or result of space-based operations, falls within the examination of the basis on which they are made available.

States can only monitor their own national satellites and those which they control;[13] a sensed state, even if subject to the visits of foreign satellites, has no authority over foreign missions flying over, but not within its airspace.[14] Outer space remains an environment not subject to national appropriation, and international law requires sensing operations to be undertaken according to its principles.[15] Developments, whereby new commercial actors seek to operate large constellations of micro-satellites for Earth observation that are designed to deliver increased data volumes in shorter times, may nevertheless also see transitions in the traditional roles and relations between sensed and sensing state, at least in relation to the availability and supply of data.

Earth observation capabilities are likely to decrease in cost, and technology is freeing up the availability of processed digital space data.[16] The field of Earth observation is also opening up to new ventures started by non-traditional space players interested in greater access to and use of processed data that can be used as a basis for development of information-driven applications and internet-based communication services.[17] While this trend does not challenge the basis of national regulation of satellite remote sensing, government and societal perceptions about the

---

10 Under Article VI OST, the obligations imposed on an international organization to comply with duties arising under the Treaty are shared between the organization and its member states.
11 M. Gerhard, Commentary on Article VI, Outer Space Treaty in Hobe, Schrogl, Schmidt-Tedd (eds), *Cologne Commentary on Space Law (CoCoSL)*, vol. I, 2009, Cologne, Heymann.
12 The position of the national licensing authority within the individual government structure varies in terms of the applicable national legislation; in some cases, it may exist in the form of discretionary powers vested in the government minister, or an administrative function allocated to a dedicated national agency or authority. In the United States, the responsible authority straddles more than one regulatory body, combining authority of both the Department of Commerce, with that of the National Office AA, known as NOAA, see p. 250.
13 See Ram S. Jakhu (2003), "International Acquisition and Dissemination of Satellite Imagery", in: *Journal of Space Law*, pp. 65–92; further, see below, 3.5, p. 255.
14 Art. XII RSP gives a sensed state a right to request access to data from its own territory, see below, p. 253.
15 Art IV RSP; A sensed state can resort to Principle XII RSP to request access to its own data, on reasonable cost terms. The direct applicability of the international Remote Sensing Principles to the commercial sector has been questioned in the past, see Ram S. Jahku, "International Acquisition and Dissemination of Satellite Imagery", n. 13, id.
16 For the example at European Union level, see the discussion on the EU Copernicus Global Monitoring for Environment and Security open platform data, p. 264, below.
17 While some developments such as Greg Wyler's OneWeb are concentrating on internet and communication services, other developments such as Planetlabs are now focusing on new methods to provide Earth observation data. Google and other platforms rely on older data, sold by government space agencies and commercial satellite operators. France's SPOT Image was able to operate commercially from the early 1980s; it belongs to the Airbus group, co-founded by CNES with other satellite manufacturers.

use and integration of Earth observation data to develop future downstream markets may alter with time. Remote sensing satellite data, when processed and integrated into other information products, are set to be a multiplier in enhancing the scope of today's digitally driven information society.[18]

1.2 Remote sensing and Earth observation activities

Data is a generic term used to describe the results collected from different satellite on orbit missions and are transmitted to a receiving Earth or ground station.[19] Remote sensing and 'Earth observation', the latter often referred to generically as 'EO', describe the gathering of data of a sensed object from a distance, using various techniques.[20] EO activities are generally classified into three main groups; monitoring, remote sensing and Earth observation. In the words of the leading authors, Francis Lyall and Paul B. Larson in their seminal work '*Space Law, a Treatise,* '*In abstract theory simple ocular observation is a form of remote sensing*'. *Remote sensing technology has developed from its early origins in photography or film-based systems, to what is now digital, 'electro-magnetic data, …emitted by an object as infra-red, 'normal' to human-vision parameters, or ultraviolet radiation, or diffracted or refracted by an objects illuminated either by natural light or by artificial radar being directed onto it and reflected*'.[21] Earth observation, in contrast, is interpreted as gathering *information* about planet Earth's physical, chemical and biological systems. The term is used to cover *the monitoring and assessment of the status of, and changes* in, the natural environment and the urban environment.[22] Earth observation data are generally acquired from remote sensing platforms such as satellites, but also aircraft, complemented and supplemented by surface and subsurface measurements and mapping.[23] 'Monitoring' is a useful, but non-dedicated generic term, describing how observing the state of a particular system over time enables parameters to be built for measuring such changes.[24]

---

18   Id., see p. 264, below; the Copernicus Programme is set to provide impetus to the development of downstream products and services developed from EO data provided free of charge by the EU. These developments are extending to encompass big data and the internet of things. The Canadian company, Urthecast, develops imagery captured from its camera on the ISS to develop new products, some of which are used in advertising and in film production, see www.urthecast.com/company (last accessed 15 December 2015).
19   Technically, data covers all results from satellite based capabilities, from positioning, navigation and tracking through to the timing facilities provided for financial data transfer, see W. Ley, K. Wittmann, W. Hallmann, *Handbook on Space Technology*, 509, 529, Wiley (2009). Only Earth observation data is discussed in this context of this chapter.
20   P.J. Gibson, *Introductory Remote Sensing: Principles and Concepts*, 1 (London: Routledge, 2000).
21   On the technology involved, see Ley, Wittmann, Hallmann, n. 21 at 530 for a discussion of the different sensor systems involved; in practice, there appears to be agreement that remote sensing involves the use of a mechanical recording medium. See further, F. Lyall & P.B. Larsen, *Space Law: A Treatise* (2009), 413.
22   See the definition of Earth Observation used at www.eo-miners.eu/earth_observation/eo_introduction.htm (last accessed 15 December 2015).
23   Id., F. Lyall and P.B. Larsen, n. 23. This chapter looks solely at space-based observation activities; drones constitute a source of aerial data, but their regulation is not examined here further. For information on geo-based data, see International Journal of Applied Earth Observation and Geoinformation www.journals.elsevier.com/international-journal-of-applied-earth-observation-and-geoinformation/ (last accessed 15 December 2015).
24   Different forms of 'monitoring' are further described in the European Union's Earth observation and monitoring programme http://europa.eu/rapid/press-release_MEMO-14-251_en.htm (last accessed 15 December 2015).

The uses to which the different types of space data are put depend largely on the type of satellite technology and techniques involved in the different types of remote sensing operations.[25] Data can be gathered for a variety of purposes, ranging from space-borne support in cases of disaster management, to meteorological information: it includes use for archeological purposes, and is increasingly delivering precedents for the use of evidence based on Earth observation data in court proceedings,[26] for example, in the delimitation of international borders.[27] The use of the data depends on their type and characteristics, their level of resolution, as well as the impact which domestic legislation governing Earth observation data has on their subsequent use and distribution.[28]

Irrespective of the actual terms used to describe the operations, enormous amounts of data are being gathered and then processed by various communities active in space. In response to these developments, new communication technologies are providing sufficient high-speed data transfer capacity to ground, in a move away from storing the data on satellites for longer periods, thereby avoiding delay in transfer from the spacecraft.[29]

National law, supported by space policies and Earth observation data policies, is therefore an important tool in mapping the national approach to satellite remote sensing capabilities and making space data available.

1.3 Data: terminology and characteristics

There is no decisive agreement at international level on a single definition of Earth observation or remote sensing data. Principle I of the Principles Relating to Remote Sensing of the Earth from Space lists three categories of data, primary data, processed data, and analyzed information, respectively.[30] The definitions introduced by the international community have, unfortunately, not furthered the development of a standard or uniform definition as to what constitutes Earth observation data. The three categories under the Remote Sensing Principles are not duplicated verbatim in national legislation or licensing practice, and differing terminology is used in the various national provisions and in the terms used when licensing Earth observation. By way of illustration, Article 23 French Law on Space Activities 2008 refers to data in the context of their spectral resolution and locations. Earth observation data are included within the scope of section 1 (c) UK Outer Space Act 1986 as 'any activity in outer space', without any further definition, and section 2 Canada's Remote Sensing Statute 2007 includes 'receiving raw data from a remote sensing satellite' as subject to approval.

The availability of data depends in any one case on a variety of factors, not least, the type of

---

25 Ley, Wittmann, Hallmann, *Handbook on Space Technology*, n. 21, 528.
26 Sa'id Mosteshar (ed.), *Evidence from Space, Study on Behalf of the European Space Agency*, London Institute of Space Policy and Law (2012).
27 Various cases heard before the ICJ have relied on space-based data, including maps, to discuss issues of territorial border, see various references to ICJ cases heard in the early twentieth century, F. Lyall, P. Larson, *Space Law*, n. 23. p. 411, n.7.
28 See pp. 253–256.
29 See the new laser driven scheme European Relay Data Scheme (ERDS), managed as a public private partnership between ESA and Airbus ADS using laser technology to enable fast transfer of data, available at www.esa.int/Our_Activities/Telecommunications_Integrated_Applications/EDRS/Ground_segment (last accessed 15 December 2015).
30 United Nations Principles Relating to Remote Sensing of the Earth from Outer Space. G.A. Res. 41/65, U.N. Doc. AIRES/41/65, 3 December 1986.

mission, the degree of processing and enhancement, alongside technical factors, some of which are referred to below.[31]

At the operative level, Earth observation data are classified or grouped according to their particular characteristics, including the process by which they are generated, the actors who generate them (including the source of mission funding, whether public, private, or mixed), users and purposes for which the data can be of use. This depends on legal title to the data, as well as the data type, and is discussed further below in the fourth section.

1.4 Remote sensing satellites – technology and capabilities

The particular features required from a satellite remote sensing mission are designed at the beginning of mission definition, and depend on the applications targeted.[32] Remote sensing satellites differ, depending on their orbital location, the payload they carry, and in terms of their imaging instruments as well as their spectral characteristics, including the swath-width of the sensors.[33] The technical aspects of programming a satellite involve consideration of the parameters determining the suitability and quality of the data required. This depends on the spatial resolution – high spatial resolution (i.e. the relation of the pixel in distinguishing it from other objects) results in a better image. A further parameter refers to their temporal resolution, the frequency with which the data are acquired, or the same geographic locations on the surface of the Earth are 're-visited'; a third, spectral resolution, refers to the narrowness of the frequency bands employed for scanning; radiometric resolution measures the gray level in relation to a black and white image.[34] Satellite remote sensing can be either active or passive. Active sensing requires the sensing device to illuminate the target being sensed electromagnetically, with the reflection captured by the sensors; passive sensing involves the sensing device collecting electromagnetic radiation emanating from the target, whether by light, heat or infra-red.[35]

These technical characteristics influence the suitability of data for particular uses, and not least, the extent to which they can undergo further degrees of processing, as well as the degree to which they can be legally protected, including the mechanisms for protection (whether statutory title, copyright or contractual agreement).[36]

1.5 Impact of commercialization on ownership regime(s) with regard to Earth observation data

Reference has been made to transitions in the market for satellite remote sensing and Earth observation data; remote sensing has developed from what was once the traditionally exclusive preserve of states to that of a new 'mixed' economy. States and intergovernmental organizations continue to operate active satellite systems and programs, with an increasing trend towards reliance on delivery by commercial satellite operators. This trend started in the early 1980s, with France enabling the former public satellite system SPOT[37] to become a largely

---

31 See p. 256, below.
32 See W. Ley, K. Wittmann, W. Hallmann, *Handbook on Space Technology*, n. 21, 529.
33 Weather satellites are generally placed in the geostationary orbit for monitoring weather on a wide scale and at high frequency.
34 F. Lyall, P. Larsen, *Space Law*, n.23, 413–414, W. Ley, K. Wittmann, W. Hallmann, Handbook on Space Technology, id. n. 21, 524.
35 Id., Lyall, Larsen n. 34, 413–414; W. Ley, K. Wittmann, W. Hallmann, id. 524.
36 See p. 256, below.
37 See n. 7, above.

commercial activity; this trend continues, latterly in Europe. Some operators handle data provided by national state systems; others launch their own satellite systems, concluding contracts with states and other commercial entities to provide remote sensing services.[38] The exact regime depends on the approach taken by national law and policy, or absence of specific capabilities at national level.

The actors who generate Earth observation data whether public, private or mixed, also have a decisive influence on the users and purposes for which the data can be put.[39] Alongside the requirements for licensing at national level, the funding of satellite remote sensing programs raises issues of principle as to data accessibility,[40] and the development of potential duopolies in former publicly-run domains.[41] There is an absence of uniformity in regulatory approach taken at national level; typical divergences also extend to details of national copyright law and the use of Earth observation data licenses, which combine together to limit the transfer of processed data and development of derivative products.

2 National Regulation of satellite remote sensing activities

The regulation of satellite remote sensing operations is generally included within the scope of statutes governing outer space activities; however, not all states have opted for dedicated satellite remote sensing regulation. The decision whether to do so depends in part on the specific capabilities of national satellite remote sensing programs.[42] Figuring high among the select states that have dedicated statutes governing operations with remote sensing data are the US, with its developed Landsat regime,[43] Canada, with its Remote Sensing Systems Act,[44] and Germany, with its Satellite Data Protection Act.[45] Other countries govern satellite remote sensing activities by applying general regulatory sources regarding licensing of space activities.[46]

---

38 F. Lyall and P.B. Larsen, *Space Law – A Treatise* (2009), n. 34, p. 414; for the state-authorized licensing arrangements in Germany, see p. 252.
39 Germany introduced its Earth observation data legislation largely as a result of the capabilities developed in the SAR synthetic aperture radar satellites, TerraSaR, a public private partnership between Airbus and DLR. Its current price list is available at www2.geo-airbusds.com/files/pmedia/public/r463_9_itd-0508-cd-0001-tsx_international_pricelist_en_issue_6.00.pdf (last accessed 15 December 2015).
40 These are addressed further below, on p. 256.
41 This discussion relating to sale and privatization of public companies has also been pursued in relation to the sale and semi-privatization of international satellite organizations, see e.g. in relation to the privatization of Inmarsat, which operates communication satellites for maritime and aviation services. F. Lyall, "The Privatisation of Inmarsat", IISL Proceedings 41st Colloquium (Melbourne, 1998), 205–223.
42 Germany introduced its space data legislation as a result of the capabilities developed in the SAR synthetic aperture radar satellites, TerraSaR, a public private partnership between Airbus and DLR whereby data can be made available for sale, subject to a sensitivity check, see current price list at www2.geo-airbusds.com/files/pmedia/public/r463_9_itd-0508-cd-0001-tsx_international_pricelist_en_issue_6.00.pdf (last accessed 15 December 2015).
43 Title 51, U.S.C., National and Commercial Space Programs, Subtitle VI, Earth Observations, formerly Title II of the Land Remote Sensing Policy Act of 1992, 15 U.S.C. § 5601, et seq.
44 Remote Sensing Systems Act, RSSA 2005, c. 45 (Canada).
45 Satellitendatensicherheitsgesetz (November 23, 2007) BGBl. I S. 2590, as amended (Germany).
46 E.g. section 1, UK Outer Space Act 1986, c. 38, France Law on Space Operations, 2008; Netherlands, Rules Concerning Space Activities and the Establishment of a Registry of Space Objects (Space Activities Act), 2006; cf. § 1 Austria, Space Law, 2011 (Weltraumgesetz BGBl., 2011, I, 132 27 December 2011).

National law therefore requires that persons subject to its jurisdiction and control may only operate a private remote sensing space system when in possession of a license.

The following section outlines the main aspects of control that are relevant to regulating the activity in question, and explains why, in today's climate of mixed public/private space economy, the issue of collection of Earth observation data, their processing and dissemination, continue to dominate policy considerations.

2.1 Jurisdiction

Satellite remote sensing activities span both on-orbit and ground segments and may appear a challenge to traditional concepts of jurisdiction. Jurisdiction has been defined to allow a combination of state control over operations located on the ground, as well as in orbit. Territorial jurisdiction applies in relation to the licensing of ground stations; in addition, Article VIII Outer Space Treaty provides the basis whereby activities in outer space, over which in terms of international space law states claim authority over their satellite operations.[47] Domestic statutes contain the conditions for exercising sovereign jurisdiction over their nationals (natural, legal persons), not only in terms of their domestic law over activities on their own territory, but also in regard to their foreign space activities, beyond the national territory. Nationality, as well as the notion of substantial link to a jurisdiction enables nationals involved in outer space activities operating out of a state other than that of their own nationality to be included within the regulatory provisions of the latter.[48] The notions of jurisdiction and control are therefore central to the entire licensing and management control of on-orbit spatial activities, under national law.

2.2 On-orbit operations and ground infrastructures

Satellites operate by transmitting and relying on radio signals within the natural spectrum. Under international law, the ITU Convention and Radio Regulations,[49] a national license is required to allow the establishment of ground stations and the use of specific frequencies by the particular satellites. The allocation of radio frequencies is regulated and coordinated at international level through the ITU, and the national state must ensure that its frequency assignments follow the main ITU allocation to the licensing state in question. The procedures applicable to frequency allocation are a complex intermix of international rules, in relation to states, and national rules, in relation to licensing.[50]

---

47 Article I, Article VIII, Outer Space Treaty 1967. The latter provision ensures that states continue to retain their jurisdiction over their space objects, even once they become dysfunctional.

48 E.g. Section 1 and 2 Outer Space Act 1986 apply to space activities whether or not carried out in the UK by British nationals; Art 23 French Space Law (LOS) 2008 applies to anyone involved in remote sensing activities falling within French jurisdiction.

49 The ITU frequency allocation tables according to regions are accessible via the ITU website; the ITU radio regulations and allotment to particular services are available www.ictregulationtoolkit.org/en/toolkit/notes/PracticeNote/2824 (last accessed 15 December 2015).

50 The increase in volume of satellite activities is also impacting on the availability of spectrum, itself a rare resource. National rules therefore specify the authority responsible for national frequency allocations. Within the EU, this is partly dictated by EU law, which has a common basis for the authorization of electronic communications networks and services, which cover satellite operations, EC Directive 2002/20/EC of the European Parliament and of the Council of 7 March 2002, OJ L 108/21 of 24 April 2002.

Ground or receiving stations are subject to national licensing in terms of national wireless or radio communications laws. Earth stations exist around the globe for telecommunication purposes, be this for air flight as well as telemetry and tracking. The traditional basis for this legislation has been Wireless Telegraphy Acts, which fall within the government's management of frequency plans for national telecommunications; these rules generally also apply to the licensing of operations of TT&C stations.[51]

3 Regulatory patterns in licensing EO satellite activities: some examples

The following section provides an overview of the main regulatory issues addressed by dedicated national remote sensing satellite legislation; it is not a comprehensive, guide, but a short overview of salient issues relating to licensing commercial remote sensing systems. These relate to designation of the competent licensing authority, the conditions attached to the license, whether there are high resolution capabilities, as well as access to Earth observation data and rights of dissemination.

The greatest distinction in national legislation governing satellite remote sensing is in the detail with which space statutes define the 'controlled (space) activity' and whether dedicated remote sensing statutes define the (various) categories of Earth observation data that fall within their scope.[52] The United States, as the first country to authorize a system of private land remote sensing through its 1984 Landsat Act,[53] has a well-developed administrative and enforcement structure for supervising and controlling private commercial satellite remote sensing activities. The Canadian Remote Sensing Systems Act 2006 owes its existence to the successor to RADARSAT, Canada's first synthetic aperture radar satellite program, launched in 1995.[54] Domestic legislation was the result of policy concerns about commercial remote sensing laid down in that agreement. The United States, Canada and Germany all have dedicated remote sensing satellite legislative instruments that are briefly outlined below.

3.1 Licensing authority

The government, represented by the responsible minister, is generally the designated authority for licensing satellite operations; the competence to license depends on the design of its ministerial portfolios, be this the ministry for economics, commerce, foreign affairs or

---

51 For a general overview, see P. Dempsey in Ram S. Jakhu (ed), *National Regulation of Space Activities* (2010), Springer, n. 6 above.

52 Section 2 Outer Space Act (UK) 1986, c. 38; Dedicated satellite remote sensing legislation includes definitions and the degree of data resolution, processing and distribution in its scope.

53 The Landsat Commercial Remote Sensing Policy Acts, 1984, 1992, were subject to further amendment after the program suffered financial failure in the attempt to commercialize the US Landsat system in 1985 through the creation of a public-private company, the Earth Observation Satellite Company (Eosat). Eosat had exclusive rights to market Landsat data, which enabled it to charge market-based prices for Landsat data, even though obliged by law to provide non-discriminatory access to unenhanced data products. By 1992, Landsat commercialization had failed. The President's US 2003 Commercial Remote Sensing Policy reinforced the Landsat 7 program, and is available at www.whitehouse.gov/files/documents/ostp/press_release_files/fact_sheet_commercial_remote_sensing_policy_april_25_2003.pdf.

54 The Canadian legislation 2006 was also a response in part to the 2000 US-Canada Agreement concerning the operation of commercial remote sensing satellite systems. Bruce. Mann, "Drafting Legislation to Regulate Commercial Remote Sensing Satellites: a How-to Guide from Canada", in IISL *Proceedings of the International Institute of Space Law*, 2006 (Valencia).

defense, for example in relation to export of data, or authorization of the sensing of third states.[55]

The most recent amendment to the United States remote sensing legislation, the National and Commercial Space Programs Act (NCSPA, or Act), 51 U.S.C § 60101 et seq. authorizes the Secretary of Commerce to license private sector operators of remote sensing systems. The authority designated to review licensing applications is the National Oceanic and Atmospheric Administration (NOAA), acting as delegated authority on behalf of the Secretary of Commerce. NOAA in turn further delegates this administrative authority to the National Environmental Satellite, Data and Information Service, NESDIS, with the Office of Commercial Remote Sensing Regulatory Affairs, entrusted with ensuring the validation and verification of licenses.[56] NOAA issues regulations establishing the requirements for the licensing, monitoring and compliance of operators of private Earth remote sensing space systems.[57] NOAA's Licensing of Private Land Remote Sensing Space Systems: Final Rule (2006)[58] codifies the US licensing practice and deals with data access, data protection, data standards, issues of national security and shutter control policy.[59] Licenses are granted on the basis of the applicant's compliance with the requirements of the Act, as well as regulations issued pursuant to its provisions, and any applicable international obligations and national security concerns of the United States. This Final Rule implements the provisions of the 2006 Act and the 2003 US Commercial Remote Sensing Policy.

The Canadian remote sensing legislation of 2006 (RSSSA) empowers the minister to license remote sensing operations, with additional powers vested in the Cabinet, and is accompanied by secondary Remote Sensing Space Systems Regulations (RSSSR).[60]

The German Satellite Data Security Act (SatDSiG)[61] was drafted in parallel to development of the first PPP-project in the SAR-sector (TerraSAR-X) as a result of security-related concerns relating to sensitive high-value data. The industrial partner and co-investor in the German PPP-project was looking to distribute the high-resolution data via a commercial chain. The German statute was designed to safeguard the security and foreign policy interests of the Federal Republic of Germany in connection with the distribution and commercial marketing of Earth remote sensing data, particularly on international markets. The authority responsible in Germany for licensing is the Ministry for Economy and Energy.[62]

3.2 Subject of license – personal scope

Space statutes regulate within their scope the notion of 'control' of a space system, a space

---

55   Space agencies operating satellites can themselves also be subject to licensing.
56   Further information on the role of NESDIS is available at www.nesdis.noaa.gov/CRSRA/files/15%20CFR%20Part%20960%20Regs%202006.pdf (last accessed 15 December 2015).
57   Title 51, U.S.C., National and Commercial Space Programs, Subtitle VI, Earth Observations, formerly Title II of the Land Remote Sensing Policy Act of 1992, 15 U.S.C. § 5601, et seq.
58   The aim of the licensing system is to facilitate the development of the US commercial remote sensing industry, promote the collection and widespread availability of Earth remote sensing data, while preserving essential US national security interests, meeting foreign policy objectives and complying with international obligations.
59   For further discussion of shutter control, see below, section 3.5.
60   The secondary rules contain a variety of technical details elaborating on the main provisions in the statute.
61   2590 Federal Gazette (BGBl.) Year 2007 Part I No. 58, Bonn, 28 November 2007.
62   Bundesministerium für Wirtschaft und Technologie (BMWi), see www.bmwi.de/EN/Service/suche.html?

object and satellite remote sensing activity, as well as the 'person' operating the system.[63] As regards natural and legal persons, the provisions of the statute depend on personal jurisdiction, founded on residence, nationality of the natural or legal person, and/or the location of space operations within its territory.[64]

Canada and the US assume personal jurisdiction over natural persons (citizens, permanent residents) and legal persons (Canadian or US corporations). This generally extends to such persons within those categories having a 'substantial connection' to Canada and the US; this is of relevance in relation to satellite remote sensing space operations. The notion of 'substantial connection' is a concept of international private law by which states found jurisdiction over foreign persons and corporations present in that state which might otherwise not be subject to its rules.[65] Whether foreign space activities undertaken in third countries by their own nationals are subject to regulation by the state of nationality can only be examined in relation to the state in question.[66] Satellite remote sensing operations implicitly include foreign sensing operations; Canada and the US, but not Germany, require remote sensing activities outside their territorial jurisdiction to be licensed. Considerations relating to national security, defense, conduct of international relations and international obligations influence the granting or amendment of a license. Both the US and Canada look not only at the applicant's ability to comply with the applicable regulations, but also to the national interests in enhancing the competitiveness of their respective remote sensing space industry in assessing licensing applications.

Germany's dedicated satellite remote sensing statute, Satellite Data Security Act, SatDSiG covers German citizens, natural and legal persons, including foreign persons with a center of administration in Germany. The German statute is limited in scope; it does not apply when satellite remote sensing systems are operated by a state bodies for example military or reporting tasks that are not governed by the law; nor does it apply where a system is operating under the laws of another EU member state that are comparable to the German statute.[67] Satellite remote sensing service providers, value-adding firms or data resellers are not included within its scope.

3.3 Subject of license – space activity

Licenses are awarded on the basis of the statutory requirements for the "controlled activities". In the US, this is contained in Chapter 51 US Code sec. 5621(a)1. relating to a 'space operation'. The US Land Remote Sensing Policy Act 1992[68] defines satellite remote sensing as the collection of data which can be processed into imagery of surface features of the Earth. This is to be read together with the definition of the raw or unenhanced Earth observation data as "land remote sensing signals or imagery products that are unprocessed or subject only to data pre-processing".[69]

---

63 See § 2.1. Austrian National Space Law, *Weltraumgesetz*, 2011, BGBl Öst, 132, 27. 12. 2011.
64 General space statutes such as the French, Austrian or UK legislation are examples of territorial and national jurisdiction.
65 For Canadian Supreme Court on the application of this doctrine, see *Éditions Écosociété Inc. et al. v Banro Corp.*, 2012 SCC 18; *Breeden v. Black 2012, SCC 19*, available online at https://scc-csc.lexum.com/scc-csc/scc-csc/en/nav_date.do (last accessed 15 December 2015).
66 See e.g. section 1, UK Outer Space Act, 1986 c. 38.
67 Nor does it apply to operations of a third state whose laws guarantee comparable security and there is a special agreement between that third state and Germany.
68 For the latest provisions on the Landsat 7 remote sensing program, data and data archiving, see 15 U.S. Code Chapter 82; also available at www.law.cornell.edu/uscode/text/15/chapter-82 http://geo.arc.nasa.gov/sge/landsat/15USCch82.html; (both last accessed 15 December 2015).
69 Chapter 82, Land Remote Sensing Policy Act § 5671–5672. Under Subchapter VI of the Land Remote Sensing Policy Act, there is a prohibition of licensing commercial weather satellites.

Further details relating to the licensing of private remote sensing space systems are contained in Subchapter II, § 5621 to 5625. The US applies the principle of non-discriminatory access to the Earth observation data, which means that, in the absence of exclusionary criteria, requests for dissemination are to be serviced.

Under the Canadian legislation, the controlled activity under sec. 2(a)–(d) RSSA 2006 covers the operation of commands to satellites, the reception of raw data, storage, processing or distribution of raw data, establishment or use of cryptography, and 'information assurance' measures. The German legislation para. 1(1) 1–2 covers the operation of the system and the handling of data until dissemination. This means it applies in the case of commands being sent to the system from German territory, as well as the handling of RS data, generated by the system, up to its distribution by data suppliers based in German territory. The German statute differentiates between two types of activities, in that it prescribes two separate types of licenses – one for operating the satellite remote sensing space system, and one for disseminating Earth observation data. Although the term "satellite remote sensing space system" is more or less identical in all statutes (in the sense that it includes space and ground segments), only the German statute applies to "high-grade" systems that (can) generate data of "particularly high information content" (para. 2(2) and subsequent details in the secondary regulations).[70] The system operator and data supplier do not have to be the same person under the German provisions, and the data supplier may obtain Earth observation data without undergoing the sensitivity test.

3.4 Conditions of license

The three national satellite remote sensing statutes discussed, the US, Canada and Germany, contain common mandatory conditions. First, licensing the management and control of the satellite remote sensing systems; second, raw data may only be communicated to authorized persons; third, each of the licensing systems enables the national government to call on the data through so-called priority access for governments.[71] This includes forbidding and closing down the system for reasons of national security, peaceful co-existence of nations and international relations.

The licensing of satellite systems is a complex process, requiring assessment of important information relating to the technical side of operations and any alterations to the operations including sale of interests, particularly to foreign interests. The relevant technical criteria include the availability of infrastructure to perform the activity; availability of qualified specialists; certification of technical equipment and technological processes that maintain reception, processing and storage of information; guaranteed protection of information from unauthorized access; the registration and storage of information from remote sensing satellites; permission to undertake the activity involving use of classified information; provision of required documents (closed list) that are evidence of fulfilling the conditions listed above.

The German legislation requires an assessment whether the operator has sufficient reliability (credibility) to guarantee safe operation of the system, and safe handling of Earth observation data: this includes the system setting, as well as control over sensors, Earth observation data transmission from the system to the ground station and data distribution directly within the system. This includes excluding third parties from access to system and Earth observation data;

---

70 Satellite Data Security Regulations, SatDSiv (Satellitendatensicherheitsverordnung) dated March 26, 2008 (www.gesetze-im-internet.de/satdsiv/BJNR050800008.html).
71 E.g. Section 15, Remote Sensing Systems Act, RSSA Canada.

those operating the system must have passed security clearance. All three systems discussed here require approval of a data protection plan, a system disposal plan and satisfactory guarantee of its fulfilment are part of the process. Details of licensing in terms of the NOAA regulation include annual audits, reporting, tasking logs from operational satellites, and, on termination of licensed operations, disposal of any satellites in space in a manner satisfactory to the President.[72] The Canadian statute provides for penalties for failure to comply with the provisions of the license, just as it can impose making the availability to a sensed state a condition of license, as a flowdown of Principle XII RSP.

Whether the license is issued for a specific term, or is linked to satellite lifetime, or for a shorter period, subject to renewal, is a question of national law.

3.5 Tasking satellites: collecting, processing and disseminating data

Sec. 5602(13) US statute regulates unenhanced, unprocessed or pre-processed signals and imagery products, the Canadian statutory definitions of Earth observation data are the most elaborate.

Under sec. 2 RSSSA, "raw data" are defined as sensor data and any auxiliary data not yet transformed into a product, and "remote sensing product" is defined as an image or any other product produced in a way that transforms raw data.[73]

Para. 2(1)2 German statute covers "data" as signals from one or more sensors and all products made from them, independent of the level of processing or the form of storage. It considers "dissemination" as bringing data into circulation or making data accessible to third parties. The grant of a dissemination license is covered by sections 11 and 12 of the Chapter 1 Part 3 ("Dissemination data"), and the provisions of its Chapter 2 define the process of data dissemination. More specifically, they focus on the important sensitivity check (section 17), the duty to provide documentation (section 18), as well as specific cases that require a permit (section 19) or collective permit (section 20). The sensitivity check constitutes a fully standardized procedure according to the criteria in the accompanying statutory regulation on the SatDSiV.[74] The data provider wishing to comply with a request for the dissemination of data of a high-grade Earth remote sensing system must examine the request for its sensitivity, as defined in the statutory ordinance under para. (3). A request is sensitive if the information content of the data obtained as a result of the sensor-operating mode and form of processing used, the target area represented by the data, the time of generation of the data and the period of time between generation of the data and compliance with the request and the ground segments to which the data are to be transmitted, when viewed as a whole, reveal the possibility of harm being caused to the vital security interests of Germany, to the peaceful co-existence of nations or to the foreign relations of Germany.

A full assessment takes account of the personal characteristics of the requesting party, as well as those persons who might prospectively come into contact with the data provided for in the request, including their usual places of residence. The data provider must check the identity of the requesting party in suitable manner and require the names of the persons who prospectively come into contact with the data as provided for in the request, including their usual places of residence.

---

72 The measures required to meet this requirement are specified in each license issued by NOAA.
73 The Canadian statute also uses "transform" to define the processing that results in substantial impossibility to reconstitute raw data from the resulting product.
74 Satellite Data Security Act (Gesetz zum Schutz vor Gefährdung der Sicherheit der Bundesrepublik Deutschland durch das Verbreiten von hochwertigen Erdfernerkundungsdaten, SatDSiG) dated March 26, 2008, www.gesetze-im-internet.de/satdsiv/BJNR050800008.html.

The German SatDSiG distinguishes between an "operator license" for a high grade Earth remote sensing system and a "dissemination license" introduced for the data provider wishing to disseminate the relevant sensitive data. The operator and data provider can be the same legal entity, so the administrative conditions (and requirements) are formulated in a similar way. A key element in obtaining the license is the reliability of the person acting, and a list of technical and organizational measures required from the particular entities. The general licenses are independent of the data dissemination as such. The SatDSIG also provides for an additional permit for purposes of dissemination of data qualified as sensitive by the security check.[75] However, a concrete administrative authorization is required only for the low percentage of data that has been qualified as sensitive.

By tasking the satellite, data can be collected by ground station controlled command. This is part of the activity that falls under more detailed provisions governing the licensing of satellite remote sensing systems and operations. The regulatory control addresses the interaction between the technical operations and the legal requirements; this includes the security-related sides of such operations.[76] The form of control best illustrating the concerns arising from the licensing and dissemination of Earth observation data can be seen in the provisions of the Canadian Remote Sensing Statute 2005, (RSSA).[77] The main objectives of governments when licensing commercial satellite remote sensing systems focus on the need to ensure maintenance of security at operative level, including all aspects of data collection, management, dissemination and data disposal. The following section illustrates the importance of accompanying governmental rights to authorize or close down sensing over territories, when required. The Canadian and US regulations emphasize the statutory limitations that can be placed on the dissemination of highly valuable raw data.[78]

The Canadian licensing provisions illustrate the high level of control on those authorized to operate satellite remote sensing systems by requiring those entities or individuals owning or operating systems to provide "identifying information"; equivalent information relating to the actual management of the generated Earth observation data is required, with details of all system participants to be notified. This includes entities having direct or indirect control over the system, whether or not they fall within the scope of the regulations.[79] Those operating the system must be eligible for security clearance.[80] Documentation must be submitted for approval relating to the tasking, receiving and storing of data.[81] This includes a command protection plan, a data protection plan, how data are to be stored and protected through the lifetime of the operations.[82] Information is also required on how raw data or data products are

---

75 This transfer must be declared suitable by the Federal Office for Information Security.
76 See in particular, Schedule 1 Remote Sensing Space System Regulations, 2007 (Canada), available at http://laws-lois.justice.gc.ca (last accessed 15 December 2015).
77 Remote Sensing Space Systems Act 2005, c. 45, together with the accompanying Remote Sensing Space System Regulations (RSSSA), 2007, available at http://laws-lois.justice.gc.ca (last accessed 15 December 2015).
78 Section 13(1), Schedule 1 Remote Sensing Space System Regulations, 2007, defines transformed data as that which does no longer enables the raw data to be identified. The German statute contains the sensitivity test in para 17 SatDSiG, but it is the operator and provider who decide whether the request is subject to sensitivity.
79 Section 1(2) Remote Sensing Space System Regulations, 2007.
80 Section 12, Remote Sensing Space System Regulations, 2007.
81 Similar provisions apply in the US remote sensing legislation, see Chapter 15 CFR part 960 on the regulation of private remote sensing systems, which are accompanied by Annexes outlining the application form and procedure, see e.g. Appendix 1, 960.4 (application process); 960.11. (condition of operations); prohibitions (960.13) and foreign agreements (960.8).
82 Section 8 Remote Sensing Space System Regulations, 2007, id.

Law relating to remote sensing

to be communicated. Canada (and the US) are among the few states imposing a duty on the licensees to make their Earth observation data available to sensed governments making a request for access.[83] Further detailed conditions are outlined in section 12, Remote Sensing Space System Regulations; these include the maintenance of operational records, and extend to a data disposal plan. Section 20(1)(g1) Canadian Act makes reference to the right of public access to archived data, but this provision is not transported down to the RSSSR regulation level.

Ensuring that there is no unauthorized third party access to Earth observation data is an essential part of the licensing process. Satellite remote sensing systems must be encrypted, and diagrams of communication links made available to the licensing authority. These provisions are to be found in the elaborate provisions of the Canadian RSSSR relating to command protection plan in Schedule 1, sections 14–21.

A further mechanism devised to manage the dissemination of Earth observation data is the concept of shutter control. Best known in relation to US satellite remote sensing operations, shutter control policy enables governments to order the cessation or restriction of licensed operations for overriding reasons of international, national or security interest. This includes prohibiting satellite remote sensing activities over specific territories or areas.[84] It encompasses programming delays in downloading data from the satellites, to imposing restrictions on the resolution of data, up to and including bans on data products.[85]

The notion of dissemination of Earth observation data cannot be understood as a general right to transfer the data acquired through a satellite remote sensing system, and specifically not in relation to raw, as opposed to processed data. Just as licenses to operate satellite remote sensing can be granted, they can be withdrawn or suspended. Interestingly, Canadian law provides a substantial difference to US and German law in relation to the dissemination of raw, unprocessed, data. In principle, dissemination of raw data is a restricted activity, as it ensures that only transformed or processed data are made available. Section 8(6) RSSA 2005 provides that dissemination of raw data may, on prior authorization by the minister, be made available to classes of persons on the basis of specified conditions. Even more significant is that this, as well as any subsequent economic activity (of further processing), is no longer a controlled activity.[86] This provision highlights the fact that, if so approved and where not prejudicial to overriding national interests, certain types of Earth observation data can be made available; introducing such a provision clarifies what otherwise falls under the open data trend. Governments can within their licensing structures pave the way to disseminate non-sensitive raw data in individual cases on the basis of legislative provisions.

---

83 This imports the provision under Pr. XII Remote Sensing Principles; sec. 8(4)(c) Canadian Act; Schedule 1 (7) (8) Remote Sensing Space System Regulations, 2007. The US regulations in sec. 960.118(10) are more detailed than the Canadian.
84 The United States operates a clear shutter control policy contained in two different public laws, by virtue of National and Commercial Space Programs Act (P.L. 111 314): "Shutter Control" as well as The Kyl-Bingaman Amendment to the 1997 National Defence Authorization Act specifies the rules with regard to Israel).
85 F. Lyall and P. Larson, Space Law, n 23 above, 428, 441–2; further, B. Mann, Drafting Legislation to Regulate Commercial Sensing Satellite: A How-to Guide from Canada, n. 54 above.
86 Section 8(6) RSSA, final sentence "The receipt, communication or processing or storage of raw data by such persons is not a controlled activity".

4 EO data: ownership, copyright and licensing

4.1 General

The content of legal norms and policy guidelines applicable to ownership, protection and conditions regarding use of Earth observation data is strongly influenced, and at times, directly determined by several factors. First, the very nature of Earth observation data needs to be taken into account when addressing their protection in form and scope. Second, today, satellite remote sensing is carried out as an economic activity by many different actors, public and private, locally, nationally or internationally. These two facts directly or indirectly affect the licenses or other mechanisms setting out conditions of access to and use of Earth observation data, and raise the issue of legal interoperability of Earth observation data available on the market. Third, the general open data trend that started with the push of government data towards unrestricted accessibility and use, is now staking its chances with private Earth observation data.

After Earth observation data are acquired by satellite – this is often done by the satellite itself, or from ground stations using computer algorithms and in situ data and have been initially processed, Earth observation data may then be made available to users for various applications. Processing data with "inputs of data and knowledge from other sources"[87] then becomes analyzed information.[88] The nature and components for such processing depend on the applications for which Earth observation data, or rather information they may contain, are used to transform them.

The United States and Canada[89] follow an approach similar to the UN Remote Sensing Principles whereby they make a verbatim distinction between raw and processed Earth observation data or imagery. Both legal acts indicate processing as the basis for this distinction. The US Land Remote Sensing Policy Act[90] differentiates between unprocessed and processed Earth observation data or imagery. By the same token the Canadian Remote Sensing Space Systems Act makes a distinction between 'raw data' and 'remote sensing product'.[91] However, most jurisdictions in Europe do not make such a distinction.[92] For instance, the German Satellite Data Security Law[93] explicitly avoids any distinction between raw and processed data or information, defining Earth observation data both as satellite signals and all products derived from them independent of the level of processing, mode of their storage or presentation.[94] The European Space Agency, while referencing the UN Remote Sensing Principles in its Data Policy, categorizes Earth observation data depending on their availability or accessibility, not

---

[87] Principle I United Nations Principles Relating to Remote Sensing of the Earth from Outer Space. G.A. Res. 41/65, U.N. Doc. AIRES/41/65, December 3, 1986.
[88] In the terminology of the UN Remote Sensing Principles; terms used in national regulations do differ.
[89] Remote Sensing Space Systems Act. S.C. 2005, c. 45. November 25, 2005.
[90] H.R.6133. 1992.
[91] See §2 "Definitions" Canadian Remote Sensing Space Systems Act.
[92] Terminology may vary, e.g. "raw" data are often called primary or unenhanced.
[93] §2 Satellitendatensicherheitsgesetz (November 23, 2007) BGBl. I S. 2590, as amended.
[94] For a more extensive analysis regarding definition of Earth observation data see C.A. Doldirina, "Rightly Balanced Intellectual Property Rights Regime as a Mechanism to Enhance Commercial Earth Observation Activities" (2010) 67 *Acta Astronautica* at 639–647.

degree of processing.[95] Another layer of legal issues linked to the protection of Earth observation data, access and their subsequent reuse is linked to the multiplicity of actors who generate Earth observation data or make Earth observation information products. These actors do not necessarily apply exactly the same conditions or restrictions on sharing and use of their Earth observation data. By analogy to technical interoperability issues that arise when Earth observation data are generated and stored using different standards, procedures or formats that prevent efficient use of such Earth observation data, varying legal conditions and restrictions of access to and use of data reduce their legal interoperability. The lower the restrictions contained in original data, the lower the restrictions in information products made with or from them. Full legal interoperability is only achieved when data are provided without any restrictions on access and use, and, by analogy, with the copyright protection regime placed in the public domain.

A working definition of legal interoperability for Earth observation and geographic data was developed by the GEO Data Sharing Working Group:

Legal interoperability among multiple datasets from different sources occurs when:

1   use conditions are clearly and readily determinable for each of the datasets,
2   the legal use conditions imposed on each dataset allow creation and use of combined or derivative products, and
3   users may legally access and use each dataset without seeking authorization from data creators on a case-by-case basis, assuming that the accumulated conditions of use for each and all of the datasets are met.[96]

Legal interoperability also implies online capability to search or track licenses and their compatibility with legal conditions of access to and use of data from various sources. When data from multiple sources are combined or otherwise used, the resulting dataset incorporates an accumulation of the restrictions imposed by each and every source. Restrictions therefore need to be tracked. Legal interoperability implies online capability to search or track licenses, as well as their compatibility with legal conditions of access to and use of data from various sources.

The open data trend particularly affects policies and regulations regarding reuse of public sector information: establishment of the full and open access principle as a default basis for sharing government-produced and -held data and information resulted in a significant increase in their accessibility and usability without any restrictions. Examples include the amended[97] or newly adopted[98] public sector information legislation in Europe, open data policies in countries

---

95   ESA Data Policy, unclassified version, October 2012, online: https://earth.esa.int/documents/10174/296006/Revised_Simplified_EO_Data_policy_03102012.pdf/7df6dcc0-fe19-428c-bbf3-4335dee70fe4?version=1.0.
96   GEO Data Sharing Working Group, Mechanisms to Share Data as part of GEOSS Data-CORE, *Draft White Paper* on file with the author (Hereinafter Draft White Paper).
97   Directive 2013/37/EU of the European Parliament and of the Council of 26 June 2013 amending Directive of 2003/98/EC on the re-use of public sector information [2013] *OJ L* 175, at 1–8.
98   Commission Decision 2011/833/EU of 12 December 2011 on the reuse of Commission documents [2011] *OJ L*, at 39–42.

like Argentina,[99] Finland,[100] Japan,[101] New Zealand,[102] the US[103] and many others, as well as the G8 Open Data Charter.[104]

4.2 Copyright

Different choices made with regard to defining Earth observation data[105] may have very specific implications on the availability and type of protection applicable to them, particularly copyright. It is often not an easy task to establish whether copyright protection criteria are met when no such distinction between raw and processed data or information is made; such an approach fails to acknowledge the technical differences between these types of data. In its turn, copyrightability of a given type of Earth observation data can affect the legal interoperability of data with similar level of processing produced by different actors or jurisdictions.

The key characteristics of the copyright protection regime include the following: it applies to works of authorship[106] without any registration formalities, and consists of exclusive economic rights enforceable for a limited time, limitations thereon, and moral rights. The exact scope of copyright protection is determined by national copyright laws that are not uniform. The key characteristics of the copyright protection regime include the following: it applies to works of authorship[107] without any registration formalities, and consists of exclusive economic rights enforceable for a limited time, limitations to them, and moral rights.

Differences regarding the content of national copyright regulatory regimes already start with its subject-matter. Article 2 of the Berne Convention[108] grants copyright protection to "literary and artistic works", of which it codifies only examples. By analogy, national legal instruments of copyright protection[109] contain open lists that sometimes differ and include those not mentioned in the Berne Convention.[110] As a result, the focus and policy priorities in one

---

99 See www1.hcdn.gov.ar/dependencias/dsecretaria/Periodo2012/PDF2012/SANCIONES/1927-D-2011.pdf.
100 Finland's Public Sector ICT Strategy 2012–2020, November 2012, online: www.vm.fi/vm/en/04_publications_and_documents/03_documents/20121112Public/name.jsp.
101 White Paper on Information and Communication in Japan in Open Data (19 April 2013), online: www.soumu.go.jp/main_sosiki/joho_tsusin/eng/Releases/Telecommunications/130419_01.html.
102 Principles for Managing Data and Information held by the New Zealand Government (8 August 2011), online: www.ict.govt.nz/programmes/open-and-transparent-government/new-zealand-data-and-information-management-princi#fn1.
103 Open Data Policy – Managing Information as an Asset (May 9, 2013), online: www.whitehouse.gov/sites/default/files/omb/memoranda/2013/m-13-13.pdf.
104 18 June 2013, online: www.gov.uk/government/publications/open-data-charter/g8-open-data-charter-and-technical-annex.
105 For further overview of Earth observation regulatory and policy framework see Dunk, F., European Satellite Earth Observation: Law, Regulations, Policies, Projects, and Programmes (2008–2009) *Creighton Law Review* 42, at 397–445.
106 That is they represent author's original expression of ideas.
107 That is they represent author's original expression of ideas.
108 Berne Convention for the Protection of Literary and Artistic Works (9 September 1886), as last amended 28 September 1979, 1161 *U.N.T.S.* 30.
109 The US Copyright Act. Title 17 US Civil Code (October 19, 1976) Pub. L. No. 94-553. 90 Stat. 2541 as amended; German Copyright Law, Urheberrechtsgesetz (September 9, 1965) *BGBl.* I S. 1273 as amended; UK Copyright, Designs and Patents Act 1988) C 48 as amended, and French Intellectual Property Code (July 1, 1992) Law No. 92-597 as amended.
110 See e.g. designer clothes as works of authorship under Art. L. 112-2(14) French Copyright Code, ibid.

jurisdiction may lead to refusal to grant protection that in other jurisdictions is considered copyrightable.

The US Copyright Act links the creation of the work to its fixation "in a copy ... for the first time",[111] while the Canadian Copyright Act requires fixation of only specific works, like phonograms,[112] German Copyright law links exploitation rights only to material copies of the works.[113] The most important, primary criterion for copyright protection in accordance with the Berne Convention is that a protectable work should be an intellectual creation. The most important, primary criterion for copyright protection under national laws and jurisprudence differs, so that creativity may reflect a variety of criteria, ranging from the personality of the author,[114] the investment of "skill, judgment and labor" or his "selection, judgment and experience."[115]

Rules regarding exceptions to the exclusive rights of authors[116] are common at national level. One example is the EU legal framework that contains a finite list of exceptions that users are allowed to perform with regard to the work, without prior permission of the author.[117] At the same time, the US, besides individually specified exceptions, widely uses the so-called fair-use doctrine[118] applicable by courts on a case-by-case basis: a system that leaves room to exempt many more uses than those codified in the European regulatory sources. In practice, this may result in a situation where a user may not apply the same actions (quote, sample, etc.) to two copyrightable works created in different jurisdictions, and may not therefore be able to create other, independent works since active clearance of right is required when the exceptions are not applicable. This can obviously reduce legal interoperability of shared data and information, particularly in the context of Earth observation data, use of which often necessitates combination of data from different sources.

Applicability of copyright to Earth observation data

Technical characteristics of the process of generating at least some types of Earth observation data may preclude their eligibility for copyright protection. One of the *de minimis* rules established by international copyright law is: factual data are excluded from the scope of protection.[119] The regulatory distinction in some jurisdictions[120] between raw and other types of Earth observation data may be interpreted as an implicit recognition of this copyright law rule. It can be argued that even in jurisdictions that do not favor such distinction, the

---

111 §101 – the definition of 'created', *supra* note 46.
112 See e.g. The definitions of "computer program", "dramatic work" and "sound recording" Sec. 2, R.S.C., 1985, c. C-42.
113 §15(1), *supra* note 46.
114 See e.g. §2(2) German Copyright Law: protected works should be personal intellectual creations (WIPO translation, online: www.wipo.int/clea/en/text_html.jsp?lang=EN&id=1008), *supra* note 46.
1155 'Original' being something that is not copied. For a discussion on the interpretation of the authorship and creativity principle, see e.g. J. Ginsburg, The Concept of Authorship in Comparative Copyright Law (2002–2003) 52 DePaul L. Rev. 1063, at 1072–1091.
116 See Articles 9(2), 10 Berne Convention, *supra* note 45 and Article 10 WIPO Copyright Treaty (December 20, 1996) 2186 *U.N.T.S.* 121.
117 Article 5 Directive 2001/29/EC of the European Parliament and of the Council of 22 May 2001 on the harmonization of certain aspects of copyright and related rights in the information society [2001] *OJ L* 10–19.
118 Codified in Section 107 US Copyright Act, *supra* note 46.
119 Arts. 2, 5 WIPO Copyright Treaty, *supra* note 54.

(non)copyrightability of raw and processed Earth observation data will still not be affected. For example, the German Satellite Data Security Law[121] states that enforcement of other laws potentially applicable to Earth observation data should not be affected by its provisions. The definition of a copyrighted work as "author's personal intellectual creation"[122] in the German Copyright Act[123] precludes protection of raw Earth observation data by virtue of copyright.

Copyright is at least applicable to some types of Earth observation data; in virtually all jurisdictions, maps[124] are recognized as copyrightable works. Sufficiently creative processing of Earth observation data (or rather information products) may result in production of a work eligible for copyright protection.[125] This is true for products that result from processing that requires "interpretation of processed data, inputs of data and knowledge from other sources".[126]

4.3 Licences and legal interoperability

In practice the use of exclusive rights granted by copyright protection occurs through licensing that authors – or other copyright owners – use as a mechanism to authorize third parties to conduct activities that are in principle reserved their preserve. Just like the criteria of copyrightability, licensing conditions can vary across jurisdictions and make transboundary use of Earth observation data problematic or at least lacking clarity. Licenses must comply with the basic principles of copyright protection and stay within their scope. Since copyright exists only within the legislative framework that created it,[127] the licensor cannot introduce 'new' rights in the license that do not exist in the copyright regulatory framework in the applicable jurisdiction.

Licenses cannot be used for data and information that are not eligible for copyright protection. In such a case, contracts may be used; their enforcement is dependent not on the regulatory source they invoke, but on the parties' agreement.[128] The most critical difference between a contract and a license is that the former only binds the parties who sign it, and does not bind third parties against the author or rightholder. Not all clauses of the licenses in use today are compatible with the principles of copyright law.

The rules regarding licensing of Earth observation data are determined by national governments through regulations or policies, and sometimes, often due to regulatory lacunae,

---

120 See the US Land Remote Sensing Policy Act (1992) H.R.6133.
121 §3(3), Satellitendatensicherheitsgesetz, *supra* note 13.
122 Author's own translation.
123 §2(2) of the German Copyright Law, *supra* note 46.
124 See e.g. *Stadtplanwerk* BGHZ 139, S. 68; *NJW* 1998, S. 3352, reconfirmed in I ZR 227/02 *GRUR* 2005, S. 854.
125 J.R.West, "Copyright Protection for Data Obtained by Remote Sensing: how the Data Enhancement Industry Will Ensure Access for Developing Countries" (1990)11 *Nw. J. Int'l L. & Bus.* 403, referring to the United States' submission at the UN COPUOS stating that enhanced data being the product of the analyzer should be considered his property. See UN COPUOS, Report of the Scientific and Technical Sub-Committee on the Work of its 15th Session (1978) U.N. Doc. A/AC.105/216 at 8.
126 Principle I Remote Sensing Principles, *supra* note 6.
127 On these characteristics of IP protection and the issues of jurisdiction over IP issues see e.g. K. Lipstein, "Intellectual Property: Jurisdiction or Choice of Law?", 61 *Cambridge Law Journal* (2002), 295ff., esp. 296–297; see also last para. *supra* § 18.2.1.
128 Here some jurisdictional differences need to be kept in mind, in particular, for example in Europe, where copyright laws contain more requirements to contracts than in the US. However, where a contract serves the purpose of enabling use, rather than restricting it, no immediate issues with it enforceability arise.

even by private actors themselves. All private companies that generate or distribute Earth observation data set up their relationships with the users through licensing agreements that consist of clauses containing permitted uses of the licensed products, ownership, as well as categorization and status of the derivative products made by the licensee.

The ownership over licensed Earth observation data remains with the licensor, since only non-transferable, non-exclusive limited rights to use Earth observation data are usually granted to the licensee.[129] Granting limited rights is in itself compatible with the relevant provisions of the copyright protection regime. However, retaining the ownership over licensed copies[130] is not, since copyright does not apply to the actual physical copies of the work, but grants rights to the use of the original expression. Transfer of data under a license is therefore a form of exercising the distribution right that does not imply transfer of control over the copies of the work.

The wording of most licenses or contracts used for Earth observation data reveals the uncertainty as to the copyrightability of the licensed subject-matter, since data are often declared trade secrets that the licensee is obliged to protect,[131] or a database protected by the *sui generis* database right.[132] Differentiation between raw Earth observation data and information products is normally omitted even by the players under the jurisdiction of states that recognize it.[133] 'Permitted uses' that the licenses refer to represent an exhaustive list of legitimate actions on the part of the licensee are often limited to the licensee's internal purposes.[134] They include installation and copying of the licensed products on different computers of the licensee,[135] as well as use of imagery contained in the licensed products.[136]

Licenses permit production and distribution[137] of derivative works and link the distribution right of the licensee over such works as to whether imagery from the licensed data is covered. If so, free distribution of such derivative works is not allowed.[138] This type of prohibition may conflict

---

129 See e.g. § 2.1, SPOT General Supply Conditions of Satellite Imagery Products, January 2011, www2.astrium-geo.com/files/pmedia/public/r1931_9_spot_generalsupplyconditions_jan2011.pdf; § 2.1, eGEOSurimage Standard Terms and Conditions of Licence, Marchy 2010, www.e-geos.it/terms/e-GEOS%20Std%20Terms%20and%20Conditions%20of%20License_May_2010.pdf; Sec. 4, GeoEye Data Single or Multiple Organization Licence, www.americaview.org/sites/default/files/importedFiles/GeoEye_SingleOrganization_license.txt.
130 Cf. e.g. SPOT General Supply Conditions of Satellite Imagery Products: "No CLIENT shall be able to claim an exclusive right of use on the PRODUCT".
131 Cf. § 2.2, SPOT General Supply Conditions of Satellite Imagery Products; § 2.4. eGEOS Standard Terms and Conditions of Licence.
132 See also Directive of the European Parliament and of the Council on the legal protection of databases, 96/9/EC, of 11 March 1996; OJ L 77/20 (1996). The situation mirrors the practice of the European Space Agency to mention all mechanisms that theoretically protect information as applicable to remote sensing data.
133 This concerns i.a. the United States.
134 Cf. § 4(b)(d), GeoEye Data Single or Multiple Organization Licence; § 2.1(c)(e), SPOT General Supply Conditions of Satellite Imagery Products; § 2.1, eGEOS Standard Terms and Conditions of Licence.
135 Cf. § 4(b), GeoEye Data Single or Multiple Organization Licence; § 2.1 (a)(b)(c), SPOT General Supply Conditions of Satellite Imagery Products; § 1 (Definitions, Use) (a)(b)(d), eGEOSurimage Standard Terms and Conditions of Licence.
136 Cf. § 4(d), GeoEye Data Single or Multiple Organization Licence; § 2.1(g)(h), SPOT General Supply Conditions of Satellite Imagery Products; § 1 (Definitions, Use) (c), eGEOS Standard Terms and Conditions of Licence.
137 Limitations apply depending on how processed the licensed data in the derivative product is.
138 Cf. § 2.1(e), SPOT General Supply Conditions of Satellite Imagery Products; § 2.2, eGEOSurimage Standard Terms and Conditions of Licence; 4(e), GeoEye Data Single or Multiple Organization Licence.

with current legislation regarding copyright protection where the licensee creates his or her own copyrightable works on the basis of the licensed data. Under copyright rules,[139] copyright in derivative works is independent from copyright in the original work, provided that the authorization was granted to make derivative works,[140] and the author of the original work is acknowledged.

Restrictive licensing clauses create an additional layer of problems for users working with Earth observation data by often rendering the combination (or other similar use) of data from various sources practically impossible. For example, if for a production of a new derivative work a user needs data or information from several providers, he will only be in the position to carry out the planned activity if all data come with exactly the same restrictions on use. Unfortunately, even the interpretation of what constitutes a derivative work differs across licensing clauses of various companies. This reduces or eliminates legal interoperability of data and the potential for reuse of Earth observation data. Yet, the wide range of applications requires use of Earth observation data from different sources. In addition, this legal non-interoperability often unreasonably hinders the development and success of international and regional open Earth observation data initiatives that pursue important or vital goals of societal well-being and growth.

4.4 Open data trend

Governments carry out satellite remote sensing activities, producing or funding the production of vast amounts of Earth observation data. This results in the applicability of regulations governing access to and use of data and information[141] to the data produced by governments or by private entities on their behalf.[142] Normally, the goal of regulations regarding status of government data is to promote and secure access to them and their use. The main principle of such regulations across jurisdictions is free, full and open access to data. More states recognize and enforce this principle having formed the so-called Open data trend that are produced by governments or by private entities on their behalf.[143]

Sufficiently independent development of this regulatory field within separate national jurisdictions leads to differences in the content of their provisions. Regulatory sources in various countries operate with different terminology using terms like information,[144] documents[145] or records[146] to describe essentially the same concepts that nevertheless have differing interpretations.

---

139 E.g. According to Art. 31–42, German Copyright Law; Secc. 90–96, UK Copyright, Designs and Patents Act 1988 (c. 48).
140 See e.g. The definition of "adaptation", Sec. 20, UK Copyright, Designs and Patents Act; 'Bearbeitungen' in Art. 23, German Copyright Law; "derivative work" in Sec. 101, 103, US Copyright Act.
141 Depending on the jurisdiction referred to as Access to Information Acts, Freedom of Information Acts or regulations regarding access to and use of public sector information.
142 This section only aims to give a very brief overview of the existing FOIA regulations. For a more extensive analysis see L.K. Smith and C. Doldirina, "Remote Sensing: The Three E's – A Case for Moving Space Data towards the Public Good" (2008) 24/1 *Space Policy Journal* 22–32.
143 This section only aims to give a very brief overview of the existing FOIA regulations. For a more extensive analysis see L.J. Smith, L.J. and C Doldirina, C. "Remote Sensing: The Three E's – A Case for Moving Space Data towards the Public Good" (2008) 24/1 *Space Policy Journal* 22–32.
144 E.g. UK Freedom of Information Act 2000, c.36.
145 E.g. Freedom of Information Amendment (Reform) Act No. 51 of 2010, as amended; Council of Europe Recommendation Rec(2002)2 on access to official documents, available at www.coe.int/T/E/Human_rights/rec(2002)2_eng.pdf, last visited 02.02.2007.
146 E.g. U.S. Freedom of Information Act, 5 U.S.C. sect. 552; Canadian Access to Information Act. R.S. 1985, c. A-1, s 3.

Law relating to remote sensing

Different treatment across jurisdictions receives another crucial concept – ownership of government data. Some governments or their agencies are data custodians,[147] others are full-fledged owners,[148] and as a result they have different sets of rights with regard to such data. This may lead to a discretionary decision-making power as to what data and according to which conditions to make available in some agencies, or obligation to release the data.[149]

Probably the most important difference with implications for access to and use of government data lies in the provisions regarding restrictions on access to certain categories of government data.[150] Often even the basis for imposing these restrictive exemptions or exceptions to full and open access to data differs, as for example absolute and discretionary exemptions in the Freedom of Information Acts of the UK[151] and Australia,[152] or nine broad categories in the US Act.[153] Furthermore, access to certain geological and geophysical information and data, which, by definition, include Earth observation data, may also be restricted.[154]

Last, but not least, is the issue of cost recovery. Even though this in itself does not affect the accessibility and usability of government data that are made available, high costs of access may be prohibitive, if users are unable or unwilling to pay them. In some jurisdictions cost recovery is allowed, as for example in many European countries, while in others, like in the US, it is not. However, the open data trend promotes abolition of the cost recovery system of accessing government data.[155] Some jurisdictions choose to specifically regulate or address access and use of Earth observation data on a policy level.

Some of the pioneers who adopted this approach are the US with regard to the Landsat satellites[156] and recently, through the National Strategy for Earth Observations,[157] the

---

147 Schedule 1, Sec. 3 Australian Freedom of Information Act, *supra* note 73; Part. 2 Interpretation New Zealand Official Information Act 1982 No. 156.
148 Like in the UK, where the Ordnance Survey is a Crown corporation, as well as in some other member states of the European Union, even though the situation has been substantially changing in recent. See H.J. Onsrud, "Geographic Information Legal Issues", in *Encyclopedia of Life Support Systems* (EOLSS) (EOLSS Publishers, Oxford, UK, 2004).
149 The example of the US federal regulations is the most prominent one, although the situation may differ on the states' level. See e.g. H.B. Dansby, *A Survey and Analysis of State GIS Legislation* (1992) GIS Law 1(1) at 7–13.
150 This is a standard approach, since most of the rules operate alongside exceptions or limitations that constrain their application. See e.g. Canadian Access to Information Act, Section 2(a): The purpose of the Act is to "allow any person a *right of access* to the records in the custody or under the control of a public body *subject to limited and specific exceptions*" (emphasis added), *supra* note 74.
151 Part II UK Freedom of Information Act, 2000 c. 36.
152 Schedule 3 Freedom of Information Amendment (Reform) Act, *supra* note 73.
153 The Freedom of Information Act 5 *U.S.C.* § 552, as amended.
154 § 552(b)(9) US Freedom of Information Act, *supra* note 74.
155 These exemptions (called also exceptions or restrictions) are quite extensive, but have to be read narrowly. This stance is in accordance with regulatory practices in other jurisdictions. For instance, in the US, disclosure of information by public bodies is the main rule as well, and "any exception to that rule will be narrowly construed in light of the general policy of openness expressed" in the Freedom of Information Act (*Ottochian v. Freedom of Info. Comm'n*, 604 A.2d 351 (Conn. 1992). For a general discussion of the impact of the new technologies on the enforcement of FOIAs and access to databases (in the US) see I. Bloom, "Freedom of Information Laws in the Digital Age: The Death Knell of Information Privacy" (2005–2006) 12:3 *Rich. J.L. & Tech.* 9; see also J. MacDonald & C.H. Jones eds, *The Law of Freedom of Information* (Oxford University Press, 2003) at 9.25–9.77.
156 Sec. 105(a) the US Land Remote Sensing Policy Act, *supra* note 60; *see* Landsat Data Distribution Policy, online: https://landsat.usgs.gov/documents/Landsat_Data_Policy.pdf.
157 Executive Office of the President National Science and Technology Council, April 2013, online: www.whitehouse.gov/sites/default/files/microsites/ostp/nstc_2013_earthobsstrategy.pdf. Earth observation data should be fully and openly available promptly, without discrimination and free of charge whenever possible.

agreements relating to the China-Brazil Earth Resources Satellites,[158] as well as the European INSPIRE Directive.[159] The introduction of the open data regime on the regulatory or policy level is not always easy to achieve, and often it contains quite a few exceptions or restrictions, and does not apply to privately generated Earth observation data. One of the recent regulatory mechanisms that well reflects the current trends and is worth highlighting is the European Commission delegated Regulation on access to Copernicus data.[160]

The Regulation on access to Copernicus data[161] establishes "full and open" free worldwide access to Copernicus data and information for lawful reproduction, distribution, communication to the public, adaptation, modification and combination with other data. In addition, as indicated in recital 7 of the Regulation, Copernicus data-sharing regime is directly linked to international open data initiatives, namely GEOSS. Copernicus is declared a European contribution to GEOSS, and its data-sharing regime is compatible with that of the GEOSS Data-CORE: a mechanism of data sharing that does not allow any restrictions on reuse (see GEOSS Data Sharing Action Plan, 2010).[162] It also introduces obligations under international agreements, conflicts with which may trigger limitation of access to Copernicus data. This provision relates to Article 2(6) of the Regulation on access to documents of EU institutions[163] that declares its provisions to be without prejudice to rights of public access to EU institution data in accordance with instruments of international law.

There is a risk that limitations can be expanded through the adoption of vertical regulatory instruments beyond the scope of those laid down in the Regulation on access to documents of EU institutions. This can be seen, for instance, in the limitations contained in the Commission Decision on document reuse, in the Regulation on access to Copernicus data, and in the Directive on public access to environmental information may seem to introduce additional limitations.

5 Space-based meteorological services

5.1 The World Meteorological Organization Convention and its implications on the national regulatory level

The World Meteorological Organization (WMO) encourages the creation of national

---

158 See J.V. Soares, J.C. Epiphanio, G. Camara, CBERS-2B For Africa, report, online: ftp://ftp.earthobservations.org/C4/Giovanni/06/06%20-%20CBERS%20revOct.doc.
159 See Directive of the European Parliament and of the Council establishing an Infrastructure for Spatial Information in the European Community (INSPIRE), 2007/2/EC, of 14 March 2007; OJ L 108/1 (2007). Cf. Also e.g. C. Doldirina, INSPIRE: a real step forward in building an interoperable and unified spatial information infrastructure for Europe? ESPI Perspectives (March 2009) online: www.espi.or.at/images/stories/dokumente/Perspectives/espi%20perspectives%2020%20doldirina.pdf.
160 Commission Delegated Regulation (EU) No1159/2013 supplementing Regulation (EU) No. 911/2010 of the European Parliament and of the Council on the European Earth monitoring programme (GMES) by establishing registration and licensing conditions for GMES users and defining criteria for restricting access to GMES dedicated data and GMES service information. *OJ L.* 309/1, 19.11.2013.
161 Id.
162 GEOSS Data Sharing Action Plan, GEO-VII Plenary, 03-04.11.2010, p.4. Online: www.earthobservations.org/documents/geo_vii/07_GEOSS%20Data%20Sharing%20Action%20Plan%20Rev2.pdf.
163 Regulation (EC) No. 1049/2001 of May 30, 2001 of the European Parliament and of the Council regarding public access to European Parliament, Council and Commission documents. *OJ L.* 145/43, 31.5.2001.

meteorological services through a national legislative act, particularly because of their importance in providing meteorological and other related services in support of the need to protect life and property, the environment, as well as ensuring the continuity of observation data at national level, to name but a few of the ongoing calls for such data.[164] This approach is chosen by more and more countries across the world. The US,[165] Germany,[166] South Africa,[167] New Zealand,[168] Japan[169] are among those jurisdictions that have adopted the relevant regulatory regime.

One of the reasons for laying down a formal regulatory regime for a national meteorological or weather service is to designate a responsible government entity to be in charge of providing data and information on weather-related hazards.[170] Some national regulatory sources give the national meteorological services bodies exclusivity to provide such kind of data and information, stressing their responsibility to provide specific weather-related data and information,[171] or the authoritative character of the information they provide.[172]

Normally relevant national regulatory sources, alongside provisions determining the functions of such a body include, rules relating to services provided for free or paid for,[173] and to intellectual property rights. As a rule, the functions include a list of situations or a basis to determine when the national meteorological service is responsible for providing weather forecasts and warnings; about compliance with the WMO rules;[174] management of weather data and their dissemination or distribution; representation in relevant international organizations and meetings. They furthermore lay down provisions with regard to the status and protection of data produced, acquired or held by meteorological services that differ from the rules established for government data in other regulatory sources.

Specific provisions of existing acts and suggestions made by the WMO or elsewhere show that the regulatory regime applicable to the functioning of national meteorological services normally do not directly address the issue of satellite remote sensing as such. This leads to the conclusion that relevant norms from other regulatory sources will be applicable in cases of necessity. This holds true in cases where for example a national meteorological service is

---

164 Preamble Convention of the World Meteorological Organisation Geneva 23 March 1950) 77 UNTS 143, online: http://library.wmo.int/pmb_ged/wmo_15-2012_en.pdf. Declaration of Thirteenth World Meteorological Congress (1999) Cg-XIII, Annex IV, online: www.wmo.int/pages/governance/policy/geneva_declaration_en.html.
165 National Weather Services Duties Act of 2005 S.786. No.100.
166 Gesetz ueber den Deutschen Wetterdienst, September 10, 1998. BGBl. I S. 2871.
167 South African Weather Service Act No. 8 of 2001.
168 Meteorological Services Act 1990.
169 Meteorological Service Act No. 165 of June 2, 1952.
170 WMO Guidelines on the Roles, Operations, and Management of National Meteorological or Hydrometeorological Services, section 2.1, online: www.wmo.int/pages/prog/dra/eguides/index.php/en/2-legal-and-institutional-form-of-an-nms/2-1-national-legal-basis.
171 E.g. Section 2 (a) US National Weather Services Duties Act.
172 See some examples of such provisions in national regulatory sources in Communications Plan on PWS activities Responsibility of NMHSs in Issuing Meteorological Information, online: www.wmo.int/pages/prog/amp/pwsp/legalstatus_en.htm.
173 Most of national meteorological services provide at least some data, information and services against fees, which goes in line with the WMO standpoint on the matter. See WMO NMS Guidelines, online: www.wmo.int/pages/prog/dra/eguides/index.php/en/5-functions/5-13-cost-recovered-and-commercial-serviceswww.wmo.int/pages/prog/dra/eguides/index.php/en/5-functions/5-13-cost-recovered-and-commercial-services.
174 See, e.g. for warning services in the WMO NMS Guidelines, online: www.wmo.int/pages/prog/dra/eguides/index.php/en/5-functions/5-5-warnings-systems.

operating its own weather satellites, large agencies like NOAA[175] or an international organization (e.g. European Organization for the Exploitation of Meteorological Satellites, EUMETSAT), in the case of Europe.[176]

From an organizational perspective, most national meteorological services are either government agencies, or organizations that carry out public tasks. Whether or not there are specific rules addressing intellectual property rights in weather data, their status, as well as conditions of access to and use, general provisions regarding access to government data apply. For instance, weather data in Canada are subject to Crown copyright,[177] by the same token as any other data eligible for copyright protection produced by the government.[178]

This chapter has already highlighted the importance of today's open data trend that directly aims at promoting free and unrestricted access to and use of government data of all types and categories. Weather data and meteorological services based thereon, by the same token as Earth observation data, logically fall under the relevant regulatory provisions sources.

6 Outlook

Satellite remote sensing and Earth observation remain key capabilities in the hands of governments, international organizations, and a growing number of commercial operators.[179] The technology enables generation of and access to various forms of raw data, from which, after value-added processing, further remote sensing products and applications can be developed, made and distributed. Not all states have satellite remote sensing capabilities, largely because of the level of investment required; however, technological development is leading the downsizing of spacecraft and, together with the advent of low-cost launches and new forms of small satellite missions with remote sensing capabilities, it is not inconceivable that interest in this technology and its availability may increase.

Satellite remote sensing is a complex activity that requires operation of spacecraft and ground facilities, as well as maintenance of secure communication and distribution networks, able to adequately respond to the growing user demand for Earth observation data and applications. Its commercialization brings new aspects that need to be addressed. These features require the regulatory regime applicable to satellite remote sensing activities to straddle various legal fields and address issues such as licensing the activity itself, security of the satellite remote sensing system and Earth observation data, principles and rules regarding generation, reception and distribution of Earth observation data. The response has been a massive duplication of data, and little cross-over exchange. Currently, dedicated satellite remote sensing legislation is only in force – and makes sense – in those states with particularly high resolution satellite remote sensing capabilities. Even though it is unlikely that, in any given jurisdiction, satellite remote sensing activity will be exclusively governed by a single dedicated legal act, consolidation of the most important principles and reference to the applicable legal norms across various legal fields is a recommended approach.

---

175 See information online: www.noaa.gov/satellites.html.
176 Convention for the Establishment of a European Organisation for the Exploitation of Meteorological Satellites (EUMETSAT), June 19, 1986.
177 See para. 4 Terms and conditions of use of Meteorological Data via RSS or WeatherLink (the "Applications") Environment Canada (October 2010), online: https://weather.gc.ca/mainmenu/disclaimer_e.html.
178 Sec.12 Canadian Copyright Act R.S.C., 1985, c. C-42.
179 See Norbert Frischauf, "Table of Satellites", in S Brünner ed, *Outer Space in Society, Politics and Law*, (New York: Springer), 2011, 210–218.

It is furthermore advisable for the jurisdictions opting to establish licensing regimes for privately run remote sensing satellite systems to take into account the practice of states that already have such regulatory sources enacted and enforced to avoid introduction of completely different principles and norms. A more harmonized approach across regulating jurisdictions will help create a rather homogeneous environment for operation or commercial remote sensing satellite systems that most certainly will ease the transboundary flow of Earth observation data that is crucial for such businesses both on supply and demand side.

From a governance perspective, remote sensing data are a strategically important environmental management, planning and security tool; administrations can rely on them to ensure that national infrastructures remain infallible. Data distribution policies and licenses have traditionally restricted making Earth observation data available – other than in true disasters and emergencies – by virtue of overriding agency and operator economic interests. This has been partly secured through IP rights, notably economic copyright, or title, as well as through highly restrictive licensing mechanisms that ensure limited modes of using and further distributing licensed Earth observation data. Such practices need to be changed to a less restrictive approach to enable better levels of legal interoperability of Earth observation data from various providers and different jurisdictions, and as a result easier subsequent use across borders and applications. In fact, the market is adapting to the more recent availability of free data, largely inspired by efforts such as the US Landsat as one of the earliest leading examples, and the European Union's flagship program, Copernicus, in the recent years. The latter sees the liberalization of access to raw data from its original Sentinel mission in the context of global environmental management and security. Earth observation data can be obtained free of charge to all those registering on its platform. The only requirement for receiving data is that the subsequent processor makes a reference to the EU branding to mark its origin. This EU regulatory development reflects the current open data trend that promotes application of free, open and unrestricted access to government data that necessarily includes Earth observation data generated through government funding or by government-run satellite remote sensing systems.

The demand side of the Earth observation data market today is focused on the development of various applications and products by virtue of processing lots of various types of data, both Earth observation and *in situ*. The value-adding activities require access to the input data with a specific set of rights that would enable the user to conduct processing and distribute the final products to subsequent users. For this reason the principles applicable to access to and use of Earth observation data in particular should adequately respond to and reflect the interests of users and providers.

14
Law related to space transportation and spaceports

Michael Gerhard and Isabelle Reutzel

Introduction

Individuals, scientific research entities, commercial companies and public institutions use space technologies on a daily basis. While space applications require that the necessary instruments are brought *into* and maneuvered *in* outer space, other activities, such as experiments carried out by humans in outer space, require that humans and cargo are brought *into* and *back* from outer space. Space transportation is therefore an indispensable and crucial element for the realization of space missions.

Recent technical evolutions enable new actors, especially private investors, to participate in space activities and make the space sector even more attractive.[1]

The following chapter deals with the regulation of space transportation, understood as the means to transport people or cargo *to, through, in* and *back from* outer space. This chapter addresses the launch phase, the flight into outer space (often also referred to as operation or guidance of space objects) and the return or removal of the object from outer space, regardless of the application or the purpose of its mission. This chapter also addresses the regulation of spaceports, as those are a necessity for space transportation and as such a prerequisite for any space operation.

Space transportation

"Transport" can be defined as a system or means of conveying people or goods from one place to another.[2] Applied to space activities, "space transportation" can consequently be understood as the means to transport people or cargo *to, through, in* and *back from* outer space. In the following, different modes of space transportation will be described to illustrate the actual technical background of space transportation. Further, the purpose of regulating such space transportation shall be introduced, as a foreword to general remarks on national legislations

---

1 Ram S. Jakhu & Yaw M. Nyampong, "International Regulation of Emerging Modes of Space Transportation" in Joseph N. Pelton & Ram S. Jakhu, eds, *Space Safety Regulations and Standards* (Oxford: Elsevier, 2010) 215 at 219.
2 Oxford Dictionary, "Transport" online: www.oxforddictionaries.com.

related to space transportation. Finally, particular aspects of national laws related to space transportation will be described.

Modes of space transportation

Space transportation can be conducted in three different contexts and for different purposes.

The first mode of space transportation concerns people or cargo transported *from* Earth *into* outer space for the purpose of getting (and staying) there in order to conduct a further activity. In this case, the transportation *into* outer space is solely a means, and the objective of the transportation is the delivery to a pre-defined station in outer space. Examples of this are the transportation of people or cargo *to* the International Space Station (ISS), or the transportation of satellites, probes or other space objects *into* their dedicated orbit.

Second, cargo that has been transported *into* outer space may itself continue its existence as transportation vehicle. This is the case for satellite buses carrying instruments for telecommunication, remote sensing or any other application. As such, satellite buses transport the mission instruments in a dedicated orbit (position) *through* outer space. In this case, the transportation is the purpose of the activity. Aspects related to this kind of transportation are irrespective of the instruments carried on the bus and the application conducted by it.[3]

Third, people or cargo can be transported *into* outer space, *through* outer space and *back to* Earth without leaving the transportation vehicle as such. The purpose of the activity is to bring people or cargo *into* outer space and *back* for a defined and limited period of time, meaning transportation is again the sole purpose of the activity. Examples for this are tourist flights; transporting fee-paying passengers *from* a point on Earth *to* an altitude regarded to be outer space, and *back to* Earth, either to the point of departure or to a different one.[4] Currently, such flights are (planned to be) carried out as suborbital flights, with a parabolic flight path through outer space, meaning those flights do not achieve an orbit around the Earth. Another example of this kind are sounding rockets, carrying experiments to be conducted in weightlessness.

It follows that one may differentiate between transportation *from* Earth *to* outer space, transportation *from* Earth *to* outer space and *back to* Earth, and transportation *within* outer space (including end of life disposal). In the first two cases, the transportation service may be provided by a third party who is different from the transported person or owner of the transported good. In the last scenario, this is not necessarily the case. In any case, a mode of transportation *into* outer space is necessary, be it as a sole purpose or a means for conducting further activity. The following shall demonstrate that different considerations can be applied with regard to these different transportation modes.

Purpose of regulating space transportation

In many jurisdictions entities conducting space transportation are subject to regulatory control, for example through certification. Every State may have its particular reasons to regulate such

---

3 The application itself and legal aspects related to it are dealt with in Chapters 6 to 8 of this handbook.
4 On this matter and a possible regulation of private human spaceflight, see Frans G. Von der Dunk, The Integrated Approach – Regulating Private Human Spaceflight as Space Activity, Aircraft Operation, and High-Risk Adventure Tourism (2013) 92 Acta Astronautica 199 at 199ff.; see also Tanja Masson-Zwaan & Rafael Moro-Aguila, "Regulating Private Human Suborbital Flight at the International and European Level: Tendencies and Suggestions" (2013) 92 Acta Astronautica 243ff. at 243.

activities, be it to ensure a certain level of safety for the people or goods on board such transportation vehicles, to ensure a certain level of safety for third parties (people and goods) on the ground or during flight (aircraft or other objects in outer space), or to ensure a level playing field among the organizations subject to the same regulations.

From an international law perspective, two other fundamental reasons for a State to regulate space transportation are to be found in the 1967 *Treaty on Principles Governing the Activities of States in the Exploration and Use of Outer Space, including the Moon and Other Celestial Bodies*[5] (OST) and especially Articles VI and VII thereof, which are discussed in greater detail below.

Description of some national laws related to space transportation

General remarks

Rules applicable to space transportation are commonly contained in more general space acts, bearing such titles as "space activities bill", "outer space act", "[State] space law", "law on space operations" or similar. In most instances, the requirements set forth by those national legislations are the same for all aspects of transportation as dealt with in this chapter, i.e. the launch, the operation and the return of the space object. Most of those acts also address other aspects of space activities (i.e. telecommunication, navigation, remote sensing or other kinds of space application), which would be outside the scope of this chapter. A dedicated act for launching activities only exists in the US (49 USC. Chapter 701 Commercial Space Launch Activities; CFR 14 III §§ 400 et seq., Commercial Space Transportation), while other space activities under US jurisdiction are regulated in other acts.[6] Similarly, the Australian Space Activities Act contains a chapter dedicated to launches (and returns).

National laws regulating space activities have been enacted in numerous States: United States, Norway, Sweden, United Kingdom, South Africa, Russian Federation, Ukraine, Australia, Hong Kong, Brazil, Belgium, South Korea, the Netherlands, France, Austria and Kazakhstan. The scope of most of these laws includes space transportation and those pieces of legislation are therefore relevant to the present chapter. References to and consolidated analysis of those acts have already been provided by numerous authors.[7] In addition to those "space laws" *stricto sensu*, some States have adopted regulation on specific aspects of space activities, such as Canada (authorization), Argentina and Spain (registration) and Italy (liability). There are cases where space applications are being legislated, even though there is no general "space law". For example, Germany has enacted an authorization procedure for the marketing of high qualified remote sensing data. This, however, does not constitute an authorization in the sense of Art. VI OST.

The purpose of the following is to provide a general overall overview of the dispositions of a number of selected jurisdictions.

---

5   *Treaty on Principles Governing the Activities of States in the Exploration and Use of Outer Space, including the Moon and Other Celestial Bodies*, 27 January 1967, 610 UNTS 205.
6   See specifically I. Marboe & F. Hafner, "Brief Overview over National Authorisation Mechanisms in Implementation of the UN International Space Treaties" in Frans G. Von der Dunk, ed, *National Space Legislation in Europe* (Leiden: Martinus Nijhoff Publishers, 2011). 29 at 41.
7   Gerhard, *supra* note 6 before MN 1; Isabelle Reutzel, *das Weltraumrecht in Europa: Eine Analyse der nationalen Regelungen zur Raumfahrt* (Bern: Peter Lang, 2014).

United States of America

In the US, the operation of launch and re-entry sites is dealt with in 49 USC Chapter 701 as further implemented by 14 CFR Chapter III, §§ 400 et seq., in particular Part 413 and Part 415 (launch license and safety), Part 431 (Reusable Launch Vehicles) and Part 437 (Experimental permits).

The Act applies to the launching of a launch vehicle or to the re-entry of a re-entry vehicle in the US. It applies to launches or to re-entries outside the US, if conducted by a US citizen or by an entity organized or existing under the laws of a US State or county. Finally, the Act applies under certain circumstances to foreign entities in which a US citizen or entity holds the controlling interest.

The Act differentiates between launch-specific licenses and launch operator licenses. Launch-specific licenses authorize the licensee to conduct one or more launches, having the same parameters, of one type of launch vehicle from one launch site. Launch operator licenses authorize a licensee to conduct launches from one launch site, within a range of launch parameters, of launch vehicles from the same family of vehicles transporting specified classes of payloads.

Launch licenses will be issued after policy and safety approvals have been obtained, after a payload review and after compliance with environmental requirements is assessed.[8] Furthermore, the applicant must demonstrate compliance with the financial responsibilities and allocation of risk requirements set forth by the Act. Licenses for a reusable launch vehicle and a re-entry license will be issued under similar requirements.[9] Experimental permits can be issued for research and development to test new design concepts, new equipment or new operating techniques, to demonstrate compliance with requirements for obtaining a license and for crew training before obtaining a license.[10] The specific requirements for commercial human spaceflight as laid down in Part 460 (are further described in Chapter 9 of this handbook).

The policy approval is subject to a determination by the FAA whether a proposed launch could jeopardize US national security or foreign policy interests, or international obligations of the US. The applicant shall identify the model and configuration of any launch vehicle proposed for launch, identify structural, pneumatic, propellant, propulsion, electrical and avionics systems used in the launch vehicle and all propellants, identify foreign ownerships and identify proposed launch vehicle flight profile(s). For its determination, the FAA consults with the Department of Defense, the Department of State and other federal agencies, including NASA. The policy approval may be applied for separately and in advance.

The safety approval is subject to a determination by the FAA whether an applicant is capable of launching a vehicle and its payload without jeopardizing public health and safety and safety of property. The applicant has to demonstrate that he maintains a safety organization, that the flight risk meets the acceptable risk level, that a flight readiness and communication plan exists and an individual responsible for flight readiness has been assigned. Additionally, the applicant must also demonstrate safety of all launch vehicle stages or components that reach Earth orbit (in particular that there will be no unplanned physical contact between the vehicle or its components and the payload after its separation and removal of stored energy), and the existence of a plan to report and respond to launch accidents, incidents or other mishaps. The safety approval may be applied for separately and in advance, as well.

---

8   Following the requirements of the *National Environmental Policy ACT*, 42 USC 4321, as further implemented by 40 CFR parts 1500–1508.
9   These requirements, as described in Part 431 and Part 435 will not be described in detail.
10 These requirements, as described in Part 437 will not be described in detail.

A payload review aims at determining whether its launch would jeopardize public health and safety, safety of property, US national security or foreign policy interests, or international obligations of the United States. It is required unless the payload is exempt from such a review. The review can be requested from the launch license applicant or from the payload owner or operator. It may be requested in advance of or apart from a launch license application. The FAA conducts its determination on the basis of the information submitted by the applicant, in particular the payload name and class, its physical dimensions and weight, its owner and operator, the orbital parameters for parking, transfer and final orbits, hazardous or radioactive material that may be contained, its intended operations during the life of the payload and delivery point in flight at which the payload will no longer be under the control of the launch licensee. For its determination, the FAA consults with the Department of Defense, the Department of State and other federal agencies, including NASA.

The licensee has the obligation to keep records and to report to the FAA. He shall also support the US government in implementing Article IV of the 1975 Convention on Registration of Objects Launched into Outer Space, by providing the necessary information about objects launched into outer space. The license can be transferred by the FAA, if the transferee has obtained the necessary approvals and determinations required, as seen above.

The licensee has the obligation to insure the lesser of the maximum probable loss of the licensed activity or $500 million (adjusted for inflation), and to indemnify the United States for liability, loss or damage sustained by the US exceeding $1.500.000.000 (also adjusted). The maximum probable loss will be determined (by the Associate Administrator for Commercial Space Transportation of the FAA) as laid down in the Act. Furthermore, the licensee has to comply with the reciprocal waiver of claim requirements as set forth in the Act.

The United Kingdom

The 1986 UK Outer Space Act[11] is applicable to launching or procuring the launch of space objects, operating a space object and any activity in outer space, if conducted by a UK national, Scottish firm or bodies incorporated under the law of the UK, irrespective of whether the activity is carried on in the UK or elsewhere. The Act does not differentiate between the launch and the operation of a space object. It remains general and sets forth the same requirements for both.

An organization conducting space transportation has to hold a license to carry out such activities. The essential requirements set forth by the Act are that the competent authority (Secretary of State and UK Space Agency) must be assured that the activity will not jeopardize public health or the safety of persons or property, will be consistent with the international obligations of the UK and will not impair the national security of the UK. The first two requirements are linked to obligations of the UK stemming from Articles VI and VII of the OST. The competent authority can grant the license subject to conditions, for instance to ensure proper oversight over the organization. The Act suggests conditions allowing the authority to inspect the licensee's facilities, to carry out inspection and testing of the licensee's equipment and to terminate the license in specific circumstances. The Act explicitly mentions conditions related to the prevention of contamination of outer space or adverse changes in the

---

11   Act to Confer licensing and other powers on the Secretary of State to secure compliance with the international obligations of the United Kingdom with respect to the launching and operation of space objects and the carrying on of other activities in outer space by persons connected with this country. The Act was amended by Section 12 of the Deregulation Act 2015.

Earth environment, as well as avoidance of interference with activities of others in the peaceful exploration and use of outer space. These are examples of conditions aimed at ensuring the UK's compliance with Article VI of the OST by confirming that the activities of the licensee are carried out in conformity with the OST (Article VI first sentence). Furthermore, the competent authority may require the licensee to obtain third-party liability insurance. This condition is targeted to also limit the risk of the UK being held liable according to Article VII of the OST. In practice, the competent authority limits the insurance cover in the majority of cases to €60 million.[12] Finally, the competent authority may require the licensee to ensure the disposal of the payload in outer space on the termination of operations. This condition related to the avoidance of space debris does not exist in many other jurisdictions.

An applicant has to pay a fee of £6,500 for the obtention of a license. The government has published the application form for such a license online, as well as guidance for applicants and a database of standards, being the criteria by which the application is judged.[13] The guidance includes a list of minimum information required and description of the licensing procedure. For space transportation issues it is noteworthy that the guidance includes particular questions related to launching activities, to which an applicant must respond.

From an administrative point of view, it is worth mentioning that the Act allows the license to be transferred with the consent of the competent authority. Furthermore, the Act entitles this authority to give enforceable directions to the licensee and to revoke, vary or suspend the license with the consent of the licensee or where it appears that a condition of the license or any regulation made under the Act has not been complied with, or if required in the interest of public health or national security, or to comply with any international obligation of the UK. It finally establishes offences under the Act.

With regard to the potential liability of the United Kingdom under Article VII of the OST for damages caused by a person to whom the Act applies, the Act establishes an obligation to indemnify the government.

Australia

The Australian Space Activities Act was adopted in 1998.[14]

The Act applies to space activities, and Part 3 of the Act specifies in detail which activities are regulated and require approval. Amongst those explicitly mentioned are launches conducted in Australia, overseas launches, if an Australian national is a responsible party for the launch, the return to Australia of Australian-launched and overseas-launched space objects and the operation of a launch facility in Australia. Different from many other laws regulating space activities, the Australian Space Activities Act only focuses on the launch and return of space objects. There are no specific requirements set forth for the operation of space objects, other than those implicitly covered by the authorization of the launch.

An organization conducting space transportation from Australia has to hold a launch permit. The competent authority (the Minister and the Space Licensing and Safety Office) may grant

---

12 UK Space Agency, "Licence to operate a space object: how to apply" online: UK Government, www.gov.uk/apply-for-a-license-under-the-outer-space-act-1986.
13 Ibid.
14 Commonwealth Consolidated Acts, "Act about space activities, and for related purposes (Act No. 123 of 1998, as last amended by Act No. 103 of 2003)" online: Austlii, www.austlii.edu.au/au/legis/cth/consol_act/saa1998167/. *The Space Activities Regulations 2001* provide further detail about the licensing regime, in particular material to be submitted with an application.

the permit if the applicant complies with the requirements set forth in the Act. The applicant has to be competent to carry out the launch, must comply with insurance requirements (covering the maximum probable loss, but at least AUS $750 million), or has to demonstrate its financial responsibility for the launch. It has to be established that the probability of the launch causing substantial harm to public health or public safety or causing substantial damage to property is as low as reasonably practicable. These requirements aim at limiting the risk of Australia being held liable according to Article VII of the OST. Furthermore, the Act contains requirements such as, for example, not to carry nuclear weapons or weapons of mass destruction, and that the competent authority does consider that the launch permit shall be granted for reasons relevant to Australia's foreign policy or international obligations. This again aims at ensuring Australia's compliance with Article VI of the OST by ensuring that the activities of the licensee are carried out in conformity with the OST. With regard to the possibility that other States are also launching States for the launch for which an application is submitted, the Act calls the competent authority to also consider whether there is an agreement between Australia and other launching State(s), under which the country assumes any liability, and indemnifies Australia, for any damage that the space object may cause. Very similar requirements are established by the Act for an Australian organization conducting space transportation from overseas.

An applicant has to pay a fee, for example AUS $10.000 for an overseas launch certificate. The Australian government has published guidelines for applicants online.[15]

The competent authority (i.e. the appointed Launch Safety Officer) is entitled to oversee the licensed launch, for example by entering and inspecting the facility and any space object at the facility, by inspecting and testing any equipment at the facility, by requesting any information and assistance and by giving directions about the launch.

Furthermore, the Act entitles the competent authority to suspend, revoke or transfer the launch permit, if the competent authority considers that there are grounds to do so. It finally establishes what are offences under the Act.

With regard to the potential liability of Australia under Article VII of the OST for damages caused by a person to whom the Act applies, the Act establishes a differentiated obligation of indemnification of the government by that person. In the first place, the responsible party has no obligation to indemnify the government for any damage exceeding the insured amount (covering the maximum probable loss, but as minimum AUS $750 million). Only if the damage exceeds AUS $3 billion is the government entitled to receive indemnification of any amount in excess.

France

The French Space Operations Act,[16] adopted in 2008 and in force from 2010 marks a turning point in the legislative field of space activities. An early space power, especially because of the good location of the launch site in Kourou in French Guiana, France had long been entertaining a legal "French paradox",[17] according to which more and more (private) space

---

15 Industry, "Australian Civil Space" online: Australian Government, Department of Industry, Innovation and Science www.space.gov.au/SPACELICENSINGSAFETYOFFICE/Pages/SpaceActivitiesGuidelines forIndustry.aspx.
16 Loi n° 2008-518 du 3 juin 2008 relative aux opérations spatiales, *Journal Officiel de la République Française* (4 June 2008).
17 Reutzel, *supra* note 10 at 72.

activities were taking place from the French territory without being subject to any specific legislation.[18] Those activities were being organized according to a set of national and contractual measures resulting mainly from France's international commitments. Besides the international space law framework, those were the Ariane Agreement of 21 September 1973 between France and the European Space Agency (ESA) about the development of the Ariane Program delegated to CNES (the French space agency) and the Declaration between the Ariane Exploitation Phase Participating States of 14 January 1980. The first consisted of specific international agreements with ESA on the facilities of the Guiana Space Centre (which became the legal basis for the safety rules ("sauvegarde") for the launch base), while in the second those States give ESA the mandate to conclude an arrangement with private operator Arianespace to implement the exploitation phase. The development phase is still governed by ESA rules. This arrangement set forth several conditions regarding the liability of the operators, which the French Space Act of 2008 builds upon. The adoption of the Act enables the French government to achieve a balance between responsibility and liability according to Articles VI and VII of the OST and the development of private space activities on and from its territory by setting up a coherent national regime to authorize and monitor space operations under French jurisdiction.

The national *corpus juris* applicable to space operations carried out under French jurisdiction and for which France is internationally liable and responsible according to international space law is composed of a main space act and three further application decrees, dealing respectively with authorization aspects,[19] the French Space Agency[20] and space-based data.[21]

The Act is applicable to space operations. Space operations encompass any activity consisting of "launching or attempting to launch an object into outer space, or in ensuring the commanding (control) of a space object during its journey in outer space (…) and, if necessary, during its returning to Earth". The definition shows there is no distinction made in principle between the different kinds of space operations and that the Act is applicable to space transportation. It is interesting to note that the Act defines the launching phase as the "period of time which starts when the launching operations become irreversible and which ends when the object to be put in outer space is separated from its launching vehicle", and the command phase as the "period of time which starts when the object to be put in outer space is separated from its launching vehicle and which ends when the first of the following events occurs: the final manoeuvers of de-orbiting and passivation activities have been completed; the operator has lost control over the space object; the return to Earth or the full disintegration of the space object in the atmosphere."

The Act requires the operator of such activities to hold an authorization or license delivered by the administrative authority (i.e. the Ministry in charge of Space Affairs, in close cooperation with the French Space Agency CNES, in charge of the technical control of the systems for which the authorization is applied for). Operations carried out in the scope of a

---

18 Marboe/Hafner, *supra* note 9 at 39.
19 Décret n° 2009-643 du 9 juin 2009 relatif aux autorisations délivrées en application de la loi n° 2008-518 du 3 juin 2008 relative aux opérations spatiales, *Journal Officiel de la République Française* (10 June 2009), text 30 of 154.
20 Décret n° 2009-644 du 9 juin 2009 modifiant le décret n°84-510 du 28 juin 1984 relatif au Centre national d'études spatiales, *Journal Officiel de la République Française* (10 June 2009), text 31 of 154.
21 Décret n°2009-640 du 9 juin 2009 portant application des dispositions prévues au titre VII de la loi n° 2008-518 du 3 juin 2006 relative aux opérations spatiales, *Journal Officiel de la République Française* (10 June 2009), text 1 of 154.

"public mission" (governmental programs, science, development of space systems) carried out by CNES are excluded from the scope of the Act. CNES nonetheless applies the technical regulations and monitors their observance through internal independent procedures on a voluntary basis, as exemplary values. It is also interesting to note that if the launch of a space object is being procured by a non-French operator through the services of a French launching operator, only the latter shall apply for an authorization to launch.[22] Furthermore, the transfer of control of a space object requires authorization, if the object has initially been authorized under the French Act. Similarly, if a French operator wishes to take control of a space object not primarily authorized under the French Act, he has to apply for an authorization to do so.

In order to be issued, an authorization operators have to demonstrate moral, financial and professional guarantees. Financial guarantees can consist either in financial autonomy or in the need to hold insurance coverage for the duration of the space operation. Regarding the amount to be insured, this element is viewed in close relationship with the question of third-party liability below. Authorizations will not be granted if the interests of national defense or international commitments may be jeopardized.

On the technical side, the dispositions of the three sets of technical regulations must be complied with.[23] They are based on the practices of CNES, improved by decades of experience in space operations. One is applicable to launch operations, the second to satellite operations (in-orbit command and re-entry) and the last concerns safety regulations at the Guiana Space Centre (*Règlement d'Exploitation des Installations du Centre Spatial Guyannais*). The main features of these regulations are set to be as close as possible to the practices of the space industry regarding the safety of persons and property, the protection of public health and of the environment. The regulations set objectives to be reached by the operators rather than mandatory procedures. They are based on international norms and standards.

The application for authorization foresees that the applicant, demonstrating a general notification of compliance with the Technical Regulation, prepares a technical file. Also an audit on the internal standards and quality management provisions must be provided. All measures taken by the applicant regarding surveys of hazard and risk control plans aimed at ensuring the safety of property and people and to protect public health and the environment must be set. Environmental impact studies and measures designed to avoid, reduce or offset harmful effects on the environment must be made, including a risk prevention plan relating to risks caused by the fallback of the space object or any fragment thereof. This plan includes a prevention plan relating to environmental damage, a space debris mitigation plan, a collision prevention plan, and a nuclear safety and/or planet protection plan (if applicable). Finally, risk management and emergency measures envisaged also must be stated. Specific technical requirements are also applicable relating to mission analysis; flight dynamics and mission robustness; onboard neutralization capacities; flight data record capacities; general safety objectives; objectives concerning nominal stages of re-entry, including the non-creation of debris, and collision risks avoidance.

In certain circumstances, operators can apply for an exemption of the technical assessment. This is the case for example for foreign launch services purchased by French operators. If the

---

22   CNES, "The French Space Operations Act," Presentation made by the French Delegation at the 48th Session of the Legal Subcommittee of the Committee on the Peaceful Uses of Outer Space, online: UNOOSA, www.oosa.unvienna.org/pdf/pres/lsc2009/pres-04.pdf.
23   B. Lazare, "The French Space Operations Act: Technical Regulations" (2013) 92 Acta Astronautica 209 at 211.

space operation is to be carried out from the territory of a foreign State, or means or facilities falling under the jurisdiction of a foreign State, the Space Department of the French Ministry for Space Affairs may exempt the applicant from all or any part of the technical regulations compliance check, when the national and international commitments of that State, as well as its legislation and internal practices, provide sufficient guarantees regarding the safety of persons and property, the protection of the public health and the environment and liability matters.

In order to facilitate the issue of an authorization, "administrative licenses" attesting the moral, financial and professional guarantees of the applicant can be issued, so that the final authorization can be granted for each single operation on a case-by-case basis on the sole control of the technical conformity. "Technical licenses" certifying the technical conformity of generic systems and procedures used can also be issued. The final authorization will then be issued on a case-by-case basis. Finally, "licenses equivalent to authorization" may also be granted in the case of orbital systems: those consist only of an obligation to inform regarding the beginning of the operation one month prior to commencement.

Once authorization has been granted, the holder of the latter has to comply with several dispositions to enable the monitoring of the space operation. The relevant provisions of the authorization and the *corpus juris* must be observed during the carrying out of the operation and CNES must be informed of any relevant events of failures. Special agents and controllers are granted prerogatives to ensure the provisions of the authorization and the Act are respected. Their prerogatives reach from compliance checks during the application procedure to permanent access to buildings, premises and facilities where operations are conducted as well as suspension of the authorization. Also diplomatic and administrative authorities are entitled to take emergency measures aiming at protecting people, property, public health and the environment, which may result for example in the destruction of the rocket if need may be. Failure to respect the provisions of the authorization or violation of the applicable legislation may result in withdrawal or suspension. In addition, the Act also prescribes fines up to €200.000 for launching or operating space objects without an authorization or in breach of relevant administrative measures. The same rules apply for taking possession or transferring command of a space object without authorization.

Regarding third-party liability, the purpose of the Act is to concentrate the burden of liability on the operator and is inspired from the concept of State liability as established by the 1972 Convention on International Liability for Damage Caused by Space Objects[24] (LIAB): the operator is absolutely liable for damages which occur on ground and in the air space, and liable in case of fault for damages caused in outer space. In this regard, the French Act introduces a differentiation between the launching phase and the command phase, which is not foreseen for State liability by the LIAB and aimed at apportioning the liability. Furthermore, the operator can be held liable only for a limited period of time. Finally, liability is apportioned between the French State and the operator: in the event of an operator – holding an authorization under the French space Act – being condemned by a domestic or foreign court, or in the event of the French State being held liable under the LIAB because of damage caused to a foreigner, a guarantee of the French State is granted for indemnification sums exceeding the amount fixed in the French Finance Law of 2008 (approximately €60 million). Logically, the French Act imposes the duty of insurance up to this ceiling (or equivalent financial guarantees).

---

24 *Convention on International Liability for Damage Caused by Space Objects*, 29 March 1972, 961 UNTS 187.

Belgium

The Belgian Law of 2005[25] supplemented by a Royal Decree[26] about the activities of Launching, Flight Operation and Guidance of Space Objects, and revised by the law of 2013 enables the Belgian Government to ensure the legality and material safety of operational space activities performed under Belgian jurisdiction. It also develops an appropriate legal framework for the development of such activities in Belgium by implementing a registry for space objects and avoiding liability that could arise under application of the OST.[27] Activities covered under the law are "launching, flight operations and guidance of space objects" carried out by natural or legal persons in the zones placed under the jurisdiction or control of the Belgian State or using installations or property (personal or real) owned by the Belgian State or which are under its jurisdiction or its control. The application of the Belgian law can be extended by the means of an international agreement to any such activities carried out by Belgians, irrespective of the location where such activities are carried out. This provision conforms to a pragmatic understanding of the OST and enables Belgium to regulate space activities that might otherwise not fall under the scope of another space law. With this scope of application, it is obvious that space transportation is at heart of the Belgian law. Next to the launch, flight operation and guidance also fall into the scope of the law, consisting of any operation related to delivery in orbit, flying conditions, navigation or evolution of the space object in outer space, such as selection, control or correction of its orbit or trajectory. The return to Earth is not explicitly stated in the application field.

Similar to other national space legislations, such activities must have prior authorization from the Minister for Science Policy through the operator having effective control of the space object. Authorizations are delivered and held personally and as such cannot be subject to transfer without prior consent by the Minister. It is explicitly stated that such activities are to be conducted according to international (space) law. The authorization regime aims at ensuring the safety of people and property, protecting the environment, ensuring the optimal use of air space and outer space, and protecting the strategic, economic and financial interests of the Belgian State. It also satisfies the Belgian State's obligations under international law. The King and the Minister in charge can add further conditions. They may in particular impose the technical assistance of a third party, lay down conditions relating to the location of the activities or the location of the main establishment of the operator or create an obligation for insurance to be taken out in favor of third parties to cover damage that may result from authorized activities.

The law foresees a list of information that must be attached to the application for authorization, for which a standard form is prepared and made available online. An initial study is to be carried out to assess the potential impact of launching or operating the space object on the

---

25 *Law of 17 September 2005 on the Activities of Launching, Flight Operation or Guidance of Space Objects* (Belgian Official Journal, 16 November 2005), revised by the *Law of 1 December 2013* (Belgian Official Journal, 15 January 2014).

26 *Royal Decree implementing certain provisions of the Law of 17 September 2005 on the Activities of Launching Flight Operations and Guidance of Space Objects* (Belgian Official Journal, 11 April 2008); see also the reprinted text in Christian Brünner & Edith Walter, *National Space law – Development in Europe – Challenges for Small Countries* (Vienna: Koln, 2008) at 195ff.

27 See further analysis in Marboe/Hafner, *supra* note 9 at 36; also J.F. Mayence, "Granting Access to Outer Space: Rights and Responsibilities for States and their Citizens, An Alternative Approach to Article VI of the Outer Space Treaty, Notably Through the Belgian Space Legislation" in Frans G. Von der Dunk, ed, *National Space Legislation in Europe* (Leiden: Martinus Nijhoff Publishers, 2011) 73.

environment of Earth or in outer space. This study has to be conducted before the authorization is granted, but also at an intermediate stage, and may also be carried out when the object returns to the Earth's atmosphere. The use of nuclear energy must be disclosed in the application.

The authorization or its refusal will be notified within 90 days of application or 120 days if additional information is required. Experts designated by the Minister are charged with controlling the activities through access to relevant documentation and facilities. In the event of an infringement of the law or of non-compliance of the conditions set forth by the authorization, the latter can be withdrawn or suspended by the Minister. This applies also in the case of imperative reasons relating to public order, the safety of people or property. When the authorization is withdrawn or suspended after the space object has been launched into outer space, the Minister shall take all necessary measures in order to guarantee the safety of the operations, both with regard to the operator and his employees and third parties, as well as to ensure the protection of property and the environment. To that end, he may call upon the services of third parties or transfer the activities to another operator to ensure the continuity of flight and guidance operations and, if necessary, take action to deorbit or destroy the space object.

Finally, the law introduces a system of sharing the liability for the damage caused by the space object between the Belgian State and the operator. This system is based on the liability of the operator, which is limited to a certain amount. Any person carrying out activities regulated by the law without authorization shall be subject to a period of imprisonment up to one year and or a fine of up to €25,000.

The Netherlands

In the Netherlands, space activities are covered by the Space Activities Act, the Rules concerning Space Activities and the Establishment of a Registry of Space Objects from 2006.[28] This Act deals with private space activities for which the Dutch State can be considered responsible and can be held internationally liable according to international space law. The Act regulates registration, authorization and supervision of national space activities and organizes the regress of the State towards the operator in case of liability.[29] The Act does not apply to the six non-European islands for which the Kingdom of Netherlands retains jurisdiction.[30] For the purpose of the Act, space activities encompass the "launch, the flight operations and the guidance of space objects in outer space", performed in or from within the Netherlands or else or from a Dutch ship or Dutch aircraft, whereas the procurement of a launch and the operation of a launch facility are not covered by the Act. The Act may also be applied to Dutch nationals in the event of space activities being conducted from the territory of a State not party to the OST.

Under the Act, space activities shall not be conducted unless the Minister of Economic Affairs issues a license for this purpose. The implementation of the Act belongs to the domain of the national Telecom Agency. The Act lists a number of regulations or restrictions that the competent authority may attach to the license, for example for the purpose of the safety of persons and goods, the protection of the environment in outer space, financial security,

---

28 *Rules Concerning Space Activities and the Establishment of a Registry of Space Objects (Space Activities Act of June 13, 2006),* Neth, see the reprinted text in BrünnerWalter, *supra* note 30 at 201.
29 For a further analysis see Marboe/Hafner, *supra* note 9 at 38.
30 Ibid.

protection of public order, security of the State and the fulfillment of international obligations of the State. Furthermore, the Act describes that the license may be refused if such a license has been revoked owing to infringement of rules laid down or pursuant to the Act or if the applicant has not discharged his obligations under a previously issued license or if the applicant does not comply with the Act. Finally, the applicant has to have and maintain a maximal possible cover for the liability arising from the space activity that can reasonably be covered by insurance as determined by the Minister.

For the issue of a license, audits are conducted regarding the technical, legal and financial state of the activity. A decision on the delivery of the license has to be made within six months. The license can be revoked for the same reasons as it can be denied or if the conditions under which the license had been obtained have changed substantially. While the license is not transferable, the name entered in the registry may be adjusted if this corresponds to the legal form of the license-holder.

In case of disasters or if an incident occurs or has occurred that may jeopardize the safety of persons and goods, environmental protection in outer space, the maintenance of public order or national security, or otherwise cause damage, the license-holder shall immediately take reasonable measures to prevent or limit the consequences of that event. Finally, penalties are also foreseen for the infringement of the law.

Regarding liability, the Act states that the State is entitled to recover from the person whose space activity has caused the damage, for any sum it has to pay under application of Article VII of the OST or of the LIAB. In consequence, the license-holder is liable for damages caused by its space activities, up to the value of the sum insured.

Analysis

The analysis of the regulations reviewed above identifies a number of commonalities – often referred to as "building blocks" – especially because of their common international law background.

This is definitely the case for the transportation *in* outer space, that is where the satellite bus being considered a transportation vehicle. *De facto*, the international law background is also relevant for transportation *from* Earth *to* outer space, though one may have doubts whether Article VI of the OST directly applies to such transportation. When the OST speaks of "activities in outer space", it is questionable whether only activities *completely* taking place *in* outer space are mentioned.[31] This would exclude launches of space objects. However, none of the national space laws analyzed above have opted for such a restrictive interpretation. All such laws are applicable to the launch of space objects and basically set the same requirements for launches as they do for activities in outer space. Contrary to this, it is very much discussed whether the OST is also applicable – at least partly – to the last mode of transportation stated, that is transportation *from* Earth *to* outer space and *back* to Earth. The present chapter will not deal with this question. However it can be noticed that one State explicitly includes this mode of transportation in its legal framework, namely the US.

National laws relating to space activities establish authorization requirements, many of which are directly related to the obligations set forth in the OST, such as the obligation to avoid harmful contamination of outer space and adverse changes in the Earth environment (Article IX second sentence OST). Furthermore, all such national laws contain a "catch-all clause"

---

31   Gerhard, *supra* note 17 at 69; Reutzel, *supra* note 10 at 91.

ensuring that all private space activities are carried out in conformity with the OST. Through this mechanism, the dispositions set forth by the OST – even though an international treaty – are relevant for private actors.[32]

In addition, the laws reviewed define a legal basis for the competent authority to assess compliance with the law as well as with any conditions set forth by the authorization. Handling means (e.g. access rights, information obligations) and reaction measures in case of non-compliance (e.g. suspension or revocation of the authorization, fines and penalties) can also be entrusted to the implementing entity. Furthermore, such laws deal with the registration of objects launched into outer space. However, this is only relevant for that form of space transportation where the transportation vehicle remains in outer space, as registration measures only apply to objects launched into an Earth orbit or beyond. A transportation vehicle that brings cargo or people into outer space without itself entering an orbit does not have to be registered. Finally, parts of the national laws are related to liability issues, including – where so felt necessary by the legislator – a legal basis for the State to take recourse against the operator in case that State had to pay compensation according to Article VII of the OST for a damage caused by a space object.[33] The implementation of an authorization mechanism in national jurisdictions is a fundamental element for the transparency of the regulation of space activities and ensures that international space law provisions are observed during all space activities. The enactment of such legislation further increases transparency as to the rights and duties of private actors conducting space activities.

Although the legislation described above consists mainly of the "building blocks" mentioned above, a number of differences exist and need to be highlighted. For instance, while all States regulate the transportation *into* as well as the transportation *within* outer space, only a few States have regulated the return *from* outer space to Earth.

Furthermore, the level of detail in the authorization requirements varies. Some States have a rather prescriptive system, while other rely more on general and high-level requirements and on a performance-based system. More experienced States draw the conditions for assessing mission safety in a much more detailed manner, mostly directly in the law. A number of States not only look at the specific transportation activity, but also take into consideration the safety performance of the applicant with the same or similar transportation vehicles. Consequently, the level of involvement of the authorizing authority may be limited where the applicant has proven a good management system and a good safety record in the past. In terms of specific authorization requirements, only few States have set forth an explicit requirement to minimize or even avoid the creation of space debris.

Following, while almost all States require the applicant to hold a third-party liability insurance, the conditions for and the amount to be insured vary immensely. In addition, some States make a clear connection to the requirements set forth for State indemnification. The combination of both may lead to totally different financial risks in case of third-party damage: while in some jurisdictions the holder of an authorization has almost no third-party liability risk (except to bear the insurance premiums), in another jurisdiction a holder may face the full liability risk directly from the damaged party as well as indirectly via the launching State. In other jurisdictions, the legislator has established a more balanced approach for sharing the third-party liability risk between the holder of the authorization and the (launching) State. This

---

32   Marboe/Hafner, *supra* note 9 at 60.
33   A more detailed description about the building blocks of such national laws can be found in: Gerhard, *supra* note 6 at 72–77, with references to many other publications describing or analyzing such legislation.

is maybe the most interesting parameter for the legislator when considering fostering its national space industry. Finally, due to national particularities in administrative law, some differences exist and need to be highlighted in terms of application and surveillance fees, duration of the authorization procedure.

With those closing remarks regarding space transportation, it is now necessary to turn to the regulation of spaceports.

Spaceports

A "spaceport" (also referred to as range, launch site or spaceport) can be regarded as the base from which spacecraft are launched.[34] Following this, the term "spaceport" may refer to facilities involving devices for transportation *to, from* and *via* outer space.

While the building and operation of airports is heavily regulated in basically every national jurisdiction, the building and operation of spaceports is only regulated in a few States. Even States bearing spaceports on their territory do not necessarily provide for regulation and only regulate space transportation. However, a couple of States have established dedicated rules for the building and operation of spaceports.

The United States

In the US, the operation of spaceports, called launch and re-entry sites, is dealt with in 49 USC Chapter 701 as further implemented by 14 CFR Chapter III, §§ 400 et seq., Part 420 (launch sites) and Part 433 (re-entry sites). The main purposes of these regulations are the protection of public health and safety, safety of property, and national security and foreign policy interests of the US. To date, the competent authority (FAA/AST) has licensed eight commercial spaceport operations in the US.[35]

Regarding the scope of application of the regulation, the operator of a launch site and the operator of a re-entry site[36] need to hold a license. The regulation applies to anybody operating a site within the US, to US citizens and entities organized or existing under the laws of the US. Where the site is located outside US territory, the regulations can apply under certain circumstances to entities organized or existing under the laws of a foreign county, namely if a US citizen or entity holds the controlling interest in such entity operating a launch or re-entry site.

In order to be issued a license, the spaceport is subject to an environmental review,[37] a location review (risk review), an explosive site review (handling and storage of propellants) and the demonstration of the ability of the operator to comply with his responsibilities, namely related to the public access to the launch site, to agreements with air traffic and coast guard and the scheduling of hazardous activities of its customers (i.e. launch operators, payload processors, etc.). Furthermore the operator has to demonstrate flight and ground safety. The operator of a re-entry site has to demonstrate that the designated location of re-entry can be wholly

---

34   Oxford Dictionary, "Spaceport" online: Oxford Dictionary, www.oxforddictionaries.com.
35   Status October 2014, see Office of Commercial Space Transportation, "About the Office" online: Federal Aviation Administration www.faa.gov/about/office_org/headquarters_offices/ast/about.
36   A "re-entry site" is defined as a location on Earth to which a re-entry vehicle is intended to return, whereas a re-entry vehicles means a vehicle designed to return from Earth orbit or outer space to Earth, or a reusable launch vehicle designed to return from Earth orbit or outer space to Earth, substantially intact.
37   Following the requirements of the *National Environmental Policy ACT*, 42 USC 4321, as further implemented by 40 CFR parts 1500–1508.

contained and that the location is of sufficient size to contain landing impacts, including debris dispersion upon impact and any toxic release.[38]

Australia

In Australia, the operation of a launch facility is regulated by the 1998 Australian Space Activities Act.[39] The license covers a particular launch facility, a particular kind of launch vehicle and particular flight paths.

The operator has to demonstrate his competence to operate the launch facility and launch vehicles of that kind, that all necessary environmental approvals under Australian law have been obtained, and that an adequate environmental plan has been made for the construction and operation of the launch facility. Furthermore, the operator has to demonstrate that he has sufficient funding to construct and operate the launch facility, that the probability of the construction and operation of the launch facility causing substantial harm to public health or public safety or causing substantial damage to property is as low as reasonably practicable, and that there are no concerns for Australia's national security, foreign policy or international obligations. The Act furthermore specifies standard conditions for the license, such as for example to provide information to the competent authority, as requested, and to allow the competent authority (i.e. the appointed Launch Safety Officer) reasonable access to the facility and to any space object at the facility.[40]

France

The French Act on Space Operations[41] and the Decrees adopted for its application do not provide for a general regime for the operation of spaceports. Instead, the legislator only set certain conditions applicable for the exploitation of the Guiana Space Centre, especially through entrusting special missions to CNES and its President. Other common law provisions applicable to hazardous industrial activities and administrative law may also find application for ground range safety as the case may be. Labour Acts dedicated to workers' occupational health and safety remain applicable, as well as pyrotechnics safety regulations. Environmental protection acts set forth to control the pollution and accidental hazards of installations involving dangerous substances and focus on protection of the environment and the public are also relevant. Finally, regulations set up to prevent major accidents for high-level industrial risk establishments may also play a role.[42] These technical regulations and the specific regulations applicable to the Guiana Space Centre must be considered together for any launch activity

---

38 A summary of these requirements has been given e.g. by Laura Montgomery, "The Role of the Federal Aviation Administration in Regulating Spaceports" (May 2010), online: UNOOSA, www.unoosa.org/pdf/pres/lsc2010/tech-06.pdf; and Michael Mineiro, "Regulations and licensing of US commercial spaceports" in Joseph N. Pelton & Ram S. Jakhu, eds, *Space Safety Regulations and Standards* (Oxford: Elsevier, 2010) 161 at 161.

39 Commonwealth Consolidated Acts, *supra* note 18. *The Space Activities Regulations 2001* provide further detail about the licensing regime, in particular material to be submitted with an application.

40 A summary of these requirements has been given e.g. by Michael E. Davis, "Space Launch Safety in Australia" in Joseph N. Pelton & Ram S. Jakhu, eds, *Space Safety Regulations and Standards* (Oxford: Elsevier, 2010) 95 at 95.

41 Loi n° 2008-518, *supra note 20*.

42 Bruno Lazare & Jean-Pierre Trinchero, "Regulations and Licensing at the European Spaceport" in Joseph N. Pelton & Ram S. Jakhu, eds, *Space Safety Regulations and Standards* (Oxford: Elsevier, 2010) 177 at 179.

from the Guiana Space Centre. The French Act on Space Operations sets forth that any entity carrying out, under its responsibility and in an independent way, a space operation, has to obtain an authorization to do so. An operator of a spaceport is therefore also subject to this obligation and has to fulfill all general personal and technical requirements set forth in the law.[43]

In application of the French Act on Space Operations and its Decrees, the statutes of CNES have been modified and new prerogatives listed in the French Research Code.[44] CNES may exercise special police powers or administrative police in the name of the French government for the safe exploitation of the facilities of the Guiana Space Centre within the range perimeter. This perimeter includes the physical territory of the range and the vicinity up to the end of neutralization ground segment capability (close field flight safety area). CNES is therefore responsible for the enforcement of safety rules, a so-called "safeguard mission" consisting of control of the technical risks related to the preparation and performance of the launches from the Guiana Space Centre with the overall mission to ensure the safety of persons, goods and environment on Earth or during a launch. These rules apply to the transportation of the space object on site and tests and operations performed.

Further to this, CNES and its President are entrusted coercive powers in order to ensure safety of property and persons, which can take the form of evacuation of facilities, ceasing of activities or administrative fines.

Finally, under the authority of the government representative in the Département of Guiana, the President of CNES is entrusted with a coordination mission intending to ensure that all companies and other entities located and operating at the Guiana Space Centre abide by the applicable regulations. Regarding the safety mission at the Guiana Space Centre, the President of CNES shall set out applicable safety rules as regards the activities of designing, preparing, producing, storing and transporting space objects and their constitutive parts, as well as the tests and operations performed within the perimeter of the Guiana Space Centre. In particular, he shall aim at ensuring the overall coherence of the design requirements of ground facilities, roads and networks. He shall also define specific rules applicable on the ground and during the flight in order to ensure the protection of persons, property, public health and the environment. He shall also determine the areas to be protected during the launch phase and the limits of the flight corridor. He is furthermore responsible for checking the technical and meteorological conditions under which a launch can be carried out. Finally, he may adopt rules dealing with the destruction of the launcher in flight. The Space Centre Agreements concerning the operational management of the site remain in force and unchanged.

Analysis

So far, only a handful of States have enacted legislation specifically regulating the building and the operation of spaceports. Different from what has been said above about the purpose for regulating space transportation, the regulation of spaceports does not implement international space law requirements into national legislation. Those international treaties applicable to space activities do not address spaceports specifically. The regulatory purpose is therefore different and focuses mostly on domestic concerns. Still, the existing national legislations do present commonalities.

---

43 Since the requirements do not differ from those applicable to other space operators, it is referred to the description of the French legal framework applicable to space transportation above.
44 See further considerations in Lazare, *supra* note 27 at 210.

First, it must be noted that a fundamental element in all three jurisdictions described above is the protection of people and property on and around the spaceport, with regards the safety of its operation. The French regulation even explicitly mentions aspects of occupational health. Closely related and worth mentioning is the aspect of storing and handling of explosive material. Further, requirements related to the protection of the environment are set forth in all jurisdictions described. Finally, the technical and in some cases financial adequacy of the spaceport operator is checked by the licensing authority.

Second, in addition to this, isolated aspects only dealt with in some of these jurisdictions were highlighted, such as aspects related to the protection of national security and foreign policies, the control of access to the spaceport and the coordination with air traffic control.

The regulation of spaceports is still in its infancy, mostly because many spaceports are still being operated by States or with major shareholders thereof. It is expected that the growing participation of private spaceport operators in the space transportation field will lead to an enhanced need to regulate such activities. With States gaining more and more experience, further national dispositions regulating spaceports will evolve and mature, just as has been the case for the regulation of private space activities. Eventually, it may be expected that States will enter into international coordination of spaceport regulations.

Problems, gaps and future challenges

A challenge for the international and national space transportation regime is launches from the high seas or from the airspace above the high seas. The initial formation of the company Sea Launch and the launches performed from a platform on the high seas has shown that the international treaties bear uncertainties relating to the responsibility for such activities. This may result in unintended gaps regarding the compensation of damages caused by space objects launched from the high seas, in the case that none of the criteria for determining the launching State(s) can apply to the Contracting States of the OST and LIAB. Since national regulations reflect the international treaties, their application will not help to bridge that gap.

Quite often a gap also exists in the coordination between the launching States of a space object, especially when the space object is operated by a private organization and launched with a non-governmental launch service provider. Very often, at least two States qualify as launching States for one space object, for example because the launch is procured by the State of the private operator and the launch takes place from the territory of another State. In such constellations, only one of the launching States is entitled to register the space object in the international register and its national registry. The other launching State(s) is/are denied the right to do the same. The launching States therefore need to agree in which national registry the space object will be registered and which State registers it in the international register. Very often, launching States do not address the registration issue, so that the actual registration depends on whether and where the operator or the launch service provider (first) notifies the space object for registration. On many occasions, the space object is in the end registered in the State of its operator. However, in the case the State from whose territory the launch has taken place registers unilaterally all payloads in the international register without prior or further agreement with (the) other launching State(s), the space object cannot be registered anymore by the State of its operator. This may have severe consequences for the operation, considering the fact that the jurisdiction and control of the object remains with the launching State in whose registry the space object is registered.

A similar gap may also arise with regard to liability. All launching States are jointly liable for any damage that may be caused by the space object. If damage occurs, full compensation may be claimed from one of the launching States. While this State can then request indemnification from the other launching States, an agreement must be found on the internal apportioning of the liability. Once damage has occurred, it is obvious that the subsequent definition of adequate apportioning may be challenging. It therefore may be recommendable to address the matter prior to the launch, taking into consideration the several phases of the space operation in which the damage can occur (e.g. during launch, separation, operation) and under whose actual control the space object will be during those phases (under the control of the launch service provider or under the sole control of the operator).

Considering these two gaps, amendment or supplementation may be considered of the international treaties requesting or recommending to launching States to enter – prior to the launch – into an agreement on registration and apportioning of liability. At the level of national regulations, States may consider making the issue of a license subject to an agreement (or the unsuccessful negotiation, as this cannot be a showstopper for the activity) with other launching States(s).

Another gap in many regulations relating to space transportation today is assessment of its consequences for aspects related to the environment. Only few national regulations include in their licensing requirements environmental considerations. Aspects such as noise and emissions of the transportation vehicle may come to the fore in the future.

The set of rules applicable to space transportation is still very basic, especially looking at the international regime. Some States have developed a more sophisticated legal regime, but many national regulations are limited to high-level requirements. With the increase of the number of space activities it can be expected that also the regulations applicable to space transportation will become larger. Accentuating for instance the aspect of safety of space transportation, existing standards will more and more be linked to the licensing requirements and new standards will have to be developed. While today, the licensing of space transportation predominantly focuses on the activity as such, future rules may bring into the picture the organizations involved in the activity beforehand. States may consider approving the manufacturer or the operator. The involvement of such approved (and controlled) organization will then become a fundamental cornerstone also for the safety licensing of the activity. In that context, the establishment and codification of concepts such as safety management systems can play an important role.

A future challenge for the rules applicable to space transportation will also be long-distance transportation. On the basis of the emerging activities of tourist space (or suborbital) flights, design organizations and operators intend to develop long-distance transportation. Such transportation will inevitably cross outer space in a parabolic flight. This activity is essentially different from the modes of space transportation presently carried out and described above. Specific new sets of rules may be developed, building on existing elements of air and space transportation regulation, enriched with new considerations.[45]

A main challenge for spaceport regulation will be achieving an internationally harmonized set of rules. The international treaties and conventions related to the exploration and use of outer space have been developed in the late 1960s and 1970s at the beginning of the space age. They were laid down in a broad manner and have a limited scope. They do not apply to spaceports. Several spaceports exist around the globe and a new type of spaceports has emerged in the context of tourist space (or suborbital) flights. In the lack of a detailed and uniform international regulatory system, including technical standards, there is no guarantee of

---

45 For further consideration, see von der Dunk, *supra* note 4 at 200.

uniformity. There is a need to provide effective safety regulations as well as responsibility and liability mechanisms. Achieving international agreement on the design and operation of spaceports shows to be even more challenging than achieving such agreements for the exploration and use of outer space. Due to the immovability of spaceports and the fact that preoccupations linked to them are *per se* local rather than international, local considerations and existing partial regulations need to be taken into account. Harmonization through common European rules for aerodromes in Europe has shown this difficulty, despite the fact that national rules were established on the basis of agreed international standards.

A new challenge for spaceport regulations will also be the emerging activity of tourist space (or suborbital) flights. So far, spaceports predominantly provide the means for a vertical lift-off of rockets or other launch vehicles and are clearly separated from any conventional airport operation. With tourist space flights entering the market, the type of space transportation vehicle will change. Many operators plan to perform such activity with hybrid vehicles that will take off horizontally like any conventional aircraft. Spaceports from which such activities will take place will have different and additional aspects to regulate, which are much closer to those of a conventional airport, such as for example runway safety. Furthermore, operators of such tourist space flights or suborbital flights in the long run may want to take off from conventional airports, which will intermix requirements set forth for the takeoff (and landing) of aircraft and of such hybrid vehicles.[46] This will for instance put more emphasis on regulations related to the protection of third parties (aircraft passengers) as well as the storage of explosive materials at the air/spaceport.

Conclusions

As a *sine qua non* requisite for the realization of space missions, space transportation is at the heart of the international and national regulation of space activities. The question of the operation of spaceports bears an equivalent relevance and becomes ever so important with the growing implication of private actors in the launching business. Several space-faring nations have enacted national space legislation on the common basis of the UN Treaties dedicated to outer space activities. Although most Acts solely focus on space operations, the regulation of spaceports does appear in the legislation of several States. Considering the launch phase is the moment where space activities bear the highest risk, it is understandable that States want to mitigate the risks and regulate the (private) activities, even though there is no international obligation to do so.

The international framework is common to all States that are party to the treaties, which explains the commonalities between their national regulations. The fact that this international framework makes the States responsible and liable for private space activities is reason enough for enacting national regulations. A number of gaps between those have been identified. Especially matters such as the regulation of launches from the high seas, the coordination between launching States, space traffic management or the safety of the operation of spaceports call for discussion and action.

It is now time to take space law a small step ("for a man"...) further.

---

46   A technical description of possible forms of lift-offs can be found in ibid at 199ff.

Part IV

National regulation of navigational satellite systems

15
Regulation of navigational satellites in the United States

Andrea J. Harrington

US Global Positioning System (GPS)

The first US satellite navigation system was launched by the Department of Defense (DoD) in 1978. It was then called NAVSTAR (short for "Navigation System with Timing and Ranging"), which became fully operational in 1993.[1] The primary reasons for the development of this system, which cost between $10 and $12 billion dollars to field, were precise weapon delivery and standardization of the use of navigation systems within the US military.[2]

GPS is now considered to be the primary system for worldwide radionavigation.[3] It is a dual-use system that provides substantial military advantage as well as a basis for essential civil services.[4] There are two levels of GPS service that are available: the Standard Positioning Service available free to all global users and the Precise Positioning Service that provides a more accurate signal to designated users (primarily US military users).[5]

The space segment of the GPS consists of a "constellation of at least 24 US government satellites distributed in six orbital planes inclined 55° from the Equator in a Medium Earth Orbit (MEO) at about 20,200 kilometers (12,550 miles) and circling the Earth every 12 hours."[6] In order to meet their commitment to operate at least 24 satellites 95 percent of the time, the US has been maintaining as many as 31 operational satellites.[7] Additionally, the Wide Area Augmentation System "provides correction and integrity information intended to

---

1 "Global Positioning System History" (27 October 2012) online: *NASA*, www.nasa.gov/directorates/heo/scan/communications/policy/GPS_History.html.
2 Rick W. Sturdevant, "NAVSTAR, the Global Positioning System: A Sampling of Its Military, Civil, and Commercial Impact" online: NASA http://history.nasa.gov/sp4801-chapter17.pdf at 332.
3 Ibid. at 459.
4 "Presidential Decision Directive NSTC-6" (28 March 1996), White House at 1.
5 Paul B. Larsen, "Regulation of Global Navigation and Positioning Services in the United States" in *National Regulation of Space Activities,* Ram S. Jakhu, ed (New York City: Springer, 2010) at 462, at 459–460.
6 "Global Positioning System" (7 April 2014) online: *NASA,* www.nasa.gov/directorates/heo/scan/communications/policy/policy_pnt.html.
7 "Space Segment" online: *GPS.gov* www.gps.gov/systems/gps/space/.

improve positioning navigation and timing (PNT) service over the United States (US) and portions of Canada and Mexico."[8]

US GPS Policy and Regulation

The long and stable history of the GPS has built a foundation upon which the scientific and commercial sectors can confidently invest and innovate in the field of GPS technology, which has had an enormous impact on the day-to-day life of the world's civilian population.[9] In President Obama's 2010 National Space Policy, it was made clear that "[t]he United States must maintain its leadership in the service, provision, and use of global navigation satellite systems (GNSS)."[10] The key elements of this policy are to maintain free global, civil access to the GPS; encourage compatibility and interoperability with foreign GNSS systems; satisfy civil and national security needs including through augmentation by foreign GNSS systems; and invest in resiliency measures for GPS as well as relevant back-up systems.[11]

It is the belief of the US GPS provider that as long as it continues to provide signals to users free of charge that it should not bear international liability for issues relating to faulty service.[12] It is possible that liability may attach for claims that arise in the US and are brought in US federal court under the US Federal Tort Claims Act (FTCA).[13] Air traffic control has been determined to be an operational act, not a discretionary act, and thus can result in liability for negligence under the FTCA.[14] It has yet to be seen whether GPS will be similarly classified, as it functionally operates very differently from air traffic control.[15] With regard to products liability claims against the satellite manufacturer, it is possible that such claims may still fall under the immunity umbrella of the US government if the satellites are built to government specifications.[16]

The military context of the GPS is immediately apparent in the placement of the relevant law in Title 10 of the US Code, which pertains to Armed Forces. Section 2281 defines the key terms relating to the GPS. The term *Basic GPS services* includes the following components operated by the DoD: the satellites; the GPS signal-producing payloads; and the ground stations, data links, and command and control facilities.[17]

Thus, the space system is not the only portion of the GPS governed by this legislation. *GPS Standard Positioning Service* is the civil and commercial service provided by the GPS, defined in the 1996 Federal Radionavigation Plan.[18] The Federal Radionavigation Plan (FRP) is a regular report jointly prepared by the Secretaries of Defense, Transportation, and Homeland Security.[19]

8 "Global Positioning System Wide Area Augmentation System (WAAS) Performance Standard" (31 October 2008) online: GPS.gov, www.gps.gov/technical/ps/2008-WAAS-performance-standard.pdf at iv.
9 "United States Policy" online: *GPS.gov* www.gps.gov/policy.
10 "2010 National Space Policy" online: Whitehouse.gov www.whitehouse.gov/sites/default/files/national_space_policy_6-28-10.pdf at 5.
11 Ibid.
12 Larsen, *supra* note 5 at 463.
13 Ibid. at 463–464 citing 28 USC §2680(1); see also, *Smith v United States,* 507 US 197 (1993).
14 *United States v Union Trust,* 350 US 907 (1955).
15 Larsen, *supra* note 5 at 464.
16 Ibid., citing *Boyle v United Technologies* 487 US 500 (1988).
17 *Global Positioning System,* 10 USC §2281(a).
18 Ibid.
19 Ibid. §2281(c). This report was originally created prior to the existence of the Department of Homeland Security, and thus was prepared jointly by only the Secretaries of Defense and Transportation.

The FRP provides a comprehensive set of guidelines and policy imperatives for the use and management of GPS from a civilian and commercial perspective.[20] It is an audit of radionavigation and "an agreed statement and description of GPS" and GPS policy."[21]

Section 2281 charges the Secretary of Defense with the sustainment and operation of GPS capabilities for military purposes, including the development of measures to prevent hostile use of the system and ensure US military ability to effectively use the system.[22] In addition, the Secretary of Defense is charged with sustaining and operating the GPS Standard Positioning Service worldwide without direct user fees for commercial, civil, and scientific uses.[23] Again calling to the military importance of the GPS, it is clearly stated that restrictions proposed by other departments that would adversely affect the military use of GPS are impermissible.[24]

Management of the GPS

The Federal Radionavigation Plan also provides a framework for the management of the GPS. Three federal agencies play key roles in managing the GPS: the DoD acquires, operates and maintains the GPS, the Department of Transportation serves as the lead for civil GPS matters, and the Department of State coordinates foreign cooperation, consultations, and agreements with regard to GPS.[25] The Departments of Transportation and Defense have entered into a memorandum of understanding to govern their relationship with regard to GPS.[26] Specific elements of responsibility within the DoD are outlined in detail in a departmental directive.[27] The permanent Interagency GPS Executive Board was established in the FRP following Presidential Decision Directive NSTC-6.[28] Ultimately, the US President is the final decision-maker with regard to GPS, generally using the vehicle of Presidential Decision Directives.[29] The structure of the Interagency GPS Executive Board that manages the system is pictured in Figure 15.1.[30]

Threats to the GPS and future considerations

The resiliency of the GPS is important not only for military capabilities but also for essential civilian services. GPS capabilities provide a significant advantage to US military forces, but degradation to those capabilities could seriously hinder such operations.[31] Satellite operations are threatened not only by potential intentional hostile acts intended to "deny, degrade, deceive,

---

20 "1996 Federal Radionavigation Plan" online: University of New Brunswick http://gauss.gge.unb.ca/us1996frp.pdf at 1–1.
21 Larsen, *supra* note 5 at 461.
22 *Global Positioning System,* supra note 17, §2281(a).
23 Ibid. (b).
24 Ibid. (b)(5).
25 Presidential Decision Directive NSTC-6, *supra* note 4 at 3.
26 Larsen, *supra* note 5 at 461.
27 Department of Defense Directive Number 4650.05 (19 February 2008).
28 Presidential Decision Directive NSTC-6, *supra* note 4 at 2.
29 Larsen, *supra* note 5 at 460.
30 *1996 Federal Radionavigation Plan, supra* note 20 at 1–2.
31 Zachary T. Eytalis, "Disaggregation of Military Space Applications: Law and Policy Considerations" (13 May 2014), submitted to the 2nd Manfred Lachs International Conference on Global Space Governance held in Montreal, Canada on 29–31 May 2014.

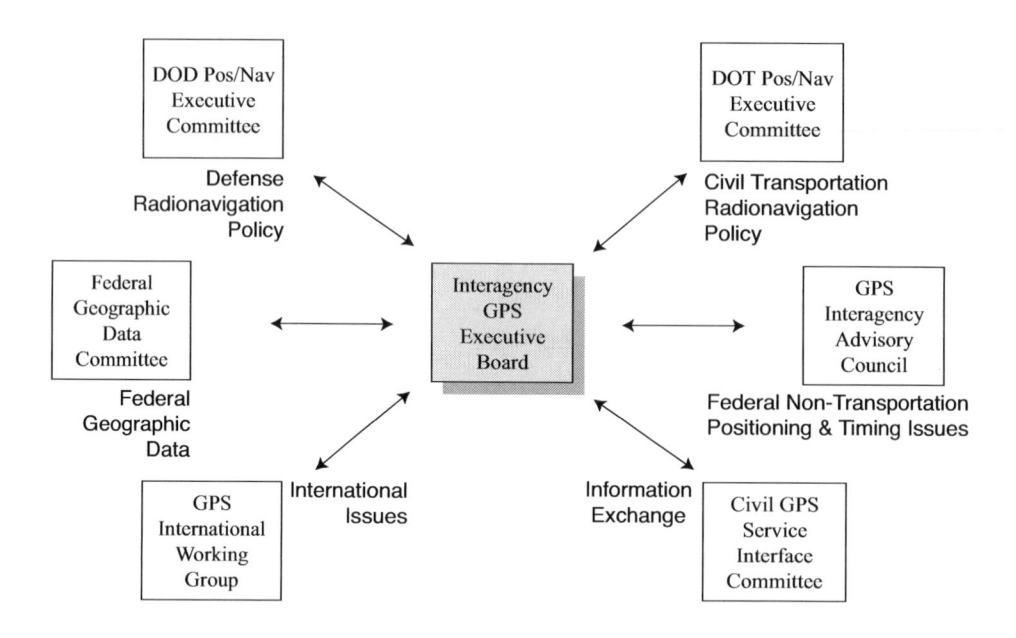

Figure 15.1 The structure of the Interagency GPS Executive Board

disrupt, or destroy space assets" but also by orbital congestion and space debris.[32] Signal encryption and strengthening technologies, physical hardening of satellites, and additional maneuvering capabilities are all traditional means of protecting space capabilities from attacks and accidental collisions or interference.

---

32   Ibid. citing U.S. Department of Defense and the Office of the Director of National Intelligence, *National Security Space Strategy*, January 2011 at 1.

16

Regulation of navigational satellites in Europe

Michael Chatzipanagiotis and Konstantina Liperi

In Europe, satellite navigation policy aims at providing the European Union (EU) with two satellite navigations systems: GALILEO and EGNOS. GALILEO will establish and operate the first GNSS for civilian use, primarily to contribute to EU's strategic autonomy. EGNOS (European Geostationary Navigation Overlay Service) improves in the European region the open signals from existing GNSS and is intended to also augment GALILEO.

GALILEO

GALILEO will consist of 30 satellites, orbiting in Medium Earth Orbit. Ten satellites will occupy each of three orbital planes, with one spare satellite in each plane. A global network of ground stations will manage the system.[1]

GALILEO will transmit radio navigation signals in four different operating frequencies: E1 (1559~1594 MHz), E6 (1260~1300 MHz), E5a (1164~1188 MHz) and E5b (1195~1219 MHz).[2] It is designed to offer five key services:[3]

(a) the Open Service (OS) will provide free improved global positioning, navigation and timing (PNT) services, mainly intended for high-volume satellite navigation applications;
(b) the Safety-of-Life (SoL) service, offered with a service guarantee,[4] will improve free OS

---

1 www.navipedia.net/index.php/Galileo_General_Introduction [All weblinks last visited on 17 Aug. 2016].
2 See UN Office for Outer Space Affairs (OOSA), *Current and Planned Global and Regional Navigation Satellite Systems and Satellite-based Augmentations Systems: International Committee on Global Navigation Satellite Systems Provider's Forum* (New York: UN, 2010) at 19–34, online: www.unoosa.org/pdf/publications/icg_ebook.pdf [UNOOSA].
3 See Art. 2(4) of *Regulation (EU) No. 1285/2013 of the European Parliament and of the Council of 11 December 2013 on the implementation and exploitation of European Satellite Navigation Systems and repealing Council Regulation (EC) No. 876/2002 and Regulation (EC) No. 683/2008 of the European Parliament and of the Council*, [2013] OJ, L 347/1[Regulation 1285/2013].
4 European Commission (EC) and European Space Agency (ESA), *Galileo: Mission High Level Definition*, 23 September 2002, para. 2.5.

signals for safety-critical applications and will also alert users, when the system fails to meet certain margins of accuracy (integrity monitoring);

(c) the Commercial Service (CS), also provided with a service guarantee,[5] is intended for professional and commercial applications, and will allow access to two additional signals for a higher data rate, offering enhanced performance compared to the OS;

(d) the Public Regulated Service (PRS) will provide, free of charge for the EU Member States (MS), encrypted signals to "government-authorized users",[6] who require high continuity of service with controlled access;

(e) the free of charge Search and Rescue (SAR) Service, a service for locating people in distress, will contribute to the international satellite system CORSPAS–SARSAT for SAR operations.[7]

GALILEO has been structured according to four different phases,[8] of which two phases have been completed: the Definition phase and the Development and Validation phase. The Deployment phase comprises the construction, establishment and protection of all space-based and ground-based infrastructure, and is scheduled to be completed by the end of 2020. The Exploitation phase includes the management, maintenance, continuous improvement, evolution and protection of system infrastructure, as well as all other activities necessary for the smooth operation of the system. This phase is scheduled to start gradually with the provision of the initial services for OS, SAR service and PRS. The target is for the system to reach Full Operational Capability (FOC) by the end of 2020.

The first four operational satellites have been constructed and launched during the In-orbit Validation phase. The rest of the satellites are scheduled to be launched during the Deployment and Exploitation phases. FOC 5 and 6 Satellites have been launched in August 2014, but were entered into a wrong orbit following an orbital injection anomaly.[9] In total, 14 satellites are now part of the constellation. The successful launch of FOC 13 and 14 satellites in May 2016, paved the way for the provision of Galileo initial services to the users by the end of 2016.[10]

EGNOS

EGNOS comprises three geostationary satellites and ground stations, and has been operational since 2009. It disseminates signals on GPS L1 frequency (1575.42 MHz), providing correction and integrity monitoring of global positioning system (GPS) services. It offers an Open Service (OS), a Safety-of-Life (SoL) service and a Commercial Service (CS).[11] The OS has been

---

5 Ibid.
6 See *Decision No. 1104/2011/EU of the European Parliament and of the Council of 25 October 2011 on the Rules for Access to the Public Regulated Service provided by the Global Navigation Satellite System established under the Galileo Programme*, [2011] OJ, L 287/1.
7 See more at http://ec.europa.eu/growth/sectors/space/galileo/sar/index_en.htm.
8 See Regulation 1285/2013, *supra* note 3, art 4.
9 www.arianespace.com/press-release/soyuz-flight-vs09-independent-inquiry-board-announces-definitive-conclusions-concerning-the-fregat-upper-stage-anomaly/. Navigation signals from these satellites are to be used for test purposes. Whether these satellites will become part of the Galileo constellation is still to be decided. See more at http://spaceref.com/news/viewpr.html?pid=49264.
10 http://ec.europa.eu/growth/tools-databases/newsroom/cf/itemdetail.cfm?item_id=8194&lang=en&tpa_id=0&title=EU-successfully-launches-two-Galileo-satellites.
11 See on EGNOS and its services www.navipedia.net/index.php/EGNOS_General_Introduction#cite_note-7.

continuously available since 2009 and provides positioning precision by correcting errors in GPS signals.[12] The SoL service mainly supports civil aviation applications and has been declared available since 2011, after the Certification of European Satellite Services Provider (ESSP) as an Air Navigation Service Provider.[13] As to the CS, the EGNOS Data Access Service (EDAS) is offered, which is a terrestrial commercial service that transmits data in real time and is the single point of access for data collected and generated by the EGNOS infrastructure over Europe and North Africa.[14]

EGNOS services cover mainly EU MS, although not all of them are covered yet. Its coverage could also extend to non-EU countries.[15]

Administration and organization

GALILEO was initially structured to be managed and operated as a Public-Private Partnership (PPP), to allow financing by both private and public funds.[16] However, after the PPP efforts failed, it was decided in 2008 to finance the system entirely by public funds.[17]

Under the new governance scheme, the EU is the owner of all tangible and intangible assets created or developed under the GALILEO and EGNOS programs.[18] The European Commission (EC) acts as the program manager on behalf of the EU and possesses the overall responsibility for the programs, while political oversight rests with the Council of the EU and the European Parliament.[19] Given that the development of the programs involves different stakeholders, the EC is also entrusted with ensuring a clear division of duties and responsibilities, in particular with the European Space Agency (ESA) and the European GNSS Agency (GSA).[20]

ESA joined forces with EU for the development of a coherent and progressive overall European Space Policy under a Framework Agreement signed in 2004.[21] Satellite navigation is one of the fields of cooperation. The initial Definition, Development and Validation phases of the GALILEO program were carried out by ESA on a co-funded basis with the EC. The deployment phase is being managed and funded by the EC, while ESA acts as design and procurement agent.[22] By virtue of delegation agreements signed with the EC, the GSA is

---

12 www.navipedia.net/index.php/EGNOS_Open_Service.
13 www.navipedia.net/index.php/EGNOS_Safety_of_Life_Service.
14 See www.egnos-portal.eu/discover-egnos/services/edas.
15 See Regulation 1285/2013, *supra* note 3, recital 12, art 2(5).
16 See Council Regulation (EC) No. 876/2002 of 21 May 2002 setting up the Galileo Joint Undertaking [2002] OJ, l 138/1.
17 See *Regulation (EC) No. 683/2008 of The European Parliament and of The Council of 9 July 2008 on the further implementation of the European satellite navigation programmes (EGNOS and Galileo)*, [2008] OJ, L196/1; *Regulation (EU) No. 912/2010 of the European Parliament and of the Council of 22 September 2010 setting up the European GNSS Agency, repealing Council Regulation (EC) No. 1321/2004 on the Establishment of Structures for the Management of the European Satellite Radio Navigation Programmes and amending Regulation (EC) No. 683/2008 of the European Parliament and of the Council*, [2010] OJ, L 276/11; *Regulation (EU) No. 512/2014 of the European Parliament and the Council of 16 April 2014 amending Regulation (EU) No. 912/2010 setting up the European GNSS Agency*, [2014] OJ, L 150/72.
18 Regulation 1285/2013, *supra* note 3, art 6.
19 Ibid., art 12.
20 Ibid.
21 *Council Decision of 29 April 2004 on the conclusion of the Framework Agreement between the European Community and the European Space Agency (2004/578/EC)*, [2004] OJ, L 261/63.
22 *Delegation Agreement between the EU, represented by the European Commission and the European Space Agency on the Deployment Phase of the European Satellite Radionavigation Programme Galileo*, 16 July 2014.

currently responsible for, *inter alia*, the commercialization and exploitation of the systems, their security accreditation, the promotion of satellite navigation applications and services, as well as the implementation in the space sector of the research program Horizon 2020.[23]

EGNOS services are currently delivered by the European Satellite Services Provider (ESSP SAS), which was founded by seven air navigation service providers.[24] The GSA has been the EGNOS program manager since 2014,[25] while ESA is the design and procurement agent working on behalf of the EC.[26]

Liability

Attributing liability for GNSS failures is complex owing to the EU's distinctive governance structure. The EU owns the GALILEO and EGNOS systems.[27] According to Article 189 of the Treaty on the Functioning of the EU (TFEU),[28] the EU enjoys a shared competence on space matters with its Member States (MS). Art. 47 of the Treaty on European Union (TEU)[29] provides that the EU has a legal personality separate from that of its MS, and a separate legal system and jurisdiction over issues of substantive European law.[30]

It is suggested that at least in the event of contractual provision of PNT services, the EU might be liable for failure to provide appropriate services or to oversee such provision.[31] The EU's contractual liability is governed by the law designated in the contract, as Article 340(1) TFEU clarifies. Eventual extra-contractual liability will be governed by Article 340(2) TFEU,[32] such claims being subject to the exclusive jurisdiction of the Court of Justice of the EU.[33] The EU, as a supranational organization with distinct legal personality, enjoys sovereign immunity; however, its exact legal basis and extent are disputed.[34]

---

23   *Delegation Agreement between the EU, represented by the European Commission and the European GNSS Agency on the exploitation of the Galileo programme*, 2 October 2014; *Delegation Agreement between the EU, represented by the European Commission and the European GNSS Agency on the implementation of Horizon 2020*, April 2014.
24   See details at www.essp-sas.eu.
25   *Delegation Agreement between the EU, represented by the European Commission and the European GNSS Agency on the exploitation of the ENGOS Programme*, 16 April 2014.
26   See ec.europa.eu/growth/sectors/space/egnos/.
27   Regulation 1285/2013, *supra* note 3, arts 12, 13.
28   *Consolidated version of the Treaty on the Functioning of the European Union* [2012] OJ, C 326/47 [*TFEU*].
29   Consolidated version of the Treaty on European Union [2012] OJ C 326/13.
30   See Lesley Jane Smith, "Legal Aspects of Satellite Navigation" in Frans von der Dunk & Fabio Tronchetti, eds, *Handbook of Space Law* (Cheltenham: Edward Elgar Publishing, 2015) 554 at 561–62.
31   See in this regard *Regulation 1285/2013*, *supra* note 3, recital 22, which recognizes explicitly the possibility of EU liability arising out of the ownership of the systems.
32   Art 340(2) provides:

   In the case of non-contractual liability, the Union shall, in accordance with the general principles common to the laws of the Member States, make good any damage caused by its institutions or by its servants in the performance of their duties.

33   Art 268 TFEU.
34   See Anna Massuti, "Legal Problems Arising from the Installation of the Galileo and EGNOS Ground Stations in Non-EU Countries" (2012) 37:1 Air & Space L 65; Ramses A Wessel, "Immunities of the European Union" (2013-2014) 10:2 Intl Organizations L Rev 395.

International agreements

The EC is responsible for managing, on behalf of the EU, relationships with third countries and international organizations.[35] In 2004, an agreement was signed with the United States on interoperability and compatibility between GPS and GALILEO.[36] Moreover, the EU has signed several cooperation agreements with various countries, e.g. China, Israel, India, Ukraine, Morocco, Korea, Norway, and Switzerland.[37]

Spectrum protection

Each EU MS is responsible for its radio spectrum management. However, national policies reflect decisions and practices proposed by European and international bodies. The Electronic Communications Committee (ECC) of the European Conference of Postal and Telecommunications Administrations (CEPT) proposes practices that contribute to spectrum harmonization, standardization and cooperation, reflecting the work done by the ITU.[38] Within the EU, the EU Radio Spectrum Committee and the EU Radio Spectrum Policy Group put forward binding decisions on harmonization and technical issues.[39] Moreover, the European Telecommunications Standards Institute (ETSI), a non-profit organization led by industry, plays a critical role in developing standards in information and communications technologies.[40]

Concerning GALILEO and EGNOS, the EU has been entrusted with the power to negotiate frequency issues, as well as to negotiate and conclude international compatibility and interoperability agreements.[41] By virtue of their competence in spectrum, the EU MS support the EU in its activities on GNSS spectrum availability and protection.[42]

Privacy protection

The EU has entrusted the EC with the protection of personal data and privacy during the design, implementation and exploitation of the European GNSS systems.[43] Moreover, all EU legislation on personal data protection is applicable to data collected during the implementation and exploitation of the systems.[44]

---

35 See *Regulation 1285/2013*, *supra* note 3, arts 12(2)(c), 29.
36 Agreement on The Promotion, Provision and Use of Galileo and GPS Satellite-Based Navigation Systems And Related Applications, signed at Dublin, on 26 June 2004.
37 www.gsa.europa.eu/galileo/international-co-operation.
38 See www.cept.org/ecc/.
39 See https://ec.europa.eu/digital-single-market/eus-spectrum-policy-framework.
40 See www.etsi.org/about.
41 See UNOOSA, *supra* note 2 at 33.
42 *Decision No. 243/2012/EU of the European Parliament and of the Council of 14 March 2012 establishing a Multiannual Radio Spectrum Policy Programme* [2012] OJ, L 81/7, art 8.
43 Regulation 1285/2013, *supra* note 3, art 31(1).
44 Ibid., art 31(2). For details on current EU legislation on data protection, see *Regulation (EC) No. 45/2001 of the European Parliament and of the Council of 18 December 2000 on the Protection of Individuals with regard to the Processing of Personal Data by the Community Institutions and Bodies and on the Free Movement of such Data*, [2001] OJ, L 8/1; *Directive 95/46/EC of the European Parliament and of the Council of 24 October 1995 on the Protection of Individuals with regard to the Processing of Personal Data and on the Free Movement of such Data*, [1995] OJ, L 281/31.

17

Regulation of navigational satellites in the Russian Federation

Olga A. Volynskaya

The GLObal NAvigation Satellite System (GLONASS) is a Russian space-based satellite navigation system, a highly intelligent product of the military production complex provided for wide application by civil users. GLONASS, as a basis of the national coordinate-time and navigation support, is designed for coordinate setting, velocity measurement, and accurate time setting by various categories of users all over the world.

Structure and main features of GLONASS

The current structure of GLONASS consists of five parts:

- space complex (including ground-based control complex);
- fundamental support systems complex;
- augmentation systems complex;
- posterior high-accuracy ephemeris computation and time correction system; and
- user equipment complex.

The orbital constellation of GLONASS is composed of 27 spacecraft, 23 of which are being used as intended, one object is performing a flight test program, one is undergoing technical maintenance, and another two are reserved in orbit.[1] Such configuration ensures a global non-stop navigation support to an unlimited number of diverse users, both mobile and fixed, throughout the year and at any time of day, irrespective of meteorological conditions, and it covers the whole Earth surface and heights up to 2,000 km.[2]

---

1 Composition of the GLONASS orbital constellation (as of 11.08.2016) www.glonass-iac.ru/GLONASS/GLONASS satellites, unlike Global Positioning System (GPS) satellites, are not synchronized with the Earth's rotation which ensures their greater stability. Thus, the GLONASS constellation does not require additional corrections during its active lifetime. Launches of new satellites in the near-future will be determined by functional necessity, The Federal Space Agency – Information Analytical Centre www.glonass-iac.ru/guide/mainsystems.php.
2 NIS GLONASS www.nis-glonass.ru/glonass/description-of-technology/

The accuracy of GLONASS has improved during the last five years and, at the moment, amounts to 2.6 meters at the global scale.[3] The improvement of this figure will largely depend on the development of a wide-zone Differential Correction and Monitoring System (DCMS), which currently unites 18 reference stations functioning in Russian territory, three stations in Antarctica, and one in Brazil.[4] Negotiations are underway on deploying up to 50 such reference stations in 36 foreign States, which would provide for the enhanced accuracy of navigational measurements up to decimeter and centimeter levels. Russian and foreign users have a guaranteed unrestricted and free access to civil GLONASS signals at any point of the Earth's surface.[5]

Russian national policy on GNSS

The progress of satellite navigation is a strategic direction of the socio-economic development of Russia[6] and one of the main priorities of the national space policy.[7] A new trend in this respect is the development of private-public partnership in the field of navigational services by promoting opportunities for the creation of commercial space navigation means.

In 2011, a new Federal Task Program "Maintenance, development and use of GLONASS for the period 2012–2020" was adopted setting forth a whole range of tasks on the enhancement of accuracy and integrity of navigation services, guaranteed solution of navigation tasks in the conditions of limited visibility of spacecraft, interferences and jamming, as well as promotion of effective applications of GLONASS in different areas. The Task Program provides for the development of all structural elements of the GLONASS system.

Sub-federal entities of Russia also implement their own regional task programs reflecting specific features of each entity targeted at the maximum effect of using GLONASS technologies.

Regulatory regime of GNSS in Russia

A variety of acts regulating different aspects related to GNSS in Russia are organized in a clear hierarchy. The top tier is formed by three Federal Laws concerning: navigation activities,[8] calculation of time,[9] and State Automated Information System ERA-GLONASS.[10] The second tier comprises over 30 more detailed regulatory acts by the President and the Government of the Russian Federation. The third tier is about 20 Acts adopted by ministries and agencies

---

3 Accuracy of GLONASS measurements, the Russian differential correction and monitoring system www.sdcm.ru/smglo/stparam?version=rus&repdate&site=extern.
4 One more station is being planned for placement in Antarctica and another one in the Crimea.
5 See *Decree of the President of the Russian Federation: On utilization of the Global Navigation Satellite System GLONASS in the interests of social-economic development of the Russian Federation*, Decree No. 638, 17 May 2007, para 1.
6 *Concept of the Long-term Socio-economic Development of the Russian Federation for the Period till 2020*, Russian Federation Government Executive Order No. 1662-r, 17 November 2008, c V, s 2.
7 *Keystones of State Policy of the Russian Federation in the Area of Space Activities for the Period till 2030 and with a Further Perspective*, President of the Russian Federation Approval No. Pr-906, 19 April 2013, paras 7b, 7f.
8 *Federal Law On Navigation Activities*, Law No. 22-FZ, 14 February 2009 [*On Navigation*].
9 *Federal Law On Calculation of Time*, Law No. 107-FZ, 3 June 2011.
10 *Federal Law On State Automated Information System ERA-GLONASS*, Law No. 395-FZ, 28 December 2013 [*On State Automated*].

within their respective areas of competence. There are also over 100 intergovernmental and national standards concerning the use of GLONASS and related issues.[11]

The Federal Law on navigation activities states that GLONASS is the property of Russia and fully financed by the federal budget.[12] All federal, regional, and local executive authorities are obliged to use GLONASS: to ensure efficient traffic management; to ensure safe transportation of passengers, as well as special and dangerous goods; and in the course of geodetic and cadastre works.[13]

In Russia, radio control is exercised by the Radio Frequency Service.[14] In order to study radiation parameters of radioelectronic means or high-frequency devices suspected of infringing the established radio frequency spectrum regime, the Radio Frequency Service is empowered to record signals from the controlled radiation source. Such recording can only serve as proof that the order of radio frequency spectrum utilization was breached. The users of the radiation source must eliminate it according to the existing legislation. Otherwise, they will be liable for the violation of privacy or breach of personal, family, commercial or other secrets protected by law.[15]

Administration of GNSS in the Russian Federation

Article 7 of the Federal Law on navigation activities provides that the President of the Russian Federation determines the main directions of State policy on GNSS, which have to be implemented by the government.[16] The GLONASS system is controlled by the Ministry of Defense. General coordination of works on maintenance, development, and use of GLONASS is organized by Roscosmos jointly with the Ministry of Defense, the Ministry of Transportation, the Ministry of Foreign Affairs, the Ministry of Communications, and other federal agencies and ministries within their powers, in accordance with Decree No. 323 of 30 April 2008 of the Government of Russia.[17]

The Joint Stock Company, "Russian Space Systems", is the leading organization in Russia responsible for the creation, production, enhancement, and target use of GLONASS.[18]

GLONASS applications

The capabilities of the modern GLONASS system are widely used in different areas of the socio-economic sphere and provide for:[19]

- navigation of ground, air, marine, river, and space vehicles;

---

11 Consultant Plus legal reference system.
12 Article 5(1) of the *Federal Law On Navigation Activities,* Law No. 22-FZ, 14 February 2009.
13 *On Navigation, supra* note 6, art 4(1); *Decree of the Government of the Russian Federation,* No. 641, 25 August 2008, para 1(d).
14 *Decree of the Government of the Russian Federation: On the Radio Frequency Service,* No. 434, 14 May 2014.
15 *Federal Law On Communications,* Law No. 126-FZ, 7 July 2003, art 25(2).
16 *On Navigation, supra* note 6, art 7.
17 *Decree of the Government of the Russian Federation: On the Authority of Federal Executive Bodies in the Area of Maintenance, Development and Use of GLONASS in the Interests of Defense and Security, Socio-economic Development of the Russian Federation and International Cooperation, as well as for Scientific Purposes,* No. 323, 30 April 2008.
18 For more information, see Russian Space Systems, "About", online: Russian Space Systems www.spacecorp.ru/en/about.
19 NIS GLONASS www.nis-glonass.ru/glonass/description-of-technology/.

- traffic control of all types of transport, including transportation of valuable or dangerous cargo;
- fisheries control in territorial waters;
- search and rescue operations;
- monitoring of the environment;
- geodetic survey and positioning of geographic objects with a centimeter precision for installation of oil and gas pipelines and power lines, as well as for construction works;
- synchronization of communications and telecommunications systems, and in the power industry;
- solution of fundamental geophysical tasks and in the mining industry;
- automated land cultivation;
- personal navigation for individual users.

In 2014, an innovation-based ERA-GLONASS project has been launched,[20] whose main task is to establish an emergency response system within the whole territory of Russia. Innovative national navigational technologies already improve transport safety and, in the near-future, will become the basis of the Russian transportation infrastructure.

International cooperation of Russia in the area of GNSS

International cooperation in the field of satellite navigation is a crucial part of the national space policy of Russia. According to the Concept of international cooperation in the area of GNSS and augmentation systems,[21] GLONASS implies special importance and responsibility of Russia, thus underscoring its increasing role in solving issues of the global sustainable development. International cooperation of Russia is targeted at promoting competitiveness of GLONASS in the world market, expanding its use all over the world and providing for its compatibility and complementarity with other GNSS.[22]

The international legal base of international cooperation of Russia on GNSS consists of cooperation agreements (with Brazil, India, Cuba, Ukraine, etc.), memoranda of understanding (with the People's Republic of China), joint statements on the joint use and development of GLONASS (with the United States), and deployment of DCMS reference stations on a mutual basis. Special attention is given to the prospective implementation of the ERA-GLONASS system (Belarus and Kazakhstan), joint ventures (Venezuela, South Africa, Turkey, and others), production of user navigation equipment and other GLONASS-based competitive products in Russia and abroad.

GLONASS has become the cornerstone of the coordinate-timing and navigational support of Russia and an inalienable element of the international GNSS infrastructure. GLONASS services are used on a wider scale each year and the system has gained international recognition. GLONASS is a strategic resource and national pride of the Russian Federation.

---

20 See *On State Automated, supra* note 8.
21 *Concept of International Cooperation in the Area of GNSS and Augmentation Systems*, Russian Federation Government Executive Order No. SI-P7-2407, 19 April 2008.
22 *Concept of International Cooperation in the Area of GNSS and Augmentation Systems*, Para. 6.

18

Regulation of navigational satellites in China

Guoyu Wang

Status

Up to 2015 the following developments concerning the Beidou System have taken place: the BeiDou System provides stable services to the Asia-Pacific area; the first next-generation BeiDou Satellite aimed at verifying new technologies has been successfully launched; the deployment of the BeiDou augmentation system for all-round scale has been completed; the construction of the rest of the BeiDou System progresses steadily. Meanwhile, China has issued a series of policies to support and guide the development of the BeiDou System and industry. By contrast, the satellite navigation legislation lags behind. The specific regulations are expected and are under extensive discussion.

The BeiDou System has been developing in line with the "three-step roadmap" and the thinking "from regional to global, and from active to passive", and forms a development path as region-highlighted, world-oriented, with its own features. The first step, 1994–2000, was about the provision of regional active services; the second step, 2004–2012, concerned the provision of regional passive services; the third step, 2013–2020, deals with the provision of global passive services.[1]

The first next-generation BeiDou Satellite was successfully launched on March 30, 2015 and the number of the constellation's satellites in-orbit reached 17. The space segment, when completed, will consist of five GEO satellites, three IGSO satellites and 27 MEO satellites around 2020, which could offer worldwide services.[2]

The BeiDou System is able to provide four types of services: open, authorized, wide area differential and short-message services. The positioning accuracy more accurate than 10 meters (the positioning accuracy is better than 5 meters in regions with low geographic latitude), the timing accuracy surpasses 20 nanoseconds and the velocity accuracy is faster than 0.2 meters per second.

---

[1] www.beidou.gov.cn/2011/12/06/20111206e06b16a3bd8846459b969277a3317e5b.html.
[2] Operation and Development of BeiDou Navigation Satellite System, China Satellite Navigation Office, Technical Presentation at the 56th UNCOPUOS Main Session, 2015.06. 10, available at www.unoosa.org/pdf/pres/copuos2015/copuos2015tech03E.pdf.

Satellite navigation regulation in China

The applications of the system focus on three aspects: industrialization of fundamental products, promoting industrial/regional demonstrative applications and mass market applications.[3]

Administration, organization and general policy framework

China Satellite Navigation Office is the authority responsible for the system administration. The objectives, fundamental policies and basic principles as to BeiDou System have been addressed by the China Satellite Navigation Office in many fora.

As for the objectives, the BeiDou System is committed:[4]

- To provide continuous, stable and reliable positioning, navigation and timing services to global users;
- To meet the requirements derived from national security, economic and social development sectors, to accelerate IT applications and the transformation of economic development methods, and to improve both economic and social benefits;
- To serve the world and benefit mankind through joint efforts with other navigation satellite systems across the globe.

As addressed by the China Satellite Navigation Office, BeiDou's fundamental policies include:

- Providing open services free of charge for users; maintaining and perfecting the system constantly, improving service performance continuously, and offering services with higher quality;
- Releasing open service performance specifications on schedule, bringing the function of government and market to full play, promoting innovation, popularization and internationalization of BeiDou/GNSS applications, and laying foundation for the national strategic emerging industries.
- Adhering to the concept of development and win-win cooperation, realizing compatibility and interoperability between BeiDou and other GNSS, fully exploiting the system efficiency and increasing users' benefits.

The Basic Principles are formulated as:

- Openness: the BeiDou System will offer open services free of charge for global users.
- Independence: develop and operate BeiDou System independently.
- Compatibility: the BeiDou System is devoted to pursuing compatibility and interoperability with other navigation satellite systems, and enables users to obtain better services.
- Speed of implementation: the BeiDou System is established step by step in the light of current Chinese technical and economic conditions.

More specific policies relevant to the promotion of the satellite navigation industry are contained in several governmental documents at different levels, such as "Some opinions on promoting the development of the satellite application industry (2007)",[5] "The Twelfth Five-

3   Ibid.
4   Ibid.
5   The Chinese version is available at: www.cnsa.gov.cn/n1081/n308674/n308957/309797.html. It is issued by the State Commission of Science and Technology for National Defense Industry and National Development and Reform Commission.

year Plan of National Strategic Emerging Industry Development (2012)",[6] "The Mid- and Long-Term Development Plan of the National Satellite Navigation Industry (2013)",[7] "Some Opinions on National Administration of Surveying, Mapping and Geoinformation on Promotion and Application of the BeiDou Satellite Navigation System (2014)".[8]

The research and formulation of navigation policies on promoting the development of BeiDou Satellite Navigation Industry is being carried on by the China Satellite Navigation Office, together with the National Development and Reform Commission, the Ministry of Industry and Information Technology, the Ministry of Science and Technology and other institutions. The National Standard System for the BeiDou Satellite (Version 1.0) has been reviewed and formulated. Eight national standards have been applied for approval, while 18 standards of the BeiDou project are expected to be published.

International agreements

The BeiDou System has been the subject of several international agreements relating to bilateral and multilateral cooperation, cooperation on applications, international standardization and technical exchanges.

The Project Committee on China-Russia GNSS cooperation has been founded and the first bilateral round table meeting on GNSS cooperation has been held. The MOU on China-Russia cooperation in the field of satellite navigation has been signed. The on-site survey has been completed including GLONASS ground stations in China and BeiDou ground stations in Russia, and the Joint Statement on compatibility and interoperability has also been released.

The first bilateral meeting of the China-U.S. civil GNSS cooperation has been held. The cooperation mechanism between BeiDou and GPS has been established, and the Joint Statement between these two systems have been signed.

The frequency coordination towards navigation frequency channel between BeiDou and GALILEO has been completed, and the cooperation mechanism between these systems is under discussion.[9]

As to multilateral cooperation, China actively undertakes international responsibility, to promote the compatibility and co-existence among navigation satellite systems. China actively participated in the 9th Meeting of the ICG, IWG, ITU and other GNSS activities organized by the United Nations and is deeply involved in the coordination of important subjects, such as the compatibility and interoperability among basic systems and satellite-bases augmentation systems, service performance parameter, GNSS monitoring and assessment, etc.

Meanwhile, the application cooperation has been conducted effectively. China advocates integrated applications of multiple systems, and is pushing forward the BeiDou services to spread abroad and benefit neighboring countries, including applying the BeiDou System to the national strategic planning of jointly building the Silk Road Economic Belt and the twenty-first-century Maritime Silk Road, namely "One Belt and One Road". In this case, China had carried out cooperation with Korea, Australia, Indonesia, Pakistan, Thailand, Singapore, the

6 The Chinese version is available at: www.china.com.cn/policy/txt/2012-07/20/content_25968625.html. It is issued by the State Council.
7 The Chinese version of this plan is available at: www.beidou.gov.cn/2013/10/11/2013101108357d7dac88404c85f9badcfd90bf49.html. It is issued by the State Council.
8 The Chinese version of this plan is available at: www.sbsm.gov.cn/article/chyw/201403/20140300008799.shtml.
9 The Chinese text of relevant news is available at: http://politics.chinaso.com/detail/20150318/1000200003270801426641843161652161_1.html (last accessed 18 March 2015).

United Arab States, Nigeria, and so on. Besides, China continues to hold the BeiDou ASEAN Tour and the BeiDou Asia-Pacific Tour, and promoting system applications.

At the level of international standardization, China actively promoted the recognition of the BeiDou System in international organizations, such as IMO, ICAO and 3GPP. The Ship-borne BeiDou-based Receivers Performance Standard has been approved by IMO, making the BeiDou System the third navigation satellite system worldwide recognized by IMO. China promoted the establishment of the BeiDou Working Group affiliated to the hundred and fourth professional committee of RTCM. Sixteen technical standards which support the positioning function of the BeiDou System have been approved by the third and fourth Generation Partnership Projects.

Regarding technical exchange, China encourages academic exchanges, hosts the China Satellite Navigation Conference, and continues to attend other international academic conferences in the field of satellite navigation. In the aspect of International Exchange and Training, the CSNO has organized three sessions of master's program specializing in satellite navigation, while 44 trainees from eight countries in the Asia-Pacific and African areas have been recruited. Three sessions of the Summer School on Frontier Technology in the field of satellite navigation have been successfully organized, and more than 200 trainees have completed their studies.

Spectrum protection

The Radio Regulation of the People's Republic of China (The Regulation) was promulgated by the State Council and the Central Military Commission in 1993.[10] The Exposure Draft of this Regulation was issued in 2014, which was drafted by the Ministry of Industry and Information Technology and the Headquarters of the General Staff.[11] The Regulation and the Exposure Draft offer a comprehensive framework and specific provisions for spectrum protection.

The state radio regulatory organ under the State Council is responsible for the nationwide management of the radio frequency spectrum,[12] while the radio regulatory organ of the Chinese People's Liberation Army is responsible for radio regulation in the military.[13]

The administrative and criminal provisions are contained in greater detail in the Exposure Draft than in the Regulation, with regard to radio jamming, the establishment and operation of an unapproved radio station, the change of authorized characteristics the transmission and/or reception of signals that are not related to its operation without permission, and so on.[14]

The relevant organs under the State Council assign frequency bands and frequencies allotted to them and notify the state radio regulatory organ or relevant local radio regulatory organs for the record.[15]

Besides, the specific regulations and standards on protection of signals and frequencies of the BeiDou System are under discussion, as highlighted and required by "The Mid- and Long-Term Development Plan of National Satellite Navigation Industry" inaugurated in 2013.[16]

10 Its non-official English version is available at: www.chinalawedu.com/news/23223/23228/23913.htm (last accessed 9 January 2016).
11 Its Chinese version is available at: www.pkulaw.cn/fulltext_form.aspx?Gid=6365 (last accessed 9 January 2016).
12 Article 8, The Exposure Draft.
13 Article 9, The Exposure Draft.
14 See Articles 43, 44, 46 of The Regulation and Articles 68–78 of The Exposure Draft.
15 Articles 22 of The Regulation.
16 See *Supra* note 7.

Privacy protection

China has no specific rules about location privacy, use of personal data involving positioning by State authorities or private entities/natural persons.

At the substantive law level, the right to privacy is protected according to the Tort Liability Law of the People's Republic of China (the Tort Law), which came into force in 2010.[17] However, it remains unclear whether location privacy is protected under this law. It is suggested that the Tort Law should be modified to clarify the scope of the privacy right, in which location privacy should be included.[18]

At the conflict-of-laws level, the characterization and compensation of tort regarding privacy is governed by the law of the State in which the injured party habitually resides.[19]

---

17 Article 6, the Chinese version is available at: www.chinadmd.com/file/o6uwstixcpxswrstz6scz3zu_1.html (last accessed 9 January 2016).
18 See Caixia Yang, *Application of Satellite Positioning Technology and Protection of Privacy Right*, 2 Journal of Harbin Institute of Technology (Social Sciences Edition) (2011), p. 47.
19 "Infringement on the right of name, portrait, reputation or privacy or other rights of personality via the Internet or by other means shall be governed by laws of the habitual residence of the infringed party." Article 46 of the law of the People's Republic of China on Application of Laws to Foreign-Related Civil Relations, entered into force in 2011.

19
Regulation of navigational satellites in Japan

Souichirou Kozuka

QZSS: Japan's regional navigational satellite system

Japan is developing its regional navigational satellite system, called the Quasi-Zenith Satellite System (QZSS) as one of its primary space projects. The project officially started in 2003, following the proposal by the Japan Business Federation (*Keidanren*) in 2001 and the subsequent report by the specialized committee of the Council for Science and Technology (now Council for Science, Technology, and Innovation) endorsing the project.[1] The most recent Basic Plan on Space Policy of Japan confirms the commitment to advance the project further for both civil and national security purposes.

The aim of QZSS is to complement and augment the Global Positioning System (GPS) of the United States (US). Its basic idea is to form a constellation of a minimum of three satellites on the geosynchronous orbit (GSO) on different planes, so that at least one of them is observed from Japan's near zenith all the time. The high elevation angle is considered important, because tall buildings in the cities and high mountains in the rural areas can hinder observation of a satellite if it is on the low elevation angle.[2] The first satellite "Michibiki" was launched on September 11, 2010 with the aim of technological validation. The current plan is to realize the constellation of four satellites by the end of the fiscal year 2017, which will be expanded to a constellation of seven by 2023.[3]

As to the legal framework, the Basic Space Law stipulates that the government shall take necessary measures to use satellites for the "improvement of the lives of the citizenry", and refers to the promotion of information systems on positioning as one of such measures.[4]

---

1 For the background of the QZSS project, see Saadia M Pekkanen & Paul Kallender-Umezu, *In Defense of Japan: From the Market to the Military in Space Policy* (Stanford, CA: Stanford University Press, 2010) at 197–201.
2 See Teruhisa Tsujino, "Effectiveness of the Quasi-Zenith Satellite System in Ubiquitous Positioning" (2005) 16 Science & Technology Trends – Q Rev (NISTEP) 88 at 94.
3 Government of Japan, *Basic Plan on Space Policy* (9 January 2015). On the Basic Plan, see generally Naohiro Kitamura, "The Impact of Japan's New Space Policy on Business", *Space Law Newsletter of the International Bar Association Legal Practice Division* 15 (October 2015) 10.
4 Japan, *Fundamental Act of Outer Space*, Law No. 43 of 2008, art 13 [Basic Space Law]. See Setsuko Aoki, "Current Status and Recent Developments of Japan's National Space Law and Its Relevance to Pacific Rim Space Law and Activities" (2009) 35:2 J Space L 363 at 378–79.

Furthermore, the Basic Act on the Advancement of Utilizing Geospatial Information (the so-called National Spatial Data Infrastructure (NSDI) Law) provides that the Japanese government shall take necessary measures to advance utilization of geospatial information by:

- using the credible positioning satellite services;
- proceeding with the research and development technology, and the feasibility study concerning satellite positioning; and
- promoting its application.[5]

Bodies responsible for the operation of QZSS

Since the Cabinet decision on September 30, 2011,[6] the Cabinet Administration Office (CAO) is responsible for the development, maintenance, and operation of the QZSS. The CAO then decided to procure the ground segment of the system, including the maintenance of the satellites, from the private sector under the Private Finance Initiative (PFI) scheme. Bids were invited in December 2012, and the group led by the NEC Corporation was nominated as the provider of the service. The group later formed Quasi-Zenith Satellite System Services Inc. (QSS) as the contractor. The procurement of three satellites with Rubidium clocks to be launched by 2017 was contracted separately by the CAO, also through a public auction.

The procurement by the PFI scheme is carried out according to the PFI Act in Japan. The Act was first enacted in 1999, but was amended to cover space projects only as late as 2011.[7] The Act enables the contractor to offer services for a fee, if it is allowed in the procurement conditions. In the case of QZSS, however, no such service is anticipated. According to the procurement conditions, the scheme is *build, own and operate* (BOO): the contractor owns the facilities, and is responsible for their renewal and maintenance, when necessary.

The PFI procurement of the ground facilities includes exploration of the potential application services. However, no agreement with the application service provider is anticipated by either the CAO or QSS. Therefore, any entity may offer services on its own, pursuant to the performance standard and interface specifications, though the latter two documents are distributed only to the members of QZS System User Society (QSUS). The membership of QSUS is open to any individual for free. In order to establish contacts with the industry, another organization named QZSS Business Innovation Council (QBIC) was established in 2013.[8]

The international and domestic framework for the use of signals

The signals of QZSS are compatible with GPS. In this sense, QZSS is complementary to GPS by adding "more satellites" to the NAVSTAR constellation. Furthermore, QZSS satellites send

---

5   Japan, *Basic Act on the Advancement of Utilizing Geospatial Information*, Act No. 63 of May 30, 2007, arts 20, 21 [NSDI Law]. See Hiroshi Murakami, "New Legislation on NSDI in Japan: 'Basic Act on the Advancement of Utilizing Geospatial Information'", *Bulletin of the Geographical Survey Institute* 55 (2008) 1.
6   Japan, *Basic Policy on the Implementation of the Operational Quasi-Zenith Satellite System (QZSS) Project*, Cabinet Decision (30 September 2011), online: Cabinet Administration Office www8.cao.go.jp/space/english/basicpolicy.html.
7   See Souichirou Kozuka, "The first PFI procurement of satellites in Japan" *Space Law Newsletter of the International Bar Association Legal Practice Division* 13 (June 2013) 17.
8   The QBIC is administered by the Satellite Positioning Research and Application Center (SPAC) as the secretariat. For the history of SPAC, see Pekkanen & Kallender-Umezu, *supra* note 1 at 199.

augmentation signals to improve precision of positioning by GPS. The Japanese Ministry of Land, Infrastructure, and Transport (MLIT) is responsible for the augmentation services by using the latter signals, as MLIT currently administers the GPS augmentation system, the Multi-Functional Transport Satellite (MTSAT) Satellite Augmentation System (MSAS).

The basis for these collaborations with GPS is the Joint Statement by the US government and the Japanese government on cooperation in the use of GPS of September 22, 1998.[9] Based on this Joint Statement, the two governments have held regular consultations at least once a year since 1998. The US government has supported the development of QZSS by Japan through these meetings. The consultation has established working groups focused on the coordination of various technical issues with regard to complementing and augmenting the GPS by QZSS.

There is no specific regulation concerning spoofing or jamming of QZSS signals. Generally, the radio signals are protected by the Radio Act under Japanese law. The user of a device that transmits radio waves must be licensed as a radio operator to operate a radio station.[10] To be duly licensed, the radio waves emitted from the radio station shall not disturb the function of other radio equipment.[11]

No specific statute exists, either, concerning civil liability that could arise in the event of errors in signals. The services will be offered subject to the disclaimer to be included in the performance standard and interface specifications, which emphasize the need for the service provider or device manufacturer to incorporate redundancies, where necessary, to avoid liabilities.

The interests of users: privacy concerns

As the use of GPS develops in Japan, the privacy of the user with respect to his or her positioning has become a big issue. There is no doubt that the track record of a person's position is personal information to be protected by the Act on the Protection of Personal Information.[12] As regards the Act's application to the telecommunication carriers, the Ministry of Internal Affairs and Communications issued Guidelines on the Protection of Personal Information in the Telecommunications Business. The guidelines are not applicable to the owner or operator of the QZSS satellites, since none of them is a telecommunication service provider. On the other hand, not only the information acquired through QZSS but also that from GPS and other GNSS is covered.

While the general rule under the guidelines requires that the carrier acquire the personal information only when it is necessary for providing a telecommunications service, the special provision on positioning information (which by its definition is limited to the information concerning the holder of a mobile device) permits acquisition of such information subject to a judicial warrant for the purposes of crime investigation as well as at the request of a rescuing

---

9   US, The White House, Immediate Release, "Joint Statement by the Government of the United States of America and the Government of Japan on Cooperation in the Use of the Global Positioning System" (22 September 1998), online: US Coast Guard Navigation Center www.navcen.uscg.gov/?pageName=whsjapan. For the background, see Tsujino, *supra* note 2 at 92.
10   See Japan, *Radio Law*, Law No. 131 of May 2, 1950, as amended most recently by Law No. 26 of 2015, art 4.
11   See ibid., art 29.
12   Japan, *Act on the Protection of Personal Information*, Act No. 57 of 2003.

agency in the event of an imminent serious danger to the person.[13] Whether the police may use the GNSS receiver without a warrant is disputed, and the decisions of the lower court are divided.[14]

---

13 Japan, *Guidelines on the Protection of Personal Information in the Telecommunications Business*, art 26.
14 See e.g. Osaka District Court, 5 June 2015 [unpublished], where the Court excluded the positioning track record acquired by attaching the GPS receiver on the car without a warrant as evidence acquired through an unreasonable search. The Court, however, later in Osaka District Court, 10 July 2015 [unpublished] held that the accused was found guilty even without the excluded evidence. Another judge of the same Court in Osaka District Court, 27 January 2015 [unpublished] earlier held that such acquisition of GPS information is not unreasonable.

20
Regulation of navigational satellites in India

Ranjana Kaul

Introduction

The importance of satellite navigation, positioning, and timing in modern economies cannot be emphasized enough. Like timing, the ability to locate one's position or the position of various objects accurately and reliably is a growing need because of wide-ranging implications for traffic management, security, the environment, the management of natural resources, and the provision of personal services (civil and commercial).

This chapter briefly describes Indian satellite navigation program, which was conceived in 2004, and its potential within the overall context of India's economic development. Importantly, the paper addresses national regulations and policies related to navigational satellites system, which comprises of GAGAN (GPS Aided Geostationary Augmentation Navigation satellite) and IRNSS (Indian Regional Navigation Satellite System).

Background

In 1947, India adopted a firmly democratic political system and an economic policy, tending towards a mixed economy.[1] The 1990 economic reforms partially de-regulated certain sectors, including the civil aviation and telecommunications sectors. However, national strategic sectors, including 'atomic energy' and 'space activities' with emphasis on self-reliance, have always remained under the direct control of the central government and its agencies.

Among five core space treaties, India has ratified the Outer Space Treaty,[2] acceded to three others,[3] and is a signatory to the Moon Agreement.[4] The Indian space agency, called Indian

---

1   See Jean Drèze & Amartya Sen, *An Uncertain Glory: India and its Contradictions* (Princeton, NJ: Princeton University Press, 2013) at 1.
2   *Treaty on Principles Governing the Activities of States in the Exploration and Use of Outer Space, Including the Moon and Other Celestial Bodies*, 27 January 1967, 610 UNTS 205 (entered into force for India on 18 January 1982) [*Outer Space Treaty*].
3   *Agreement on the Rescue of Astronauts, the Return of Astronauts and the Return of Objects Launched into Outer Space*, 22 April 1968, 672 UNTS 119 (India acceded on 9 July 1979) [*Rescue Agreement*]; *Convention on the International Liability for Damage Caused by Space Objects*, 29 March 1972, 961 UNTS 187 (India acceded on 9 July 1979) [*Liability Convention*]; *Convention on Registration of Objects Launched into Outer Space*, 14 January 1975, 1023 UNTS 15 (India acceded on 1982) [*Registration Convention*].

Space Research Organization (ISRO),[5] conducts space activities, under the supervision of the Department of Space (DOS)[6] and the Space Commission of India.[7] Under the purview of the Prime Minister's Office (PMO), the space program gradually expanded in the development and validation of indigenous space capability. Thus, even in the absence of a national space policy and national space law, the national space program progressed in a planned manner. The Citizen Charter[8] is the only document, which outlines the national vision of India, informs this State's space program.

Indian Satellite Navigation Program

The Planning Commission approved the national satellite navigation space program during the eleventh Five Year Plan (2007–12) period, given the importance and potential of commercial and strategic applications of satellite-based Positioning, Navigation, and Timing (PNT) systems.[9]

Mission goals

The two specific goals for the Indian Satellite Navigation Program are:[10]

A. Implementation of the Indian Satellite Based Augmentation System (SBAS) – GAGAN – for civil aviation over the Indian airspace and flight information region (FIR) at an estimated cost of approximately Rs. 7.74 billion (US$ 120 million); and (ii) Development of a Global Navigation Satellite System (GNSS) compatible receiver, and promotion of position, navigation and timing services for a variety of application areas in India.
B. Implementation of the Indian Regional Navigation Satellite System (IRNSS) for critical national applications.

GAGAN for CNS/ATM and GNSS

International Civil Aviation Organization (ICAO)[11] has endorsed worldwide implementation of GNSS[12] to facilitate seamless navigation across geographical boundaries. GSAT-8 and GSAT-

---

4   *Agreement Governing the Activities of States on the Moon and Other Celestial Bodies*, 18 December 1979, 1363 UNTS 3 (India signed the Agreement on 18 January 1982) [*Moon Agreement*].
5   To learn more about the Organization, see Indian Space Research Organization, online: ISRO www.isro.org.
6   To learn more about the Department, see India, Department of Space, online: DOS www.dos.gov.in.
7   To learn more about the Commission, see Indian Space Research Organization, "Space Commission", online: ISRO www.isro.gov.in/about-isro/space-commission.
8   See India, Department of Space, "Citizen Charter", online: DOS dos.gov.in/node/25.
9   See Indian Space Research Organization, *Report of Working Group on "Space" on the Eleventh Five Year Plan Proposals 2007–2012 for Indian Space Programme* (Bangalore: ISRO) at 24–27, online: Department of Science and Technology of India www.dst.gov.in/sites/default/files/rep-space.pdf.
10 See ibid. at 25.
11 International Civil Aviation Organization (ICAO) is a specialized UN Agency and is headquartered in Montreal, Canada. To learn more about ICAO, see online: ICAO www.icao.int/Pages/default.aspx.
12 ICAO, *Global Air Navigation Plan*, 4th ed, ICAO Doc 9750-AN/963 (Montreal: ICAO, 2013), online: ICAO www.icao.int/publications/Documents/9750_4ed_en.pdf.

Satellite navigation regulation in India

10 GAGAN[13] payloads were launched successfully from Kourou, French Guiana in 2011, on board Ariane-5 launch vehicles. The two-channel GAGAN payloads provide SATNAV services with accuracy and integrity required for civil aviation applications over Indian airspace and FIR. When GAGAN is fully operational, India will be the fourth country in the world to offer safety-of-life space based satellite navigation services for civil aviation.

ICAO APV 1 certification[14] for GAGAN SIS is cardinal for improving operational efficiency of the State's ailing civil aviation sector.[15] The SBAS will provide civil aviation with communication, navigation, surveillance and air traffic management (CNS/ATM) service resulting in improved safety for approaches through vertical guidance, especially in adverse weather conditions.

GAGAN also provides service for non-civil aviation end users, facilitating acceleration of economic development across India. Applications of GAGAN will include:

(i) navigation and safety enhancement of the Indian railways, roadways, ships, and spacecraft;
(ii) geographic data collection;
(iii) natural resource and land management; and
(iv) location based services for mobile, tourism, adventure sports, etc.

In July 2014, the Indian government constituted an Inter-Ministerial Group under the chairmanship of the Ministry of Civil Aviation to examine sector-specific utilization of the GAGAN system for its use in non-aviation sectors, and to develop appropriate work programs using GAGAN signals that could benefit a variety of users.[16]

Indian Regional Navigation Satellite System (IRNSS)

The IRNSS is an independent regional navigation satellite system, capable of providing equivalent stand-alone position accuracies, which will function under civil control. It consists of seven satellites – three in the geostationary (GSO) orbit and four in a non-GSO orbit – inclined at 29 degrees to the equator, the ground segment, and user receivers.[17] The IRNSS

---

13   GAGAN is the acronym for the Indian GPS Aided Geo Augmented Navigation system. India Satellite Based Augmentation System (SBAS) GAGAN was certified by DGCA-to RNP0.1 (Required Navigation Performance, 0.1 Nautical Mile) service level on December 30, 2013. The certification will enable any aircraft fitted with SBAS equipment to use the GAGAN signal in space for En-Route Navigation and Non-Precision Approaches without vertical guidance over Indian air space. See online: ISRO www.isro.org.
14   Regulatory Approach Interoperability implementing rule on Performance Based Navigation: *(SES/IOP/PBN/REGAP/1.0: Annexure A)* APV1 and APV 2 (Approach Vertical) guidance Certification is issued by ICAO. These certifications are important to achieve global interoperability for civil aviation.
15   See "India's airlines are heading for another big loss in FY2015 – but good news may be around the corner" in Centre for Aviation (CAPA), *Aviation Outlook Report for India* (2014). Although airlines expanded on the back demand in 2014, India's airlines lost an estimated US$ 10.6 billion in the last seven years and have a combined debt of US$ 15.83. Clearly, the sector is growing, but not profitably.
16   Jitesh, "IMG constituted to examine potential of GAGAN in Non-Aviation Sectors", *Jagran Josh* (8 July 2014), online: Jagran Josh www.jagranjosh.com/current-affairs/img-constituted-to-examine-potential-of-gagan-in-nonaviation-sectors-1404797426-1.
17   The full constellation of seven IRNSS navigation satellites have been launched. These are IRNSS 1A on 1-7-2013; IRNSS 1B on 4-4-2014; IRNSS 1C on 10-11-2014; IRNSS 1D on 28-3-2015; IRNSS 1E on 16-1-2016; IRNSS 1F on 10-3-2016; and IRNSS 1G on 28-4-2016. www.isro.gov.in.

provides two types of services to users with accurate position information service, both within Indian territory and in an area extending beyond 1,500 km from India's territorial boundary: (i) Standard Positioning Service (SPS); and (ii) Restricted Service (RS), with a position accuracy of better than 20 m in the primary service area.

Emphasis on self-reliance is the primary reason for developing IRNSS, the indigenous regional navigation satellite system. This was, in particular context to easing dependence on foreign navigation systems, accelerated by failure to secure military grade signals from the European navigational program GALILEO, in which India had initially planned to participate.[18]

International and domestic regulatory regime

International liability in space

India is internationally responsible and liable for damage caused in outer space in terms of the Outer Space Treaty[19] read with the Liability Convention.[20] As such, if fault for damage caused in outer space is attributed to Indian assets, the government is liable to pay damages/compensation to the affected State party to these international instruments. In this context, it is necessary to recall that international treaties are not self-executing under four specific circumstances enumerated in the Exceptions to Article 51 of the Constitution of India.[21] Exception 1 is related to the government's ability to fulfill international obligation related to liability provisions discussed above. This Exception postulates the mandatory requirement of a specific domestic law to entitle government to withdraw money from the Consolidated Fund of India (federal treasury) to make payment to a foreign power to fulfill India's international treaty obligation.[22]

The GAGAN payloads are jointly owned by ISRO and Airports Authority of India (AAI), although the operational functions are clearly demarcated: ISRO to operate the space segment; and air navigation signal provider (ANSP) as the GAGAN SIS service provider to end users, both government and private entities. No information is available in public domain as to attribution of liability between the two entities in the context of GAGAN space assets, if any. In any event, the ownership of the space assets lies in the government of India which remains internationally liable and responsible for damage caused in outer space by GAGAN and IRNSS assets.[23]

---

18 Seema Singh, "ISRO's Very Own GPS is Ready", *Forbes [India]* (1 July 2013), online: Forbes forbesindia.com/printcontent/35511.
19 See *Outer Space Treaty*, *supra* note 2, arts VI, VII.
20 See *Liability Convention*, *supra* note 3.
21 *The Constitution of India*, art 51:

> The State shall endeavour to—
> (a) promote international peace and security;
> (b) maintain just and honourable relations between nations;
> (c) foster respect for international law and treaty obligations in the dealings of organized peoples with one another; and
> (d) encourage settlement of international disputes by arbitration.

22 See ibid. Exception 1 to Article 51 was upheld in the decision of the Allahabad High Court in *Moti Lal v U.P.*, 1951 All.257 F.B.
23 See *Outer Space Treaty*, *supra* note 2, arts VI, VII; *Liability Convention*, *supra* note 3.

GNSS: liability of air navigation signal provider (ANSP)

ICAO has debated the question of whether liability can be or should be attributed to the GNSS CNS/ATM signal provider and to the GNSS CNS/ATM augmentation signal service provider in the case of international civil aviation. The issue remains unsettled. Admittedly, the consequences of deficiency in or absence of the service, for any reason or in any manner whatsoever, will result in financial loss and damage of incalculable proportions to the user. Ordinarily, principles of the law of contract would indicate that failure on the part of a signal provider to provide signals at the contracted level, causing the user to suffer damage, would trigger liability to pay compensation for loss caused to the user, in terms of the agreement or governing law. However, the unique circumstance in which global satellite navigation CNS/ATM is contemplated to be made available to users around the world has rendered problematic, if not impossible, establishment of a framework to govern the legal liability of the GNSS/SBAS signal providers. The United States (US) and the European Union (EU) have adopted contrary positions. The US opposes the establishment of an international convention on GNSS on the ground that, because global positioning system (GPS) is being provided free of cost, no liability could be attached for loss caused or damage suffered by users on account of failure/absence/degradation/inaccuracy of the GPS. The US is supported by a number of developing countries, non-EU States among others who are setting up their own global (China) or regional satellite navigation systems (India, Japan, Brazil). The EU, however, favors strongly an international convention for GNSS. This is because, unlike the US GPS, the GALILEO GNSS system is designed as a commercial enterprise, as such will impose a user charge. For the EU, therefore, the issue of 'liability' and 'compensation' are important and critical.

Liability of the Airports Authority of India (AAI)

The *liability* principle qua GAGAN is accepted as being within the domain of 'signals-in-the-sky' (SIS), and not within the domain of traditional earth-based radar/station systems currently used for aeronautical navigation service in India. The AAI, the national ANSP, will provide GPS augmented GAGAN SIS for CNS/ATM to civil aviation users in Indian airspace and FIR. AAI will also provide service to non-civil aviation users. The AAI is also the national airport operator.

The Airports Authority of India Act (AAI Act)[24] governs AAI operations as airport operator and as ANSP,[25] without demarcating functional responsibilities. As such, ANSP is viewed as adjunct to AAI's principal function as an airport operator. In this context, the protection against prosecution granted to ANSP/AAI officers and employees, under provisions of sections 32 and 33 of the AAI Act[26] continues to be a matter of concern. In fact, the defense under those sections advanced by the AAI in *Geetha Jethani* case[27] was struck down by the Supreme Court

---

24 *Airports Authority of India Act, 1994*, No. 55 of 1994 (India) [*AAI Act*].
25 Ibid. Under *AAI Act, ibid*, s 12, treaty obligations relevant to air navigation service provision contained in the *Convention on International Civil Aviation*, 7 December 1944, 15 UNTS 295, ICAO Doc 7300/9 [*Chicago Convention*], arts 15, 28, have been harmonized. Thus, the AAI is the national ANSP for civil aviation within Indian airspace and also within the Flight Information Region (FIR) as required by ICAO, and charges a user fee on a non-discriminatory basis.
26 See *AAI Act, supra* note 24, ss 32, 33.
27 *Geetha Jethani v Airport Authority of India and Ors*, 2004 (3) CPJ 106 (Indian National Consumer Disputes Redressal Commission).

of India, which held AAI to be *a service provider* for the purpose of definition under section 2(o) of the Consumer Protection Act.[28] The Supreme Court directed AAI to pay compensation for the wrongful death of the eight-year-old international passenger at Delhi airport, in terms of the limit prescribed in the First Schedule of the Carriage by Air Act, 1972.[29]

Geetha Jethani is significant when we consider liability of AAI, in its capacity as the ANSP; particularly, as the service provider of GAGAN SIS. Even otherwise, ANSP imposes user charge for providing air navigation signals in Indian FIR[30] bringing it under the Consumer Protection Act. It is clear that the obvious absence of an appropriate or relevant legal mechanism to govern ANSP in the AAI Act makes the statute wholly inadequate for regulating ANSP that provides satellite navigation services via GAGAN SIS for CNS/ATM. Going ahead, it is suggested that a new law will be required to regulate satellite navigation based ANSP, providing therein a fault based liability regime, with burden of proof on the claimant. It is difficult to foresee whether India will set out new laws which will attribute liability for damage caused on account of deficiency or defective service of GAGAN SIS service provided to end users, irrespective of whether the US GPS signals, provided free of cost to GAGAN, were inherently deficient or defective.

IRNSS policy and legal regime

A policy on distribution of IRNSS signals has not yet been announced. A responsive law and procedural regime would best serve to realize the full potential of IRNSS and GAGAN non-civil aviation end users. A robust commercial satellite navigation sector depends on certainty and predictability of policy and regulations.

Conclusion

India recognizes that satellite navigation will be one of the key enabling technologies in the twenty-first century, albeit this State does not have a legal regime in place to govern satellite navigation activities. Presently, the full contours of the multimodal dimensions of the GAGAN and GNSS are not known. Be that as it may, in defining the contours of policy and legal regime to be made applicable to the national ANSP, the Inter-Ministerial Group and the Ministry of Civil Aviation of India will be required to address several issues, preparatory to the roll out of GAGAN. The opportunity to allow the growth of a robust space industry beckons, especially keeping in mind that a growing number of young entrepreneurs are providing useful products in India based on GPS signals.

---

28 *Consumer Protection Act*, 1986 (India).
29 *Carriage by Air Act*, 1972 (India) (First Schedule harmonizes Warsaw Convention 1929 in context to carrier liability).
30 See *Chicago Convention, supra* note 25, arts 15, 28.

Part V
Commercial aspects of space law

21
Law related to intellectual property and transfer of technology*

Yun Zhao

Introduction

Space activities are no longer a field monopolized only by States; more and more private entities and individuals show great interest and many have already set their feet in the field. The participation of private entities no doubt adds to the complexity in the regulatory regime for such activities, especially with regard to the civil and commercial aspects of the legal regime. Intellectual property protection is one major issue requiring serious consideration. It offers private entities the exclusive right to use and profit from the use of their own inventions and creations. Through years of development, a complete set of rules has already been put in place to provide a transparent regime for intellectual property protection; however, it is not clear whether these rules apply to activities conducted in outer space, where no State can claim sovereignty. This situation is not conducive to the development of space activities and the participation of private entities, as one of their major concerns would be the possibility to retrieve profits from their investments and contribution to space activities. Consequently, a timely discussion and clarification on either the possible application of the existing intellectual property rules to outer space or the necessity of separate rules for space activities is extremely important and beneficial for the continued involvement of private entities in the field.

One fundamental issue arises from the important concepts of "for benefit and in the interests of all countries" and "province of all mankind" defined in the Outer Space Treaty.[1] One may argue on this basis that the inventions and economic returns cannot be monopolized by the State or entity carrying out the space activities. However, this has been widely considered to be detrimental to the development of space technologies and activities; without fair economic returns, no States or entities would be interested in the potentially exorbitant and risky investment in outer space. Accordingly, the intellectual property regime is necessary for space activities; the issue of licensing on fair and reasonable terms to other States or entities could be

---

* Part of this chapter derives from the article "Intellectual Property (IP) Protection in Outer Space" by Yun Zhao, to be published in *Queen Mary Journal of Intellectual Property*, Volume 6.
1 *Treaty on Principles Governing the Activities of States in the Exploration and Use of Outer Space, including the Moon and Other Celestial Bodies [Outer Space Treaty]*, 27 January 1967, 610 UNTS 205, art I.

negotiated at a later stage between parties.[2] In the end, an appropriate intellectual property regime should be able to encourage invention and competition; for this purpose, "an optimum balance is needed between the interests of the inventor, the State concerned, and those who improve space technology."[3]

Reconciling territoriality of IPR with non-Territoriality in outer space

Intellectual property rights are essentially territorial in nature; the protection offered is limited to a specific geographical area where they are registered for a certain period of time. The territorial nature drastically differs from the non-territorial nature of space law. As defined in the Outer Space Treaty, outer space is free from national appropriation; no States can claim national sovereignty over any part of outer space, either by means of use or occupation or by any other means.[4] States are barred from exercising their territorial jurisdiction, control and authority over outer space.

The protection of intellectual property rights relies on State enforcement; outer space, however, lacks the concept of State sovereignty. Thus, the protection of intellectual property rights in outer space requires special consideration. While non-appropriation of outer space has been wide accepted by the international society, we cannot miss another provision in the same treaty that the activities of the non-governmental entities shall require the authorization and continuing supervision by an appropriate State.[5] The treaty further provides that the State of registry has jurisdiction and control over space objects as well as personnel launched into outer space.[6] The act of registration entails important legal implications by assuming jurisdiction and control over the space object and the personnel therein in outer space.[7]

The Registration Convention further develops the responsibility provision in the Outer Space Treaty and elaborates on the arrangement for the international registration of space objects. Several elements deserve attention here. A State of registry must be a launching State which launches or procures the launching of a space object, or a State from whose territory or facility a space object is launched.[8] In case there are two or more launching States, they should jointly determine which one should register the space object. Such a State of registry shall be the one that maintains jurisdiction and control over the space object under the Outer Space Treaty. As such, while the non-appropriation principle applies, the space law regime provides relevant connections between the State of registry and the space object, and the space activities carried out in the space object. This would be one important and useful arrangement for the current discussion, especially in considering possible reconciliation of the space law regime with the intellectual property law regime.

The Registration Convention provides the opportunity for an international intergovern-

---

2   Harry M. Saragovitz, "The Law of Intellectual Property in Outer Space" (1975) 17 PTC Journal of Research and Education 95.
3   Ruwantissa Abeyratne, *Space Security Law* (Berlin: Springer-Verlag, 2011) at 96. See also *Hilton-Davis Chemical Co. v. Waner-Jenkinson Co. Inc.* 62F (3d) 1512 at 1531–1532 (Fed Cir 1995).
4   *Outer Space Treaty, supra* note 1, art II.
5   *Outer Space Treaty, supra* note 1, art VI. See further Christopher Miles, "Assessing the Need for an International Patent Regime for Inventions in Outer Space" (2008) 11 Tulane Journal of Technology & Intellectual Property 62.
6   *Outer Space Treaty, supra* note 1, art VIII.
7   Saragovitz, *supra* note 2 at 90.
8   *Convention on Registration of Objects Launched into Outer Space*, 14 January 1975, 1023 UNTS 15, art 1(a).

mental organization to register a space object under certain conditions.[9] This may cause difficulty in the determination of an applicable legal regime for intellectual property protection. In this regard, the member States within an international intergovernmental organization could reach an agreement beforehand in dealing with the issue of intellectual property.[10] Useful reference can be made to the International Space Station Intergovernmental Agreement (ISS IGA) with regard to the arrangements for intellectual property protection within the European Partner States that are represented by the European Space Agency (ESA), which will be discussed further in the next part.[11]

Accordingly, we may make reference to the legal regimes for international space where no States can claim for sovereignty. Obviously, the high seas would be one ideal example for reference. Quasi-extension of national territory has been applied, much like registration of spacecraft under the Outer Space Treaty and Registration Convention, for activities carried out on high seas by vessels holding the registration of that State. This means that the activities carried out in a vessel would be considered to be in the territory of the State where the vessel is registered, and the law of the flag shall apply. The United Nations Convention on the Law of the Sea provides that "every State shall fix the conditions for the grant of its nationality to ships, for the registration of ships in its territory, and for the right to fly its flag. Ships have the nationality of the State whose flag they are entitled to fly. There must exist a genuine link between the State and the ship."[12] This Convention further provides that "every State shall effectively exercise its jurisdiction and control in administrative, technical and social matters over ships flying its flag."[13]

The nationality standards implemented can create the territorial connecting points for the jurisdiction and control by the State of registry. As such, the territorial connection can be naturally created for the protection of intellectual property rights in outer space for the activities carried out in a spacecraft, which will be considered as territory of the State where the spacecraft is registered. This would be a useful means to the resolve the dilemma.

The application of the quasi-extension of national territory requires that space objects be properly registered with a State in accordance with the Registration Convention. However, besides the traditional concerns over the ambiguous definition of "space object", the application of the Registration Convention faces other challenges in the era of space commercialization, especially in the case of on-orbit transfer of space objects. This issue has been widely discussed in the space law circle, which led to the adoption of a UNGA resolution in 2004.[14]

In case relevant activities are carried out in outer space outside spacecraft, relevant nationality or domicile of the person shall be a starting point to study the protection of intellectual property for certain activities conducted and results achieved by that person. This nationality approach shall apply only when no quasi-territorial connection can be determined.

---

9   Ibid., art VII.
10 See Manfred Lachs, *The Law of Outer Space: An Experience in Contemporary Law Making* (Leiden: Sijthoff, 1972) at 70. Lachs observes that "in cases of joint launching, agreement between the parties is required as to which of them is to be deemed the 'State of Registry'. A similar agreement is also necessary when a launching is carried out by an international organization."
11 *Agreement Among the Government of Canada, Governments of Member States of the European Space Agency, The Government of Japan, The Government of the Russian Federation, and the Government of the United States of America concerning cooperation on the civil international space station [ISS IGA]* (29 January 1998), art 21.
12 *United Nations Convention on the Law of the Sea*, 10 December 1982, 1933 UNTS 397, art 91(1).
13 Ibid., art 94(1).
14 *Application of the concept of the "launching State"*, UNDOC A/RES/59/115 (2004).

Relevant international legal regime for intellectual property protection

WIPO regime

The World Intellectual Property Organization (WIPO) is a specialized international governmental organization under the UN framework responsible for the promotion of the protection of intellectual property throughout the world. The WIPO oversees several important international regimes governing the protection of various types of intellectual property, including patent, trademark, copyright and neighboring rights. It administers around 26 treaties in the field, which are categorized into three groups: intellectual property protection treaties, global protection system treaties, and classification treaties.[15]

The WIPO Copyright Treaty (WCT) was concluded in the Internet era.[16] Accordingly, it contains provisions regarding the protection of computer programs and the compilation of data or other materials. More importantly, the WCT establishes the regime for the broad protection of communication rights, both online and offline.[17] As such, signals and relevant data transmitted from a spacecraft in outer space enjoy copyright protection under the WCT.

TRIPs regime within the WTO

The establishment of the World Trade Organization (WTO) in 1995 brought major changes to the legal regime for intellectual property protection. Trade related intellectual property protection became one major pillar of the WTO. The Agreement on Trade Related Aspects of Intellectual Property Rights (TRIPs)[18] brings in all major international treaties in the field, reflecting "a synergy between States in the establishment of a uniform regime that would harmonize intellectual property rights within member states of WTO."[19] However, the members are free to individually decide on the appropriate methods to implement their commitments under the TRIPs within their own legal system and practice.[20]

The TRIPs defines the following as its main principles: minimum levels of protection; effective procedures and remedies for enforcing intellectual property rights; non-discrimination (national and most-favored-nation treatment); and enforcement through WTO dispute settlement.[21]

Similar to the treaties mentioned above, the TRIPs does not address the issue of intellectual property protection in outer space. But to a certain extent, however this agreement expresses similar consideration as the Outer Space Treaty that space exploration shall be for the benefit of all mankind, by providing that "In order to facilitate the implementation of this agreement, developed country members shall provide, on request, and on mutually agreed terms and conditions, technical and financial cooperation in favor of developing and least developed country members."[22]

---

15   See further "WIPO-Administered Treaties," online: World Intellectual Property Organization www.wipo.int/treaties/en/.
16   *The WIPO Copyright Treaty (WCT)*, 12 April 1997, WIPO Doc. CRNR/DC/94.
17   Ibid., art 8.
18   *Agreement on Trade Related Aspects of Intellectual Property* (TRIPS), 15 April 1994, 33 ILM 81 (1994).
19   Abeyratne, *supra* note 3 at 92.
20   TRIPs, *supra* note 18, art 1(1).
21   "Intellectual Property (TRIPS): Negotiations, implementation and TRIPS Council work," online: World Trade Organization www.wto.org/english/thewto_e/minist_e/min99_e/english/about_e/10trips_e.htm.
22   TRIPS, *supra* note 18, art 67.

Intellectual property

It would be interesting to note that the agreement provides that the location of invention shall not affect the patent rights,[23] which directly leads to the deduction that inventions arising from space activities shall similarly enjoy patent protection. WTO Members shall not discriminate on the patentability of an invention, no matter whether a first-to-file system or a first-to-invent system is adopted in a particular State.[24] So within a domestic legal regime, a State should make sure that patent protection shall not be refused simply because of the location of the invention in outer space.

Selected bilateral and multilateral legal regimes for IP protection

International space cooperation is one fundamental principle defined in the Outer Space Treaty. The States are free to adopt any mechanisms to carry out space cooperation, the conclusion of bilateral and multilateral agreements being one major mechanism for the purpose of space cooperation. It would be important to examine the arrangements of the existing major agreements in the field of intellectual property protection. It would be impossible to examine all existing agreements; therefore two agreements are selected for illustration below.

The Intergovernmental Agreement (IGA) for the International Space Station (ISS) in 1998 is the first and most successful multilateral agreement for conducting a cooperative space project. The arrangements in the IGA provide a successful example for space cooperation in the field of intellectual property protection. The IGA is the only international agreement providing clear wording on intellectual property protection, with one long provision devoted for this purpose. It adopts the quasi-territorial approach by providing that an activity occurring in or on an ISS flight element should be deemed to have occurred only in the territory of the Partner State of that element's registry.[25] The IGA further defines the application of relevant national intellectual property law to such an activity.[26] As such, the relevant domestic legal regime shall govern the creation, use and transfer of intellectual property. The same approach has also been retained and applied for the issue of criminal jurisdiction.

However, the temporary presence in the territory of a Partner State of an article, including the components of flight elements, in transit between any place on Earth and any flight element of the Space Station registered by another Partner State or the European Space Agency (ESA) should not in itself form the basis for any patent infringement proceedings in the first Partner State.[27]

Despite the adoption of the quasi-territorial approach, a Partner State shall not apply its own laws on secrecy of inventions to prevent a person who is not its national or resident from filing a patent application in any other Partner State that provides for the protection of the secrecy of patent applications containing information that is classified or otherwise protected for national security purposes.[28] This arrangement is different from normal practice in that it requires an inventor to apply for patent protection in the State where the inventor is a resident

---

23 *TRIPS, supra* note 18, art 27(1).
24 Daniel Gervais, The TRIPS Agreement: Drafting History and Analysis (London: Sweet & Maxwell, 1998) at 147.
25 *ISS IGA, supra* note 11, art 21(2).
26 Ibid.
27 Ibid., art 21(6). See also International Bureau of WIPO, "Intellectual Property and Space Activities" (April 2004) online: World Intellectual Property Organization, www.wipo.int/export/sites/www/patent-law/es/developments/pdf/ip_space.pdf at 20, para 76.
28 *ISS IGA, supra* note 11, art 21(3).

or where the invention is made. This special arrangement is understandable for the purpose of international cooperation among Partner States in such a large cooperative project.

As far as the European Partner States are concerned, since the ESA is delegated to register the ESA flight elements, any European Partner State may deem relevant activity to have occurred within its territory for ESA registered elements.[29] For the purpose of enforcement, a person or entity could bring proceedings and obtain compensation only in one State even if the intellectual property is protected in more than one European Partner State.[30] To prevent possible multiple proceedings against the same act of infringement by two or more persons or entities, the IGA provides that a court may grant a temporary stay of proceedings for actions filed later pending the outcome of the earlier action; it further provides that satisfaction of an earlier action shall bar any pending or future actions based on the same act of infringement.[31]

In case of licensing, the effect of a license under the law of any one European Partner State shall not be refused recognition in any other European Partner States. Such an arrangement is based on the existing framework of the ESA and helps to promote further cooperation among the Member States of the ESA. One space lawyer raised an issue regarding the difficulty with intellectual property enforcement caused by the legal privileges and immunities endowed upon the ESA and its staff members by the ESA Convention.[32] The enforcement of intellectual property is a practical issue. We may overcome the technical difficulty caused by the existence of privilege and immunity by referring to the existing systems of compulsory licensing and fair use.

A provision establishing cross-waivers of liability is inserted in the IGA for the purpose of closer cooperation among the Partner States. However, this provision shall not apply to intellectual property claims.[33] Accordingly, any intellectual property claims arising out this cooperative project does not need to be waived between and among the Partner States, which partly demonstrates the importance of intellectual property issue in spite of the essential nature of cooperation in the ISS project.

It can be seen from the above examples that the existing agreements do not intend to go into basic concepts of intellectual property rights; instead they focus more on the procedural aspects of how to prevent infringements of existing property rights and protect the exclusive rights of the original right owners. Consequently, we can deduce from the above arrangement that the existing substantive and procedural arrangement would similarly apply to the protection of intellectual property rights in outer space. With regard to outer space, we will focus on how to promote space cooperation in the field and how to correlate the connecting points in outer space to satisfy the geographical feature of traditional regimes for intellectual property protection.

Domestic legal regimes for intellectual property protection

Protection of industrial property rights

As discussed earlier, several international regimes have been set up to deal with industrial property rights. However, the domestic regimes for the protection of industrial property rights

---

29 Ibid., art 21(2).
30 Ibid., art 21(4).
31 Ibid., art 21(4).
32 Arnold Vahrenwald, "Industrial Property on the Space Station FREEDOM" (1993) 15 European Intellectual Property Review at 441–445.
33 *ISS IGA*, *supra* note 11, art 16(3)(d)(4).

are far from harmonized. This can be well exemplified by the co-existence of the first-to-file and first-to-invent regimes in different countries for patent protection. The United States adopts the first-to-invent system, while many other States adopt the first-to-file system.[34] National regimes also differ in the determination of patentability, namely, the understanding of novelty, inventive step (non-obviousness) and industrial applicability (utility).[35]

Furthermore, if actual reduction to practice happened on a US-controlled space object in outer space, "it would be as-if it was an actual reduction to practice within the US."[36] As such, it is clear that a quasi-territorial approach has been adopted by the United States for the protection of inventions in outer space. It is to be noted that the United States also uses registration, not launching, as a connecting factor in determining the element of jurisdiction and control.[37]

Even before the above provision was enacted, case law in the United States also confirmed the possible extra-territorial reach of U.S. patent law to space activities. The judge in *Decca Limited v. United States* justified the application of the U.S. patent law taking into consideration of the three factors: ownership of the equipment, control of the equipment and the actual beneficial use of the system within the United States.[38] The first two factors have been again cited in the *NTP v. Research Motion* case.[39] The court has taken further opportunities to analyze what constitutes "within the United States" in the *Hughes Aircraft Co. v. United States* case[40] through the examination of the existence of a direct control point in the United States. As Smith correctly observes, "No appropriation of any area is necessary by a granting State to enforce patent rights in favor of an individual. Rather, what is required is the ability to control conduct of individuals; this can be facilitated through the exercise of jurisdiction over the space object on which their activities are based."[41]

Nevertheless, the law provides two exceptions for its application, even if the United States is in control of the space object. The U.S. patent law shall not apply to the space object if it is specifically identified and otherwise provided for by an international agreement to which the United States is a party,[42] or if it is carried on the registry of another State in accordance with the Registration Convention.[43]

At the current stage, many States carry out space activities to conduct experiments and

---

34 Leo B. Malagar & Marlo Apalisok Magdoza-Malagar, "International Law of Outer Space and the Protection of Intellectual Property Rights" (1999) 17 Boston University International Law Journal at 362–363.
35 TRIPS, *supra* note 18, art 27.1.
36 35 USC §106. See further David Irimies, "Promoting Space Ventures by Creating an International Space IPR Framework" (2011) 33 European Intellectual Property Review 43.
37 B. Sandeepa Bhat, "Inventions in Outer Space: Need for Reconsideration of the Patent Regime" (2010) 36 Journal of Space Law 13.
38 *Decca Limited v. United States*, 210 Ct Cl 546 at 552–553, 544 (Ct Cl 1976).
39 *NTP, Inc. v. Research in Motion, Ltd.*, 418 F (3d) 1282 (Fed Cir 2005). See further Kurt G. Hammerle & Theodore U. Ro, "The Extra-Territorial Research of U.S. Patent Law on Space-Related Activities: Does the 'International Shoe' Fit as We Reach for the Stars?" (2008) 34 Journal of Space Law at 259–261.
40 *Hughes Aircraft Co. v. United States*, 29 Fed Cl 197 (1993).
41 Tim Smith, "A Phantom Menace? Patents and the Communal Status of Space" (2003) 34 Victoria University Wellington Law Review 553.
42 S Rept 101–266 (101st Congress, 1989–1990) at 6.
43 35 USC §105(a) (1990). For further discussion, see Theodore U. Ro, Matthew J. Kleiman & Kurt G. Hammerle, "Patent Infringement in Outer Space in Light of 35 U.S.C. §105: Following the White Rabbit Down the Rabbit Loophole" (2011) 17 Boston University Journal of Science & Technology Law 213.

scientific research. While States may have different ways to define and understand the meaning of scientific research and experiments, these activities generally fall within the area of either fair use or compulsory licensing in the patent regime. The continued application of fair use and compulsory licensing in the space field is important in encouraging relevant entities to carry out space exploratory work for further advancement of space technologies.

There is yet another concern regarding a possible barrier created by patent for further development of subsequent research and space activities. For example, patenting technologies that would cover a system or method of satellite communication using certain useful orbits may in effect limit the access to these orbits by other parties.[44] In this regard, we may again consider the application of compulsory licensing to balance the exclusive rights of the owner and public interests. Many States may even go further to define certain inventions that are necessary for the protection of public order or morality that are therefore not patentable. This provision is also specifically allowable under TRIPs.[45]

Copyright protection and other intellectual property rights

Among all types of intellectual property rights, copyright protection has the lowest standards of originality. The Berne Convention and the WCT have harmonized very well the legal regime for copyright protection. The substantive requirements for copyright protection are almost the same around the world, though the threshold of originality may differ from State to State. It has been well accepted that copyright and data rights can be applied to protect relevant data and materials in the space field.[46]

It is also simplified because the nationality of the author defines the legal regime for copyright protection. Only in case of non-protected authors will the place of first publication play a role in determining the applicable legal regime. One would thus only need to examine the application of the current copyright protection regime for several types of materials arising out of space activities.

Direct broadcasting services (DBS) create programs which no doubt enjoy copyright protection. Remote sensing, together with satellite imagery, has been widely used in our daily lives in the fields of Earth observation, disaster mitigation and management, weather broadcasting, mining, and so on. Copyright protection for remote sensing data has been one major issue for consideration. Under the 1996 UNGA resolution on remote sensing,[47] remote sensing data are differentiated into three levels: primary data, processed data and analyzed data.[48]

44 Alain Pompidou, "The Ethics of Space Policy" (2000) online: UNESCO, http://unesdoc.unesco.org/images/0012/001206/120681e.pdf at 134.
45 *TRIPS, supra* note 18, art 27(2) provides that "members may exclude from patentability inventions, the prevention within their territory of the commercial exploitation of which is necessary to protect order public morality, including to protect human, animal or plant life or health or to avoid serious prejudice to the environment, provided that such exclusion is not made merely because the exploitation is prohibited by their law."
46 Lee Ann W. Lockridge, "Intellectual Property in Outer Space: International Law, National Jurisdiction, and Exclusive Rights in Geospatial Data and Database" (2006) 32 Journal of Space Law 357.
47 *The Principles Relating to Remote Sensing of the Earth from Outer Space (Remote Sensing Principles)*, UN Doc A/RES/41/65 (1986) ann. at 2.
48 Ibid., Principle 1. "Primary data" refer to those raw data that are acquired by remote sensors borne by a space object and that are transmitted or delivered to the ground from space by telemetry in the form of electromagnetic signals, by photographic film, magnetic tape or any other means; "processed data" refer to the products resulting from the processing of the primary data, needed to make such data usable; "analyzed data" refer to the information resulting from the interpretation of processed data, inputs of data and knowledge from other sources.

Similarly, the United States and Canada differentiate remote sensing data by the level of processing from raw data to remote sensing product.[49] The Russian Resolution on the Order of Acquisition, Use and Provision of Geo-Spatial Information, however, defines all data as "primary data" under the above UNGA resolution.[50]

There is no problem in finding that processed data and analyzed data enjoy copyright protection. However, when it comes to primary data, it would be difficult to argue for copyright protection.[51] Fortunately, we note that some States have extended intellectual property protection through a *sui generis* regime.[52] A database right was created and granted to the owner, forbidding unauthorized extraction or re-utilization of all or a substantial part of the database contents.[53] This was implemented in European countries, such as the United Kingdom.[54] As long as there is a substantial investment in obtaining, verifying or presenting the contents of the database, the owner of the database shall enjoy a property right in the database, no matter whether the database or any of its contents is a copyrighted work.[55]

The Copyright Act in the United States sets up a statutory copyright license for the distribution of point-to-multipoint television station signals over DBS through the payment of copyright fees to the programming copyright owners.[56]

Aside from the above traditional categories of intellectual property rights, we should also note other special types of products for intellectual property protection. Integrated circuits are important for the functioning of spacecraft, vehicles and facilities. Due to the special environment in outer space, scientific experiments often lead to the production of new plant species. This is another area of intellectual property rights worthy of attention. In this regard, many States have already formed their own legal regimes for the protection of integrated circuits and new plant species.

Legal controls over transfer of space technology

The role of export controls in international trade regime

Advanced space technologies are indispensable for space exploratory activities. These space technologies are normally considered to be highly sensitive and relevant to national security.

---

49 US Land Remote Sensing Policy Act of 1992, HR 6133, Section 2; Canadian Remote Sensing Space Systems Act, S.C., 2005, c. 45, Section 2.
50 *The Russian Resolution on the Order of Acquisition, Use and Provision of Geo-Spatial Information (Russian Remote Sensing Resolution)*, No. 326 (28 May 2007), § 2.
51 See further Catherine Doldirina, "A Rightly Balanced Intellectual Property Rights Regime as a Mechanism to Enhance Commercial Earth Observation Activities" (2010) 67 Acta Astronautica at 642–643.
52 For example, the Council of the European Union passed Directive No. 96/9/EC of 11 March 1996 on the legal protection of databases, which introduced separate legal rights for certain computer records, known as database rights.
53 EC, European Parliament and the Council Directive 96/9/EC of 11 March 1996 on the legal protection of databases [1996] O.J. L 77/20 at 20–28.
54 UK Copyright and Rights in Databases Regulations (1997) S.I. 1997/3032; UK Copyright, Designs and Patents Act (1988) C 48 as amended. See further Sa'id Mosteshar, "Regulation of Space Activities in the United Kingdom," in Ram S. Jakhu, ed, *National Regulation of Space Activities* (Dordrecht: Springer, 2010) at 371.
55 UK Databases Regulations, *supra* note 54; UK Copyright Act, *supra* note 54.
56 17 USC §§ 119 & 122. See further Petra A. Vorwig, "Regulation of Satellite Communications in the United States" in Ram S. Jakhu, ed, *National Regulation of Space Activities* (Dordrecht: Springer, 2010) at 432.

Thus, international community has already reached consensus on the necessity of export controls over some space technologies and products. In the trade area, States adopt various measures, including licensing and quotas, to control the export of certain products and technologies. Such measures can similarly apply to the space field.

To facilitate international cooperation in the space field, however, States have reached some consensus on the transfer of technical data and goods. The IGA provides an obvious example in this regard. Technical data and goods for transfer are limited to those that are "considered to be necessary to fulfill the responsibilities of that Partner's Cooperating Agency under the relevant MOUs and implementing arrangements."[57] The Partners shall encourage and facilitate the expeditious transfer of these technical data and goods.[58]

However, even under such a cooperative framework, national laws or regulations must be strictly followed, including those regarding export controls. The IGA further sets restrictions that may be identified by the furnishing Cooperating Agency, which may mark with a notice or otherwise specifically identify the technical data or goods to be protected for the purposes of export control, proprietary rights, or national security.[59] Other Partner States shall take appropriate measures "to prevent unauthorized use, disclosure, or retransfer of, or unauthorized access to, such technical data or goods."[60]

Similar arrangements can also be found in the APSCO Convention. The Member States shall reach agreements on technology safeguarding measures to prevent "any unauthorized access to protected information, items and related technologies."[61] Furthermore, Member States shall respect national export control laws and regulations.[62]

International and national export control regimes

Due to the high sensitivity of space products and technologies, the international community has formed different export control regimes to deal with different types of products and technologies. The 1996 Wassenaar Arrangement coordinates national regulations and policies on export controls for conventional weapons and sensitive dual-use goods and technologies.[63] It serves as "an export control transparency arrangement".[64] The Missile Technology Control Regime (MTCR) established an international regime for export controls over missiles and missile-related products and technologies.[65] As a supplement to the MTCR, the International Code of Conduct against Ballistic Missile Proliferation (Hague Code of Conduct) was concluded with the aim to curb ballistic missile proliferation worldwide.[66]

---

57 *ISS IGA, supra* note 11, art 19(1).
58 Ibid., art 19(2).
59 Ibid., art 19(3).
60 Ibid., art 19(4).
61 *The Convention on the Asia-Pacific Space Cooperation Organization (APSCO Convention)*, 28 October 2005, 2423 UNTS 127, art 23(1)–(2).
62 Ibid., art 23(3).
63 *Wassenaar Arrangement on Export Controls for Conventional Arms and Dual-Use Goods and Technologies*, online: Wassenar, www.wassenaar.org/.
64 Michael C. Mineiro, *Space Technology Export Controls and International Cooperation in Outer Space* (Dordrecht: Springer, 2012) at 24.
65 *Missile Technology Control Regime*, online: MTCR, www.mtcr.info/english/index.html.
66 See Bureau of Nonproliferation, *International Code of Conduct Against Ballistic Missile Proliferation*, Washington, DC, (6 January 2004) online: US Department of State www.fas.org/asmp/resources/govern/ICOC-6January2004.html.

Along with the above international export control regimes, States have also established their own national legal regimes for export controls. The United States has formulated a complete set of rules for export controls, including the 1917 Trading with the Enemy Act, the 1946 Atomic Energy Act, the 1949 Export Control Act, the 1951 Mutual Defense Assistance Control Act, the 1969 Export Administration Act, and the 1976 Arms Export Control Act.[67] Necessary export control measures may be taken under the consideration of national security, foreign policy and short supply.[68] The Export Administration Regulations list commodities, software and technologies and nations that are subject to export controls.[69] A "presumption of approval" for export license is adopted under the Export Administration Regulations.[70] "Goods" are defined as "any article, natural or manmade substance, material, supply or manufactured product, including inspection and test equipment, and excluding technical data."[71] "Technology" is defined as

> the information and know-how (whether in tangible form, such as models, prototypes, drawings, sketches, diagrams, blueprints, or manuals, or intangible form, such as training or technical services) that can be used to design, produce, manufacture, utilize, or reconstruct goods, including computer software and technological data, but not the goods themselves.[72]

The Directorate of Defense Trade Controls (DDTC) is the entity within the Department of State in charge of the issuance of export licenses for defense articles and defense services under the International Traffic in Arms Regulations (ITAR).[73] The U.S. Munition List provides the details of defense articles and defense services subject to export controls, with spacecraft (including communications satellites) included in its Category XV.[74]

The Export and Import Permits Act (EIPA),[75] together with Export Permits Regulations and Import Permits Regulations,[76] is the major legislation in Canada dealing with export controls and transfer of technologies and goods. In accordance with the EIPA, the Canadian government issues an Export Control List (ECL) and an Area Control List (ACL), providing detailed lists of technologies, goods and countries for export controls through the issuance of permits.[77]

The Foreign Trade Law in China sets up a legal regime for export controls, which is further concretized in other regulations for specific types of technologies and goods. The Regulations

---

67 See Ram S. Jakhu & Joseph Wilson, "The New United States Export Control Regime: Its Impact on the Communications Satellite Industry" (2000) 25 Annals of Air & Space Law 157.
68 50 USC § 2402(2) (2004). See further Paul Stephen Dempsey, "Overview of the United States Space Policy and Law" in Ram S. Jakhu, ed, *National Regulation of Space Activities* (Dordrecht: Springer, 2010) at 399–400.
69 15 CFR Parts 730–773 (2004).
70 50 USC § 2403(d) (2009).
71 50 USC § 2415(3) (2009).
72 50 USC § 2415(4) (2009).
73 22 CFR Parts 120–130 (2004).
74 22 CFR § 120.7 (2004). See further Petra A. Vorwig, "Regulation of Private Launch Services in the United States" in Ram S. Jakhu, ed, *National Regulation of Space Activities* (Dordrecht: Springer, 2010) 417–419.
75 *Export and Import Permits Act*, Canada, RSC E-19 (1985).
76 *Export Permits Regulations*, Canada, SOR/97-204 and *Import Permits Regulations*, Canada, SOR/79-5.
77 *Export and Import Permits Act*, supra note 75, s 7(1).

on Control of Military Products Export and the Regulations on Export Control of Missiles and Missile-related Items and Technologies are the two major documents dealing with export controls of space-related technologies and goods. Exporters are required to obtain licenses for the export of the above items and technologies.[78]

Conclusion

The WIPO provides two reasons for the necessity of intellectual property protection, that is, "to give statutory expression to the moral and economic rights of creators in their creations and such rights of the public in access those creations" and "to promote, as a deliberate act of Government policy, creativity and the dissemination and application of its results and to encourage fair trading which could contribute to economic and social development."[79] These two reasons also apply to the protection of intellectual property in outer space.

The privatization and commercialization of outer space calls for an appropriate legal regime for the protection of the highly sophisticated space technologies and data arising from space activities. Without clear and strong protection for intellectual property rights, private entities will be hesitant and in the end likely lose interest in investing in space activities.[80]

While the current intellectual property regime shall continue to apply to any scientific and research results, we will need to find ways to reconcile the territorial intellectual property protection regime and the non-territorial outer space regime. Only with sufficient protection for space technologies and data in place will private entities be willing to participate in space activities, which will further stimulate the development of space technologies in general.[81]

The above discussions show that the conflicting features of the two regimes are not irreconcilable. Since the existing regime for intellectual property is relatively mature, we need to create a connecting point linking outer space with the current intellectual property regime. As such, this mission is not impossible. The intellectual property and space principles have been in co-existence before and will continue to be so in the future.[82]

While upholding the principle of international cooperation in the peaceful uses of outer space, we can be optimistic that the States are able to find the appropriate connecting point to extend the current intellectual property regime to outer space and establish an appropriate national regime for the protection of intellectual property, including the regime for the transfer of space technologies. As such, an optimum balance can be reached "between the interests of the inventor, the State concerned, and those who improve space technology."[83]

---

78   *Regulations on Control of Military Products Export*, PRC, (2002), art 2; *Regulations on Export Control of Missiles and Missile-related Items and Technologies*, PRC, (2002), art 2.
79   World Intellectual Property Organization, *Introduction to Intellectual Property: Theory and Practice* (London: Kluwer, 1997) at 3.
80   Barbara Luxenberg & Gerald J. Mossinghoff, "Intellectual Property and Space Activities" (1985) 13 Journal of Space Law 8.
81   Jocelyn H. Shoemaker, "The Patents in Space Act: Jedi Mind Trick or Real Protection for American Investors on the International Space Station?" (1998–1999) 6 Journal of Intellectual Property Law at 396–397.
82   Julie D. Cromer, "How on Earth Terrestrial Law Can Protect Geospatial Data" (2006) 32 Journal of Space Law 291.
83   Ruwantissa Abeyratne, "The Application of Intellectual Property Rights to Outer Space Activities" (2003) 29 Journal of Space Law 20.

22
Commercial satellite programs

Henry R. Hertzfeld and Alexis M. Sáinz

Introduction

The commercial satellite industry has changed dramatically over the past 20 years from mainly involving telecommunications satellites (fixed point voice, data, and services), and direct broadcast television and radio satellites to an industry that now also includes: mobile services, machine-to-machine communication networks, asset tracking systems, private networks, hosted payloads and "condosats", and private remote sensing systems that have real-time capabilities. In the near-term horizon there are also likely to be other new emerging technologies and services, such as private weather satellites and satellites that can perform on-orbit activities such as refueling, repairing and servicing other satellites. In addition, there has been a rapid development of privately financed small satellite systems with a large numbers of satellites that can operate independently and/or synchronize their systems and services.

A number of these and other technologies will likely enter the commercial realm fairly quickly since many evolve from the R&D and operational programs already incorporated into existing government space systems. There are other past examples of this evolution, but it still should be noted that commercial operations are different from government R&D or mission spacecraft and do require significant innovations, cost-saving technologies, and market development. Commercial operations ultimately need to be predicated on market demand and a demonstrated business case. Hosted payloads, joint procurements and multi-satellite constellations also introduce new sets of complexities. Each of these new technological capabilities will require attentiveness to specialized risks and interdependencies in the contractual arrangements between manufacturers and satellite operators, satellite operators and customers, satellite operators and lenders, as well as in governmental licensing procedures.

Understanding the commercial and legal risks associated with commercial satellite programs has become increasingly important in this developing area of the law. Financing of such programs and understanding the interdependencies of and related risks among the underlying arrangements between satellite operators and their key counterparties in a satellite program is critical, and the mitigation of such risks must ultimately impact the arrangements between satellite operators and their lenders or investors.

Some of the future legal challenges in contracting for commercial satellite programs are predictable, but many will depend on market developments, consumer demands, emerging business models, sources of financing, and other factors. Those other factors may even include non-space substitutes and complements to existing services. Such systems could be, for example, commercially developed high-altitude platforms that would provide regional communications and Earth observation services similar to those performed by satellites but located within altitudes legally under the jurisdiction of an existing government. Other services could be a combination of terrestrial equipment interacting with instruments on airplanes, sub-orbital rockets, and future reusable hypersonic transport vehicles. Although this may sound more like science fiction, enabling technologies for all of these types of systems are in the research and development stages today.

The legal and procurement issues can differ greatly among the various types of satellites and services offered, as well as the type of financing used. In the context of a single satellite program, the entity that undertakes to contract for the manufacture, launch, operation and financing of a satellite, ultimately serving as the satellite operator, will take on many roles in relation to its counterparties. It will be a purchaser under its satellite manufacturing contract, a customer under its launch services contract and Telemetry, Tracking and Command ("**TT&C**") contract (if it is not flying the spacecraft itself), a borrower under its loan documentation or an investment vehicle to its investors, and a service provider to its customers, and perhaps a partner to another satellite operator in the context of a hosted payload and/or condosat. This chapter will, at a high level, introduce the basic contractual issues involved with the procurement and financing of commercial satellite programs and highlight recent examples of programs that illustrate the importance of select concepts described. The focus will be on introducing these concepts in the context of a geosynchronous telecommunications satellite program undertaken by a single satellite operator, but we will also introduce certain significant differences among the newer services being offered. Given the complexity of the contracts and the legal issues involved, a full treatment is not possible here on the breadth of issues or the intricacies associated with negotiating each. Instead, we will focus on certain areas that have become more visible in the current commercial space environment.

The commercial satellite industry

The commercial satellite industry has more than doubled over the past ten years and, while there have been some dips in revenue along the way, it continues to be resilient and show robust economic growth in revenues.[1] Today, on a worldwide basis, annual revenues from all satellite services total more than $200 billion. This total includes manufacturing, launch, broadcast and other private sector sales. Over 40 percent of those sales are U.S. based. However, the largest annual growth rate is in non-U.S. sales. The largest component of the revenues is in direct broadcast television/direct to home, which accounts for 77 percent ($97.8 billion) of all satellite services revenue. Although the relationship between fixed and mobile satellite services is increasingly becoming intermixed and complex, each grew at 4 percent annually. Interestingly, there was also a noticeable and significant increase in the rate of growth of Earth observation services of 10 percent between 2014 and 2015, representing a new trend in private sector interest as well as governmental interest in developing new Earth observation applications.

---

1   These, as well as the subsequent figures, are taken from: Satellite Industry Association *State of the Satellite Industry Report,* September 2016.

Of the nearly 1,400 operating satellites in space, about 38 percent are for commercial communications, 14 percent for Earth observation and the rest divided among government satellites used for many purposes ranging from communications to navigation, research and exploration. Additionally, even government-sponsored programs often involve contracting with private satellite manufacturers and launch services providers, and they have been financed by sources other than by the host government, and so they too are operating in a satellite manufacturing ecosystem that largely features commercial actors.

Also of note is the re-emergence of the idea of satellite constellations and the rapid growth of very small satellites from private companies. The number of these satellites launched rose from a handful in 2012 and preceding years to about 100 in 2014, indicating a new and very interesting future trend in this industry. Most of those satellites were designed for Earth observation and are still in the research and development stage, having not yet advanced to a robust commercial market.

Additionally, the advent of the next push in both government and commercial space technology is beginning to become apparent with the growth of proposals to perform new types of operations in space. Companies are developing the ability to refuel, repair, and service satellites in space. These abilities range from the ability to approach satellites and observe their functioning (or non-functioning in the case of satellites needing repairs), to docking with space assets to refuel, repair, move, or otherwise change their location, operations, or functioning. At the same time, the financing of satellite programs has also continued to evolve. For example, in recent years, export credit agency financing has played an increasingly important role.

What are the key commercial and legal risks associated with commercial satellite programs and the financing of such programs, and how can satellite operators mitigate those risks to make their programs more attractive to investors and lenders? How should lenders diligence such programs? How do lenders and investors view these programs differently from other infrastructure projects? This chapter introduces some of the most salient issues and introduces some of the critical considerations, viewed through the lens of a satellite operator/borrower and lender or investor in a commercial satellite program. There are certainly many other considerations, and solutions are necessarily program specific and must be understood and considered in the context of the individualized satellite program.

Procurement of satellite programs and the key associated contracts

A procurement of a new commercial satellite involving a single geosynchronous satellite must begin about three to five years in advance of the planned launch of the satellite. The usually key drivers of timing include: (1) the two to three year manufacturing period for a satellite using mostly existing technology, as well as (2) establishing a window for launch on the manifest of one of the launch services providers. For a new program, the overall key steps include establishing a strong base case model containing the financial projections for the program, gaining access to an orbital slot and associated radio frequency spectrum, negotiating the satellite manufacturing contract, negotiating the launch services contract, negotiating or otherwise provisioning for TT&C, insuring the manufacture, launch and in-orbit functioning of the satellite, executing customer contracts, and identifying the investment or financing source for the program. From the perspective of the satellite operator, the key commercial participants are the satellite manufacturer, the launch services provider, the TT&C provider, the customers, and the investors and/or lenders.

Manufacturing and launch services contracts have to be tailored to address specific program risk issues and considerations, as well as variations arising from programs involving, for example, multiple payloads, new intellectual property, constellation programs, creative partnerships between satellite operators, technology transfer from a manufacturer to a satellite operator, and many other variations. The ultimate impact on the "bankability" of such programs must be understood by a satellite operator seeking to package manageable risk for the potential lender or investor. Without considering these issues early on, the satellite operator risks having to renegotiate contracts from a much weaker position relative to the bargaining power the satellite operator has early on in negotiations, requesting concessions from its counterparty after all other arrangements have been bargained for and the counterparty is well aware that the requested modification is one upon which the satellite operator's financing might rely, potentially resulting in the satellite operator having to make concessions that could have been avoided at the outset. Legal practitioners will need to continue to evolve in their approach to drafting these contracts and addressing issues associated with new technology and business models as well as in helping to identify risk mitigants in connection with these. The underlying finance and commercial legal concepts have not changed, but the implementation of these certainly has, and there will be a continued need for creative problem-solving as new issues arise.

Contract for the manufacture of the satellite

The contract for the procurement of the satellite is typically called the "Satellite Purchase Agreement". The satellite operator is the purchaser under the Satellite Purchase Agreement, and its counterparty for this agreement is the satellite manufacturer. As commercial contracts, these arrangements are subject to the same underlying legal principles and requirements as other commercial contracts, but the specific provisions are highly specialized. Some of the specialized key provisions in a Satellite Purchase Agreement include, at a high level:

- **Scope of work and deliverables**: satellite manufacturer agrees to provide the necessary personnel, material, services and facilities to design, manufacture, test and ship the satellite, along with other deliverable items;
- **Price and payment terms**: specifies timing of payments, which are usually milestone based and may be tailored to parallel costs paid out by the satellite manufacturer in connection with components and long-lead items, since initially most of the activity will be in the design phase and will not require significant outlays of funds to component manufacturers; invoicing mechanism; late fees; treatment of taxes;
- **Launch vehicle compatibility**: satellite manufacturer to maintain compatibility with a set of candidate launch vehicles and down-selection timing of same; satellite manufacturer's obligation to provide assistance and to communicate and cooperate with the launch services provider to support integration of the satellite with the designated launch vehicle; treatment of launch base support services and costs associated with specific launch vehicles;
- **Delivery of the satellite, acceptance and ground equipment**: satellite operator/purchaser will conduct a review of the satellite prior to shipment or the satellite's entry into storage, referred to in the industry as the "Satellite Pre-Shipment Review";
- **Delivery schedule and the ability to make adjustments**: contracts vary in flexibility associated with the parties' rights to make changes to the delivery schedule, subject to agreement on modification of impacted terms such as price and schedule, among others; a stop work provision may sometimes be included; treatment of excusable delays;
- **Transfer of title and risk of loss** (as modified by type of delivery, i.e. on-ground versus in-orbit): title to and risk of loss or damage to the satellite passes from satellite

manufacturer to satellite operator/purchaser at the time of intentional ignition of the launch vehicle used to launch the satellite; transfer of title of non-satellite deliverable items to occur when such items have been accepted by the satellite operator/purchaser;

- **Orbital performance incentives or a payback scheme in connection with the performance of the satellite**: the satellite manufacturing contract may provide that the purchaser pays to the manufacturer orbital performance incentives after a specified time after in-orbit testing, with the amount adjusted based on the performance of the satellite at such time, or there may be provisions for an incentive payment or payback, of such incentives if the satellite later does not continue to perform to such levels, depending on whether the failure to perform can be attributable to the satellite manufacturer; such orbital performance incentives and warranty payback provisions become part of the overall economic transaction, and satellite operator/purchaser requirement for significant orbital performance incentives or a warranty payback may result in a different negotiated price and other terms;
- **Warranties and limitations of liability**: satellite manufacturer warrants that the satellite will be manufactured and will perform in accordance with agreed specifications at the time of delivery, with warranty terminating at the time of intentional ignition; warranty for ground system customarily extends beyond such time;
- **Authorizations**: responsibility for preparing, coordinating and filing applications, registrations, reports, licenses, permits and authorizations with the applicable regulatory authorities and with any other national governmental agencies having jurisdiction over the satellite operator, for the construction, launch and operation of the satellite; satellite manufacturer support in connection with same; radio frequency coordination; compliance with export control laws;
- **Regime for liquidated damages for late delivery and early delivery incentives**: in the event of a late delivery of the satellite by the satellite manufacturer, the parties agree to a pre-established regime for liquidated damages to be paid by the satellite manufacturer to the satellite operator/purchaser; conversely, the satellite may be delivered before the scheduled delivery date, and such early delivery may result in the satellite operator/purchaser making an agreed incentive payment to the satellite manufacturer;
- **Satellite operator/purchaser right to terminate for convenience**: the satellite operator/purchaser's right to terminate for convenience will be subject to a scheduled termination liability, based on when in the performance of the contract the termination occurs; if the satellite operator/purchaser has made payment for such work pursuant to such terms, then there may be a provision by which completed work would pass to the satellite operator/purchaser;
- **Termination for satellite manufacturer default:** the satellite operator/purchaser will have a right to terminate the contract if the satellite manufacturer fails to deliver the satellite by the established date of delivery plus an additional period of time; the termination liability will generally be based on amounts paid on the contract to date, with certain carve-outs; there may also be a provision in which the satellite operator could have the option to obtain title to the work-in-process at a negotiated price;
- **Termination for satellite operator/purchaser default**: the satellite manufacturer will have the right to terminate for satellite operator/purchaser failure to pay or for other material breaches; termination liability for satellite operator/purchaser failure may be based on the amounts paid for satellite operator/purchaser's termination for convenience or may be separately established;

- **Indemnity for personal injury and property damage, and waiver of subrogation**: the satellite manufacturer will customarily agree to indemnify the satellite operator/purchaser, affiliates and subcontractors against any losses, damages and other liabilities adjudicated to be owing to a third-party claimant if the losses of such parties were caused by, or resulted form, a negligent act or omission or willful misconduct of the satellite operator or the satellite operator's employees or representatives; the satellite manufacturer will not assume any liability for third-party loss caused by the satellite after delivery to the satellite operator/purchaser; the satellite operator/purchaser undertakes a parallel indemnity for losses caused by its employees or representatives; certain inter-participant waivers will be required; the parties undertake to obtain a waiver of subrogation and release any right of recovery against the other party and from any insurer providing coverage for the risks subject to indemnification;
- **Property insurance**: manufacturer commits to insure the satellite up to delivery to the satellite operator/purchaser, and the satellite operator/purchaser agrees to obtain subrogation waivers from its launch and in-orbit insurers;
- **Intellectual property rights**: the satellite manufacturer will generally indemnify the satellite operator/purchaser against third-party claims or suits based on an allegation that the manufacture or use of the satellite or any other deliverable item infringes on any third party's intellectual property rights; treatment of existing versus created intellectual property, including jointly created intellectual property, if applicable;
- **Assignment and security interests**: typically bar against assignment of contract, unless to affiliates with sufficient financial resources to fulfill the assigning party's obligations; satellite operator/purchaser should be able to assign without the manufacturer's consent if in connection with obtaining financing for the satellite; there may be other exceptions as well;
- **Post-launch anomaly support and corrections**: satellite manufacturer will investigate anomalies during the in-orbit life of the satellite and undertake satellite anomaly resolution support and provide software upgrades as applicable (with price terms negotiated); and
- **Mission operations support services**: describes services related to the satellite which continue for the life of the satellite.

The foregoing provisions can be highly negotiated, each in connection with the others, and each program requires its own overall balance based on the commercial imperatives of the purchaser, negotiating leverage of the parties and the underlying economics of the project. For example, a satellite manufacturer may be more willing to provide a shorter production schedule if the liquidated damages scheme is more favorable and adequately scales up over time and there is an otherwise longer long-stop date after which the purchaser's termination rights arise, as well as whether the program is one involving new or existing technology and whether the satellite operator/customer is one with experience in the industry and that will be a known good partner over the multi-year period in which the satellite is constructed.

While there is a great deal of discussion that could be had regarding each one of the provisions in a satellite manufacturing contract, we highlight below two specialized topics related to satellite purchase agreements, focusing on important satellite-specific issues and emerging areas of the law with respect to the commercial satellite industry.

In-orbit delivery contracts

A critical differentiator between types of satellite purchase agreements is whether the satellite will be delivered by the manufacturer to the satellite operator at the time of launch or whether delivery will occur after in-orbit testing of the satellite (an "**IOD Contract**"). An IOD Contract provides for the manufacture, launch and insuring of the satellite(s) in a single contract between the satellite operator and the satellite manufacturer. A sophisticated purchaser may wish to have control over launch and insurance, rather than having the satellite manufacturer run the launch services and insurance process. A newer or first-time satellite operator, however, may prefer to pay a premium for end-to-end service. And a lender or investor to a satellite operator with an IOD Contract may be willing to relax covenants or equity contingencies associated with covering the risks that must be otherwise mitigated – especially if this is a new satellite operator. IODs comprise a relatively small portion of satellite procurements, and it is important to understand the trade-offs involved with such an approach.

Intellectual property arrangements

Many satellite programs involve existing technology in which the satellite manufacturer licenses its existing technology to the satellite operator/purchaser. In some instances, there may be a collaborative effort between the satellite operator and the satellite manufacturer. For example, Skybox Imaging contracted with Space Systems Loral to build 13 small high-resolution Earth observation satellites using a Skybox Imaging design for which SSL had been given an exclusive license.[2] In a satellite program involving existing technology, the satellite manufacturer will license its existing intellectual property ("**IP**") to the satellite operator, to the extent needed to operate the satellite and for the operational life of the satellite, and the satellite operator will require that the manufacturer indemnify the satellite operator against third-party claims or suits related to contracted-for use of IP. For programs involving new IP, the parties will need to carefully consider the treatment of IP that is delivered during the course of the satellite manufacturing program. For example, will the satellite operator be contributing IP to the program? If so, does the manufacturer have the right to use such IP on other programs? Will IP be jointly developed? If so, what rights does each party have to further develop and grant licenses to such IP to other parties? Chapter 21 provides an in-depth review of intellectual property issues with respect to satellite programs.

Contract for the launch of the satellite

The contract for the launch of the satellite is typically called the "Launch Services Contract". The counterparty for this agreement is the launch services provider. A number of governments license and regulate private launch services providers. In the United States, the US Federal Aviation Administration's Office of Commercial Space Transportation licenses and regulates launch services providers and the operation of commercial launch and reentry sites,[3] as authorized by the Commercial Space Launch Act of 1984 (the "**CSLA**").[4]

A few of the specialized key provisions in a Launch Services Contract include:

---

2   "SSL to Build 13 Imaging Satellites for Skybox". *SpaceNews*. Peter B. de Selding. February 10, 2014. http://spacenews.com/39452ssl-to-build-13-imaging-satellites-for-skybox/.
3   *2015 Commercial Space Transportation Forecasts*. April 2015. FAA Commercial Space Transportation (AST) and the Commercial Space Transportation Advisory Committee. Federal Aviation Administration. p. i.
4   CFR 4.041 (Scope). 51 U.S.C. 50901-50923.

- **Description of services**: number of launches, options for additional launches, the time at which contractual performance by the launch services provider is deemed complete, launch site location and whether alternate sites are available;
- **Price and payment terms**: whether payments are made on a fixed date or on a milestone basis; invoicing mechanisms, late fees, treatment of taxes;
- **Customer rights to additional payload and performance capacity**: may involve additional significant cost and may not be determined until such time as final launch preparations are underway;
- **Launch services schedule and adjustments to schedule, delays**: designation of launch period, launch slot, launch interval and launch date during which the launch services will take place, circumstances under which the customer can be rescheduled (such as for government pre-emption), customer's rights to postpone the launch services, treatment of customer and contractor delays;
- **Reflight option**: whether customer can purchase an additional launch service in the event of a launch failure and the timing and costs associated with the reflight;
- **Representations and warranties**: for example, the launch services provider might represent that it shall maintain certain certifications and standards and otherwise abide by common standards, practices, methods and procedures in the commercial aerospace industry;
- **Licenses and regulatory clearances**: identification of parties responsible for obtaining licenses, authorizations, clearances, approvals and/or permits for obligations; compliance with government requirements including export and import laws, regulations, rules, licenses and agreements;
- **Non-recurring or recurring launch vehicle qualification criteria**: process for qualifying new and untested or significantly reconfigured launch vehicles, qualification after a launch failure;
- **Limitations on liability and disclaimer of warranties, risk allocation for launch site activities**;
- **Cross-waivers of liability and indemnification**: Each party agrees not to sue or otherwise bring a claim against the other party, related third parties or the U.S. government or its contractors or subcontractors for any injury, death, property loss or damage in connection with activities relating to the launch, and to indemnify the other party to the extent that claims of liability by such related third parties are not covered by third-party liability insurance. These are requirements in connection with the CSLA, as further discussed below;
- **Security interests**: whether customer may grant a security interest in its rights under the contract to a lender that provides financing for the performance by the customer of its obligations under the agreement (i.e. payment);
- **Termination rights by each party**: termination for convenience, termination for delay.

Technical issues, including satellite encapsulation and integration, are contained in the Statement of Work and Interface Control Document and are typically included as exhibits to the Launch Services Contract.

There are core interdependencies between the Satellite Purchase Agreement, the Launch Services Contract, the customer contracts and the financing terms for a commercial satellite program. For example, late delivery of the satellite would result in the satellite operator losing revenue that it would otherwise have received through the provision of satellite capacity to its customers as of the anticipated date of commencement of operations. The satellite operator may have an obligation under its customer contracts to commence services as of a certain date, the failure of which could result in the contract being terminated. The satellite operator may have a long-stop date under its financing, after which the satellite operator will be in default and the loan will be subject to acceleration.

Key lender-specific provisions include assignment rights and, potentially, lender access to the project. Lenders will be concerned with an overall "bankability" analysis, understanding how, for example, late delivery might be mitigated with liquidated damages and linkages to customer contracts. Certain unmitigated risks at the program level might be addressed via additional contingent equity or other additional credit support.

Recent trends and developments

An important recent development having an impact on the provision of launch services has been the resurgence of low-Earth orbiting constellations. These programs involve significant manufacturing undertakings, with groupings of satellites being built and launched together. Such programs may involve more than one launch services provider, and/or a back-up launch services provider. There are significant contracting differences between manufacturing and launching a single geosynchronous satellite versus issues that arise in the context of a constellation. A launch services contract for a constellation of satellites would include the provisions introduced above but would be significantly modified to reflect complications associated with payload delivery of multiple satellites, and scheduling launch services for the program. This would include making provision for a much more complicated set of sequencing issues and interdependencies between, for example, the timing of the delivery of the satellites and the launch of the satellites, including treatment of launch postponements at the individual and/or full schedule level, and issues such as whether the launch of multiple satellites will be grouped on a single launch. Payment schedule, termination schedule and many other provisions are necessarily more complicated. Constellation replenishment must also be considered. Many of these constellations involve or have involved new launch services providers or new vehicles. How are these providers and/or vehicles qualified as flight ready, to the satisfaction of the satellite operator and its lenders or investors? How is schedule risk managed? How is the insurance program organized? All of these issues must be carefully considered and understood as it relates to the overall program.

Another trend in recent years has been creative partnering between satellite operators seeking to develop new programs. This has stemmed from the need to share financial or other resources. For example, the joint procurement of four all-electric Boeing 702-SPs by two regional satellite operators, Asia Broadcast Satellite and Satmex (now Eutelsat Americas), was the first time electric thrusters were to be used to carry a satellite from initial transfer orbit to final geostationary position. By joining forces, the regional satellite operators were able to achieve an economy of scale in satellite and rocket production usually reserved for larger satellite operators.[5] The purchase and delivery of the satellites was reportedly governed under a joint procurement agreement.[6] Another example is the Horizons 3e satellite, a joint effort between JSAT and Intelsat, in which Intelsat contributed the orbital slot at 169E, and part of an ongoing 10 year cooperation and joint venture with Horizons 3e representing the fourth

---

5   Selding, Peter B. "ABS, Satmex Banding Together for Boeing Satellite Buy". *Space News*. March 13, 2012. http://spacenews.com/abs-satmex-banding-together-boeing-satellite-buy/.

6   "ABS and Satmex jointly buy all-electric Boeing satellites". *Satellite Finance*. March 13, 2012. www.satellitefinance.com/insights/abs-and-satmex-jointly-buy-all-electric-boeing-satellites.

joint satellite project between them.[7] Other examples involve hosted payloads and various forms of shared ownership of satellites, sometimes dubbed "condosats" – a moniker some consider descriptive and others misleading. Other creative approaches have involved satellite manufacturers sharing risk through providing vendor-financing.

Each of these joint efforts have the same program considerations in a procurement by a single entity, but with varying complications of certain terms that necessarily involving another layer of background coordination and negotiation of rights and responsibilities between the companies. The following questions often arise: How do satellite operators involved in a joint procurement negotiate the various factors associated with program schedule? How do lenders to a program with a hosted payload or condosat arrangement assess counterparty risk? What does "ownership" of a satellite mean on a jointly-flagged satellite, and how are issues such as program management and oversight during the manufacturing process negotiated? What elements are commonly owned in such programs, and how are spare component redundancy and power sharing addressed? How are issues such as lender assignability negotiated when multiple parties are involved? How does one owner ensure that they have quiet enjoyment rights and non-disturbance rights, if the other owner has a lender and that lender wishes to enforce its security interest? How are licensing and coordination issues addressed? How are these programs insured? How do these arrangements impact other program risks and relationships? Each of these and many other factors must be carefully considered and explored.

Insuring satellite programs

Satellite operators will typically insure the cost of the satellite, the launch services and the cost of the insurance premium in the event of a partial or total failure of the satellite. Key coverages on the satellite will include (1) pre-launch insurance, (2) launch and initial operations insurance and (3) in-orbit insurance. Additionally, third-party liability is customarily procured. A satellite operator must ensure that insurance coverage in connection with ground coverage during pre-launch, attachment of launch-risk coverage and a terminated ignition or pad abort event are seamless, since the satellite operator bears the risk of an uninsured loss arising from gaps in coverage. As a result, it is critical that the project contracts and policy language regarding the terms "intentional ignition", "total loss" and "partial loss" are aligned, otherwise there could be a gap in coverage.

Pre-launch insurance includes all-risks and transit of the satellite, up to the time of "intentional ignition" of the satellite, and such insurance is almost always procured by the satellite manufacturer as a requirement under the satellite manufacturing contract. Risk of Loss passes from the satellite manufacturer to the satellite operator at intentional ignition of the satellite.

Launch insurance is typically procured by the satellite operator and covers all risks of physical loss of or damage to a satellite arising out of the launch process, at the moment of intentional ignition, until the satellite has separated from the launch vehicle. The named insured changes because risk of loss of the satellite passes from the manufacturer to the satellite operator at the time of delivery. For a financed satellite program, the lender will be the loss payee – the party entitled to receive the insurance proceeds in the event of a loss. Launch insurance may also include the first 12 months of operations of the satellite while it is in orbit, the arrangement deemed "Launch + 1" in the industry.

7   "JSAT and Intelsat to jointly own Asia Pacific-focused Epic satellite." *Satellite Finance*. November 4, 2015. www.satellitefinance.com/insights/jsat-and-intelsat-jointly-own-asia-pacific-focused-epic-satellite.

Launch liability insurance usually addresses damage, harm or death in space, in airspace or on the ground, and will name the launch services provider as the named insured. Additional insureds typically include the supplier, the satellite operator, lenders and the government of the launching state. Third-party liability insurance is the insurance to protect against any liabilities brought in any jurisdiction for bodily injury to third parties and damage to third-party property incurred anywhere in the World.[8]

For U.S. launch services providers, the Commercial Space Launch Act requires launch vehicle operators to have liability insurance up to a required threshold.[9] A licensee is not required to obtain insurance or demonstrate financial responsibility of more than $500,000,000 for claims by a third party for death, bodily injury, or property damage or loss resulting from an activity carried out under the license.[10] The launch services provider is required to make a reciprocal waiver of claims with its contractors, subcontractors, and customers, and contractors and subcontractors of its customers, involved in the launch services under which each party agrees to be responsible for property damage or loss it sustains, or for personal injury to, death, property damage or loss by its own employees resulting from the launch activities.[11]

Title I, Section 102 of the recent H.R. 2262, U.S. Commercial Space Launch Competitiveness Act, passed by Congress and signed by the President in November 2015, includes two important provisions relating to commercial satellite launches and insurance. The first provision, §102(b), directs the Administration to reevaluate the calculations necessary to determine the maximum probable loss from a launch and specifically includes a desire of Congress to balance the potential impact on Federal liabilities with the necessary amount of insurance that a private company needs to purchase. The second provision, §102(d), extends the Federal indemnification for launch liability until 30 September 2025.

Financing of satellite projects

There is a great diversity in the sources and types of financing available in connection with a satellite program. Potential sources include venture capital, private equity and debt, commercial banks, capital markets, export credit agencies, vendor-financing and anchor-tenant financing. Types of financings range from investments, to unsecured debt, to corporate financing, to project financing, among others. Broadly speaking, in a corporate financing in which the satellite operator as a going concern is receiving financing, the significance of certain program-level risks are reviewed globally in order to determine whether the potential outcomes could result in a material impact on the company, as a whole, and which would affect the company's ability to pay back its debt. Conversely, in a project financing, the lender looks to the revenues of the project, any insurance proceeds, the project contracts and, in some cases, the work in process, as the source of collateral during construction with limited resourse to the project sponsors. As such, the risks associated with the individual project assume greater importance.

---

8   It should be clearly noted that nations that have launch operations have a treaty obligation that specifically requires that launching state to ultimately indemnify any other nation for third-party injury claims arising out of launch operations or the re-entry of vehicles or their parts (Outer Space Treaty, Art. VII). Because of this, nations impose insurance and indemnification requirements on commercial launch and payload companies. In the United States this obligation is incorporated into the Commercial Space Launch Act and the subsequent regulatory actions of the Department of Transportation (FAA).
9   Public Law 98-575-Oct. 30, 1984. 49 USC app 2513. Section 16 ("Liability Insurance").
10   51 U.S. Code § 50914(a)(3)(A)(i).
11   51 U.S. Code § 50914(b)(i).

The sources and types of financings available to a satellite operator will vary, depending on the credit-worthiness of the satellite operator and the type of project, among many other factors. Each approach comes with different trade-offs. While public capital markets often offer a lower cost of capital than private markets, as well as less restrictive covenants,[12] accessing public capital markets comes with a whole set of other requirements and may not be an option for a new market entrant. Equity investors and lenders will have the same considerations, but may view risks through a different lens. Take, for example, pre-launch sales of satellite capacity. While pre-sold capacity establishes a strong market proposition for a program, capacity sold two or three years prior to a satellite even being launched may be heavily discounted when compared to capacity sold on an existing satellite that can provide services today. A lender's primary concern will be repayment of debt. They will not be sympathetic to an argument that there are additional margins to be found by holding off on sales, while an equity investor who benefits from the upside of the profits may take a different view – but both will be equally concerned with market horizon. Equity investors may also be more likely to support a program with newer, less proven technology if the upside may be great. Lenders will typically prefer a proven technology and will be more likely to seek to minimize risks across the program. A strong satellite operator/borrower with other financing options usually will have more leverage and accordingly will generally be able to negotiate a lighter covenant package with a lower percentage of pre-sold capacity on the satellite, all other things being equal.

Satellite operators with an established track record may view extensive lender involvement as potentially detrimental or at least as hampering their ability to nimbly respond to market considerations. They may press for a lighter covenant package such that lender control is only triggered if certain events occur or ratios are not complied with. A new satellite operator may not have the negotiating strength to obtain such a covenant package; in that case, they may use more restrictive financing early on and then refinance debt once the risk profile has improved, such as after in-orbit testing of the satellite or once financial ratios and percentage of pre-sales creates a stronger credit risk profile. Satellite operators should carefully review their covenant packages with experienced counsel in order to understand how their financing documentation can impact the operations of the company as well as future flexibility of the company's activities.

Investor/lender due diligence of satellite programs

As part of the legal diligence process, lenders will review, among others, credit, legal, technical and market risk. They will also seek to confirm that adequate insurance requirements have been established and complied with, and that lender-specific endorsements have been obtained prior to the first disbursement of funds. Along with legal counsel, lenders may engage a technical consultant, market consultant and insurance consultant. Lenders will review the satellite manufacturing contract, the launch services contract, the key customer agreements, insurance and documentation of existing debt, along with many other aspects of the program. A full review of lender analysis of satellite operator/borrower risk is beyond the scope of this chapter, but key considerations include the satellite operator's credit profile, foreign exchange earnings relative to currency debt burden, credit rating of customer parties, assets, liquidity, business profile and management ability, strength of financials, country risk, credit-worthiness

---

12 Mark L. Mandel, James H. Ball, Jr., Rod Miller, Brett Nadritch, Arnold B. Peinado III, Manan Shah. *The IPO and Public Company Primer: A Practical Guide to Going Public, Raising Capital and Life as a Public Company.* RR Donnelley. 2014. p. 1.

obligors, the repayment period and the drawdown period.[13] Lenders will also diligence the satellite manufacturer, the launch services provider and key revenue generating customers, among others, and may require financial statements and other information about these parties. As part of their due diligence inquiry, lenders will seek to understand the key milestones and provisions for delay by the manufacturer in the satellite manufacturing contract and how these align with the satellite operator's rights to change schedule in the launch services contract, as well as the satellite operator's obligations under the customer contracts and the key customers' rights to terminate in the event of delay. Lenders will also seek to understand, among other risks, what the impact of delay will be on the overall program, and gaps in liability between contractual obligations that would fall to the satellite operator and, ultimately, to the lender as the lender ultimately bears the credit risk and default risk of the satellite operator.

Insurance from the perspective of the lender

Lenders will often require as a condition to loan disbursement that the insurances described earlier in this chapter be in place with premiums paid, and that the underwriters or insurance companies meet certain ratings requirements. Loan documentation will also typically contain an ongoing covenant requiring the borrower to maintain such insurances, as long as the insurance is available on reasonable and customary terms. There may be instances when such insurance is not available. Pre-launch satellite property insurance premium rates and the maximum per-launch coverage fluctuate with the market, based on recent claims. A satellite operator may need to negotiate with its lenders for an appropriate waiver resulting from the satellite operator's inability to procure the required insurances as a result of market forces. In the event of a total loss, loan documentation associated with the financing of a single satellite will likely require that all insurance proceeds in respect of the total loss be applied to the mandatory prepayment of the credit. In some cases, including loans in which the loan obligor is a sufficiently creditworthy going concern, the loan proceeds may be able to be applied to a replacement program in accordance with a lender-approved replacement plan. In the event of a partial loss, there is typically a threshold amount below which the satellite operator may apply the proceeds as it sees fit, and above which it must use the funds towards a mandatory prepayment or towards a lender-approved replacement plan. This is similar to what might be seen in the context of a non-satellite infrastructure financing.

Collateral

In a secured financing, collateral is used to secure the repayment of the satellite operator/borrower's debt. The customary collateral package includes, during manufacture includes: the Satellite Purchase Agreement (including IP and support after launch), the Launch Services Contract, insurance proceeds, TT&C Contract, or ground facility and associated real property, customer contracts, and governmental authorizations.

Once the satellite is in orbit and operating, the core collateral customarily includes the satellite, the TT&C facility, including the real property upon which the TT&C facility is located, and the ground segment infrastructure, including gateways, network operation center

---

13   For example, see Ex-Im Bank's "Credit Classification Definitions for Non-Financial Institution Risk: Qualitative Descriptions of Non-Financial Institution Risk for FIBC, Medium and Long-Term Transactions". www.exim.gov/tools-for-exporters/exposure-fees/credit-classification-definitions. Last accessed December 4, 2015.

and interconnection facilities. The lender will also be concerned with governmental authorizations and the licenses needed to operate the space and ground systems in the event the lender must take possession of the satellite.

The value of a satellite (and of the underlying contracts to manufacture and launch the satellite), is limited without the associated revenue-generating customer contracts. There are limited alternative applications for satellites that are far along in the manufacturing process or that are already launched into space. Similarly, a customer contract, by itself, is not of value unless it can be assigned to a satellite operator with similar coverage and parameters that can fulfill the same customer requirements.[14]

Pre-sales of capacity will be a key differentiator to lenders and to investors. Customer contracts are the life blood of the satellite project, and they are the core security assuming the lender has all of the other rights it needs to step into the project in the event of a default.

Direct agreements with key contractual counterparties

Direct agreements are sometimes a requirement of lenders lending on a project financing basis, where the lenders look to the program for security rather than to the ongoing commercial credit of the satellite operator. The company's contractual rights to manufacture and launch the satellite are the key assets of the project company during the manufacturing phase. Direct agreements establish a direct line of privity between a lender and a satellite operator's counterparty. Lenders will customarily seek to have such agreements with the satellite manufacturer, the launch services provider, and other key project participants, covering, among other things, lender cure rights in the event of a satellite operator's breach, the counterparty's consent to the assignment of the contract as collateral and acknowledgment of the lender's security interest in the satellite operator's rights to the contract, and the obligation that the counterparty provide copies of all notices. A customer will be concerned with preserving its access to the capacity such that the customer would not, as a result of the satellite operator's security agent enforcing any security over the satellite or taking any physical action over the satellite, lose the contractual benefits of the capacity agreement or be disturbed by the security agent or the senior creditors in receiving access to capacity pursuant to, and in accordance with, the terms of the capacity agreement. The customer would expect, so long as the underlying capacity agreement has not been terminated, that it will continue to have exclusive rights to possession and control of its transponders.[15]

The lenders may resist a provision allowing the customer to continue to have and enjoy the benefits of the capacity agreement and not be disturbed in receiving the performance thereof notwithstanding any default or breach on the part of the satellite operator under the loan documentation, because in so doing, they effectively make it impossible to move the satellite to another orbital slot. However, under most circumstances, the greatest value of an in-orbit satellite is in the orbital slot for which it is designed and for which existing pre-sold capacity agreements have been contracted for.

There are features of certain satellite programs, especially geostationary programs, that make it more difficult for a customer to seek services elsewhere. For example, in a direct-to-home

---

14   Peter Nesgos, Presentation: What Makes Satellite Financing Different, Challenging and Unpredictable? April 4, 2013.
15   Peter Nesgos, "Satellites and Transponders." *Equipment Leasing*. Ed. Jeffrey J. Wong. Matthew Bender & Co. 2010.

program, it would be difficult for the customer to re-point each satellite dish, for each of its customers, at a new satellite. Because customers are somewhat captive, a direct agreement may be less critical than if the customer were completely free to choose another provider of capacity.

Creation and perfection of security interests under the U.C.C.

The process and associated formalities of creating and perfecting a security interest is determined by the laws under which the security interest is governed. In the United States, versions of Article 9 of the Uniform Commercial Code (the "**U.C.C.**"), which governs the creation and perfection of security interests, have been adopted in all of the states, including New York.[16] Article 9 applies to a transaction, regardless of form, that creates a security interest in personal property.[17] A "security interest" is defined under the U.C.C. As "an interest in personal property ... which secures payment or performance of an obligation."[18] A satellite would be deemed personal property under Article 9.[19] Thus a security interest in a satellite can be created in the United States by contract, and such security interest will be governed under Article 9.

The creation and perfection of a security interest in other jurisdictions, however, must be carefully researched. A new international convention sponsored by UNIDROIT would create a uniform international system to register security interests in satellites.[20] However, as discussed below, some industry participants are skeptical about the purpose and benefits of the Convention.

Perfection of security interests: unidroit space assets protocol as an alternative

The International Institute for the Unification of Private Law (UNIDROIT) is an independent intergovernmental Organization with its seat in the Villa Aldobrandini in Rome. Its purpose is to study needs and methods for modernizing, harmonizing and coordinating private and in particular commercial law as between States and groups of States and to formulate uniform law instruments, principles and rules to achieve those objectives.[21]

Approximately 20 years have elapsed since this international organization began developing a legal regime for protecting large mobile equipment that either crosses international borders or would be located in outer space (a geographic location designated to be without sovereignty by treaty). At the time of the commencement of this initiative, asset-based financing was how many airplanes, railroad cars and communications satellites were financed and there was a need for developing a trans-national system to protect lenders and the owners of assets.

The Cape Town Convention on Interests in Mobile Equipment was drafted in 2001 and was designed to protect lenders and owners of large, valuable assets that are easily moved across

---

16 James J. White and Summers. *Uniform Commercial Code*. West Group Practitioner Treatise Series. Fifth Edition. Vol. 4. West Group. 2002. 30–1(a).
17 U.C.C. § 9-109(a)(1).
18 U.C.C. § 1-201(35).
19 See U.C.C. § 9-102(a)(44), defining "Goods" under Article 9.
20 Panahy, Dara and Raman Mittal. "The Prospective UNIDROIT Convention on International Interests in Mobile Equipment as Applied to Space Property." *Uniform Law Review*. NS – Vol. IV. UNIDROIT. 1999–2.
21 www.unidroit.org/about-unidroit/overview accessed 27 November 2015.

borders during normal activities. The main issue was, of course, the protection of the ownership and collateral security in that asset when it is moved from the country with direct jurisdiction over the asset and company to another jurisdiction with possibly different collateral security and enforcement laws and regulations. The Convention and its supporting Protocols have five basic objectives:

1. to provide for the creation of an international interest which will be recognized in all Contracting States;
2. to provide the creditor with a range of basic default remedies and, where there is evidence of default, a means of obtaining speedy interim relief pending final determination of its claim on the merits;
3. to establish an electronic international register for the registration of international interests which will give notice of their existence to third parties and enable the creditor to preserve its priority against subsequently registered interests and against unregistered interests and the debtor's insolvency administrator;
4. to ensure through the relevant Protocol that the particular needs of the industry sector concerned are met;
5. by these means to give intending creditors greater confidence in the decision to grant credit, enhance the credit rating of equipment receivables and reduce borrowing costs to the advantage of all interested parties.[22]

The Convention itself entered into force on 3 January 2006 and currently has 69 contracting states.[23]

Three different protocols were drafted under this Convention. One was for aircraft, one for railroad cars, and one for space assets. Only the protocol covering aircraft has been signed by enough nations (currently 59) to be in force.

This short description focusing on space assets will not attempt to trace all of the history of these protocols, but only illustrate that over time a number of both financial and technical conditions have changed and what once looked like a very promising international protocol and a stimulus for commercial and private space operations has ended up as a stalled agreement with only four nations as signatories and no ratifications.

However, it should be clearly noted that the business of space-based telecommunications has been, and continues to be, a thriving and profitable business venture for a number of private companies. The existence of a commercial market has contributed to the establishment of rapid global communications to many peoples and nations that otherwise would not have had these opportunities.

During the 1980s and 1990s there was a rapid growth of new private telecommunications satellites. Space-based capabilities grew rapidly, particularly in the use of the geosynchronous orbit for wide area coverage of communications. Today there is terrestrial ground receiving equipment also improved, particularly for small, inexpensive consumer/home receiving antennae. This, combined with more powerful, longer-lasting, and larger satellites enabled a fast development of many services.

The largest revenue generating satellites quickly became those broadcasting television directly to consumers. The financing of new satellite systems was sometimes asset-based, with

---

22 www.unidroit.org/overview-2001capetown, accessed 27 November 2015.
23 www.unidroit.org/status-2001capetown, accessed 27 November 2015.

lenders holding financial interests in the space-based assets, either as a whole or for specific transponders incorporated into the asset but dedicated to a specific customer or user. Addressing treatment was part of the backdrop to the Convention.

In asset-based financing, a creditor's ability to have prompt recourse to the underlying assets in the event of a default is a principal factor in determining how the transaction's risks, and overall costs, are calculated. Where national legal rules for the recognition and enforcement of security interests present impediments to such prompt recourse, or are materially different from rules in other jurisdictions, the risks (or perceived risks) for the creditor can increase, particularly if, as in the case of aircraft objects, the asset will be moving through different jurisdictions and possibly become subject to such national legal rules at the time of default. The costs of finance tend to be higher as a result of the increased risks. The Convention addresses this issue by establishing an international legal framework for the creation, recognition, registration and enforcement of "international interests" in high-value mobile equipment.[24]

Over time the largest companies involved in satellite services have matured to the point where other forms of financing expensive space assets are available. This has led to a division among space communication companies between the powerful large companies and the smaller newer entrants (as well as less industrialized nations). The large satellite operating companies, the space insurance industry, and the satellite manufacturers, as a group, now strongly oppose the ratification of the Space Protocol of the Cape Town Convention.[25] They argue that it is not necessary since there have been no serious financing issues, and it would increase costs and regulatory burdens unnecessarily. Some also argue that the Convention is directed toward mobile assets, which for these purposes are assets moving across national borders, and that satellites as space objects under the Outer Space Treaty always remain under the jurisdiction and control of one nation.[26,27] Others still advocate for its acceptance and for States to become contracting parties to the Protocol.

One interesting aspect of this Protocol is the definition of a space asset. Article 1 states that a:

(k) "space asset" means any man-made uniquely identifiable asset in space or designed to be launched into space, and comprising
  (i) a spacecraft, such as a satellite, space station, space module, space capsule, space vehicle or reusable launch vehicle, whether or not including a space asset falling within (ii) or (iii) below;
  (ii) a payload (whether telecommunications, navigation, observation, scientific or otherwise) in respect of which a separate registration may be effected in accordance with the regulations; or
  (iii) a part of a spacecraft or payload such as a transponder, in respect of which a separate registration may be effected in accordance with the regulations, together with all installed, incorporated or attached accessories, parts and equipment and all data, manuals and records relating thereto.

---

[24] Unidroit, *DEPOSITARY REPORT* 1 January 2012–31 December 2013, DC9/DEP-Doc.11, August 2014.
[25] See, for example, Neil Stephens, *The Cape Town Convention Space Protocol, An Insurance Underwriter's Perspective,* Atrium Space Insurance Consortium, 9 February 2011.
[26] Outer Space Treaty, Articles VI and VIII.
[27] Sa'id Mosteshar, *Financing Space Assets: The Unidroit Solution Examined,* London Institute of Space Policy and Law, Practitioner and Industry Workshop, 9 February 2011.

It is interesting to note that although the Protocol specifically deals with "interests in mobile equipment" the discussion surrounding the Protocol was oriented toward communication satellites, which, in 2001 was virtually the only commercially financed category of space assets. However, the original and the slightly amended definition of space assets includes all types of equipment and makes no distinction between government, civil, or privately owned spacecraft. It still is an open question as to how this agreement would be enforced – would governments be obligated to register their satellites? Would components on hosted payloads be registered separately? Or, would the Supervisory Authority and Registry only apply to equipment that was financed through asset-based contracts?

Similarly there are also questions concerning liability, salvage, jurisdiction, and the relationship of provisions of the Protocol with respect to specific national laws, such as the export control regime of the United States, that need to be clarified.[28]

For purposes of the Protocol, this definition sets up the establishment of a new registration process and system for space assets. Although this has been deemed not to duplicate or interfere with the existing Outer Space Treaty or the Convention on the Registration of Space Objects and the UNOOSA register of space objects,[29] it nevertheless does add a potential new burden on the current space regulatory process. And, it should be noted that the treaty definition of a space object is quite vague.[30] And, the UNOOSA Registry associates space objects with the launching state (of which each object may have more than one), not with any financing designation and it has no formal method of reflecting the sale, transfer, lease, or other change in ownership. In fact, it does not even require a State to notify the registry when the space object has reached its end-of-life.

But, the UN registry of space objects has proven to be a useful base for identifying most satellites and other objects launched into space, even if it is not a basis for a legal/ownership/financial interest identification or dispute.[31]

Finally, although there have been international discussions about the formation of a new registry under this Protocol, it has not been implemented, nor is it likely to be completed any time soon. The Protocol also calls for the formation of a Supervisory Authority to oversee its implementation. The Supervisory Authority as well as the registry would be fee-based and self-financing. Although international organizations such as the International Telecommunication Union have expressed interest in hosting such a registry, no formal processes have begun to implement this. Many nations have also expressed reservations focused on the imposition of yet another organization for space activities that includes overlapping jurisdiction with the existing UN and ITU space offices as well as with national law.

In spite of the objections, the *Protocol to the Convention on International Interests in Mobile Equipment on Matters Specific to Space Assets* was signed at a meeting in Berlin, Germany on 9 March 2012. However, only four nations have signed this Protocol and none has ratified it. Subsequent to the Berlin Agreement, the ITU has issued a report detailing activities to be discussed under the protocol including the establishment of a new Supervisory Authority and

---

28 Larsen, Paul, *Report on the UNIDROIT Space Project Protocol*, IAC-06-E6.2-A04, September 2006.
29 Op. cit.
30 Henry Hertzfeld, Fault Liability for Third Party Damage in Space: Is Article IV(1)(b) of the Liability Convention Useful Today?, IAC-10.E7.3, Paper presented at IISL Prague, CZ, September 2010.
31 An interesting and current discussion of these topics can be found in: Bruce Cahan, Irmgard Marboe, Henning Roedel, *Outer Frontiers of Banking: Financing Space Explorers, and Safeguarding Terrestrial Finance*, IAC-15,E6,1,5x29408, Jerusalem, Israel October 2015.

Registry.[32] To date, although meetings and discussions have been held, no concrete action has been taken to establish any new legal regime.

Looking forward and other areas of inquiry

This chapter has introduced some of the critical components of a commercial satellite program as well as some of the key current topics impacting such programs. There are basic requirements and contractual arrangements associated with any program, but these are necessarily tailored to each individual program. Many of the issues that concern a satellite operator will also be important to potential lenders and investors, although the ways in which the risks are viewed and addressed vary. There are additionally different sources and types of financing, each with different considerations. Fully describing and analyzing the proper structuring of a satellite financing arrangement is beyond the scope of this chapter. It is, nonetheless, important to emphasize that understanding the risks and the points of leverage in the various negotiations between investors and lenders as well as the different financial and legal formats of satellite projects is central to a successful financing arrangement. These additional factors should also be fully understood by all parties to such a negotiation and transaction.

Acknowledgement

I would like to thank Peter Nesgos and Dara Panahy for their thoughtful input and comments to this chapter, along with their ongoing support and guidance over the years.

---

32   ITU Plenipotentiary Conference PP-14, 20 October to 7 November 2014, *ITU'S Role as Supervisory Authority fo the International Registration System for Space Assets under the Space Protocols,* Document 62-E, 8 August 2014.

Index

4-D trajectories 176
49 USC Chapter 701 271, 282

ABM Treaty (Treaty between the US and the USSR on the Limitation of Anti-Ballistic Missile Systems) 205, 206
absolute liability 65–6
Activation for Asia Pacific 155
Active Debris Removal (ADR) 79–80, 189
active sensing 246
Activities of Launching, Flight Operation or Guidance of Space Objects (2005, Belgium) 278–9
Act on the Protection of Personal Information (2003, Japan) 311
adjudication 103–4
adjudicative jurisdiction 43
ADS-B 176
advance publication information (API) procedure 122–3; Article 9 124, 125, 126
adverse changes 80, 81
Agreement on Civil Aircraft 168
Agreement on Government Procurement 167
Agreement on Trade in Civil Aircraft 167
Airbus 242n9
Airports Authority of India (AAI) 163, 316; liability of 317–18
air space 27; delimitation of 27, 27n17; demarcation line with outer space 28
American Arbitration Association (AAA) 102
ANS (Air Navigations Services) 175, 176
ANSP (air navigation signal provider) 316; liability to GNSS 317, 318
Antarctic Treaty 202
Antrix 102
AP30A (Appendix 30A): Annex 1 132, 133; Article 2A 133; Article 4 130, 131, 132, 133; Article 5 131; Articles 9 and 9A 129, 130
AP30 (Appendix 30): Annex 1 132, 133; Article 2A 133; Article 4 130, 131, 132, 133; Article 5 131; Articles 10 and 11 129, 130
AP30B (Appendix 30B) 134; 6.17 136; Annex 1 134; Annex 3 135; Annex 4 136; Article 6 135, 136, 137, 139; Article 7 137, 139; Article 8 136; Article 10 134
AP I (Additional Protocol I to the 1949 Geneva Convention) 221, 222; Article 35 (3) 223; burden of proof 223
appropriate state, status of 46–7
APSCO Convention 330
ARABSAT 37
arbitral tribunals 99
arbitration 101–3
Area Control List (ACL) 331
Argentina 213; discovery and return of private spacecraft 48
Ariane Agreement (1973) 275
Ariane Program 275
Arianespace 275
armed conflict, law of see LOAC (law of armed conflict)
arms control: ad hoc Committee 207; CBM ideas 212–14; de-weaponization proposals 210; difficulty defining weaponization of space 208–9; existing agreements relevant to PAROS 209; existing proposals and future initiatives 209; partial approach 212; program of work 206–7; prohibited actions 211–12; TCBM efforts 215–17; weaponization of space v. military use of space 207–8
Arms Export Control Act (1976) 331
Article 38 (ICJ Statute) 5, 18; customary law 5,

Index

8–9; general principles 5, 9–10; hierarchy of sources 15–16; judgements and case law 5, 10–11; "the most highly regarded publicists" 11–12; treaties 5, 6–7
ASAT (anti-satellite) weapons 205, 207, 209; attacks 223; existing proposals and future initiatives 209; partial ban 212; Russian moratorium 213; tests 197–8
Asia Broadcast Satellite 341
Asian Disaster Reduction Centre 155
Asia Pacific Space Cooperation Organization (APSCO) 37
Assembly and Command Ship 51
assertion 3
asset-based financing 348–9
associated bodies 156, 158
Astrium 102
ATM Modernization 176
Atomic Energy Act (1946) 331
Australia: liability for space transportation 274; spaceports 283; space transportation 273–4
Australia Group (AG) 218
Australian law: outer space borders 54
Australian Space Activities Act (1998) 270, 273–4, 283
Austrian Federal Law 83
Authorized Users (AUs) 155, 157
authors 259
Avanti Communications 102
aviation: and GNSS 175; safety 177

backward contamination 80, 81
Basic Space Law (Japan) 309
BeiDou 2 – COMPASS 161, 162
BeiDou ASEAN Tour 307
BeiDou Asia-Pacific Tour 307
BeiDou Satellite Navigation Industry 306
BeiDou System: administration, organization and general policy framework 305–6; international agreements 306–7; objectives 305; principles 305; privacy protection 308; services 304; spectrum protection 307–8; status 304–5; three-step roadmap 304
BeiDou Working Group 307
Belgium 58; liability 279; space transportation 278–9
beneficiary bodies 156
Benefit Principles 21
Berne Convention on Copyright 169, 259, 328; Article 2 258; copyright 328–9
bilateral agreements 163–4
bodies of law: hierarchies 16
Boeing Company 48, 52, 62, 102
BOO (build, own and operate) 310
BR IFIC (International Frequency Information Circular of the Radiocommunication Bureau) 123, 130, 138, 139; PART III-S 128; PART II-S 128
broadcasting satellites 232–3
BSS (broadcasting satellite service) 126, 233; and associated feeder-link Plans 129–30; List 130; procedure for implementation of Plan or List assignments (Article 5) 131; procedures for modifications 131, 131–3
Bureau (Radiocommunication Bureau of the ITU) 115, 117–18, 122; allotment examinations 137; assignment notifications 131; coordination requests 124, 125, 126; cost recovery 138–9; due diligence information 138; examination of submissions 131–2, 135; notification examination 128; notification of frequency assignments 127; regulatory requirements for small satellites 140–1; required agreements 136; technical examinations 132

Cabinet Administration Office (CAO, Japan) 310
Canada: dissemination of raw data 255; distinction between raw and processed EO data 256; licensing of data 252, 253; licensing provisions 254–5; militarization of outer space 205; PAXSAT-A proposal 214; personal jurisdiction over natural persons 251; satellite remote sensing operations 251
Canadian Remote Sensing Act (2005) 79
Cape Town Convention on Interests in Mobile Equipment (2006) 347–9; Space Protocol 349–51
Carter, President 204
case law 10–11; domestic 11
CBM (confidence building measures) 212–13; amending the Registration Convention 213; declaration of non-deployment of weapons in outer space 213; elaboration of a code of conduct 214; ISI proposals 213–14; keep-out zones 214; satellite monitoring systems 214
CD (Conference on Disarmament): ad hoc Committee 207; arms control efforts 206–17; CBM ideas 212–14; de-weaponization proposals 210; difficulty defining weaponization of space 208–9; existing agreements relevant to PAROS 209; existing proposals and future initiatives 209; partial approach 212; program of work 206–7; prohibited actions 211–12; TCBM efforts 215–17; weaponization of space v. military use of space 207–8
celestial bodies 29; peaceful purposes 34
Centre National d'Études Spatiales (CNES) *see* CNES
certification 269–70
Charter of the United Nations (UN) *see* UN Charter

353

Index

Cheng, Professor B. 12, 64
Chicago Convention 56, 61, 176
China: ASAT tests 198; definition of weaponization 209; GNSS 161, 162; international agreements on satellite navigation 306–7; militarization of outer space 205; National Industry Standard 79; privacy protection 308; satellite navigation *see* BeiDou System
China-Brazil Earth Resources Satellites 264
China Satellite Navigation Conference 307
China Satellite Navigation Office (CSNO) 305, 306; training 307
Chinese People's Liberation Army 307
Christol, Professor C. 12
Civil Aviation Authority (CAA) 57
civilian satellites 222
Claims Commission 68
climate change 148
CNES 78, 275–6, 277, 283, 284; Standard 78
CNS/ATM 317
Cold War 226
collateral 345–7
collision avoidance manoeuvres 189
commercial remote sensing 148
Commercial Remote Sensing Policy (2003) 250
commercial satellites 333–4; collateral 345–7; contracts for the launch of 339–41; contracts for the manufacture of 336–8; creation and perfection of security interests under the U.C.C. 347; direct agreements 346–7; financing of projects 343–5; industry of 334–5; insurance 342–3, 345; intellectual property arrangements 339; investor/lender due diligence 344–5; in-law, delivery contracts 338–9; manufacturing and launch services contracts 335–6; procurement of satellite programs and key associated contracts 335–42; recent trends and developments 341–2
Commercial Service (CS) 296, 297
Commercial Space Launch Act (CSLA, 1984) 39, 62, 339, 343
Commercial Space Launch Amendments Act (2004) 39, 54
Commercial Space Launch Competitiveness Act (2015) 343
Commission Directive 145
Common Heritage of Mankind (CHM) 33–4
common spaces: laws governing 27
compatibility 163
compensation 61, 64; dispute settlement mechanism 68; financial 69; launching States 70; *restitutio in integrum* 69
Comprehensive Test Ban Treaty (1996) 6
conciliation 100–1
concurrent jurisdiction 43

Conference on Disarmament (CD) *see* CD (Conference on Disarmament) 20
conflicts *see* disputes and conflict
conjunctions 191
consultation and negotiation 96–8
contamination 80, 81
contracts, commercial satellites 336–8
Convention on Broadcasting (1936) 235
Convention on International Interests in Mobile Equipment 142
Convention on International Liability for Damage Caused by Space Objects (LIAB) 277
Convention on Registration of Objects Launched into Outer Space (1975) 150; Article IV 272
cooperating bodies 156
cooperation principle 35–7; Principles XIII and XIV 152
coordination procedures 121, 123; action upon requests for 126; requirement and request for 124–5
coordination requests (CRs) 123
Copernicus data 264, 267
copyright 169, 170, 258–9, 328–9; Canada 259; EO data 259–60; licensing and 260–2; maps 260; United States of America (US) 259
Copyright Act (Canada) 259
Copyright Act (US) 259, 329
copyright law (Germany) 259
CORPAS-SARSAT system 161
cosmic navigation systems 178–9
Cosmos 954 (USSR) 11, 86, 96–7, 100
COSPAR (Committee on Space Research) 81–2
COSPAS-SARSAT 236
cost recovery 138–9; data 263
criminal jurisdiction 50
crisis victims 156
cross-waivers, liability 105, 326
CS (Constitution of the ITU): Article 14 115; Article 28 112; Article 31 110; Article 44 114; Article 45 113
Cuba 213
CubeSats 188
Curaçao 58
customary international law 8–9; delimitation of air space and outer space 54; Draft Articles on State Responsibility 14
CV (Convention of the ITU) 110, 112, 187; Article 11 116–17; right to privacy of correspondence by electronic means 231; on the RRB 115–16

damage: definition 67
damage liability *see* liability
data: collecting, processing and disseminating

354

253–5; Copernicus data 264, 267; cost recovery 138–9, 263; definition 244; dissemination of 253–5; Earth observation *see* Earth observation data; ephemeris 191; government 263; licensing of 251–2; open data trend 262–4, 267; ownership of 263; priority access to the government 252; raw 255; remote sensing and 151–2; space data 245; terminology and characteristics 245–6; *see also* primary data; processed data
DBS (direct broadcasting service) 233, 328, 329
Decca Limited v. United States case (1976) 327
Declaration between the Ariane Exploitation Phase Participating States (1980) 275
Declaration on International Cooperation in the Exploration and Use of Outer Space for the Benefit and in the Interest of All States, Taking into Particular Account the Needs of Developing Countries (1996) 21
decolonization 227
Decree No. 323 (2008) 302
Definition phase (Galileo) 296, 297
de lege ferenda 174–5
Delta II 48
Democratic People's Republic of Korea (DPRK) 17
Dempsey, Professor P. 194
Department of Space (DOS, India) 314
Devas Corporation 102
developed States 227–8; cooperation principle 36
developing States 227–8; cooperation principle 36
Development and Validation phase (Galileo) 296, 297
Differential Correction and Monitoring System (DCMS) 301
Digital Globe 231
direct agreements 346–7
Direct Broadcasting Principles 232; prohibition of propaganda 235
direct causation theory 65
Directorate of Defense Trade Controls (DDTC) 331
direct satellite broadcasting 232, 233
Direct Television Broadcasting 21
disarmament: Conference on Disarmament (CD) 20; Eighteen Nation Committee on Disarmament (ENDC) 201; GCD (general and complete disarmament) 200; Moon Agreement 205; space disarmament 198, 200
Disaster Charter 144, 145, 152–4; Article 1 156; Article IV – contributions by the parties 157; Article V – associated bodies 158; Article VI – accession 158; Article VII – entry into force, expiry and withdrawal 158; Article VIII – implementation 158; data and information availability 145; intent of 154; mechanisms to activate 155–7; membership 153; national implementation 158–9; objectives 153; organization of cooperation 157; protection of mankind 154; purpose and operation of 156–7; purpose and terms of 154–5; scenario writing 157; scope of 156; Secretariat 156, 157; *see also* Remote Sensing Principles
disasters *see* Disaster Charter; Remote Sensing Principles
disputes and conflicts 90–2; arbitration and adjudication 101–4; conciliation 100–1; definition 90; dispute avoidance 98–100; negotiation and consultation 96–8; particularities 104–6; PPPs (public-private partnerships) 95–6; preventative diplomacy 99; private enterprises 95; procedural mechanisms 92; resistance of states to adjudication 95; techniques 96–104; typology of 92–6; UN Charter 91
Dispute Settlement Understanding 167
dissemination licence 254
dissemination of data 253–5
doctrine 11, 12
domestic legal systems: sources of law 3
Draft Articles on Responsibility of International Organizations 14
Draft Articles on State Responsibility 14
Draft Articles on Transboundary Harm 14
Draft Treaty on the Prevention of the Placement of Weapons in Outer Space, the Threat or Use of Force against Outer Space Objects 54
Dual-Use Goods and Technologies List 219
dual-use satellites 222
due diligence 74, 344–5; administrative 137–8
due regard principle 73–4, 75, 183

Earth observation 147, 155, 241–2; activities 244–5; definition 244; licensing of data 251–2; micro-satellites 243; openings for new ventures 243–4
Earth observation data 244, 245–7, 256–8, 259–60, 266–7; analyzed information 256; contributors to 257; copyright 259–60; legal interoperability 257, 262; licences 260–2; open data trend 262–4; *see also* licensing
Earth stations 124
Eastern Carelia case (1923) 91–2
EC (European Commission) 161; international agreements 299; negotiation and consultation 97; privacy protection 299; programme manager of Galileo and EGNOS 297–8
EchoStar 102
ECOSOC (Economic and Social Council) 228
EGNOS Data Access Service (EDAS) 297
EGNOS (European Geostationary Navigation Overlay Service) 97, 162, 164, 178, 296–7,

Index

298; administration and organization 299
Eighteen Nation Committee on Disarmament (ENCD) 201
electromagnetic pulse (EMP) 84; radiation 200
electromagnetic radiation 147–8
Electronic Communications Committee (ECC) 299
enforcement jurisdiction 42–3
ENMOD Convention (Convention on the Prohibition of Military or Any Other Hostile Use of Environmental Modification) 204
environmental law 15
ephemeris data 191
ERA-GLONASS project 303
ESA (European Space Agency) 7, 37, 50, 78, 161, 297–8; dispute settlement 99; EO data 256; European Space Policy 297–8; IPRs (intellectual property rights) 325–6; Planetary Protection Policy 83; space transportation agreements with France 275
EU (European Union) 161; access to documents of institutions 264; Code of Conduct 22–3; cooperation agreements 299; Council Directive on Television without Frontiers 235; draft code of conduct 216; EGNOS (European Geostationary Navigation Overlay Service) 296–7; Galileo 63–4; GNSS 161–2, 162; International Code of Conduct (ICoC) 23; owner of Galileo and EGNOS assets 297; Radio Spectrum Committee 299; Radio Spectrum Policy Group 299; regulation of navigational satellites 295–7; SST (Space Surveillance and Tracking) system 192; support for international convention on GNSS 317
EUMETSAT 7, 37
European Code of Conduct for Space Debris Mitigation 78
European Conference of Postal and Telecommunications Administrations (CEPT) 299
European Convention on Transfrontier Television 235
European Directive 145
European Geostationary Navigation Overlay Service (EGNOS) *see* EGNOS (European Geostationary Navigation Overlay Service)
European GNSS Agency (GSA) 297, 298
European Satellite Services Provider (ESSP) 297, 298
European Telecommunications Standards Institute (ETSI) 299
European Tripartite Group 97
Eutelast vs Alcatel Space case (2004) 102
EUTELSAT 37
exclusive jurisdiction 43
exoneration 67

Exploitation phase (Galileo) 296
exploration: freedom of 31, 32
Export Administration Act (1969) 331
Export Administration Regulations 331
Export and Import Permits Act (EIPA) 331
Export Control Act (1949) 331
Export Control List (ECL) 331
export controls 330–2
Export Permits Regulations and Import Permit Regulations 331

FAA/AST 282
Factory at Chorzow 93
fair-use doctrine 259
fault liability 66–7, 72
Federal Aviation Administration (FAA) 3–4, 39, 186; Human Space Flight Requirements (2006) 54, 57, 58; Office of Commercial Space Transportation (AST) 52; payload review 272; safety approval of launch vehicles 271
Federal Law on Navigation: Article 7 302
Federal Radionavigation Plan (FRP) (1996) 292–3
Federal Republic of Yugoslavia 197
Federal Tort Claims Act (FTCA) 292
Finland: *Eastern Carelia* case (1923) 91–2
First Schedule of the Carriage by Air Act (1972) 318
fixed-satellite service (FSS) *see* FSS (fixed-satellite service)
foreign entities 190
Foreign Trade Law 331
formalist school of thought 18
Fractional Orbital Bombardment Systems (FOBS) 201–2
Framework Agreement (2004) 297
France: guarantees 276; liability for space transportation 277; national space law 38; protection of launch operators 71; safety approval 276, 277, 284; space operations 275; spaceports 283–4; space transportation 274–7; Technical Regulation 276; transfer of ownership 72
freedom of exploration 31, 32; limitations 32
freedom of expression, right to 232–3
Freedom of Information Acts (Australia) 263
Freedom of Information Acts (UK) 263
freedom of scientific investigation 31, 32
freedom of use 31; limitations 32
French Space Operation Act (2008) 78
frequency allocation 166
Frequency Allotment Plans 233
frequency assignments 121–2, 124, 126; notification procedures 127; procedure for effecting coordination of 123
frequency spectrum management authority 120–1

356

FSS (fixed-satellite service) 121, 233; associated feeder-link Plans 129–30
FSS Plan: associated List of assignments 134; and associated procedures 134–7; procedure for implementation of allotment in the Plan or introduction of an additional system 134–5; procedure for inclusion of assignment in the List (Article 6) 135–6; procedure for inclusion of assignment in the MIFR (Article 8) 136–7; procedure for the addition of a new allotment for a new Member (Article 7) 137
Full Operational Capability (FOC) 296

GAGAN (GPS Aided Geostationary Augmentation Navigation Satellite) 163, 315, 317; applications of 315; joint ownership of 316
Galileo 63–4, 161, 161–2, 162, 164, 295–6; administration and organization 297–8, 299; phases 296
GATS (General Agreement on Trade in Services) 167, 168
GATT (General Agreement on Tariffs and Trade) 167, 168
GCD (general and complete disarmament) 198
Geetha Jethani v Airport Authority of India and Ors case (2004) 317–18
General Secretariat (ITU) 119
GEO Data Sharing Working Group 257
GEO (Geostationary Earth's Orbit) 30, 74, 187; limited natural resources 187; operating satellites 188
GEOSS 264
Germany: conditions of licensing 252–3; copyright law 259; data legislation 253; dissemination 253; licensing of data 252; SatDSiG 254; satellite remote sensing operations 251
GGE (Group of Governmental Experts): TCBM Report 215–16
GLONASS (GLObal NAvigation Satellite System) 161; administration of GNSS in the Russian Federation 302; applications 302–3; international cooperation of Russia 303; regulatory regime of GNSS in Russia 301–2; Russian national policy on GNSS 301; structure and main features 300–1
GNSS (Global Navigation Satellite Systems) 160; applicable law 172; ATM Modernization 176; augmentation systems 161, 162–3; authorization and supervision 164; aviation law 175; basis and form of liability 172–3; bilateral agreements 163–4; Chicago Convention 176; civil application 161; CNS/ATM 317; competent court 171–2; core-constellation systems 161–2; cosmic navigation systems 178–9; definition and applications 160–1; frequency allocation 166–7; global regulation in aviation 176–7; GPS and 292; ICAO policy principles 177; IMO policy 177–8; insurance 174–5; intellectual property rights (IPRs) 168–9; International Committee 163; international trade law 167–70; IPR aspects 170; liability 164–6, 170–1, 175; liability chain – persons liable 173; liability of their navigation signal provider 317; market access 167; negligence/fault 174; particularities of the open signal 174; PBN AND 175–6; recognition and enforcement of judgements 172; registration and return of space objects 166; regulatory regime in Russia 301–2; Russian national policy on 301; SARPs 177; sovereign immunity 171; space law 164; technical overview 160–4; and WTO treaties 168
good faith 9
good Samaritan laws 145
GPA (Government Procurement Agreement) 97, 168
GPS (Global Positioning Systems) 161; liability 292; management of 293; Policy and Regulation in the US 291–2; Precise Positioning Services 291; space segment 291; Standard Positioning Service 291; threats and future considerations 293–4; United States of America (US) 291–2
gross negligence (*faute lourde*) 67
Group on Earth Observation (GEO) 152, 156
GSO (Geostionery-Satellite Orbit) 114, 117, 118, 125
Guiana Space Centre 276, 283–4; Agreements 284

Hague Code of Conduct against Ballistic Missile Proliferation (HCOC) 185, 215, 330
Hague V Convention 222
hardware malfunctions 172–3
harmful affection 81
harmful contamination 74
harmful interference 166; Bureau (ITU) 117; dispute between France and Iran 98; ITU dispute resolution 112–13
HCOC (Hague Code of Conduct) 185, 215, 330
Highly Elliptical Orbit (HEO) 162
high seas: launching from 51
Horizons 3e satellite 341
Hubble Space Telescope 148
Huber, M. 27n17
Hughes Aircraft Co. v. United States case (1993) 327
Hughes Network Systems 102

357

Index

human rights: movement 227; right of information 232–4; right to freedom of expression 232–3; right to honour and reputation 231; right to peace 230; right to privacy 231; sovereign right to natural resources 234; twin covenants of 1966 227; UN Charter 227; *see also* international human rights law
Human Rights Committee 228
human rights law 15
human spaceflight 56–8
Human Space Flight Requirements (2006) 54

IAA (International Academy of Astronauts) 181, 182, 185; international agreement on STM 194; study 194
IADC (Inter-Agency Space Debris Coordination Committee): debris mitigation guidelines 22; Space Debris Mitigation Guidelines 76–7
ICAO (International Civil Aviation Organization) 171, 182, 314; APV 1 certification 315; existing jurisdiction 194; Global Aeronautical Distress and Safety System 175; GPS 161; jurisdiction of 56; policy principles 177; responsibilities 194
ICCPR (International Covenant on Civil and Political Rights) 227; Article 1(2) 234; Article 19 232; Article 20 234; prohibition of propaganda 235
ICESCR (International Covenant on Economic, Social and Cultural Rights) 227; Article 1(2) 234; international cooperation 236
ICJ (International Court of Justice): Article 38 5–12; Article 59 10; creation and purpose of 5; nuclear weapons, definition of 85; *South West Africa* cases 100
ICOC (international code of conduct) 216–17
IGA (Intergovernmental Agreement on the International Space Station) 49, 50, 325, 330; Article 5 49; Article 21 (2) 50; Article 22 50; cross-waivers of liability 326
IHL (international humanitarian law) 221
ImageSat 105
immunity 190
IMO (International Maritime Organization) 161, 183; BeiDou System 307; policy 177–8
incidental damage 222
indemnification 67
India: economic deregulation 313; Exceptions to Article 51 of the Constitution 316; Five Year Plan 314; GNSS 161, 162, 163; international liability in space 316; mission goals satellite navigation 314; Planning Commission 314; satellite navigation 313–14; satellite navigation program 314–16
Indian Space Research Organization (ISRO) *see* ISRO (Indian Space Research Organization)
individual rights: in outer space 30–1
industrial property rights 169, 326–8
information 156; right of 232–4
Inmarsat 192
INSPIRE Directive 264
Institute and Centre for Research of Air and Space Law xviii
insurance: commercial satellites 338, 342–3, 345; GNSS 174–5
Intelsat 37, 192, 236, 341
Interagency GPS Executive Board (US) 293, 294
intercontinental ballistic missiles (ICBMs) 201, 202
Intergovernmental Agreement on the International Space Station (IGA) *see* IGA (Intergovernmental Agreement on the International Space Station)
Intermediate-Range Nuclear Forces Treaty (INF Treaty) (1987) 206
International Aeronautical Federation 28
international arbitration 101
International Association for the Advancement of Space Safety (IAASS) 22
International Atomic Energy Agency (IAEA) 88
International Bill of Rights 230
International Chamber Of Commerce (ICC) 102
International Code of Conduct against the Proliferation of Ballistic Missiles 185, 215, 330
International Code of Conduct (ICoC) 23
International Committee on GNSS (ICG) 163
international cooperation 236–7
International Disasters Charter *see* Disaster Charter
international disputes 101
international environmental law: space debris 73–6
international humanitarian law 14
International Institute for the Unification of Private Law (UNIDROIT) *see* UNIDROIT (International Institute for the Unification of Private Law) 171
international law: application to space activities 75; arbitration 101; Article 38 of the ICJ Statute 5–12; hierarchy of sources 15–18; non-traditional notes of regulation 18–24; outer space 228; remote sensing activities 149; soft law norms 19–24; space law as part of 12–15; standards and guidelines 22; states and non-states 4; traditional sources of 5–18; traditional understanding of 4; transparency and confidence building measures 22–4
International Law Association (ILA): Model Space Law 39–41

International Law Commission 14
international law subjects 92
international organizations: responsibility for space activities 37
international persons 92
international registry 143
International Registry for Space Assets 143
international satellite broadcasting 232
international space law *see* space law
International Space Research Organization (ISRO) 102
International Space Station (ISS) 49–50, 67, 269, 323; *see also* IGA (Intergovernmental Agreement on the International Space Station)
international telecommunications law 186–8
International Telecommunications Union (ITU) *see* ITU (International Telecommunications Union)
International Traffic in Arms Regulations (ITAR) 331
international tribunal 91
interoperability 163
IOD Contract 339
IPRs (intellectual property rights) 50, 145, 332; aspects of GNSS 170; bilateral and multilateral legal regimes 325–6; commercial satellites 338, 339; first-to-invent system 327; general principles 169–70; IGA (Intergovernmental Agreement) 325; industrial 326–8; most favored state 169; national treatment/assimilation 169; non-territoriality of outer space 323, 332; Partner States 325–6; private entities 321; procedural rules and priority 170; territoriality of 169, 322, 323, 332; TRIPS regime within the WTO 324–5; WIPO regime 324, 332; *see also* technology transfer
IRNSS (Indian Regional Navigation Satellite System) 161, 162, 314, 315–16; regional policy and legal regime 318
ISI (international space inspectorate) 213–14
ISO (International Standards Organization) 22; debris mitigation ISO-24113:2011 77; remote sensing data and information 149–50
ISRO (Indian Space Research Organization) 163, 313–14; joint ownership of GAGAN 316
ITU (International Telecommunications Union) 4, 37, 109–10; action upon requests for coordination 126; administrative due diligence 137–8; allocation structure 119–21; BSS plans and associated procedures (Appendices 30/30A) 129–33; Constitution and Convention 6; cost recovery 138–9; Council 113–14, 118; dispute resolution 112–13; dispute settlement 94; frequency allocation 166; Frequency Allotment Plans 233; FSS Plan and associated procedures (Appendix 30B) 134–7; General Secretariat 119; geographic regions 114; GNSS 167; harmful interference 65; ITU-R study 139–40; major principles 111; membership 111–12, 114; notification and recording (Article 11) 127–9; notification examination 128; organizational structure of 113–14; overview 111–12; pico, nano and small satellites 139–41; privacy rights 231; procedures 9.7, 9.11 and 9.21 126–7; procedures applying to non-planned services 121–7; purposes and objectives of 110; regulations governing frequencies and orbits 121; requirement and request for coordination 124–5; Space Protocol 142–4; STM (space traffic management) 180, 187; Table, the 120–1; time limits for notifications 128
ITU-R (Radiocommunication Sector of the ITU) 114, 117, 166; bodies of 114–15; study using nanosatellites and picosatellites 139–40

Jakhu, R.S. 113
Japan: GNSS 162; GPA agreement 97; Joint Statement with the US 311; Ministry of Transport (MoT) 97; navigational satellites *see* QZSS (Quasi-Zenith Satellite System)
Japan Business Federation 309
JAXA 83
Jennings, Sir R. 20
Joint Functional Component Command for Space (JFCC Space) 191
Joint Statements 164
JSAT 341
JSPOC (Joint Space Operations Center) 191
jurisaction 43
jurisdiction 42–6, 50; satellite remote sensing activities 248; spacecraft 50; state of registry 43–5, 46, 50; transfer of ownership 45–6
jurisfaction 43
jus ad bellum 13–14
jus cogens norms 16–17
jus in bello 14

keep-out zones (KOZ) 214
Kosmos 945 66

labor law 16
Lachs, Judge, M. 12
la doctrine 11
Lagrange points 55
Land Remote Sensing Policy Act (1992) 251, 256
Landsat 242, 247, 267
Landsat Act (1984) 249

Index

launch and re-entry sites 282–3
launching authorities 52
launching operators 70–1
launching States 51–2, 60, 61; compensation 68; control of private activities 69; joint liability 70; liability 65; NPS Principles 87; registration of space objects 150; sharing of risk 69–70; United States of America 62
launch insurance 342
launch liability insurance 343
launch operator licenses 271
launch services 50–2
Launch Services Contract 339–40, 345
launch sites *see* spaceports
launch-specific licenses 271
Law of the Sea 323
Law on Licensing of Certain Activities 39
Law on Space Activities (1993) 39
legal interoperability 257, 262
LEO (Low Earth Orbit) 181, 187; increasing number of satellites 188; space debris 197–8
lex posterior rules 17
lex specialis 18, 60
liability 64–5; absolute 65–6; Airports Authority of India (AAI) 317–18; Belgian space transportation 279; consequences of 69–72; damage 67; dispute settlement mechanism 68; Dutch space transportation 279, 280; exoneration 67; fault 66–7, 72; French space transportation 274, 277; GPS (Global Positioning Systems) 292; kinds of 65–7; legal sources for damage caused by space activities 59–60; navigational satellites 298; responsibility for 60–3; scope of 63–5; space transportation 285–6
Liability Convention (1972) 6, 7, 11, 17, 37; Article I 165; Article III 66; Article IV 69–70; Article V 61, 70; Article VII 101; Article VIII 94, 100; claims 166; compensation 68–9; conciliation 100; Cosmos 954 (USSR) 96–7; damage 67; definition of launching state 52; definition of space objects 53, 63; dispute settlement 94; drafting and adoption of 60; final wording 63; GNSS 165; kinds of liability 65–7; launching State 60, 61; limitations of 72; multiple states 49; state liability 47; strict liability 165; *travaux préparatoires* 165; types of damage 165–6
licenses/licensing 248–9; Australian spaceports 283; Australian space transportation 273–4; authority 249–50; Belgian space transportation 279; conditions of license 252–3; copyright and 260–2; dissemination licence 254; Dutch space transportation 279–80; EO licenses 260–2; French space transportation 275–6, 277; launch operator 271; launch-specific 271; operator license 254; provisions in Canada 254–5; satellite systems 252; space transportation records 272; subjects of license – personal scope 250–1; subjects of license – space activity 251–2; UK space transportation 272–3; US spaceports 282; US space transportation 271, 272
Limitation of Underground Nuclear Weapon Tests Treaty (TTBT) (1974) 206
limited natural resource 187
LOAC (law of armed conflict) 14, 18; applicability to armed conflicts in space 220–1; law of neutrality 223–4; prohibited methods or means of warfare 223; satellites as military objectives 222–3
Lockheed Martin Space Systems 102
London Court of International Arbitration (LCIA) 103
Long March rockets 79
Long Beach (California) 62
Loral vs Acatel Space case (2003) 102
Low-Earth Orbits (LEOs) 74
Lyall, F. and Larson, P.B. 244

mankind: Common Heritage of Mankind (CHM) 33–4; province of 32–3
maps 260
Maritime Differential GPS System 178
maritime law 177–8
Maritime Silk Road 306
Mavrommatis Concessions cases 90
McGill University Faculty of Law xviii
Member National Scientific Institution (COSPAR) 82
MEO (Medium Earth Orbits) 160, 161, 187
meteorological services 264–6
MFN (Most Favored Nation) principle 168
Michibiki 309
MIFR (Master International Frequency Register of the Bureau) 110, 117, 127; harmful interference 187; Lists 130; recording of examination 128, 129
military objectives 222–3
military remote sensing 147
military satellites 204, 222
military use of space 199, 207–8
Minero, Dr. M. 194
Minister and the Space Licensing and Safety Office (Australia) 273–4
Minister for Science Policy (Belgium) 278–9
Minister of Economic Affairs (Netherlands) 279
Ministry for Economy and Technology (Germany) 250
Ministry of Land, Infrastructure, and Transport (MLIT, Japan) 311
Mir Space Station 97
missile defense systems 209
Model Space Law (ILA) 39–41

Moon Agreement (1979) 6, 7; Article 1(2) 205; Article 4 32; Article 11 29, 30, 33–4; Article 11 (7) 34; Article 15 96; Common Heritage of Mankind (CHM) 33; cooperation 36; demilitarization of outer space 205; dispute settlement 94; planetary protection 81
most favored state 169
MTCR (Missile Technology Control Regime) 217–18, 330; Annex 218; Guidelines 218
MTSAT Satellite Based Augmentation System (MSAS) 97, 162
multinational space objects 48–52
Munition List (US) 219, 331
Mutual Defense Assistant Control Act (1951) 331

nanosatellites 139–41
NASA (National Aeronautics and Space Administration) 82; definition of planetary protection 80; dispute settlement 98–9; Gravity Recovery and Climate Experiment (GRACE) 147–8; Office of Planetary Protection 82; orbital debris mitigation guidelines 77–8; Planetary Protection Policy 82; planetary protection requirements 83; Policy Directive 8710.3A 186
NASA Policy Directive (NPD): "Biological Contamination Control for Outbound and Inbound Planetary Spacecraft" 82
NASA Policy Instruction (NPI): "NASA Policy on Planetary Protection Requirements for Human Extraterrestrial Missions 82–3
NASA Procedural Requirements (NPR): "Planetary Protection Provisions for Robotic Extraterrestrials Missions" 82
NASDA (National Space Development Agency) 78
National and Commercial Space Programs Act (NCSPA) 250
National Environmental Satellite, Data and Information Service (NESDIS) 250
National Imagery and Mapping Agency (NIMA) 197
National Industry Standard (China): "Requirements on Space Debris Mitigation" 79
national law 245; satellite remote sensing activities 247–9
national law, space transportation 270; Australia 273–4; authorization requirements 280–1; Belgium 278–9; building blocks 280, 281; catch-all clause 280–1; France 274–7; liability 281; Netherlands 279–80; registration 281; UK 272–3; US 271–2
National Oceanic and Atmospheric Administration (NOAA) 250, 253, 265, 266
National Reconnaissance Office (NRO) 197

National Research Council: Space Studies Board 83
national space law: France 38; ILA Model Space Law 39–41; Russia 39; state responsibility for 38; STM (space traffic management) 185–6; United States of America (US) 39
National Space Policy (2010, US) 192–3, 292
National Spatial Data Infrastructure (NSDI) Law 310
National Standard of the Russian Federation: "General Requirement to Design and Operation of Spacecraft and Orbital Stages on Space Debris Mitigation" 78
National Standard System (China) 306
National Strategy for Earth Observations 263
National Treatment principle 168
natural resources, sovereign right to 234
navigational satellites: administration and organization 297–8; in China see BeiDou System; EGNOS (European Geostationary Navigation Overlay Service) 296–7; European Union (EU) 295–7; Galileo 295–6; in India 313–18; international agreements 299; in Japan see QZSS (Quasi-Zenith Satellite System); liability 298; management of GPS 293; privacy protection 299; in Russia see GLONASS (GLObal NAvigation Satellite System); Russian national policy on GNSS 301; spectrum protection 299, 307–8; threats to GPS and future considerations 293–4; US Global Positioning System (GPS) 291–2; US GPS Policy and Regulation 291–2
NAVSTAR (Navigation System with Timing and Ranging) 291, 310
Near Earth Objects (NEOs) 85
NEC Corporation 310
negligence 174
negotiation and consultation 96–8
Netherlands: liability 279, 280; space transportation 279–80
neutrality, law of 222; in space armed conflicts 223–4
New Skies 102
Nextgen 176
no harm principle 75
non-appropriation principle 29–30
non-governmental entities 47
Non-Proliferation Treaty (1968): Article VI 19
norms, peremptory 16–17
notification and recording (Article 11): examination by the Bureau 128; MIFR (Master International Frequency Register of the Bureau) 127; notification procedures 127; responsibilities of the notifying administration 129; time limits 128
NPS Principles 86–8

361

Index

NTMs (national technical means of verification) 206
NTP v. Research Motion case (2005) 327
nuclear power sources (NPS): IAEA documents 88; NPS Principles 86–8; nuclear power sources (NPS) 86; outer space treaties 86; regulation of 86–8
Nuclear Suppliers Group (NSG) 218
nuclear testing 83–6, 89; cessation of 84; Outer Space Treaty (1967) 85–6; Partial Test Ban Treaty 83–4
nuclear weapons 85

objective liability 65
obligations *erga omnes* 7
Odyssey Launch Platform 51
Office of Commercial Remote Sensing Regulatory Affairs 250
Office of Commercial Space Transportation (AST) 39, 52
Office of Planetary Protection, NASA: NASA Procedural Requirements (NPR) 82
OHCHR (Office of the High Commissioner for Human Rights) 228
open data trend 262–4, 267
Open Service (OS) 295, 296–7
open signals 174
operator licence 254
opinio juris 8–9
Optional Protocol on the Compulsory Settlement of Disputes Relating to the Constitution and Administrative Regulations (ITU) 112
Optional Rules, PCA 102, 103, 113
on-orbit operations 248
orbit/spectrum resources and management 111, 121
outer space: boundaries 27–9; Common Heritage of Mankind (CHM) 33–4; definition 211; delimitation of 27, 27n17, 31, 53–4; demarcation line with air space 28; as a domain of human activity 25–6; freedom of exploration 31, 32; freedom of scientific investigation 31, 32; freedom of use 31; freedoms of 30–1; international cooperation 49–50; international law 228; legal status 27–34; limitations 34; military uses of 34; non-appropriation principle 29–30; province of mankind 32–3; regulation of 226; space debris 73–6
Outer Space Act (1986, UK) 83, 272–3
Outer Space Treaty (1967) 6, 8, 26; Article I 30–1, 32, 33, 36, 146, 149, 183; Article II 13, 29, 30; Article III 12, 17, 34, 75, 80–1, 86, 96, 228, 235; Article IV 34, 85, 183, 201–2; Article IX 9, 35–6, 40, 73, 74, 82, 85, 94, 96, 180, 183, 184; Article VI 7, 14, 30, 37, 44, 46, 47, 60, 66, 69, 71, 164, 243, 273, 280; Article VII 37, 41, 60, 69, 164–5, 243; Article VIi 273; Article VIII 43–4, 45, 46, 243, 248; Article XI 150, 184; Article XIII 30, 94, 96; assessment of the different interpretations of 203–4; brief drafting process 201–2; cooperation principle 35; delimitation of outer space 53; dispute settlement 94; exploration 32; freedom of scientific investigation 32; interpretations for peaceful purposes 202–3; limitations 32; nuclear testing 85–6; opening paragraph of 227; planetary protection 80; preamble 226; on propaganda 234; responsibility of states 92–3; space debris removal 79–80; transfer of ownership 71
outward contamination 80

pacta sunt servanda 7
Paris Convention on Industrial Property 61, 169
PAROS (Prevention of an Arms Race in Outer Space) 207, 209, 230; existing agreements relevant to 209
Partial Test Ban Treaty (PTBT) 6, 83–4, 200–1; Article I 85
Partner's Cooperating Agency 330
passive sensing 246
patents 170, 328
PAXSAT-A proposal 214
PBN (Performance Based Navigation) 175–6
PCA (Permanent Court of Arbitration) 10; Optional Rules 102, 103, 113
Peaceful Nuclear Explosions Treaty (PNET) (1976) 206
peaceful purpose doctrine 230
peace, right to 230–1
peremptory norms 16–17
Permanent Court of Arbitration (PCA) *see* PCA (Permanent Court of Arbitration)
Permanent Court of International Justice (PCIJ) 9, 11, 90; *Eastern Carelia* case (1923) 91–2; *Factory at Chorzow* case (1928) 93
persistent object, position of 8–9
persons liable 173
picosatellites 139–41
planetary protection 89; COSPAR (Committee on Space Research) 81–2; definition 80; international regulations 80–2; Moon Agreement 81; national and regional regulations 82–3; Outer Space Treaty (1967) 80–1
Planetary Protection Officer (PPO), NASA 83
Planetary Protection Policy (COSPAR) 81, 82
Ploughshare Innovations 170
PNT (Position, Navigation and Timing) 160, 161
PP (ITU Plenipotentiary Conference) 113, 114

PPPs (public-private partnerships): dispute settlement 95–6
PPWTs (Prevention of Placement of Weapons in Outer Space) 20, 23, 24, 210, 211, 212
precautionary principle 15
Precise Positioning Services 291
pre-launch insurance 342
Preparatory Commission 143
prescriptive jurisdiction 42, 44
Presidential Decision Directive NSTC-6 293
preventative diplomacy 99
primary data 147, 148
primary jurisdiction 50
principle of cooperation 35–7
Principles and Guidelines for Human Missions to Mars, COSPAR 81
Principles Governing the Use by States of Artificial Earth Satellites for International Direct Television Broadcasting (1982) 21
Principles Relating to Remote Sensing of Earth from Outer Space (1986) 21
Principles Relevant to the Use of Nuclear Power Sources in Outer Space (1992) 21, 86–8
a priori planning procedures 121
privacy, right to 231
private enterprises: dispute settlement 95, 104
private entities: intellectual property 321; sharing of risk 70
Private Finance Initiative (PFI) scheme 310
Private Land Remote Sensing Space Systems: Final Rule (2006) (NOAA) 250
private spacecraft: application of international law to 47–8; supervision of 47
processed data 148
production systems 218
Project Committee on China-Russia GNSS cooperation 306
Project West Ford (1963) 97
propaganda, prohibition of 234–6
Protocol on Matters specific to Aircraft Equipment (2012) 142
Protocol to the Convention on International Interests in Mobile Equipment on Matters Specific to Space Assets (2012) 349–51
province of mankind 32–3
public capital markets 344
public international law: STM (space traffic management) 182–3
Public Regulated Service (PRS) 296
pulsars 178–9
Putin, President 161

QSS (Quasi-Zenith Satellite System Services Inc.) 310
Question of the Peaceful Use of Outer Space 199

QZSS (Quasi-Zenith Satellite System) 162–3, 309–10; aim of 309; bodies responsible for the operation of 310; collaborations with GPS 311; privacy concerns 311–12; signals 310–11
QZS System User Society (QSUS) 310

racial hatred 234, 235
RADARSAT 249
Radiocommunication Advisory Group, ITU 115, 116–17
radiocommunication assemblies (RA) 114
Radiocommunication Study Groups 114, 116, 117
radio frequencies 248
Radio Frequency Service 302
radio navigation 291
Radio Navigation Satellite Services (RNSS) 167
Radio Regulation, China 307
Radio Regulations (RR) see RR (Radio Regulations of the ITU)
Radio Spectrum Committee, EU: Radio Spectrum Policy Group 299
Radio Spectrum Policy Group, EU 299
RA (Radiocommunications Assembly) 114, 116
raw data 255
Receivers Performance Standard 307
Registration Convention 184, 185, 222, 322–3, 323; Article II 49–50; transfer of ownership 71
Registration Convention (1974) 6, 7, 44–5; amending 213; Article II (1) 64–5; Article IV 39; definition of space objects 53; GNSS 166; launching 51; private activity 47; space objects 43
Registry (international) 143
Regulations on Control of Military Products Export 331–2
Regulations on Export Control of Missiles and Missile-related Items and Technologies 332
religious hatred 234, 235
remote sensing 241, 266–7; activities 244–5; commercial 148; copyright 328; definition 244; military 147; national regulation 247–9; parties, responsibilities and interests 242–4; security-related 148; space-based meteorological services 264–6; UN Principles relating to 146–7; see also Earth observation data; licensing
Remote Sensing Principles 144, 145, 146, 159; data and information availability 145; definitions 147–8; natural disasters 151; primary and processed data 148; Principle IV 149; Principle IX 150; Principles II and III 149; Principles V and VI 149–50; Principles VII and VIII 150; Principles X and XI 150–1; Principles XIII and XIV 152; Principle XII

Index

151–2; Principle XV 152; protection of mankind 151; protection of the environment 151; right of information 233; *see also* Disaster Charter
Remote Sensing principles 21
remote sensing satellites 231; technology and capabilities 246
Remote Sensing Space System Regulations: section 12 255
Remote Sensing Space Systems Act (RSSSA) 250, 256; section 2 253
Remote Sensing Space Systems Regulations (RSSSR) 250
Remote Sensing Statute (2005) 254
Remote Sensing Statute (2007) 245
Remote Sensing Systems Act (2005) 247
Report of Resolutions (UNISPACE III) 153
Republic of Serbia v *Imagesat International NV* case (2009) 104–5
Rescue Agreement (1968) 6, 47–8; Article 2 48; GNSS 166; private spacecraft 48; return to launching authority 52
Resolution 1348 60
restitutio in integrum 67, 69
right of information 232–4
right to freedom of expression 232–3
right to honour and reputation 231
right to peace 230–1
right to privacy 231
RNAV (Area Navigation) 176
RNP (Required Navigation Performance) 176
rocket systems 218
RRB (Radio Regulations Board) 114, 115–16, 117; Appendix 4 125; frequency management 120–1; notification examination 128; notification of frequency assignments 127
RRCs (Regional Radiocommunication Conferences of the ITU) 115, 117
RR (Radio Regulations of the ITU) 5, 110, 123, 124; allowances 233; Appendices 30/30A *see* AP30A (Appendix 30A); AP30 (Appendix 30); Appendix 4 122, 132, 133; Appendix 30B *see* AP30B (Appendix 30B); Article 15 98; Article 21 135; Article 22 135; derogation of provisions 233; objectives 112
Rules concerning Space Activities and the Establishment of a Registry of Space Objects (2006) 279
Russia: ABM Treaty 205, 206; ASAT tests 198; Cold War 226; GNSS 162; as launching state 51; Legal Subcommittee (LSC) 200; militarization of outer space 205; moratorium on ASAT weapons 213; national policy on GNSS 301; national space law 39; navigational satellites *see* GLONASS (GLObal NAvigation Satellite System); nuclear arms control agreements with US 206; proposal for de-weaponization 211; Question of the Peaceful Use of Outer 199; *see also* Soviet Union
Russian Aviation and Space Agency: Space Debris Mitigation Standard 78
Russian Bock DM Upper 62
Russian Federal Space Agency (ROSCOSMOS) 78
Russian Resolution on the Order of Acquisition, Use and Provision of Geo-Spatial Information 329
Russian Space Systems 302

SABS (Satellite Based Augmentation System) 314
Safety Framework for Nuclear Power Source Applications in Outer Space 88
Safety-of-Life (SoL) service 296, 297
SALT I (Interim Strategic Arms Limitation Treaty) 206
SARPs (Standards and Recommended Practices) 177
SAR (Search and Rescue) 161, 296
SatDSiG 254
satellite buses 269, 280
satellite communications services 197
Satellite Data Protection Act (2007) 247
Satellite Data Security Act (SatDSiG) 250
Satellite Data Security Law 256, 260
satellite monitoring systems 214
satellite navigation *see* navigational satellites
satellite operators 344, 345
Satellite Purchase Agreement 336–8, 340, 345
satellite remote sensing activities: jurisdiction 248; national regulation of 247–9; *see also* licensing
satellites 28–9, 139–41; civilian 222; de-registration 46; dual-use 222; MEO (Medium Earth Orbits) 160; military 204, 222; as military objectives 222–3; military use 197; remote sensing 246; small, characteristics of 140–1; testing emerging technologies 140; *see also* commercial satellites
Satmex 341
SATMS (Space and Air Traffic Management System) 186
Scientific and Technical Subcommittee, UNCOPUOS: space debris reduction guidelines 184–5
scientific investigation: freedom of 31, 32
SDA (Space Data Association) 192
Sea Launch 50–2, 62, 102, 285
Search and Rescue (SAR) Service 161, 296
secondary jurisdiction 50
Second World War 226
security interests 347; perfection of 347–51
self-defense 13

self-determination 227
Sentinel Asia 155
Serbia 104–5
SES 192
shutter control 255
signal defects 173
signals 310–11
signals-in-the-sky (SIS) 317
Silk Road Economic Belt 306
Single European Sky (SES) 176
Skybox Imaging 339
SLVs (space launch vehicles) 215
SmallSats 187, 188
Smith, T. 327
soft law 19–20, 24; standards and guidelines 22; transparency and confidence building measures 22–4; UN General Assembly resolutions 20–2
software defects 173
sources of law 3
South Africa: discovery and return of private spacecraft 48; law on outer space borders 54
South West Africa cases 100
sovereign immunity 171
sovereign right to natural resources 234
Soviet Union: cessation of nuclear testing 84; *Eastern Carelia* case (1923) 91–2; Fractional Orbital Bombardment Systems (FOBS) 201–2; liability position 59; *see also* Russia
Space Activities Act (Netherlands) 279
space arms race 230
space assets 53, 349
Space Benefits Declaration (1996) 36
Space Commission of India 314
spacecraft 42; authorization and continuing supervision by the appropriate state party 46–7; definition of space object 63, 64; disposing of 188; International Space Station (ISS) 49–50; jurisdictional rules 50; jurisdiction over space objects 42–6; legal status of multinational space objects 48–52; private, application of international law to 47–8; Sea Launch 50–2; suborbital spaceplanes 52–8
space data 156; collection of 243
space debris 40, 67, 72, 88–9; ASAT attacks 223; harmful contamination 74; IADC 76–7; law of outer space and international environmental law 73–6; legal issues concerning active removal of 79–80; LEO (Low Earth Orbit) 197–8; national and regional regulations 77–9; Scientific and Technical Subcommittee, UNCOPUOS 184–5; STM (space traffic management) 188–9; UNCOPUOS 76–7
space disarmament 198, 200
space facilities 156

space law: contextualizing 3–5; cooperation principle 35–7; international sources of 26–7; law-making processes in the domestic context 3–4; law-making processes in the international context 4–5; non-territorial nature of 322; as part of general international law 12–15; peaceful nature of outer space 230; STM (space traffic management) 183–5; trusteeship of the United Nations 228
space objects *see* spacecraft
Space Operation Functions (SOF) 133
Space Operations Act (2008, France) 274–6, 277, 283–4
spaceplanes: air law vs. space law 53–6; definition of space objects 53; delimitation of outer space 53–4; domestic regulation of human spaceflight 56–8; functionalist theory 55; jurisdiction of ICAO 56; private companies 52–3; spacialist theory 54–5
Space Policy of Japan 309
spaceports 282; Australia 283; France 283–4; international agreement on design and operation of 287; legislation 284–5; licenses 282, 283; regulation 285; safety approval 284; tourist space flights 287; United States of America 282–3
Spaceport Sweden 58
Space Protocol 142–4
Space Report of the Space Foundation (2015) xviii
space safety *see* STM (space traffic management)
SpaceShipOne 183
Space Shuttle 189
space signals 64–5
Space Surveillance Network (SSN) 73, 192
Space Surveillance System (SSS) 192
Space Systems Loral 339
space technology: export control measures 220; legal controls over the transfer of 329–30; missile technology control regime 217–18; Wassenaar Arrangement (WA) 219–20
space transportation 268–9, 287; Australia 273–4; Belgium 278–9; command phase 275, 277; coordination between launching states 285; environmental consequences and considerations 286; France 274–7; guarantees 276; international harmonization of rules 286–7; launching from high seas 285; launching phase 275, 276, 277, 287; liability 274, 277, 279, 280, 285–6; licenses 271, 272, 272–3, 273–4, 275–6, 277, 279, 279–80; long-distance 286; modes of 269; national laws *see* national laws, space transportation; Netherlands 279–80; payload review 272; purpose of regulation 269–70; safety approval 271, 274, 276, 277, 278; United Kingdom 272–3; US 271–2

365

Index

space weapons 208–9
Spanish law: spaceflight regulation 57
spectrum protection 299
sponsor Authorized Users 155
SPOT satellites 242n7, 246–7
Spurring Private Aerospace Competitiveness and Entrepreneurship Act (2015) 30
Sputnik I 27, 198, 226, 237
SSA (Space Situational Awareness): agreements 190; contents of agreements 191; definition 189; global networks 192; immunity 190; information to foreign entities 190; international context 193; international measures to increase 190; notification of operators of possible conjunctions 191; private efforts to increase information sharing 192; as a public-private partnership 191
SST (Space Surveillance and Tracking) system 192
Standard Positioning Service 291
State Administration of Science, Technology and Industry for National Defense, China 79
Statement of Work and Interface Control Document 340
state of registry 43–5, 50, 322; de-registration 46; GNSS 166
state(s): consultation regime 74–5; due regard 73–4; international responsibility 37; launching 51–2, 60, 61; model law 39–41; national space law 38–9; no harm principle 75; position as persistent object 8–9; remote sensing 146; responsibility for space activities 37–41; supervision of private operations 47; *see also* launching States
Statute on Licensing of Space Activities 39
STM (space traffic management) 180, 192–3, 195–6; congestion in space 188; definition 180–2; implementing a global system 193–4; international agreement on 195–6; international collaboration 193; international space law 183–5; international telecommunications law 186–8; national space law 185–6; private system 195; public international law 182–3; role for existing organisations 194–5; space debris 188–9; SSA (Space Situational Awareness) 189–93
Stratcom 191; Joint Functional Component Command for Space (JFCC Space) 191; JSPOC (Joint Space Operations Center) 191
Strategic Arms Reduction Treaty (START 1) (1991) 206
strict liability 61, 100, 174
subjects of States 92
suborbital spaceplanes 52–8
substantial connection, notion of 251
Summer School on Frontier Technology 307
Supervisory Authority 143, 144

Sweden: spaceflight regulation 58
Swiss Space Systems 52
System for Differential Corrections and Monitoring (SDCM) 162

Table of Frequency Allocations 127, 136, 137
tasking satellites 253–5
TBT (Technical Barriers to Trade Agreement) 168
TCBMs (transparency and confidence building measures) 22–4, 190; HCOC 215; ICOC (international code of conduct) 216–17; UN GGE 215–16
technology transfer: international and national export control regimes 330–2; space technology, legal controls over 329–30; *see also* IPRs (intellectual property rights)
Telecommunication Development Sector, ITU 117, 118–19
Telecommunication Standardization Sector, ITU 118
Telemetry, Tracking and Command ("TT&C") contract 334, 345
territoriality, IPR 169
third-party liability insurance 343
Thuraya D1 102
Tort Liability Law, China 308
tourist space flights 269, 287
Trade Policy Review Mechanism 167
trade secrets 170
Trading with the Enemy Act (1917) 331
Transparency and Confidence Building Measures (TCBMs) *see* TCBMs (transparency and confidence building measures)
treaties: ABM Treaty 205, 206; Antarctic Treaty 202; Article 38 (ICJ Statute) 6–7; Comprehensive Test Ban Treaty (1996) 6; interpretations 13; Non-Proliferation Treaty (1968) 19; obligations 15; outer space 86; satellite-based mutual monitoring mechanisms 206; Vienna Convention on the Law of Treaties (VCLT) 6; *see also* Outer Space Treaty (1967); Partial Test Ban Treaty (PTBT)
Treaty on Conventional Armed Forces in Europe (CFE Treaty) (1990) 206
Treaty on Principles Governing the Activities of States in the Exploration and Use of Outer Space Including the Moon and Other Celestial Bodies *see* Outer Space Treaty (1967)
Treaty on the Functioning of the EU (TFEU) 298
TRIPS Agreement (Trade-Related Aspects of Intellectual Property Rights) 167, 169; Article 4 169; within the WTO 324–5

UAVs (unmanned aerial vehicle systems) 218

Index

UDHR (Universal Declaration of Human Rights) 227; Article 12 231; Article 19 232; preamble 230
UK Outer Space Act (1986) 185; section 1 (c) 245
UN Charter 6; Article 2(7) 4, 13; Article 51 13, 212; Article 103 13, 17; human rights 227; purpose of 13; resolution of disputes and conflict 91
UNCITRAL Arbitration Rules 102–3
UNCLOS (United Nations Convention on the Law of the Sea) 30, 182
UN Commission for Conventional Armaments 204
UN Committee on Economic, Social and Cultural Rights 16
UN Committee on the Peaceful Uses of Outer Space (UNCOPUOS) *see* UNCOPUOS
UN Convention on the Law of the Sea (UNCLOS) 30, 182
UNCOPUOS (UN Committee on the Peaceful Uses of Outer Space) 19, 20; damage liability for space activities 60; dispute settlement 99–100; IADC space debris mitigation guidelines 22; Legal Subcommittee Working Group on National Legislation 10; peaceful purposes doctrine 230; peaceful uses 199; remote sensing in disaster management 144; right of information 233; Safety Framework for Nuclear Power Source Applications in Outer Space 88; space debris guidelines 76–7; STM (space traffic management) 194–5
UN Declaration of Legal Principles Governing Activities of States in the Exploration and Use of Outer Space (1963) 8
UNESCO: Declaration of Guiding Principles on the Use of Direct Broadcasting by Satellite 232
UNGA (United Nations General Assembly): HCOC 215; No First Placement of Weapons in Outer Space (2014) 24; outer space resolution 198; PAROS (Prevention of an Arms Race in Outer Space) 230; recommendations only 20; Resolution 37/92 94, 96; Resolution 41/65 94, 96; Resolution 47/68 94, 96; Resolution 61/75 216; Resolution 62/101 184; Resolution 110 (II) 234, 234–5; Resolution 1148 (XII) 198–9; Resolution 1348 (XIII) 199; Resolution 1472 (XIV) 199; Resolution 1721A (XVI) 199; Resolution 1721 (D) 236; Resolution 1803 (XVII) 234; Resolution 1884 (XVIII) 200; Resolution 1962 201; Resolution 1962 (XVIII) 94, 199; Resolution 1962 (XVIII) (Principle 6) 96; Resolution on Remote Sensing Principles 146; resolutions as soft law 20–2; Space Principles Declaration (1963) 20

UNIDROIT (International Institute for the Unification of Private Law): General Assembly 143; purpose 347
Uniform Commercial Code (U.C.C.) 347
UNISPACE III 153
UNITAR/UNOSAT 155
United Kingdom (UK): as launching state 52; Partial Test Ban Treaty 84; space transportation 272–3
United Nations Commission on International Trade Law (UNCITRAL) Arbitration Rules 102
United Nations Convention on Jurisdictional Immunities of States and Their Property 171
United Nations Principles Relating to Remote Sensing of the Earth from Space 245
United Office for Outer Space Affairs (UNOOSA) *see* UNOOSA (United Nations Office of Outer Space Affairs)
United States of America (USA): ABM Treaty 205, 206; ASAT tests 198; bilateral GNSS agreements 164; Cold War 226; Copyright Act 329; distinction between raw and processed EO data 256; first-to-invent system 327; GNSS 161, 162; GPS (Global Positioning Systems) 291–2; GPS Policy and Regulation 291–2; Joint Statements 164, 311; as launching State 62; as launching state 51–2; management of GPS 293; national space law 39; nuclear arms control agreements with Russia 206; opposition to international convention on GNSS 317; Partial Test Ban Treaty 84; personal jurisdiction over natural persons 251; private rights in outer space 30; protection of launch operators 71; Question of the Peaceful Use of Outer 199; satellite remote sensing operations 251; Section 2281 292, 293; space debris regulations 77–8; spaceports 282–3; space transportation 271–2
UN Online Index of Objects Launched into Outer Space 52
UNOOSA (United Nations Office for Outer Space Affairs) 17, 155, 228, 237; Registry 350
UN Security Council (SC) 17, 219; Article 42 13; binding resolutions 20; Resolution 1540 220; Resolution 1718 220
UN Spider 241
UN (United Nations): General Assembly Resolution 61/111 163; NPS Principles 86–8; trusteeship of space law 228
US Air Force 54
US Department of Defense (DOD) 190
US FAA/AST 186
US Federal Communications Commission (FCC) 78
U.S. NAVSTAR: Global Positioning System (GPS) 161

367

Index

US Orbital Debris Mitigation Standard Practices 78
US Strategic Command (Stratcom) 191
UTC (Coordinated Universal Time) 160
utility models 170

Venezuela: definition of weaponization 209; proposal for de-weaponization 211
Very High Resolution (VHR) data 148
Vienna Convention on the Law of Treaties (VCLT) 6
Virgin Galactic 52, 58; SpaceShipTwo 53
von Kármán line 28, 53, 54, 55
Voyager missions 148

WAAS (Wide Augmentation System) 162, 178
war propaganda 234
warranties 337
Wassenaar Arrangement (WA) 219–20, 330; catch-all controls 219, 220
weaponization of space 207–8; difficulty defining 208–9
weather-related hazards 265
Wide Area Augmentation System 291–2
wilful misconduct (*faute intentionnelle*) 67
WIPO Copyright Treaty (WCT) 324
WIPO (World Intellectual Property Organization) 169, 324, 332
Wireless Telegraphy Acts 249
WMD (weapons of mass destruction) 85, 204; definition 204; MTCR (Missile Technology Control Regime) 217–18
World Conferences on International Telecommunications (ITU) 114
World Meteorological Organization (WMO) 264–5, 265–6
World Radiocommunication Conferences (WRC) 114
world telecommunication development conference (WTDC) 114
world telecommunication standardization assembly (WTSA) 114
WRCs (World Radiocommunication Conferences of the ITU) 114, 115, 118, 127, 166; orbit/spectrum management 121; Resolution 49 137; Resolution 91 138; Resolution 552 138; WRC-12 128, 139; WRC-15 133; WRC-97 137
WTO (World Trade Organization): Commitments 168; and GNSS treaties 168; human rights 16; Multilateral Agreements 167; negotiation and consultation 97; principles and structure of 167–8; Schedules 168; TRIPS regime 324–5

XCOR 52; Lynx 58; lynx 53
X-ray pulsar navigation 179

Zenit Rocket 62

Printed in Great Britain
by Amazon